MUSIC FOR
PATRIOTS, POLITICIANS,
AND PRESIDENTS

Our Country's Songs

Star Spangled Banner.
Hail Columbia.
Stand by the Flag.
Columbia rules the sea.
Our Union right or wrong.

Yankee Doodle.
Red, White & Blue.
Vive l'America.
Unfurl the glorious Banner.
America.

NEW YORK.
PUBLISHED BY FIRTH, POND & C.º 547 BROADWAY

ALBANY. J.H. HIDLEY.

CINCINNATI C. Y. FONDA

Music for Patriots, Politicians, and Presidents

HARMONIES AND DISCORDS
OF THE FIRST HUNDRED YEARS

Vera Brodsky Lawrence

MACMILLAN PUBLISHING CO., INC.

NEW YORK

COLLIER MACMILLAN PUBLISHERS

LONDON

Graphic concept by Vera Brodsky Lawrence

Macmillan Publishing Co., Inc.
866 Third Avenue, New York, N.Y. 10022
Collier Macmillan Canada, Ltd.

Library of Congress Cataloging in Publication Data
Lawrence, Vera Brodsky.
Music for patriots, politicians, and presidents.
Bibliography: p.
Includes index.
1. Music—United States—History and criticism.
2. Patriotic music, American—History and criticism.
3. Political ballads and songs, American—History and
criticism. 4. Music, American. I. Title.
ML3551.L29   784.7'1973   75-28041
ISBN 0-02-569390-5

First Printing 1975

Printed in the United States of America

For Lester S. Levy,
gratefully and affectionately

CONTENTS

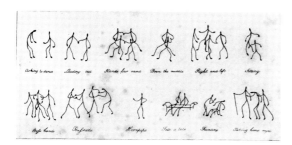

PRELUDE

This book started out in 1971 to be a collection of presidential campaign songs in facsimiles of old sheet music editions. Primarily intended to be played and sung for entertainment, it was also meant to be a reminder—now that Americans seem to have lost the knack for setting their politics to music—of the politically and historically illuminating odes and obbligatos with which our forefathers were wont to celebrate our Great Quadrennial Rites.

Straying into the seductive bypaths that crisscross history research, I soon came to realize that the campaign songs—beguiling as they are—represent but a tiny segment of a vast and fascinating literature of related sociopolitical, patriotic, and (after 1789) presidential words-and-music that embody, albeit in an unfamiliar dimension, a step-by-step narrative of American history. From the first stirrings of colonial resistance in 1765, American bards and balladeers faithfully recorded and interpreted the great and small events and issues of our evolving national destiny. It seemed to me that a representative selection of their work, assembled from the treasure of musical documentation accrued since the eighteenth century in newspapers, broadsides, almanacs, pamphlets, songsters, and, of course, sheet music with wonderfully evocative pictorial cover art, would provide a much-needed, fresh perspective on the American past and its inhabitants; it would permit us, in a sense, to hear history happen again. To help listen is the revised purpose of *Music for Patriots, Politicians, and Presidents.*

⁓

In the following pages, the above symbol is used to denote the omission of a stanza or stanzas. Archaic or idiosyncratic spellings and punctuation have largely been retained for their contemporary flavor, but, to avoid clutter and interruption of the text, they are not indicated by the word *sic* in square brackets. For the same reason, citations, dates, and source references are given within the body of the text, not in footnotes. Obsolete words are defined; as far as possible, people are identified; and background events are sketched in with the lightest of light pencils when required to explain the meaning of the songs. To satisfy the demands of layout and the limitations of space, a few omissions of well-known songs were regrettably unavoidable.

ACKNOWLEDGMENTS

Of the many people and institutions whose help and cooperation enabled me to realize this book, my first thanks are given to the Rockefeller Foundation, through whose assistance I accomplished my initial research in 1971, and to Lester S. Levy, who unstintingly proffered not only his magnificent collection of American sheet music but also his rare scholarship, wisdom, and warm interest. Mr. Levy's contribution to this book is nothing less than staggering. Other private sources to whom I am indebted are James J. Fuld, Harry Dichter, William Ryden, Ruth Shaw Wylie, and the Collection of Ambassador and Mrs. J. William Middendorf II.

I am also deeply indebted to James J. Heslin and his staff, serving in various departments of the New-York Historical Society: James Gregory, Sue A. Gillies, Roger N. Mohovich, Wendy Shadwell, Jan B. Hudgens, and former staff member Wilson G. Duprey.

For her extraordinary help and her incredible patience, my sincere thanks are expressed to Norma Jean Lamb, Music Division, Buffalo and Erie County Public Library.

I am abidingly grateful for their assistance to Thomas R. Adams, John Carter Brown Library, Brown University; Malcolm Freiberg, Massachusetts Historical Society; Harold Samuel, John Herrick Jackson Music Library, Yale University; Herbert R. Collins and Edith P. Mayo, Political History Division, Smithsonian Institution; Oliver Lloyd Onion, Alexandria-Washington Lodge No. 22, A.F.& A.M.; Neda M. Westlake, Charles Patterson Van Pelt Library, University of Pennsylvania; Lillian Tonkin, Library Company of Philadelphia; Geneva Warner, Lilly Library, Indiana University; Georgia B. Bumgardner, American Antiquarian Society; Karol A. Schmiegel, Henry Francis duPont Winterthur Museum; Richard Harrington, Anne S. K. Brown Military Collection; John H. Stanley, John Hay Library, Brown University; P. William Filby, Maryland Historical Society; and Donald Gormley, Art Commission of the City of New York. At the New York Public Library: Maude Cole and Peter Rainey, Rare Book Division; Elizabeth Roth, Prints Division; and Richard Jackson, Music Division. At the Library of Congress: Milton Kaplan, Prints and Photographs Division; Julia Harty, Rare Book Division; and Peter Fay, Music Division.

Grateful acknowledgment is also given to the Boston Public Library; Boston Museum of Fine Arts; Metropolitan Museum of Art; Cornell University Library; Lewis Walpole Library; Yale University Library; Yale University Art Gallery; the Philip H. and A. S. W. Rosenbach Foundation; Fort Ticonderoga Museum; United States Department of State; National Gallery of Art; Vermont Historical Society; Henry E. Huntington Library and Art Gallery; Historical Society of Pennsylvania; Thomas Jefferson Memorial Foundation; Special Collections, Columbia University Library; Pierpont Morgan Library; New York State Historical Association; and Cincinnati Historical Society.

For their assistance in history, newspaper, and picture research, I owe great thanks to Davida Tennenbaum Deutsch, Elizabeth Pierce, and, particularly, to Elaine A. Frezza.

VERA BRODSKY LAWRENCE

*MUSIC FOR
PATRIOTS, POLITICIANS,
AND PRESIDENTS*

The effect of popular songs and airs, especially in times of alarm and danger, has been long known; and they have often been employed, both by patriot and traitor, to inspire resolution, and rouse to heroism . . .

United States' Gazette, for the Country
October 25, 1805

I.

The LIBERTY SONG. In F

Come join hand in hand brave A-me-ri-cans-all, And rouse your bold hearts ... press your just claim, Or stain with dishonour A-me-ri-ca's name., In Free... live, Our pur-ses are rea-dy, Steady, Friends, Steady.

Our worthy Forefathers--Let's give them a cheer
To Climates unknown did courageously steer;
Thro' Oceans, to deserts, for freedom they came,
And dying bequeath'd us their freedom and Fame.
  In Freedom we're born &c.
Their generous bosoms all dangers despis'd,
So highly, so wisely, their *Birthrights* they priz'd;
We'll keep what they give, we will piously keep,
Nor frustrate their toils on the land and the deep.
  In Freedom we're born, &c.
The Tree their own hands had to liberty rear'd;
They liv'd to behold growing strong and rever'd;

With transport they cry'd, "now our wishes
For our children shall gather the fruits of ou
  In Freedom we're born &c.
Swarms of placemen and pensioners soon
Like locusts deforming the charms of the
Suns vainly will rise, Showers vainly des
If we are to drudge for what others shall
  In Freedom we're born &c.
Then join hand in hand brave Americans
By uniting we stand, by dividing we fall
In so Righteous a cause let us hope to su

Overture to Revolution

1764-1775

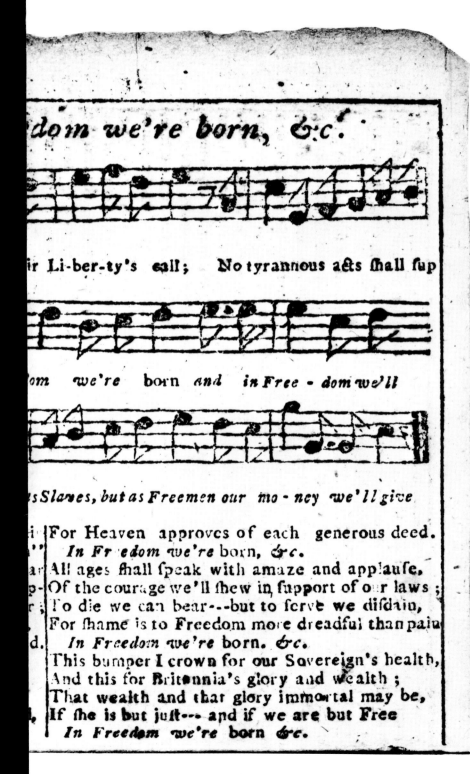

dom we're born, &c.

ir Li-ber-ty's call; No tyrannous acts shall sup

om we're born and in Free - dom we'll

s Slaves, but as Freemen our mo - ney we'll give

For Heaven approves of each generous deed.
    In Freedom we're born, *&c.*
All ages shall speak with amaze and applause.
Of the courage we'll shew in support of our laws ;
To die we can bear---but to serve we disdain,
For shame is to Freedom more dreadful than pain
    In Freedom we're born. *&c.*
This bumper I crown for our Sovereign's health,
And this for Britannia's glory and wealth ;
That wealth and that glory immortal may be,
If she is but just--- and if we are but Free
    In Freedom we're born *&c.*

The first patriotic music to be published in America was John Dickinson's "Liberty Song," which swept the colonies in 1768. Like all American resistance songs of the eighteenth century, Dickinson's stirring words were sung to a popular British tune, in this instance "Heart of Oak."

THE Boſton- AND COUNTRY Gazette, JOURNAL.

Containing the freſheſt Advices, Foreign and Domeſtic.

MONDAY, March 12, 1770.

Masthead of the Boston-Gazette, and Country Journal, *a Patriot newspaper,*
in whose columns the Stamp Act and later British taxation measures were opposed

At the curtain-raising Stamp Act Riot in Boston on August 14, 1765, the opening scene disclosed—hanging from the branches of the "Great Tree" (thenceforward known as the "Liberty Tree")—two effigies: one of Andrew Oliver, the newly appointed stamp distributor for the Province of Massachusetts Bay, and the other representing the recent British prime minister, Lord Bute, in the form of a boot (a visual pun on his name), out of which peeped his accomplice, the Devil. With or without diabolical collaboration, Bute was generally believed in America to have been the author of the infamous Stamp Act, the first oppressive British taxation measure to arouse violent resistance in the colonies. Americans, who proudly regarded themselves as full-fledged British subjects, signified their outrage at this assault on their "natural" constitutional rights by spontaneously organizing into militant groups called "Sons of Liberty." Throughout the thirteen colonies they reenacted, with inspired improvisations, the vivid deeds that were committed at the prototypal Boston event. British collaborators and sympathizers were "persuaded"—by molestation, intimidation, and coercion— to mend their ways. Their effigies were hanged wholesale from local liberty trees, and were often given mock funeral rites, after which they were burned. In most cases these lawless proceedings were conducted to the zestful accompaniment of the "liberty songs," sung to popular British tunes, that spontaneously began to materialize in newspapers and broadsides, or handbills.

Taking as its title the Sons of Liberty battle cry, "Liberty, Property, and No Excise," a broadside poem-cantata (two sections apparently were meant to be sung) commemorated Boston's thrilling August 14 premiere. In a blend of lofty and earthy verse it expressed both defiance and loyalty to the king, lauded America's supporter, William Pitt, and made a variety of puns on the word *stamp*. It was decorated with a minute engraving of Lord Bute's effigy, and it opened with these ringing lines:

> Let *Albion's* sons in praise their tongues employ;
> *New-England* smile, and *Boston* shout for joy:
> Despite of knaves, their politics and wit,
> She still enjoys her *LIBERTY* and *PITT*.
> She rests secure from ev'ry foreign foe,
> Derides their plots, and sees their overthrow;
> And soon shall see the wretch completely curs'd
> Who strove to *STAMP* her glory in the dust.
> "Freedom, (she cries) I cannot cringe to knaves,
> "My sons are free, and never will be slaves:"

The crowd that collected to gaze at the wonders in the tree was moved to express its satisfaction in song.

> This pleasing prospect entertains the throng,
> All join as one, and thus begin their song,
> "With grateful joy, O *Boston*, now behold
> "Those truths fulfill'd, which lately were foretold!
> "With thankful hearts now see the villains swing,
> "Who hate their country, and would sell their king:
> "Behold the man, *whose heart* was set on gain,
> "And view the wretch, who wish'd some tyrant's reign."

Liberty, Property, and no Excise.

A Poem,

Compos'd on occasion of the SIGHT seen on the GREAT TREES, (so called) in BOSTON, NEW-ENGLAND, on the 14th of AUGUST, 1765.

LET *Albion*'s sons in praise their tongues employ ;
New-England smile, and *Boston* shout for joy :
Spite of knaves, their politics and wit,
She still enjoys her *LIBERTY* and *PITT*.
She rests secure from ev'ry foreign foe,
Derides their plots, and sees their overthrow ;
And soon shall see the wretch completely curs'd
Who strove to *STAMP* her glory in the dust.
" Freedom, (she cries) I cannot cringe to knaves,
" My sons are free, and never will be slaves :"
Let tyrants rule with arbitrary sway,
Villains command, and whining fools obey :
Let dastards live in infamy and shame,
While *Britons* fight for liberty and fame :
Let all her foes like bees prepare to swarm ;
Old *Pluto* rage, and *Purgatory* storm :
Let *Charon* raise his oars and long-boat take,
And force with fury down the torrid lake.
Speak *Proserpine*, thy will shall be obey'd,
Bid ev'ry fiend forsake the gloomy shade :
Give these commands to each infernal ghost,
" Go spit your venom on the *British* coast ;
" Haste there and spread contention wide and far,
" Perplex her isle, and set her sons at war :
" Then to *America* with vengeance go,
" Let them in slavery own the powers below."
Suppose this done, and all the winged bands
At this new world with thunder in their hands :
Our hardy youth would still their force repel,
Defeat their wiles and drive them back to hell ;
These sons of *Mars* their courage would confound,
A conquest gain and still maintain their ground.
Then would e'en devils be compell'd to own
Our sovereign lives and God supports his throne :
Thus blast his foes in ev'ry base design
All-gracious heaven, and bless the royal line.
O give us favor in our monarch's eyes,
Defend our rights, remove the late *EXCISE* :
Let truth prevail and fierce oppression cease,
And bid our Prophet speak the words of peace.
Lo ! here he comes, softly he seems to tread,
Now rolls his eyes, now bows his rev'rend head :
He like a God appears in form divine,
Whose very aspect speaks some deep design ;
Hither he comes, on purpose to relate
Each sacred truth and tell some hidden fate,
" *Boston*, (he cries) your woes are at an end,
" Your foe shall fall and times shall quickly mend ;
" With shame o'erwhelm'd he soon shall hide his face,
" Then hark while I predict the time and place.
" The day now dawns, the gloomy night is spent,
" And soon your eyes shall see the grand event.
" See fair *Aurora* from her couch arise,
" Whose chearful blushes paints the morning skies :
" The shades are chac'd, the ling'ring stars are fled,
" And yonder *Phœbus* lifts his golden head :
" (Then cries the Prophet) I must haste away,
" The Gods command and mortals must obey."
No more I heard from out his sacred mouth,
He took his leave and went towards the *South* :
Then I beheld amazing wonders there,
Saw human shapes and monsters in the air.
A stately elm appear'd before my eyes,
Whose lofty branches seem'd to touch the skies ;
It's limbs were bent with more than common fruit,
It bore the Devil, *O——r*, and *B--te*.
Well then, said I, my doubts are wholly fled,
I find the truth of what the father said :
But while I stood to gaze upon the tree,
Another and another came to see ;
Each moment I beheld a diff'rent face,
For on they prest 'till thousands fill'd the place,
Here stands a child and looks with wond'ring eyes,
And there a champion of gigantic size ;
Yonder a maid at humbler distance stands,
And here a jilt with lifted eyes and hands.

This pleasing prospect entertains the throng,
All join as one, and thus begin their song,
" With grateful joy, O *Boston*, now behold
" Those truths fulfill'd, which lately were foretold !
" With thankful hearts now see the villains swing,
" Who hate their country, and would sell their king :
" Behold the man, *whose heart* was set on gain
" And view the wretch, who wish'd some tyrant's reign."
Thus I observ'd they entertain'd the day,
In songs and chat they past the hours away ;
Now *Sol* retires, and journies down the West,
And weary nature seems in sable dress.
And now a hero lifts his voice aloud,
Stretches his hand, and speaks to all the crowd.
" Hear me, (he cries) and be not too severe,
" Curst be the man that leaves the bodies here
" Expos'd to all the dangers of the night,
" Then bear them hence with every fun'ral right."
Thus having spoke, they all with willing hands
Began to execute their chief's commands :
With rapid haste some to the tree repair,
And on their shoulders bear a ladder there.
One draws his knife, and running to their aid,
Ascends the limbs, that bear each lifeless shade
Then cuts the ropes in presence of them all,
And as he cuts the ghastly *objects* fall.
Down on the earth in horrid form they lie ;
A frightful sight to each beholding eye :
What now, (said I) is all compassion fled ?
Can none be found, that will relieve the dead ?
Their chief reply'd, " Go place them on the bier ;
" Prepare yourselves and quickly bring them here."
This done, he cries, " Let ev'ry man resort
" In solemn order with the corps to *court*.
" March then, (said he) in one united throng,
" And as you march, be this the fun'ral song.
" Great *Jove* decrees, and go these mortals must ;
" 'Tis earth to earth, and *STAMP* 'em in the dust."
Then as they move, the words are sung by all,
Down to the *court* and thro' the pompous *hall* :
Soon after this arose a grand debate,
(Such oft' attend the fun'rals of the great)
And wild disorder seizes all the band ;
Forth some advance, while others make a stand.
One bids them halt, another " still march forth
" And visit all the region of the *North*."
A third proclaims, " Let these be first convey'd
" In peaceful silence to the dreary shade."
Then spake their head, (the regent of the night)
" Alas ! our host is in a shameful plight :
" Is this the way to get a hero's name ?
" The road to honor and immortal fame ?
" Cease wrangling then, let each in order stand,
" Join arm to arm, like one eternal band ;
" Then here (he cries) be all contention fled,
" Come follow on, your chief is at the head."
Thus having spake, all hear the wond'rous *man*,
And forth they move ; (the champion leads the van)
All seem impatient to obey his will,
And bend their course for the appointed *hill*,
Whose lofty summit once contain'd a *fort*,
To this they haste and quickly leave the *court*.
Freedom and friendship centers in each soul,
They shout and sing without the least controul :
Here then we find no obstacles arose,
Noise could offend, and nothing dare oppose,
(Nothing) except a stately *EDIFICE*,*
This stops their course, but soon they down with this ;
Low in the dust they made the structure lay,
Then *STAMPT* the bricks, and bore the wood away,
Now from the ruins ev'ry one retire,
Up to the *mount* and raise the fun'ral fire.

* Supposed to be built for a STAMP-OFFICE.

John Singleton Copley's cartoon "The Deplorable State of America," derived from a British cartoon of the same name, was described in the Massachusetts Gazette Extraordinary *(October 31, 1765) as "A caricatura, being a Representation of the Tree of Liberty, and the Distress of the present Days."*

Under the inspired guidance of such wizards of political propaganda as James Otis and Samuel Adams, the Sons of Liberty became the major political force in pre-Revolution America. Adams, who was described by the historian Samuel Eliot Morison as "the Western world's first orchestra leader of revolution," well understood how to captivate and activate the emotionally attuned public imagination. With virtuoso skill he devised and wielded a wide repertory of picturesque symbolism and ritual that came to dominate the politico-patriotic scene in the colonies. The Liberty Tree—and this meant everybody's local liberty tree—became the shrine for patriotic and community activities of all kinds. Not only was it used for hangings in effigy and harassment of officials, but it was also the scene of patriotic demonstrations, protest meetings, celebrations, denunciations of tyranny, picnics, drinking of patriotic toasts, dancing, feasting, and the singing of liberty songs. Sometimes the liberty tree was the scene of violence; the British resented its significance and occasionally made good their reiterated threats to cut it down.

Paul Revere's portrait of Samuel Adams, engraved in 1774, is framed by symbols of freedom as well as a musical cherub.

This Boston scene is described in the Boston Evening-Post (February 24, 1766) as "a Stage erected under LIBERTY TREE, having two Effigies thereon, one of them representing B--e, dressed in Plaid [Bute was a Scotsman], the other a Representation of G--e [General Thomas Gage, the British commander in chief for the colonies]; over them a Gallows, on which appeared the D---l [wearing a boot] handing a S---p A-t to B--e, and uttering these Words, Force it; to which he replies, We can't do it. . . ."

A n instant replay of the Boston drama was staged (with minor revisions) at Newport. In reviewing it the *Boston Evening-Post* reported (September 2, 1765) that "the populace brought forth the effigies of three persons in a cart . . . each of them with a rope around their necks, and carried them to a gallows about 20 feet high, placed near the townhouse on which they were exhibited to public view the whole day, where great numbers of people resorted. . . . On one of the Posts out of Reach, *Whoever attempts, in any Way whatsoever, to render ineffectual this Mark of public Contempt, will be deem'd an Enemy to Liberty, and incur the Resentment of the Town.*—On the other, at the same Height, the following SONG."

HE who for a Post, or base sordid Pelf,
His Country betrays, makes a Rope for himself;
Of this an Example before you we bring,
In these infamous Rogues, who in Effigy swing.

Huzza, my brave Boys!—every man stand his ground,
With Liberty's Praise let the Welkin resound;
Eternal Disgrace on those miscreants fall,
Who thro' Pride or for Wealth would ruin us all.

Let us make wise Resolves, & to them let's stand strong,
(Your Puffs and your Vapours do never last long)
To maintain our just Rights ev'ry measure pursue.
To our King we'll be loyal—to ourselves we'll be true.

Those Blessings our Fathers obtain'd by their blood,
We are justly oblig'd as their Sons to make good;
All internal Taxes let us then nobly spurn,
These Effigies first—next the Stamp Paper burn.

CHORUS. *Sing Tantarara, burn all, burn all,
Sing Tantarara, burn all.*

This issue of William Bradford's Pennsylvania Journal; and Weekly Advertiser *(October 31, 1765) announced suspension of publication because of the "insupportable Slavery"—newspapers were required to be printed on taxed, stamped paper. November 1, 1765, the day the obnoxious tax was scheduled to go into effect, was observed colonywide as a day of mourning, and funeral ceremonies for Liberty were enacted everywhere. The* Newport Mercury *(November 4, 1765) reported one of these "funerals," at which Liberty miraculously and symbolically revived at the moment of interment. His resurrection was celebrated with "Rejoicing, and Bells ringing . . . and the Evening Song was:*

The Birthright of Britons is FREEDOM,
The contrary is worse than Death's pangs:
　　HUZZA *for* GEORGE *the Third.*

CHORUS. *Britannia's Sons despise Slavery,
And dare to nobly free."*

Songs to celebrate repeal of the Stamp Act extolled King George and Pitt, while Lord Bute, Sir George Grenville (the British prime minister), and their villainous henchmen were execrated. They were usually consigned to the Devil who, incidentally, was widely credited with having helped to mastermind the whole abominable scheme. The following song, published in Philadelphia in 1766, featured a cast of characters that not only included Grenville, Bute, and the Devil, but also John Huske and Eve. Huske was a former Bostonian who had emigrated to England some years before and, surprisingly, become a member of Parliament. He was suspected by many Americans of having been the true author of the Stamp Act, and his effigy had inhabited its share of liberty trees during the recent troubles. Eve's involvement in the plot was purely incidental. In the text, the reference to Pitt's eloquence as "cheek music" is particularly beguiling.

A NEW SONG.

On the Repeal of the Stamp-Act.

Tune, A late worthy old Lyon.

Of old times we read how the De'il tempted Eve
And told her fine stories, which she did believe;
How in eating the apple, 'twould open her eyes,
And make her quite happy, as well as quite wise.
    Taral Laddey, &c.

She eagerly listen'd and gap'd at the fruit,
And swallow'd it down, but alas! 'twould not suit:
The Devil was victor, be that as it will,
He tempted her just as he tempted Gr.nv.ll.
    Taral Laddey, &c.

Quoth the Devil to Gr.nv.ll I've drawn up a plan,
And think in my conscience that thou art the MAN;
When e'er I intend any evil to do
You may always be sure I will pitch upon you.
    Taral Laddey, &c.

O'er-joy'd at the news like a courtier polite,
He thanked the Devil, and thought all was right;
Expecting large share, of the profits in fact,
Arising by virtue of the *Noble Stamp-Act—*
    Taral Laddey, &c.

This tickled his fancy, he tho't it would suit,
To commune with his *friends,* such as H.sk and dear B.te.
Who pleas'd with the *Scheme,* on wickedness bent,
All three to the Devil they lovingly went.
    Taral Laddey, &c.

The Devil surpriz'd and almost struck mute
Yet rejoic'd at the sight of his *old friend,* J.hn B.te:
He kindly receiv'd them for better or worse,
And told them be sure put the Stamp-Act in *force.*
    Taral Laddey, &c.

Recommended it strongly as a *Scheme* that would fit,
But told them like Devils to *out-brazen* PITT,
And not fail to oppose *him* on ev'ry occasion,
Else his *tongue* like the serpents would beguile the
  whole nation.
    Taral Laddey, &c.

Now alas! it is truth tho' odd it doth seem,
From old Devils, young Devils certainly came;
The old Devil *plann'd* it, but H.sk, Gr.nv.ll and B.te
Three Devils *incarnate* were to execute.
    Taral Laddey, &c.

But behold! *one* arises, unrival'd in MERIT!
With *eloquence* fitted to his noble spirit:
With the sound of *cheek music,* this politick *Messiah,*
Knock'd Gr.nv.lle quite stiff, as did *David, Goliah.*
    Taral Laddey, &c.

Now rejoice ye *Americans,* they're left in the lurch,
Fairly slung by the *Devil,* no friend to the *church;*
Conspicuous PITT! stands and displays truth as his shield,
Come give him a bumper, *the Stamp-Act's repeal'd.*
    Taral Laddey, &c.

Long life to great PITT see the bumpers do smile,
A *statue erect* for his *labour* and *toil;*
Let his name be *immortal* and ne'er be forgot,
Whilst those of his *foes* do corrupt, stink and rot.
    Taral Laddey, &c.

A bumper ye SONS of LIBERTY ALL,
Let's drink and let's pray, ye great and ye small,
May the *gout* and the *stone* and whatev'r ye will,
Leave the GOOD patriot PITT, and take *root* in Gr.nv.lle,
    Taral Laddey, &c.

Now jointly with PITT let's bid Gr.nv.lle defiance,
And laugh at their *Devilish quadruple* alliance:
May they now in *good earnest* not in effigy swing,
Then we LIBERTY's SONS will *triumphantly* sing.
    Taral Laddey, &c.

Thus you see from whose *hands* the *Stamp-Act* first came,
And which of those *four Devils* was most to blame:
The old serpent plann'd, but H.sk, Gr.nv.lle and B.te,
Two *Traytors,* and a *Rebel,* beat old *Cloven-foot.*
    Taral Laddey, &c.

From an undated broadside

When the Stamp Act was repealed the news
was received in the colonies with unbounded
jubilation. Cannon were fired, bells rung,
flags flown, feasts held, toasts drunk
(particularly to George III and William
Pitt, who had argued in Parliament for repeal),
and great celebrations were held beneath
festively decorated liberty trees, where, of
course, liberty songs were sung.

Resistance songs—however subversive—were as a matter of course sung to popular or traditional British tunes. To the English colonists this music was a part of their cultural heritage, just as singing it for political protest was a part of their natural birthright. Topical texts were sung in eighteenth-century America to just about every conceivable variety of British tune, from hymns to bawdy ditties to "God Save the King." If this seems incongruous, we should remember that we still sing "My Country, 'tis of Thee" to the tune of the British national anthem, and what's more, our own national anthem is set to an eighteenth-century English drinking song, "To Anacreon in Heaven."

Stormy local political issues were fought out not only in debates but in bitter newspaper and pamphlet wars and in vicious lampoons in verse and song. A broadside, *The Election, A Medley, Humbly Inscribed to Squire Lilliput, Professor of Scurrillity*, both graphically and musically chronicles the events of the hotly contested 1764 election in Pennsylvania. Written in fourteen separate sections to nine different popular tunes (five were reprised), it also shows, in a vivacious cartoon, the assembled voters (among them Benjamin Franklin) at the polling place, the State House in Philadelphia. The scurrilous "Squire Lilliput" was James Dove, a Philadelphia schoolmaster and libelous pamphleteer, who had been locked in mortal pamphlet-combat with Isaac Hunt (the future father of Leigh Hunt). Hunt is believed to have written *The Election, A Medley*. Franklin, who missed reelection to the Assembly by twenty-five votes, is lauded in two sections of the medley, both set to the versatile tune of "God Save the King." One of them goes:

O Lord our God Arise!
  Scatter our Enemies.
And make them fall:
  Confound their Politicks,
Frustrate such Hypocrites;
  Franklin, on thee we Fix,
  God save us all.

*This manuscript copy of "God Save the King,"
from* John Greenwood's Book, *dates from the Revolution.*

22

After the fashion of the period, this portrait of James Otis on the frontispiece of Bickerstaff's Boston Almanack *for 1770 was flanked by allegorical figures symbolizing liberty. The Phrygian liberty cap on a spear was an omnipresent prop in contemporary graphics of a political nature.*

In turbulent Massachusetts Bay Province the larger political conflict with the mother country was closely intertwined with violent local politics and politicking. Important behind-the-scenes political manipulation took place at meetings of the "Caucus Club" in Tom Dawes's garret, the prototype of the smoke-filled room. There, according to John Adams, tobacco was smoked, flip drunk, and selectmen, assessors, and representatives were chosen. A disgruntled former member had somewhat vindictively referred to it as the "Cork-ass." Boston's radical leaders, Samuel Adams and James Otis, were, of course, principal members. Just before the spring elections of 1765 James Otis, who was running for reelection in the Massachusetts House of Representatives, was outrageously attacked in a song, "Jemmibullero," that appeared in the *Boston Evening-Post* (May 13, 1765). The lampoon was attributed to Samuel Waterhouse, an alcoholic Boston customsman and Tory, who was described by a contemporary as "the most notorious scribbler, satirist, and libeller in the service of the conspirators against the liberties of America." The title of his song referred to "Lilliburlero," the old tune with a nonsense refrain that had played a subversive role in seventeenth-century England and that was now a subject of a pamphlet squabble between Otis and Martin Howard, a Tory lawyer from Newport.

In the text, the reference to "Jemmy" as a "Cooper's vessel" is a pun on the name of Otis's political colleague, William Cooper, the Boston town clerk; "Jemmy's Dad" is Colonel Otis, who had been in and out of political office a number of times. He was currently in, and it was generally believed that he had gained his appointment through his son's complicity, a belief that nearly cost the younger Otis the election.

"Jemmibullero" is a parody of "Lilliburlero" in name only; the tune does not fit, and Waterhouse did not specify to which British music his song should be sung.

A FRAGMENT OF AN
ODE OF ORPHEUS;

Freely translated from the original Tongue, and
adapted to British Music.

BY PETER MINIM, Esq;

And Jemmy is a silly dog, and Jemmy is a tool.
And Jemmy is a stupid cur, and Jemmy is a fool,
And Jemmy is a madman, and Jemmy is an ass.
And Jemmy has a leaden head, & forehead spread with brass.
   Sing tititumti, tumtititi, tititumti, tee,
   And tumtititi, tititumti, tumtiprosodee.

And Jemmy is a lying dog and Jemmy is a thief,
And Jemmy is a jury-mouther,—Jemmy spouts his brief,
And Jemmy is a grammar-smith, and Jemmy is a grub,
And Jemmy is a Cooper's vessel—Jemmy is a tub.
   Sing tititumti, tumtititi, tititumti, tee,
   And tumtititi, tititumti, tumtiprosodee.

Jemmy's a town-meeting-man, & Jemmy makes a speech,
Jemmy swears that LIBERTY and LIBERTY he'll preach,
And Jemmy's in the CAUCUS, and Jemmy's with the REPS,
And all who'd rise as Jemmy rose must tread in Jemmy's steps.
   Sing tititumti, tumtititi, tititumti, tee,
   And tumtititi, tititumti, tumtiprosodee.

And Jemmy is a surly dog, and Jemmy is a clown,
And Jemmy is an ugly whelp as e'er a one in town,
And Jemmy's a malicious dog,—you see it in his look,
And Jemmy's scribbled politics, & Jemmy's burnt his book.
   Sing tititumti, tumtititi, tititumti, tee,
   And tumtititi, tititumti, tumtiprosodee.

And Jemmy's an abusive dog, and Jemmy has been bang'd,
And Jemmy's had a bloody nose, & Jemmy has been hang'd,
And Jemmy's been dissected, and Jemmy's been explor'd
And Jemmy is detested as Jemmy was ador'd.
   Sing tititumti, tumtititi, tititumti, tee,
   And tumtititi, tititumti, tumtiprosodee.

~~~

As Jemmy is an envious dog, and Jemmy is ambitious,
And rage and slander, spite and dirt to Jemmy are delicious,
So Jemmy rail'd at *upper folks* while Jemmy's DAD was out,
But Jemmy's DAD has now a *place*, so Jemmy's turn'd about.
   Sing tititumti, tumtititi, tititumti, tee,
   And tumtititi, tititumti, tumtiprosodee.

~~~

And Jemmy thinks his counter-talk will render Jemmy safe;
But Jemmy is a stupid fellow—Jemmy is a calf:
Tho' Jemmy was outrageous, Sir, yet Jemmy will get clear,
For Jemmy's most contemptible where Jemmy's most severe.
   Sing tititumti, tumtititi, tititumti, tee,
   And tumtititi, tititumti, tumtiprosodee.

Since Jemmy loves no music, and Jemmy hates a song,
'Tis Jemmy may have music and music all day long:
For Jemmy is a filthy scunk, and Jemmy's a rackoon,
And I cou'd Jemmy, Jemmy, Jemmy, Jemmy it till noon.
   Sing tititumti, tumtititi, tititumti, tee,
   And tumtititi, tititumti, tumtiprosodee.

~~~

In 1768 Waterhouse again invoked his malevolent muse against Otis, who by now was organizing American resistance against the latest British taxation inequities, the Townshend laws. In a new song, "Jemmicumjunto," Waterhouse lived up to his pseudonymous role of "Surveyor and Controller of the Fire-Works" by unleashing a dazzling display of syllabic pyrotechnics. In a "general grand chorus" to end all general grand choruses he concocted a masterpiece of nonsense syllables, employing a technique known as "fa-la" in the sixteenth century and "scat-singing" in the twentieth. In the text, a *chamade* is a signal given by beat of drum or sound of trumpet to invite parley with the enemy. From the *Boston Evening-Post* (January 11, 1768):

JEMMICUMJUNTO,
An ODE

FOR the NEW-YEAR 1768.
BY HENRY SCRATCH'EM, Esq.
Director General of the Ordnance, and
Surveyor and Controller of the Fire-Works.

When *Jemmicumjunto* first drew out his blade,
   Tod*dletum*, tod*dletum*, tod*dletum*, *toddy*!
He swore that he never wou'd beat the chamade:
   Tod*dletum*tum, *tum*tum*toddle*, *oddy*!
But ah when the Crisis of trial is come
He puts up his dagger and muffles his drum.
   Tul*der o*! lud*dy*, tul*der o*! *luddy*,
   Tud*dletum*tum, *tum*tumder*uddle luddy*!

While flaunting & taunting & flashing & show!
   Tod*dletum*, tod*dletum*, tod*dletum*, *toddy*!
How much he wou'd do, and how far he wou'd go!
   Tod*dletum*tum, *tum*tum*toddle oddy*!
Ah! what is become of his skips & his hops,
His huffs & his dings & his puffs & his pops?
   Tul*der o*! lud*dy*, tul*der o*! *luddy*,
   Tud*dletum*tum, *tum*tumder*uddle luddy*!

He'd *write* and he'd *fight*, and he'd *die* for us all,
   Tod*dletum*, tod*dletum*, tod*dletum*, *toddy*!
Our freedom he'd raise, and the GREAT he wou'd maul!
   Tod*dletum*tum, *tum*tum*toddle*, *oddy*!
But alas! things are suffer'd to keep their old course,
And we must still take them for better or worse!
   Tul*der o*! lud*dy*, tul*der o*! *luddy*,
   Tud*dletum*tum, *tum*tumder*uddle luddy*!

~~~

Since this our *wild* BOOBIES have dealt all-along,
   Tod*dletum*, tod*dletum*, tod*dletum*, *toddy*!
We'll express our contempt of the *Jemmy-joined* Throng,
   Tod*dletum*tum, *tum*tum*toddle*, *oddy*!
We despise all their *Tricks*! all their *Cant*! & their *Trade*!
Their clatter and spatter, huzza! and parade!
   Tul*der o*! lud*dy*, tul*der o*! *luddy*,
   Tud*dletum*tum, *tum*tumder*uddle luddy*!

~~~

GENERAL GRAND CHORUS.
Sing riddletum, tiddletum, fiddletum, fag!
Twiddletum, thriddletum, quiddletum quiddy;
And niddletum, diddletum, briddletum brag!
Thwiddletum, squiddletum, giddletum giddy!
With a rattletum, twattletum, tittletum tat,
And a battletum, flattletum, spittletum spat!
   Tulder o! luddy, tulder o! luddy,
   Tuddletumtum, tumtumderuddle, luddy!

John Dickinson's twelve *Letters from a Farmer in Pennsylvania to the Inhabitants of the British Colonies* exerted an overwhelming impact on American political thought and emotions during the crisis over the Townshend taxes. Dickinson, a conservative establishment lawyer in Philadelphia and a gentleman farmer by avocation, surprisingly introduced the radical ideology that Britain had no right to impose taxes of any kind on the colonies. His *Farmer's Letters*, first published serially in 1767–1768 in the *Pennsylvania Chronicle, and Universal Advertiser*, were instantly reprinted in virtually every newspaper in the thirteen colonies. As a pamphlet the collected *Farmer's Letters* were printed and reprinted, devoured, and argued about not only in America but in England and on the Continent as well. Americans regarded the *Farmer's Letters* as political gospel and the "Farmer" as a hero. "By uniting we stand, by dividing we fall" was his credo, and when he set it to music, all America fervently sang his words.

In his editor's preface to Bickerstaff's Boston Almanack for 1769, Isaac Bickerstaff—a pseudonym borrowed from Dean Jonathan Swift by the well-known astronomer and almanac maker (not the painter) Benjamin West—pridefully noted the inclusion of "the new and Favourite Liberty Song, neatly engraved and set to Musick for the Voice, to which are added the words." If the "neatly engraved" notes look primitive to twentieth-century eyes, it should be remembered that this is one of the first American publications, if not the very first, of secular music. Until the late 1780s music-printing technology in America was minimal, as were composers. Like all topical songs of the period, Dickinson's song was meant to be sung to a familiar tune, in this case "Heart of Oak," a stirring air originally composed in 1759 by William Boyce to words by David Garrick. With Dickinson's words the tune became America's first national hymn, even before she became a nation.

26

This frontispiece portrait of John Dickinson appeared in some copies of the third pamphlet edition of his Letters from a Farmer in Pennsylvania.

At the height of the furor over his *Farmer's Letters*, Dickinson astutely commented on the value of sung propaganda in a letter to James Otis (July 4, 1768). He wrote: "I inclose you a song for American freedom . . . songs are frequently very powerful on certain occasions. . . . Cardinal de Retz always inforced his political operations by songs." Adding that he hoped his own song would not offend by its "boldness," the conservative Dickinson apparently already had misgivings. Only two days later he forwarded "a corrected copy, which I like better," to Otis, saying that he thought the first version, "composed in great haste . . . rather too bold." In case it had already gone to press, he asked that a retraction be published together with the new version, which contained an added stanza. Whatever other changes he might have made remain a tantalizing mystery since no copy of a bolder first version is known to have been found.

John Dickinson created as forcible an impact with his "Liberty Song" as he had with his *Farmer's Letters*. By popular insistence it was printed and reprinted throughout the colonies. The "Liberty Song" became an obsession, being sung everywhere: at political demonstrations, protest meetings, patriotic celebrations, dedication ceremonies for liberty trees, for pure enjoyment, and also for nuisance value to enrage the British and their American sympathizers. Without the added stanzas, but otherwise apparently approved by Dickinson, its text was first published as a broadside by the Philadelphia printers Hall and Sellers; it was immediately reprinted, appearing simultaneously in the *Pennsylvania Gazette* and the *Pennsylvania Journal* (July 7, 1768) and in New York and Boston newspapers later that month. At Dickinson's request the complete "Liberty Song" appeared in the *Pennsylvania Chronicle* (July 11, 1768). The new stanza, inserted after stanza four, seems no less "bold" than the others.

> How sweet are the labors that Freemen endure,
> That *they* shall enjoy all the Profit, secure—
> No more such sweet Labors AMERICANS know
> If Britons shall *reap* what Americans sow.
> In FREEDOM we're BORN, &c.

Mein and Fleeming, the publishers of Bickerstaff's Boston Almanack, *advertised an earlier sheet music publication of the "Liberty Song" in the* Boston Chronicle *(August 29–September 5, 1768), but no copy seems to have survived.*

27

Paul Revere engraved this cartoon depicting the infamous Seventeen (one of them pig-headed) being assisted by two devils into the fearsome portals of their rightful abode, Hell. The ironic verse beneath the engraving is ironic in a double sense: its author, Dr. Benjamin Church, was eventually discovered to be a less than pure American Patriot.

By the time the "Liberty Song" had begun to sweep the colonies, Boston was in the throes of a new series of crises. Early in June of 1768 irate Bostonians had so riotously protested when John Hancock's sloop *Liberty* was seized on a charge of smuggling that the members of the British Establishment were forced to flee for safety to Castle William, the fortress in Boston harbor. There they remained, awaiting the arrival of the military protection that an alarmed Governor Sir Francis Bernard had requested from the home government. Passions, already at fever pitch, were further exacerbated when the Massachusetts Assembly was dismissed by order of Lord Hillsborough, the secretary of state for the colonies. Defying the ministry's command that they rescind a circular letter in which they had urged the united resistance of the other twelve colonies to the oppressive Townshend laws, the Assembly voted ninety-two to seventeen against rescission. Their consequent dismissal provided the creative leaders of the Sons of Liberty with superb material for a new set of ritualistic patriotic symbols, a numerology in which the number ninety-two was exalted as a sublime symbol of freedom, while seventeen was despised as a mark of treason.

The "Gentlemen belonging to the Insurance-Office" in Salem who commissioned this patriotic silver bowl from Paul Revere dedicated it with a "genteel Entertainment, and invited a Number of Gentlemen of Distinction in the Town, when 45 Toasts were drank, and the whole concluded with a new Song, the Chorus of which is, In Freedom we're born, and in Freedom we'll live, &c." Salem's Essex Gazette (August 2–9, 1768) further reported that the "Liberty Bowl" weighed forty-five ounces and held forty-five jills.

The numerology was applied in extraordinary ways. At a dedication of a liberty tree at Petersham, the *Boston Evening-Post* (September 26, 1768) reported that the Sons of Liberty convened "at forty-five Minutes past two o'clock, P.M. . . . having made the choice of a beautiful young Elm, they cut off [and burned] 17 useless Branches," leaving, by a happy coincidence, ninety-two perfectly formed and admirable branches, under which the "Liberty Song" was duly performed. In Charlestown (now Charleston), South Carolina, according to another story reprinted in the *Boston Evening-Post* (November 7, 1768), when the "principal Mechanicks" of the town met to consecrate a live oak to liberty, the ceremonies began with a rendition of the "celebrated Liberty Song. . . . at dark the tree was ornamented with 45 lights, and fireworks played off. . . ." After "suitable toasts" they marched off, "preceded by 45 of their number, each carrying a lighted candle. . . . opposite the house of the Lieut. Governor, they drew up before the door, and . . . gave the toast of the *Massachusetts Ninety-Two* . . . they proceeded to Dillon's tavern . . . where 45 candles were placed on the table, and 92 glasses were applied in resounding the voices of as many loyal toasts." The party broke up, the *Evening-Post* restrainedly concluded, in "mirth and jollity." And the numerology made a social as well as a patriotic impact. At a wedding ball in New London, again reported by the *Boston Evening-Post* (June 26, 1769), ninety-two gentlemen and ladies attended and danced ninety-two "jiggs," forty-five minuets, and seventeen hornpipes. The company retired at forty-five minutes past midnight.

A song in praise of the immortal Ninety-two was inevitable; it appeared in the *Pennsylvania Journal* (August 4, 1768), and it was, of course, widely reprinted in New England newspapers. Preceded by an epigraph comprising some of William Pitt's most stirring pro-American words, it glorified the brave Sons of Liberty (one of whom was its author) in its first stanza, and lauded the "glorious Ninety-two" and the "Beloved Farmer" while it vividly damned the despicable Seventeen in its last.

A SONG.

Addressed to the SONS OF LIBERTY on the Continent of America; particularly to the illustrious, glorious, never to be forgotten NINETY-TWO of BOSTON.

"The Americans are the Sons, not the Bastards
"of England; the *Commons* of *America*, represented
"in their several Assemblies, have ever been in
"Possession of the Exercise of *this their Con-*
"*stitutional Right*, of GIVING and GRANTING their
"own Money; they would have been SLAVES if they
"had not enjoyed it."
Mr. PITT'S *Speech.*

Tune "Come, Jolly Bacchus," &c.
or "Glorious first of August."

Come, jolly SONS OF LIBERTY—
  Come ALL, with Hearts UNITED,
Our motto is, "WE DARE BE FREE,"
  Not easily affrighted!
Oppression's Band we must subdue,
  Now is the Time, or *never*;
Let each man PROVE this Motto true,
  And SLAV'RY from him sever.

Now, FARMER dear, we'll fill to you,
  May Heav'n its Blessings show'r,
As on the glorious NINETY-TWO,
  But Seventeen devour—
Mean abject *Wretches!—Slaves in Grain!*
  How dare ye shew your Faces?
To latest days *go drag your Chain!*
  Like *other* MULES or ASSES!
A SON OF LIBERTY.

Forty-five was added to the numerology in honor of John Wilkes, the radical English journalist and member of Parliament, who was regarded as a hero in the colonies for his ardent championship of American causes. When he was imprisoned for having criticized the king and Parliament in the forty-fifth issue of his periodical the North Briton, *he adopted the number forty-five as his talisman, and it was immediately embraced in the colonies as yet another emblem of opposition to tyranny. This portrait of Wilkes, surrounded by appropriate symbols of freedom, appeared as the frontispiece of Bickerstaff's* Boston Almanack *for 1769.*

Tory feelings, outraged by the unremitting repetition of Dickinson's "Liberty Song," found release in a bitterly scurrilous parody that was simultaneously published in the *Boston Gazette* and the supplement extraordinary to the *Boston Evening-Post* (September 26, 1768), just a few days before the British troops arrived in Boston in response to Governor Bernard's summons. Becoming known simply as "The Parody," it was, of course, intended to be sung to the tune of "Heart of Oak." The *Evening-Post* sardonically referred to its supposed place of origin, Castle William, with the caption: "A Parody upon the well known LIBERTY SONG (Said to be in great Vogue at a certain Fortress, where it was compos'd)."

"A View of Castle William By Boston in New England . . . ,"
line engraving credited to William Burgis

In the text: "Belzee" is a pet name for Beelzebub; "Tyburn' is the British place of execution; *Bunters* are low women a *regale* is a choice refreshment. The *Boston Gazette* version was headed:

Last Tuesday the following SONG
made its Appearance from the Garret
at C-st-e W-----m.

Come shake your dull Noddles, ye Pumpkins and bawl,
And own that you're mad at fair Liberty's Call.
No scandalous Conduct can add to your Shame.
Condemn'd to Dishonor, Inherit the Fame—
 In Folly you're born, and in Folly you'll live,
  To Madness still ready,
  And Stupidly steady,
 Not as Men, but as Monkies, the Tokens you give.

Your Grandsire, old Satan, now give him a Cheer,
Would act like yourselves, and as wildly would steer;
So great an Example in Prospect still keep,
Whilst you are alive, old Belzee may sleep.
 In Folly, &c.

Such Villains, such Rascalls, all Dangers despise:
And stick not at Mobbing, when Mischief's the Prize.
They burst thro' all Barriers, and Piously keep,
Such Chattels and Goods the vile Rascalls can sweep.
 In Folly, &c.

The Tree which the Wisdom of Justice hath rear'd,
Should be stout for their Use, and by no Means be spar'd:
When fuddled with Rum, the mad Sots to restrain,
Sure Tyburn will sober the Wretches again.
 In Folly, &c.

Your Brats and your Bunters, by no Means forget,
But feather your Nests, for they're bare enough yet;
From the insolent Rich, sure the poor Knave may steal,
Who ne'er in his Life knew the Scent of a Meal.
 In Folly, &c.

When in your own Cellars you've quaff'd a Regale,
Then drive, tugg, and stink the next House to assail.
For short is your Harvest, nor long shall you know,
The Pleasure of Reaping what other Men sow.
 In Folly, &c.

Then plunder, my Lads, for when Red Coats appear,
You'll melt like the Locusts, when Winter is near:
Gold vainly will glow; Silver vainly will shine:
But, Faith you must skulk, you no more shall purloin.
 In Folly, &c.

Then nod your poor Numbskulls, ye Pumpkins & bawl,
The De'il take such Rascalls, Fools, Whoresons and all.
Your cursed old Trade of purloining must cease,
The Curse and the Dread of all Order and Peace.
 In Folly, &c.

All Ages shall speak with Contempt and Amaze,
Of the vilest Banditti that swarm'd in those Days:
In Defiance of Halters, of Whips, and of Chains,
The Rogues would run Riot, damn'd Fools for their Pains.
 In Folly, &c.

Gulp down your last Dram, for the Gallows now groans,
And Order depress'd her lost Empire bemoans;
While we quite transported and happy shall be,
From Mobs, Knaves, and Villains, protected and free.
 In Folly, &c.

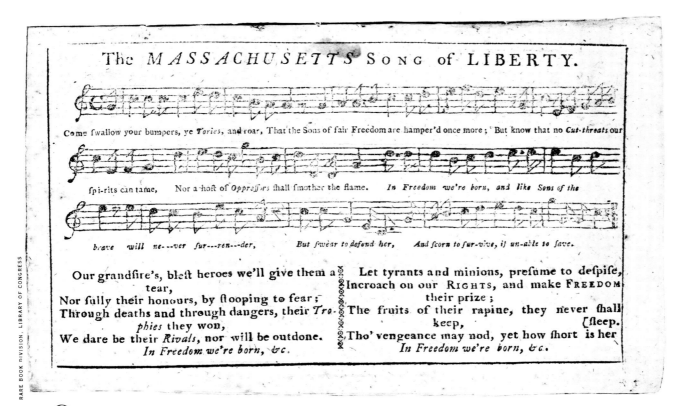

The MASSACHUSETTS SONG of LIBERTY.

Come fwallow your bumpers, ye *Tories*, and roar, That the Sons of fair Freedom are hamper'd once more; But know that no *Cut-throats* our

fpi-rits can tame, Nor a hoft of *Oppreffors* fhall fmother the flame. *In Freedom we're born, and like Sons of the*

brave will ne---ver fur---ren---der, But fwear to defend her, And fcorn to fur-vive, if un-able to fave.

Our grandfire's, bleft heroes we'll give them a
tear,
Nor fully their honours, by ftooping to fear;
Through deaths and through dangers, their *Tro-*
phies they won,
We dare be their *Rivals*, nor will be outdone.
In Freedom we're born, &c.

Let tyrants and minions, prefume to defpife,
Incroach on our RIGHTS, and make FREEDOM
their prize;
The fruits of their rapine, they never fhall
keep, [fleep.
Tho' vengeance may nod, yet how fhort is her
In Freedom we're born, &c.

Only a few days after firing the first salvo, both the *Boston Evening-Post* and the *Boston Gazette* (October 3, 1768) discharged another volley in the parody war: "The Parody Parodiz'd," also called "The Massachusetts Liberty Song," again to "Heart of Oak." Its author was the highly respected Patriot physician and writer Dr. Benjamin Church, who had composed the verse for Revere's cartoon "A Warm Place—Hell" (see page 28). It later astoundingly turned out that Dr. Church had all along been a traitor masquerading in patriot's clothing. He is believed to have written Tory rebuttals to a number of patriotic American writings and songs, some of them his own. Becoming active as a British agent after hostilities broke out in 1775, Church's treason was discovered, and he was tried and found guilty at a court martial presided over by George Washington. Too ill to be imprisoned, Church was paroled and eventually was granted permission to leave the country. The ship on which he sailed for the West Indies was lost at sea. It is intriguing to speculate whether Dr. Church might not himself have written the parody that he parodied.

As the number two Patriot song hit—it never quite equalled the phenomenal success of Dickinson's song—"The Massachusetts Liberty Song" appeared in musical score when the astute editor of Bickerstaff's Boston Almanack superimposed Dr. Church's words on his "neatly engraved" music plate of the year before and published it in his 1770 issue.

John Adams, in his Diary, *reported hearing both Dickinson's and Church's liberty songs at a great political rally: "Dined with three hundred and fifty Sons of Liberty, at Robinson's, the sign of the Liberty Tree, in Dorchester. . . . After dinner was over and the toasts drunk . . . we had . . . the Liberty Song—that by the farmer, and that by Dr. Church, and the whole company joined in the chorus. This is cultivating the sensations of freedom." John Norman engraved this portrait of Adams for the* Boston Magazine *(February 1784).*

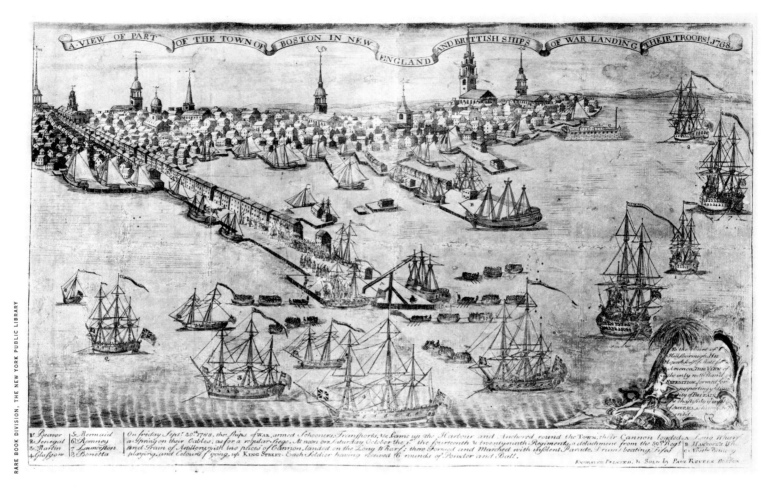

Paul Revere accompanied his famous engraving (published in 1770) of the arrival of the British troops at Boston with a vivid description of the landing. On disembarking, he wrote, they "formed and marched with insolent Parade, Drums beating, Fifes playing, and Colours flying. . . ." In all probability the fifers were tootling "Yankee Doodle." The New-York Journal; or, the General Advertiser *(October 13, 1768) reported:*

"The Fleet was brought to anchor near Castle William; that evening [September 29, 1768] there was throwing of Sky Rockets, and those passing in boats observed great Rejoicing, and that the Yankey Doodle Song [at that time considered a bitter insult to Americans] was the Capital Piece in their Band of Music."

It is impossible to determine just when and how the British acquired their predilection for needling the colonists with "Yankee Doodle." Even the origin of the tune and title has stubbornly defied discovery, despite the massive scholarly research and controversy "Yankee Doodle" has provoked through the centuries. Ascribed to a variety of sources—English, Dutch, Irish, Hungarian, Hessian, Basque, and Indian, to name a few—we still don't know where "Yankee Doodle" really came from. Wherever or whenever it first appeared in America, and whatever its ancestry, we do know that the British insulted Americans to its merry strains in the 1760s (perhaps even earlier) until the merry strains alone—even without words—came to be regarded as an affront. Which offensive words were used, however, is not known, since "Yankee Doodle" was for a long time disseminated only by oral transmission, undergoing many unrecorded extemporaneous changes.

The generally supercilious British attitude toward the colonists is recorded in both fact and legend. A popular but apocryphal tale, dating from the early nineteenth century, credited a Dr. Shuckburgh, a surgeon supposedly attached to General Amherst's (or General Abercrombie's) staff in the 1750s, during the French and Indian War, with having been so amused by the unmilitary, ragamuffin appearance of the colonial soldiers assigned to his regiment that he composed a mocking little song about them ("Yankee Doodle") to entertain his elegant messmates. Perhaps a more realistic clue to an earlier American text is offered by the first publication of "Yankee Doodle" as sheet music, which was not until 1775, when a variant version of the tune was brought out, of all places, in London (see page 52). Issued just after the battles of Lexington and Concord, and conceived as anti-American propaganda, it began with a derisive stanza in a nasal, mock-Yankee dialect about a Yankee coward back in the time of the French and Indian War. If this is an example of the kind of words the British sang during their occupation of Boston in 1768, it is understandable that the mere sound of the tune would have caused the Yankees, who were proud of their brave showing in Canada, to cringe.

Brother Ephraim sold his Cow
 And bought him a Commision,
And then he went to Canada
 To fight for the Nation;
But when Ephraim he came home
 He proved an arrant Coward,
He wou'd'n't fight the Frenchmen there
 For fear of being devour'd.

This unfavorable comment on the quality of Yankee participation in the French and Indian War is thought by some scholars to have been derived from some earlier narrative ballad version or versions that might have been sung in America as early as the 1740s or '50s, but no surviving contemporary documentation has been found to prove it. A later undated broadside, "Yankee Song," probably published in the early nineteenth century (see next page), closely resembles the unflattering British version in its opening stanzas, while in others it suggests textual elements of a number of different "Yankee Doodle" versions believed to have originated during the Revolution. Which version really came from which, or when it originated, remains a typically tantalizing "Yankee Doodle" mystery. Whatever its vintage, "Yankee Song" offers a unique refrain. In the text, the "lasses" that were lapped at the "lection" festivities at "uncle Chace's" were the kind from which rum was distilled; apparently the printer couldn't decide on a consistently satisfactory spelling for the word *father*.

Just when Yankee Doodle first came riding on his pony into town is not known. His trip was not recorded in print in America until well into the nineteenth century. Oscar Sonneck, the great musicologist, tells us, however, that back in

the time of Oliver Cromwell an air was sung, called "The Roundheads and the Cavaliers," that resembled "Yankee Doodle" in structure and meter, but not in tune. It had an alternate set of lyrics which went:

Nankee Doodle came to town
 Upon a little pony,
With a feather in his hat
 Upon a macaroni.

Macaroni was an eighteenth-century term for fop. Sonneck also reports a nonsense stanza of uncertain origin that has since been quoted in varying versions:

Yanker didel, doodel down
 Didel, dudel lanter,
Yanke viver, voover, vown
 Botermilk und tanther.

In occupied Boston in 1769 the untrammeled occupiers indulged their infatuation with "Yankee Doodle" in curious ways. The *Boston Evening-Post* (March 20, 1769) reported:

The *court concert* of the last evening was it seems, turned topsy turvy. . . . Some officers of the army were for a little *dancing* after the music, and being told that G------r B-----d did not approve of their proposal, they were for sending him home to eat his *bread* and *cheese*, and otherwise treated him as if he had been a mimick G------r; they then called out to the band to play the *Yankee Doodle* tune . . . and not being gratified they grew noisy and clamorous; the candles were then extinguished, which instead of checking, completed the confusion; to the no small terror of the *weaker sex*, who made part of the company. The old honest music master . . . was roughly handled by one of those sons of Mars; he was actually in danger of being *throatled*, but *timeously* rescued by one who soon threw the officer on lower ground than he at first stood upon. . . .

Detail of a page with " 'Yankey' Doodle" from a manuscript tune-book belonging to the Reverend James Pike, a pastor in Somersworth, New Hampshire, in 1730

YANKEE SONG.

THERE is a man in our town,
I'll tell you his condition,
He sold his Oxen and his Cows
To buy him a commission.
CHORUS.
Corn-stalk twist your hair off,
Cart-wheel frolic round you,
Old fiery dragon carry you off,
And mortar pestle pound you.

When a commission he had got
He prov'd to be a coward,
He durst not go to Canada
For fear of being devoured.

But farther and I went down to camp
Along with Captain Goodwin,
And there we saw the men and boys
As thick as Hastypudding.

And there they had a little kegg,
The heads were made of leather,
They knock't upon't with little clubs
To call the folks together.

There I saw a swamping gun
As big's a log of maple,
Put upon two little wheels
A load for Father's cattle.

Every time they fired it off
It took a horn of powder,
It made a noise like Farther's gun
And rung a nation louder.

I went so nigh to get a peep
I saw the under-pinning—
Father went as nigh again,
I thought the duce was in him.

Brother Si he grew so bold
I thought he would have cock'd it,
He hook't around the other side
And hung by Father's pocket.

There they had another thing,
Father call'd a mortar;
It look'd like mother's porrage pot,
It held a pail of water.

I saw a man a talking there
You might heard to the barn sir,
Hallooing and scolding too—
The deal of one would do.

There he kept a riding round
Upon a spanking Stallion,
And all the people standing round,
A thousand or a million.

He had a ribbon on his hat,
It looked nation fine sir!
I wanted it most ducedly
To give to my Jemima.

My Jemima's very sick,
I'm sure there's something aile
She use'd to eat her supper
But now her stomach fails

Brother Si is gone to town
With a load of shingles,
And if he can't have lasses for't
He says he'll break a window.

For brother Jo is come to town,
He's gon't to nock them all off,
He plays upon a swamping fiddle
As big as Father's hog trough.

Husking time is coming on
They all begin to laugh sir—
Father is a coming home
To kill the heifer calf sir.

Lection time is now at hand,
We're going to uncle Chace's,
There'l be some a drinking round
And some a lapping lasses.

Now husking time is over
They have a duced frolic,
There'l be some as drunk as sots
The rest will have the cholic.
CHORUS.
Corn stalks twist your hair off,
Cart wheel frolic round you,
Old fiery dragon carry you off,
And mortar pestle pound you.

YANKEE SONG.

There is a man in our town,
I'll tell you his condition,
He sold his Oxen and his Cows
To buy him a commission.

   CHORUS.
Corn-stalks twist your hair off,
Cart-wheel frolic round you,
Old fiery dragon carry you off,
And mortar pessel pound you.

When a commission he had got
He prov'd to be a coward,
He durst not go to Canada
For fear of being devoured.

But farther and I went down to camp
Along with Captain Goodwin,
And there we saw the men and boys
As thick as Hastypudding.

And there they had a little kegg,
The heads were made of leather,
They rapt upon't with little clubs
To call the folks together.

There I saw a swamping gun
As big's a log of maple,
Put upon two little wheels
A load for Father's cattle.

Every time they fired it off
It took a horn of powder,
It made a noise like Farther's gun
And rung a nation louder.

I went so nigh to get a peep
I saw the under-pinning—
Father went as nigh again,
I thought the duce was in him.

Brother Si he grew so bold
I thought he would have cock'd it,
He hook't around the other side
And hung by Father's pocket.

There they had another thing,
Father call'd a mortar;
It look'd like mother's porrage pot,
It held a pail of water.

I saw a man a talking there
You might heard to the barn sir,
Hallooing and scolding too—
The deal of one would answer.

There he kept a riding round
Upon a spanking Stallion,
And all the people standing round,
A thousand or a million.

He had a ribbon on his hat,
It looked nation fine sir!
I wanted it most ducedly
To give to my Jemima.

My Jemima's very sick,
I'm sure there's something ails her
She use'd to eat her supper up
But now her stomach fails her.

Brother Si is gone to town
With a load of shingles,
And if he can't have lasses for't
He vows he'll breed a wrangle.

For brother Jo is come to town,
He's gon't to nock them all off,
He plays upon a swamping fiddle
As big as Father's hog trough.

Husking time is coming on
They all begin to laugh sir—
Father is a coming home
To kill the heifer calf sir.

Lection time is now at hand,
We're going to uncle Chace's,
There'l be some a drinking round
And some a lapping lasses.

Now husking time is over
They have a duced frolic,
There'l be some as drunk as sots
The rest will have the cholic.

   CHORUS.
Corn stalks twist your hair off,
Cart wheel frolic round you,
Old fiery dragon carry you off,
And mortar pessel pound you.

*Dr. Joseph Warren, after a portrait
by John Singleton Copley*

Dr. Joseph Warren, the luminous Boston patriot, vividly captured the intrepid Boston spirit of the time in his ringing, swinging song, set to the tune of "The British Grenadiers." "The New Massachusetts Liberty Song" was another great popular success, and it enjoyed a long life, being reprinted in songsters as late as the mid-nineteenth century. Dr. Warren's song was performed by the versatile New England musician Josiah Flagg at Boston Concert-Hall on February 13, 1770, as we learn from Edes and Gill's *North American Almanack; and Massachusetts Register for the Year 1770,* where it was reprinted, along with Dickinson's and Church's liberty songs. America pronounced "Amerikay" was a frequently used rhyming device. Dr. Warren's song was brutally parodied:

In Bedlam, lofty Numbers discordant Yankies sing,
And twang in awful Ditty, God save our Gracious King
May they leave off their canting, and with devotion pray,
Have Mercy, Mercy, Mercy Lord on poor America.

An early English edition of "The British 'Granadiers'"

THE NEW *MASSACHUSETTS*

LIBERTY SONG,

[*To the Tune of the* Britilh Grenadier.]

I.

THAT Seat of Science ATHENS, and Earth's great Miltrefs ROME,
    Where now are all their Glories, we fcarce can find their Tomb :
Then guard your Rights, AMERICANS ! nor ftoop to lawlefs Sway,
Oppofe, oppofe, oppofe, oppofe,——my brave AMERICA.

II.

Proud ALBION bow'd to *Cæfar*, and num'rous *Lords* before,
To *Picts*, to *Danes*, to *Normans*, and many Malters more :
But we can boalt AMERICANS ! we never fell a Prey ;
Huzza, huzza, huzza, huzza, for brave AMERICA.

III.

We led fair FREEDOM hither, when lo the *Defart* fmil'd,
A Paradife of Pleafure, was open'd in the Wild ;
Your Harveft bold AMERICANS ! no Power fhall fnatch away,
Affert yourfelves, yourfelves, yourfelves, my brave AMERICA.

IV.

Torn from a World of Tyrants, beneath this weftern Sky,
We form'd a new Dominion, a *Land* of LIBERTY ;
The World fhall own their Malters here, then haften on the Day,
Huzza, huzza, huzza, huzza, for brave AMERICA.

V.

GOD blefs this maiden Climate, and thro' her vaft Domain,
Let Holts of Heroes clufter, who fcorn to wear a Chain :
And blaft the venal Sycophant, who dares our Rights betray,
Preferve, preferve, preferve, preferve my brave AMERICA.

VI.

Lift up your Heads my Heroes ! and fwear with proud Difdain,
The Wretch who would enflave you, fhall fpread his Snares in vain ;
Should EUROPE empty all her Force, wou'd meet them in Array,
And fhout, and fhout, and fhout, and fhout, for brave AMERICA.

VII.

Some future Day fhall crown us, the Malters of the Main,
And giving Laws and Freedom, to fubject FRANCE and SPAIN ;
When all the ISLES o'er Ocean fpread, fhall tremble and obey,
Their Lords, their Lords, their Lords, their Lords of brave AMERICA.

[A]n Account of a late Military Maſſacre at Boſton, or the Conſequences of Quartering Troops in a populous well-regulated Town, taken from the [Bo]ſton-Gazette, of March 12, 1770.

BOSTON, March 12, 1770.

THE Town of Boſton affords a recent and melancholy Demonſtration of the deſtructive Conſequences of quartering Troops among Citizens in a Time of Peace, under a Pretence of ſupporting the Laws and aiding Civil Authority; every conſiderate and unprejudic'd Perſon among us was deeply impreſt with the Apprehenſion of theſe Conſequences when it was known that a Number of Regiments were ordered to this Town under ſuch a Pretext, but in Reality to inforce oppreſſive Meaſures; to awe and controul the legiſlative as well as executive Power of the Province, and to quell a Spirit of Liberty, which however it may have been baſely oppos'd and even ridicul'd by ſome, would do Honor to any Age or Country. A few Perſons amongſt us had determin'd to uſe all their Influence to procure ſo deſtructive a Meaſure with a View to their ſecurely enjoying the Profits of an American Revenue, and unhappily both for Britain and this Country they found Means to effect it.

It is to Governor Bernard, the Commiſſioners, their Confidents and Coadjutors, that we are indebted as the procuring Cauſe of a military Power in this Capital—The Boſton Journal of Occurrences, as printed in Mr. Holt's York Gazette, from Time to Time, afforded many ſtriking Inſtances of the Diſtreſſes brought upon the Inhabitants by this Meaſure; and ſince thoſe Journals have been diſcontinued, our Troubles from that Quarter have been growing upon us: We have known a Party of Soldiers in the face of Day fire off a loaden Muſket upon the Inhabitants, others have been prick'd with their Bayonets, and even our Magiſtrates aſſaulted and put in Danger of their Lives, when Offenders brought before them have been reſcued; and why thoſe and other bold and baſe Criminals have as yet eſcaped the Puniſhment due to their Crimes, may be ſoon Matter of Enquiry by the Repreſentative Body of this People—It is natural to ſuppoſe that when the Inhabitants of this Town ſaw thoſe Laws which had been enacted for their Security, and which they were ambitious of holding up to the Soldiery, eluded, they ſhould more commonly reſent for themſelves—and accordingly it has ſo happened; many have been the Squabbles between them and the Soldiery; but it ſeems their being often worſted by our Youth in thoſe Rencounters, has only ſerv'd to irritate the former—What paſſed at Mr. Gray's Rope-walk, has already been given the Public, and may be ſaid to have led the Way to the late Cataſtrophe—That the Rope-walk Lads when attaked by ſuperior Numbers ſhould defend themſelves with ſo much Spirit and Succeſs in the Club-way, was too mortifying, and perhaps it may hereafter appear, that even ſome of their Officers were *unhappily* affected with this Circumſtance: Divers Stories were propagated among the Soldiery, that ſerv'd to agitate their Spirits; particularly on the Sabbath, that one Chambers, a Serjeant, repreſented as a ſober Man, had been miſſing the preceeding Day, and muſt therefore have been murdered by the Townſmen; an Officer of Diſtinction ſo far credited this Report, that he enter'd Mr. Gray's Rope-walk that Sabbath; and when required of by that Gentleman as ſoon as he could meet him, the Occaſion of his ſo doing, the Officer reply'd, that it was to look if the Sergeant ſaid to be murdered had not been hid there; this ſober Sergeant was found on the Monday unhurt, in a Houſe of Pleaſure—The Evidences already collected ſhew, that many Threatnings had been thrown out by the Soldiery, but we do not pretend to ſay that there was any preconcerted Plan, when the Evidences are publiſhed, the World will judge—We may however venture to declare, that it appears too probable from their Conduct, that ſome of the Soldiery aimed to draw and provoke the Townſmen into Squabbles, and that they then intended to make Uſe of other Weapons than Canes, Clubs or Bludgeons.

Our Readers will doubtleſs expect a circumſtantial Account of the tragical Affair on Monday Night laſt; but we hope they will excuſe our being ſo particular as we ſhould have been, had we not ſeen that the Town was intending an Enquiry and full Repreſentation thereof.

On the Evening of Monday, being the 5th Current, ſeveral Soldiers of the 29th Regiment were ſeen parading the Streets with their drawn Cutlaſſes and Bayonets, abuſing and wounding Numbers of the Inhabitants.

A few minutes after nine o'clock, four youths, named Edward Archbald, William Merchant, Francis Archbald, and John Leech, jun. came down Cornhill together, and ſeperating at Doctor Loring's corner, the two former were paſſing the narrow alley leading to Murray's barrack, in which was a ſoldier brandiſhing a broad ſword of an uncommon ſize againſt the walls out of which he ſtruck fire plentifully. A perſon of a mean countenance armed with a large cudgel bore him company. Edward Archbald admoniſhed Mr. Merchant to take care of the ſword, on which the ſoldier turned round and ſtruck Archbald on the arm, then puſhed at Merchant and pierced thro' his cloaths inſide the arm cloſe to the arm-pit and grazed the ſkin. Merchant then ſtruck the ſoldier with a ſhort ſtick he had, and the other Perſon ran to the barrack and bro't with him two ſoldiers, one armed with a pair of tongs the other with a ſhovel: he with the tongs purſued Archbald back thro' the alley, collar'd and laid him over the head with the tongs. The noiſe bro't people together, and John Hicks, a young lad, coming up, knock'd the ſoldier down, but let him get up again; and more lads gathering, drove them back to the barrack, where the boys ſtood ſome time as it were to keep them in. In leſs than a minute 10 or 12 of them came out with drawn cutlaſſes, clubs & bayonets, and ſet upon the unarmed boys and young folks, who ſtood them a little while, but finding the inequality of their equipment diſperſed.—On hearing the noiſe, one Samuel Atwood, came up to ſee what was the matter, and entering the alley from dock-ſquare, heard the latter part of the combat, and when the boys had diſperſed he met the 10 or 12 ſoldiers aforeſaid ruſhing down the alley towards the ſquare, and aſked them if they intended to murder people? They anſwered Yes, by G—d, root and branch! With that one of them ſtruck Mr. Atwood with a club, which was repeated by another, and being unarmed he turned to go off, and received a wound on the left ſhoulder which

The BLOODY MASSACRE perpetrated in King-Street BOSTON on March 5th 1770 by a party of the 29th REGT

Unhappy BOSTON! ſee thy Sons deplore,
Thy hallow'd Walks beſmear'd with guiltleſs Gore:
While faithleſs P—n and his ſavage Bands,
With murd'rous Rancour ſtretch their bloody Hands;
Like fierce Barbarians grinning o'er their Prey,
Approve the Carnage, and enjoy the Day.

If ſcalding drops from Rage from Anguiſh Wrung,
If ſpeechleſs Sorrows lab'ring for a Tongue,
Or if a weeping World can ought appeaſe
The plaintive Ghoſts of Victims ſuch as theſe;
The Patriot's copious Tears for each are ſhed,
A glorious Tribute which embalms the Dead.

But know, FATE ſummons to that awful Goal,
Where JUSTICE ſtrips the Murd'rer of his Soul:
Should venal C—ts the ſcandal of the Land,
Snatch the relentleſs Villain from her Hand,
Keen Execrations on this Plate inſcrib'd,
Shall reach a JUDGE who never can be brib'd.

The unhappy Sufferers were Meſs.rs SAM.L GRAY, SAM.L MAVERICK, JAM.S CALDWELL, CRISPUS ATTUCKS & PAT.K CARR *Killed. Six wounded; two of them* (CHRIST.R MONK & JOHN CLARK) *Mortally*

reached the bone and gave him much pain. Retreating a few ſteps, Mr. Atwood met two officers and ſaid, Gentlemen, what is the matter? They anſwered, you'll ſee by and by. Immediately after, thoſe heroes appeared in the ſquare, aſking where were the boogers? where were the cowards? But notwithſtanding their fierceneſs to naked men, one of them advanced towards a youth who had a ſplit of a raw ſtave in his hand, and ſaid damn them here is one of them; but the young man ſeeing a perſon near him with a drawn ſword and good cane ready to ſupport him, held up his ſtave in defiance, and they quietly paſſed by him up the little alley by Mr. Siſby's to Kingſtreet, where they attacked ſingle and unarmed perſons till they raiſed much clamor, and then turned down Cornhill ſtreet, inſulting all they met in like manner, and purſuing ſome to their very doors. Thirty or forty perſons mostly lads, being by this means gathered in King ſtreet, Capt. Preſton, with a party of men with charged bayonets, came from the main guard to the commiſſioners houſe, the ſoldiers puſhing their bayonets, crying, Make way! They took place by the cuſtom-houſe, and continuing to puſh to drive the people off, pricked ſome in ſeveral places; on which they were clamorous, and, it is ſaid, threw ſnow-balls. On this, the Captain commanded them to fire, and more ſnow-balls coming, he again ſaid, Damn you, Fire, be the conſequence what it will! One ſoldier then fired, and a townſman with a cudgel ſtruck him over the hands with ſuch force that he dropt his firelock; and ruſhing forward aimed a blow at the Captain's head, which graz'd his hat and fell pretty heavy upon his arm: However, the ſoldiers continued the fire, ſucceſſively, till 7 or 8, or as ſome ſay 11 guns were diſcharged.

By this fatal manœuvre, three men were laid dead on the ſpot, and two more ſtruggling for life; but what ſhewed a degree of cruelty unknown to Britiſh troops, at leaſt ſince the houſe of Hanover has directed their operations, was an attempt to fire upon or puſh with their bayonets the perſons who undertook to remove the ſlain and wounded!

Mr. Benjamin Leigh, now undertaker in the Delph Manufactory, came up, and after ſome converſation with Capt. Preſton, relative to his conduct in this affair, adviſed him to draw off his men, with which he complied.

The dead are Mr. Samuel Gray, killed on the ſpot, the ball entering his head and beating off a large portion of his ſkull.

A mulatto man, named Criſpus Attucks, who was born in Framingham, but lately belonged to New-Providence and was here in order to go for North-Carolina, alſo killed inſtantly; two balls entering his breaſt, one of them in ſpecial goring the right lobe of the lungs, and a great part of the liver moſt horribly.

Mr. James Caldwell, mate of Capt. Morton's veſſel, in like manner killed by two balls entering his back.

Mr. Samuel Maverick, a promiſing youth of 17 years of age, ſon of the Widow Maverick, and an apprentice to Mr. Greenwood, Ivory-Turner, mortally wounded, a ball went through his belly, and was cut out at his back: He died the next morning.

A lad named Chriſtopher Monk, about 17 years of age, an apprentice to Mr. Walker, Shipwright; wounded a ball entered his back about 4 inches above the left kidney, near the ſpine, and was cut out of the breaſt on the ſame ſide; apprehended he will die.

A lad named John Clark, about 17 years of age, whoſe parents live at Medford, and an apprentice to Capt. Samuel Howard of this town; wounded, a ball entered juſt above his groin and came out at his hip, on the oppoſite ſide, apprehended he will die.

Mr. Edward Payne, of this town, Merchant, ſtanding at his entry-door, received a ball in his arm, ſhattered ſome of the bon[es].

Mr. John Green, Taylor, coming up Leverett's Lane, received a ball juſt under his hip, and lodged in the under part of his thigh, which was extracted.

Mr. Robert Patterſon, a ſeafaring man, who was the perſon that had his trowſers ſhot through in Richardſon's affair, wounded; a ball went thro' his right arm, and he ſuffered great loſs of blood.

Mr. Patrick Carr, about 30 years of age, who work'd with Mr. Field, Leather-Breeches-maker in Queen-ſtreet, wounded, a ball enter'd near his hip and went out at his ſide.

A lad named David Parker, an apprentice to Mr. Eddy the Wheelwright, wounded, a ball entered in his thigh.

The People were immediately alarmed with the Report of this horrid Maſſacre, the Bells were ſet a Ringing, and great Numbers ſoon aſſembled at the Place where this tragical Scene had been acted; their Feelings may be better conceived than expreſs'd; and while ſome were taking Care of the Dead and Wounded, the Reſt were in Conſultation what to do in thoſe dreadful Circumſtances.—But ſo little intimidated where they, notwithſtanding their being within a few Yards of the Main-Guard, and ſeeing the 29th Regiment under Arms, and drawn up in King-Street; that they kept their Station and appear'd as an Officer of Rank expreſs'd it ready to run upon the very Muzzles of their Muſkets.—The Lieut. Governor ſoon came into the Town-Houſe, and there met ſome of his Majeſty's Council, and a Number of Civil Magiſtrates; a conſiderable Body of the People immediately entered the Council Chamber, and expreſſed themſelves to his Honor with a Freedom and Warmth becoming the occaſion. He uſed his utmoſt Endeavours to pacify them, requeſting that they would let the Matter ſubſide for the Night, and promiſing to do all in his Power that Juſtice ſhould be done, and the Law have its Courſe; Men of Influence and Weight with the People were not wanting on their part to procure their Compliance with his Honor's Requeſt by repreſenting the horrible Conſequences of a promiſcuous and raſh Engagement in the Night, and aſſuring them that ſuch Meaſures ſhould be entered upon in the Morning as would be agreeable to their Dignity, and a more likely way of obtaining the beſt Satiſfaction for the Blood of their Fellow-Townſmen.—The Inhabitants attended to theſe Suggeſtions, and the Regiment under Arms being ordered to their Barracks, which was inſiſted upon by the People, they then ſeparated and returned to their Dwellings by One o'Clock, at 3 o'Clock Capt. Preſton was committed, as were the Soldiers who fir'd, a few Hours after him.

Tueſday Morning preſented a moſt ſhocking Scene, the Blood of our Fellow Citizens running like Water thro' King-Street, and the Merchants Exchange the principal Spot of the Military Parade for about 18 Months paſt. Our Blood might alſo be track'd up to the Head of Long-Lane, and through divers other Streets and Paſſages.

At eleven o'clock the inhabitants met at Faneuil-Hall, and after ſome animated ſpeeches becoming the occaſion, they choſe a Committee of 15 reſpectable Gentlemen to wait upon the Lieut. Governor in Council, to requeſt of him to iſſue his Orders for the immediate removal of the troops

The Meſſage was in theſe Words:

THAT it is the unanimous opinion of this meeting that the inhabitants and ſoldiery can no longer live together in ſafety; that nothing can rationally be expected to reſtore the peace of the town and prevent further blood and carnage, but the immediate removal of the Troops; and that we therefore moſt fervently pray his Honor that his power and influence may be exerted for their inſtant removal.

His Honor's Reply, which was laid before the Town then Adjourn'd to the Old South Meeting-Houſe, was as follows,

Gentlemen,

I AM extremely ſorry for the unhappy differences between the inhabitants and troops, and eſpecially for the action of the laſt evening, and I have exerted myſelf upon that occaſion that a due enquiry may be made, and that the law may have its courſe. I have in council conſulted with the commanding officers of the two regiments who are in the town. They have their orders from the General at New-York. It is not in my power to countermand thoſe orders. The Council have deſired that the two regiments may be removed to the Caſtle. From the particular concern which the 29th regiment has had in your differences, Col. Dalrymple who is the commanding officer of the troops has ſignified that that regiment ſhall without delay be placed in the barracks at the Caſtle until he can ſend to the General and receive his further orders concerning both the regiments, and that the main guard ſhall be removed, and the 14th regiment ſo diſpoſed and laid under ſuch reſtraint that all occaſion of future diſturbances may be prevented.

The foregoing Reply having been read and fully conſidered—the queſtion was put, Whether the Report be ſatisfactory? Paſſed in the Negative, (only 1 diſſentient) out of upwards of 4000 Voters.

It was then moved & voted that John Hancock, Eſq; Mr. Samuel Adams, Mr. William Molineux, William Phillips, Eſq; Dr. Joſeph Warren, Joſhua Henſhaw, Eſq; and Samuel Pemberton, Eſq; be a Committee to wait on his Honour the Lieut. Governor, and inform him, that it is the unanimous Opinion of this Meeting, that the Reply made to a Vote of the Inhabitants preſented his Honor in the Morning, is by no means ſatisfactory; and that nothing leſs will ſatisfy, than a total and immediate removal of all the Troops.

The Committee having waited upon the Lieut. Governor agreeable to the foregoing Vote; laid before the Inhabitants the following Vote of Council received from his Honor.

His Honor the Lieut. Governor laid before the Board a Vote of the Town of Boſton, paſſed this Afternoon, and then addreſſed the Board as follows.

Gentlemen of the Council,

"I lay before you a Vote of the Town of Boſton, which I have juſt now received from them, and I now aſk your Advice what you judge neceſſary to be done upon it.

The Council thereupon expreſſed themſelves to be *unanimouſly* of opinion, "that it was abſolutely neceſſary for his Majeſty's ſervice, the good order of the Town, and the Peace of the Province, that the Troops ſhould be immediately removed out of the Town of Boſton, and thereupon adviſed his Honor to communicate this Advice of the Council to Col. Dalrymple, and to pray that he would order the Troops down to Caſtle-William." The Committee alſo informed the Town, that Col. Dalrymple, after having ſeen the Vote of Council, ſaid to the Committee, "That he now gave his word of Honor that he would begin his Preparations in the Morning, and that there ſhould be no unneceſſary delay until the whole of the two Regiments were removed to the Caſtle."

Upon the above Report being read, the Inhabitants could not avoid expreſſing the high Satisfaction it afforded them.

After Meaſures were taken for the Security of the Town in the Night by a ſtrong Military Watch, the Meeting was Diſſolved.

The 29th Regiment have already left us, and the 14th Regiment are following them, ſo that we expect the Town will ſoon be clear of all the Troops. The Wiſdom and true Policy of his Majeſty's Council and Col. Dalrymple the Commander appear in this Meaſure. Two Regiments in the midſt of this populous City; and the Inhabitants juſtly incenſed: Thoſe of the neighbouring Towns actually under Arms upon the firſt Report of the Maſſacre, and the Signal only wanting to bring in a few Hours to the Gates of this City many Thouſands of our brave Brethren in the Country, deeply affected with our Diſtreſſes, and to whom we are greatly obliged on this Occaſion—No one knows where this would have ended, and what important Conſequences even to the whole Britiſh Empire might have followed, which our Moderation and Loyalty upon ſo trying an Occaſion, and our Faith in the Commander's Aſſurances have happily prevented.

Laſt Thurſday, agreeable to a general Requeſt of the Inhabitants, and by the Conſent of Parents and Friends, were carried to their *Grave* in Succeſſion, the Bodies of *Samuel Gray, Samuel Maverick, James Caldwell,* and *Criſpus Attucks*, the unhappy Victims who fell in the bloody Maſſacre of the Monday Evening preceeding!

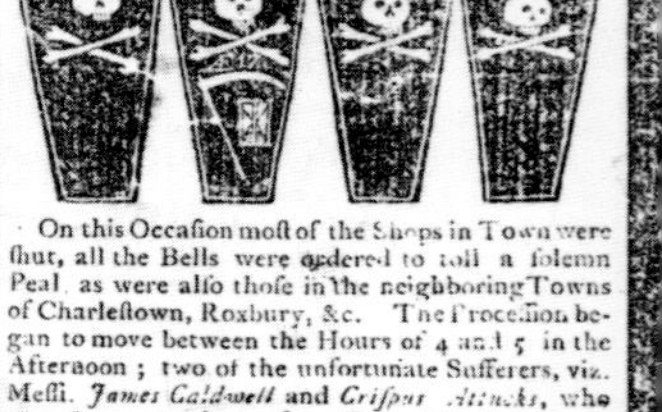

On this Occaſion moſt of the Shops in Town were ſhut, all the Bells were ordered to toll a ſolemn Peal, as were alſo thoſe in the neighboring Towns of Charleſtown, Roxbury, &c. The Proceſſion began to move between the Hours of 4 and 5 in the Afternoon; two of the unfortunate Sufferers, viz. Meſſ. *James Caldwell* and *Criſpus Attucks*, who were Strangers, borne from Faneuil-Hall, attended by a numerous Train of Perſons of all Ranks; and the other two, viz. Mr. *Samuel Gray*, from the Houſe of Benjamin Gray, (his Brother) on the North-ſide the Exchange, and Mr. *Maverick*, from the Houſe of his diſtreſſed Mother Mrs. *Mary Maverick*, in Union-Street, each follow'd by their reſpective Relations and Friends: The ſeveral Hearſes forming a Junction in King-Street, the Theatre of that inhuman Tragedy! proceeded from thence thro' the Main-Street, lengthened by an immenſe Concourſe of People, ſo numerous as to be obliged to follow in Ranks of ſix, and brought up by a long Train of Carriages belonging to the principal Gentry of the Town. The Bodies were depoſited in one Vault in the middle Burying-ground: The aggravated Circumſtances of their Death, the Diſtreſs and Sorrow viſible in every Countenance, together with the peculiar Solemnity with which the whole Funeral was conducted, ſurpaſs Deſcription.

BOSTON, March 19.

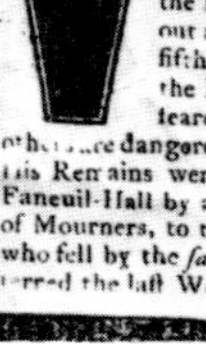

Laſt Wedneſday Night died, *Patrick Carr*, an Inhabitant of this Town, of the Wound he received in King-Street on the bloody and execrable Night of the 5th Inſtant—He had juſt before left his Home, and upon his coming into the Street received the fatal Ball in his Hip which paſſed out at the oppoſite Side; this is the fifth Life that has been ſacrificed by the Rage of the Soldiery, but it is feared it will not be the laſt, as ſeveral others are dangerouſly languiſhing of their Wounds. His Remains were attended on Saturday laſt from Faneuil-Hall by a numerous and reſpectable Train of Mourners, to the *ſame* Grave, in which thoſe who fell by the *ſame* Hands of Violence were interred the laſt Week.

NEW-YORK HISTORICAL SOCIETY

After nine months of essentially military rule General Thomas Gage, the British commander in chief, unwisely decided that Boston had been sufficiently tamed, and he transferred two of his regiments to Halifax. The remaining troops were given a hard time by the Bostonians, whose original hostility was further incited by dreadful atrocity stories circulated by Samuel Adams. Clashes repeatedly broke out, culminating in serious violence on March 5, 1770, when troops were goaded into firing at a mob of "Liberty Boys" and waterfront toughs, with whom they had been brawling. Five men were killed and a number of others wounded in what immediately became known as the "Boston Massacre." Patriot leaders demanded that the remaining troops be removed for "the good order of the Town, and the Peace of the Province" (*Boston Gazette*, October 12, 1770). The troops were duly sent to Castle William.

While interned at Castle William, one Briton took out some of his frustrations in a wistful, saber-rattling little song, published in the *Boston Gazette* (March 26, 1770), with special rancor directed against John Hancock.

A NEW SONG.
(Lately compos'd on Castle Island)
At present said to be much in Vogue among the *Caledonians.*

You simple Bostonians, I'd have you beware,
Of your Liberty Tree I would have you take Care:
For if that we chance to return to the Town,
Your Houses and Stores will come tumbling down.
 Derry down, down, hey, derry down.

If you will not agree to Old England Laws,
I fear that K--g H-----k will soon get the yaws:
But he need not fear, for I swear we will,
For the want of a Doctor, give him a hard Pill.
 Derry down, &c.

A brave Reinforcement, we soon think to get;
Then we will make you poor Pumpkins to sweat:
Our Drums they'll rattle, and then you will run
To the Devil himself, from the sight of a Gun.
 Derry down, &c.

Our Fleet and our Army, they soon will arrive,
Then to a bleak Island, you shall not us drive.
In every House, you shall have three or four,
And if that will not please you, you shall have half a score.
 Derry Down, &c.

John Hancock was Boston's leading capitalist and a staunch supporter of the Sons of Liberty. These credentials entitled "King Hancock," as the British derisively called him, to a preferred position on their "enemies list." This portrait of Hancock was engraved by Paul Revere in 1774.

Paul Revere's famous reportage of the Boston Massacre was "borrowed" from an original design by Henry Pelham. On the same black-bordered page of the Boston Gazette *(March 12, 1770) where it first appeared were five coffins to commemorate the five victims of the tragedy.*

In February 1770 the New York Sons of Liberty purchased a site for their new Liberty Pole when the City Corporation refused them permission to raise it where the old one had stood. The original pole, erected to commemorate the repeal of the Stamp Act, had been cut down and the pieces vindictively piled up in front of Liberty Hall by British troops after the bloody fighting at Golden Hill on January 18, 1770. The raising of the new pole was satirized in a wicked medley, The Procession, With the Standard of Faction. Pierre Eugène Du Simitière's cartoon of the new Liberty Pole, raised after the postelection violence in New York, shows a wolf in sheep's clothing (presumably a visual pun on the name of the New York Patriot leader John Lamb) plaintively bleating at the base of the pole.

Alexander McDougall, one of the leaders of the New York Sons of Liberty, was imprisoned for sedition in February 1770, when his fiery broadside attacking the newly elected conservative Assembly, To the Betrayed Inhabitants of the City and Colony of New York, was "secretly" circulated all over town. In prison he was so greatly lionized by Patriots that he was forced to set up a schedule of visiting hours to accommodate the hordes of admirers who clamored to see him. Dubbing him the "American Wilkes," the number forty-five was invoked in his honor, and it was exercised in exceptional ways. For example, the New-York Journal (March 22, 1770) reported that a delegation of forty-five New York virgins paid him their respects in prison. After partaking of suitable refreshments of tea and chocolate, they serenaded him with a timely adaptation of the forty-fifth psalm. McDougall's portrait is a miniature on ivory by John Ramage.

THE
PROCESSION,
WITH THE
STANDARD
OF
FACTION:
A CANTATA.

RECITATIVE.

'TWAS on the Morn when *Virtue* wept to see
 Discord stalk forth in Robes of *Liberty*,
The Sons of FACTION met, (a ghastly Band!)
To fix their *Standard* in our bleeding Land.
Pleas'd with the *Play Thing* roar'd the youthful Train,
Wond'ring their Parents had grown *young* again.
High o'er the rest bra' *Champion* SAWNEY stood,
The *brazen Trumpet* of the *Factious Brood*;
He wav'd his Hand, ... three Times hem'd aloud,
And thus in soothing Strains address'd the Crowd:
AIR. (*Thro' the Wood, Laddie.*)
I.
'Guid People, it grieves your poor SAWNEY to tell,
 How much it did teize me,
 And sadly displease me,
Prepar'd for a Meeting when t'other *Pole* fell.
How thro' the *Fields*, Laddies, I wander'd mysel.
II.
But now with what Joy shall I daily espy,
 This Pole gaily standing,
 Attendance commanding,
When *Ketch*, proudly hanging his Victims hard by,
Shall not have as many Spectators as I.
III.
Bra' *Johnny* has often complain'd with a Sigh,
 At our slender Banditti,
 The Dregs of the City;
But now with our Numbers we'll give Fame the Lie,
As thro' the *Fields*, Laddies, we noisily hie.
IV.
O Laddies, pray silence starch B******'s loud Knell,
 Tho' Fate in his *Caput*,
 Has naething at a' put,
Yet still Night and Morning, he rattles pell mell,
As if not a *Creature* cou'd speak but himsel.

To the Sons of Liberty in this City.

GENTLEMEN,

IT'S well known, that it has been the Custom of all Nations to erect Monuments to perpetuate the Remembrance of grand Events. Experience has proved, that they have had a good Effect on the Posterity of those who raised them, especially such as were made sacred to Liberty. Influenced by these Considerations, a Number of the Friends to Liberty in this City, erected a Pole in the Fields, on Ground belonging to the Corporation, as a temporary Memorial of the unanimous Opposition to the detestable Stamp-Act; which having been destroyed by some disaffected Persons, a Number of the Inhabitants determined to erect another, made several Applications to the Mayor, as the principal Member of the Corporation, for Leave to erect the new Pole in the Place where the old One stood. The Committee that waited on him the last Time, disposed to remove every Objection, apprehensive that some of the Corporation might be opposed to the Erection of the Pole, from a Supposition that those Citizens who were for its being raised, were actuated solely by a Party Spirit, offered when the Pole was finished to make it a Present to the Corporation, provided they would order it to be erected either where the other stood or near Mr. Van De Bergh's, where the two Roads meet. But even this, astonishing as it may seem to Englishmen, was rejected by the Majority of the Corporation, and the other Requisitions denied. We question whether this Conduct can be paralleled by an Act of any Corporation in the British Dominions, chosen by the Suffrages of a free People.

And now, Gentlemen, seeing we are debarred the Privilege of public Ground to erect the Pole on, we have purchased a Place for it near where the other stood, which is full as public as any of the Corporation Ground. Your Attendance and Countenance are desired at Nine o'Clock on Tuesday Morning the 6th Instant, at Mr. Crommelin's Wharf, in order to carry it up to be raised.
By Order of the Committee.

New-York, February 3, 1770.

The Sons of Liberty were summoned by this broadside to assist at the raising of the new Liberty Pole. A New York newspaper story reprinted in the New-Hampshire Gazette *(February 23, 1770) reported that "the Pole was raised without any accident, while the French Horns played God save the King."*

The first known parody on "Yankee Doodle"—in the eighteenth century any alternate text was called a parody—was a nonpolitical, slightly naughty ditty in Andrew Barton's spicy ballad opera *The Disappointment*, published in New York in 1767. The tune's first known political parody—thousands were to follow—was part of the extraordinarily malignant medley *The Procession, With the Standard of Faction* that was found under the doors of a great many houses in New York on the morning of March 15, 1770. Comprising spoken recitatives and scathing lyrics to four popular tunes, this elaborate exercise in scurrility mercilessly ridiculed the Patriot leaders in New York who had assisted at the raising of the new Liberty Pole. Section 2, set to the tune of "Yankee Doodle," satirized the tempestuous shipmaster Isaac Sears, who played a vivid role in New York before and during the Revolution. In the text, Captain Sears is represented as speaking in the first person.

THE PROCESSION,
WITH THE STANDARD OF FACTION:
A Cantata.

AIR. (*Yankee doodle.*)

Good neighbors, if you're not afraid,
Be not in Trepidation,
Tho' our great Loss before did raise
Prodigious Consternation.
 Yankee doodle, &c.

Let ev'ry Body laugh and sing,
And be a very gay Soul;
For we have got *another* POST
As big as any MAY POLE.
 Yankee doodle, &c.

~~~

My Mammy, when she *carried* me,
Dream'd of a wondrous *something*,—
She dream'd she bore a great *Mushroom*,
As large as any *Pumpkin*.
 Yankee doodle, &c.

Which grew, she thought, into a Tree,
(I *veaw* 'twould make a Dog laugh!)
Whose Body was as big and long
As Daddy's swineging *Hog-Trough*.
 Yankee doodle, &c.

"Ah, Dame, (the Neighbours cry'd) your Son!
"No Hero will be greater;
"It signifies he'll make a wise
"And marvellous *Whorator*.
 Yankee doodle, &c.

"The Tree that from a Root so mean
"So nimbly upwards vaulted,
"Does *tipifie* your Son shall die
"In Station high exalted."
 Yankee doodle, &c.

~~~

O then a great Man will be I,
And all my Foes be worsted;
I'll be a *Lord*,—and *Pumpkin Pie*
Devoaur until I'm *bursted*.
 Yankee doodle, &c.

~~~

The Mother Country. A SONG.

We have an old Mother that peevish is grown;
She snubs us like Children that scarce walk alone;
She forgets we're grown up and have Sense of our own;
   Which no body can deny, deny,
    Which no body can deny. —

If we don't obey Orders, whatever the Case;
She frowns, and she chides, and she loses all Patience; and sometimes she hits us a Slap in the Face,
    Which no body can deny, &c.

Her Orders so odd are, we often suspect
That Age has impaired her sound Intellect:
But still an old Mother should have due Respect,
    Which no body can deny, &c.

Let's bear with her Humours as well as we can:
But why should we bear the Abuse of her Man?
When Servants make Mischief, they earn the Rattan,
    Which no body should deny, &c.

Know too, ye bad Neighbours, who aim to divide
The Sons from the Mother, that still she's our Pride;
And if ye attack her we're all of her side,
    Which nobody can deny, &c.

We'll join in her Lawsuits, to baffle all those,
Who, to get what she has, will be often her Foes:
For we know it must all be our own, when she goes,
    Which nobody can deny, deny,
     Which nobody can deny.

While in England, Benjamin Franklin wrote down (c.1771) the words of "The Mother Country," a song sharply illustrating the parent-child allegory that was widely used in written and graphic political satires of the contentious British-American relationship at that time. Surviving in his handwriting, this song text has been attributed to Franklin, who is known to have written a number of song lyrics, but there is no proof that he composed it. Although the refrain seems familiar, the tune is not identified.

THE MOTHER COUNTRY.
A Song.

We have an old Mother that peevish is grown,
She snubs us like Children that scarce walk alone;
She forgets we're grown up and have Sense of our own;
 Which nobody can deny, deny,
 Which nobody can deny.

If we don't obey Orders, whatever the Case;
She frowns, and she chides, and she loses all Patience, and sometimes she hits us a Slap in the Face,
 Which nobody can deny, &c.

Her Orders so odd are, we often suspect
That Age has impaired her sound Intellect:
But still an old Mother should have due Respect,
 Which nobody can deny, &c.

Let's bear with her Humours as well as we can:
But why should we bear the Abuse of her Man?
When servants make Mischief, they earn the Rattan,
 Which nobody can deny, &c.

Know too, ye bad Neighbors, who aim to divide
The Sons from the Mother, that still she's our Pride;
And if ye attack her we're all of her side,
 Which nobody can deny, &c.

We'll join in her Lawsuits, to baffle all those,
Who, to get what she has, will be often her Foes:
For we know it must all be our own, when she goes,
 Which nobody can deny, deny,
 Which nobody can deny.

In this cartoon illustrating the popular eighteenth-century parent-child allegory, Britain was symbolized as a lady of fashion and her recalcitrant daughter America as an Indian princess.

T E A,

DESTROYED BY INDIANS.

YE GLORIOUS SONS OF FREEDOM, brave and bold,
That has stood forth----fair LIBERTY to hold ;
Though you were INDIANS, come from distant shores,
Like MEN you acted-----not like savage Moors.

CHORUS.

Bostonian's SONS keep up your Courage good,
Or Dye, like Martyrs, in fair Free-born Blood.

Our LIBERTY, and LIFE is now invaded,
And FREEDOM's brightest Charms are darkly shaded :
But, we will STAND---and think it noble mirth,
To DART the man that dare oppress the Earth.

Bostonian's SONS keep up your Courage good,
Or Dye, like Martyrs, in fair Free-born Blood.

How grand the Scene !----(No Tyrant shall oppose)
The T E A is sunk in spite of all our foes.
A NOBLE SIGHT---to see th' accursed TEA
Mingled with MUD----and ever for to be ;
For KING and PRINCE shall know that we are FREE.

Bostonian's SONS keep up your Courage good,
Or Dye, like Martyrs, in fair Free-born Blood,

Must we be still--- and live on Blood-bought Ground,
And not oppose the Tyrants cursed sound ?
We Scorn the thought- --our views are well refin'd
We Scorn those slavish shackles of the Mind,
" We've Souls that were not made to be confin'd."

Bostonian's SONS keep up your Courage good,
Or Dye, like Martyrs, in fair Free-born Blood.

Could our Fore-fathers rise from their cold Graves,
And view their Land, with all their Children SLAVES ;
What would they say ! how would their Spirits rend,
And, Thunder-strucken, to their Graves descend.

Bostonian's SONS keep up your Courage good,
Or Dye, like Martyrs, in fair Free-born Blood.

Let us with hearts of steel now stand the task,
Throw off all darksome ways, nor wear a Mask.
Oh ! may our noble Zeal support our frame,
And brand all Tyrants with eternal SHAME.

Bostonian's SONS keep up your Courage good,
And sink all Tyrants in their GUILTY BLOOD.

After the repeal in 1770 of the Townshend duties (with the exception of a token three pence per pound on tea), the colonies enjoyed an interlude of prosperity and calm—a calm disquieting to Patriot leaders, who feared that the euphoria might lull America into irretrievable submissiveness. With the passage of the Tea Act, awarding the British East India Company a monopoly in the tea-addicted colonies, Parliament itself supplied the weapon to rekindle the flames of resistance. By the time the first tea ships arrived in December 1773, Americans were prepared to resist, but none so spectacularly as the Bostonians. On December 16, 1773, they staged the superextravaganza that succeeded in finally shoving the tottering British-American relationship over the brink.

The "Indians" who conducted the tea show at Boston were lauded in extravagant song, as this ballad broadside illustrates. In more mundane terms the *Massachusetts Gazette: and the Boston Weekly News-Letter* (December 23, 1773) reported that on that fateful evening, "just before the Dissolution of the [town] Meeting, a Number of brave and resolute Men, dressed in the Indian Manner, approached near the Door of the Assembly, gave the War-Whoop . . . [then] repaired to the Wharf where the Ships lay that had the Tea onboard." The affair was by no means a secret. They "were followed by Hundreds of People, to see the Event. . . . the Indians immediately repaired onboard Capt. Hall's Ship . . . and emptied the Tea overboard. . . ."

The famous doings at the Boston tea party were vividly captured (except for the omission of the "Indians") by a musical Philadelphian and published in the *Philadelphia Packet* (January 3, 1774).

A NEW SONG,
To the plaintive tune of Hosier's Ghost.

As near beauteous Boston lying
  On the gently swelling flood,
Without jack or pendant flying
  Three ill-fated Tea-ships rode.

Just as glorious Sol was setting,
  On the wharf a numerous crew,
SONS OF FREEDOM, fear forgetting,
  Suddenly appear'd in view.

Arm'd with hammer, ax, and chissels,
  Weapons new for warlike deed,
Towards the herbage-freighted vessels,
  They approached with dreadful speed.

⌁

"Soon, they cry'd, your foes will banish,
  "Soon the triumph shall be won;
"Scarce shall setting Phoebus vanish,
  " 'Ere the deathless deed be done."

Quick as thought the ships were boarded,
  Hatches burst and chests display'd;
Axes, hammers, help afforded;
  What a glorious crash they made!

Squish into the deep descended
  Cursed weed of *China's* coast—
Thus at once our fears were ended:
  British rights shall ne'er be lost.

Captains! Once more hoist your streamers,
  Spread your sails, and plow the wave!
Tell *your* masters they were dreamers
  When they thought to cheat the BRAVE.

To the Public.

THE long expected TEA SHIP arrived last night at Sandy-Hook, but the pilot would not bring up the Captain till the sense of the city was known. The committee were immediately informed of her arrival, and that the Captain solicits for liberty to come up to provide necessaries for his return. The ship to remain at Sandy-Hook. The committee conceiving it to be the sense of the city that he should have such liberty, signified it to the Gentleman who is to supply him with provisions, and other necessaries. Advice of this was immediately dispatched to the Captain; and whenever he comes up, care will be taken that he does not enter at the custom-house, and that no time be lost in dispatching him.

New-York, April 19, 1774.

Public notices, published as handbills, alerted Americans to the latest developments in the tea situation. In 1773–1774 the tea issue swept the colonies. After the Boston episode, "tea parties" became the fashion, being given in a number of other ports, and the "cursed weed" was unanimously boycotted everywhere.

CHOICE

Bohea Tea,

By the Chest, Hundred or Dozen, Just Imported in Captain Stevens from LONDON, TO BE SOLD BY

Thomas Walley,

At his Store on Dock-Square.
Where he has also to sell,
All Sorts of Groceries as usual.
‡‡‡ Whereas in the late Fire sundry Things that were removed from said Walley's Store are still missing, viz.
4 or 5 Casks of Raisins.
1 Barrel of Flour.
Part of a Box of 18 Inch Pipes, T. D.—&c.
It is desired if any Person knows where they are, they would inform him; and if any suspected Persons should offer them for Sale, that they might be stopped.

BEST HYSON TEA,
Fresh imported in the Pennsylvania Packet, Captain Falconer, to be SOLD by
FRANCIS HOPKINSON,
At his Store, in Walnut-street;
ALSO a few Family Medicine Chests, very suitable for Country Physicians. They are thought to be the most complete of their Kind of any that have been put up in this Way; containing a large and useful Assortment of Medicines, curiously disposed. They may be intirely depended upon, the Drugs being the very best that could be procured. In each Case there is a List of the Contents, with a Book of Directions.

Tea had long been a staple of life in the colonies. These pre-tea-party advertisements, announcing the arrival of tea shipments, appeared (above) in the Boston Gazette *(February 29, 1768) and (below) in the* Pennsylvania Gazette *(May 19, 1768). Francis Hopkinson, the Philadelphia advertiser, claimed to be America's first composer, which he most probably was. He was a signer of the Declaration of Independence as well.*

To punish Boston, and at the same time provide an object lesson to the other colonies, an enraged Parliament passed the four laws that Americans called the "Coercive," or "Intolerable," Acts. The first of these, the Boston Port Act (passed in June 1774), closed the port of Boston to all trade until indemnity for the destroyed tea would be paid to the British East India Company. Far from intimidating the colonies, the Coercive Acts bound them more closely together and impelled them toward a showdown with England, inevitable since their first resistance to the Stamp Act. In a spontaneous display of unity and concern over Boston's predicament, gifts of food and money were sent by all the colonies, and great public demonstrations of sympathy were held everywhere.

William Billings, the great American composer, movingly expressed his sorrow over the plight of his native city in an anthem, "Lamentation Over Boston," after the 137th Psalm. A tanner by trade, Billings dedicated his financially deprived life to the service of his all-consuming passion, music. "Lamentation Over Boston" was included in his second tunebook, *The Singing Master's Assistant*, published in Boston in 1778.

LAMENTATION OVER BOSTON.

By the Rivers of Watertown we sat down & wept,
We wept, we wept, we wept
When we remembered thee, O Boston;
As for our Friends, Lord God of Heaven,
Preserve them, defend them, deliver them
And restore them unto us;
Preserve them, defend them & restore them to us again.
For they that held them in Bondage
Required of them to take up arms against their Brethren.
Forbid it Lord God, forbid!
Forbid it Lord God that those who have sucked Bostonian Breasts
Should thirst for American Blood!
A voice was heard in Roxbury
Which ecchoe'd thro' the Continent,
Weeping for Boston because of their Danger.
Is Boston my dear Town, is it my native Place?
For since their Calamity I do earnestly remember it still;
If I forget thee, yea if I do not remember thee
Then let my numbers cease to flow, Then be my Muse unkind;
Then let my Tongue forget to move & ever be confin'd.
Let horrid Jargon split the Air & rive my nerves asunder,
Let harmony be banish'd hence and Consonance depart;
Let dissonance erect her throne and reign within my heart.

Paul Revere engraved the frontispiece for the first of Billings's six tune-books,
The New-England Psalm-Singer, or The American Chorister *(1770)*.

"*The Bostonians in Distress*," *a cartoon published in England in 1774, exemplified the hardships brought about by the British blockade.*

In New England, as British reprisals became a reality, the mood grew somber. In an affecting song commemorating the Boston Massacre, a new seriousness is expressed, and the first glimmering of a new concept is perceived: an American America, not a British one. From the *Newport Mercury* (March 14, 1774):

A SONG for the 5th of MARCH.
To the Tune of Once the Gods of the Greeks, &c.

When the *Foes* of the Land, our Destruction had plan'd,
 They sent *ragged* TROOPS for our *Masters*:
But from former Defeat they must now understand,
 Their *Wolves* shall not prowl in our PASTURES.

Old *History* shows and AMERICA knows,
 That *Tyrants* make Carnage their Food;
But that we will oppose all such insolent Foes;
 Experience hath wrote it in Blood.

No Traitor to come, as we dare to presume,
 Will solicit an Army for BOSTON;
New-England's brave HEROES denounce their sad doom,
 That *Britain* will mourn she has lost one.

But the *Banner of Freedom* determin'd we'll stand,
 Waving high o'er our *Countrymen*'s Graves;
From the deep vault of Death they give forth the Command,
 "Revenge us, or live to be Slaves."

Awaken'd, we learn, 'tis a common Concern,
 All AMERICA swarms to the Field;
Not a Coward that wastes one mean tho't on his Life,
 Not a Wretch that has Life, and would yield.

Blest FREEDOM's the Prize, thither bend all their Eyes,
 Stern Valour each Visage inflames;
The Lands they have won, and still Claim as their own,
 And no Tyrant shall ravish their Claims.

A ray of bright Glory now Beams from afar,
 Blest dawn of an EMPIRE to rise;
The AMERICAN Ensign now sparkles a Star,
 Which shall shortly flame wide thro' the Skies.

Strong knit is the Band, which unites the blest Land,
 No *Damon* the Union can sever;
Here's a Glass to fair *Freedom*, come give us your Hand;
 May the ORATOR flourish for ever.

THE

ASSOCIATION, &c.

OF THE

Delegates *of the* Colonies,

AT THE

GRAND CONGRESS,

Held at PHILADELPHIA, Sept. 1, 1774,

VERSIFIED, and adapted to MUSIC,

CALCULATED

For GRAVE and GAY DISPOSITIONS ;

WITH A SHORT

INTRODUCTION.

By BOB JINGLE, Efq;
POET LAUREAT *to the* CONGRESS,

" *I fing the* Men, *read it who lift,*
" Bold *Trojans true, as ever p-ft.*   Cotton's Virg. Trav.

Printed in the Year M,DCC,LXXIV.

The title page of this anti-Congress tract, "to be either sung or said," credited its authorship to "Bob Jingle," a pseudonym often used by Francis Hopkinson. It is highly unlikely that the patriot Hopkinson was responsible for this lampoon of the Association, which Congress appointed to enforce the boycott of trade with England.

Uniting in the resolve that the cause of a single colony was the cause of all, delegates from every colony except Georgia met at Carpenters' Hall at Philadelphia on September 5, 1774, to deliberate on how to oppose the Coercive Acts. Inevitably, the first Continental Congress evoked an outpouring of versified and vocalized reaction, both Patriot and Tory. To the tune of "Smile Britannia," the Patriots sang:

> The Delegates have met
> For wisdom all renown'd,
> Freedom we may expect
> From politicks profound;
> Illustr'ous Congress! may each name
> Be crowned with immortal fame!

While the Tories, in *The Poor Man's Advice to His Poor Neighbors,* a concoction of eighty-seven virulent stanzas to the tune of "Chevy Chace," earthily countered with:

> Arise! shake off the Congress yoke;
> Act as Freemen becomes.
> Their book is bluster all, and smoke,
> Ah! Wipe it with your b-ms.

Line engraving by John Norman (1781) of John Hancock, president of the Continental Congress in 1774 and 1775

Spin-off songs from Congress reflected a wide range of political opinion, but the prevailing attitude in America at that time is perhaps best expressed in the bold parody on "Rule, Britannia" published in the *Pennsylvania Gazette* (October 19, 1774) only a week before Congress adjourned. Quoting the text of the original first and fourth stanzas verbatim, the song transmits, particularly in its powerful paraphrasing of the refrain, the extent to which America's developing national consciousness had grown.

An AMERICAN PARODY on the old Song of RULE BRITANNIA.

When Britons first, by Heaven's Command,
  Arose from out the azure Maine,
This was the Charter of the Land,
  And Guardian Angels sung this Strain:
    Rule Britannia, rule the Waves,
    Britons never will be Slaves.

To spread bright *Freedom's* gentle Sway,
  Your isle too narrow for its Bounds,
We traced wild Ocean's trackless Way,
  And here a safe Asylum found.
    Rule Britannia, rule the Waves,
    But rule us justly—*not like Slaves.*

While we were simple, you grew great;
  Now swelled with *Luxury* and *Pride,*
You pierce our peaceful free Retreat,
  And haste t'enslave with Giant-stride.
    Rule Britannia, rule the Waves,
    But rule us justly—*not like Slaves.*

Thee haughty Tyrants ne'er could tame,
  All their Attempts to pull thee down,
Did but arouse thy gen'rous Flame,
  And work their Woe, and thy Renown.
    Rule Britannia, rule the Waves,
    Britons then *would ne'er be Slaves.*

Let us, your Sons, by Freedom warm'd,
  Your own Example keep in view,—
'Gainst Tyranny be ever arm'd,
  Tho' we our Tyrant find—*in you,*
    Rule Britannia, rule the Waves,
    Britons then *would ne'er be Slaves.*

With *Justice* and with *Wisdom* reign.
  We then with thee will firmly join,
To make thee Mistress of the Main,
  And ev'ry shore it circles thine.
    Rule Britannia, rule the Waves,
    But ne'er degrade your Sons to Slaves.

~~~

Our *Youth* shall prop thy tott'ring Age;
  Our *Vigour* nerve thy feeble Arm:
In vain thy Foes shall spend their Rage,—
  We'll shield thee safe from ev'ry Harm.
    Rule Britannia, rule the Waves,
    But never make your Children Slaves.

For thee we'll toil with chearful Heart,
  We'll labour—*but we will be free*—
Our *Growth* and *Strength* to thee impart,
  And all our Treasures bring to thee.
    Rule Britannia, rule the Waves,
    We're Subjects—*but we're not your Slaves.*

The first edition of Dr. Thomas Arne's "Rule, Britannia," published in England in 1740; (opposite) a 1775 liberty song, published as a broadside

American-Liberty

A New Song.

AWAKE, awake Americans,
  Put chearful courage on,
If tyrants then shall you oppress,
  Arise and say be-gone.

II
O, let no papists bear the sway,
  Nor tyrants ever reign,
Treat such infringments of our rights,
  With resolute disdain.

III.
Yet we will loyal subjects be,
  To any loyal King;
And in defence of such a Prince,
  Spend ev'ry precious thing,

IV.
But when our Prince a Tyrant grows,
  And Parliament grows worse,
New-England's blood will never bear,
  The ignominicus Curse.

V.
Then let Lord North, and Hutchinson,
  And Bernard do their worst,
Their hated Names, thro' ev'ry age,
  forever shall be curs'd

VI.
But mortal tongue can ne'er express,
  The praise that shall descend,
Upon the head of ev'ry one,
  Who proves New-England's friend.

VII.
Tho' Navies do around us lie,
  And Troops invade our land,
Yet we'll defend our Liberty,
  As long as we can stand.

VIII.
Tho' fighting be our last address,
  We'll bravely let them know,
That we will fight with all our might,
  Before our Rights shall go.

IX.
All for the sake of Liberty,
  Our Fathers first came here,
And hunger underwent and cold,
  And hardships most severe.

X.
Then let no haughty Tyrant think,
  We're such a wretched brood,
As to give up that Liberty,
  Our Fathers bought with blood.

XI.
We gladly will consent to peace,
  On reasonable terms,
Our Liberties, once well secur'd,
  We will lay down our arms.

XII
But never will resign those Rights,
  Our Fathers purchas'd so,
Whilst any of their noble blood,
  Within our veins does flow.

XIII.
Domestic Enemies we have,
  Almost in ev'ry Town,
Whose names to unborn ages shall,
  Be always handed down,

XIV.
With Infamy; dishonour's yoke,
  Shall sink them in disgrace,
Amongst the Sons of Liberty,
  Till time itself shall ceate.

XV
Unite, Unite Americans,
  With Purse, with Heart and hand,
Divided we shall surely fall,
  United we shall stand.

XVI.
And let our hearts be all as one,
  And all our Veins be free,
To Fight; and rather bleed, and die,
  Than lose our Liberty.

XVII.
Come, come O brave Americans,
  Let's drink a loyal bowl
May the dear sound of Liberty,
  Sink deep in ev'ry Soul.

XVIII.
Here's a health to North-America,
  And all her noble boys,
Their Liberty and Property,
  And all that she enjoys.

YANKEE DOODLE, or
(as now Christened by the SAINTS of New England)
THE LEXINGTON MARCH

NB. The Words to be Sung thro' the Nose, & in the West Country drawl & dialect.

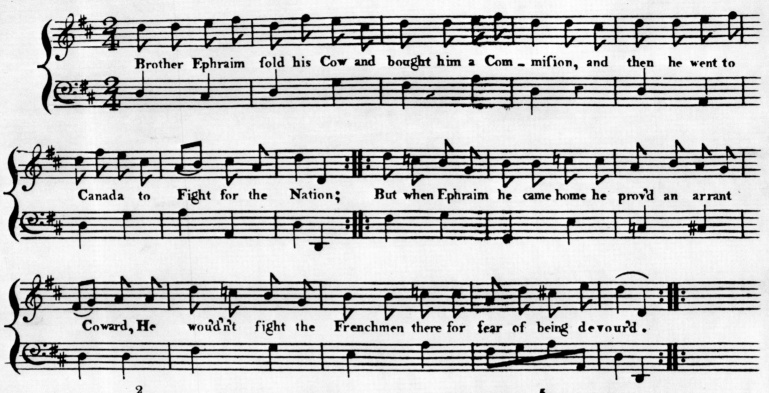

Brother Ephraim sold his Cow and bought him a Com-mission, and then he went to Canada to Fight for the Nation; But when Ephraim he came home he prov'd an arrant Coward, He woud'nt fight the Frenchmen there for fear of being devour'd.

2
Sheep's Head and Vinegar
  Butter Milk and Tanſy,
Boſton is a Yankee town
  Sing Hey Doodle Dandy:
Firſt we'll take a Pinch of Snuff
  And then a drink of Water,
And then we'll ſay How do you do
  And that's a Yanky's Supper

3
Aminadab is juſt come Home
  His Eyes all greaſ'd with Bacon,
And all the news that he cou'd tell
  Is Cape Breton is taken:
Stand up Jonathan
  Figure in by Neighbour,
Nathen ſtand a little off
  And make the Room ſome wider

4
Chriſtmas is a coming Boys
  We'll go to Mother Chaſes,
And there we'll get a Sugar Dram,
  Sweeten'd with Melaſſes:
Heigh ho for our Cape Cod,
  Heigh ho Nantaſket,
Do not let the Boſton wags,
  Feel your Oyſter Baſket.

5
Punk in Pye is very good
  And ſo is Apple Lantern,
Had you been whipp'd as oft as I
  You'd not have been ſo wanton:
Uncle is a Yankee Man
  'Ifaith he pays us all off,
And he has got a Fiddle
  As big as Daddy's Hogs Trough.

6
Seth's Mother went to Lynn
  To buy a pair of Breeches,
The firſt time Vathen put them on
  He tore out all the Stitches;
Dolly Buſhel let a Fart,
  Jenny Jones ſhe found it,
Ambroſe carried it to Mill
  Where Doctor Warren ground it.

7
Our Jemima's loſt her Mare
  And can't tell where to find her,
But ſhe'll come trotting by and by
  And bring her Tail behind her
Two and two may go to Bed;
  Two and two together,
And if there is not room enough,
  Lie one a top o'to'ther.

THE LEXINGTON MARCH

Sk:

But when our country's cause the Sword demands,
And sets in fierce array, the warrior bands;
Strong martial music, glorious rage inspires,
Wakes the bold wish and fans the rising fires.

The Boston Chronicle
October 23–26, 1769

2. *Martial Music*

1775-1781

At home the perverse British fascination with "Yankee Doodle" persisted despite the Provincials' success at Lexington and Concord. Shortly after the surprising news reached England, "Yankee Doodle" was published in London as sheet music (for the first time). With a derisive new title and a highly satirical pseudo-Yankee text that contained an outrageous insult to Dr. Joseph Warren, who died at Bunker Hill at just about the time that "The Lexington March" was published, this version appears to have enjoyed a huge success in England.

"Yankee Doodle" was a first (if miscast) participant in the American Revolution. A Worcester, Massachusetts, newspaper account (May 10, 1775) of the fighting at Lexington and Concord on April 19, 1775, reported that "when the second brigade marched out of Boston to reinforce the first [the British had not fared well in their pre-dawn 'surprise' at Lexington] nothing was played by the fifes and drums but *Yankee Doodle.*" It added exultantly: "Upon their return to Boston [barely a jump ahead of the hotly pursuing minutemen] one [Briton] asked his brother officer how he liked the tune now,— 'D--n them, returned he, *they made us dance it till we were tired.*'—Since which *Yankee Doodle* sounds less sweet to their ears." As an anonymous versifier wrote, in the character of General Gage, whose blockaded city was now besieged by the Provincials, ". . . [we'll] mowe, like grass, the rebel Yankees/ I fancy not those *doodle* dances. . . ."

*William Rush's portrait in wood of
Benjamin Franklin, who sometimes turned
his fluent quill to sharp versifying*

The Battle of Lexington was not neglected by American balladeers. No less an author than Benjamin Franklin was credited with having written an oblique ballad, ridiculing the classic perplexity of the traditionally trained British regulars when confronted with unconventional fighting techniques. Beginning with a review of past British military ineptitudes, the last seven stanzas of this fifteen-stanza ballad are devoted to a highly satirical treatment of the regulars' sorry performance at Lexington. The free meter of the text follows the distinctive style of the English song it parodies, in which long stretches of patter are freely spoken or chanted over a single held note or chord. A contemporary described it as "a kind of recitativo, like the chaunting of the prose in cathedrals." The song first appeared in the *Boston Gazette* (November 27, 1775) and continued to be reprinted until well into 1776. In the text, "Lord Percy" refers to the commander of the unavailing reinforcements that so arrogantly marched out from Boston to "Yankee Doodle"; "Sandwich" is the Earl of Sandwich, no friend to America.

The Kings own REGULARS;
And their Triumphs over the *Irregulars.*

A New SONG,

To the Tune of,
*An old Courtier of the Queen's,
and the Queen's old Courtier.*

Since you all will have singing, and won't be said, nay,
I cannot refuse where you so beg and pray;
So I'll sing you a song—as a body may say,
'Tis of the King's Regulars, who ne'er run away.
    O the old soldiers of the King, and the King's own Regulars.

Grown proud at reviews, great George had no rest;
Each grandsire, he had heard, a rebellion supprest.
He wish'd a rebellion, look'd round and saw none,
So resolv'd a rebellion to make of his own—
    With the old soldiers, &c.

The *Yankees* he bravely pitch'd on, because he thought they would not fight,
And so he sent us over to take away their right,
But least they should spoil our review clothes, he cried braver and louder,
"For God's sake, brother kings, don't sell the cowards any powder."
    O the old soldiers, &c.

Our General with his council of war did advise,
How at Lexington we might the *Yankees* surprise.
We marched—and re-marched—all surpriz'd at being beat;
And so our wise General's plan of *surprise* was complete.
    O the old soldiers, &c.

For fifteen miles they follow'd and pelted us, we scarce had time to pull a trigger;
But did you ever know a retreat performed with more vigour?
For we did it in two hours, which sav'd us from perdition,
'Twas not in *going out* but in *returning*, consisted our *expedition.*
    O the old soldiers, &c.

Says our General, we were forced to take to our arms in our own defence;
For *arms* read *legs*, and it will be both truth and sense.
Lord Percy (says he) I must say something of him in civility,
And that is, "I can never enough praise him for his great—agility."
    O the old soldiers, &c.

Of their firing from behind fences, he makes a great pother,
Ever'y fence has two sides; they made use of one, and we only forgot to use the other.
That we turn'd our backs and ran away so fast, don't let that disgrace us;
'Twas only to make good what Sandwich said, "that the *Yankees* could not face us."
    O the old soldiers, &c.

As they could not get before us, how could they look us in the face?
We took care they should not, by scampering away apace;
That they had not much to brag of, is a very plain case,
For if they beat us in the fight, we beat them in the race.
    O the old soldiers of the King, and the King's own Regulars.

During the short interval between the Battles at Lexington/Concord and Bunker Hill, an exuberant patriotic parody of Dr. Arne's popular hunting song, "The Echoing Horn," appeared in the *New-Hampshire Gazette and Historical Chronicle* (May 26, 1775). First titled merely "A Song," it traveled south via the newspaper route, eventually arriving at the *North-Carolina Gazette* (July 7, 1775), where it acquired a new title, "American Freedom."

AMERICAN FREEDOM.
A new Song.

Hark! 'tis Freedom that calls, come Patriots awake;
To Arms, my brave Boys, and away;
'Tis Honour, 'tis Virtue, 'tis Liberty calls,
And upbraids the too tedious Delay.
What Pleasure we find in pursuing our Foes.
Thro' Blood and thro' Carnage we'll fly;
Then follow, we'll soon overtake them, huzza!
The Tyrants are seized on, they die.

Triumphant returning, with Freedom secur'd.
Like men, we'll be joyful and gay,
With our Wives and our Friends we will sport, love and drink,
And lose the Fatigues of the Day.
'Tis Freedom alone gives a relish to Mirth,
But Oppression all Happiness sours;
It will smooth Life's dull Passage, 'twill slope the Descent,
And strew the Way o'er with Flowers.

"*The Echoing Horn," from* Thomas and Sally *by*
Thomas A. Arne, was published in its original version in
The American Musical Miscellany *(1798).*

A
SONG,

Composed by the British Butchers, after the Fight
at BUNKER-HILL, on the Seventeenth of June, 1775.

IT was on the seventeenth by break of day, the Yankees did surprize us,
With their strong works they had thrown up, to burn the town and drive us;
But soon we had an order came, an order to clear them,
Like rebels stout they stood it out, and thought we ne'er could beat them.

The caption of this pro-British broadside ballad commemorating
the Battle of Bunker Hill is illustrated by a primitive woodcut
depicting the battle and the burning of Charlestown. Despite its
content, the subtitle suggests that the broadside was
published by a Patriot printer.

"The late Magnanimous and Heroic Gen.
Joseph WARREN, Slain fighting in the Cause
of LIBERTY, at BUNKER HILL." (1776)

56

A slightly variant broadside version of the same song omits the British Butchers. Although no date or tune was given for either broadside, it is reasonable to assume that both appeared shortly after the battle and that their tune was "Yankee Doodle."

BUNKER'S HILL,
A NEW SONG.

The seventeenth of June, at Break of Day,
 The Rebels they surpriz'd us,
With their strong Works, which they'd thrown up,
 To burn the Town and drive us.
But soon there was an Order came,
 An Order to defeat them,
Like rebels stout, they stood it out,
 And thought we ne'er could beat them.

About the Hour of Ten next Day,
 An Order came for marching,
With three good Flints and sixty Rounds,
 Each Man was to discharge them.
Then we march'd down to the Long Wharf,
 Our Boats were ready waiting,
With Expedition we embark'd,
 Our Ships were cannonading.

From Cops-Hill Batt'ry, near Charles Town,
 The Twenty-fours they played,
And from three Frigates in the Stream,
 Who very well behaved
The Glasgow Frigate clear'd the Shore,
 All at the Time of landing,
With her Grape Shot and Cannon-Balls,
 No Rebels near could stand them.

But when our Boats all filled were
 With Officers and Soldiers,
Of as good Troops as England had,
 We car'd not who oppos'd us.
But when our Boats all filled were,
 Drawn up in Line of Battle,
Like show'rs of Hail the Shot did fly,
 And Cannons loud did rattle.

With five Battalions of us there,
 We very well behaved,
And every Man did Honour get,
 For Hardships he received.
But when the Rebels scal'd their Walls,
 We did put them to Flight,
Some of them roll'd in their own Blood,
 Now Bunker's Hill deny't.

But when we landed on the Shore,
 And formed all together,
The Rebels they all mann'd their Works,
 And thought we'd ne'er gone thither.
But soon we did perceive brave Howe.
 Great Howe, our brave Commander,
With Grenadiers and Infantry,
 We made them to surrender.

But as for our Artillery,
 They all behaved gently,
And while they Ammunition had,
 They gave it to them plenty.
Their Conductor did get broke,
 For Misconduct, I'm sure,
The Shot he sent for twelve-pound Guns,
 Was made for twenty-four.

Brave Howe was so considerate,
 That to prevent all Dangers,
He allowed us Half a Pint a Day,
 To Rum we're now no Strangers.
Long may he live, by Sea or Land,
 For he's belov'd by many;
The Name of Howe the Rebels dread,
 I see it very plainly.

Some people in the Town did say,
 (Poor Rogues their Hearts were quaking)
We went to kill their Countrymen,
 As they their Hay were making.
But such damn'd Whigs I never saw,
 To hang them all I'd rather,
Or mow their Hay with Musket-Balls
 And Buck-Shot mix'd together.

But now my Song is near an End,
 To compleat my Ditty,
It is the poor and ignorant,
 And only them, I pity.
But as for that King Hancock,
 And Adams, if they're taken,
Their Heads for signs, up high we'll hang,
 Upon a Hill call'd Bacon.

After the brilliant American performance at Bunker Hill, the "doodle dances" became less amusing to British ears. Although the Americans were not the tactical victors, they emerged from the ordeal triumphant both strategically and spiritually. And they no longer cringed at the sound of "Yankee Doodle." From then on they reclaimed the tune and exulted in it. With a variety of texts it became the principal American battle theme of the Revolution, and eventually it came to be a greater symbol of humiliation to the British than it had ever been to Americans. Thomas Anburey, a British officer, is quoted (by Oscar Sonneck) on the American reclamation of "Yankee Doodle": "The name of Yankee has been more prevalent since the commencement of hostilities. The soldiers at Boston used it as a term of reproach, but after the affair at Bunker's Hill, the Americans gloried in it."

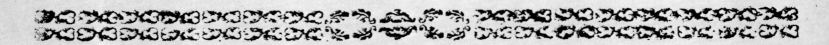

THE AMERICAN HERO.

Made on the battle of Bunker-Hill, and the burning of Charlestown.

WHY should vain mortals tremble at the sight of
Death and destruction in the field of battle,
Where blood and carnage clothe the ground in crimson,
    Sounding with death groans?

Death will invade us by the means appointed,
And we must all bow to the king of terrors;
Nor am I anxious, if I am prepared,
    What shape he comes in.

Infinite goodness teaches us submission;
Bids us be quiet under all his dealings:
Never repining, but forever praising
    God our Creator.

Well may we praise him—all his ways are perfect;
Though a resplendence, infinitely glowing,
Dazzles in glory on the sight of mortals
    Struck blind by lustre.

Good is Jehovah in bestowing sun-shine,
Nor less his goodness in the storm & thunder,
Mercies and judgments both proceed from kindness;
    Infinite kindness.

O then exult, that God forever reigneth;
Clouds, which around him hinder our preception,
Bind us the stronger to exalt his name, and
    Shout louder praises,

Then to the wisdom of my Lord and Master,
I will commit all that I have or wish for;
Sweetly as babes sleep will I give my life up
    When call'd to yield it.

Now, Mars, I dare thee, clad in smoky pillars,
Bursting from bomb-shells, roaring from the cannon,
Rattling in grape shot, like a storm of hail-stones,
    Torturing æther!

Up the bleak heavens let the spreading flames rise,
Breaking like Ætna thro' the smoky columns,
Low'ring like Egypt o'er the failing city,
    Wantonly burnt down.

While all their hearts quick palpitate for havoc,
Let slip your blood-hounds, nam'd the British lions,
Dauntless as death stares; nimble as the whirlwind;
    Dreadful as demons.

Let oceans waft on all your floating castles,
Fraught with destruction, horrible to nature;
Then with your sails fill'd by a storm of vengeance,
    Bear down to battle!

From the dire caverns made by ghostly miners,
Let the explosion, dreadful as volcanoes,
Heave the broad town, with all its wealth and people,
    Quick to destruction.

Still shall the banners of the King of heaven
Never advance where I'm afraid to follow:
While that precedes me, with an open bosom,
    War, I defy thee.

Fame and dear freedom lure me on to battle,
While a fell despot, grimer than a death's head,
Stings me with serpents, fiercer than Medusa's
    To the encounter.

Life for my country, and the cause of freedom,
Is but a trifle for a worm to part with;
And if preserved in so great a contest,
    Life is redoubled.

Nathaniel Niles, a New England theologist and preacher, commemorated Bunker Hill in a powerful and religious "Sapphick Ode." Set to equally stirring music by his fellow New Englander, the composer and hymnodist Andrew Law, it was widely sung during the Revolution. Under the title "The American Hero," the ode was published as a broadside.

GEN. WASHINGTON takes Command of the
American Army at Cambridge July 3ᵈ 1775.

From the Monthly Military Repository (1796)

*Washington's camp at Cambridge furnished the locale for what
became the "official" American text of "Yankee Doodle."
Attributed to Edward Bangs, a sophomore at Harvard who had
served at Lexington as a minuteman, these words—with slight
variations—were often reprinted during the later eighteenth
and early nineteenth centuries. The broadside opposite,
probably dating from 1775 or 1776, is the earliest known printing
of this version. In the text, the Yankee locutions* taring *and*
pockily, *like* tarnal, *indicate intensity of expression.*

O nly three weeks after Lexington and Concord, the second
Continental Congress met primarily to deal with the country's most urgent need, the creation of a unified Continental
Army. They unanimously appointed George Washington
as its commander in chief, and he immediately left for his
new headquarters at Cambridge. While still on the way, he
learned of the Battle of Bunker Hill.

Both Washington's appointment as commander in chief
and his trip to Cambridge were ridiculed to the tune of
"Yankee Doodle" by an anonymous Tory. The references
in the text to Washington as "the country's papa" and to his
crossing over Jersey would date the composition of this
parody as later than 1775; it was probably one of the
loyalist ballads that proliferated during the Revolution.

ADAM'S FALL:
THE TRIP TO CAMBRIDGE.

When Congress sent great Washington,
　All clothed in power and breeches,
To meet old Britain's warlike sons
　And make some rebel speeches;

'Twas then he took his gloomy way
　Astride his dapple donkeys,
And travelled well, both night and day,
　Until he reach'd the Yankees.

Away from camp, 'bout three miles off,
　From Lily he dismounted,
His sergeant brush'd his sun-burnt wig,
　While he the specie counted.

All prinked up in *full* bag-wig;
　The shaking notwithstanding,
In leathers tight, oh! glorious sight!
　He reach'd the Yankee landing.

The women ran, the darkeys too;
　And all the bells, they tolléd;
For Britain's sons, by Doodle **doo**,
　We're sure to be—consoléd.

Old mother Hancock with a **pan**
　All crowded full of butter,
Unto the lovely Georgius ran,
　And added to the splutter.

Says she, "Our brindle has just calved,
　And John is wondrous happy.
He sent this present to you, dear,
　As you're the 'country's papa.' "—

"You'll butter bread and bread butter,
　But do not butt your speeches.
You'll butter bread and bread butter,
　But do not grease your breeches."

Full many a child went into camp,
　All dressed in homespun kersey,
To see the greatest rebel scamp
　That ever cross'd o'er Jersey.

The rebel clowns, oh! what a sight!
　Too awkward was their figure.
'Twas yonder stood a pious wight,
　And here and there a nigger.

Upon a stump, he placed (himself),
　Great Washington did he,
And through the nose of Lawyer Close,
　Proclaimed great Liberty.

The patriot brave, the patriot fair,
　From fervor had grown thinner,
So off they march'd, with patriot zeal,
　And took a patriot dinner.

The Farmer and his Son's return from a visit to the CAMP.

FATHER and I went down to camp,
　Along with Captain Gooding,
And there we see the men and boys
　As thick as hasty pudding.

Yankey doodle keep it up, yankey doodle
　dandy,
Mind the music and the step,
And with the girls be handy.

And there we see a thousand men,
　As rich as 'squire David,
And what they wasted every day,
　I wish it had been saved.
　　Yankey doodle, &c.

The 'lasses they eat every day,
　Would keep an house a winter;
They have as much that I'll be bound,
　They eat it when they're mind to.
　　Yankey doodle, &c.

And there we see a swamping gun,
　Large as a log of maple,
Upon a ducid little cart,
　A load for father's cattle.
　　Yankey doodle, &c.

And every time they shoot it off,
　It takes a horn of powder,
And makes a noise like father's gun,
　Only a nation louder.
　　Yankey doodle, &c.

I went as nigh to one myself,
　As 'Siah's underpinning;
And father went as nigh again,
　I thought the duce was in him.
　　Yankey doodle, &c.

Cousin Simon grew so bold,
　I thought he would have cock'd it;
It scar'd us so I shriek'd it off,
　And hung by father's pocket.
　　Yankey doodle, &c.

And captain Davis had a gun,
　He kind of clapt his hand on't,

And stuck a crooked stabbing iron
　Upon the little end on't.
　　Yankey doodle, &c.

And there I see a pumpkin shell,
　As big as mother's bason,
And every time they touch'd it off,
　They scamper'd like the nation.
　　Yankey doodle, &c.

I see a little barrel too,
　The heads were made of leather,
They knock upon with little clubs,
　And call'd the folks together.
　　Yankey doodle, &c.

And there was captain Washington,
　And gentlefolks about him,
They say he's grown so tarnal proud,
　He will not ride without them.
　　Yankey doodle, &c.

He got him on his meeting clothes,
　Upon a flapping stallion,
He set the world along in rows,
　In hundreds and in millions.
　　Yankey doodle, &c.

The flaming ribbons in his hat,
　They look'd so taring fine ah,
I wanted pockily to get,
　To give to my Jemimah.
　　Yankey doodle, &c.

I see another snarl of men,
　A digging graves they told me,
So tarnal long, so tarnal deep,
　They 'tended they should hold me.
　　Yankey doodle, &c.

It scar'd me so I hook'd it off,
　Nor stopt as I remember,
Nor turn'd about 'till I got home,
　Lock'd up in mother's chamber.
　　Yankey doodle, &c.

The stirring events in Massachusetts and Philadelphia during the summer of 1775 inspired many authors to write freedom songs. One of these, "Liberty Tree," attained great and long-lasting popularity. First published in the *Pennsylvania Magazine: or American Monthly Museum* for July 1775, it was signed "Atlanticus," a pseudonym often used by the magazine's illustrious editor, Thomas Paine, the high priest of revolution. Although written in the stilted, allegorical style popular at the time, Paine's song, in its last stanza, nevertheless comes to grips with reality and openly accuses the king of being as culpable as his ministers—an accusation which was generally avoided until that time. This last stanza has been regarded as a direct precursor of Paine's *Common Sense*, which in 1776 so powerfully propelled the colonies toward independence.

The words and tune ("Once the Gods of the Greeks") appeared in The American Patriotic Songbook (1813).

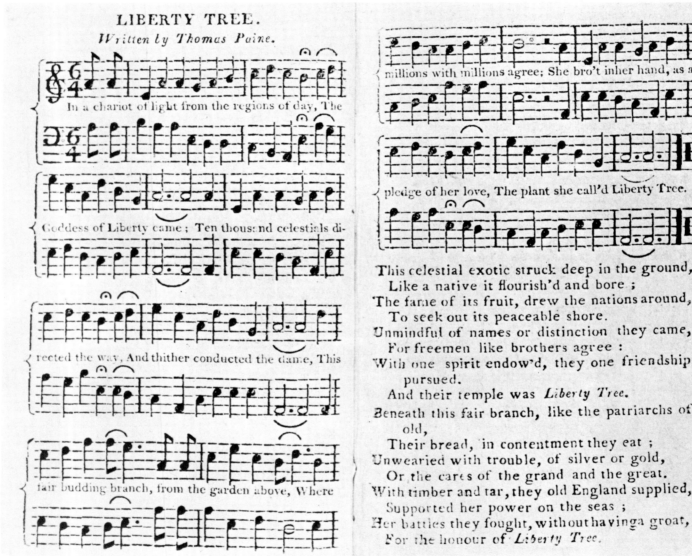

This celestial exotic struck deep in the ground,
　　Like a native it flourish'd and bore ;
The fame of its fruit, drew the nations around,
　　To seek out its peaceable shore.
Unmindful of names or distinction they came,
　　For freemen like brothers agree :
With one spirit endow'd, they one friendship
　　pursued.
　　And their temple was *Liberty Tree.*
Beneath this fair branch, like the patriarchs of
　　old,
　　Their bread, in contentment they eat ;
Unwearied with trouble, of silver or gold,
　　Or the cares of the grand and the great.
With timber and tar, they old England supplied,
　　Supported her power on the seas ;
Her battles they fought, without having a groat,
　　For the honour of *Liberty Tree.*

But hear, O ye swains, ('tis a tale most profane)
　　How all the tyrannical powers,
King, Commons, and Lords, are uniting amain,
　　To cut down this guardian of ours;
From the east to the west, blow the trumpet to arms,
　　Thro' the land let the sound of it flee,
Let the far and the near,—all unite with a cheer,
　　In defense of our LIBERTY TREE.

Early in 1776, while Washington was still deviling the besieged British in Boston, one of the first major ballads of the American Revolution began to spread over the country. Variously titled "Washington," "Gen. Washington," "War and Washington," and even "Ward [General Artemas Ward] and Washington," it was composed by Jonathan Mitchell Sewall, a lawyer and minor poet from Portsmouth, New Hampshire, with a knack for writing gravestone epitaphs. Referring to Washington as "godlike" for possibly the first time in a song—it was later to become standard practice—the ballad was issued with slight textual variations in broadside versions. It also hit the newspaper circuit, appearing as far afield as Dixon and Hunter's *Virginia Gazette* as early as February 24, 1776.

The tune and opening lines of "War and Washington," from Henry Brown's manuscript book of poetry and music

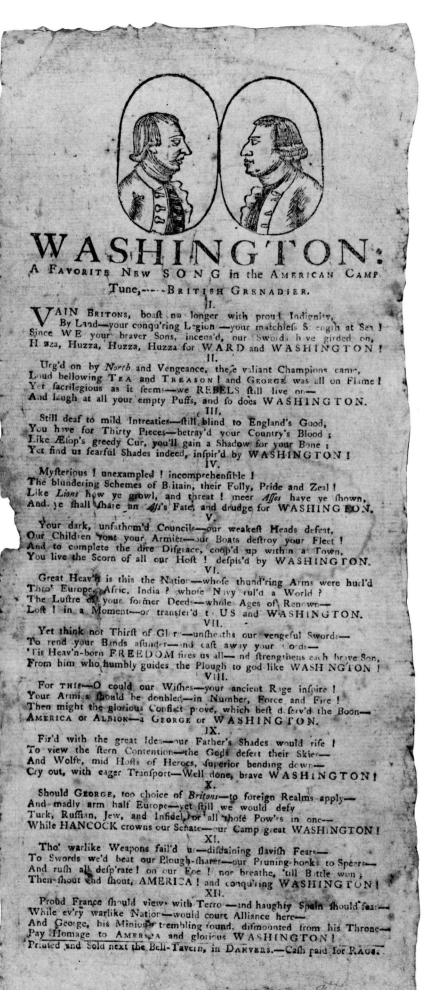

WASHINGTON:

A FAVORITE NEW SONG in the AMERICAN CAMP.
Tune,——BRITISH GRENADIER.

I.

VAIN BRITONS, boast no longer with proud Indignity,
   By Land—your conqu'ring Legion—your matchless Strength at Sea!
Since WE your braver Sons, incens'd, our Swords have girded on,
Huzza, Huzza, Huzza, Huzza for WARD and WASHINGTON!

II.

Urg'd on by *North* and Vengeance, these valiant Champions came,
Loud bellowing TEA and TREASON! and GEORGE was all on Flame!
Yet sacrilegious as it seems—we REBELS still live on—
And laugh at all your empty Puffs, and so does WASHINGTON.

III.

Still deaf to mild Intreaties—still blind to England's Good,
You have for Thirty Pieces—betray'd your Country's Blood;
Like Æsop's greedy Cur, you'll gain a Shadow for your Bone;
Yet find us fearful Shades indeed, inspir'd by WASHINGTON!

IV.

Mysterious! unexampled! incomprehensible!
The blundering Schemes of Britain, their Folly, Pride and Zeal!
Like *Lions* how ye growl, and threat! meer *Asses* have ye shown,
And ye shall share an *Ass's* Fate, and drudge for WASHINGTON.

V.

Your dark, unfathom'd Councils—our weakest Heads defeat,
Our Children rout your Armies—our Boats destroy your Fleet!
And to complete the dire Disgrace, coop'd up within a Town,
You live the Scorn of all our Host! despis'd by WASHINGTON.

VI.

Great Heav'n is this the Nation—whose thund'ring Arms were hurl'd
Thro' Europe, Afric, India? whose Navy rul'd a World?
The Lustre of your former Deeds—whole Ages of Renown—
Lost! in a Moment—or transfer'd to US and WASHINGTON.

VII.

Yet think not Thirst of Glory—unsheaths our vengeful Swords—
To rend your Bands asunder—and cast away your Cords—
'Tis Heav'n-born FREEDOM fires us all—and strengthens each brave Son,
From him who humbly guides the Plough to god-like WASHINGTON!

VIII.

For THIS—O could our Wishes—your ancient Rage inspire!
Your Armies should be doubled—in Number, Force and Fire!
Then might the glorious Conflict prove, which best deserv'd the Boon—
AMERICA or ALBION—a GEORGE or WASHINGTON.

IX.

Fir'd with the great Idea—our Father's Shades would rise!
To view the stern Contention—the Gods desert their Skies—
And Wolfe, mid Hosts of Heroes, superior bending down,
Cry out, with eager Transport—Well done, brave WASHINGTON!

X.

Should GEORGE, too choice of *Britons*—to foreign Realms apply—
And madly arm half Europe—yet still we would defy
Turk, Russian, Jew, and Infidel, or all those Pow'rs in one—
While HANCOCK crowns our Senate—our Camp great WASHINGTON!

XI.

Tho' warlike Weapons fail'd us—disdaining slavish Fears—
To Swords we'd beat our Plough-shares—our Pruning-hooks to Spears,
And rush all desp'rate! on our Foe! nor breathe, 'till Battle won;
Then shout and shout, AMERICA! and conqu'ring WASHINGTON!

XII.

Proud France should view with Terror—and haughty Spain should fear—
While ev'ry warlike Nation—would court Alliance here—
And George, his Minions trembling round, dismounted from his Throne—
Pay Homage to AMERICA and glorious WASHINGTON!

Printed and Sold next the Bell-Tavern, in DANVERS.—Cash paid for RAGS.

Two favorite SONGS,

made on the Evacuation of the Town of BOSTON,

by the *Britiſh Troops*, on the 17th of March, 1776.

IN ſeventeen hundred and ſeventy ſix,
On March the eleventh, the time was prefix'd,
Our forces march'd on upon Dorcheſter-neck,
Made fortifications againſt an attack.

The morning next following, as Howe did eſpy,
The banks we caſt up, were ſo copious and high,
Said he in three months, all my men with their might,
Cou'd not make two ſuch Forts as they've made in a night.

Now we hear that their Admiral was very wroth,
And drawing his ſword, he bids Howe to go forth,
And drive off the YANKEES from Dorcheſter hill :
Or he'd leave the harbour and him to their will.

Howe rallies his forces upon the next day,
One party embark'd for the Caſtle they ſay,
But the wind and the weather againſt them did fight,
On Governor's Iſland it drove 'em that night.

Then being diſcourag'd they ſoon did agree,
From Bunker and Boſton, on board ſhip to flee :
Great Howe loſt his ſenſes, they ſay for a week,
For fear our next fort ſhould be rais'd in King-ſtreet.

But yet notwithſtanding the finger of God,
In the wind and the weather which often occurr'd ;
Still Howe, Pharaoh like, did harden his heart,
Being thirſty for victory to maintain his part.

He gives out freſh orders on Thurſday it's ſaid,
Forms his men in three branches upon the parade ;
Acknowledging it was a deſperate caſe,
In their ſituation the YANKEES to face :

Yet neverthelefs being haughty of heart,
On Friday one branch of his men did embark :
A ſecond ſtood ready down by the ſea ſide :
His Dragoons were mounted all ready to ride.

Great Howe he now utters a deſperate oration,
Saying fight my brave boys for the crown of our nation :
Take me for your pattern, and fight ye as I,
Let it be 'till we conquer, or elſe 'till we die.

But all of a ſudden, with an Eagle ey'd glance,
They eſpied a fire being kindled by chance,
In a barrack at Cambridge, as many do know,
And then in confuſion they ran to and fro.

Moreover as Providence order'd the thing,
Our drums beat alarm, our bell it did ring,
Which made them cry out O the YANKEES will come ;
O horror ! they'll have us, come let us begone.

Then hilter ſkilter they ran in the ſtreet,
Sometimes on their heads and ſometimes on their feet,
Leaving cannon and mortars, pack ſaddles and wheat,
Being glad to eſcape with the ſkin of their teeth.

Now off goes Pilgarlick with his men in a fright,
And altho' they ſhow cowards, yet ſtill they ſhow ſpite,
In burning the Caſtle, as they paſs along,
And now by Nantaſket they lie in a throng.

Let 'em go, let 'em go, for what the will fetch,
I think their great Howe is a miſerable wretch ;
And as for his men, they are fools for their pains,
So let them return to Old-England again

IT was'nt our will that Bunker Hill
From us ſhould e,er be taken ;
We thought 'twould never be retook,
But we find we are Miſtaken.

The ſoldiers bid the hill farewell,
Two images left ſentreis,
This they had done all out of fun
To the American Yankees.

A flag of truce was ſent thereon,
To ſee if the hill was clear,
No living ſoul was found thereon,
But theſe images ſtood there.

Their hats they wave, come if you pleaſe.
There's none here to moleſt us,
Theſe wooden men that here do ſtand,
Are only to defy us.

Theſe images they ſoon threw down,
Not one man's life was loſt then,
No ſooner they were on the hill
But they landed into Boſton.

The women come, and children run,
To brave PUTNAM rejoicing,
Saying now is your time to man your lines
For the ſoldiers have left Boſton.

The troops you fairly ſcar'd away,
On board the ſhips they're quarter'd,
The children laugh'd, ſaying over the wharf
They threw their beſt bomb mortar.

With the blazing of your guns that night,
And roaring of your mortars,
The ſoldiers cry'd the Yankees come
To tear us all in quarters.

The barracks being ſet on fire,
Which made the ſoldiers quiver,
They ſoon embark on board their ſhips,
May they ſtay there forever.

Soon after this the fleet fell down,
It's what we long deſir'd,
I think the Gen'rals were afraid
That they'd be ſet on fire.

The ſhipping now have all ſet ſail,
No cauſe have we to mourn,
But ſeem afraid becauſe 'tis ſaid
That they will ſoon return.

Some ſay they're ſail'd for Halifax,
And others for New York ;
Howe let none know where he was bound,
When the ſoldiers did embark.

Where they are bound there's none can tell,
But the great GOD on high,
May all our heads be cover'd well,
When cannon balls do fly.

Washington scored his first triumph of the Revolution when he forced the British to evacuate Boston on March 17, 1776. After painstakingly accumulating enough ammunition to sustain an offensive action, he seized Dorchester Heights, from where he could effectively smoke out the British troops and fleet. General Sir William Howe, who had taken over the British command from General Gage, realized his vulnerability and lost no time in departing for Halifax. Large numbers of loyalist refugees left under his protection.

Shortly before independence was declared, the *Pennsylvania Gazette* (June 19, 1776) advertised the publication of a new play by John Leacock, *The Fall of British Tyranny: or, American Liberty Triumphant*, in which George Washington figured as a dramatized character for the first time. Although it seems never to have been performed, the play was widely read and highly successful. It included at least one hit song, "In Praise of St. Tammany, the American Saint," which was published in advance in the *Pennsylvania Evening Post* (April 30, 1776) as a salute to May First, St. Tammany's Day. The "Sons of St. Tammany" was a patriotic society related to the Sons of Liberty, whose patron saint was a legendary, exemplary Delaware Indian chief named Tammanend, or Tammany. The organization was run by thirteen "sachems," and its rituals were patterned on Indian customs. This early Tammany society was not the ancestor of later Tammany organizations.

SONG.
Tune: The hounds are all out &c.

Of St. *George*, or St. *Bute*, let the poet laureat sing,
Of *Pharaoh* or *Pluto* of old,
While he rhimes forth their praise, in false, flattering lays,
I'll sing of St. Tamm'ny the bold, my brave boys.

~~~

In freedom's bright cause, Tamm'ny pled with applause,
And reason'd most justly from nature;
For this, this was his song, all, all the day long:
Liberty's the right of each creature, brave boys.

Whilst under an oak his great parliament sat,
His throne was the crotch of the tree;
With Solomon's look, without statutes or book,
He wisely sent forth his decree, my brave boys.

His subjects stood round not the least noise or sound,
Whilst freedom blaz'd full in each face:
So plain were the laws, and each pleaded his cause;
That might BUTE, NORTH and MANSFIELD disgrace,
  my brave boys.

No Duties, nor Stamps, their blest liberty cramps,
A *King*, tho' no tyrant, was he;
He did oft'times declare, nay sometimes wou'd swear,
The least of his subjects were free, my brave boys.

~~~

When fourscore years old, as I've oft times been told,
To doubt it, sure, would not be right,
With a pipe in his jaw, he'd buss his old squaw,
And get a young saint ev'ry night, my brave boys.

As old age came on, he grew blind, deaf and dumb,
Tho' his sport, 'twere hard to keep from it,
Quite tired of life, bid adieu to his wife,
And blaz'd like the tail of a comet, brave boys.

What country on earth, then, did ever give birth
To such a magnanimous saint?
His acts far excel all that history tell,
And language too feeble to paint, my brave boys.

Now, to finish my song, a full flowing bowl
I'll quaff, and sing all the long day,
And with punch and wine paint my cheeks for my saint,
And hail ev'ry First of sweet May, my brave boys.

Music for St. Tammany by Samuel Low, from the New York Magazine *(May 1790)*

"American Independence. Declared July 4th, 1776"
*was graphically conceived as thirteen hands grasping
a continuous chain.*

In the infant republic a new political numerology had
supplanted 92–45–17, and the number thirteen was even
more imaginatively and insistently celebrated. The *Pennsylvania Evening Post* (June 28, 1777) tells us that just before
the first birthday of the Declaration of Independence:

At a meeting of a lodge of Free Masons . . . it accidently happened that exactly thirteen members met, that at dinner they
had thirteen dishes of meat on the table; they drank thirteen loyal
American toasts, sang thirteen songs; their bill for liquor was
thirteen bottles of wine, and thirteen bowls of toddy; their
reckoning thirteen pounds, and they spent thirteen hours, viz.
from eight o'clock in the morning until nine o'clock in the evening, in the greatest harmony and good humour, which caused
it to be remarked that it was in some degree emblematical of the
union, friendship, harmony, and freedom of the thirteen United
States of America.

On July 3, 1776, the *Pennsylvania
Gazette* tersely announced: "Yesterday the Continental Congress declared the United Colonies Free and
Independent States." The great rejoicing that followed in the newly
created states often took the form of
songs to the unlikely tune of "God
Save the King." From the *New-York
Packet* (August 1, 1776):

Hail! O America!
Hail now the joyful day!
    Exalt your voice.
Shout, George is King no more,
Over this Western shore;
Let him his loss deplore,
    While we rejoice.

Now in thy banner set,
Transtulet sustinet;*
    God is our King.
Who does in mercy deign,
Over us for to reign,
And our just rights maintain,
    His praises sing.

O may he deign to bless
The Great and each Congress,
    Of this land.
With wisdom from on high,
And unanimity,
To save our liberty
    Nobly to stand.

And on the virt'ous head,
Abundant blessings shed.
    Of Washington;
Give him to know thy will,
Fill him with martial skill,
His station to fill,
    'Till glory's won.

And may our Gen'rals all,
Officers great and small,
    Be Heaven's care:
Within the hostile field,
Guard them with thy own shield.
While they the sword do wield,
    In this great war.

~~~

* He who transported us hither
will support us.

On the bitterly cold morning of December 26, 1776, Washington at last reversed the tide of defeats that had kept him and his tattered army barely one jump ahead of the enemy during the latter half of 1776. Crossing the icy Delaware, the Continental Army surprised the Hessians, in whose charge the hedonistic General Sir William Howe had left his camp at Trenton, and who were sleeping off their collective Christmas hangover. As the Patriot dramatist Hugh Henry Brackenridge sang in his 1777 play, *The Death of General Montgomery*:

> For our sons, in noble rage,
> O'er their native Delaware
> Hasten swiftly to engage,
> And turn back the infernal war.

Seventy-one years later, Americans were still singing about it. In a song for male quartet, published in New York in 1847, Seba Smith's words reflect another century's response to the event.

WASHINGTON
CROSSING THE DELAWARE.

Dark and gloomy was the hour,
    And freedom's fire's burnt low
For twenty days had Washington
    Retreated from the foe;
And his weary soldiers' feet were bare
As he fled across the Delaware.

Hearts were fainting thro' the land,
    And patriot blood ran cold;
The stricken army scarce retain'd
    Two thousand men, all told,
While British arms gleamed every where
From the Hudson to the Delaware.

Cold and stormy came the night;
    The great chief rous'd his men;
Now, up, brave comrades, up and strike
    For freedom once again.
For the lion sleepeth in his lair,
On the left bank of the Delaware.

By the darkling river's side
    Beneath a wintry sky,
From that weak band forlorn and few,
    Went up the patriot cry,
O land of freedom, ne'er dispair,
We'll die or cross the Delaware.

How the strong oars dash the ice,
    Amid the tempest's roar
And how the trumpet voice of Knox
    Still cheers them to the shore!
Thus in the freezing midnight air
Those brave hearts cross'd the Delaware.

In the morning gray and dim,
    The shout of battle rose;
The chief led back his valient men
    With a thousand captive foes,
While Trenton shook with the cannon's blare,
That told the news o'er the Delaware.

"Washington's March at the Battle of Trenton" is believed to have been written during the Revolution; this edition, combined with "Yankee Doodle," was published about 1812.

German mercenaries in the British Army, indiscriminately known as "Hessians," were universally hated for their cruelty.

The Hessians were as renowned for their musical ability as they were notorious for their brutality. Upon their first arrival in New York in 1776, the British-controlled *New-York Gazette* (October 28, 1776) reported that the Hessians "debarked from their respective Ships . . . in the highest Spirits imaginable . . . making the Hills resound with Trumpets, French Horns, Drums, and Fifes, accompanied by the Harmony of their Voices." When they were captured at Trenton, Major-General Heath wrote to Governor Jonathan Trumbull of Connecticut that among the plunder were ". . . 12 Drums, a number of Trumpets, Clarionets &c . . ." and among the prisoners: ". . . 20 drummers, 9 musicians. . . ." The captured Hessians' musical talents were enlisted at the first Fourth of July anniversary celebration at Philadelphia, where, at an "elegant dinner," reported in the *Pennsylvania Evening Post* (July 5, 1777): "The Hessian band of music, taken in Trenton the 26th of December last, attended and heightened the festivity with some fine performances suited to the joyous occasion."

"The Hessian Camp" was included in John Greenwood's manuscript book of popular tunes, given to him by a friendly, captured British fifer-major sometime between the Battles of Bunker Hill and Trenton. The time can be pinpointed because Greenwood's entire career as an army fifer was spanned by these two events. Resigning after the Battle of Trenton when he was sixteen years old, Greenwood ultimately studied dentistry and became famous as the "Father of Scientific Dentistry in America." He was George Washington's favorite dentist, and he fashioned several sets of Washington's celebrated dentures.

The atrocity stories circulated in the newspapers concerning the inhumane treatment of American prisoners of war by their British and Hessian captors are substantiated in the *Journal* of Elias Boudinot, the eminent New Jersey statesman, who was appointed by Washington to negotiate with the British on relief for Americans imprisoned in New York. The pitiable plight of these men is movingly described in a broadside ballad of thirty-four stanzas, the first part of which is devoted to an unrelated topic, privateering. Although no tune is indicated, the ballad can be sung to "Chevy Chase," or "Nancy Dawson," or even "Yankee Doodle." Some of the stanzas devoted to the prisoners are given here.

A New Privateering *SONG:*
Concluding with some Remarks upon
the Cruelty exercised by the Regulars and Hessians
Upon our poor Prisoners in New-York.

The regulars and hessians too,
  Assisted by the tories,
Did an exploit some time ago,
  In which they seem to glory.

Some of our bravest men they took,
  By accident surprized,
And over them the dagger shook,
  And proudly tyrannized.

Then to *New York* they were convey'd
  While tories did deride them,
And in a stinking dungeon laid,
  All sustenance denied them.

They stript them of their cash & clothes,
  Deny'd them any fuel,
Poor creatures, many of them dy'd,
  The devil's not more cruel.

But some of them do yet survive,
  Beyond their expectation,
And were permitted just alive,
  To visit their relation.

But some of those who were releas'd,
  With poison were infected,
That many of them are deceas'd,
  And some have been distracted.

They who survive and still remain,
  Their sufferings are many;
I fear they'll ne'er return again,
  But very few if any.

For though they bore the want of food,
  While pinching cold annoy'd them,
By the small-pox the cruel foe,
  Endeavour'd to destroy them.

Was ever cruelty so great,
  As is practised by them;
Yet tis a truth, what I relate,
  Nor can I well bely them.

I've read the records often times,
  Of many heathen nations,
Yet never read such horrid crimes
  With so great aggravations.

Doubtless a double-'prenticeship,
  To satan they have served,
For from his rules they never step,
  Or ever yet have swerved.

No Indian ever took the field,
  Or Assiric sooty nation,
But to their captives if they yield,
  Would grant some mitigation.

This witty commentary on the cataclysmic year 1776, set to the old tune "Derry Down," did not appear in the *Pennsylvania Evening Post* until April 17, 1777.

The HEADS, or the Year 1776.

Ye wrong heads, and strong heads, attend to my strains;
Ye clear heads, and queer heads, and heads without brains,
Ye thick sculls, and quick sculls, and heads great and small,
And ye heads that aspire to be heads over all.
    Derry down, &c.

Ye ladies (I would not offend for the world!)
Whose bright heads, and light heads, are feather'd and curl'd,
The mighty dimensions dame Nature surprise,
To find she'd so grosly mistaken the size.
    Derry down, &c.

And ye petits maitres, your heads I might spare,
Encumber'd with nothing but powder and hair,
Who vainly disgrace the true monkey race,
By transplanting the tail from its own native place.
    Derry down, &c.

Enough might be said, durst I venture my rhymes.
On crown'd heads, and round heads, of these modern times;
This slippery path let me cautiously tread,
The neck else will answer perhaps for the head.
    Derry down, &c.

The heads of the church, and the heads of the state,
Have taught much, and wrote much, too much to repeat;
On the neck of corruption uplifted, 'tis said,
Some rulers, alas, are too high by the head.
    Derry down, &c.

Ye schemers and dreamers of politic things,
Projecting the downfall of Kingdoms and Kings,
Can your wisdom declare how this body is fed,
When the members rebel and wage war with the head.
    Derry down, &c.

Expounders, confounders, and heads of the law,
I bring case in point, don't point out a flaw;
If reason be treason, what plea shall I plead?
To your chief I appeal, for your chief has a head.
    Derry down, &c.

On Britannia's bosom sweet liberty smil'd,
The PARENT grew strong whilst she Foster'd the CHILD;
Ill treating her offspring, a fever she bread,
Which contracted her limbs, and distracted her head.
    Derry down, &c.

Ye learned state doctors, your labors are vain,
Proceeding by bleeding to settle her brain;
Much less can your art the lost members restore,
Amputation must follow, perhaps something more.
    Derry down, &c.

Pale Goddess of Whim! When with cheeks lean or full,
Thy influence seizes an Englishman's scull,
He blunders, yet wonders, his schemes ever fail,
Though often mistaking the head for the tail.
    Derry down, &c.

The predominant eighteenth-century flair for satirical versification was given full play in a great number of the songs written during the American Revolution by both Patriots and Tories. The enemy's foibles, failings, and failures were seized upon and mercilessly probed and ridiculed in deft verse, often pretending to be written in the first person, as in this song, apocryphally reprinted from a London source and ascribed to Sir Peter Parker. Parker was the naval commander of the unsuccessful British attempt to invade Charleston, South Carolina, in June 1776. Both he and Sir Henry Clinton, who commanded the land forces, had been ignominiously repulsed at Sullivan's Island in Charleston harbor by Colonel William Moultrie and a small band of men having only thirty-one guns. The song appeared in the *Pennsylvania Journal; and the Weekly Advertiser* (February 26, 1777).

A NEW WAR SONG,
By Sir Peter Parker.
Written, and Printed in LONDON.

Tune—"Well met Brother Tar."

My Lords, with your leave,
  An account I will give,
That deserves to be written in metre;
  For the *Rebels* and I
  Have been pretty nigh,
Faith *almost too nigh* for Sir Peter.
  With much labour and toil
  Unto Sullivan's Isle,
I came, fierce as Falstaff or Pistol;
  But the *Yankies* (odd rat 'em)
  I could not get at 'em,
Most terribly maul'd my poor *Bristol!*
  Bold Clinton by land
  Did quietly stand,
While I made a thund'ring clatter;
  But the channel was deep.
  So he only could peep.
And not venture over the water.
  De'el take 'em, their shot
  Came so swift and so hot,
And the *cowardly dogs* stood so stiff, Sirs,
  That I put ship about,
  And was glad to get out,
Or they would not have left me a skiff, Sirs.
  Now, bold as a Turk,
  I proceed to New-York,
Where with Clinton and Howe you may find me;
  I've the wind in my tail
  And am hoisting my sail,
To leave Sullivan's Island behind me.
  But my Lords do not fear,
  For before the next year,
(Altho' a *small Island* could fret us)
  The *continent whole*
  We shall take, by my soul—
If the *cowardly Yankies* will let us.

Early in June 1777 Lieutenant General John Burgoyne embarked southward from Canada with a great force of British troops, German mercenaries, and Indians. His plan was to invade upper New York State and New England by way of Lake Champlain and the Hudson River, and then join forces at Albany with General Howe. After some initial successes Burgoyne's fortunes shifted, and he was repeatedly defeated, largely through Benedict Arnold's brilliant strategy. Finally, finding himself hopelessly trapped at Saratoga, Burgoyne had no choice but to ask for terms of surrender. The extraordinary terms, called a "convention," not a capitulation, stipulated that Burgoyne and his army would be returned to England on parole not to serve again. As a result of this stunning victory, France decided openly and actively to enter the war on America's side.

American victory music at Saratoga consisted chiefly of "Yankee Doodle." Oscar Sonneck quotes the British officer Thomas Anburey, a member of the surrendered army, who wrote from his subsequent internment at Cambridge on November 27, 1777: "*Yankee Doodle* is now their paean, a favorite of favorites, played in their army, esteemed as warlike as the Grenadier's March—it is the lover's spell, the nurse's lullaby. After our rapid successes, we held the Yankees in great contempt, but it was not a little mortifying to hear them play this tune, when their army marched down to our surrender."

Benedict Arnold's inspired tactics with a homemade fleet on Lake Champlain succeeded in thwarting British strategy in 1776, the year C. Randle painted this watercolor.

The *Boston Gazette* (December 1, 1777) brought out a song dealing with the Burgoyne fiasco to "Yankee Doodle," now referred to—perhaps sardonically—as "The Lexington March."

SONG.

[*To the Tune of* "Lexington March"]

As Jack the King's Commander,
　　Was going to his Duty,
Thro' all the Crowd he smil'd and bow'd,
　　To ev'ry blooming Beauty.

The City rung of Feats he'd done,
　　In Portugal and Flanders;
And all the town tho't he'd be crown'd
　　A second Alexander.

To Hampton Court he first repair'd,
　　To kiss great George's Hand, Sir,
Then to harangue on state Affairs
　　Before he left the Land, Sir.

The Lower House sat mute as Mouse,
　　To hear his grand Oration,
And all the Peers, with loudest Cheers,
　　Proclaim'd him thro' the Nation.

Then straight he went to Canada,
　　Next to Ticonderoga;
And passing those, away he goes
　　Straightway to Saratoga.

With grand Parade his March he made,
　　To gain his wish'd for Station,
Whilst far and wide his Minions try'd
　　To spread his Proclamations.

"To such as stay'd he Offers made,
　　"Of Pardon on Submission,
"But Savage Bands should waste the Lands
　　"Of All in Opposition."

But ah! the cruel Fate of War!
　　This boasted Son of Britain,
When mounting his triumphal Car,
　　With sudden Fear was smitten.

The Sons of Freedom gather'd round,
　　His hostile Bands confounded,
And when they'd fain have turn'd their Backs,
　　They found themselves surrounded.

In vain they fought; in vain they fled,
　　Their *Chief*, humane and tender,
To save the rest, he thought it best,
　　His Forces to surrender.

Thus may America's brave Sons,
　　With Honor be rewarded;
And be the Fate of all her Foes
　　The same as here recorded.

The American Revolution was a civil war on two planes: it was not only a struggle to sever ties with the mother country, but also a bitter interior conflict between Americans of opposing principles and allegiances—the Loyalists, whom the Patriots called "tories," and the Patriots, whom the Loyalists called "rebels." When an occupation of a city impended, as at Philadelphia in 1777—or an evacuation, as at Boston in 1776 or New York in 1783—an exodus of political refugees would occur; and people of opposing political loyalties who remained behind were faced with adjusting to the new order, or appearing to. But the conflict nevertheless went on. Of course, there were always some willing collaborators on both sides who expediently bent with the prevailing wind. One of these was that Jekyll and Hyde among newspaper publishers, Benjamin Towne, who twice changed his political skin (when the British arrived at Philadelphia and after they departed) in order to maintain publication of his *Pennsylvania Evening Post* uninterrupted, intact (except ideologically), and in Philadelphia. When General Howe took the city in September 1777, a number of Loyalist bards surfaced, and Towne's newspaper provided a hospitable vehicle for their songs.

The most prominent Loyalist poets at this time were Joseph Stansbury and Dr. Jonathan Odell, both talented and prolific versifiers. Stansbury's beguilingly satirical verses were more adaptable for singing than Odell's, which tended to be massive and serious. Both men shared an avocation that appears to have been endemic to the breed of Loyalist balladeers—following the example of Dr. Benjamin Church, they were British agents. Stansbury and Odell later became implicated in the Benedict Arnold/Major John André treason plot; both were prosecuted by the American government; and both escaped, first to British-held New York and then to England.

The chameleonlike Mr. Towne published a song in the *Pennsylvania Evening Post* (December 2, 1777) that vividly evokes the atmosphere in captured Philadelphia, where the inhabitants had suffered from wartime shortages and inflation. Using a feminine pseudonym, "Flirtilla," Stansbury charmingly tempts the Philadelphians, to a nursery jingle, with a catalog of the good things of life available if only they would cooperate and yield up their hard money. Apparently New York, under British domination throughout the Revolution, was well supplied.

A NEW SONG.

Tune, "Come, my kitten, my kitten," &c.

Come all ye good people attend,
   Pray hear what a newcomer offers;
I've all sorts of good things to vend,
   If you will but open your coffers.
     Here we go up, up, up,
       And here we go down, down down–e
     Here we go backwards and forwards,
       And here we go round, round, round–e.

Here is a fleet from New York,
   And here the dry goods shall abound–e;
Here is both butter and pork,
   And all just now come around–e.
     Here, &c.

Here you have salt for your broth,
   And here you have sugar and cheese–e;
Tea without taxes or oath,
   But down with your *gold*, if you please–e.
     Here, &c.

Here is an end to your rags,
   Your backs shall no longer go bare–e:
Farewel to the sneers of the wags,
   But your *gold*, sir, must first take air–e.
     Here, &c.

Here you have good Irish beef,
   And here you have pepper and spice–e;
Here you may part with your grief,
   For *gold* we have plumbs for mince pies–e.
     Here, &c.

Here you have topknot and tete,
   Too big for a bushel to hold–e;
Here you may dress like the great,
   And all for a trifle of gold–e.
     Here, &c.

Here you have catgut and gauze,
   And cambrick and lawn very fine–e;
Mits, hose, and a thousand kickshaws,
   For which let your *silver* be mine–e.
     Here, &c.

Here you have trinkets so fine,
   And baubles to hang by your side–e.
Here you may glitter and shine,
   For gold you may look like a bride–e.
     Here, &c.

Then spurn at the wise old dons,
   Who make for their *paper* a rout–e;
Here's goods for your *gold* at once,
   Come out with your *gold*, come out–e.
     Here, &c.

You'll Ruin The Land, We Know,
   By joining with what we've told–e;
But since all your wealth must go,
   We'll strive to encircle your gold–e.
     Here, &c.

Come, surely I've told you enough!
   We have all that you want and wish–e;
But pray give us no paper stuff,
   We come here for the loaf and the fish–e.
     Here, &c.

The notorious Tory publisher James Rivington reprinted Stansbury's "Flirtilla" song in his New York Royal Gazette *(February 16, 1780).*

In 1775 irate Patriots had hanged Rivington in effigy, despite his protests that he faithfully maintained an impartial editorial policy in his New-York Gazetteer; *later that year, headed by Isaac Sears, they destroyed his printing press, then marched off to the tune of "Yankee Doodle."*

[NEW-YORK, SATURDAY, July 26, 1783.] THE [No. 713.]

R O Y A L GAZETTE.

PUBLISHED BY JAMES RIVINGTON, PRINTER   TO THE KING's, MOST EXCELLENT MAJESTY

Rivington went to England in 1776 and returned the following year with new printing equipment and an appointment as King's Printer. Appropriately changing his newspaper's name, and unimpeded by any further constraint to pretend impartiality, he resumed publishing in the congenial atmosphere of occupied New York.

Loyalists deplored the harsh treatment of Quakers by American Patriots, who regarded Quaker pacifism as a cloak for collaboration with the enemy. This concern is expressed by Stansbury in a serious song published from manuscript in 1860 by Winthrop Sargent (*The Loyalist Verses of Joseph Stansbury and Dr. Jonathan Odell*). In an editor's note Sargent explained that the Quakers' "willingness to remain at Philadelphia when the city was threatened by Howe . . . and when every one . . . on the American side was flying with his effects to the country, confirmed the suspicions already entertained against them. In March, 1777, John Adams writes from Philadelphia that 'more than one half of the inhabitants have removed into the country. . . . The remainder are chiefly Quakers, as dull as beatles. From these neither good is to be expected nor evil to be apprehended. . . .'"

A NEW SONG.

Tune: "Caesar and Pompey were both of them," &c.

When Britain determined to tax us at pleasure,
We rose as one Man, and opposed the measure;
Not liking the Pilgrammage, I can assure ye,
Of going to England for Trial by Jury.
   Therefore for Freedom alone we are fighting:
   For that sort of Freedom was not so inviting.

To Edicts of Britain subjection refusing,
We set up a Government of our own chusing.
The guardians of Freedom resolv'd to maintain it,
And published a long Bill of Rights to explain it.
   For it's for Freedom alone we are fighting:
   The name of all names which true Freemen delight in.

We fondly imagin'd that all future Story
Should tell of our Justice, our Freedom and Glory:
We laughed at Oppression, not dreaming or fearing
That Men would be banish'd without charge or hearing:
   For Freedom indeed we supposed we were fighting;
   But this sort of Freedom's not very inviting.

If they with our Enemies have been partakers,
Then prove it in God's name, and punish the Quakers:
But if there is nothing alleged but suspicion,
What honest Man's safe from this State-Inquisition?
   If such be the Freedom for which we are fighting,
   This sample, good Folks, is not very inviting.

The good men are seiz'd on, who boldly defie all
The malice of Hell, and demand a fair Trial—
The cause of refusal you vainly dissemble:
"The churchmen must bend, and the Quakers shall tremble."
   Since this is the Freedom for which we are fighting.
   The old-fashioned Freedom was much more inviting.

When Quakers and Churchmen have suffer'd your pleasure—
Their Worship and Consciences shap'd to your measure—
The Catholics then may expect Penal laws,
Whereby we shall have one Religion and Cause.
   This, this is the Freedom for which we are fighting:
   And let all who think so, call it inviting.

As 1777 drew to a close, Loyalist ballads proliferated in the compliant pages of the *Pennsylvania Evening Post*. The following song, supposedly smuggled out of a Boston jail, appeared on December 4. In the text, "Jemima" refers to "my Jemima" in "Yankee Doodle"; *bundle* refers to bundling, a charming eighteenth-century premarital exercise, not confined to America.

A new SONG,

Composed by a prisoner in a Boston jail.

Tune, Black Sloven.

Americans swarming by thousands on shore,
Grew mighty in mischief, were subjects no more.
   Fa la, &c.

Held George in defiance, his friends they trepann'd,
The loyal imprisoned, and rav'd through the land.
   Fa la, &c.

They boasted Great Britain no more dare oppose,
And those who dissented, they treated as foes.
   Fa la, &c.

Independence proclaimed, each tailor look'd big,
Flung his measure aside, became colonel and Whig.
   Fa la, &c.

His majesty frown'd at their folly and rage,
But his pity prevail'd, he was loth to engage.
   Fa la, &c.

Be easy and happy, my children, he cried.
Their madness was boundless, his mercy defy'd.
   Fa la, &c.

Go forth then, brave Howe, and the rebels chastise,
He spoke while soft pity sat drenched in his eyes.
   Fa la, &c.

Go bear provok'd vengeance, but rather forgive,
Should the rebels submit, then spare and let live.
   Fa la, &c.

Howe fled o'er the ocean, and bounced on his prey,
Whole colonies swarmed, as assur'd of the day.
   Fa la, &c.

But what are e'en numbers, when Britons arise?
They run on sure ruin: who meets them but dies?
   Fa la, &c.

~~~

The rebels retreat and their bulwarks they shun,
To the woods nimbly skulk with their brave Washington.
   Fa la, &c.

~~~

Their impregnable fortress, Long-Island is taken,
And York and Kingsbridge are forever forsaken.
   Fa la, &c.

Now where will the Yankies retreat in their flight?
To Jemima, be sure, better bundle than fight.
   Fa la, &c.

Come on ye brave heroes, proceed, Boston assail,
Relieve the poor Tories, who languish in jail.
   Fa la, &c.

~~~

Although this Congress-hating song was supposed to have been "wrote" in 1776, while Congress was debating the Declaration of Independence, it did not see the light of day until the British were well ensconced in Philadelphia, when it appeared in Towne's *Pennsylvania Evening Post* (December 20, 1777).

A SONG.

Wrote in the Spring of the year 1776.
Tune: "Nancy Dawson"

Ye Tories all rejoice and sing
Success to George our gracious King,
The faithful subjects tribute bring,
  And execrate the congress.

Those hardy knaves and stupid fools,
Some apish and pragmatic mules,
Some servile acquiescing tools;
  These, these, compose the congress.

When Jove resolv'd to send a curse,
And all the woes of life rehearse,
Nor plague, nor famine, but much worse,
  He curs'd us with a congress.

∼∼∼

With freemen's rights they wanton play;
At their command we fast and pray,
With worthless paper they us pay;
  A fine device of congress.

∼∼∼

Time serving priests to zealots preach,
Who King and parliament impeach,
Seditious lessons to us teach,
  At the command of congress.

∼∼∼

With puffs and flams and gasconade,
With stupid jargon they bravade,
We transports take, Quebec invade;
  With laurels crown the congress.

Our mushroom champions they dragoon,
We cry out hero, not poltroon,
The next campaign we'll storm the moon,
  And there proclaim the congress.

∼∼∼

Clinton, Burgoyne, and gallant Howe,
Will soon reward our conduct true,
To ev'ry traitor give his due;
  Perdition waits the congress.

∼∼∼

There's Washington and all his men,
Where Howe had one, the goose had ten,
March'd up the hill, and down again,
  And sent returns to congress.

Prepare, prepare, my friends prepare,
For scenes of blood, the field of war,
To royal standard we'll repair,
  And curse the haughty congress.

Huzza! Huzza! We thrice huzza,
Return peace, harmony, and law,
Restore such times as once we saw,
  And bid adieu to congress.

After the British departed from Philadelphia, the changeable Benjamin Towne, seen above in an engraving after Rowlandson (1809), once again became a dedicated publisher of American liberty songs. This advertisement in his Pennsylvania Evening Post *(January 29, 1780) solicited contributions for a pamphlet collection of patriotic songs.*

†✚† A variety of fongs to be fold by the printer, who would be much obliged to ladies and gentlemen for copies of fuch American LIBER-TY fongs as he has not yet printed.

Francis Hopkinson, in two senses the author of "The Battle of the Kegs," has been called, "next to Franklin, the most versatile American of the eighteenth century." Besides being America's first composer—and an accomplished performing musician as well—he was a gifted writer of prose and poetry, an inventor, an artist and designer (he is believed to have designed the American flag), and a philosopher. As a lawyer, Hopkinson occupied a number of official positions, many of them judicial. He was a signer of the Declaration of Independence, and a friend of Benjamin Franklin, Thomas Jefferson, and George Washington, to whom he dedicated a group of songs. His portrait is an engraving after the well-known painting by Robert Edge Pine.

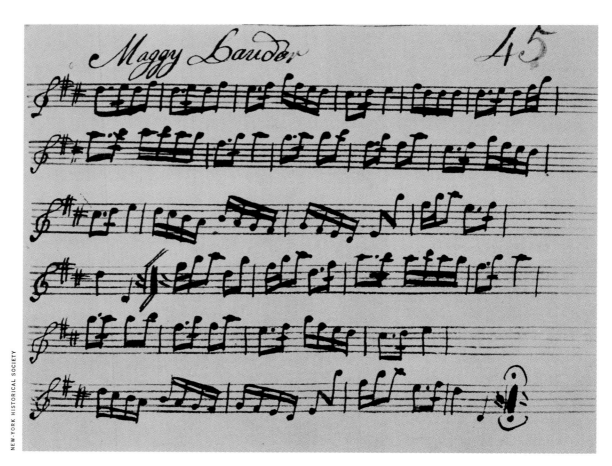

"Maggie Lauder," from John Greenwood's Book

In the winter of 1778, during the occupation of Philadelphia, Hopkinson, as chairman of the Navy Board, engaged in a fantastic and innovative experiment with David Bushnell, the inventor of the torpedo and "Father of the Submarine." Floating mines made to resemble wooden kegs, which would blow up on contact, were released on the Delaware, where a large number of British ships were anchored. Because of freezing weather the plan miscarried: the intended targets had been docked to avoid floating ice. The juicy propaganda potential of the incident was not neglected, however. Understandable British bafflement over these unidentified floating objects was ridiculed in a delightful spoof of the incident that appeared disguised as a news story in the *New-Jersey Gazette* (January 21, 1778). Its author was Francis Hopkinson.

Converting his prose satire to a ballad set to the popular tune "Maggie Lauder," Hopkinson provided much-needed relief to the hard-pressed Americans at a time of great crisis. James Thacher wrote (*Journal of the American Revolutionary War*) that at camp: "Our drums and fife afforded us a favorite amusement till evening, when we were delighted with the song composed by Mr. Hopkinson called the 'Battle of the Kegs' sung in the best style by a number of gentlemen." The song first appeared in the *Pennsylvania Packet* (March 4, 1778). In the text, "Sir William" is, of course, General Howe; his sleeping partner is the notorious Mrs. Joshua Loring; "Sir Erskine" is Sir William Erskine, a member of Howe's staff.

THE BATTLE OF THE KEGS.
Tune, "Maggie Lauder"

Gallants attend, and hear a friend
    Trill forth harmonious ditty;
Strange things I'll tell, which late befel
    In Philadelphia city.

'Twas early day, as poets say,
    Just when the sun was rising;
A soldier stood on a log of wood,
    And saw a sight surprising.

As in amaze he stood to gaze,
    The truth can't be deny'd, sir;
He spy'd a score of kegs, or more,
    Come floating down the tide, sir.

A sailor too, in jerkin blue,
    This strange appearance viewing,
First damn'd his eyes, in great surprise,
    Then said—"Some mischief's brewing.

"These kegs now hold the rebels bold
    "Pack'd up like pickl'd herring:
"And they're come down to attack the town,
    "In this new way of ferrying."

The soldier flew, the sailor too,
    And scar'd almost to death, sir;
Wore out their shoes to spread the news,
    And ran till out of breath, sir;

Now up and down, throughout the town,
    Most frantic scenes were acted;
And some ran here and others there,
    Like men almost distracted.

Some fire cry'd, which some deny'd,
    But said the earth had quaked:
And girls and boys, with hideous noise,
    Ran through the streets half naked.

Sir William he, snug as a flea,
    Lay all this time a snoring,
Nor dreamed of harm, as he lay warm
    In bed with mrs. Loring.

Now in a fright he starts upright,
    Awak'd by such a clatter;
First rubs his eyes, then boldly cries,
    "For God's sake, what's the matter?"

At his bed side he then espy'd
    Sir Erskine at command, sir;
Upon one foot he had one boot,
    And t'other in his hand, sir.

"Arise, arise," sir Erskine cries,
    "The rebels—more's the pity!
"Without a boat are all afloat,
    "And rang'd before the city.

"The motley crew, in vessels new,
    "With Satan for their guide, sir;
"Pack'd up in bags, and wooden kegs,
    "Come driving down the tide, sir.

"Therefore prepare for bloody war,
    "These kegs must all be routed,
"Or surely we despis'd shall be,
    "And British valour doubted."

The royal band now ready stand,
    All rang'd in dread array, sir,
On ev'ry slip, in ev'ry ship,
    For to begin the fray, sir.

The cannons roar from shore to shore,
    The small arms make a rattle;
Since wars began, I'm sure no man
    E'er saw so strange a battle.

The *rebel* dales—the *rebel* vales,
    With *rebel* trees surrounded;
The distant woods, the hills and floods,
    With *rebel* echoes sounded.

The fish below swam to and fro,
    Attack'd from ev'ry quarter;
Why sure, thought they, the De'il's to pay
    Among folks above the water.

The kegs, 'tis said, tho' strongly made
    Of *rebel* staves and hoops, sir,
Could not oppose their powerful foes,
    The conqu'ring British troops, sir.

From morn to night these men of might
    Display'd amazing courage;
And when the sun was fairly down,
    Retir'd to sup their porridge.

One hundred men with each a pen
    Or more, upon my word, sir,
It is most true, would be too few
    Their valour to record, sir.

Such feats did they perform that day
    Against these wicked kegs, sir.
That years to come, if they get home,
    They'll make their boasts and brags, sir.

Benjamin Franklin was a member of the American commission that signed two treaties of alliance with France in 1778. One treaty pledged mutual amity and commerce; the other promised military alliance in case France's recognition of the United States brought her to war with Great Britain, which soon transpired. With recognition, Franklin became the first American minister to France—or anywhere—and a French minister was appointed to the United States. Franklin's portrait was painted by Jean-Baptiste Greuze in 1782.

GOD SAVE AMERICA.

God save America, Free from tyrannic sway,

Till time shall cease: Hush'd be the din of arms,

And all proud war's alarms ; Follow in

all her charms, Heaven born peace.

In the new United States, "God Save America" replaced "God Save the King" in everything but tune. From the American Patriotic Songbook *(1813).*

When the glorious news of the alliance with France began to spread through the thirteen states, there was great rejoicing and celebration everywhere. At Washington's camp at Valley Forge, according to the *North-Carolina Gazette* (May 29, 1778), there was a "triple discharge from thirteen pieces of cannon. . . . Universal joy appeared in every countenance; and great plenty of liquor was given to the populace. . . ." In Baltimore the alliance was celebrated in song. The tune? "God Save the King." From the *Maryland Journal, and the Baltimore Advertiser* (May 12, 1778):

The following SONG was composed *ex Tempore*,
on receiving the TREATIES from *France*.

God save *America*,
Free from despotic sway.
   Till time shall cease.
Hushed be the Din of Arms,
Also fierce War's Alarms,
And follow in all her charms,
   Heaven-born Peace.

Next in our Song shall be,
Guardian of Liberty,
   Louis the King.
Terrible God of War,
Plac'd in victorious Car,
Of *France* and of *Navarre*,
   Louis the King.

God save great *Washington*,
Fair FREEDOM's chosen son;
   Long to command.
May ever'y Enemy,
Far from his Presence fly,
And be grim Tyranny,
   Bound by his Hand.

France's overt participation in the American Revolution began with the arrival in July 1778 of a fleet under the command of Count Charles-Hector d'Estaing. In August he sailed for Rhode Island to assist General John Sullivan in an attempt to dislodge the British from Newport, which they had held since 1776. D'Estaing was met by a British fleet under Lord Howe, and as they prepared to do battle, a storm of such furious violence arose that both fleets were dispersed far and wide. By the time d'Estaing collected his scattered and battered forces, he decided to make for Boston instead of returning to support Sullivan. This fiasco inspired a ditty of derogation to the tune of "Yankee Doodle" that appeared in Rivington's *Royal Gazette* (October 3, 1778).

In the text, "Lewis" is Louis XVI of France; "Monsieur Gerard" is Conrad Alexandre Gérard, the first French minister to the United States, who arrived with d'Estaing; *Begar* is a euphemism for *by God*, and, according to the *Oxford English Dictionary*, is "not in polite use"; "bold Pigot" is Sir Robert Pigot, the British commander in chief for Rhode Island; "Jonathan" (also "Brother Jonathan") was a nickname, or symbol, first for Yankees, then for all Americans. It is said to have originated during the Revolution when General Washington referred to his friend Governor Jonathan Trumbull of Connecticut as "Brother Jonathan." Jonathan continued to symbolize America until the early nineteenth century, when he was replaced by "Uncle Sam."

Admiral Lord Howe

YANKEE DOODLE's *Expedition to Rhode-Island.*
Written at Philadelphia.

From Lewis, Monsieur Gerard came
To Congress in this town Sir,
They bow'd to him, and he to them,
And then they all sat down, Sir.
    CHORUS. Yankee Doodle, &c.

Begar said Monsieur one grand *Coup*
You shall *bientot* behold Sir,
This was believ'd as Gospel true,
And Jonathan *felt bold* Sir.

So Yankee Doodle did forget
The sound of British drum Sir,
How oft it made him quake and sweat
In spite of Yankee Rum Sir.

He took his wallet on his back,
His Rifle on his shoulder,
And *veow'd* Rhode Island to attack
Before he was much older.

In dread array their tatter'd crew,
Advanc'd with colours spread Sir,
Their fifes play'd Yankee Doodle doo,
King Hancock at their Head Sir.

What numbers bravely cross'd the seas,
I cannot well determine,
A swarm of Rebels and of fleas,
And every other vermin.

Their mighty hearts might shrink they tho't;
For all flesh only grass is,
A plenteous store they therefore brought,
Of Whisky and Molasses.

They swore they'd make bold Pigot squeak,
So did their good Ally, Sir,
And take him prisoner in a week;
But that was all *my eye*, Sir.

As Jonathan so much desir'd,
To shine in martial story,
D'Estaing with politesse retir'd
To leave him all the glory.

He left him what was better yet;
At least it was more use Sir,
He left him for a quick retreat,
A very good excuse Sir.

To stay, unless he ruled the sea,
He thought would not be right Sir,
And Continental Troops, said he,
On Islands should not fight Sir.

Another cause with these combin'd
To throw him in the dumps Sir,
For CLINTON's name alarmed his mind
And made him stir his stumps Sir,
    Sing Yankee Doodle Doodle doo.

When the principal arena of the war shifted to the South in the autumn of 1778, the North Carolina-born general Robert Howe was put in command of the Southern Continental forces, an appointment that stirred up great controversy in South Carolina, where he was unpopular. The dispute culminated in the resignation of his rival, the South Carolinian general Christopher Gadsden, and the two generals eventually settled their differences in a bloodless duel. This singular incident was ridiculed in yet another song to "Yankee Doodle" that pretended to have been written in Charleston. More probably it originated in New York; its author was the talented and versatile Major John André, who was stationed there. The song appeared in a pamphlet published by Rivington in 1780.

On the Affair Between the
Rebel Generals

HOWE and GADDESDEN,

Written at *Charlestown.*

It was on Mr. *Peroy*'s land,
   At Squire *Rugeley*'s corner,
Great H and G met, sword in hand,
   Upon a point of honour.
     Yankee Doodle, doodle doo, &c.

G went before with Col'nel E
   Together in a carriage,
On horseback followed H and P,
   As if to steal a marriage.

On *chosen* ground they now alight,
   For battle duly harness'd,
A *shady* place, and *out* of *sight,*
   It shew'd they were in *earnest.*

They met, and in the usual way,
   With hat in hand saluted,
Which was, no doubt, to shew how they
   Like *Gentlemen* disputed.

And then they both made
   This honest declaration,
That they came there—by *honor* led,
   But—not by *inclination.*

That if they fought, 'twas not because
   Of rancour, spite or passion,
But only to obey the laws
   Of custom and of fashion.

The pistols then, *before their eyes,*
   Were fairly prim'd and loaded!
H wish'd, and so did G likewise,
   The custom was exploded!

But as they now had gone so far
   In such a *bloody business,*
For action straight they both prepare
   With—mutual forgiveness.

But lest their courage should exceed
   The bounds of moderation,
Between the seconds 'twas agreed
   To fix them each a station.

The distance stepp'd by Colonel P.
   'Twas only eight short paces,
Now, gentlemen, says Colonel P,
   Be sure—to keep your places.

Quoth H to G—Sir, please to fire,
   Quoth G—no, pray begin, Sir;
And, truly, one must needs admire
   The temper they were in, Sir!

We'll fire both at once, said he,
   And so they both presented;
No answer was returned by G,
   But silence, Sir, consented.

They *paus'd* awhile, these gallant foes,
   By turns politely grinning,
Till after many cons and pros,
   H made a *brisk* beginning.

He miss'd his *mark,* but not his *aim,*
   The shot was well directed;
It sav'd them both from *hurt* and *shame;*
   What more could be expected!

Then G, to shew he meant no harm,
   But hated jars and jangles,
His pistol fired, across his arm,
   From H—almost [at] angles.

H now was call'd upon by G
   To fire another shot, Sir,
He *smil'd,* and—"after this" quoth he,
   "No, truly, I cannot, Sir."

Such honour did they both display,
   They highly were commended;
And thus, in short, this gallant fray
   Without mischance was ended.

No fresh dispute, we may suppose,
   Will e'er by them be started,
For now the Chiefs, no longer foes,
   Shook hands, and—so they parted.
     Yankee Doodle, doodle doo, &c.

By far the most musically significant song of the American Revolution is William Billings's "Chester," for which he wrote new patriotic words in 1778. In its original form "Chester" had been set to an exquisite spiritual text by Dr. Isaac Watts and published in the first of Billings's six tune-books, *The New-England Psalm-Singer, or American Chorister* (1770). With its stirring new text it was included in his second book, *The Singing Master's Assistant* (1778), and it immediately became a favorite Revolutionary anthem. "Chester" is outstanding, not only because it is the first authentically American patriotic musical statement we know of, but because it is an authentic work of musical genius for any age.

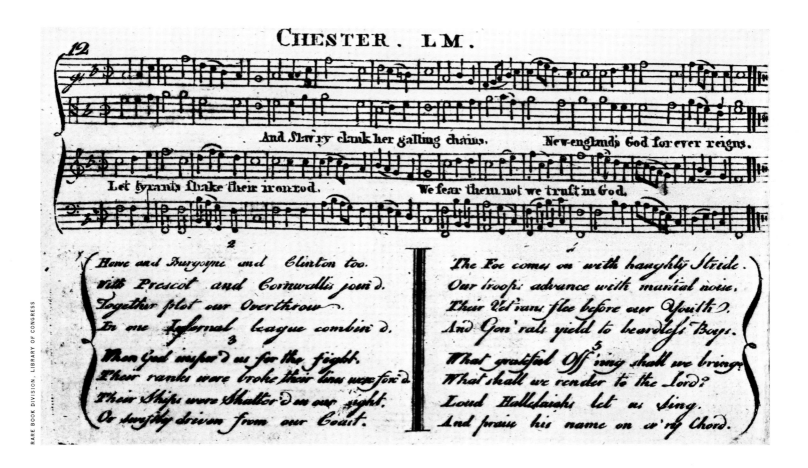

Let tyrants shake their iron rod
And Slav'ry clank her galling chains,
We fear them not, we trust in God,
New-England's God for ever reigns.

Howe and Burgoyne and Clinton too,
With Prescott and Cornwallis join'd,
Together plot our Overthrow,
In one Infernal league combin'd.

When God inspir'd us for the fight,
Their ranks were broke, their lines were forc'd,
Their Ships were Shatter'd in our sight,
Or swiftly driven from our Coast.

The Foe comes on with haughty Stride,
Our troops advance with martial noise,
Their Vet'rans flee before our Youth,
And Gen'rals yield to beardless Boys.

What grateful Off'ring shall we bring?
What shall we render to the Lord?
Loud Halleluiahs let us Sing,
And praise his name on ev'ry Chord.

"Mad" Anthony Wayne's spectacular midnight capture of the British stronghold at Stony Point, New York, on July 16, 1779, was celebrated in prose and verse, some of it sung. Straining the limits of exuberant eighteenth-century journalistic passion, the *Connecticut Gazette, and the Universal Intelligencer* (August 4, 1779) exclaimed: "The firm coolness with which they [Wayne's men] marched up to the attack of what our Enemies stiled the *American Gibralter*, was never exceeded by any troops whatever, ancient or modern." The Loyalist Justice Thomas Jones wrote (*History of New York during the Revolutionary War*): "The commandant of the fort and a select company of friends were devoting themselves to pleasure, and pouring down large libations to the 'jolly god' . . . when Wayne entered the room and made them all prisoners."

General Anthony Wayne

"On General Wayne's taking Stoney Point," found in an undated pamphlet collection of liberty songs, gives a sprightly and fairly accurate account of the exploit except for the date. In the text, "Johnson" is Colonel Johnson, the British commander of the fort; "Fleury, Stewart, Knox," and "Gibbons" are Wayne's officers. The tune, slyly titled "One night as Ned stept into bed," scans suspiciously like "Yankee Doodle."

ON GEN. WAYNE'S TAKING STONEY POINT.

Tune: One night as Ned stept into bed.

July, they say, the fifteenth day,
  In glittering arms arrayed,
That gen'ral Wayne and his brave men
  The British lines essayed;
Just twelve at night, if I am right,
  And honestly informed,
Both wings at once they did advance,
  And Stoney Point they stormed.

  With ascents steep, morasses deep,
This boasted place abounded,
Strong abettees, of forked trees,
  Were doubly placed around it;
"In this strong place the rebel race
"Us never dare come nigh, sir,
"Great Washington, and all his train,
"I, Johnson do defy, sir."

  But mark the fate of Johnson's hate,
How quickly he was humbled,
When light'ning like, bold WAYNE did strike,
  His pride and glory tumbled;
See FLEURY brave the standard wave,
  Which strongly was defended,
And from his foes; 'midst of their blows,
  Most gallantly did rend it.

  Let STEWART's name in books of fame
For ever be recorded,
Through show'rs of balls he scaled their walls,
  And danger disregarded;
O'er stones and rocks heroic KNOX,
  To charge the foe he pushed,
In gallant fight, with eagle's flight,
  O'er their strong ramparts rushed.

  And GIBBONS, gay as chearful May,
His duty well discharged,
He dealt his foes such deadly blows,
  That left their walls unguarded.
May war's alarms still rouse to arms
  The gallant sons of brav'ry,
Who dare withstand a tyrant's band,
  And crush infernal slav'ry.

General Waynes New March
— Stoney Point & Yanky doodle —

Published at B. Carrs Musical Repositories Philadelphia, New York & J. Carrs Baltimore (Price 12 Cents)

In 1780, a desperate year for America, the British commander in chief Sir Henry Clinton and his second in command Lord Cornwallis embarked on a massive offensive in the South. On May 12 they took Charleston from General Benjamin Lincoln. The surrender was attended by a singular, musical clash of wills between the opposing commanders. As related by an eyewitness, General William Moultrie (*Memoirs of the American Revolution*), the seventh of Lincoln's Articles of Capitulation, submitted on May 8, proposed: "The Garrison shall . . . march out with shouldered arms, drums beating and colours flying, to a place agreed on, where they will pile their arms." The following day the British commanders, General Clinton and Admiral Arbuthnot, for some reason imposed a restriction on the music to be played: ". . . the drums are not to beat a British march . . . or colours to be uncased." Although he had not previously suggested that the American bands play a British march, General Lincoln unaccountably found this restriction "inadmissable." He insisted: "This article to stand as first proposed [which it hadn't been]; the drums beating a British march." It was now General Clinton's turn to find this inadmissable, and so, according to General Moultrie, the battle was resumed with "cannon balls whizzing and shells hissing continually amongst us." On May 11 Lincoln was forced to capitulate again and to accede to Clinton's musical prohibition. A German staff captain of the Jäger Corps, attached to Clinton's army, wrote in his journal (quoted in Bernard A. Uhlendorf's *Siege of Charleston*): "The moment the British grenadiers came under the gate the oboists played 'God Save the King.'" He then recounted the final act of the bizarre musical comedy: the American garrison "were permitted to march off with drums beating and trumpets sounding, but their colors had to be cased. Since they were not allowed to play an English march, they played the Turk's march. . . ."

General Benjamin Lincoln

After the capture of Charleston, Congress appointed General Horatio Gates to command the Southern Continental forces, and on August 16 he was vanquished by Cornwallis in a fierce engagement near Camden. The hero of Saratoga distinguished himself by executing a spectacular personal retreat on horseback, galloping nonstop as far as Charlotte—some seventy miles from the battlefield—and, incidentally, galloping out of the active army as well. A fairly elaborate vocal concoction in duet form, dealing with Gates's fiasco, was published in the *Royal Gazette* on September 27, 1780, and reprinted in the *South Carolina and American General Gazette* in once-again Loyalist Charleston.

A PASTORAL ELEGY,

Set to Music by Signora Carolina.

JONATHAN.   ISAAC.

ISAAC. *(Allegro.)*
O Wherefore brother Jonathan,
  So doleful are your features?
Say, are you rather poorly, man,
  Or have you lost your creatures?

JONATHAN. *(Piano.)*
Ah, wou'd to Heaven that were all!
  But worse I have to mention,
For Gates, our gallant general
  Has made a new convention.

ISAAC. *(Vivace.)*
Then Jonathan prick up your ears;
  Why don't you smile and caper?
Why, we'll enlist the Regulars,
  And pay them with our paper.

JONATHAN. *(Piano.)*
The regulars prescribed the terms,
  Nor staid for long orations;
They forc'd our troops to ground their arms
  And eke their corporations.

ISAAC. *(Moderato.)*
O! that is grievous! I mistook,
  Tho' your lank phiz did bode ill,
How pert will ev'ry Tory look—
  And sneer at Yankee Doodle!

JONATHAN. *(Piano.)*
A thousand slaughtered friends we've lost,
  A thousand more are taken;
Horatio's steed, which gallop'd past,
  Has saved his rider's bacon.

DUETTO *(Affettuoso.)*
Now mourn, with sackcloth cover'd o'er,
  Our Israel forsaken!
So many slain—while such a Boar
  As Gates shou'd save his bacon.

Music to celebrate British military successes

In September 1780 both America and Europe were stunned at the shocking disclosure that the brilliant American general Benedict Arnold was a traitor. The incredible details—Arnold's treason; his defection to the British; and the concomitant capture and execution of his young British accomplice, the gifted and personable Major André—were the dominant topic everywhere. *The Connecticut Courant, and the Weekly Intelligencer* (October 3, 1780) wrote: ". . . a most horrid plot was discovered, the infamous Gen. Arnold at the heart of it; who, it is supposed, has been corrupted by the influence of British gold, having agreed to deliver up the Fort at West Point; for which purpose he drew a plan of all the works at the Point, and gave it to a spy, Major John André, Adjutant General of the British army, and First Aid of Sir Henry Clinton."

A victim of conspiring fate and bad judgment, Major André was caught while trying to get back to New York, having missed connections with his ship after his meeting with Arnold at West Point. He was tried and sentenced to be executed as a spy. British pressures on General Washington to obtain his release were unavailing, as was André's letter begging Washington to allow him to die before a firing squad instead of being hanged as a common spy.

The *Connecticut Courant* (October 10, 1780) commented on André's execution: "His unhappy fate was much regretted, though his life was justly forfeited by the law of nations. . . he died like a brave soldier . . . in the bloom of life [he was twenty-nine years old], Major André, the pride of the British army. . . ." Despite his acknowledged guilt, André's fate somehow aroused great pity and romantic sentiment among Americans. While Arnold was universally execrated (he was not greatly loved by his new British colleagues, either), André—handsome, young, doomed—has continued over the years to inspire tears, sighs, poems, and songs.

A pen and ink self-portrait of Major John André, made in prison (October 1, 1780) shortly before his execution

Bizarre processions, complete with effigies and devils reminiscent of Stamp Act days, took place to commemorate Arnold and André's infamy. The Smith who shared with André the double-faced effigy shown here is Joshua Hett Smith, an American who was implicated in André's attempted escape. According to the Independent Chronicle *(October 19, 1780) the parade was accompanied by appropriate music, "The Rogues' March," played by drums and fifes, as we see in this illustration from the* Amerikanischer Haus und Wirtschafts Calender auf das 1781ste Jahr Christi. . . , *Philadelphia (1780).*

Death of Major Andre.

COME all you brave Americans I pray you lend an ear,
I will sing you a short ditty your spirits for to cheer,
Concerning a young gentleman whose age was twenty-two,
He is fit for North America, with a heart that's just and true.

The British took him from his lodging and did him close confine
They in strong prison bound him & kept him there sometime,
But he being something valient resolv'd there not to stay,
He got himself at liberty and from them come away.

And when that he had returned home to his own country,
There was many a plan contriving to undo America;
Plotted by General Arnold, and his bold british crew,
They tho't to shed our innocent blood and America to undue.

It was of a scouting party that sail'd from Tarrytown,
They met a British officer of fame and high renown;
And sail to this young gentleman you are of the british core,
And I trust that you can tell me if the dangers are all o'er.

O then up steps John Spalding saying you must dismount,
And where you are agoing you must give a strict account;
I am a British flag sir, I've a pass to go this way,
Upon an expedition in North America.

O then up steps John Spalding saying you must dismount,
And where you are agoing give me a more strict account;
For I will have you searched before that you pass by—
On a strict exammation he was found to be a British Spy!

" There take my gold and silver and all I have in store,
And when down to New. York I come will send you thousands
        more!
I scorn your gold and silver, I've enough of it in store,
And when my mouey it is gone I will bodily fight for more.

O then he found that all his plans were like to be bro't to light,
He call'd for pen and paper and begged leave to write
A line to General Arnold to let him know his fate,
He begged of him assistance but alas, it was too late!

When Arnold he this letter read it made his heart relent,
He called for his barge, down to New York quickly went;
There he is amongst the Britons a fighting for his king
He has left poor Major Andre on the gallows for to swing!

If you are a man from Britain with courage stout and bold,
I'le fear no man of valour tho' he be cloth'd in gold;
This place it is improper our valour for to try,
And if we take the sword in hand one of the two must die!

When he was executed he being both meek and mild,
Around on the spectators most pleasantly did smile,
' fill'd each one with terror and caus'd their hearts to bleed,
They wished that Andre was set free and Arnold in his stead.

Success unto John Spalding, let his health be drank around,
Likewise to those brave heroes who fough against the crown
Here is a health to every Soldier who fought for liberty,
And to the brave and gallant Washington of North America·

Printed and Sold at N0, 25, High Street, PROVIDENCE, where may be obtained 100 other kinds.

WASHINGTON'S MARCH

AS PERFORMED

at the

New Theatre.

PHILADELPHIA

Published and Sold at G. Willig's Musical Magazine.

By the summer of 1781 the Continental forces under General Nathanael Greene, Gates's successor, had regained all of the South except Charleston and Savannah. By meticulous planning, superb teamwork, and prompt action, Washington, Count Rochambeau, and Admiral de Grasse, with split-second precision, brought

Quick Step Composed by R. Taylor.

the combined allied forces together at Yorktown, where Cornwallis had succeeded in painting himself into a corner. On October 17, 1781, exactly four years from the day Burgoyne had capitulated at Saratoga, Cornwallis asked for terms of surrender.

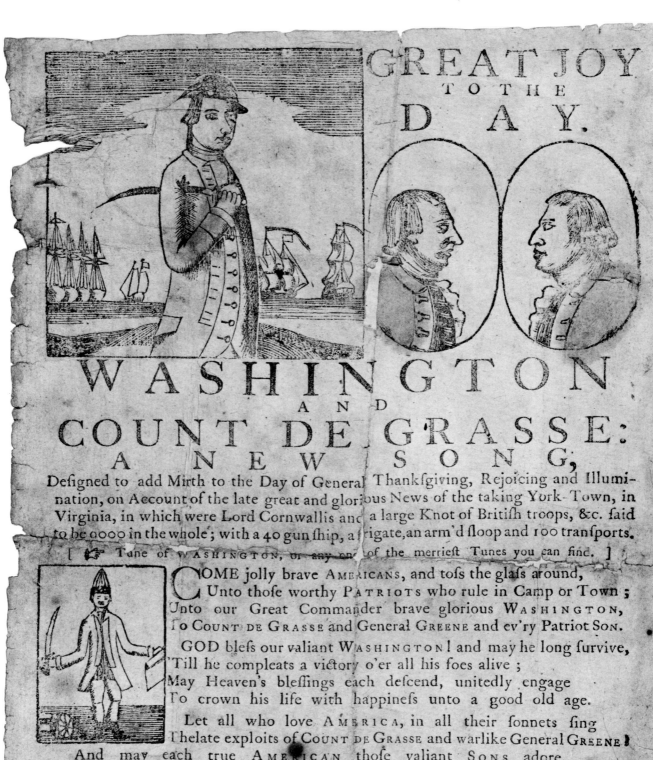

GREAT JOY TO THE DAY.

WASHINGTON AND COUNT DE GRASSE:
A NEW SONG,

Designed to add Mirth to the Day of General Thanksgiving, Rejoicing and Illumination, on Account of the late great and glorious News of the taking York-Town, in Virginia, in which were Lord Cornwallis and a large Knot of British troops, &c. said to be oooo in the whole; with a 40 gun ship, a frigate, an arm'd sloop and 100 transports.

[☞ Tune of WASHINGTON, or any one of the merriest Tunes you can find.]

COME jolly brave AMERICANS, and toss the glass around,
Unto those worthy PATRIOTS who rule in Camp or Town;
Unto our Great Commander brave glorious WASHINGTON,
To COUNT DE GRASSE and General GREENE and ev'ry Patriot Son.

GOD bless our valiant WASHINGTON! and may he long survive,
'Till he compleats a victory o'er all his foes alive;
May Heaven's blessings each descend, unitedly engage
To crown his life with happiness unto a good old age.

Let all who love AMERICA, in all their sonnets sing
The late exploits of COUNT DE GRASSE and warlike General GREENE!
And may each true AMERICAN those valiant SONS adore,
For all their brave heroic deeds 'till time shall be no more.

O what a noble capture 'twas! must ev'ry one confess,
Of valiant COUNT DE GRASSE of late, and each the Hero bless;
His conqu'ring pow'r by sea display'd, forc'd British ships to strike,
One hundred sail of transports yield to the Blue and White:

Besides three British men of war were captur'd by his hand,
Struck to this noble ADMIRAL's flag, and bow'd at his command.
Nine thousand of their armed troops were conquer'd all in one,
Huzza! for Admiral COUNT DE GRASSE and glorious WASHINGTON.

GOD bless our noble GOVERNOR! long may he yet survive,
A scourge to all base Tories who wickedly connive
To undermine fair FREEDOM's walls, with all her noble train;
Huzza! for all our PATRIOT Sons, let FREEDOM ever reign.

Sold at RUSSELL's Printing-Office, near Liberty-Stump. (Pr. 4 Cop.) ☞ At the same Place may be had, cheap to Travelling-traders, &c. BICKERSTAFF's BOSTON ALMANACK for 1782.

90

3. Grand Triumphal March 1781-1788

The appealing tale that Cornwallis's regimental bands slowly and mournfully played a tune called "The World Turned Upside Down" as they lay down their arms at Yorktown is strictly hearsay. Originating only in 1828, the story caught on, and it is still generally accepted, although it does not appear in contemporary accounts of the occasion. However, there was no failure to mention "Yankee Doodle," which was continuously played at Yorktown, but not by the British. Possibly in retaliation for the episode at the surrender of Charleston the year before, they were forbidden to play an American or a French march. Just about every newspaper in the United States reported that ". . . General Lincoln received the captured Lord Cornwallis; and . . . the army played up Yankey doodle, when the British army marched to lay down their arms." For reasons of haste or economy, the printer of this broadside to celebrate Yorktown, "Great Joy to the Day," used the same engraving of two men in profile to represent Washington and de Grasse that had appeared on the broadside "War(d) and Washington" (see page 63). The tune, designated as "Washington," is "The British Grenadiers."

His Excelly GEORGE WASHINGTON, Esqr.

GENERAL and COMMANDER in CHIEF of the Allied Armies,

Supporting the Independence of AMERICA.

Taken from an Original Picture in posession of his Exy Govr Hancock
Published by John Coles, Boston, March 20.1782

From the Americ shore,
The vast Atlantic o'er,
   Shout—"WASHINGTON!"
Americans all unite
To do the hero right,
Our glory—boast—delight
   High in renown.

See o'er the British Peer
He rides the grand career
   Of Victory.
At his advance the foe
Lay their proud standards low,
And, by these tokens, show
   America's free.

An army in parade
Captives, at length are made;
   The deed is done.
America triumphs free;
Laws, Rights, and Liberty,
Next God, we owe to thee,
   Great WASHINGTON.

~~~

From a song in the New-Jersey Journal
(December 26, 1781) to the
tune of "God Save the King";
the portrait of Washington
engraved by John Norman (1782).

At Yorktown "Yankee Doodle" was supremely vindicated. A French observer, A. Levasseur, later wrote (*Lafayette in America in 1824 and 1825*) that when the British General O'Hara (standing in for the unsporting Cornwallis, who "pleaded indisposition") attempted to offer his sword to General Rochambeau instead of Washington, Lafayette "revenged himself in a very pleasant manner. He ordered the music of the light infantry to strike up *Yankee doodle*, an air which the British applied to a song composed to ridicule the Americans at the beginning of the war, and which they uniformly sung to all their prisoners. This pleasantry of Lafayette was so bitter to them, that many of them broke their arms in a rage in grounding them on the glacis."

After Yorktown a flood of songs deriding Cornwallis—mostly to the tune of "Yankee Doodle"—descended on the land. For example, the *Pennsylvania Packet* (November 27, 1781) published the following ballad.

Marie Joseph Paul Yves Roch Gilbert du Motier,
Marquis de Lafayette

THE DANCE.

A Ballad, to the tune of "Yankey Doodle."

CORNWALLIS led a country dance
 The like was never seen, sir,
Much retrograde, and much advance,
 And all with General Greene, sir.

They rambled up, and rambled down,
 Join'd hands, then off they run, sir,
Our General Greene to Charleston,
 The earl to Wilmington, sir.

Greene, in the south, then danced a set,
 And got a mighty name, sir,
Cornwallis jigg'd with young Fayette,
 But suffer'd in his fame, sir.

Then down he figur'd to the shore,
 Most like a lordly dancer,
And on his courtly honour swore,
 He would no more advance, sir.

Quoth he—my guards are weary grown,
 With footing country dances,
They never at Saint James's shone,
 At capers, kicks or prances.

Though men so gallant ne'er were seen,
 While saunt'ring on parade, sir,
Or wriggling o'er the park's smooth green,
 Or at a masquerade, sir.

Yet are red heels, and long lac'd skirts,
 For stumps and briars meet, sir,
Or stand they chance with hunting shirts,
 Or hardy vet'ran feet, sir.

Now hous'd in York he challenged all,
 At minuet or all'mande,
And lessons for a courtly ball,
 His guards by day and night conn'd.

This challenge known, full soon there came,
 A set who had the *bon ton*,
De Grasse, and Rochambeau, whose fame,
 Fut brillant pour un long tems.

And Washington, Columbia's son,
 Whom easy nature taught, sir,
That grace, which can't by pains be won,
 Or Pluto's gold be bought, sir.

Now hand in hand they circle round,
 This ever dancing peer, sir,
Their gentle movements soon confound,
 The earl as they draw near, sir.

His music soon forgets to play—
 His feet can move no more, sir,
And all his hands now curse the day,
 They jigg'd it to our shore, sir.

Now tories all, what can ye say?
 Come—is not this a griper?
That while your hopes are danc'd away,
 'Tis you must pay the piper.

CORNWALLIS *turned* NURSE, *and his* MISTRESS *a* SOLDIER.

A Prifoner from Virginia's coaft,
  Cornwallis has return'd, fir;
Toolong, toolong he rul'd the roaft
  And for our ruin burn'd, fir.
Before he was, in wretched plight,
  By armed men furrounded,
He fhow'd himfelf a man of might
  And every thing confounded.
But when they thunder'd at his door
  He prov'd by this difafter,
His race was run, his battles done
  And Wafhington his mafter.
His miftrefs in a paffion cry'd,
  She could have acted bolder;
So put his fword upon her fide,
  His mufquet on her fhoulder.

Like Hercules, renown'd of old,
  The diftaff is his calling;
And while he hears his miftrefs
  fcold,   [ing.
  He keeps her brat from bawl-
Behold him here and fhed a tear,
  Sir Henry and Knyphaufen;
And Arnold too may quake with
  fear,
  Whom Satan has his claws on.
Each valiant chief fhall fee with
  grief,
  Their horrid revolution;
Cornwallis forc'd to fpin for
  bread,
  Burgoyne to thump a cufhion.

Cornwallis was depicted as a nursemaid and his mistress as a soldier in this cartoon and song (to the meter of "Yankee Doodle") that appeared in the Continental Almanac *for the year 1782.*

94

A Political Concert; the Vocal parts By —
1. *Miss America*. 2. *Franklin*. 3. *F-x*. 4. *Kepp-ll*. 5. *M.*^{rs} *Brittania*. 6. *Shelb-n*. 7. *Dun-i-g*. 8. *Benidick Rattle Snake*.

In 1782 an American peace commission composed of John Adams, John Jay, and Benjamin Franklin negotiated a peace treaty with Britain, and on November 30 the preliminary articles of peace were signed at Paris and the war was formally over. The Definitive Treaty of Peace—the Peace of Paris—was not signed until September 3, 1783. This British cartoon, "A Political Concert," treated the peace negotiations as a musical performance. On the far right, Benedict Arnold is depicted as a rattlesnake, standing beneath his "coat of arms," a gallows presided over by a devil.

In all strata of American society peace was acclaimed with great manifestations of joy, with feasting, and with music. An advance copy of the ode "On the Peace—Designed for Music" was sent to George Washington in April 1783 and he responded with a note, calling the song "elegant," and adding: "The accomplishment of the great object we had in view, in so short a time, and under such propitious circumstances, must I am confident, fill every bosom with the purest joy; and for my own part I will not strive to conceal the pleasure I already anticipate from my approaching retirement to the placid walks of domestic life." The ode, written in the favored lofty style, appeared in the *Boston Gazette* (June 9, 1783) and was subsequently reprinted in a large number of newspapers. The music for which it was "designed" is not known.

ON THE PEACE: *AN ODE.*
Designed for Music.

At length WAR's sanguine scenes are o'er;
Her dire alarms are heard no more
    Thro' all COLUMBIA's Plain:
Sweet PEACE descends with balmy wings
And heaven born *independence* brings
    With *freedom* in her train.
    Hail! heaven descended guests, all hail!
Peace, Independence, Freedom, hail!

Ruler of Kings! thy mandate shook
The fated monarch's throne; and struck
    The JEWEL from his crown:
The wisdom the rude statesman taught,
With aid divine the soldier fought;
    The weak an empire won.
    Hail! sovereign Wisdom, Goodness, hail!
    Peace, Independence, Freedom, hail!

Her darling SON, *Columbia*'s boast!
Envy and dread of Albion's host!
    Her patriot faulchion sheaths:
Celestial meeds in ample flow,
Crown the DELIVERER!—bind his brow
    With Honor's endless wreaths!
    Hail Washington! Deliverer hail!
    Peace, Independence, Freedom, hail!

Now let the loud shrill clarions play,
Triumphant peals proclaim the day,
    The UNITED STATES are free!
While round all chearing music floats,
And echoing hills rebound the notes,
    GOD's firm and just DECREE!
    CHORUS.
    Halleluja, &c. &c.

As early as 1781 Washington's birthday, February 11, old style (transposed to February 22 when Britain adopted the Gregorian calendar in 1752), had been publicly celebrated. In 1784 New Yorkers celebrated Washington's birthday with a political dinner at which a special birthday song was sung. It was printed the next day (February 12—apparently the old date was still being observed) in the *Independent Gazette; or The New-York Journal Revived* together with a passionate editorial reflecting the incredibly high esteem in which Washington was held by his contemporaries in America: "... I shall ask one question of my fellow citizens —After the Almighty Author of our existence and happiness, to whom, as a people are we under the greatest obligations? I know you will answer to Washington." The song, to be sung to the tune of "God Bless America" ("God Save the King," of course) went:

> AMERICANS rejoice,
> While songs employ each voice,
>   Let trumpets sound.
> The thirteen stripes display,
> In flags and streamers gay,
> 'Tis WASHINGTON's birth day,
>   Let joy abound.
>
> From scenes of rural peace,
> From affluence and ease,
>   At Freedom's call;
> A hero from his birth,
> Great Washington stands forth,
> The scourge of George and North,
>   And tyrants all.
>
> The silver trump of fame
> His glory shall proclaim,
>   Till Time is done.
> Genius with taste refin'd,
> Courage with coolness join'd,
> 'Bove all, an honest mind,
>   Has WASHINGTON.

~~~

> Long may he live to see
> This land of Liberty
>   Flourish in Peace;
> Long may he live to prove
> A grateful people's love,
> And, late, to Heaven remove.
>   Where joys ne'er cease.
>
> Fill the glass to the brink,
> WASHINGTON's health we'll drink,
>   'Tis his birth-day.
> Glorious deeds he has done,
> By him our cause was won,
> Long live great WASHINGTON,
>   Huzza! Huzza!

Jean-Antoine Houdon's superb life mask of George Washington emphasizes the divine attributes bestowed on the hero by an adoring nation. At the peak of the extraordinary Washington-worship that swept America during and after the Revolution, he was regarded by many as being next in importance to God. A song for his birthday in 1788 went (to the tune of "God Save the King"):

> *Hail Godlike Washington!*
> *Fair Freedom's chosen son,*
> *   Born to command:*
> *While this great globe shall roll,*
> *Thy deeds from pole to pole,*
> *Shall shake Columbia's soul*
> *   With virtuous praise.*

Private enterprise was both practiced and lauded in the optimistic young republic. In 1786, when the imposing new bridge over the Charles River was opened, a Boston newspaper writer (June 19, 1786), reprinted in the *Independent Chronicle* (June 22), commented: ". . . whilst it exhibits the greatest effect of private enterprise within the United States, [it] is a most pleasing proof how certainly objects of magnitude may be obtained by spirited exertions." The bridge, opening on June 17, the eleventh anniversary of the Battle of Bunker Hill and the burning of Charlestown, had been "compleated" in thirteen months. Its opening was a spectacular affair, illustrating America's love of a terrific party: ". . . the company invited, moved in procession [to]

a Band of Musick, accompanied with Drums and Fifes. . . . Thirteen cannon were discharged from Copp's Hill, while they were passing over the Bridge. . . ." The story went on to describe the joyous occasion: "The Streets, windows, and eminences in the neighborhood of the Bridge swarmed with spectators, to the amount of at least twenty thousand, and the ladies were peculiarly attractive."

The account of the ceremonies for the opening of Charlestown Bridge continued: "After dinner . . . toasts were drank. . . . After the 4th toast was given, the following ODE [by Thomas Dawes, Esquire] was sung by Mr. Rea, and several other gentlemen, accompanied with the Band."

ODE.
Tune: "God Save the King"

Now let rich Musick sound
And all the Region round
    With Rapture fill.
Let the full Trump of Fame
To Heaven itself proclaim
The everlasting Name
    Of Bunker Hill.

Beneath his sky-wrapt Brow
What Heroes sleep below;
    How dear to Jove!
Not more belov'd were those
Who toil'd celestial Foes
When the old Giants rose
    To Arms above.

Now scarce eleven short years
Have roll'd their rapid spheres
    Thro' Heaven's high Road;
Since o'er yon swelling tide
Pass'd all the British pride,
And water'd Bunker's side
    With foreign Blood.

Then Charlestown's gilded Spires
Felt unrelenting Fires,
    And sunk in Night.
But, Phoenix-like, they'll rise
From where their ruin lies,
And strike the astonish'd Eyes
    With Glories bright.

Meand'ring to the Deep,
Majestick Charles shall weep
    Of War no more.
Fam'd as the Appian Way,
The World's first Bridge, To-Day
All Nations shall convey
    From Shore to Shore.

On our bless'd Mountain's Head
The festive Board will spread
    With Viand's high,
Let Joy's broad Bowl go round,
With publick Spirit crown'd;
We'll consecrate the Ground
    To LIBERTY.

This engraving of the bridge appeared in the Massachusetts Magazine *(September 1789).*

It was a really terrific party. The report concluded: "Joy crowned the day, and in the evening the lamps were lighted on the bridge, and produced not only a happy effect on the eye, but were useful in directing the steps of some of the votaries of the *rosy deity* who returned to town between 10 and 11, with a band of music before them, inspired by the collective pleasure of the scene, but above all by the generous draughts they had taken, to *commemorate* this *auspicious occasion.*"

With the coming of peace, America in the 1780s began to try her fledgling cultural wings. Activity developed in the arts, the sciences, education, and international commerce. The dismal aftermath of war was in some measure offset by the optimism of an evolving nation. As Columbia exultantly proclaimed in "A CANTATA for the FOURTH of July, 1786," (*Pennsylvania Packet*, July 21, 1786):

> Commerce with her·sedgy crown,
> Honor, arts and bright renown,
> Agriculture with her spade,
> Join'd to science (glorious maid)
> By her side philosophy,
> Darts her penetrating eye,
> Pointing still to Heav'n and earth,
> Designative of her birth,
> The Muses——

The 1780s abounded in patriotic, self-congratulatory poems and songs in the lofty style. Many were contributed by members of the "Hartford Wits," a group of talented young poets and writers who celebrated America. One of these, Dr. Timothy Dwight, who had served as a chaplain during the Revolution and would later become the president of Yale, wrote both the words and music for one of the best known of these songs, "Columbia." The words were first published in the *American Museum* (June 1787); with the music it appeared in *The American Musical Miscellany* (1798).

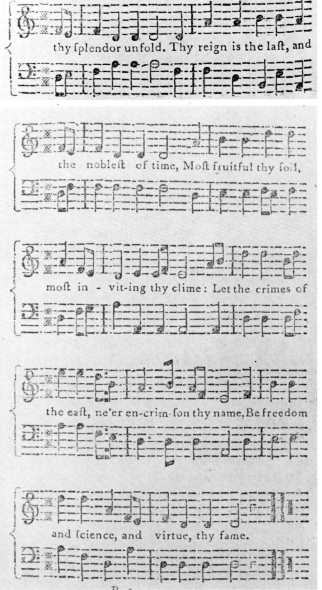

Despite their newfound national optimism and cultural expansion, Americans in the 1780s were faced with acute hardships resulting from the severe economic depression that followed the Revolution. Many were subjected to imprisonment because there was simply no money to be had for the payment of their debts and taxes. In Massachusetts, where the situation was particularly drastic, armed insurgents, led by the Revolutionary veteran Daniel Shays, took the law into their own hands in August 1786 and employed force to intimidate the state legislature into issuing paper money. Upon the inability of an impoverished Congress to respond to Massachusetts's plea for help, General Benjamin Lincoln raised private funds to support a militia and put down the rebellion. Shays and his principal colleagues were condemned to death; they escaped to Vermont and were subsequently pardoned. The widespread concern for the country's economic plight and for the preservation of her law and order was soon reflected in a number of ballads, both serious and satirical. The *Massachusetts Centinel* (March 7, 1787) published a song that lampooned not only the lawlessness of the episode, but also neighboring Rhode Island's questionable solution to the money problem: creditors were required by law to accept state-issued, inflated paper currency in payment of debts— a solution that sent many Rhode Island creditors into hiding from their debtors. In the text, *gauntlope* is a variant of *gauntlet*, as in "running the gauntlet"; the various gentlemen named are Shays's confederates. Of course, the opportunity to rhyme Shays with "Days" (Luke Day was a leader in the rebellion) was an irresistible versifier's delight. The footnotes are part of the original text.

A SONG.

(Tune—*Black Sloven*.)

Come, come, my bold boxers, 'tis liberty calls,
Hark, hark, how she lustily bawls, and bawls!
It is high time, if ever for mobbing 'twas time;
To mobbing, ye chicks of dame Liberty run;
Scour up the old *whinyard*, and brush the old *gun*;
    Freedom we'll chime,
    While Tag, Rag, and Bobtail,
    Lead up our decorum, Huzza!

Sure these are the plaguiest of all plaguy times,
When *villains* must hang for their crimes, their crimes,
And debtors a gauntlope of bailiffs must run;
When *rulers* will *govern*, and we must *obey*,
And *law* down our gullets is cramm'd every day—
    Rap, Rap, 'tis a dun!
    The sheriff's behind him,
    We'll gag him and bind him, Huzza!

When the *rum* is all out, and the *cyder* runs low,
And the taverns won't sell for *ditto*, *ditto*,
And a man for his victuals must work like a dog;
Paper-money, and *cheating my law*, have both fled,
To Rhode-Island to hive in their Governor's head.
    Come, come, t'other mug!
    Here's a health to our master;
    Talk less and drink faster, Huzza!

Then haste to our chiefs, such as never were seen,
With hats* and with *noddles*, so *green*, so *green*,
There's the *Hind*† that's let loose of true Naphtal breed
There are *Shayses* and *Dayses* and such pretty things,
And *Grovers* and *Wheelers* and *Parsons* and *Kings*,
    Yet, dismal to read!
    Our poor brother *Shattuck*,
    Was felled with a mattock, Heigh ho!

~~~

The Senate and Courts to our friend Beelzebub,
We'll drive with the musket, and club, and club,
And in *apron* and *jerkin* our governor dress;
To set in the saddle we've men that know how,
And make all your ruffle-shirts foot it and bow;
    The World shall confess
    We've spirits in *hogsheads*,
    And cunning in *fox-heads*, Huzza!

Thus no longer with *stocks*, and with *pillories* vex'd
Nor with work, jail, or sheriff perplex'd, perplex'd,
The mobmen shall rule, and the great men obey,
The world upon wheels shall be all set agog
And blockheads and knaves hail the reign of King *Log*;
    Under his sway,
    Shall Tag, Rag, and Bobtail,
    Lead up our decorum, Huzza!

---

* A green bough is the badge of the Mob.
† Hind of Greenwich, famous for giving godly words.

Rhode Island's perversely unilateral monetary policy inspired a waggish commentary in the form of an "advertisement" for a new musical invention that appeared in the *Massachusetts Centinel* on July 18, 1787.

ADVERTISEMENT EXTRA.

Wanted immediately, a number of likely, young CATS, for the express purpose of making a *Categorical Instrument of* MUSICK.—As this Instrument will be calculated chiefly for Martial Musick, those Cats whose voices can be occasionally grum and shrill will have the preference. None will answer unless they squall forthwith on having their tails pinched. A double price will be given for those with Two tails.—Any person inclining to furnish said cats will be generously paid in the PAPER MEDIUM of Rhode Island, in which State the instrument is first to be tried, by way of thorough Bass to the Proceedings of their Legislature, and ('tis thought the CORDS will be excellent) from thence it will be sent to General SHAYS, to play up for Volunteers for the next Winter's Campaign. For further particulars, inquire of the *Mintors*.

Warblington, July 15th, 1787.
An explanation of the CATegorical *Instrument.*

Eight cats, representing the eight notes of musick, are to be put into a wooden box, in which eight separate holes are to be made, at a convenient distance from each other. Through each hole a *tail-single* is to be thrust.—This instrument is to be played upon like a spinnet or organ, the musician siting in front, and pinching the tail of the particular cat which he would wish to have squeal. Thus, by a quick transition from tail to tail, an artist may make the musick of this instrument very pleasing, and critically adapted to the musical ear of those *harmonious politicians* who are to enjoy the first fruits of its labour—A few PIGS, by way of CHORUS, might possibly be an addition.

In 1785 John Adams had been appointed as the first American minister to Great Britain. It was rumored that while there he had become enamored of "monarchical" customs, even going so far as to suggest that it might be a good thing if they were adopted at home. In 1787 the *Pennsylvania Packet* (August 20) published a representative response to this rumor; it was set to an old tune labeled with an alternate title.

*Portrait of John Adams,
from the* European Magazine
(September 1783)

A NEW SONG.

Tune, "A cobler there was, and he liv'd in a stall."

A Plan is propos'd, and it comes from Great Britain,
The prettiest scheme that ever was hit on!
Our minister there has told us fine things
Of the parliament house and advantage of kings.
    Derry down, down, down, derry down.

Who alone can controul the people's mad whim,
And in tempests the state boat can rig, man and trim;
In the wars which he makes, who else but a king
The troops can so early into the field bring?
    Derry down, &c.

And who can so well the brave fellows reward,
Whom he presses to fight both at home and abroad;
Who else upon earth can do them such good,
Bedeck them with honours, ennoble their blood?
    Derry down, &c.

Besides, when religion is at a dead list,
What else but a King can make a good shift;
Who else under God can keep virtue alive,
And from our citizens wickedness drive?
    Derry down, &c.

Who else can establish and rebuild the church,
Which its friends in old England left in a sad lurch;
Or, who else can do, what perhaps is much better,
Reform our laws, and absolve ev'ry debtor?
    Derry down, &c.

But then, my brave fellows, I very much doubt
This plan will not do greater taxes without.
For to what we now have we must add a long string
Of a new civil list the new monarch must bring.
    Derry down, &c.

The lords of his houshold and guards at his gate,
With all the regalia and trappings of state,
With pensions and bribes, our army and fleet
Will increase our taxes some millions complete.
    Derry down, &c.

Besides, though with gold he may lure us to fight,
And on a parade may shew a grand sight,
Our pockets, our barns, our daughters and wives
Will all pay for that as sure as our lives.
    Derry down, &c.

Then let us no longer to Adams attend,
But 'gainst his king projects our country defend;
Let's support our Congress with might and with main,
And treaties observe with France, Holland and Spain.
    Derry down, &c.

Let's remember how nobly our freedom we bought,
Oh, never forget for this Washington fought,
From Concord to Georgia remember who bled;
Warren, Mercer and Kalb are among the brave dead!
    Derry down, &c.

May nations whose necks are still under the yoke,
Whose monarchical chains have never been broke,
Feel them lighter and lighter whilst us they admire,
And when ever press'd hard to like freedom aspire.
    Derry down, &c.

But should we return to our slavish condition,
Their spirits must sink, and their tyrants' ambition
Must rise, till he bow their necks down to the ground,
And no trace of freedom on earth can be found.
    Derry down, &c.

Where then is the wretch who'd change Congress [for] Kings,
And degrade all our freemen to pitiful things;
Let feathers and tar be that fellows lot—
Call him Tory, and let his true name be forgot.
    Derry down, down, down, derry down.

In 1787 and 1788 all America was absorbed by the supremely vital issue of the federal Constitution and its ratification by the thirteen states. Federalists and Anti-Federalists locked in mortal verbal combat, and an avalanche of songs variously urged, discouraged, congratulated, or wryly commented as states ratified or hung back. Only a few weeks after the Constitutional Convention adjourned, one of the first Federalist songs appeared in the *Massachusetts Centinel* (October 6, 1787). It was set to a tune that had served before to impel Americans toward unity, but it had been known then as "Heart of Oak."

THE GRAND CONSTITUTION:
Or, The PALLADIUM of COLUMBIA:
A New FEDERAL SONG.

Tune—"Our Freedom We've Won," &c.

From scenes of affliction—Columbia opprest—
Of credit expiring—and commerce distrest,
Of nothing to do—and of nothing to pay—
From such dismal scenes let us hasten away.
 Our Freedom we've won, and the prize let's maintain
  Our hearts are all right—
  Unite, Boys, Unite,
 And our EMPIRE *in glory shall ever remain.*

The Muses no longer the cypress shall wear—
For we turn our glad eyes to a prospect more fair:
The soldier return'd to his small cultur'd farm,
Enjoys the reward of his conquering arm.
 "Our Freedom we've won," &c.

Our trade and our commerce shall reach far and wide,
And riches and honour flow in with each tide
Kamschatka and *China* with wonder shall stare,
That the *Federal* Stripes should wave gracefully there.
 "Our Freedom we've won," &c.

With gratitude let us acknowledge the worth,
Of what the CONVENTION has call'd into birth,
And the Continent wisely confirm what is done
By FRANKLIN, the sage, and by brave WASHINGTON.
 "Our Freedom we've won," &c.

The wise CONSTITUTION let's truly revere,
It points out the course of our EMPIRE to steer,
For oceans of bliss do they hoist the broad sail,
And *peace* is the current, and plenty the gale.
 "Our Freedom we've won," &c.

With gratitude fill'd—let the great Commonweal
Pass round the full glass to Republican zeal—
From ruin—their judgment and wisdom well aim'd,
Our liberty, laws, and our credit reclaim'd.
 "Our Freedom we've won," &c.

Here Plenty and Order and Freedom shall dwell,
And your *Shayses* and *Dayses* won't dare to rebel—
Independence and culture shall graciously smile,
And the *Husbandman* reap the full fruit of his toil.
 "Our Freedom we've won," &c.

That these are the blessings, Columbia knows—
The blessings the Fed'ral CONVENTION bestows.
O! then let the People confirm what is done
By FRANKLIN the sage, and by brave WASHINGTON.
 Our Freedom we've won, and the prize will maintain
  By Jove we'll Unite,
  Approve and Unite—
 And huzza for Convention *again and again.*

The Federalist era had dawned.

A bold triumphal Arch *you see,*
Such as by antiquity
Was raised to Rome's great heroes, who
Did the rage of war subdue.

The Arch *high bending doth convey,*
In a hieroglyphic way,
What in noble stile like this,
Our United Empire is.

The Pillars *which support the weight,*
Are each of them a mighty State:
Thirteen and more the vista shews.
As to vaster length it grows:
For new states shall added be,
To the great Confederacy.

The United States Magazine
January 1779

THE

tates Magazine,

Delaware,
Maryland,
Virginia,
North-Carolina,
South-Carolina,
Georgia.

EMBER 1779.

The Federal Constitution, boys,
And liberty forever . . .

Mr. Milns

Tune: "Yankee Doodle"
1798

4. Federalist Fanfares
1788-1800

PART I

In 1788 the metaphor of the federal edifice was graphically translated as a colonnade, to which a new column was added as each state ratified the Constitution. Running as a series of cartoons in the *Massachusetts Centinel* (where this one appeared on August 2, 1788) and numerous other newspapers, the visualization acted not only as propaganda to promote the Constitution but also as a distinctive graph to record the progress of its adoption. Delaware, Pennsylvania, and New Jersey became the first three pillars to support the federal edifice when they ratified the Constitution in December 1787.

REDEUNT SATURNIA REGNA.

On the erection of the Eleventh PILLAR of the great National DOME, we beg leave most sincerely to felicitate "OUR DEAR COUNTRY."

Rise it will.

The foundation good—it may yet be SAVED.

The FEDERAL EDIFICE.

☞It WILL yet rise.

The RAISING:
A NEW SONG FOR FEDERAL MECHANICKS.

I.
COME muster, my lads, your mechanical tools,
  Your Saws and your Axes, your Hammers and Rules;
Bring your Mallets and Planes, your Level and Line,
And plenty of Pins of American Pine;
    For our roof we will raise, and our song still shall be—
    A government firm, and our citizens free.

II.
Come, up with *the Plates,* lay them firm on the wall,
Like the people at large, they're the ground-work of all;
Examine them well, and see that they're found,
Let no rotten parts in our building be found;
    For our roof we will raise, and our song still shall be—
    Our government firm, and our citizens free.

III.
Now hand up *the Girders,* lay each in his place,
Between them *the Joists* must divide all the space;
Like Assembly-men, *these* should ly level along,
Like *Girders,* our Senate prove loyal and strong;
    For our roof we will raise and our song still shall be—
    A government firm, over citizens free.

IV.
The Rafters now frame—your *King-Posts* and *Braces,*
And drive your Pins home, to keep all in their places;
Let wisdom and strength in the fabrick combine,
And your Pins be all made of American Pine;
    For our roof we will raise and our song still shall be—
    A government firm, over citizens free.

V.
Our *King-Posts* are Judges—how upright they stand,
Supporting the *Braces,* the laws of the land—
The laws of the land, which divide right from wrong,
And strengthen the weak, by weak'ning the strong;
    For our roof we will raise and our song still shall be—
    Laws equal and just for a people that's free.

VI.
Up! Up with the Rafters—each Frame is a State!
How nobly they rise! their Span, too how great!
From the north to the south, o'er the whole they extend,
And rests on the Walls, while the Walls they defend,
    For our roof we will raise and our song still shall be—
    Combined in strength, yet as citizens free.

VII.
Now enter the *Purlins,* and drive your Pins through,
And see that your Joints are drawn home, and all true;
The *Purlins,* will bind all the Rafters together,
The strength of the whole shall defy wind and weather;
    For our roof we will raise and our song still shall be—
    United as States, but as citizen free.

VIII.
Come, raise up the Turret—our glory and pride—
In the centre it stands, o'er the whole to preside;
The sons of *Columbia* shall view with delight
Its PILLARS and ARCHES, and towering height;
    Our Roof is now rais'd, and our song still shall be—
    A Federal Head, o'er a people still free.

IX.
Huzza! my brave boys, our work is complete,
The world shall admire *Columbia's* fair seat;
Its strength against tempests and time shall be proof,
And thousands shall come to dwell under our Roof.
    Whilst we drain the deep bowl, our toast still shall be—
    Our government firm, and our citizens free.

Francis Hopkinson set the federal edifice allegory to music when he adapted his song "The Raising" from his prose parable "The New Roof." "The Raising" became one of the most popular of the countless songs to participate in the general Constitutional debate in 1788. It first appeared in the Pennsylvania Gazette *(February 6, 1788); by March 1, when "The Raising" was reprinted in the* Massachusetts Centinel, *six states, including Massachusetts, had ratified the Constitution, as can be seen from the number of pillars that headed the stanzas. No tune was given in either publication.*

In a disdainful little song, Pennsylvanians, smug over their own prompt acceptance of the Constitution, made fun of Boston's "Grand Procession," which had followed Massachusetts's somewhat reluctant ratification on February 6, 1788. First appearing in Philadelphia, it was reprinted in the *Massachusetts Centinel* (March 5).

"THE GRAND FEDERAL EDIFICE."

The motion for ratifying was declared in the affirmative, by a majority of nineteen, in Boston. In consequence of which the Boston folks had a grand procession—

> There they went up, up, up,
> And there they went down, down, downy,
> There they went backwards and forwards,
> And poop for Boston towny!

This *grand intelligence* reached Philadelphia, on Saturday evening last, when the bells of Christ Church were rung—

> Here they rung, rung, rung,
> And here they bobb'd about, pretty,
> Here were *doubles* and *majors* and *bobs,*
> And heigh for 'delphia city.

"In answer to the above scrap of antifederal wit," the *Massachusetts Centinel* in the same issue countered with a laudatory, versified review of the proceedings of both the Massachusetts Constitutional Convention and the following celebratory grand procession. The thirteen symbolic stanzas, consisting of equal parts of indigenous Yankee lingo and "Yankee Doodle," were reprinted from the *Pennsylvania Mercury* (apparently not all Pennsylvanians were equally scornful of Boston). In the text, *woundy* is a superlative, i.e., Squire Hancock made a top-notch fed'ral speech; *deucid* (deuced) means devilish; *nation* is eighteenth-century American slang for damnation, i.e., it was a damned fine procession; and John Foster Williams, who created such a stir among the lasses, was a distinguished Boston naval officer of the Revolution. His surprising conveyance in the procession was a symbolic ship placed on a carriage drawn by horses. The "federal ship" was a principal feature at all ratification parades; an ambulatory printing press in full operation was another.

YANKEE SONG.

The 'Vention did in Boston meet,
    But State-House could not hold 'em,
So then they went to Fed'ral street,
    And there the truth was told 'em—
        Yankee Doodle, keep it up!
          Yankee doodle dandy,
        Mind the musick and the step,
          And with the girls be handy.

They ev'ry morning went to prayer,
    And then began disputing,
'Till opposition silenc'd were,
    By arguments refuting.
        Yankee doodle, keep it up! &c.

Then 'squire Hancock like a man,
    Who dearly loves his nation,
By a council'atory plan
    Prevented much vexation.
        Yankee doodle, &c.

He made a *woundy* fed'ral speech,
    With sense and elocution;
And then the 'Vention did beseech
    T' adopt the Constitution.
        Yankee doodle, &c.

The question being outright put,
    (Each voter independent)
The Fed'ralists agreed t' adopt,
    And then propose amendment.
        Yankee doodle, &c.

The other party seeing then
    The people were against 'em,
Agreed like honest, faithful men,
    To mix in peace amongst 'em.
        Yankee doodle, &c.

The Boston folks are *deucid* lads,
    And always full of notions;
The boys, the girls, their 'mams and dads,
    Were filled with joy's commotions.
        Yankee doodle, &c.

So straightway they procession made,
    Lord! how *nation* fine, Sir!
For ev'ry man of ev'ry trade,
    Went with his tools—to dine, Sir.
        Yankee doodle, &c.

JOHN FOSTER WILLIAMS in a ship,
    Join'd in the social band, Sir,
And made the lasses dance and skip,
    To see him sail on land, Sir.
        Yankee doodle, &c.

Oh then a whopping feast begun,
    And all hands went to eating;
They drank their toasts—shook hands and sung,
    Huzza! for 'Vention meeting.
        Yankee doodle, &c.

Now Politicians of all kinds,
    Who are not yet decided;
May see how Yankees speak their minds;
    And yet are not divided.
        Yankee doodle, &c.

Then from this sample let 'em cease,
    Inflammatory writing,
For FREEDOM, HAPPINESS, and PEACE,
    Is better far than fighting.
        Yankee doodle, &c.

So here I end my Fed'ral song,
    Composed of thirteen verses,
May agriculture flourish long,
    And commerce fill our purses!
        Yankee doodle, keep it up!
          Yankee doodle dandy,
        Mind the musick and the step,
          And with the girls be handy.

The *Pennsylvania Mercury* (February 21, 1788) completed its vindication of Boston with yet another song to "Yankee Doodle"—"The Federal Ship," of which the final stanza went:

    Come, come, my lads, send round the can,
        And drink to Boston city—
    They are the boys began the plan—
        How beautiful, how pretty!

The SHIP Fœderal UNION.

Every ratification parade had its federal ship. This one, the Union, *later sailed in the great Philadelphia constitutional procession on July 4, 1788. From the* Pennsylvania Journal, *and the* Weekly Advertiser *(July 12, 1788).*

the Conventions of nine States, ſhall be ſufficient for the eſtabliſhment of this

ACTUM EST.

" The ratification of

NINTH and the SUFFICIENT PILLAR.

If it hath not—
it will riſe.

Conſtitution. A R. Vii.

" Yeſterday morning, a repeated inſtance of the uncer-

*With New Hampshire's ratification (the decisive ninth) on June
21, 1788, the Constitution became law (for the nine consenting
states). In jubilant words, a Portsmouth newspaper proclaimed:
"We have, in effect, laid the top stone to the grand FEDERAL
EDIFICE, and happily raised the Ninth pillar." The Massachusetts
Centinel (July 2, 1788) exultantly commemorated the erection
of the "Ninth and Sufficient Pillar" in its series.*

In keeping with Federalist grand procession tradition, representatives of every conceivable trade and profession, carrying the tools and implements of their respective callings,
paraded at Portsmouth. The parade was led by a "Band of
Musick in an open Coach"; it included, according to the
Independent Gazetteer (July 7): "Printers . . . and . . .
compositors at work; pressmen, with Mr. Benjamin Dearborn's new invented printing press (named the American
Press) employed during the whole procession, in striking
off and distributing . . . songs in celebration of the ratification of the federal constitution by the State of New Hampshire." Presumably one of these was the song comprising a
medley of three tunes that was reprinted in the *Pennsylvania
Packet* (July 18, 1788). Its first section, to the tune of "He
Comes, He Comes," went like this:

FEDERAL SONG.

Sung at the Grand Procession
at Portsmouth, New Hampshire, after dinner.

It comes! it comes! high raise the song!
The bright Procession moves along;
From pole to pole resound the NINE,
And distant worlds the chorus join.

In vain did Britain forge the chain,
While countless squadrons hid the plain,
Hantonia, foremost of the NINE,
Defy'd their force, and took Burgoyne.

The fourth section lauded love to the tune of "When
Britons First &c.":

See each industrious ART moves on,
    To ask protection, praise and fame;
The *Ploughman* by his tools is known,
    And *Vulcan, Neptune*, join their claim;
Allow them all—and wisely prove,
Nought can exist long without LOVE.

LOVE binds in peace the universe;
    By LOVE societies combine;
LOVE prompts the Poet's rapt'rous verse,
    And makes these humble lays divine:
Then shout for Union, heav'n-born dame!
And crown the goblet to her name.

The stellar attraction of Philadelphia's mammoth constitutional parade—delayed until July 4, 1788, after the tenth
state, Virginia, was safely in the Union—was the Constitution itself. Occupying the thirteenth place in the procession
and heralded by a band of music, the Constitution, according to the *Pennsylvania Gazette* (July 9, 1788), was "framed
and fixed on a staff, crowned with the cap of Liberty—the
words, 'The PEOPLE' all in gold letters, on the staff." The
precious document was held by Chief Justice Thomas Mc-
Kean who, with two other "honorable judges," all in their
"robes of office," rode in a "lofty Car, in the form of a large
eagle." Francis Hopkinson, who designed and staged the
brilliant spectacle, no doubt had planned that the musicians
would proclaim the Constitution with Alexander Reinagle's
"Fœderal March," especially composed for the occasion.
When "The Fœderal March" was published, soon after, it
too was symbolically adorned with the "cap of liberty" on
a pole, grandly mounted on the terrestrial globe; this is the
earliest known example of a graphic decoration to appear
on a piece of American sheet music.

In its review of the parade, the *Pennsylvania Journal, and the
Weekly Advertiser* (July 12, 1788) reported that the federal
ship *Union*, attended by her full crew of officers and men,
had sailed along atop a carriage whose wheels were concealed by canvas "painted to represent the waves of the sea."
So faithfully was realism pursued that when the parade route
rounded corners, the sails of the *Union* were accordingly
trimmed. Other allegorical floats included "The New Roof,
or the Grand Federal Edifice," represented as an elegant
building supported by thirteen white pillars, three of which
were left unfinished to symbolize the three states that had
not yet ratified the Constitution. The federal edifice was
drawn by ten symbolic horses and attended by a number of
gentlemen and "house carpenters."

Of the many wonders witnessed by Philadelphians at the July 4 parade, perhaps the most unusual was the debut of the United States air mail service. The *Pennsylvania Gazette* (July 9, 1788) described the event, the props of which were "a stage 9 feet square, drawn by four horses . . . the Federal Printing office, furnished with a Printing-press complete . . . by ten Printing offices united. On the stage men at work, in the different branches of the profession. Mr. Durant, in the character of MERCURY, in a white dress, ornamented with red ribbands, having real wings affixed to his head and feet, and a garland of blue and red flowers round his temples. During the procession the pressmen were at work, and struck off many copies of the following Ode, composed for the occasion by Francis Hopkinson, Esq."

AN ODE

FOR THE 4TH OF JULY 1788.

Oh for a muse of fire! to mount the skies
And to a list'ning world proclaim—
Behold! behold! an empire rise!
An Æra new, Time, as he flies,
Hath enter'd in the book of fame.

〜〜〜

See! where Columbia sits alone,
And from her star-bespangled throne,
Beholds the gay procession move along,
And hears the trumpet, and the choral song—

〜〜〜

The *Gazette* continued: "This Ode, together with one in the German language . . . was thrown among the people as the procession moved along. Ten small packages, containing the foregoing Ode . . . addressed to the ten states in union respectively . . . were tied to ten pidgeons, which at intervals rose from Mercury's cap, and flew off, with the acclamations of the admiring multitude."

Advertisement in the Pennsylvania Packet *(July 17, 1788) for "The Federal March"*

The frontispiece of Bickerstaff's Boston Almanack, or the Federal Calendar *for 1788 depicted Washington and Franklin conducting the "Federal Chariot," drawn by thirteen men symbolizing the thirteen states.*

Despite Washington's retirement from public life and Franklin's advanced age, there seems to have been no question in the minds and hearts of Americans that they were the men to lead the federal union. From the *Pennsylvania Packet* (August 5, 1788):

A NEW FEDERAL SONG.

No more shall Anarchy bear sway,
  Nor petty states pursue their way,
But all united firm as one,
  Shall seek the gen'ral good alone.
      Great Washington shall rule the land,
      While Franklin's council aids his hand.

The gilded toys of Europe's shore
  Shall rob us of our wealth no more,
Imposts their dang'rous progress stop,
  And premiums bear industry up.
      Great Washington shall rule the land,
      While Franklin's council aids his hand.

The wasted soil its strength renews,
  Collecting from the rains and dews;
With proper tillage stronger grows
  Such skill true agriculture knows.
      Great Washington shall rule the land,
      While Franklin's council aids his hand.

Thus Halcyon days shall bless our life,
  And party rage forget its strife,
Like children of one parent still,
  Under our vine and fig tree dwell.
      Great Washington shall rule the land,
      While Franklin's council aids his hand.

The symbolic number thirteen was employed in extraordinary ways. For example, an advertisement in the *Pennsylvania Packet* (July 8, 1788) announced an "exhibition" to take place at the university, at which would be heard "an ORATION on the *Independence of the United States*, to be delivered by thirteen young Gentlemen, who will speak at once, with Voices perfectly United." Music was also promised at the exhibition: "A song—God Save America" and "General Washington's March."

In New York, where enthusiasm for the Constitution was less than unanimous, thirteen local patriotic gentlemen met at Mr. Dawson's tavern "in the town of Brooklyne" to celebrate the Fourth of July and to urge in song the benefactions of a "fed'ral" government. The *New-York Daily Advertiser* (July 5, 1788) published their song but not its tune; it was probably the tune of the earlier St. Tammany song (see page 65), after which this "Federal Song" was patterned. In the text, *ant's* is presumably contemporary slang for antis, or Anti-Federalists.

A FEDERAL SONG.
Composed for the 4th of July, 1788.

Of their tutelar saints let the nations be vain,
　And call their mock saintships divine;
Let them bow, if they will, to the ideal train;
　We sacrifice not at their shrine:
There's Andrew, George, Patrick—I can't tell each name,
　A groupe of such fictitious pow'rs,
Whose votaries celebrate yearly their fame;
　But the FOURTH OF JULY shall be our's.

Oh, day of delight, to Columbians so dear,
　Long may thy rich benefits last!
May this signal period in each circling year,
　Be kept and enjoy'd like the past.
Here thirteen are met with a patriot design
　To honor an æra so great,
Here freedom and similar sentiments join—
　May such concord pervade every state.

In freedom and blest independence secure,
　Our prosperity scarce is alloy'd;
So vast a profusion of favors, is sure
　More than country has ever enjoy'd.
But one thing is needful; a government free,
　Just and fed'ral, efficient and strong,
This land must adopt, or, alas! we shall see
　An end to its greatness ere long.

Ye well approv'd patriots, whose talents and worth
　Our most grateful expressions demand,
On this awful occasion we challenge you forth,
　In defence of the union to stand;
Those ant's arrest, in their daring career,
　Who for gain would their country undo;
From them we have ev'rything evil to fear,
　And all things to hope for from you.

Now let the charg'd glasses go chearfully round,
　Thro' this little republican band—
In such friendship and firm unanimity bound,
　May the thirteen fair pillars e'er stand.
In hilarity thus while we spend this blest day,
　While we raise the bright bumpers on high,
(Our hearts full as our glasses) let each of us say
　Here's again to the FOURTH OF JULY.

New-York, July 29.

ELEVENTH PILLAR!

'On Saturday evening about 9 o'clock arrived the joyful tidings of the adoption of the New Constitution, at Poughkeepsie, on Friday, July 25, Yeas 30, Nays 25, Majority 5.——The bells in the City were immediately set a ringing, and from the Fort and the Federal Ship Hamilton, were fired several salutes. The Merchants at the Coffee House testified their joy by repeated huzzas; and a large body of citizens, headed by a number of the first characters, went to the houses of the members of the Convention, and gave three cheers. as a testimony of their approbation of the glorious EVENT brought about by their united, unremitted, and toilsome exertions.—In short, a general joy run through

Alexander Hamilton and his phenomenal eloquence are credited with having overcome New York's strong opposition to the Constitution at the stormy state convention at Poughkeepsie. When New York became the eleventh state to ratify, the New-York Packet *(July 29) reported that "a general joy run through the whole city, and several of those who were of different sentiments drank freely of the* Federal Bowl, *and declared they were now perfectly reconciled to the New Constitution."*

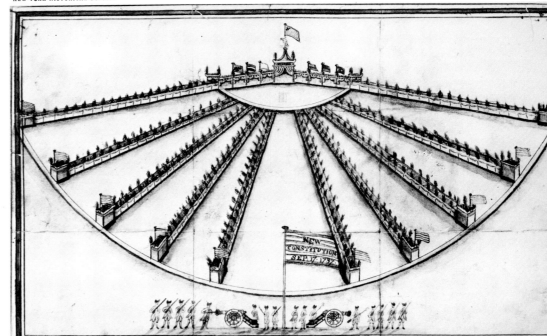

Major Pierre Charles L'Enfant, a veteran of the Revolution, designed this banqueting pavilion, where six thousand New Yorkers assembled after the parading was over to feast and listen to speeches in praise of the Constitution and, presumably, to music.

The two following Odes were printed at the Federal Printing Press, as it mov-ed along in the Procession, on Wednes-day last, and distributed among the mul-titude.

An O D E
On the adoption of the FEDERAL CONSTITUTION.
Composed by Dr. S.———. Set to music.
Tune, *The Dauphin.*
CROWN'D with auspicious light,
Columbia's Eagle rise;
Thine emblems bless our sight,
Thine honors greet our eyes!
Nations admire thy rising dawn, and shall salute thy day,
While generations yet unborn, receive the genial ray.
Chorus.   An Empire's born!—Let cannon roar!
Bid echo rend the sky:
Let ev'ry heart adore,
High Heav'n, our *Great Ally!*
II.
Illustrious Æra, hail!
Thy stars in union grow;
Opposing mists dispel
And with fresh splendor glow.
Thy glories burst upon the gloom, where darkness drag'd her chain,

Submissive she that Pow'r ador'd,
The Sovereign Universal Lord,
Almighty, wise and good!
Whose eye omniscient saw 'twas right,
We should attain that glorious height,
Through Seas of kindred blood.
III.
And, lo! the all-important period's nigh,
And swells the mighty theme—
An Æra, greater than the golden age
Of which the Poets dream;
And adds a wond'rous, an illustrious page
To this terrestial Globe's vast history.
Begin oh Muse,
And far diffuse
Th' inspiring news
To Earth's remotest bound:
Throughout the world let joy like ours be found,
And Echo catch the animating sound,
Now all our highest hopes are crown'd.
Through time's incessant round,
Fame shall resound
This long desir'd event,
And tell what mighty blessings Heav'n has sent;
Immortal Fame,
Whose loud acclaim
Is deathless as the Poet's song,

Headed by a handsome emblematical eagle, the two odes that had been distributed during the Constitutional parade were published in the New-York Packet *(July 25, 1788).*

Too impatient to wait for confirmation of the vote at Poughkeepsie, New Yorkers held their grand procession on July 25, three days before official notification arrived. The New York parade, a huge affair, included all the appurtenances of a proper grand constitutional gala: elaborate floats, allegorical tableaux, a federal ship (named *Hamilton*, in honor of New York's favorite son), and representatives of the arts, trades, and professions. The customary printing press was in operation: ". . . during the procession many hundred copies of a song, and an Ode, adapted to the occasion were struck off, and distributed . . . among the multitude." In contrast to the rather stately official odes, the *New-York Journal, and Daily Patriotic Register* (July 28, 1788) published a waggish commentary on the Poughkeepsie convention by an anonymous Anti-Federalist songsmith.

A SONG.

What means their wisdoms roving to Poughkeepsie,
Their heads with politics are surely tipsey!
Why to the Druids ancient haunts be trotting,
Where naught but acorns on the ground lie rotting?
The oracles long since have left their oaks,
And minded now no more than pigs in pokes,
And laughed to scorn by every John a Nokes:
Unmask your faces then, and one and all
Sing *falderal* and *anti-falderal.*

CHORUS.
Federal, falderal, federalist.
Your thumb to your mouth, and your nose to your fist,
Federal, falderal, federal tit.
Beware of the dainty, the savory bit,
Keep fast all behind you or you're sur[e]ly b-t
Sing falderal, federal, ant's and yeomen,
Beware of the snare as you're truemen and freemen,
Federal, falderal, fiddle de day,
Falderal tit, and tit falderay.

PART II

God *save Columbia's son!*
God *bless great* Washington!
Crown him with bays!
Shout, shout America—
Wide over earth and sea,
Shout in full harmony,
Washington's *praise!*

Tune: "God Save the King"
Columbian Centinel
July 13, 1793

Washington was praised in marble by Jean-Antoine Houdon.

George Washington's reception at the Trenton Bridge

George Washington's historic journey from Mount Vernon to New York to be inaugurated as the first president of the United States was accompanied by universal manifestations of joy: cheering crowds, receptions, banquets, eulogies, military exhibitions, ringing of church bells, firing of cannon, escorts on horseback, prayers, flowers, triumphal arches, and music. At Trenton a lavishly decorated arch was erected at the bridge. According to the *Pennsylvania Packet* (May 1, 1789), it was "supported by 13 columns—each column entwined with wreaths of evergreens. . . . On the front of the arch the following motto was inscribed in large gilt letters—*'The Defender of the mothers will also protect the daughters.'* . . . A numerous train of ladies, leading their daughters, were assembled at the arch. . . . As the General passed under the arch, he was addressed in the following SONATA, composed and set to music for the occasion, by a number of young ladies. . . ."

The oddly named "Sonata" was renamed a "Chorus" when it was published late in 1789 with a dedication to Mrs. Washington. Its composer was Alexander Reinagle, the versatile British-born musician whose "Federal March" had been played at the great constitutional parade in Philadelphia. The authenticity of Reinagle's "Chorus" has been questioned by some musicological sceptics, who cannot reconcile the bass clef notation of its lowest part with the sex of its performers at Trenton. While it is likely that Reinagle would rewrite his composition to appeal to a larger range of performers, it is most improbable that a man of his prominence would claim a spurious work and, what's more, dedicate it to the president's wife. Since there is no specific reference to any other original music performed for Washington during his inaugural journey, it may be assumed that Reinagle's "Chorus" is the first music to have been composed for a president of the United States.

The inside title page of Reinagle's "Chorus" gives the charming details of the singular serenade to Washington by the matrons and maidens of Trenton. An eyewitness wrote (*Pennsylvania Packet*, May 1, 1789): "When his excellency came opposite the little female band, he honored the ladies by stopping until the Sonata was finished. The scene was truly grand—universal silence prevailed—nothing could be heard but the sweet notes of the songsters—and the mingled sentiments—bathed many cheeks with tears." Presented with a copy of the "Sonata," Washington was moved to express his gratitude in a "card," or newspaper announcement, as follows:

General Washington cannot leave this place, without expressing his acknowledgements to the matrons and young ladies, who received him in so novel and grateful a manner at the triumphal arch in Trenton, for the exquisite sensation he experienced in that affecting moment. The astonishing contrast between his former and actual situation at the same spot; the elegant taste with which it was adorned for the present occasion; and the innocent appearance of the *white-robed choir* who met him with the gratulatory song—have made such an impression on his remembrance, as, he assures them, can never be effaced.

Trenton, April 21, 1789

CHORUS.

Sung by a number of young Girls, dreſſed in white, decked in wreaths and Chaplets, holding Baſkets of flowers in their Hands, as General Waſhington paſſed under the Triumphal Arch raiſed on the Bridge at Trenton April 21ſt, 1789.---On his Way to New-York in Character of Preſident of the United States of America, there to meet the Congreſs then aſſembled under the New Conſtitution.

> Welcome mighty chief! once more
> Welcome to this grateful ſhore:
> Now no mercenary Foe
> Aims again the fatal blow.
>
> Virgins fair and Matrons grave,
> Thoſe thy conquering Arms did ſave,
> Build for thee Triumphal Bowers
> Strew, ye fair, his way with flowers,
> Strew your Hero's way with Flowers.

As they ſung theſe lines, they ſtrewed the flowers before the General, who halted until the CHORUS was finiſhed.---- The aſtoniſhing contraſt between his former and actual ſituation *on the ſame ſpot.*-------The elegant taſte with which the Triumphal Arch was adorned at the time, and the innocent appearance of the white-robed Choir, who met him with this gratulatory Song, made a lively and ſtrong Impreſſion on his mind.

On April 23 Washington reached Elizabethtown Point, New Jersey, where he boarded a gorgeously decorated barge and was rowed across the bay on the final lap of his journey by thirteen distinguished retired sea captains. The brilliance of the voyage is made immediate through the words of Elias Boudinot, a member of the presidential party. Boudinot, who made up in vividness for what he lacked in punctuation, wrote: ". . . a number of Boats with a great variety of superb Flags came up to us. and dropped in our wake. . . . Boat after Boat & Sloop after Sloop added to our little fleet gaily dressed with every naval Armament— we began to make a most elegant appearance."

Incongruously, Washington was welcomed to New York to the tune of "God Save the King." Boudinot continued:

Before we got to Bedlars Island a large Sloop. came. with full sail on our Starboard Bow, when about 20 Gentn & Ladies rose up. and with excellent & melodious Voices sung an Eloquent Ode appropriate to the occasion. & set to the Music of "God save the King," welcoming their Great Chief to the Seat of Government. At the conclusion we gave them our Hats, and then they with the surrounding Boats., gave three Hurra's which made the neighboring shores rebound with Joyful acclamation Soon after another Boat came under our Stern and threw in amongst us a number of Copies of another Ode. and immediately about a dozen Gentn began to sing it in parts as we passed along. Our Worthy President was greatly affected with these tokens of profound respect and gratitude.

The ode to "God Save the King" was the work of Samuel Low, a quasi-official New York odesmith.

"Salute to Gen Washington in N. Y. Harbor" by L. M. Cooke (undated)

O D E,

TO BE SUNG ON THE ARRIVAL OF THE

PRESIDENT of the UNITED STATES.

TUNE—"GOD SAVE, &c."

Composed by Mr. L**.

HAIL thou auspicious day !
　Far let America
　Thy praise resound :
Joy to our native land !
Let ev'ry heart expand,
For WASHINGTON's at hand,
　With Glory crown'd !

Thrice blest Columbians hail !
Behold, before the gale,
　Your CHIEF advance ;
The matchless HERO's nigh !
Applaud HIM to the sky,
Who gave　L iberty,
　With gen'rous France.

Illustrious Warrior hail !
Oft' did thy Sword prevail
　O'er hosts of foes ;

Come and fresh laurels claim,
Still dearer make thy name,
Long as Immortal Fame
　Her Trumpet blows !

Thrice welcome to this shore,
Our Leader now no more,
　But Ruler thou ;
Oh, truly good and great !
Long live to glad our State,
Where countless Honors wait
　To deck thy Brow.

Far be the din of Arms,
Henceforth the Olive's charms
　Shall War preclude ;
These shores a HEAD shall own,
Unsully'd by a throne,
Our much lov'd WASHINGTON,
　The Great, the Good !

Contemporary broadside of Mr. Low's "Ode" to welcome Washington

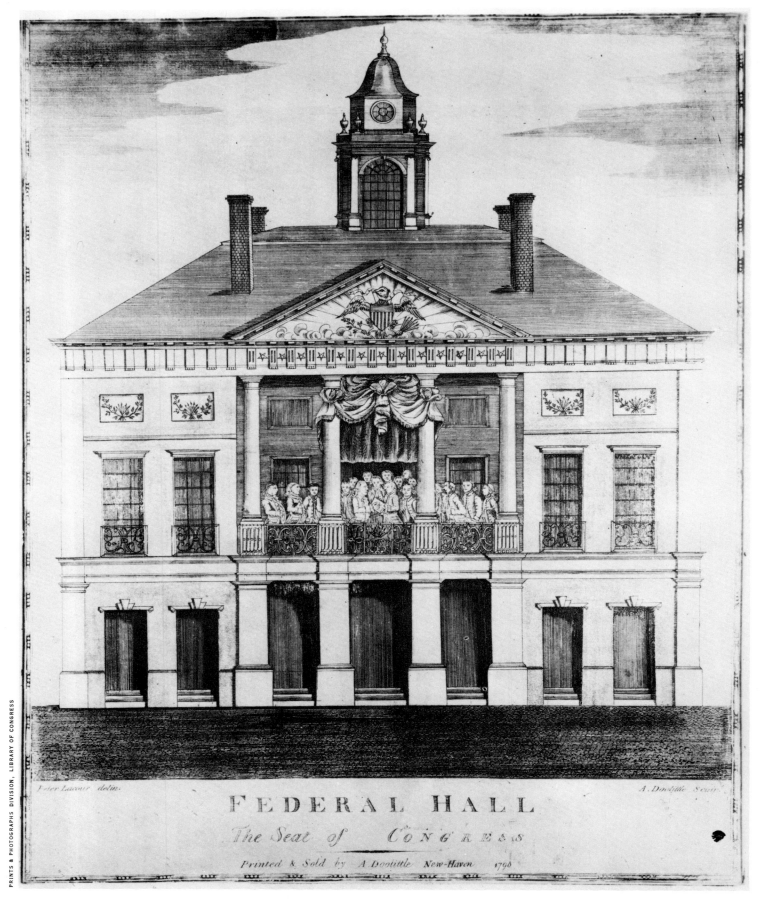

Peter Lacour delin.

A. Doolittle Sculp.

FEDERAL HALL
The Seat of CONGRESS

Printed & Sold by A Doolittle New-Haven 1790

George Washington taking the oath of office at Federal Hall
on April 30, 1789; engraving by Amos Doolittle.

Fragment of flag carried at Washington's inauguration ceremonies

Button or medal to commemorate Washington's inauguration

Aside from "God Save the King," there seems to be no clear record of what music was performed at Washington's inaugural ceremonies, but it is believed that "The President's March" (following page), attributed to Philip Phile, was composed for the occasion. Phile, of German origin, was an itinerant violinist and composer who settled in Philadelphia in 1789. Even allowing for the flexibilities of eighteenth-century spelling, his name underwent an unusual number of transformations: he was variously known (according to Oscar Sonneck) as Fyles, Fayles, Pfeil, Pfyle, Pfazles, Pfaltz, Phylz, Thyla, Phyla, Phylo, Phyles, and Phile. Little more is known about him except that he died at Philadelphia in 1793, the year his "President's March" was published.

"Ça Ira," the French revolutionary song printed with the "President's March," had been for a time tremendously pop-ular in the United States, where it was even called the "French Yankee Doodle." Americans were at first enthusi-astically in support of the enlightened principles of the French Revolution. With the advent of the Reign of Terror, however, they vehemently took sides, and "Ça Ira" became the subject of great partisan controversy. The phrase *Ça Ira*, literally translated "it will go"—colloquially meaning something more like "we shall overcome"—was attributed to Benjamin Franklin. While living in France during the American Revolution, he is supposed to have responded to adverse news from home with this philosophical little motto. The French, who loved Franklin, adopted his slogan; and Lafayette, later remembering the words during the fateful early days of the French Revolution, is supposed to have suggested them to the popular singer and balladeer Ladré, who wrote the song.

PRESIDENTS MARCH AND CA IRA

Price 12 Cents

Prefidents March

Carr & Co.

When Joseph Hopkinson wrote patriotic words to Philip Phile's "President's March"
in 1798, it gained immortality under a new name, "Hail Columbia."

the New
PRESIDENT'S MARCH

NEW YORK Sold at J. PAFF's Music Store

WASHINGTON'S MARCH

*Two other popular marches for Washington, supposedly of Revolutionary origin, are
seen here in a publication that appeared sometime between 1798 and 1811.
"Washington's March" is also known as "Washington's March at the Battle of Trenton."*

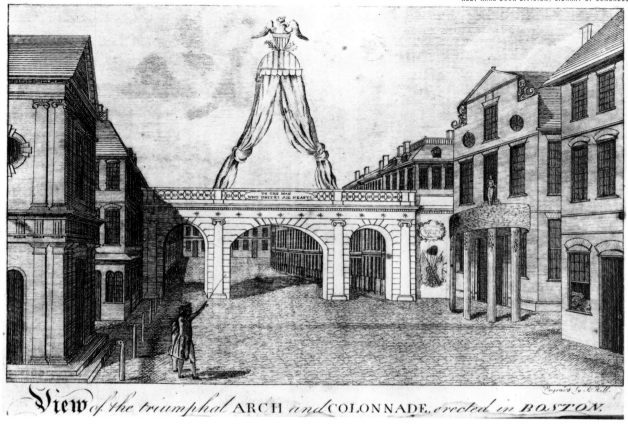

View of the triumphal ARCH *and* COLONNADE, *erected in* BOSTON.

When President Washington made his tour of New England in October 1789, he was royally feted everywhere, but at Boston, where he had gained his first victory of the Revolution, he received the most tremendous welcome of all. Met at the edge of town by a grand procession led by "musick," he rode between two facing columns of citizenry to the State House, where a handsome triumphal arch and colonnade awaited him and where he was given "three huzzas from the citizens." Samuel Hill's engraving of the arch and colonnade appeared in the *Massachusetts Magazine* (January 1790).

In addition to huzzas, Washington was serenaded at the State House with delightful original music, composed for the occasion by the outstanding New England composer Oliver Holden and sung by the Independent Musical Society. The score of Holden's "Ode to Columbia's Favourite Son" was published in the *Massachusetts Magazine* (October 1789) along with another musical eulogy, an "Ode to the President of the United States," with words by "a lady" and music by another local composer, Hans Gram.

View of Faneuil-Hall, in Boston, Massachusetts.

Seat of the Muses. 571

FOR THE MASSACHUSETTS MAGAZINE.

WASHINGTON.

Set by S. HOLYOKE.

When Al - ci - des, the fon of O - lym-pian Jove, Was call'd from the

earth to the re - gions above, The fet-ters grim Tyranny twift from his hand,

And with rap - ine and mur-der u - furp'd the command; While Peace, love - ly

maiden, was fcar'd from the plains, And Lib - er - ty, cap - tive, fat wail - ing in

chains; Her once gal-lant offspring lay bleeding around, Nor on earth could a

Among the musical tributes and lavish entertainments that were heaped upon Washington in Boston was "a sumptious and elegant dinner" at Faneuil Hall, at which Vice-President John Adams was present. On his subsequent tour through New England, Washington's musical endurance must have been severely tried; at Kittery, Maine, the *Massachusetts Centinel* (November 11, 1789) reported that "A number of young gentlemen who compose the band . . . anxious to afford our illustrious and beloved President all the entertainment in their power followed him (i.e. on a harbour excursion) in a barge and performed several pieces of musick on the water."

As early as 1789 the *Massachusetts Magazine*, a periodical devoted to a wide range of cultural subjects, published original music in full score by a newly emerging group of New England composers. One of them, S. Holyoke, composed this musical laud of Washington, which appeared in the magazine's issue for September 1790.

No.V.] Massachusetts Magazine, [Vol. II.

ERIPUIT CÆLO FULMEN; SCEPTRUMQUE TYRANNIS.

B. FRANKLIN. L.L.D. F.R.S.

On April 17, 1790, Benjamin Franklin died at the age of eighty-four, and on April 22 all Philadelphia turned out to pay homage to the memory of their greatest son and to mourn at his funeral. The *Gazette of the United States* (April 28, 1790) reported that "not less than 20,000 persons attended and witnessed the funeral." The incalculable extent of Franklin's contribution to America throughout his long and prodigious life was well understood and appreciated by his contemporaries; indeed Franklin was the only other man of his era who was as highly regarded as George Washington.

At commencement ceremonies on July 17, 1790, the College of Philadelphia (now the University of Pennsylvania) paid tribute to Franklin, who had been largely responsible for its founding in 1751, with an ode to be sung to the old tune "Thou Soft Flowing Avon." The touching stanzas were widely reprinted in newspapers, but it remained for Isaiah Thomas, the most innovative American publisher of his time after Franklin himself, to devote front-page space to both the words and music of the ode in the columns of his *Massachusetts Spy: Or, the Worcester Gazette* (September 2, 1790), with its notable multilingual motto.

Ye Sages contending in virtue's fair course,
   Ye Patriots striving for freedom and laws,
Suspend for a while your labours and care,
   And to the green grave of your Franklin repair.

Bring with you sweet flow'rets from grove and from stream—
   Of things more than *mortal* your Franklin did dream—
And beings not *mortal* shall lend you their aid,
   To deck the green *grave* where your FRANKLIN is laid.

The earth, wrapp'd in fire, from her orbit shall roll,
   The heavens folded up, shall depart, as a scroll;
But he who the lightning controll'd with his rod,
   Unhurt, thro' the flames, shall ascend to his God.

THOMAS's
Maſſachuſetts SPY: Or, The Worceſter Gazette.

"The Liberty of the Preſs is eſſential to the Security of Freedom."—*La Liberté de la Preſſe eſt eſſentielle au ſoutien de la Liberté Publique.*
ΨΗ του εμφανίζοντος δόξας τας ίδίας αναγκαία ιστί τη ασφάλεια τῆς ελευθερίας.—*A facultate loquendi palam, vel ſcribendi, pendet Reipublicæ Libertas.*

VOL. XIX.] *WORCESTER,* THURSDAY, SEPTEMBER 2, 1790. **[No. 909.**

Miſcellanies.

From the UNIVERSAL ASYLUM.
AN EXERCISE,

Performed at the PUBLICK COMMENCEMENT, *in the College of Philadelphia, July 17, 1790, containing an* ODE, *ſacred to the memory of Dr.* FRANKLIN. *The Dialogue ſpoken by Mr.* WILLIAM MEREDITH *and Mr.* JAMES COXE, *and the Ode ſung by the Rev. Mr.* BLAGROVE*.

M.

PEACE with your fiddling there—it muſt be
   ſpoke;
To loſe our fineſt piece would be no joke—
A piece ſo full of learning and of fun—
Come, come good JAMES—I ſay, it muſt be done.

Done—what! I ſpeak before ſo many ladies!
Not I indeed—for ſpeaking not my trade is—
I'm ſlow of tongue—my genius but a jade is:
I've try'd her often, and have cauſe to doubt her;
Though I, with all my might ſhould ſpur and
   clout her,
I'm ſure, I ne'er ſhall be a——*publick ſpouter!*
Whene'er I try—my memory is ſo frail—
My fears and baſhfulneſs ſo much prevail
Before the *ladies*—conſtantly I fail,
Of my beſt ſpeeches I forget one half,
And, quite confounded, like an awkward calf,
Around me raiſe an univerſal laugh—
—Go, you, *good* WILLIAM, with your mincing
   paces,
Your tongue ſo flippant, and your pretty faces,
And ſhew the ladies how you've learn'd the graces.
Play well your part, and ſuit it to the time,
With fine preambles, bows and legs—in rhyme,
Scholaſtick tropes, and nonſenſe moſt ſublime!
—For me—I've no ſuch talents to diſplay,
But wit enough to keep myſelf away,
And not expoſe my weakneſſes to day—
M. [*Catching hold of his gown to prevent his eſcape.*]
  Stop! Stop!—By your allegiance to the *College*,
Come back—They'll think you wholly void of
   knowledge—
I ne'er *rehears'd* it—But you oft have ſpoke it;
And more than this—you have it in your pocket—
What ſhould you fear? you know our wiſer tutors
Forbid us to be mean and cringing ſuitors—
The *fair* their cenſure to your years will ſuit,
Nor nip the bloſſom, when they with the fruit—
He comes—O ladies! ſpare him in his fright—
He comes—like ſome coy maiden on her wedding
   night.

C.

Well, if I *muſt*—why, then, I ſurely *muſt,*
By way of ſpeaking, try to raiſe a duſt—
Fair gentlemen and ladies—Pugh! That's wrong—
Fair ladies and gentlemen—attend my *ſong—*
  " To-day you've heard full many a learned ſpeech,
Good ſenſe, no doubt, but ſenſe beyond your reach.
And firſt you heard a Latin declamation!
Were you not wiſer made by that oration?
O yes!"—DOCTRINA UNIVERSITATIS!
High ſounding words, all charming and all *gratis*—
Language ſublime, and well deliver'd too!
With ſenſe and meaning, what had ye to do?
Merit, to day, we by amuſement meaſure,
We come not for inſtruction, but for pleaſure—
Sounds more than ſenſe, you know, enchant the ear;
There are but few who *think*—but all can hear.
Then follow'd *wranglings* LOGICAL, and doubts,
By ſome call'd *ſyllogiſtical* diſputes.
ORATIONS PHILOSOPHICAL came next,
With bows and ſcrapes, the prologue to each text—
Engliſh 'tis true—the things were well enough,
But how can ladies like ſuch ſerious ſtuff?
Pray, did you mark that learned dialogue,
Upon a doctrine mightily in vogue,
" That all things are *fair,* alike are *free,*
Children alike of heaven and liberty!
That what we *ſee* and *feel* and beauty call,
Is Nature's ſlight of hand—deception all;
That *white* is *black,* if we can think it ſo,
And *black* is *whiter* than the driven ſnow;
That features and the tinctures of a ſkin,
Make not the difference of a ſingle pin!"
  Ah! then, what boots it, that yon bluſhing maid,
In all the tints of beauty ſtands array'd!
Her glowing cheek, her lips of coral dye,
Her ſnowy boſom and her ſparkling eye
Art all deluſions—(ſo theſe men have taught)
Exiſting only in her lover's thought!
Ceaſe then, thou phantom of an amorous ſwain,
And ſigh no more imaginary pain,
Since all thy fancied joys can only prove—
Ideal raptures of *ideal* love!
  Oh! rare PHILOSOPHY! Oh! ſkill divine!
Pray ladies is not this extremely fine?
To ſuch high learning none can make pretence,
But thoſe who leap the bounds of common ſenſe;
Stretch wide the wings of ſeeming demonſtration,
And ſoar in regions of their own creation—
But, ladies! not to tire you longer, ſay—
What ſhall we call th' *amuſement* of this day?
Is it a COMEDY?—Oh, no!
For the whole world, we muſt not call it ſo.
'Tis a COMMENCEMENT—that I think's the
   name,
Or general JAIL DELIVERY—much the ſame—
Or if they will excuſe an odd conceit,
Albeit this tedious *ſcientifick* treat,
It may be liken'd, in my poor opinion,
Exactly to the *peeling* of an ONION—

* This Exerciſe conſiſts of lines partly original, and partly ſelected or altered from former ſimilar compoſitions in the College. As they were haſtily thrown together, for the occaſion of the preſent Commencement, it is hoped that they will be received with the uſual indulgence of a candid publick.

Skin after ſkin .... knowledge,
All ſmelling ...... of LEARNING ..... the COL-
   LEGE
If you ... in hopes a core to find—
Alas! there's little more than ſkin and rind,
But ſomething follow'd ſtill ... rather ſerious
A ceremony ſolemn and myſterious
DEGREES were next beſtow'd ...... power,
Of many a toilſome, tedious ... hard
Honours to gratify ... learned ...,
And dub each ſcholar *Batchelor of Arts;*
You ſaw PROFESSORS ſit in due decorum,
The LADS all ſtanding in a row before 'em—
Our PROVOST ſpoke to each of them in Latin,
Were you not charm'd—it came ſo very pat in—
" *Authoritate qua fui conſtituta*—
You've been good boys—of this there is no doubt a
" *In cujus rei*"—Here it is my lad o
Hoc little ſcroll of parchment—" *tibi trado.*"
  This done—a ſpeech ſucceeded—a ſad ditty,
Call'd VALEDICTORY—to move your pity,
You ſaw the orator, with tragick grace
Screw up to ſeeming woe his rueful face—
  " Adieu, ye dear companions of my youth,
With whom I trod the flow'ry paths of truth!
One parting tear"—and here a tear had come,
Had he not left his handkerchief at home!
It matters not—ſuch was the mournful ſtyle,
You weep'd, perhaps—but I could only ſmile—
Laſt from the PULPIT—

M.

  Hold, my friend, forbear—
The PULPIT CHARGE permits no *ſporting* here!
Enough of frolick wit hath been allow'd
O'er ſcenes which *Athens* felt with joy had view'd—
" Science triumphant, and a land refin'd,
Where once rude Ignorance ſway'd th' untutor'd
   mind;"
The *wiſe,* the *good,* the *fathers* of the ſtate,
Conven'd to dignify the Muſes' ſeat!—
All hail! and welcome, ye who grace this dome!
" To Wiſdom's ſchools ſo throng'd the ſons of
   Rome—
When by their arms each neighbouring ſtate was
   ſway'd,
And kings an homage to their warriors paid—
Ev'n then thoſe chiefs who all the world ſubdu'd,
Lower'd their proud faſces to the *learn'd* and *good;*
Nor with leſs glory, in the rolls of Fame,
Shone every *ſage's* than each hero's name."—
" In Egypt's climes fair Learning firſt begun,
It roſe and travell'd with the weſtward ſun;
Enraptur'd Athens catch'd the burning ray,
Her courtly ſons inhal'd the gladſome day.
Next Rome, her features rough with many a ſcar,
Drank the pure luſtre of the orient ſtar;
Here virtuous NUMA form'd his godlike thought,
Here TULLY, PISO, ANTONINUS taught,
And ſacred VIRGIL, lab'ring with his theme,
With melting muſick charm'd Tiberia's ſtream."
  In Albion next fair SCIENCE rais'd her head,
Wiſdom and Virtue bleſs'd where ſhe led.
There BACONS, SIDNEYS, BOYLES advanc'd
   to light;
Reaſon's gay beams diſpell'd the ſhades of night.
Laſt NEWTON roſe—and, borne on eagle wings,
Collected knowledge from a thouſand ſprings,
Bound down the planets in the blue expanſe,
And would have pierc'd all NATURE at a glance,
Had not the Goddeſs, in her dread decree,
Reſerv'd, for FRANKLIN's hand, the *golden key*
That opes her inmoſt doors—O laſt and beſt
Of *Patriots* and *Philoſophers* confeſs'd,
Whoſe ever waking comprehenſive mind
Labour'd alone to benefit mankind!
All hail, COLUMBIA, to you favourite ſon!
All hail, theſe happy walls! your FOUNDER own!
With grateful ſtrains, ye *ſons of Science,* come,
While trembles with his DIRGE this hallow'd
   dome!

ODE.
[AIR. " *Thou ſoft flowing Avon, &c.*"]

Ye Sages cen-

tending in vir-tue's fair cauſe; Ye Pa-triots

ſtriv-ing for freedom and laws; and laws, and

laws; for freedom and laws;

Suſpend for a

moment your la——bours and care, And

to the green grave of your Franklin re-

Suſpend for a moment your labours

and care, And to the green grave of your

Frank-lin repair.

II.

Bring with you ſweet flow'rets from grove and
   from ſtream—
Of things more than *mortal* your Franklin did
   [dream—
And beings not *mortal* ſhall lend you their aid,
To deck the green *grave* where your FRANKLIN
   is laid.

III.

The earth, wrapp'd in fire, from her orbit ſhall
   roll,
The heavens folded up, ſhall depart, as a ſcroll;
But he who the lightning controll'd with his rod,
Unhurt, thro' the flames, ſhall aſcend to his God!

C.

How ſweet the power of *muſick* and of ſong,
To lighten woe, and ev'ry joy prolong!
" Muſick the fierceſt pangs of grief can charm,
And the ſevereſt rage of fate diſarm;
Can ſooth the ſavage, ſoften pain to eaſe,
And bid even ſad deſpair and anguiſh pleaſe."
—Proceed we then to cloſe this feſtive day—
To SONG and SCIENCE give the parting lay.
Hail Science, hail! how glorious is thy reign!
Sweet *Peace* and ev'ry virtue in thy train!
" On thy ſmooth brow, no rugged helmet frowns,
An olive wreath thy ſhining temple crowns;
Tutor'd by thee, the world ſhall know repoſe,
And warring nations bluſh that they were foes;
Stern chiefs no more their crimſon'd blades ſhall
   wield,
Nor deadly cannon bellow o'er the field!
Satiate of war, the battle breathing ſteed,
Harmleſs ſhall range the grove and verdant mead;
No drum ſhall animate the ſoldier's breaſt,
Nor piercing fife arouſe him from his reſt;
The trump ſhrill ſounding and the clang of arms,
Shall ſhake the world no more with dire alarms;
The uſeleſs rampart ſhall its ſtrength reſign,
And o'er the baſtion ſpread the curling vine;
Th' aſpiring ivy o'er old towers ſhall ſtray,
And in the trenches harmleſs *lambkins* play;
The chryſtal ſtreams ſhall flow without a ſtain,
In ſpotleſs beauty bloom each flow'ry plain;
In the ſame field where groves of lances roſe,
The furrow'd grain ſhall golden ranks compoſe!"
  Far to the *Weſt,* fair Science ſhall explore
The tawny chief on ERIE's diſtant ſhore;
Or trace his paths among the foreſts wide,
That deep imbrown the vaſt ONTARIO's tide,
And bid him quick his deadly bow unbend,
" For now deſtructive war is at an end;"
While mighty *Miſſiſſippi,* as he runs,
Proclaims aloud to all his ſwarthy ſons—
" That to earth's end fair Science ſhall increaſe,
And form one reign of KNOWLEDGE and of
   PEACE;
Where pure RELIGION's precepts ſhall prevail,
Impartial JUSTICE poiſe her balanc'd ſcale.
Bright LIBERTY exulting in each breeze,
Innoxious PLEASURE, *philoſophick* eaſe,
Heart cheering MIRTH, and PLENTY ever gay,
And roſy HEALTH—ſhall all attend her ſway.
M.

" Rapt with the thought, my ſpirits mount anew;
It comes, it comes—it ruſhes to my view!
Smit deep, I antedate the golden days,
And ſtrive to paint them in ſublimer lays—
New ſeats of *Science* riſe, new beauties pleaſe;
Commerce unfurls her canvaſs to the breeze,
On purple hills the cluſt'ring vines abound,
And laviſh culture ſpreads profuſion round;
Rich fruitage blooms, majeſtick gardens glow
That vie with Eden, or delightful Stow;
Gay Attick manners mark the fauntleſs taſte,
And Rome revives amid the deſert waſte;
Her heroes, patriots, ſages live anew,
And paſs before my eyes in long review:
For every ancient *chief,* behold a SON!
For CINCINNATUS, ſee a WASHINGTON!
Alike amidſt the ſtorms of WAR renown'd,
In PEACE with a ſuperiour glory crown'd:
Not thron'd in the proud pageantry of ſtate,
But in the boſoms of the good and great;
The firm avenger of his country's cauſe,
Guardian of JUSTICE, LIBERTY and LAWS!
A thouſand other worthies crowd my ſight—
Lo other TULLIES, VIRGILS ſpring to light!
Lo the wild Indian ſoftened by their ſong,
Emerging from his arbors, bounds along
The green Savannah, patient of the lore
Of dove eyed Wiſdom—and is rude no more!
Hark! even his babes MESSIAH's praiſe proclaim,
And fondly learn to liſp JEHOVAH's name!
O Science! onward thus thy reign extend,
O'er realms yet unexplor'd, 'till time ſhall end;
'Till death like Ignorance forſake the ball,
And life endearing Knowledge cover all!
'Till wounded SLAVERY ſeek her native hell,
'Midſt kindred fiends eternally to dwell.
Not trackleſs deſarts ſhall thy progreſs ſtay,
Rocks, mountains, floods, before thee muſt give way;
Sequeſter'd vales at thy approach ſhall ſing,
And with the voice of cheerful Labour ring;
Where wolves now howl, ſhall poliſh'd villas riſe,
And towery cities grow into the ſkies.
" Earth's diſtant ends our glory ſhall behold,
" And the new world give freedom to the old."—
DUET.
I.
PEACE and SCIENCE! heav'nly maids!
  Still extend your boundleſs ſway,
    Widely o'er yon weſtern ſhades,
    Pour the light of *civil day.*
II.
FREEDOM, mankind's ſafeſt guide,
  Shall attend your joyous reign;
    Truth and *Juſtice* by her ſide,
    Golden Commerce in her train.
M.
Well! now the buſineſs of the day is o'er,
And we, perhaps, ſhall tread this ſtage no more—

Portrait of John Jay by Joseph Wright (1786)

John Jay was one of the eighteenth-century men of conscience who deeply deplored slavery. It was outlawed in Rhode Island as early as 1774; Vermont followed in 1777, and Massachusetts in 1781. By the end of the century slavery was abolished by law in all the northern states except New Jersey, and abolitionist societies had sprung up everywhere, both in the North and the South. From time to time songs expressing abhorrence of slavery were published. One such song, "The Negroes Complaint," which appeared in the *New-York Daily Advertiser* (September 6, 1792), was dedicated to John Jay, the chief justice of the United States and head of New York's Society for Promoting the Manumission of Slaves, and to "other members of [the] laudable Society, for putting an end to slavery in this country." The tune given was "Welcome, Welcome, brother debtor."

> Forc'd from home and all its pleasures,
> Afric's coast I left forlorn;
> To increase a stranger's treasures,
> O'er the raging billows borne.
> Men from England bought and sold me,
> Paid my price in paltry gold;
> But tho' theirs they have enrol'd me,
> Minds are never to be sold.

Antislavery songs were to be expected in Rhode Island, the earliest stronghold of racial enlightenment in America. A Providence journal with an imposing name, the *United States Chronicle: Political, Commercial, and Historical* (August 2, 1792), published a plea for universal brotherhood, set to unidentified music, which blended cosmic tolerance with good old New England righteousness in a beguiling attempt at Negro dialect.

SONG.

> Dear Yanko say, and true he say,
>   All mankind, one and t'other,
> Negro, Mulatto and Malay,
>   Through all the world be broder:
>
> In black, in yellow, what disgrace,
>   That scandal so he use 'em,
> For dare no virtue in de face,
>   De Virtue in de Bosom.
>   *Dear Yanko say, &c.*
>
> Whatever harm dare in shape or make,
>   What harm in ugly feature?
> Whatever colour, form, he take
>   De Soul Make Human Creature:
>   *Dear Yanko say, &c.*
>
> Den black and copper both be friend;
>   No colour he bring beauty;
> For beauty, Yanko, say, attend,
>   On Him Who Do Him Duty.
>   *Dear Yanko say, &c.*

Advertisement for a slave sale in the Pennsylvania Journal, and Weekly Advertiser *(July 25, 1765)*

TO BE SOLD,
On Saturday the 27th inſtant, at the London Coffee houſe;
Twelve or Fourteen
Valuable NEGROES,

Conſiſting of young men, women, boys and girls. They have all had the ſmall pox, can talk Engliſh, and are ſeaſoned to the country. The ſale to begin at twelve o'clock.

THE DESPONDING NEGRO.

On Afric's wide plains where the li-on now roaring, With freedom ftalks forth the vaft de-fert ex-ploring, I was dragg'd from my hut and enchain'd as a flave, In a dark floating dungeon up--on the falt wave, Spare a halfpenny, Spare a halfpenny, Spare a halfpenny to a poor Negro.

Tofs'd on the wild main, I all wildly defpairing,
Burft my chains rufh'd on deck with my eyeballs
  glaring,   (day,
When the lightnings dread blaft ftruck the inlets of
And its glorious bright beams fhut forever away.
    Spare a halfpenny, &c.

The defpoiler of man then his profpeft thus lofing,
Of gain by my fale, not a blind bargain choofing,
As my value compar'd with my keeping was light,
Had me dafh'd overboard in the dead of night.
    Spare a halfpenny, &c.

And but for a bark to Britannia's coaft bound then,
All my cares by that plunge in the deep had been
  drown'd then,   (wave,
But by moonlight defcry'd, I was fnatch'd from the
And reluftantly robb'd of a watery grave.
    Spare a halfpenny, &c.

An antislavery song, published in
The American Musical Miscellany *(1798)*

Surprisingly, some antislavery songs were written and published in the South during the eighteenth century. This eloquent early indictment of slavery from the Charleston *City Gazette, or the Daily Advertiser* (November 18, 1789) provides an unusual insight into a liberal southern attitude at that time.

FAVORITE SONG.
—Tune, "*The son of Alknomack.*"
By Mr. C*******

The power that created the night and the day
Gave his image divine to each model of clay:
Tho' on different features the god be imprest,
One spirit immortal pervades ev'ry breast.
    And nature's great charter the right never gave
    That one mortal another should dare to enslave.

The same genial rays that the lily unfold
Gave the rose its full fragrance, the tulip its gold;
That Europe's fond bosoms to rapture inspire,
Warm each African breast with as gen'rous a fire,
    And nature's, &c.

May the head be corrected, subdu'd the proud soul,
Who would fetter free limbs and free spirits controul!
Be th' gem or in ebon or in ivory enshrin'd,
The same form of heart warms the whole human kind.
    And nature's, &c.

May freedom, whose rays we are taught to adore,
Beam bright as the sun, and bless ev'ry shore;
No charter that pleads for the rights of mankind
To invest these with gold, those in fetters can bind.
    And nature's, &c.

SONG L.

AN ODE FOR THE FOURTH OF JULY.

Come all ye sons of song, Pour the full sound along

In joyful strains; Beneath these western skies,

See a new empire rise, Bursting with glad surprise

Ty - ran-nic chains.

Liberty with keen eye,
Pierc'd the blue vaulted sky,
Resolv'd us free;

In keeping with eighteenth-century usage in choral writing, the melody of "God Save the King," to which this "Ode for the Fourth of July" was set, appears in the tenor part. The four-part arrangement was included in The American Musical Miscellany *(1798).*

Despite the emergence of native patriotic music in America, the reliance on "God Save the King" as a melodic catchall persisted. It served as an inexhaustible vehicle for everything from innumerable odes for the Fourth of July and countless paeans to Washington to praise of Thomas Paine's *Rights of Man*. If our forefathers chose to salute the sublime revolutionary social concepts of their times to the bromidic strains of "God Save the King," it merely signifies that their musical awareness had not kept pace with their recognition of the noble principles that they were celebrating. William Billings, for example, might have provided more fitting music for the song about the *Rights of Man* that appeared in the *Providence Gazette* (May 25, 1793).

A NEW SONG.
To the Tune of "God save the King."

God save—"THE RIGHTS OF MAN:"
Give him a heart to scan
   Blessings so dear;
Let them be spread around,
Wherever Man is found,
And with the welcome sound
   Ravish his ear!

See from the Universe
Darkness and clouds disperse:
   Mankind awake!
Reason and truth appear,
Freedom advances near,
Monarchs with terror hear,
   See how they quake!

Sore have we felt the stroke;
Long have we borne the yoke,
   Sluggish and tame;
But now the Lion roars,
And a loud note he pours,
Spreading to distant shores
   LIBERTY's flame.

First English edition of the "Anacreontic Song" (1779–1780)

When the popular "Anacreontic Song" emigrated from England in the late eighteenth century, it soon began to contend with "God Save the King" as a vehicle for American patriotic and political song texts. Its original words were by Ralph Tomlinson, president of the Anacreontic Society, a popular drinking club in London, whose patron saint was Anacreon, the "convivial bard of Greece," and whose "sprightly" membership, according to a contemporary, was dedicated to "wit, harmony, and the God of Wine." The identity of the song's composer, whose name was omitted when the "Anacreontic Song" was first published in 1779–1780, has been the subject of another of those periodic disagreements among musicologists. After long dispute, the general consensus has settled on John Stafford Smith, a well-known British composer of the eighteenth century, although the even better known Samuel Arnold still has some supporters. Comparatively few people now recognize the tune by its original title, but it has played a unique role in American history. Of the numberless textual transformations to which it has been sung, one is called "The Star-Spangled Banner."

Among the earliest American parodies on the "Anacreontic Song" was a Federalist indictment of the flamboyant first minister sent by the French Republic to the United States, Edmond-Charles Genêt, and of his American Republican supporters. Genêt's dangerously irresponsible tactics had added fuel to the partisan fire that already was raging in America. Despite Washington's outspoken disapproval of dissenting political parties, two distinctly opposing partisan groups, exemplifying the eternal conflict between conservative and liberal, had come into being during his first administration. The Federalists, by now a moneyed, elitist, pro-British party, headed by Alexander Hamilton, denounced the violent regime in France, while the democratic Republicans (not to be confused with today's Republicans), led by Thomas Jefferson, condoned and even applauded it. When Genêt first arrived in April 1793, he was feted by admiring Francophile Republicans, who signified their approval of the French Revolution by adopting French manners and styles of dress, celebrating Bastille Day, addressing each other as "Citizen" and "Citizeness," and singing "Ça Ira." Before long, however, Genêt's recall was demanded by President Washington, over whose head he had attempted to enlist popular American support. At the peak of the Genêt excitement, this early Anacreontic parody was published in the *Columbian Centinel* (December 4, 1793). Apparently the tune—often maligned in later years—was well enough thought of when it was new in America. In the text, "Jay, Wilcocks and King" are the eminent Federalists John Jay, William Wilcocks, and Rufus King; "Pacificus" is a pen name often used by Alexander Hamilton; the "Antis" are, of course, the Anti-Feds; *Jacobins* is the derogatory term applied to them by the Feds because of their French sympathies.

PARODY.

Of the excellent Song, "To Anacreon in Heaven."

To G***t in *New-York*, where he reigns in full glee,
    Some *Anti's* have lately prefer'd their petition,
That he their *Inspirer* and *Champion* would be;
    When this answer arriv'd from this Chief of Sedition.
        Of Jay, Wilcocks, and King,
        Let us make the world ring,
    I'll lend you my Pascal, (so fit for the string,)
And besides I'll instruct you how you may convey,
All Columbia's *Glory* and *Freedom* away.

The news through *Columbia* immediately flew,
    Pacificus rose, and thus vented his cares:
"If these traitors are suffer'd their schemes to pursue,
    "Like France we shall soon be a nation of bears:
        "Hark! already they cry,
        "In transport of joy,
    "Away to G***t let us instantly fly—
"And this Chief will assist us, that we may convey,
"All Columbia's *Glory* and *Freedom* away."

~~~

Then Freedom rose up, with her cap and her spear,
    "And swore, by *Columbia* she ever would stand,
"That her sons should receive not a[n] insult nor sneer,
    "While her laws should drive *Anarchy* out of the land:
        "Then while transports resound,
        "And Discord's fast bound,
    "And American brows are with laurels hung round,
"We free and united, our laws will obey—
"And rive from Columbia, the *Faction* away."

~~~

Francis Scott Key was by no means the first American to set patriotic words to the Anacreontic air; more likely it was the anonymous "Citizen of the United States," whose song embellished the lustrous occasion reported in the *Philadelphia General Advertiser*, later the *Aurora* (January 9, 1796).

SONG.

For the Fourth of July, 1795;
The Anniversary of American Independence.

Sung at an elegant Entertainment given by James Munroe, the American Minister at Paris, in presence of a numerous party of French and American Citizens, convened at his house, to celebrate the day. Written at Paris, 2d July, 1795, by a Citizen of the United States.

In climes where fair Freedom, secure from her foes,
Sees millions who bow at her shrine with devotion.
Where vet'ran patriots in laurel'd repose,
Lament to see arrogance crimson the ocean:
        Where order pervades
        The mountains and glades,
    Where Columbia reclines in her own native shades,
Hark! millions of Freemen with joy hail the day
Which rescu'd their Country from Tyranny's sway!

~~~

"*The Ladies Patriotic Song*" (1798) is by no means what its title implies, at least not by twentieth-century standards. Women were restricted mainly to decorative or utilitarian roles in eighteenth-century American society. The contemporary songsmith's ideal patriotic lady appears to have been one who freely offered the enticements of Love, Beauty, and Innocence to inspire patriotic gentlemen to commit nationally beneficial deeds of valor and to emulate George Washington. This socially unimaginative anonymous songsmith set his "Ladies Patriotic Song" to the tune of "Washington's March at the Battle of Trenton."

During the controversial year 1795 a surprising revolutionary social concept of major dimension was enunciated when the *Philadelphia Minerva* (October 17, 1795) published a song, "Rights of Woman," to the tune of "God Save the King." Motivated and inspired by the first great feminist document, Mary Wollstonecraft's *Vindication of the Rights of Woman*—published in England in 1792, right on the heels of Thomas Paine's *Rights of Man*—this astonishing Declaration of Women's Independence, written by an anonymous "Lady," is as radical a statement for its time as anything ever written by Paine. Whoever the visionary lady was, she must be regarded as the Founding Mother of American women's liberation.

RIGHTS OF WOMAN,
by A Lady.

Tune, "God Save America."

God save each Female's right,
Show to her ravish'd sight
    Woman is free;
Let Freedom's voice prevail,
And draw aside the vail,
Supreme Effulgence hail,
    Sweet Liberty.

Man boasts the noble cause,
Nor yields supine to laws
    Tyrants ordain;
Let woman have a share,
Nor yield to slavish fear,
Her equal rights declare,
    And well maintain.

Come forth with sense array'd,
Nor ever be dismay'd
    To meet the foe,—
Who with assuming hands
Inflict the iron bands,
To obey his rash commands,
    And vainly bow.

O Let the sacred fire
Of Freedom's voice inspire
    A Female too;—
Man makes the cause his own,
And Fame his acts renown,—
Woman thy fears disown,
    Assert thy due.

Think of the cruel chain,
Endure no more the pain
    Of slavery;—
Why should a tyrant bind
A cultivated mind
By Reason well refin'd
    Ordained Free.

Why should a Woman lie
In base obscurity,
    Her talents hid,
Has providence assign'd
Her soul to be confin'd;
Is not her gentle mind
    By virtue led?

—•—

Let snarling cynics frown,
Their maxims I disown,
    Their ways detest;—
By man, your tyrant lord,
Females no more be aw'd.
Let Freedom's sacred word,
    Inspire your breast.

Woman aloud rejoice,
Exalt thy feeble voice
    In chearful strain;
See Wolstonecraft, a friend,
Your injur'd rights defend,
Wisdom her steps attend,
    The cause maintain.

Political expediency suggested a gesture in the direction of women's liberation when, for a brief period during the astonishing 1790s, financially qualified women were permitted to vote in New Jersey. An obvious Federalist ploy to pad ballot boxes, this short-lived nod in the direction of equal rights engaged both the news media (the story was carried as far away as Edenton, North Carolina) and the topical bards. A tongue-in-cheek story in the Newark *Centinel of Freedom* (October 25, 1797) covered the unusual election proceedings at Elizabeth-town under the title:

RIGHTS of WOMEN

At the late election in this town, the FEMALES asserted the privilege granted them by the laws of this state, and gave in their votes for members to represent them in the state legislature.

Though it is a general opinion that females ought not to intermeddle in political affairs, yet the Emperor of Java never employs any but women in his embassies, and those are generally widows. The court of Java is persuaded, that women are better calculated than men for negociation, that they are more accustomed to dissimulation and constraint, that they have more address and ascendency, and that they possess greater resources of a creative fancy, as well as fertility in expedients.

A correspondent asks—is it not probable that we should have obtained better terms in a certain treaty, had some WIDOW been appointed to negociate it, instead of an *extraordinary* MALE *minister* [John Jay].

An unmistakably Republican spoof of the Federalists' vote-expanding device was set to a popular tune and published in the Republican *Centinel of Freedom* (October 18, 1797).

BATTLE OF THE KEGS.

Gallants attend, and hear a friend, Trill forth harmonious ditty, Strange things I'll tell which late befel, In Phi-la-del-phia city, 'Twas early day, as poets say, Just as the sun was rising, A soldier stood on a log of wood, And saw a sight sur-pris-ing.

NEW-YORK HISTORICAL SOCIETY

From the American Patriotic Songbook *(1813)*

The FREEDOM of ELECTION.
A NEW SONG.

To the Tune of—The Battle of the Kegs.

New Jersey hail!—thrice happy state!
 thy genius still befriends thee;
The *Arts* obedient round thee wait,
 and Science still attends thee:
In freedom's cause you gain'd applause,
 and nobly spurn'd subjection;
You're now the *Oracle* of *Laws*,
 and *Freedom* of *Election*!

Let Democrats, with senseless prate,
 maintain the softer sex, sir,
Should ne'er with politics of state
 their gentle minds perplex, sir;
Such vulgar prejudice we scorn;
 their sex is no objection.
New *trophies* shall our *brows* adorn,
 by *Freedom* of *Election*!

What tho' we read, in days of yore,
 the woman's occupation,
Was to direct the wheel and loom,
 not to direct the nation:
This narrow-minded policy
 by us hath met detection;
While woman's bound, man can't be free,
 nor have a *fair Election.*

This ray of light, which shines so bright,
 beam'd first upon that land, sir,
Where *David* lately prophecy'd,
 and gave us God's command, sir:
He did declare, with solemn air,
 Melennial state was near, sir!
Strange things, and new, should strike our view,
 and lo! it doth appear, sir.

Oh! what parade those widows made!
 from marching cheek by jole, sir;
In stage, or chair, some beat the air,
 and press'd on to the *Pole*, sir.
While men of rank, who play'd this prank,
 beat up the widows' *quarters*;
Their hands they laid on every maid,
 and scarce spar'd wives, or daughters.

This precious clause of section laws
 we shortly will amend, sir;
And women's rights, with all our might,
 we'll labour to defend, sir:
To Congress, lo! widows shall go,
 like metamorphos'd witches!
Cloath'd with the dignity of state,
 and eke, in coat and breeches!

Then Freedom hail!—thy powers prevail
 o'er prejudice and error;
No longer shall men tyrannize,
 and rule the world in terror:
Now one and all, proclaim the fall
 of Tyrants!—Open wide your throats,
And welcome in the *peaceful* scene,
 of government in petticoats!!!

Vocalized commentary on the controversy over the ratification of Jay's Treaty was published in the *City Gazette & Daily Advertiser* (September 3, 1795) in the form of a Yankee dialect song laden with homely political advice to "Brother Jon'than" to the tune of "Yankee Doodle." In the text, both "Georgy" and "George" refer to President Washington; the "riggling pole" is the helm of a ship; "Grenville" and "Pitt" are the two British ministers with whom Jay had so unsuccessfully negotiated; the reference to "merchants" concerns compensation for wholesale British seizures of American merchant ships; the "Western Posts" are the frontier posts within the boundary lines awarded to America in the peace treaty but held by the British.

*John Jay burned in effigy,
from an undated print*

When Chief Justice John Jay, who had been sent to England to resolve the many complications and grievances in Anglo-American relations, brought back a distinctly less-than-satisfactory treaty, the ensuing public demonstrations against its ratification recalled the violence of Stamp Act days. Alexander Hamilton was stoned when he attempted to defend Jay's Treaty, and in a number of places Jay was burned in effigy. Newport reverted to its protest patterns of former days, but with marching music added. A Newport story reprinted in the Charleston *City Gazette & Daily Advertiser* (September 23, 1795) told how a procession had "moved in great order through the Main street . . . having in their front the effigy of the late chief justice, exalted in a cart, drawn by a *white horse*, and decorated with the usual and proper ornament, a *purse*." The *Gazette* added a cultural note: "During the procession . . . the music was excellent, and the gentlemen were happy to recognize their old favorite tune, Yanky Doodle. . . ."

SONG.—Tune, *Yankey Doodle.*

Brother Jon'than, what are you 'bout,
 What the nation ails you?
Why with treaty make such *rout!*
 '*Vow*, your reason fails you.
  Chorus—Yankey Doodle, keep it up,
   Yankey Doodle, dandy;
   Sure you've had a *pow'rful* cup,
   'Lasses mix'd with brandy.

Sure, if treaty is not right,
 Georgy will not sign it;
'Till't has teeth it cannot bite—
 To him then resign it.
  Yankey Doodle, &c.

Grenville is a st--king hound,
 So is sh---poke Pitt, too—
Crowing dung-hills, I'll be *bound*,
 Bragging Jay has bit you.
  Yankey Doodle, &c.

George is at the *riggling pole*,
 Sure the vessel's right, *you*;
He'll see the merchants are made whole,
 Tipping *Yankey-bite*, you.
  Yankey Doodle, &c.

Treaties, they are solemn things,
 Deacon Ziba told us;
But if broken once by Kings,
 Broke, how can they hold us!
  Yankey Doodle, &c.

    ～～～

Mind your bread and butter, *you*,
 Quit this *tarnal mouthing*:
France is rising full to view—
 Britain's *Hag* is *southing*.
  Yankey Doodle, &c.

Let's treat on then, get our cash.
 Get our Western Posts, too;
When her fleet is gone to *smash*,
 Tickle up her hosts, you.
  Yankey Doodle, &c.

Perhaps the ultimate in Washington-worship was reached by a devoutly Federalist songwriter who referred to Washington's birthday as America's "political Christmas." In his introductory note to his "Christmas" carol, adapted from "God Save America," a song that had first appeared in 1789 in *The Philadelphia Songster*, the author emotionally continued:

Begin with the infant in his cradle, let the first word he lisps be WASHINGTON; and let the gray-headed sire, expire with this prayer upon his trembling lips, "Giver of good! long, long indulge this country with thy WASHINGTON."

Some of the stanzas, published in the *Columbian Centinel* (February 20, 1796), went:

A SONG.

While others sing of Kings,
And *suchlike titled things*;
  To praise in songs,
HEROES, in battle slain,
STATESMEN, who still remain
Our glory to maintain,
  To us belongs.

GOD save great WASHINGTON!
Bellona's noblest son,
  Long to command;
May every enemy,
Aw'd by his virtues, flee,
And be grim tyranny
  Bound by his hand.

God save America!
Free from despotic sway,
  'Till time shall cease;
Long hath the din of arms
Been hush'd; to war's alarms
Follow'd in all its charms,
  Heaven-born PEACE.

〜〜〜

And fain, great patriot JAY,
Would we a tribute pay,
  To worth like thine;
While all the good and wise,
Thy late proceedings prize,
In vain to blind our eyes,
  Shall knaves combine.

Wilt though great HAMILTON!
Genius and Virtue's son,
  Accept these lays;
Altho' thy treasury
Of fame, exhaustless be,
We give, from penury
  One mite of praise.

But time itself would fail,
Should we attempt to hail
  The FEDERAL BAND:
Long may Columbia know,
What joys from freedom flow,
And ne'er may any foe
  Distress our land.

GENERAL WASHINGTON'S JACK ASS.

THIS is the true picture of that Celebrated Animal, which his Most Catholick Majesty the King of Spain Bought with his own money and Shipped at his own Expence, for a present to our beloved General.

Hero merit takes, and Gallant Actions shine
Or Mighty Sir, this Afs had ne'er been thine,
Though droll the Gift, yet from a King tis' good;
Afses, Kings, Minifters are all one blood.

In 1785 Charles III of Spain as a mark of "great favour" had sent Washington the appropriately named Royal Gift, whose picture appeared in Weatherwise's Town and Country Almanack *for 1786. He was soon followed by another highly superior jackass, Knight of Malta, and two anonymous jennets; all were imported at farmer Washington's behest to found an improved new breed of donkey in the United States. Both Royal Gift and Knight of Malta were objects of ridicule in a caustic satire of adulatory Washington's birthday songs.*

The Anti-Federalist Philadelphia *Aurora* (February 20, 1796) chose to take a heretical view of America's political Christmas. Sharply satirizing the accepted "classical" Washington's birthday ode, muses and Olympian gods were invoked in a slyly wicked lampoon of the current Federalist regime: its events, personalities, donkeys, and even the foibles of quasi-royal etiquette practiced at the Washingtons' levees. In the text, "Caesar," of course, refers to Washington; "Amphibious Tim" is Timothy Pickering, who as secretary of war served as head of the navy as well as the army; "Ye Sons of Whiskey" refers to the insurgents in the Whiskey Rebellion.

FOR THE AURORA.
Written for the 22d of Feb. 1796.

I sing the day—tho' often sung before,
  On which Fame's trumpet (so the Fates ordain'd)
With blasts more loud than bursting *Ætna*'s roar,
  Glad tidings to the universe proclaim'd.

Ye sacred Nine! vouchsafe my pray'r to grant
  And bottle up, from Hippocrates' pure stream,
One doz'n, or two, or three—nay, all I want
  To make my stanzas equal to my theme.

Let *Malta*'s knight—let *royal gift* rejoice,
  And with harmonious paeans rend the skies—
Let ev'ry brother-brayer raise his voice,
  Whilst echo from each distant hill replies.

Excisemen, Senators, and Army-Hectors,
  All hail the day in clear or squalid notes;
Place-hunters too, with lordly Bank-directors,
  Loud in the gen'ral concert strain their throats.

The splendid LEVEE too, in some degree,
  Must CAESAR's dignity and pow'r display:
There Courtiers smooth, approach with bended knee,
  And hoary Senators their homage pay.

He, gratifi'd beyond his heart's desire,
  Whilst *loyal subs* their duty thus perform,
Vouchsafe's to smile upon his trusty 'Squire,
  Amphibious TIM—"successor but in form."

Tho' "faction most detestable"—most vain,
  Hath on JAY's Treaty curses dire conferr'd—
What! self-created SCUM! dare ye complain,
  Or say *infallibility* hath err'd?

Against that rock—that adamantine wall,
  Ye Sons of Whiskey, aim your puny blows—
Slanders against great CAESAR's name must fall
  "Like pointless arrows shot from broken bows!"

Tho' some have strove (with impudent allusion)
  From trammels of idolatry to free us—
Ye *partizans of war and fell confusion!*
  "Avaunt! ye cannot say 'twas"

BOWZYBEUS

In 1794 Washington's Masonic brothers commissioned the artist William Williams to paint this candid portrait of him.

In Washington's undelivered but widely published farewell address, he gave his reasons for refusing a third term; expressed his disapproval of political parties; advised America on economic policy; and, most memorably, admonished her to shun involvement in foreign quarrels. This final counsel was singled out by songwriters, who continued to observe Washington's birthday even after John Adams became president. Just after Washington left office, the *Columbian Centinel* (March 15, 1797) published a topical Washington's birthday song that commented on his retirement and referred to his foreign policy.

SONG:

Sung at *Plymouth*, on the late celebration of
GEORGE WASHINGTON's birth day:

[*Composed and set to music by* Mr. Benj. M. Seymour.]

Hark! what plaintive soft murmurs, far westward I hear;
'Tis *Columbia* grown pensive and thoughtful I fear;
See great GEORGE now retires from the helm of state,
Revered by his country, admired by the great.

Cloth'd with honor, in peace may he free from alloy
Find the peaceful retirement he seeks to enjoy:—
To his counsel *Columbia* shall ever adhere;
Banish foreign intrigue, and be free without fear.

PART III

Hark, the loud Drums, hark
The shrill Trumpet calls to Arms,
Come Americans, come,
Prepare for War's Alarms.

The Freeman's Journal, or
New-Hampshire Gazette
April 12, 1777

In 1794 the tune of "Yankee Doodle" was published in America for the first time
when the composer-publisher Benjamin Carr included it in his "Federal Overture,"
a nonpartisan potpourri of political and nonpolitical popular tunes, with something
to please every taste. Besides "Yankee Doodle," it comprised "The Marseilles March"
("La Marseillaise"), "Ça Ira," "La Carmagnole," "Oh Dear! What Can the Matter
Be!" "The Irish Washerwoman," and "The President's March."

THE

Launch,

A FEDERAL SONG.

YE Sons of COLUMBIA, your ardour display,
    With true Federal Spirit, on this joyful day :
When the MERRIMACK, in speed is bending her course,
The Trade of COLUMBIA, to protect by main force.

Let true Federal mirth be seen in each face,
No *Jacobin* or *Traitor* your company disgrace ;
But shew your dislike to such characters as these,
And tell them they're welcome to the *Fraternal Squeeze.*

See the Eagle assuming her right for to reign,
Her wings on a flutter, those rights to maintain ;
While commerce denotes the pursuits we explore—
The Seas of the World from America's shore.

See *Justice*, the guide by which we'll maintain
Our *rights* on the Land, and our *claim* on the Main—
By Justice we make all *our* actions to square,
Whether Peace be our fortune, or destiny—WAR.

With *Barry* and *Nicholson*, and brave Captain *Brown*,
We've nothing to fear from *Talleyrand's* frown ;
His millions demanded—we'll pay in a scroll,
Well tinctur'd with Powder, and display'd by a Ball.

Let the French & the Dutch, their own contracts attend,
And *Talleyrand* with *rescriptions* his *associates* befriend ;
While ADAMS and WASHINGTON stands at the helm,
We'll mind our own business, and leave their's to them.

To confide in the wisdom of patriots thus try'd,
(Tho the French and all Europe, their virtues deride)
Is the duty of all, whose wish is to share
A right in the glory of COLUMBIA so fair.

The Directory of France, with all their deceit,
May sound false alarms—our spirits to defeat ;
Still we've men at the helm, who with wisdom can shie
And track them in Council, as well as in field.

Our Constitution and laws, by our father's design'd
To render us happy—and useful and kind ;
We'll freely support—with our lives and estates,
Without hesitation or lengthy debates.

By three captur'd Frenchmen, safe lodg'd on our sho
Some pence is recover'd, to replenish our store ;
Tho' millions beside have been robb'd from our land,
We'll make them to tremble, *and refund cash in hand.*

No peace with such robbers, 'till down on their knees,
They beg of us pardon—and pay for the SQUEEZE ;
'Till all their proud hearts are melted as one,
And promise us treble for mischief they've done.

And now, my brave friends, let's each one unite,
In wishing the MERRIMACK a sure and quick flight ;
From the cradle to that element—design'd for her station,
To bravely oppose the proud foes of our Nation.

FINIS.

*Launchings were frequent in the late 1790s; this broadside ballad
concerns the launching of the Merrimack in 1798.*

During John Adams's administration, the dormant American navy was reactivated and the navy department created. In 1797 the *Constitution*, one of six frigates ordered by Washington in 1794, was completed; she was finally launched at the Boston shipyard on October 21, 1797, after two unsuccessful earlier attempts. Federalists, who enthusiastically supported naval rearmament, accused Republicans, who equally enthusiastically opposed it, of somehow being responsible for the *Constitution*'s earlier reluctance to take to the seas—a not unreasonable suspicion after the official Republican poet Philip Freneau had exclaimed: "O frigate *Constitution*! Stay on shore!"

A folksy Yankee ballad, wonderfully re-creating the excitement attending one of the *Constitution*'s frustrated launches, was reprinted in the *Aurora* (October 12, 1797) from the Newburyport *Impartial Herald*. The tune "Lexington March" is, of course, "Yankee Doodle."

TRIP TO LAUNCHING.
Tune—"*Lexington March.*"

Says BOB to DICK, come let us go
  To Boston town, to launching;
'Twill be grand times, for all the world
  In flocks are thither prancing.
    CHORUS.—*Yankee Doodle, &c.*

There's Parson TRIG, with his spruce Wig,
  And eke the Parson's Lady,
Are thither gone, with 'Squire PRIM,
  His WIFE, his DOG, and BABY.

The PRESIDENT, that wondrous Man,
  Will grace the celebration;
I long to see that famous chief,
  He's done *much* for the nation.

Our GOVERNOR, 'tis also said,
  —Will there be instate, sir,
And *Feds* and *Antifeds* will join,
  The Day to celebrate, sir.

'Twas said, some *Jacobinic* fiends
  Of this had been the cause sir;
Who wish the "*Constitution*" dead,
  And eke our *Federal Laws*, sir.

While others, with more truth, assert,
  Which all but sceptics see, sir;
Miss "*Constitution*" rest a while;
  The times are bad at sea, sir!

Then heigh for *Constitution launch*!
  And heigh for *Federal Navy*!
And may all those who laugh and sneer,
  Take lodgings with *Old Davy*.

The *Frigate* she is mighty large,
  And without diminution,
'Tis said, may fitly be compar'd
  To "*Federal Constitution*."

There's our *Nab*, and *Moll*, and *Bett*,
  Will join us in the party;
And 'Squire BUMPKIN's bouncing *Doll*,
  That laughs and sings so hearty.

Then straight they tackled up their *Nags*,
  And mounted them in haste, sir;
Then jogg'd along with decent pace,
  Of time made little waste, sir.

But when to Boston town they came,
  O, what uproar was there, sir.
The *Horses* neigh'd, the *Asses* bray'd,
  Moll scarce could curb her *Mare*, sir.

The people too, in every street,
  Were on each other pressing;
The *Dogs* ran here—the *Cats* mew'd there
  'Twas sure a scene distressing.

Some on houses—some on wharves,
  And some in boats were squeezing;
Sir, by your leave—an equal chance—
  Lord, sir, *you're very teasing*.

It was sweat, & rub, & thump, & kick,
  Each strove to push 'fore t'other;
Indeed, ne'er did the *Boston Cits*
  Behold so great a pother.

But language fails to close the scene,
  Just as it chanc'd to hap, sir,
For "*Constitution*" still, it seems,
  In *Cradle* wish'd to *nap*, sir.

Nor could the noisy clam'rous shouts
  From her repose once shake her;
She still *slept* on—and seem'd to *laugh*
  At those who wish'd to *wake* her!

Then after having gap'd a while,
  The num'rous croud retir'd;
Some *few* were pleas'd—but *more* by far
  Were with resentment fir'd.

Matthew Lyon, the Irish-born, maverick Republican congressman from Vermont, created a considerable flurry in 1797 when he made a fiery speech opposing the appointment of a committee to "wait upon" President Adams for the purpose of being told where and when the president would be pleased to receive Congress's formal reply to the annual presidential message. Lyon condemned this aristocratic ceremonial, saying that he "believed the president should always be ready to receive important communications." Both Washington and Adams followed royal British custom and delivered their annual messages before the assembled Congress "as if from a throne."

Because he was a foreigner of humble origins, the controversial Lyon became a prime target for Federalist intolerance and snobbishness. When a fellow congressman from Connecticut (probably Lyon's later adversary, Roger Griswold) observed during a debate that he "hoped there would be *American* blood enough [in Congress] to carry the question," Lyon was goaded into replying, according to Claypoole's *American Daily Advertiser* (June 5, 1797), that

He had no pretention to *high blood*, though he thought he had as *good blood* as any of them, as he was born of a hale, healthy woman. Before yesterday, he never heard of gentlemen boasting of their blood at that house. He could not say, it was true, that he was descended from the bastards of Oliver Cromwell, [or his] courtiers, or from the Puritans, who switched the horses for breaking the Sabbath, [or] from those who persecuted the Quakers and hanged the witches. He could, however, say that this was his country because he had no other; and he owned a share of it, which he had bought by means of honest industry; he had fought for his country.

The juicy episode was gleefully seized upon by the Federalist press at home, where it was translated into a deft song in low-comedy Irish dialect, emanating from the "shop of Colon and Spondee" and published in the *Farmer's Weekly Museum, Newhampshire and Vermont Journal* (June 26, 1797). "Colon and Spondee" was a writing collaboration of two of the most gifted American writers of the time, Joseph Dennie, who later became the editor of the *Farmer's Weekly Museum*, and Royall Tyler, the author of *The Contrast*, one of the best known of early American plays. Their song not only satirized every detail of Lyon's outburst in Congress, but it also resurrected an old calumny in which Lyon was accused of having been cashiered out of the American army by Horatio Gates for failing to defend a post on the Onion River in 1776. It had been rumored that Gates had ordered Lyon to wear a wooden sword as he was drummed out of camp to the ignominious music of "The Rogue's March."

A NEW SONG.

To the tune of "O dear what can the matter be."

[As sung with applause at *Congress Gardens*.]

Come hones of Congress, pray do not be smoking me,
With your well borns, and ill borns, pray do not be poking me,
For what you call complaisance always is choking me;
    If you know me, pray how should it fail;
For Och blood anouns, what can the matter be,
That Congress with high blood all should full fatten'd be;
O gramachree, you had better have rattan'd me;
    I'm bother'd from head to the tail.

When first I bog trotted to Congress, dear Spaiker,
I thought a Rep, like a pig, was a liberty creature,
Who might nuzzle and grunt in his own pretty nature,
    And quarrel like felons in jail;
But Och blood anouns, what can the matter be,
With breeding and complaisance thus to bespatter me,
And thus to be putting the gentleman after me;
    I'm bother'd from head to the tail.

And as to this answer *here* to our ould President
Why can't we all carry it, while we are here *resident*?
For Fait, my politeness shall ne'er draw a precedent;
    To the old fowl myself will turn tail;
For Och blood anouns, what can the matter be,
That to bow and to scrape you will beflatter me.
And on both sides of the House thus so bother and batter me,
    I'm bother'd, Fait, how should I fail.

With your high blood and well born, pray do no more rack us;
But hear that sweet soul, honest Horace O'Flaccus,
Who says that good blood will most damnably thwack us,
    Och honies, O how should it fail!
But Och blood anouns, what can the matter be,
That Congress with high blood should thus all fatten'd be?
O gramachree, you had better have rattan'd me;
    I'm bother'd from head to the tail.

Here is *I* my nown self, who was born of my mother,
A hale hearty wench, and my father's another,
Whose blood ran as low as the wash of the gutter;
    Och honies, O how should it fail!
Then Och blood anouns, what can the matter be,
That with your high blood you still will bespatter me;
I fear my dear blarneys you are after to flatter me;
    I'm bother'd from head to the tail.

My father ne'er hang'd a witch of a woman,
Or beat a poor baiste, who made Sunday common,
For why, his own self was tuck'd up at Roscommon,
    Och honies, O how should he fail!
But Och blood anouns, what can the matter be,
That with ould Noll Cromwell you will bespatter me
And give me more daddies than ever went after me;
    I'm bother'd from head to the tail.

Did you know how I fought on the sweet Onion river,
It would cause all your bowels to caper and quiver,
With my big wooden sword: daddy Gates was the giver,
    Och honies, O how should I fail;
Och blood anouns, what can the matter be,
That in your two ditches you will thus bespatter me,
I'm sick of your nonsense and long to bescatter ye;
    I'm bother'd from head to the tail.

Now take your fine spaiches and all go and read them;
Let the house go before, maister Spaiker precede them,
While I'll stay behind, like a fowl that loves freedom,
    Och honies, O how should I fail;
Och blood anouns, what can the matter be,
That with your civilities, thus you'l bespatter me,
Fait honies, you can't to a GENTLEMAN flatter me,
    You are bother'd from head to the tail.

"He in a trice struck Lyon thrice/ Upon his head, enrag'd, sir/ Who seiz'd the tongs to ease his wrongs/ And Griswold thus engag'd, sir."

"Lord save us, the Congress are fighting!" sang Americans early in 1798 to the tune of "The night before Larry was stretched," and indeed Congress had been fighting! All America was titillated by the sensational duel with mixed weapons—hickory stick versus fire tongs—that had erupted during a session of Congress when Roger Griswold, the gentleman from Connecticut who had earned a spit in the face through his too-frequent references to a wooden sword, vengefully confronted Matthew Lyon, the gentleman from Vermont who had done the spitting. Far from attempting to restrain the combatants, their congressional colleagues happily spurred them on, as we see from this cartoon, "Congressional Pugilists," which was embellished by lines from another topical ballad, "The Battle of the Wooden Sword," to the tune of "Yankee Doodle."

"Peter Porcupine" (William Cobbett, the infamous editor of *Porcupine's Gazette*) published a ballad in his newspaper (May 5, 1798) that not only ridiculed Matthew Lyon but also satirized the celebrated writers' group, the Hartford Wits. Except for its nonsense refrain in satirical imitation of Irish fa-la refrains, it fits the meter of "Yankee Doodle."

The Wits of Connecticut are putting LYON's *Speeches into verse.*

ORATION 1.

The LION commenceth his oration by asserting his independence. . . . He speaketh much of pedigree, and showeth his own, negatively and positively. The LION remarketh on the fondness of some gentlemen for forms and ceremonies—expresseth his dislike there of; and withall, concludeth his oration by declaring his resolution to abide with Pompey, the Hallsweeper, while the House should wait on the President.

> *As still as mice the members sat,*
> *Expecting royal fun, sir;*
> *The Speaker gently moved his hat,*
> *And L--- thus begun, sir.—*

I'm rugged Mat, the Democrat,
   Berate me as you please, sir;
True Paddy-Whack ne'er turn'd his back,
   Or bow'd his head to Caesar.

> *Horum, scorum, rendum, roarum,*
>   *Spittam, spattam, squirto;*
> *Tag, rag, derry, merry, raw head and*
>   *bloody bones,*
>   *Sing Langolee, nobody's hurt, O!*

The Yankey crew long since I knew—
   At home I drill them daily;
There's not a man of all their clan
   But knows my old Shelalee.
      Horum, &c.

These gentry spout of *ancient blood*—
   It reddens all their speeches:
Zounds, sir! my veins contain as good
   As theirs who hang'd the witches.
      Horum, &c.

'Tis true my grandam never smirk'd
   And toy'd with the Protector;
Nor did she spill the beer that worked
   While folks were gone to lecture.
      Horum, &c.

My dam, sir, was a buxom lass—
   Her milk was rich and good, sir;
No cow that's fed on clover grass
   Can boast of purer blood, sir.
      Horum, &c.

My sire he was a strapping buck
   As ever girl sat eye on;
What wonder then they had the luck
   To bring the world a Lion!
      Horum, &c.

The blue skin'd lads are vastly fond
   Of 'lection, shows and raising;
They love to strut, like geese from pond,
   And set the fools a gazing.
      Horum, &c.

We Lions bold abominate
   To court the great and wealthy;
I did it not in Vermont State—
   I sha'nt in Philadelphia.
      Horum, &c.

Nor was I to this Congress sent
   To dress like coxcombs fine, sir—
To cringe before the President,
   And taste his cake and wine, sir.
      Horum, &c.

Go you, who like such royal cheer,
   And stalk in long procession;
I'll stay and eat my luncheon here,
   As at the extra session.

> *Horum, scorum, rendum, roarum,*
>   *Spittam, spattam, squirto;*
> *Tag, rag, derry, merry, raw head and*
>   *bloody bones,*
>   *Sing Langolee, nobody's hurt, O!*

The engraving contains state insignia and statistics. Visible labels include:

NEW HAMPSHIRE — 2 Senators 4 Representatives, 183,858 Inhabitants
VERMONT — 2 Senators 2 Representatives, 106,923 Inhabitants
MASSACHUSETTS — 2 Senators 15 Representatives, 422,845 Inhabitants
CONNECTICUT — 2 Senators 7 Representatives, 251,002 Inhabitants
RHODE ISLAND — 2 Senators 2 Representatives, 69,122 Inhabitants
NEW YORK — 2 Senators 11 Representatives, 332,170 Inhabitants
PENSYLVANIA — 2 Senators 14 Representatives, 602,365 Inhabitants
NEW JERSEY — 2 Senators 5 Representatives, 11,114 Inhabitants
MARYLAND — 2 Senators 9 Representatives, 300,635 Inhabitants
DELAWARE — 2 Senators 1 Representatives, 64,273 Inhabitants
VIRGINIA — 2 Senators 23 Representatives, 878,959 Inhabitants
NORTH CAROLINA — 2 Senators 11 Representatives, 378,005 Inhabitants
SOUTH CAROLINA — 2 Senators 9 Representatives, 248,591 Inhabitants
GEORGIA — 2 Senators 3 Representatives, 162,686 Inhabitants
TENNESSEE — 2 Senators Representatives, 97,680 Inhabitants
KENTUCKY — 2 Senators 4 Representatives, 229,955 Inhabitants

MILLIONS FOR OUR DEFENCE NOT A CENT FOR TRIBUTE

JOHN ADAMS President of the United States

A New DISPLAY of the UNITED STATES

In this engraving by Amos Doolittle, John Adams is surrounded by the insignia and statistics of the sixteen United States. The militant-looking eagle surmounting the composition is grasping in its talons a ribbon inscribed with the famous slogan of 1798.

"Millions for defense, but not a cent for tribute" became America's rallying cry in 1798, after public disclosure of the scandalous "XYZ" incident. The slogan, credited to Charles Cotesworth Pinckney, was in fact a paraphrase of his indignant exclamation "No! No! Not a sixpence!" when he and his fellow commissioners to France, John Marshall and Elbridge Gerry, were confronted by three unofficial representatives of the French Directory, mysteriously known as X, Y, and Z, who coolly demanded a *douceur* (bribe) of a quarter of a million dollars to arrange a meeting with the French minister Talleyrand. The commission had been appointed by President Adams to seek peaceful means of resolving the serious strife arising from French spoliation of American shipping.

The blaze of patriotic passion ignited by the XYZ scandal was stoked by the incitant patriotic songs that appeared almost daily in the press and increasingly frequently as sheet music. In large measure they were set to the tune of "Yankee Doodle," which appears to have supplanted "God Save the King" as an all-purpose, nonpartisan musical vehicle. Memorable among the myriad "Yankee Doodle" songs written during the "undeclared war" with France is this Federalist version recounting in ballad fashion the details of the XYZ affair and adding a number of pertinent side comments. It appeared in the *Commercial Advertiser* (June 29, 1798) and subsequently in a number of other publications. In the text, *cinq Têtes* refers to the five-man French Directory; *trappan* (trepan) is an archaic term for trap; "Benny Faction" is Benjamin Franklin Bache, Benjamin Franklin's Francophile, Republican grandson, who was the publisher of the Anti-Federalist newspaper, the *Aurora*; the insulting reference to "Aurora's mill" is a paraphrase of the rude insult to Dr. Joseph Warren in "The Lexington March" (see page 52); "Venice" and "Dutch bugs" refer to Napoleonic exploits. The footnotes appear in the original.

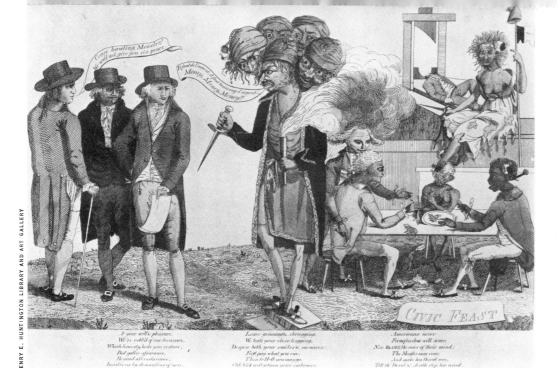

A 1799 cartoon of the five-headed monster, representing the French Directory, in the act of extorting money from the three American commissioners

NEW VERSES—To an old Tune.

Sing Yankee Doodle, that fine tune,
  Americans delight in;
It suits for peace, it suits for fun,
  It suits as well for fighting.
Chorus: Yankee doodle (mind the tune)
    Yankee doodle dandy,
    If Frenchmen come with naked bum,
    We'll *spank* 'em hard and handy.

To Ca ira and Carmagnole,
  Direct'ry dance like Neroes;*
But Frenchmen's songs, so full of wrongs
  Are scorn'd by Yankee heroes.
    Yankee doodle, &c.

The President, with good intent,
  Three Envoys sent to Paris,
But cinq Têtes,† would not with 'em treat,
  Of honor France so bare is.
    Yankee doodle, &c.

Thro' X and Y, and Madam Sly,
  They made demand of money;
For as we're told, the French love gold,
  As stinging bees love honey.
    Yankee doodle, &c.

Nebuchadnezzar long ago,
  Set up a golden image,
Shadrach, Mechach, Abednego,
  Would not go down in homage.
    Yankee doodle, &c.

Just so cinq Têtes, with pride elate,
  Of Marshall, Pinckney, Gerry,
Demand that they, adore and pay,
  The piper to make merry.
    Yankee doodle, &c.

That Talleyrand might us trappan
  And o'er the country sound it;
He sent his pill, t'Aurora's mill,
  And Benny Faction ground it.
    Yankee doodle, &c.

But Marshall came with trump of fame,
  And brought the noble answer;
Without a joke, he had in soak,
  A rod for Talleyrand, Sir.
    Yankee doodle, &c.

With fraud and he, Directory,
  Deal in deceit and evil;
Who Venice sold, for pow'r and gold,
  Would sell us to the Devil.
    Yankee doodle, &c.

Their 'fernal hugs, may squeeze Dutch bugs
  But we will have no master;
And while the Swiss, Sans Culottes** kiss,
  We'll spread a blister plaister.
    Yankee doodle, &c.

Americans then fly to arms,
  And learn the way to use 'em:
If each man fights, to 'fend his rights,
  The French can't long abuse 'em.
    Yankee doodle, &c.

Bold Adams bid in seventy six,
  Our Independence sign, Sir;
And he will not, give up a jot,
  Tho' all the world combine, Sir.
    Yankee doodle, &c.

Let every man, adopt his plan,
  Like brothers stick together;
Then all the threats of vile cinq Têtes,
  Will never weigh a feather.
    Yankee doodle, &c.

If we are firm, peace will return,
  Sweet peace, the very dandy;
May they that flinch a single inch,
  Ne'er taste the sugar candy.
    Yankee doodle (mind the tune)
    Yankee doodle dandy,
    If Frenchmen come with naked bum,
    We'll *spank* 'em hard and handy.

---

* Nero fiddled while Rome was burning.
† Pronounced sank tate.
** i.e., wedding breeches.

Portrait of Joseph Hopkinson by Gilbert Stuart

Mrs. John Adams, seen here in a portrait by an unknown eighteenth-century artist, wrote of the first performance of "Hail Columbia" that the applause "was enough to 'stund' one."

Of the countless songs that contributed to the patriotic exaltation of 1798, one achieved immortality. "Hail Columbia," for which Joseph Hopkinson wrote stirring Federalist words to Philip Phile's "President's March" (see page 120), for more than a century competed with "The Star-Spangled Banner" (written in 1814) as our national anthem; it was only in 1931 that the "Banner" was given official status by proclamation of President Hoover. In 1798 "The President's March" became a supreme favorite among Federalist tunes; when it was played at the theatre in Philadelphia (presumably the New Theatre) in response to a "general clamor" for it, *Porcupine's Gazette* (April 10, 1798) reported that "the uproar and applause from all quarters of the house were so general, so loud and incessant that very little of the tune was heard." This ovation, great as it was, was exceeded on April 25, when "Hail Columbia," was sung for the first time at the New Theatre by Gilbert Fox, the versatile young English-born actor-singer and engraver. Fox is supposed to have asked Hopkinson (the son of Francis Hopkinson) to write patriotic words to "The President's March" for him to sing at his benefit, but according to the first lady, Abigail Adams, who attended the performance "in cogg," the words were written in response to partisan public demand.

In a letter to her sister, Mrs. Adams wrote that "their had been for several Evenings at the Theatre something like disorder, one party crying out for the Presidents March and Yankee Doodle, whilst Ciera [Ça Ira] was vociferated from the other. It was hisst off repeatedly. The Managers were blamed. Their excuse was that they had not any words to the Presidents March—Mr. Hopkinson accordingly composed these to the tune." The first audience was electrified; repeated encores were demanded from Mr. Fox, and Mrs. Adams wrote that "the last time, the whole . . . Audience broke forth in the Chorus whilst the thunder from their Hands was incessant, and at the close they rose, gave 3 Huzzas, that you might have heard a mile—My head aches in concequence of it."

Gilbert Fox engraved this idyllic "View of the City of Philadelphia" as well as the handsome exterior view of the New Theatre, where he sang the historic first performance of "Hail Columbia." The interior view of the theatre was published in the New York Magazine *(April 1794).*

A circular portrait of John Adams, surrounded by the popular quotation from its text, "Behold the Chief who now commands!" identifies the rare first publication of "Hail Columbia." Announced by Benjamin Carr only two days after its sensational premiere, it first appeared under the lackluster, if descriptive, title of "The favorite new Federal Song, Adapted to the President's March," but before the year was out—and several editions later—it was renamed. It swept the country, arousing patriotic emotions as fervent as Dickinson's "Liberty Song" had done in 1768.

At the second performance of "Hail Columbia," *Porcupine's Gazette* (April 27, 1798) wrote: ". . . it was called for again and again . . . and encored every time. At every repetition it was received with additional enthusiasm, 'till, towards the last [a] great part of the audience, pit, box, gallery, actually joined in the chorus. . . . no sooner were the words, 'Behold the CHIEF WHO NOW COMMANDS,' pronounced, than the house shook to its very centre, the song and the whole scene were drowned in the enthusiastic peals of applause, and were obliged to stop and begin again and again in order to gain a hearing. . . ." Republican journalists blasted "Hail Columbia," calling it an "aristocratic tune," full of "ridiculous bombast, the vilest adulation to the anglo-monarchial party [the Federalists] and the two Presidents." When it was performed, they wrote, "the extacy of the party knew no bounds, they encored, they shouted, they became 'mad as the Priestess of the Delphic God'" (quoted in *Porcupine's Gazette*, April 27, 1798).

Brothers joind peace and safety we shall find.

2

Immortal Patriots rise once more
Defend your rights — defend your shore
    Let no rude foe with impious hand
    Let no rude foe with impious hand
Invade the shrine where sacred lies
Of toil and blood the well earnd prize
    While offering peace sincere and just
    In heav'n we place a manly trust
    That truth and justice will prevail
    And every scheme of bondage fail
        Firm — united &c

3

Sound found the trump of fame
Let Washingtons great name
    Ring thro the world with loud applause
    Ring thro the world with loud applause
Let every clime to Freedom dear
Listen with a joyful ear —
    With equal skill with godlike pow'r
    He governs in the fearful hour
    Of horrid war or guides with ease
    The happier times of honest peace —
        Firm — united &c

4

Behold the Chief who now commands
Once more to serve his Country stands
    The rock on which the storm will beat
    The rock on which the storm will beat
But arm'd in virtue firm and true
His hopes are fix'd on heav'n and you —
    When hope was sinking in dismay
    When glooms obscur'd Columbias day
    His steady mind from changes free
    Resolved on Death or Liberty —
        Firm — united &c

For the FLUTE or VIOLIN

2d time Chorus

Dramatized presentations of popular patriotic songs now took the public by storm. *Porcupine's Gazette* (May 5, 1798) discussed a forthcoming production of "Hail Columbia" at a New York theatre that would provide "every assistance that true love of country and ardour for the American cause can inspire. . . . the *American Standard* is to be *planted*, guarded by Messrs. Martin, Hallam, jun, &c. as American officers." Porcupine editorialized, ". . . we have no doubt but the zeal of the performers will awaken the audience to that pitch of enthusiasm which so animating a subject must at this critical moment inspire." The same newspaper had advertised (April 27, 1798) an added attraction to the bill at the Philadelphia theatre: ". . . a new song of the tune of *Yankee Doodle*, replete with patriotism, and well adapted to the spirit of the times . . . sung by [Mr. Blisset] in the character of a Yankee Sailor." This "Yankee Doodle" song became a successful vehicle for the celebrated actor-singer Mr. Hodgkinson as well, as we learn from the sheet music.

2
The only way to keep off war,
And guard 'gainst perfection,
Is always to be well prepar'd,
With hearts of resolution
    Yankee Doodle, let's Unite,
    Yankee Doodle Dandy,
As patriots, still maintain our right,
    Yankee Doodle Dandy.

3
Great WASHINGTON, who led us on,
And Liberty effected,
Shall see we'll die or else be free—
We will not be subjected
    Yankee Doodle, guard your coast,
    Yankee Doodle Dandy—
Fear not then nor threat nor boast
    Yankee Doodle Dandy.

4
A Band of Brothers let us be,
While ADAMS guides the nation;
And still our dear bought Freedom guard,
In ev'ry situation.
    Yankee Doodle, guard your coast
    Yankee Doodle Dandy —
Fear not then or threat or boast,
    Yankee Doodle Dandy

5
May soon the wish'd for hour arrive,
When PEACE shall rule the nations—
And Commerce, free from fetters prove
Mankind are all relations
    The Yankee Doodle, be divine,
    Yankee Doodle Dandy—
Beneath the Fig tree and the Vine,
Sing Yankee Doodle Dandy.

Flute

The sheet music of "Adams and Liberty," published in 1798 by the Boston printers Thomas and Andrews, is believed to be the first publication in America of the tune of our future national anthem.

ADAMS AND LI

The Boston Patriot

Written by THOMAS PAIN

ALLEGRETTO.

Ye fons of Columbia, who bravely have fought, For thofe rig

fcended, May you long tafte the bleffings your valour has bou

fathers defended. Mid the reign of mild peace, May

glory of Rome, and the wifdom of Greece; And ne'er may the fons

earth bears a plant, or the sea rolls its waves.

Next to "Hail Columbia," the greatest song hit of 1798 was Thomas Paine's "Adams and Liberty," set to the air of the "Anacreontic Song." Paine (not the Thomas Paine who wrote *Common Sense* and *The Rights of Man*) was commissioned by the Massachusetts Charitable Fire Society to write the song. It is said that when a host refused him a glass of wine unless he would add a stanza about Washington, Paine, who had a drinking problem, seized a pen and dashed one off.

ERTY.

Song.

. M.

...unftain'd from your Sires had de-

...your fons reap the . foil, which your

nation   increafe,   With the

...OLUMBIA   be   flaves, While the

II.

In a clime, whofe rich vales feed the marts of the world,
  Whofe fhores are unfhaken by *Europe's* commotion,
The *Trident* of Commerce fhould never be hurl'd,
  To incenfe the *legitimate* powers of the ocean.
      But fhould *Pirates* invade,
      Though in thunder array'd,
  Let your *cannon* declare the *free charter* of TRADE.

For ne'er fhall the fons of COLUMBIA *be flaves,*
While the earth bears a plant, or the fea rolls its waves.

III.

The fame of our arms, of our laws the mild fway,
  Had juftly ennobled our nation in ftory,
Till the dark clouds of *Faction* obfcur'd our young day,
  And envelop'd the fun of American glory.
      But let TRAITORS be told,
      Who their *Country* have fold,
  And barter'd their *God,* for his image in gold—

That ne'er will the fons of COLUMBIA *be flaves,*
While the earth bears a plant, or the fea rolls its waves.

IV.

While FRANCE her huge limbs bathes recumbent in *blood,*
  And *fociety's bafe* threats with wide diffolution ;
May PEACE, like the *Dove,* who return'd from the flood,
  Find an *Ark* of abode in our mild CONSTITUTION !
      But though PEACE is our aim,
      Yet the boon we difclaim,
  If bought by our SOV'REIGNTY, JUSTICE, or FAME.

For ne'er fhall the fons of COLUMBIA *be flaves,*
While the earth bears a plant, or the fea rolls its waves.

V.

'Tis the fire of the *flint,* each American warms ;
  Let *Rome's* haughty victors beware of *collifion !*
Let them bring all the vaffals of *Europe* in arms,
  WE'RE A WORLD BY OURSELVES, and difdain a *divifion !*
      While, with patriot pride,
      To our LAWS we're allied,
  No foe can fubdue us—no faction divide.

For ne'er fhall the fons of COLUMBIA *be flaves,*
While the earth bears a plant, or the fea rolls its waves.

VI.

Our mountains are crown'd with imperial *Oak,*
  Whofe *roots,* like our *Liberties,* ages have nourifh'd :
But long ere our nation fubmits to the yoke,
  Not a *tree* fhall be left on the field where it flourifh'd.
      Should *invafion* impend,
      Every *grove* would defcend
  From the *hill-tops* they fhaded, our *fhores* to defend.

For ne'er fhall the fons of COLUMBIA *be flaves,*
While the earth bears a plant, or the fea rolls its waves.

VII.

Let our Patriots deftroy *Anarch's* peftilent *worm,*
  Left our Liberty's *growth* fhould be check'd by *corrofion* ;
Then let clouds thicken round us, we heed not the ftorm ;
  Our realm fears no *fhock,* but the earth's own explofion.
      Foes affail us in vain,
      Though their FLEETS *bridge* the main,
  For our *altars* and *laws* with our lives we'll maintain !

And ne'er fhall the fons of COLUMBIA *be flaves,*
While the earth bears a plant, or the fea rolls its waves.

VIII.

Should the TEMPEST OF WAR overfhadow our land,
  Its bolts could ne'er rend FREEDOM's *temple* afunder ;
For, unmov'd, at its *portal,* would WASHINGTON ftand,
  And repulfe, with his BREAST, *the affaults of the* THUNDER !
      His *fword,* from the fleep
      Of its *fcabbard,* would leap,
  And conduct, with its *point,* every *flafh* to the deep.

For ne'er fhall the fons of COLUMBIA *be flaves,*
While the earth bears a plant, or the fea rolls its waves.

IX.

Let FAME to the world found AMERICA's voice ;
  No INTRIGUE *can her fons from their* GOVERNMENT *fever* ;
Her PRIDE *is her* ADAMS—*his* LAWS *are her* CHOICE,
  And fhall flourifh, till LIBERTY *flumber forever* !
      Then unite, heart and hand,
      Like *Leonidas'* band,
  And fwear to the GOD of the ocean and land,

That ne'er fhall the fons of COLUMBIA *be flaves,*
While the earth bears a plant, or the fea rolls its waves.

In 1798, at the peak of the war frenzy, the four laws were passed that earned the Adams administration the name of the "Federalist Reign of Terror." The Naturalization, Alien, and Sedition Acts gave the Jeffersonian Republicans the collective weapon with which they ultimately defeated the Federalists. Of these oppressive statutes, the Sedition Act imposed fines and imprisonment on anyone who wrote or said anything against the president or the government. This assault on basic personal liberties and the freedom of the press was caustically protested to the innocent tune of "Nancy Dawson" in the dauntless Republican newspaper, the Newark *Centinel of Freedom* (August 14, 1798). In the text, "Master Rawle" is William Rawle, United States attorney for Pennsylvania; "Charley Lee" is the attorney general of the United States (both were stalwart Federalists); "George" is, of course, George III; "Dickerson" is John Dickinson, the beloved farmer of former days; *mumchance* means silent, tongue-tied.

AMERICAN LIBERTY;
or, the
SOVEREIGN RIGHT OF THINKING.

A new Song. Tune—Nancy Dawson.

Since we're forbid to speak or write,
A word that may our Betters bite,
I'll sit Mum-chance from morn to night,
    But pay it off with *thinking*.

One word they ne'er shall fish from me,
For *Master Rawle*, or *Charley Lee*;
Yet, if they'll let my thoughts be free,
    I'll pay them off with *thinking*.

When *George* began his tyrant-tricks,
And Ropes about our necks would fix,
We boldly kickt against the Pricks,
    Nor sat Mum-chance a *thinking*.

We freely spoke, and freely thought,
And freely told him what we sought,
Then freely seiz'd our swords and fought,
    Nor dream'd of silent *thinking*.

If *Hancock* and great *Washington*,
Had nothing *said*, and nothing done,
His race the Tyrant would have run,
    Whilst we were *mum* a *thinking*.

Had *Dickerson* not *dar'd to write*,
Had *Common-Sense* not spit his spite,
Our Soldiers had not dar'd to fight,
    But set down *mum* a *thinking*.

We swore that *thoughts* and *words* were *free*,
And so the *press* should ever be,
And that we fought for Liberty,
    Not *Liberty* of *thinking*.

But Liberty to write and speak,
And vengeance on our foes to wreak;
And not like mice in cheese, to squeak,
    Or, sit down *mum* a *thinking*.

Again, on *Constitution Hill*,
We swore the sov'reign People's will
Should never want a *press* or *quill*,
    Or *tongue* to speak as *thinking*.

That still we're *sovereign*, who'll deny?
For though I *dare not speak*; yet I,
One sovereign right will still enjoy,
    The sovereign right of thinking.

Portrait of Matthew Lyon
by an unknown artist

Public outrage became focused on the shameful victimization of Matthew Lyon, who had violently fought the Alien and Sedition Acts on the House floor. A predestined victim (he was high on the administration's enemy list), Lyon was to all intents and purposes framed when a Federalist newspaper in Vermont printed a too-candid letter in which he had said, among other things, that the president was "importing corruption in his appointment of men of office" and that he was "devoted to fondness for 'ridiculous pomp, idle parade, and selfish avarice.'" Lyon's observations merely reflected what most Republicans felt. The presidential predilection for monarchist ritual had furnished an inexhaustible source for Republican criticism—criticism that was even sung to the tune of "Yankee Doodle." As the "Aristocratic Song" in the *Centinel of Freedom* (May 29, 1798) so felicitously put it:

> See Johnny at the helm of state,
> Head itching for a crowny;
> He longs to be like Georgy great,
> And pull Tom Jeffer--- downy.
> Yankee doodle, etc.

The too-outspoken Lyon was prosecuted for sedition; he was sentenced to four months in prison at Vergennes, Vermont, and fined one thousand dollars. Friends and sympathizers—among them Thomas Jefferson—subscribed a reported twelve thousand dollars in Lyon's behalf, and he was reelected to Congress directly from jail. His rousing welcome on being released from the "Federal Bastile'" included a song in the *Centinel of Freedom* (March 5, 1799).

PATRIOTIC EXULTATION on LYON's
release from, the Federal Bastile, *in*
Vergennes.—Sung at Bennington, (Vermont)
the third day of release, Feb. 12, 1799.

Tune—"Black Sloven."

Ye peasants who live by the sweat of the brow,
Who lop the rude forests and follow the plough,
Unite in the chorus with music and glee,
To hallow the strains of the happy and free.

Fair FREEDOM benignantly greets us to day,
Then let us adore her, and woo her to stay,
And pray for the millions are bleeding to gain
The sunshine of Freedom, and break off their chain.

Our FRIEND is restor'd to our cordial embrace,
While *Fitches** and fiends sink to equal disgrace,
Of despotic rage who the horrors can tell
But subordinate tyranny's HELL upon HELL.

Columbia be jealous, your Liberty prize,
Shun the fangs of Great-Britain and curst Hessian flies,
Those tyrants abroad, and the tyrants at home,
Are equally hostile to Liberty's Dome.

The *freedom* of *speech* to discuss and debate,
On the deeds of our servants who govern the state,
We'll never resign to the sticklers for power,
Though courtiers and sycophants frown and look sour.

While taxes are *equal*, be ready to pay,
But guard with due caution each venal essay,
To wring from your coffers the fruits of your care,
And bring you to poverty, woe, and despair.

Thus freedom shall reign and run even with time,
Inviting her worthies to his happy clime,
'Till the spheres shall run down and the system decay,
And man be translated to regions of day.

---

* The name of the Federal Marshall.

In May 1798 President Adams, accelerating the preparations for war against France, created the navy department, naming Benjamin Stoddert as the first secretary of the navy; and on July 2 he appointed George Washington as lieutenant general and commander in chief of the American armies. Washington's willingness to forsake his longed-for retirement at Mount Vernon when duty called was duly lauded in a song, doubly appropriately set to "Hail Columbia" (after all, the tune had originally been written for Washington). *From the Federal Gazette & Baltimore Daily Advertiser (August 4, 1798):*

> Attend, *Columbians*, join the song,
> We'll sing th' immortal *Washington*;
>   Behold he leaves his blest abode,
>   Behold he leaves his blest abode,
> Where (quitting honor's splendid seat)
> He lately sought a calm retreat.
> Mount Vernon's shades he now forsakes,
> In toils of war again partakes;
> He glads the heroes of the land,
> And 'midst their plaudits takes command.
>   The godlike hero lends his aid,
>   No ruffian band shall dare invade;
>   In deeds of valor let us vie,
>   And win the cause, or bravely die.

Despite the army's illustrious commander in chief, recruitment limped unenthusiastically along. To stimulate flagging interest, brilliant military displays were mounted, and even "Yankee Doodle" was enlisted to encourage enlistments. Vocal recruitment propaganda to *Yankee Doodle* appeared in the *Centinel of Freedom* (June 11, 1799).

A SONG,

Adapted to the Recruiting Service,
which is about to commence.

> Come ye Lads who wish to shine
>   Bright in future story—
> Haste to arms, and form the line
>   That leads to Martial glory!
>
> CHORUS.
>   Beat the drum, the trumpet sound,
>   Manly and United;
>   Danger face, maintain your ground,
>   And see your country righted.

In 1799, to celebrate Washington's return to the army, timely new words were set to "Washington's March," and the sheet music was issued together with Francis Hopkinson's 1778 tribute to Washington, "A Toast." Benjamin Carr apparently changed his mind about the price of his publication after it was printed, raising it from thirty-two to thirty-seven cents.

If army recruitment lagged during this strange quasi-war, the budding navy covered itself with glory, capturing great numbers of French vessels and protecting American shipping from French spoliation. When news reached home of Commodore Thomas Truxtun's brilliant victory in the frigate Constellation *over the French frigate* l'Insurgente *on February 9, 1799, celebratory songs materialized by the score.*

Songs to celebrate Truxtun's victory were elaborately dramatized in the Philadelphia and New York theatres. When the Philadelphia production was presented at New York, the advertisement in the *New-York Gazette* (May 24, 1799) promised: "In the course of the entertainment, an exact representation of the Chase, and the late Action between the Constellation and the insurgente Frigates. The whole to conclude with the Original Song, by Mr. Tyler." At the Philadelphia performances, the song "Huzza for the Constellation," a catchy chantey in minor, was sung by Mr. Fox, who is believed to have engraved the beautiful vignette of ships that appeared on Benjamin Carr's sheet music.

HUZZA for the CONSTELLATION.

Come join my hearts in jovial glee
   While I sing strains of victory
And boast our prowess on the sea
   In the brilliant Constellation.
A Frigate fine Commander brave
As ever cut Atlantic wave
    With Sailors bold
    And hearts of gold
Who conquer with Columbian stripes
And shout whene'er the boatswain pipes
  All hands in the Constellation
CHORUS.—*All hands in the Constellation.*

An exhilarating exception to the accepted, stuffy, "classical" July Fourth ode appeared in the *Massachusetts Mercury* (July 30, 1799). In Royall Tyler's sparkling song, the "Sage of Quincy" refers to President Adams.

FEDERAL CONVIVIAL SONG.

By R. Tyler, Esq.
Sung at Windsor, (Vermont), July 4, 1799.
TUNE—"Here's to our Noble Selves, Boys."

Come fill each brimming glass, boys,
　Red or white has equal joys,
Come fill each brimming glass, boys,
　And toast your country's glory;
Does any here to fear incline,
And o'er Columbia's danger whine,
Why let him quaff this gen'rous wine,
　He'll tell another story.

Here's WASHINGTON, the brave, boys,
　Source of all Columbia's joys,
Here's WASHINGTON, the brave, boys,
　Come rise and toast him standing;
For he's the hero firm and brave,
Who all our country's glory gave,
And once again he shall us save
　Our armies bold commanding.

Here's to the gallant Tar, boys,
　Whose cannon's roar our foe annoys,
Here's to the gallant Tar, boys,
　His country's cause defending;
For warlike TRUXTON's noble name,
Like NELSON's shall extend his fame,
And loud through all the earth proclaim,
　His glory never ending.

Here's to our native land, boys,
　Land of liberty and joys,
Here's to our native land, boys,
　Your glasses raise for drinking.
And he that will not drink this toast,
May he in *France* of freedom boast,
There dangling on a lanterne post.
　Or in the *Rhone* be sinking.

Here's to our Vermont FAIR, boys,
　Pledges bright of Fed'ral joys,
Here's to our Vermont FAIR, boys,
　Fill high to Love and Beauty!
For while we toast their glowing charms,
Their virtue ev'ry bosom warms,
We'll die to guard them safe from harms,
　It is a Fed'ral duty.

Here's to Vermont State, boys,
　And all her manly rustic joys,
Here's to Vermont State, boys,
　Columbia's brave defender;
For while our pines ascend on high,
And while our *Mountains* mock the sky,
Our Independence, Liberty,
　We never will surrender.

Here's to the SAGE of *Quincy*, boys,
　Legal head of all our joys,
Here's to the SAGE of *Quincy*, boys,
　Who guards us while we're drinking;
For while we quaff the boozy wine,
And sense and tipsy mirth combine,
With temp'rate head he sits sublime,
　And for our good is thinking.

Now come join hand in hand, boys,
　Mistic type of Fed'ral joys,
Now come join hand in hand, boys,
　Like brother, brother greeting;
For while our union we pursue,
'Tis he and he, and you and you,
One pleasure all may yet renew,
　At our next Fed'ral meeting.

*This commemorative portrait of Washington decorated the 1811 edition
of a popular but unrelated piece of music, "The Battle of Prague,"
a programmatic battle sonata by the Bohemian composer Franz Kotzwara.*

When George Washington suddenly died on December 14, 1799, a shocked nation abandoned itself to an orgy of mourning that surpassed in emotional extravagance even the adulation that had been lavished upon Washington the god-hero in earlier days. Simulated funerals were held throughout the nation, and not only were memorial services celebrated in churches, but elaborately dramatized funereal rites were enacted in theatres. In addition to universal tributes in prose and verse, unlimited varieties of memorial objects were turned out by artists and artisans, from paintings and sculpture to ceramics and mourning jewelry. Little girls executed apotheoses in needlework; memorial wallpapers were hung; and floods of odes, elegies, monodies, threnodies, psalms, anthems, and dead marches were composed, published, and performed everywhere.

Funeral Dirge

Adopted for & Play'd by the Alexandria BAND at the FUNERAL

of

GEN.ˡ GEO. WASHINGTON.

Engr.ᵈ by A. Lynn.   Price 25 Cᵗˢ.   by J. Decker.

Washington was buried at Mount Vernon just before sunset. As a vessel in the Potomac fired minute guns, wrote a correspondent to the Gazette of the United States (December 23, 1799), the mourners took up their solemn procession to "a band of music [which] with mournful melody melted the soul into all the tenderness of woe."

In addition to Benjamin Carr's "Dead March and Monody," a great deal of other music was heard at the Lutheran Church on December 26. The *Aurora* (December 27, 1799) reported that "the religious solemnity commenced with music, and [with] an anthem by a female band placed on the organ loft behind the pulpit. . . . The funeral anthems were performed by Mr. Darley and the band of female performers with accompaniments very happily executed. . . . After the . . . eulogium, several soft airs were performed; with additional anthems. The ceremonial being concluded, the full band accompanied by kettle drums performed several solemn martial airs. . . ."

Dramatized mourning for Washington—in theatres, churches, and processions—exemplifies eighteenth-century America's proneness to participate in emotional extravaganzas. At the New Theatre in Philadelphia a popular mourning spectacle was repeatedly presented around a "Monody" composed by Alexander Reinagle and Raynor Taylor, the score of which regrettably has vanished. The production, which unbelievably shared the bill with a comedy, is memorably described in J. Russell's *Gazette* (January 9, 1800):

The house which, was "full to overflowing," displayed a scene calculated to impress the mind with the utmost solemnity and sorrow. The pillars supporting the boxes were incircled with black crape, the chandeliers were decorated with the insignia of woe, and the audience, particularly the Female part, appeared covered with the badges of mourning. About 7 o'clock the band struck up "*Washington's March*," after which, a solemn dirge was played, when the curtain slowly rising, discovered a Tomb in the centre of the stage in the Grecian style of Architecture. . . . In the center was a portrait of the General, incircled by a wreath of oaken leaves; under the portrait a sword, shield and helmet and the colours of the United States. The top was in the form of a Pyramid, in the front of which appeared the American Eagle, weeping tears of blood for the loss of her General, and holding in her beak a scroll, on which was inscribed, "a *nation's tears*."

Among the airs comprising Reinagle and Taylor's "Monody," the following stanzas were sung:

> Slowly strike the solemn bell;
>   Nature, sound thy deepest knell—
> Pow'r of Music! touch the heart,
>   Nature there will do her part.
>
> God of Melancholy, come,
>   Pensive o'er the Hero's tomb;
> In saddest strains his loss deplore,
>   With piercing cries rend ev'ry shore,
>   For Washington's no more!

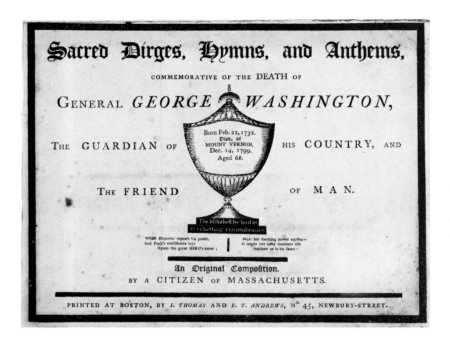

Oliver Holden, whose "Ode to Columbia's Favorite Son" had greeted Washington on his triumphal visit to Boston in 1789, compiled this memorial volume of Sacred Dirges, Hymns, and Anthems, of which "An Ode for the 22d February" was his own composition. President Adams had officially proclaimed Washington's birthday a day of national mourning.

He broke the fetters of the land;
He taught us to be free;
He raised the dignity of man,
He bade a nation be.

A National Dirge.
Anthony Pasquin and
Oliver Holden
February 22, 1800

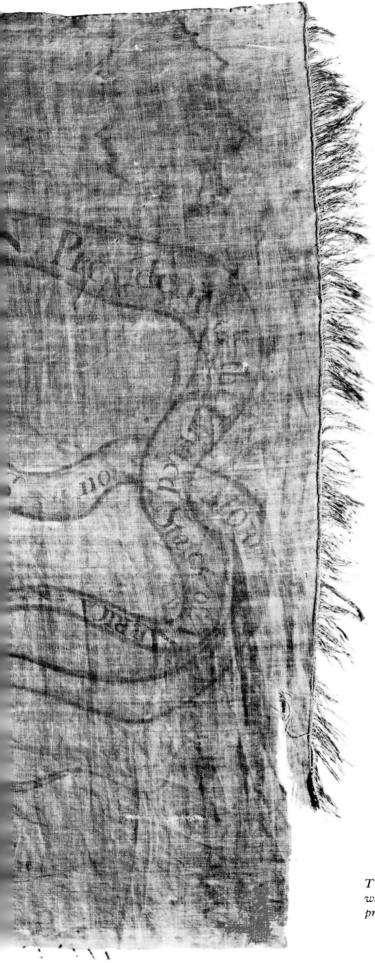

While some on rights and some on wrongs
  Prefer their own reflections,
The People's right demand our songs
  The Right of free Elections.

Song: "Election the People's Right"
John I. Hawkins
March 1801

5.
Two-Party
Invention
1800–1809

This banner for Thomas Jefferson
was probably waved during the
presidential election campaign of 1800.

By the summer of 1800, the first full-fledged bipartisan battle for the presidency was in full swing and gaining momentum. Because electioneering by presidential candidates was considered unseemly, the bitter contest was waged largely through the press, where innumerable songs, consisting chiefly of name-calling and defamatory misrepresentation, faithfully reflected party propaganda. The Republicans referred to Adams—who shared the Federalist ticket with Charles Cotesworth Pinckney—as a monarchist, an autocrat, a Tory, a tool of Britain, and a tyrant; and his administration was habitually referred to as a reign of terror. The Federalists, on the other hand, branded Jefferson—whose running mate was Aaron Burr—an atheist, an anarchist, a Jacobin, a tool of France, and a bloodthirsty revolutionary who would destroy the nation. The opposing ideologies were embodied in microcosm in a pair of songs, set to the nonpartisan tune of "Yankee Doodle," that complemented each other as precisely as a pair of Siamese twins. The Federalist version appeared in the *Gazette of the United States, and Philadelphia Daily Advertiser* (May 28, 1800); the Republican reply in the *Centinel of Freedom* (July 15, 1800).

Federalists! be on your guard,
  Look sharp to what is doing:
Your foes you see are working hard
  To bring about your ruin.
    Yankee-Doodle, &c.

There's not a man among you all
  But what sincerely glories,
To help—effect the destin'd fall
  Of *Democrats* and Tories.
    Yankee-Doodle, &c.

Then rally strong, and you'll defeat,
  Their schemes of wicked action,
And trample down beneath your feet
  The *Jeffersonian* faction.
    Yankee-Doodle, &c.

Be staunch and true on freedom's side,
  And keep a firm connexion;
Let not the *Democrats* divide
  Your votes, at next election.
    Yankee-Doodle, &c.

～～～

A NEW SONG TO AN OLD TUNE.

Republicans, be on your guard;
Look sharp to what is doing;
The *Feds* you see are working hard
To bring about your ruin
    Yankee Doodle, here's a cup,
    Take a little Brandy.
    Twill serve to keep your spirits up
    Drinking is the dandy.

There's not a man among us all,
But tells his vaunting story,
Of JOHNNY QUINCY's destin'd fall—
That cursed British tory.
    Yankee Doodle, push the glass,
    Send about the brandy,
    He that flinches is an ass.
    JEFFERSON's the DANDY.

Then rally strong, and you'll defeat
Their schemes of wicked action;
And trample underneath your feet,
The Royal British faction.
    Yankee Doodle turn 'em out,
    Places are the dandy,
    What the Devil are you about
    Send us round the Brandy.

Be staunch and firm on freedom's side,
And keep a close connection;
Let no Aristocrats divide
Your votes at next election.
    Yankee Doodle, keep it up,
    Push about the Brandy,
    Johnny Quincy's out of luck,
    Jefferson's the dandy.

The cry for war has no release,
But hot and hotter waxes;
Then vote him in, he'll give us peace
And pay off all our taxes.
    Yankee Doodle *Jeffer*doo,
    Son—y, doodle dandy,
    Son—y, doodle, *Jeffer* do
    Sink the price of Brandy.

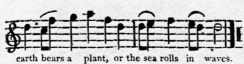

JEFFERSON AND LIBERTY.

Ye sons of Columbia who cherish the prize, The

arms of your fathers so valiantly gain'd, Like the

sun unobscur'd may your glory arise, And your

lib - erties flourish forev-er unstain'd, While

Mars clad in gore, bids the far thunders roar, May

freedom and peace bless our dear native shore, And

ne'er may the sons of Columbia be slaves, While the

earth bears a plant, or the sea rolls in waves.

By art more than arms our foes have long try'd,
  To lead the brave sons of Columbia in slav'ry,
Their force we've withstood, and their power
    defy'd,
And repuls'd each attack with republican
    brav'ry.
    Though our internal foes,
    May our freedom oppose,
Our firmness and zeal, to the universe shows,
        That ne'er will, &c.

The agents of Briton like fiends in disguise,
  Have kindled the fire of faction around us ;
Yet unaw'd by the flame we united arise,
  To pull down the Babel that strove to con-
    found us.
    All intrigue is in vain,
    We'll united remain ;
And our rights and our liberties ever maintain.
        And ne'er shall, &c.

Calumny and falsehood in vain raise their voice,
  To blast our republican's fair reputation,
But Jefferson still is American's choice,
  And he will her liberties guard from inva-
    sion.

The final stanza of this election song for Jefferson, printed in the *American Patriotic Songbook* (1813), is a paean in praise of a basic tenet of Jeffersonian democracy: the freedom of political choice. It was sung to the tune of the "Anacreontic Song."

> Remember *election* is liberty's base,
> By which noble *charter* our freedom we cherish:
> At the helm of our nation then Jefferson place,
> That our free *Constitution* and *rights* ne'er may perish.
>   Still America's pride
>   In her cause has been try'd,
>   And he in her councils was born to preside.
> That ne'er may the sons of Columbia be slaves,
> While the earth bears a plant, or the sea rolls in waves.

In 1800 Washington City, as it was called, although still a primitive, frontierlike town, became the nation's capital. John Adams moved into the President's House—what there was of it—on November 1, and Congress met for the first time in the partially completed Capitol building on November 17. Although an insufficient number of congressmen appeared in Washington on opening day to make up a quorum in either house, the event inspired greater euphoria in other localities. The *Boston Gazette* (December 4, 1800), for example, was impelled to wax lyrical over the "Central Spot." No tune was given.

SONG.
ON THE MEETING OF CONGRESS
AT WASHINGTON CITY.

Hail! hail! thou bright auspicious day,
  Which ne'er by us can be forgot,
Let every freeman homage pay
  To the attractive *Central Spot.*

Great Constantine a corner chose,
  We all have learnt Rome's fatal lot,
And Petersburgh shall soon disclose,
  'Tis wrong to leave the *Central Spot.*

Our Washington's expanded mind,
  (Whose name's exempt from ev'ry blot)
The States in unity to bind,
  Directed to the *Central Spot.*

Then let us firm, united be,
  Scorning each foe's distracting plot,
The manly Sons of Liberty
  Will always love the *Central Spot.*

In 1800, recalls Margaret Bayard Smith, the inimitable nineteenth-century social commentator (*The First Forty Years of Washington Society,* Gaillard Hunt, editor), Sunday worship was held at the "Hall of Representatives" in the unfinished Capitol building because no adequate church existed in Washington City at that time. Soon transformed into a chic social function, the services were attended by "the youth, beauty and fashion of the city, Georgetown and environs." Mrs. Smith observes that "the gay company who thronged the H. R. looked very little like a religious assembly." She adds: "This sabbath-day-resort became so fashionable, that the floor of the house offered insufficient space, the platform behind the Speaker's chair, and every spot where a chair could be wedged in was crowded with ladies in their gayest costume and their attendant beaux . . . who led them to their seats with the same gallantry as is observed in a ball room." Of the "musick" provided for these unorthodox occasions, Mrs. Smith observes that it was "as little in union with devotional feelings, as the place. The marine-band, were the performers. Their scarlet uniform, their various instruments, made quite a dazzling appearance in the gallery. The marches they played were good and inspiring, but in their attempts to accompany the psalm-singing of the congregation, they completely failed and after a while, the practice was discontinued,—it was *too* ridiculous."

Senate wing of the Capitol in 1800

Jefferson's victory was so confidently anticipated by his fellow Republicans in 1800 that they sang politically exultant songs even before the actual voting took place. This "Impromtu" from the *Centinel of Freedom* (December 16, 1800) paraphrased the Federalists' own hymn in an election song that reiterated Republican campaign issues and referred to Jefferson as "the people's friend," his most widely used and politically significant campaign slogan.

An *IMPROMTU* of the moment,
*from a correspondent,
on hearing the news favorable
to Jefferson's election.*

To the Tune of "Hail Columbia."

Awake ye trimmers hail the throng,
Come and join our side that's strong,
    Let no base fear of Britain's pow'r,
    Let no base fear of Britain's power,
Appal you now for freedom reigns,
And Jefferson a triumph gains;
    'Tis he, the people's friend will rule,
    In him no Monarch finds a tool,
    Our would be nobles now may mourn,
    That terror's reign cannot return.
        "Firm united let us be,
        Rallying round our liberty,
        As a band of brothers join'd,
        Peace and safety we shall find."

Drawing of Thomas Jefferson by the engineer and architect Benjamin Henry Latrobe, whom he engaged to design public buildings in Washington

Another before-the-fact, Republican victory song was to become the most remembered of all Jefferson songs. First published in the *Aurora* (January 24, 1801) with the optimistic title "A Patriotic Song, for the Glorious Fourth of March, 1801," it was supposed to have been sung to a tune with the unlikely title of "Willy Was a Wanton Wag." The song has endured as "Jefferson and Liberty," another Republican campaign slogan, and the tune to which it is sung is known as "The Gobby-O."

JEFFERSON AND LIBERTY.

The gloomy night before us flies,
    The reign of Terror now is o'er;
Its Gags, Inquisitors and Spies,
    Its herds of Harpies are no more!
        Rejoice! Columbia's Sons, rejoice!
        To tyrants never bend the knee,
        But join with heart and soul and voice,
        For *Jefferson* and *Liberty*.

~~~

His Country's Glory, Hope and Stay,
    In Virtue and in Talents try'd
Now rises to assume the sway,
    O'er Freedom's Temple to preside.
        Rejoice! Columbia's Sons, &c.

~~~

No Lordling here with gorging jaws
    Shall wring from Industry the food,
Nor fiery Bigot's holy Laws,
    Lay waste our fields and streets in blood.
        Rejoice! Columbia's Sons, &c.

Here strangers from a thousand shores,
    Compell'd by Tyranny to roam,
Shall find amidst abundant stores,
A nobler and a happier home.
        Rejoice! Columbia's Sons, &c.

Here Art shall lift her laurel'd head,
    Wealth Industry and Peace divine,
And where dark pathless Forest spread,
    Rich Fields and lofty Cities Shine.
        Rejoice! Columbia's Sons, &c.

From Europe's wants and woes remote,
    A dreary waste of waves between,
Here Plenty cheers the humblest Cot,
    And smiles on every village-green.
        Rejoice! Columbia's Sons, &c.

From Georgia to Lake Champlain,
    From Seas to Mississippi's Shore,
Ye Sons of Freedom loud proclaim,
    The Reign of Terror is no more.
        Rejoice! Columbia's Sons, rejoice!
        To tyrants never bend the knee,
        But join with heart and soul and voice,
        For *Jefferson* and *Liberty*.

Jefferson was elected after a suspense drama unrivalled in the history of American presidential elections. On counting the presidential electors' ballots on February 11, 1801, it was discovered that the two Republican candidates, Jefferson and Burr, had tied for first place. Since the man having the most votes was awarded the presidency and his runner-up the vice-presidency, it became necessary for the House of Representatives to hold a runoff vote by states to determine who would be president; a majority of one vote was needed to win the election. Seizing upon this unexpected opportunity to eliminate their hated adversary Jefferson, Federalist congressmen launched into a series of last-minute cabals to gain the presidency for the Machiavellian Burr, whom they regarded as the lesser of two Republican evils. But Burr declined. The ensuing wheeling and dealing on both sides resulted in a stalemate that stubbornly refused to be broken, and it was not until February 17 and thirty-six ballots later that Jefferson finally became the new president.

Thomas Jefferson was the first president to be inaugurated in Washington, taking his oath of office in the Senate Chamber, where, according to an eyewitness report reprinted in Poulson's *American Daily Advertiser* (March 9, 1801), "there were about 1000 persons . . . besides the members of the legislature and not less than 150 ladies." The story tersely concluded: "Mr. Adams left town at 4 o'clock this morning." Adams's precipitate departure was not lost on Republican bards, one of whom commemorated it in a biting ballad to a Yankee Doodlish meter, giving as the name of the tune, "I followed him to Glasgow town." Braintree (now Quincy), Massachusetts, was Adams's birthplace. The song appeared in *The American Republican Harmonist* (1803). In the text, "Lyon" is presumably Matthew Lyon, Adams's old adversary; "Poor Robbins' sprite" is the ghost of Jonathan Robbins, a seaman who had been sentenced to be hanged during Adams's presidency and who consequently became the subject of great Federalist-Republican controversy; "Harper" is the anti-Jeffersonian Robert Goodloe Harper, who had voted for Burr in the recent presidential deadlock; "Pickering," "Bee," and "Chase" are presumably Timothy Pickering, Thomas Bee, and Samuel Chase, staunch Federalists all.

Not only did John Adams vindictively refuse to attend Jefferson's inauguration, but he spent the last night of his presidency making his famous "midnight appointments," bequeathing to his successor the legacy of a Federalist judiciary—a legacy Jefferson would later try to disown by means of impeachments. This likeness of Adams was engraved by T. Johnson after a portrait by Gilbert Stuart.

THE DUKE'S RETREAT TO BRAINTREE.

John Adams was a President,
  And fain he would again be;
But Jefferson we chose instead,
  But sent the Duke to Braintree.
    Tol lol der rol.

John Adams was with anger fraught,
  Scarce his anger could sustain he,
That he should be regarded naught;
  And so he went to Braintree.
    Tol lol der rol.

The fourth of March 'twas early morn,
  As in story you may plain see,
He rose dejected and forlorn,
  And scurried away to Braintree.
    Tol lol der rol.

To see the honours of that day
  Conferr'd, could not sustain he,
So th' Duke arose, and don'd his clothes,
  At four in the morn for Braintree.
    Tol lol der rol.

Not so his predecessor great,
  For took him by the hand he,
And led him to the chair of state;
  E'en this same Duke of Braintree.
    Tol lol der rol.

Now, Lyon kindly did advise
  Him, to go round by main sea;
And sure I think had he been wise,
  He'd gone that way to Braintree.
    Tol lol der rol.

His houshold furniture was gone,
  E'en the horses that had train'd he,
And as for coach, he now had none,
  So he went in th' stage for Braintree.
    Tol lol der rol.

While cypress did his brows adorn,
  Pale envy did contain he,
'Twas in his breast a rankling thorn;
  He carried it on to Braintree.
    Tol lol der rol.

When he to Philadelphia came,
  The tories did him again see,
With wine and beer, they did him cheer,
  And wish'd him safe to Braintree.
    Tol lol der rol.

Sad thoughts by day, while on the way,
  And sleeping he could plain see,
Poor Robbins' sprite on ev'ry night,
  He journey'd on to Braintree.
    Tol lol der rol.

At Hartford in Connecticut,
  Was his *Highness* complimented;
Yet their address he open'd not,
  But return'd it as presented.
    Tol lol der rol.

So Doctor Slop, when by a flirt,
  (As we're told by Tristram Shandy)
His horse had thrown him in the dirt,
  Treated Obadiah's congee.
    Tol lol der rol.

And when to Quincy he was come,
  The Yankees did him again see,
And tho' with grief they all were dumb,
  They welcomed him to Braintree.
    Tol lol der rol.

O the snubs and drubs and jeering rubs,
  'Tween Washington and Braintree,
Had he been wise, he'd ta'en advice,
  And then gone home by main sea.
    Tol lol der rol.

Of Harper, Pickering, Bee, and Chase,
  And colleagues, does complain he,
As cause of all his sad disgrace,
  And his retreat to Braintree.
    Tol lol der rol.

God prosper long this land of fame,
  And long may we remain free;
And God prevent as President,
  The Duke's return from Braintree.
    Tol lol der rol.

One hundred years or more to come,
  But yet I would not vain be,
This song may chance again be sung,—
  Call'd the Duke's retreat to Braintree.
    Tol lol der rol.

A great deal of specially composed music was performed at Philadelphia's spectacular inauguration day festivities. During the parade, which recalled the grandeur of the great Philadelphia constitutional parade in 1788, "Jefferson's March merited and received distinguished applause," reported the *Aurora* (March 6, 1801) in its account of the celebration.

When the paraders reached the German Reformed Church, they found "500 Ladies who had received tickets of admission" already seated. The ceremonies began and closed with "Jefferson's March," and the Declaration of Independence was read in honor of its author. Among the prayers, orations, and music heard at the church was "The People's Friend," sung by a chorus. Its composer, the scientist and inventor John Isaac Hawkins, had first met the music-loving Jefferson in connection with the sale of an improved pianoforte of Hawkins's devising. The "Citizen" who wrote the democratic words was the renowned artist Rembrandt Peale (see following two pages).

JEFFERSON'S MARCH

Performed at the Grand Procession at Philadelphia on the 4th
of March 1801

Sold & Printed by G: Willig No 185 Market St.

THE PEOPLE'S FRIEND

Written & Composed for the Celebration of the 4th of March 1801

Words by a Citizen   Music by John I. Hawkins

Philadelphia Printed by G : Willig

Moderato

No more to subtle arts a prey, which, fearful of the eye of day a nations ruin plan'd

Now en _ t'ring on th'auspicious morn in which a people's hopes are born what joy o'erspreads the Land.

2
While past events portended harm,
And rais'd the spirit of alarm,
   Uncertain of the end;
E're all was lost, the prospect clear'd,
And, the bright Star of Hope appear'd
   The People's chosen friend.

3
Devoted to his Country's cause
The Rights of Men and equal laws,
   His hallow'd pen was given;
And now those Rights & Laws to save
From sinking to an early grave,
   He comes employed by Heaven.

4
What joyful prospects rise before!
Peace, Arts and Science hail our Shore,
   And thro' the Country spread —
Long may these blessings be preserv'd
And by a virtuous Land deserv'd,
   With JEFFERSON our head.

HAIL COLUMBIA.

Hail, Columbia, happy land, Hail, ye heroes,

Heav'n born band! Who fought and bled in freedom's

cause, Who fought and bled in freedom's cause, And

when the storm of war was gone, Enjoy'd the

peace your valour won. Let Independence be our boast,

Ev - er mindful what it cost, Ev - er grateful

for the prize, Let its altar reach the skies.

Firm—united— let us be, Rallying round our

lib - er - ty, As a band of brothers join'd,

Peace and safe - ty we shall find.

Immortal Patriots! rise once more,
Defend your rights, defend your shore;
Let no rude foe with impious hand,
Let no rude foe with impious hand,

Not all Republican postelection singing was pitched at an exalted level. Referring to Alexander Hamilton's frustrated military ambitions, the *Aurora* (March 11, 1801) gloatingly published:

A NEW "HAIL COLUMBIA."
"HOW ARE THE MIGHTY FALLEN."

~~~

See the Hamiltonian Feds,
How they hang their jaw-locked heads,
Mourning now their fallen chief,
In whom they hop'd to find relief—
Who with an army at command,
Thought soon to rule this happy land.
But now their hopes are all destroy'd,
Their wicked schemes are null and void;
   The fed'ral rats have left the ship,
   And we in turn will take a trip.

    Thro' the rough "tempestuous sea,"
    We'll safely guard our liberty:
    Stop the leaks, the rigging clear,
    And to a peaceful haven steer.

~~~

July 4, 1801, the first Fourth to be celebrated in Washington City, was officially observed at a state dinner, during which the Marine Band, in an adjacent room, "played patriotic and festive airs," among them "Jefferson's March." After a toast to "the day and those who value it," Captain Thomas Tingey proceeded, "with happy animation," virtuously to reprehend the drinking of toasts, to the tune of "Hail Columbia." His musical sermon concluded, the toasts were resumed, after which, as Poulson's *American Daily Advertiser* (July 10, 1801) tells us, "the remainder of the day was enlivened by the cheerful circulation of the glass, by an excellent selection of instrumental music, and by animating songs from different citizens. . . ." Captain Tingey sang:

All party toasts we *here* disclaim,
Which join'd with wine the soul inflame,
   And prove the source of civil broils,
   And prove the source of civil broils,
Let us this day that made us free,
Devote to social harmony.
   So rapidly our States increase,
   Cherish'd by freedom, nurs'd in peace,
If bumpers to each state we take,
Uproar might all our country shake.
   Firm United let us be,
   Rallying round our liberty.
   As a band of brothers join'd,
   Peace and safety we shall find.

~~~

The perennial national song, "Hail Columbia," as it was published in the American Patriotic Songbook *(1813)*

EXCELSIOR

THE
4TH. OF JULY
A
Grand Military
SONATA
for the
Piano Forte
Composed in Commemoration of that
GLORIOUS DAY
AND
Dedicated to Mdlle Sansay
by
JAMES HEWITT

Price 10/b.

Rollinson sculp.

New York Printed & Sold at J. Hewitt's Musical Repository Nº 59 Maiden Lane & at D. Bowen's Columbian Museum Boston

Jefferson validly assessed the radical change brought about by the Republican victory when he referred to it as the "Revolution of 1800": "as real a revolution in the principles of our government as that of 1776 was in its form." It was indeed nothing short of revolutionary that an opposing, popular party should supplant, by nonviolent means, the elitist group of "the rich and the well-born" that had controlled the government since the founding of the republic. By establishing the right of a dissenting party not only to dissent but to win, Jefferson contributed to America the essential basis of democracy. As president he was even more despised by the Federalists than before. No longer inhibited by the now lapsed Sedition Act, his enemies went beyond all bounds in traducing him, his political and personal philosophies, even his physical characteristics and his private life. In a song published in the *Washington Federalist* (February 8, 1802), Jefferson was mercilessly lampooned for just about every conceivable reason: his inaugural address, his "atheism," his propensity for revolution, his conflict with the judiciary, and more besides. In the text, "T. I." represents Jefferson—the letters *J* and *I* were interchangeable in eighteenth- and early nineteenth-century typography; *crater*, in the mock-Irish dialect of the song (foreigners—especially the Irish—were hated by the chauvinistic Federalists), apparently means creature. No tune is given.

THE MAN OF THE PEOPLE,
A NEW SONG.

Let us sing my brave boys to the man of the People,
    That can do what he pleases, the wonderful crater;
He can twist like an Eel, tho' he looks like a steeple;
    He's the child of us all, and we are all his Creator.
Then huzza, jolly boys, let us constantly cry,
    A long life to the wonderful crater, T.I.

How he humbugg'd the Feds with a touch of the fashion,
    On the day he was chosen to work our Salvashon;
They were fools to belaave him, or get in a passion,
    For the spaache that he made 'em was all augurashon.
Then huzza, &c.

Oh, he's brought us, brave boys, to a charming condition,
    Where there can be no perjury, murder nor traason;
Neither can their be harm in a little sedition,
    When we're free from all faith, and govern'd by raason.
Then huzza, &c.

All our creditors owe us, you know, many grudges;
    'Tis becaase we don't pay; but we've now better times;
Now the man of the people will put down their Judges;
    For there need not be courts, where there cannot be crimes.
Then huzza, &c.

Let the Feds go and grumble; the best constitution
    Is that where the people do just what they plaaze;
For what signifies freedom without revolution?
    Sure it cannot beam bright, till we're all in a blaze.
Huzza, &c.

*Portrait of Jefferson by A. B. Doolittle
in* verre églomisé, *engraving
on gold applied to a glass surface*

News of the repeal of the Judiciary Act of 1801, which had paved the way for Adams's midnight appointments of Federalist judges, was greeted with jubilation by the Republican press and with dirges in Federalist newspapers. The *National Intelligencer* (March 5, 1802) exulted: "On this event we congratulate those friends of the Constitution who are friends to liberty," while the *Washington Federalist* (March 8, 1802) lamented: "The Constitution is no more. . . . He [the president] has gratified his malice toward the judges, but he has drawn a tear into the eye of every thoughtful patriot." On December 8, 1802, the *Washington Federalist* reprinted from *The Wasp* an accusatory song to the tune of "Who Killed Cock Robin" in which the "murderers" of the judiciary—the Republican congressmen who had supported repeal of the Judiciary Act of 1801— were sardonically enumerated. In the text, Jefferson is referred to as "Tom Gestion" in a gibe at *gestion*, a term he had used in a speech. It had earlier been ridiculed by the Federalist press when the *Boston Gazette* (April 1, 1802) had printed:

AN IMPROMPTU.

In one of his late answers to an address,
Mr. Jefferson promises his addressers the utmost fidelity
*in the "*Gestion *of their affairs."*

A few days since an honest swain
    Propos'd this simple question—
"What can Sage Monticello mean,
    "By this *new* word called "gestion."
A stranger who the problem heard,
    At once resolv'd the question—
"He thinks our *state affairs* too *hard*
    "For ought but *his di* "gestion."

Among the Republican congressional characters in the text of "Poor Jude": "Stout John" is probably an ironical reference to the attenuated form of John Randolph of Roanoke; "Giles Smart" is William Branch Giles; "Beau Dawson" is John Dawson; "Proud Sam" is Samuel Mitchill; "Friar Bacon" is John Bacon, a clergyman as well as a congressman; "Jo Nick" is either John Nicholas or Joseph Hopper Nicholson; "Matt Clay" is Matthew Clay; and "Sir Ned" might be Edwin Gray, "The Bird, for his Wisdom preferred" and "Mahomet" have eluded identification.

POOR JUDE,
OR THE DEATH OF THE JUDICIARY.

An amplified Parody *of the celebrated*
Song Cock-Robin.

Here lies Poor Jude! and how he fell,
This mournful Song shall quickly tell.

Who kill'd poor Jude?
    Alas! such a band
    As disgraces the land!—
    Poor murder'd Jude!

Who gave the word?
    'Twas I, says Tom Gestion,
    Without further question,
    I gave the word.

Who knock'd him down?
    'Twas I, says Stout John
    With my "Sling and Stone,"
    I knock'd him down.

Who pierc'd his heart?
    'Twas I, says Giles Smart,
    With my poison'd dart,
    I pierc'd his heart.

Who caught his blood?
    'Twas I, says Beau Dawson,
    In my little Bason,
    I caught his blood.

Who saw him die?
    'Twas I, says the Bird,
    For his Wisdom preferr'd,
    I seen him die.

Who spurned the corse?
    'Twas I, says Proud Sam,
    Who Am What I Am,
    I spurn'd the corse.

Who spit in his face?
    'Twas I, says Mahomet,
    Tho' the speaker—G-d d--n it!
    Does he think me an ass?

Who "brake his legs?"
    'Twas I, says Friar Bacon,
    If I'm not mistaken,
    I "brake his legs."

Who gave the shroud?
    'Twas I, says Jo Nick,
    Tho' the worst I could pick,
    I gave the shroud.

Who dug the grave?
    'Twas I, says Matt Clay,
    As 'twas all in my way,
    I dug the grave.

Who toll'd the bell?
    'Twas I, says Sir Ned,
    With the *tongue* in my head,
    I toll'd the bell.

Who danc'd at the grave?
    Alas! such a throng,
    As would damn any song,
    Danc'd at the grave.

Such were the hands by which he fell!—
And so, Poor Jude, farewell!—farewell!

*Line drawing of Jefferson
by an unknown French artist*

President Jefferson was virulently attacked in 1802 when the Federalist press released a flood of infamy concerning his supposed relations with his quadroon slave, Sally Hemings. The story had been circulated by the malevolent journalist James Thomson Callender in retaliation for Jefferson's refusal to yield to his extortion attempts and threats of blackmail. Gleefully seizing on Callender's slanders, Federalist newspapers embroidered upon them and rebroadcast them throughout the United States, not only in prose but in verse and song.

Sally Hemings was fourteen years old in 1787, when she accompanied the widowed Jefferson's younger daughter Maria to France, where Jefferson was serving as United States minister. In later years Madison Hemings—one of the five children Sally Hemings was rumored to have borne Jefferson—wrote that she soon became Jefferson's "concubine," and that she was pregnant when they returned to America in 1789. Gossip had it that her children—four of whom survived—bore a striking resemblance to Jefferson; and that he freed them when they reached the age of twenty-one, a condition that Sally Hemings is supposed to have exacted as the price of her return to America in 1789. She remained Jefferson's slave until his death in 1826, and received her freedom two years later from his daughter, Martha Randolph. The Jefferson-Hemings story offers an area of hot disagreement among Jefferson scholars, most of whom find it incompatible with the historic evidence of Jefferson's essential grandeur, while others find it a moving revelation of vulnerable humanity and a capacity for enduring devotion—the affair is reputed to have lasted thirty-nine years. With no firsthand documentation having come to light (written proof, if it ever existed, might have been destroyed by Jefferson or his descendants), the tale presents a fascinating enigma. There was nothing enigmatic, however, about the abusive racist songs that appeared during the Federalist orgy of calumny in 1802. The *Boston Gazette* (September 23, 1802) published:

A PHILOSOPHIC LOVE SONG.
TO SALLY.

Let poets sing, and striplings sigh,
   For damsels bright and fair,
The ruby lip, the sapphire eye,
   The silken, auburn hair.

My philosophic taste disdains
   Such paltry charms as those;
Scorns the smooth skin's transparent veins,
   And cheeks that shame the rose.

In glaring red, and chalky white,
   Let others beauty see;
Me no such tawdry tints delight—
   No! *Black's* the hue for me!

What though my *Sally's* nose be flat,
   'Tis harder then to break it—
Her skin is sable—what of that?
   It's smooth as oil can make it.

If down her neck no ringlets flow,
   A fleece adorns her head—
If on her lips no rubies glow,
   Their thickness serves instead.

Thick pouting lips! how sweet their grace!
   When passion fires to kiss them!
Wide spreading over half the face
   Impossible to miss them.

Thou, *Sally*, thou my house shalt keep,
   My widow'd tears shall dry
My virgin daughters—see! they weep—
   Their mother's place supply.

Oh! *Sally*! hearken to my vows!
   Yield up thy swarthy charms—
My best beloved! my more than spouse,
   Oh! take me to thy arms!

An even more offensive song was reprinted in the *Boston Gazette* (October 11, 1802) from the Philadelphia *Port Folio*. Pretending to have been written by Jefferson, it quotes, in a footnote, an incriminating passage from his *Notes on the State of Virginia*. The song's authorship has been ascribed to Joseph Dennie, the talented but malicious Federalist editor of the *Port Folio*, who was later indicted for libel. The venomous Callender, who had instigated the whole lamentable episode, died a curious death: in July 1803 he was found drowned in three feet of water in the James River.

A SONG.
Supposed to have been written by
The Sage of Monticello.

Tune—Yankee Doodle.

Of all the damsels on the green,
　On mountain, or in valley,
A lass so luscious ne'er was seen
　As Monticellean Sally.
　　Yankee Doodle, who's the noodle?
　　What wife were half so handy?
　To breed a flock, of slaves for stock.
　　A blackamoor's the dandy.

Search every town and city through,
　Search market, street and alley;
No dame at dusk shall meet your view,
　So yielding as my Sally.
　　Yankee Doodle, &c.

When press'd by loads of State Affairs,
　I seek to sport and dally,
The sweetest solace of my cares
　Is in the lap of Sally.
　　Yankee Doodle, &c.

Let Yankee Parsons preach their worst—
　Let tory Witling's rally!
You men of morals! and be curst,
　You'd snap like sharks for Sally.
　　Yankee Doodle, &c.

She's *black* you tell me—grant she be—
　Must colours always tally?
Black is love's proper hue for me—
　And white's the hue for Sally.
　　Yankee Doodle, &c.

What though she by the glands secretes;
　Must I stand shill-I shall-I?
Tuck'd up between a pair of sheets
　There's no perfume like Sally.*
　　Yankee Doodle, &c.

You call her slave—and pray were slaves
　Made only for the galley?
Try for yourselves, ye witless knaves—
　Take each to bed your Sally.
　　Yankee Doodle, who's the noodle?
　　Wine's vapid, tope me brandy—
　For still I find to breed my kind,
　　A negro-wench the dandy!

---

* *They (the blacks) secrete less by the kidneys and more by the glands of the skin, which gives them a very strong and disagreeable odor.*

A VIEW of NEW ORLEANS TAKEN FROM THE PLANTATION of MARIGNY

Early in 1803, while the grievous Hemings scandal was still raging, President Jefferson dispatched James Monroe to France to negotiate with Napoleon for the purchase of the vast Louisiana territory. By the end of April the treaty was signed, granting the United States, for the payment of approximately fifteen million dollars, "full right to and sovereignty over New Orleans and the whole of Louisiana. . . ." —an area which more than doubled the size of the United States. The changeover, attended by impressive ceremonial and a great deal of music, took place at New Orleans the following December. A detachment of American troops (some in Kentucky hunting dress!) marched to the American consul's house to receive an American flag, which, according to the New Orleans *Telegraphe* (December 21, 1803), was duly "wrapped around the waist of the officer of the detachment." The Americans next proceeded to the parade ground, where they were awaited by a company of French troops. The flag was "affixed to the haliards of the staff from which the French colors were flying . . . the French flag was lowered half way down the staff and the American hoisted till both flags met, in this state both remained for five minutes (the pause being the mark of reciprocal respect)—at length the French flag was entirely lowered, and the American hoisted to the top. During this truly interesting ceremony the American music played *Hail, Columbia*, accompanied by Huzzas." As the French withdrew, their "national flag folded around the waist of a French officer," they played "La Marseillaise."

drop   of blood shed   Great JEFFERSON adds to the wealth of a   Nation.

2

The disdainful may foam, and the malecontents rail
At thy measures, O Chief, fram'd in wisdom & zeal
Pro publico bono — so fam'd in old Story
For the welfare of all — or the Whig or the Tory!
We admire the calm Sage, who presides o'er a Nation
Of Freemen (no titles) each Man in his Station.
  Without Arms — without dread —
  Or a drop of blood shed —
Great JEFFERSON adds to the wealth of a Nation.

4

Bright Reason, clear sighted, discerns that a State
Can boast of her Sinews — assert She is great,
When a large Congregation of Citizens join,
(From the Globes various regions) at Freedom's wide shrine.
We admire the calm Sage, who presides o'er a Nation
Of Freemen, united, each Man in his Station.
  Without Arms — without dread —
  Or a drop of blood shed —
Great JEFFERSON adds to the wealth of a Nation.

3

Tho' the man of weak nerves may conceive it a danger,
To admit to thy shores, O Columbia the Stranger!
Who flies from proud Tyranny's uplifted rod,
To seek an Asylum — a safer abode.
We admire the calm Sage, who presides o'er a Nation
Of Freemen (a Bulwark) each Man in his Station.
  Without Arms — without dread —
  Or a drop of blood shed —
Great JEFFERSON adds to the wealth of a Nation.

5

Let Fame sound her Clarion of praise thro' the land
'Tis the meed of desert — tis high Heav'n's command,
And faction expiring, forget all its rage,
'Midst th'applause of a Nation conferr'd on her Sage.
We admire the wise Chief, who presides o'er a Nation
Of Freemen (a Rampart) each Man in his Station.
  Without Arms — without dread —
  Or a drop of blood shed —
Great JEFFERSON adds to the wealth of a Nation.

The peaceable acquisition of Louisiana was festively celebrated in official Washington, and a "great national festival to be held throughout the union" was promoted by William Duane, the editor of the *Aurora*, and kindred Republican editors. Despite the deprecations of the Federalist press, many local celebrations were joyously observed. In Philadelphia, the *Aurora* (May 14, 1804) reported, the festivities were held "in a manner which must have communicated to every lover of American happiness and prosperity, feelings and emotions the most impressive." In addition a special song was written, which Duane, in his capacity of book-seller, advertised in his *Aurora* (May 9 and 10) as: "Just published. A National Song. (Set to animated music) entitled 'The Acquisition of Louisiana' . . . written by Michael Fortune for the purpose of expressing a nation's joy ON THIS GREAT AND GLORIOUS EVENT." The advertisement wound up in a blend of partisan editorializing and salesmanship: "Which reflects high honor on our patriotic chief and the present administration; and for sale by Messrs. M. Carey and Wm. Duane, Market Street (and other places). . . ."

William Rollinson's stipple engraving of Alexander Hamilton was published shortly after Hamilton's death. The portrait of Aaron Burr by Charles Fevret de Saint-Mémin is undated.

The nation was astounded when Alexander Hamilton, one of the principal architects of the republic, was fatally shot in a duel with the vice-president of the United States, Aaron Burr. The shocking affair, which took place on the cliffs of Weehawken in the early morning of July 11, 1804, had climaxed a long-continuing drama of high intrigues and personal conflicts. Burr had justifiably blamed Hamilton for his loss of the recent New York gubernatorial election; Hamilton had justifiably blocked his election: Burr was believed to be implicated with extremist New England Federalists in a secession conspiracy.

Six weeks after Burr lost the election, he demanded that Hamilton retract certain damaging political and personal statements that had found their way into the press. On receiving no satisfaction, Burr challenged Hamilton to a duel. After considerable evasion, Hamilton accepted; for a man of honor to have refused would have been to lose face.

This ode by Dr. George K. Jackson, the English-born composer, was sung at Hamilton's obsequies in New York.

A week before the duel, at a Fourth of July banquet in New York attended by both Hamilton and Burr, Hamilton is supposed to have jumped up on a table and sung a lively Scots ballad, "The Drum," as Burr looked reflectively on. The historian Roger Butterfield asserts (in The American Past*) that by then all the arrangements for the duel had been completed. This version of "The Drum" was included in* John Greenwood's Book.

Hamilton was accorded elaborate memorial honors, not only in New York, where the funeral ceremonies rivalled those for Washington, but elsewhere in the country as well. Great processions were held, flags were flown at half-mast, mourning was worn, and bells were tolled. The Federalist *New-York Evening Post*, which Hamilton had founded, ran a series of black-bordered memorial issues for a full month after his death. Later its editor William Coleman, a dedicated Hamilton man, at Mrs. Hamilton's request compiled a pamphlet, *Collection of the Facts and Documents Relative to the Death of A. Hamilton; with comments: Together with the Various orations, Sermons, and Eulogies that Have Been Published or Written on His Life & Character*. This imposingly titled document contained a song written in a Scots accent in deference to Hamilton's Scottish origins. It was addressed to the vice-president, who had departed from the local scene; he was under indictment for murder in New York and New Jersey.

ON THE MURDER OF HAMILTON.

A SCOTCH BALLAD.

Tune—"Good night, and joy be wi' ye a'!"

Oh! wo betide ye, Aaron Burr!
　May mickle curse upo' ye fa'!
Ye've kill'd as brave a gentleman
　As e'er liv'd in America.

Wi' bloody mind ye ca'd him out,
　Wi' practis'd e'e did on him draw,
And wi' deliberate, murderous aim,
　Ye kill'd the flower o' America.

A nobler heart, an abler head,
　Nor this, nor any nation saw;
He was the Country's hope and pride,
　The darling of America.

Wha now, like him, wi' temper'd fire,
　His country's "sword will strongly draw";
And, mid the furious onset, spare
　The vanquish'd foes o' America?

Wha now, like him, wi' honest zeal,
　Will argue in the Senata ha,'
And 'lighten wi' his genius' rays,
　The interests of America?

Mild, mild was he, o' tenderest heart,
　Kind and sincere without a flaw;
A loving husband, father, friend;
　And oh! he lov'd America.

Torn by a murderer's desperate arm,
　Frae midst his friends and family a,'
He's gone—the first of men is gone—
　The Glory of America!

Where'er ye go, O! Aaron Burr!
　The worm of conscience ay will gnaw;
Your haunted fancy ay will paint
　Your bloody deed in America.

But though ye flee o'er land and sea,
　And 'scape your injur'd country's law,
The red right hand of angry Heaven
　Will yet avenge America.

O save us, Heaven! frae faction's rage;
　Our headstrong passions keep in awe!
And frae ambition's hidden arts,
　O God! preserve America.

THE
SIEGE OF TRIPOLI

An Historical Naval Sonata for the

Piano Forte.

Composed by B. Carr.

Price 1 Dollar 25 Cents

Philadelphia, published by Carr & Schetky and sold at the following Music Stores. J. Carr. Baltimore. G. Blakes Philad. J. Hewitts New York. F. Mallets. Boston.

The Bashaw of Tripoli declared war on the United States in 1801 when President Jefferson indignantly rejected his demand for increased tribute payments. Since the inception of the republic, the American government had paid out more than two million dollars in ransoms and protection money to the piratical Barbary states: Morocco, Tunis, Algiers, and Tripoli. The Tripolitan war was not seriously pursued until 1803, when a task force commanded by Commodore Edward Preble appeared in the Mediterranean. In 1804 Preble blockaded Tripoli, and Benjamin Carr promptly translated the event into a programmatic "historical naval sonata" that included a detailed scenario of the fighting, copious references to the United States Marines, and a rondo-finale on "Yankee Doodle."

The negotiated peace with Tripoli, signed in June 1805, was treated in America as a brilliant victory, and the returning heroes were lavishly feted. At a grand dinner for Stephen Decatur in his home city Philadelphia, the *Washington Federalist* (January 18, 1806) reported, transparencies depicting his exploits in the war were exhibited and a specially composed song was sung by Mr. Robbins of the theatre. The transparencies (paintings on cloth or paper illuminated from behind) and the song both celebrated Decatur's daring feat in February 1804, when he penetrated Tripoli harbor with a small band of men on board the captured ketch *Intrepid*. Boarding the frigate *Philadelphia*, in Tripolitan hands since she had gone aground during a battle the previous October, Decatur's party had overpowered the native crew (most of whom dived overboard to escape), set fire to the ship, and made a deft getaway. In the text of this song, for which no tune was given by the anonymous gentleman of Philadelphia who wrote it, "Brave Bainbridge" is William Bainbridge, the commander of the *Philadelphia*, who with his crew had been captured and imprisoned by the Tripolitans when they took his ship.

SONG.

Allur'd by the wealth which Columbia possess'd;
Mistaking the smiles which Her countenance dress'd;
The plundering Turk did on tribute insist,
And swore that mere merchants would never resist.

Our Genius, indignant at outrage so base,
Determin'd to punish the treacherous race:
Her orders are issued—her sons fly to arms,
And Tripoli's tyrant is shook with alarms.

His hopes are reviv'd, when, thrown on his coast,
Brave *Bainbridge*, and all his companions, are lost:
But short is the hope—for *Decatur* appears—
His prize wrapt in blazes, rekindles his fears.

The gun-boats are mann'd, and advance to the walls;
Decatur, still leading, the tyrant appals:
Tho' four times our number, yet nought can withstand,
The valour impelling our brave little band.—

~~~

The carnage is past, but our honors remain
Pure, bright and exalted, untouch'd by a stain:
The heroes return'd, with delight we receive,
And those that are gone, shall in gratitude live.

The first edition cover of Benjamin Carr's piano sonata "The Siege of Tripoli" (c. 1804–1805) handsomely depicts Preble's flagship the Constitution *firing on a fortress in Tripoli harbor.*

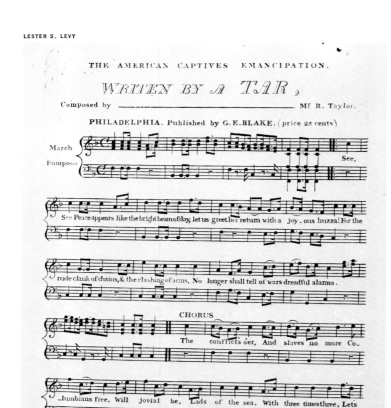

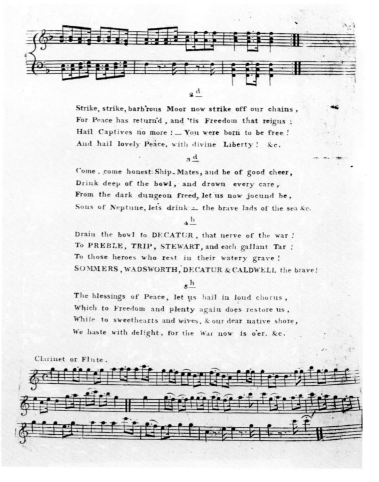

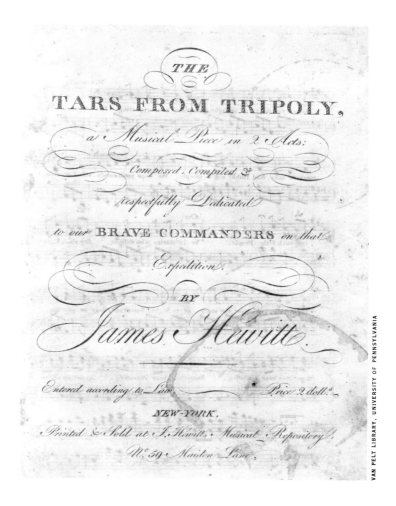

Before the peace treaty with Tripoli was signed, great public concern had been felt for the imprisoned American seamen, who were undergoing great hardships. A letter from Jonathan Cowdery, ship's surgeon of the captured *Philadelphia*, addressed to his father and published in the *Boston Gazette* (August 29, 1805), tells in poignant terms—no less poignant in the twentieth century—what life was like for prisoners of war:

Tripoli (in Barbary), Nov. 7th, 1804
My dear Father: No doubt, you have often heard of the loss of the frigate Philadelphia, and the capture of its whole crew (by the barbarians) among whom is your unfortunate son. We were taken . . . and entirely robbed of property, even the greatest part of the clothes on our backs were taken from us. Our seamen were immediately put to hard labour, without mercy. . . . five have paid their last debt to nature, and five have turned Turks. . . . We live in hopes of being liberated. . . .

When the released prisoners finally returned home, they were greeted with joyous celebrations and songs of welcome.

The 1806 hit musical *The Tars from Tripoly* shared the bill with a Gothic chiller, *Castle Spectre*, when it opened at the Park Theatre in New York on February 24. James Hewitt, a versatile musician with his finger on the topical pulse, handily adapted it from *The Naval Pillar*, a successful English ballad opera glorifying English naval heroes by Thomas Dibdin and John Moorhead. Transposing the locale and circumstances to fit the present occasion, Hewitt eulogized the American heroes of the recent war to many of the same tunes and often in identical words. He added his own overture, which includes a number of popular airs, some hornpipes, and of course the ubiquitous "Yankee Doodle." Hewitt himself published the score in 1806.

Duplicating the finale of *The Naval Pillar* (below), *The Tars from Tripoly* concluded with the music of "The Anacreontic Song," anticipating "The Star-Spangled Banner" by eight years. It was spectacularly staged at the Park Theatre, according to an advertisement in the *New-York Evening Post* (February 27, 1806):

The piece to conclude with A TRIUMPHANT NAVAL PILLAR Inscribed to the "Mediterranean Heroes" adorned with appropriate Trophies, &c. &c. At the termination of the Dance, Columbia descends supported by *LIBERTY* and *JUSTICE With an occasional Address*. After which she ascends, the TRIPOLITANS bending to her decree.

*Woodcut (1812) depicting
an episode of Lewis and Clark's
journey by Patrick Gass,
a member of the expedition*

Peaceful territorial expansion and the exploration of the vast, mysterious West were among Jefferson's happiest achievements as president. Even before the purchase of Louisiana, he had planned to send an expedition to explore the unknown lands of the West, and in 1803 Meriwether Lewis, Jefferson's former secretary, set out with William Clark on the epoch-making journey of exploration that took them as far as the Pacific and back again.

Lewis and Clark were warmly welcomed when they returned from their journey in 1807. The *National Intelligencer* (January 16, 1807) tells of "an elegant DINNER . . . given to CAPT. MERIWETHER LEWIS, by the Citizens of Washington, as an expression of their personal respect and affection, of their high sense of the services he has rendered his country, and of their satisfaction at his return to safety into the bosom of his friends." It was regretted that Captain Clark, for whom the dinner had been delayed, was after all unable to be present. "After partaking of the gratifications of a well-spread table," the *Intelligencer* went on, "toasts were drank interspersed with appropriate songs and instrumental music."

A rather stuffy laudatory poem, composed especially for the occasion by the eminent Democratic poet and statesman Joel Barlow, was soon ridiculed in an anonymous Federalist ditty to the meter of "Yankee Doodle," in which even Sally Hemings was lampooned. John Quincy Adams was rumored to have been its author; the rumor was exhumed to Adams's detriment during the bitter presidential election campaign of 1828. In the text, the "Indian tribe from Welchmen straight descended" refers to a mythical tribe supposed to have been founded in the twelfth century by legendary Welsh explorers in America; Lewis had hoped to discover them on his travels. The song was published in the *Monthly Anthology and Boston Review* (March 1807).

ON THE DISCOVERIES OF CAPTAIN LEWIS.

GOOD people, listen to my tale,
 'Tis nothing but what true is;
I'll tell you of the mighty deed
 Atchiev'd by Captain Lewis—
How starting from the Atlantick shore
 By fair and easy motion,
He journied, *all the way by land*,
 Until he met the ocean.

Heroick, sure, the toil must be
 To travel through the woods, sir;
And never meet a foe, yet save
 His person and his goods, sir!
What marvels on the way he found
 He'll tell you, if inclin'd, sir—
But *I* shall only now disclose
 The things he *did not* find, sir.

He never with a Mammoth met,
 However you may wonder;
Not even with a Mammoth's bone,
 Above the ground or under—
And, spite of all the pains he took
 The animal to track, sir,
He never could o'ertake the hog
 With navel on his back, sir.

And from the day his course began,
 Till even it was ended,
He never found an Indian tribe
 From Welchmen straight descended:
Nor, much as of Philosphers
 The fancies it might tickle;
To season his adventures, met
 A Mountain, sous'd in pickle.

～

Let dusky Sally henceforth bear
 The name of Isabella;
And let the mountain, all of salt,
 Be christen'd Monticella—
The hog with navel on his back
 Tom Pain may be when drunk, sir—
And *Joël* call the Prairie-dog,
 Which once was call'd a Skunk, sir.

～

True—Tom and Joël now, no more
 Can overturn a nation;
And work, by butchery and blood,
 A great regeneration;—
Yet, still we can turn inside out
 Old Nature's Constitution,
And bring a Babel back of *names*—
 Huzza! for REVOLUTION!

Committed to peace, President Jefferson did not yield to the popular clamor for war with England after the frigate *Chesapeake*, commanded by Commodore James Barron, was fired upon by the British ship of war *Leopard* (June 22, 1807). Barron had refused the British commander's demand to board and search the *Chesapeake* for British deserters. In the ensuing shooting, three of Barron's crew were killed, eighteen wounded, and four men—one indeed a deserter—were seized; the deserter was hanged. British impressment of American seamen was not new, but it had been increasing alarmingly since the turn of the century. Federalists and Republicans alike demanded war after the *Chesapeake* episode, but the president countered—in the name of "peaceable coercion"—by signing the disastrous Embargo Act, a measure that in theory would subdue England (and France) through the imposition of economic sanctions. In reality the Embargo boomeranged: the cessation of foreign commerce caused a serious economic depression in America, while at the same time it encouraged a thriving and unabashed black market that supplied American goods to both England and France.

"Jemmy" Madison, unkindly referred to in longhand on this broadside ballad, was Jefferson's supportive secretary of state.

THE EMBARGO,

A SONG COMPOSED AND SUNG AT DOVER. JULY 4th, 1808.

[*TUNE—Come let us prepare—*

DEAR Sirs, it is wrong
 To demand a *New Song*;
 I have let all the breath I can spare, go;
With the Muse I've confer'd,
And she won't say a word,
 But keeps laughing about the EMBARGO.

I wish that I could
Sing in *Alegro* mood,
 But the times are as stupid as *Largo*;
Could I have my choice,
I would strain up my voice,
 'Till it snapt all the strings of EMBARGO.

Our great politicians,
Those dealers in visions,
 On *paper* to all lengths will dare go;
But when call'd to decide,
Like a *turtle* they hide,
 In their own pretty shell the EMBARGO.

In the time that we try,
To put out Britains *eye*,
 I fear we shall let our own *pair* go;
But yet we're so wise,
We can see with French eyes,
 And then we shall like the EMBARGO.

A French privateer
Can have nothing to fear;   [go;
 She may load, and may hear or may there
Their friendship is such
And we love them so much,
 We let them slip thro' the EMBARGO.

Our ships all in motion
Once whiten'd the ocean;
 They sail'd and return'd with a Cargo;
Now doom'd to decay,
They are fallen a prey,
 To Jefferson, worms, and EMBARGO.

Left Britain should take
A few men by mistake,
 Who under false colors may dare go;
We're manning their fleet
With our Tars, that retreat
 From poverty, sloth, and EMBARGO.

What a *fuss* we have made,
About rights and *free trade*,
 And swore we'ed not let our own share go;
Now we can't for our souls
Bring a Hake from the *shoals*,
 'Tis a breach of the *twentieth* EMBARGO.

Our Farmers so gay,
How they gallop'd away,
 'Twas money that made the old mare go;
But now she wont stir,
For the whip or the spur,
 'Till they take off her *clog*, the EMBARGO.

If you ask for a debt,
The man turns in a *pet*,
 " I pay sir? I'll not let a hair go;
" If your officer comes,
" I shall put up my thumbs,
 " And clap on his breath an EMBARGO."

Thus Thommy destroys,   (or Jemmy)
A great part of our joys;
 Yet we'll not let the beautiful fair, go;
They all will contrive
To keep commerce alive,
 There's nothing they hate like EMBARGO.

Since rulers design,
To deprive us of wine,
 'Tis best that we now have a *rare go*;
Then each to his post,
And see who will do most,
 To knock out the blocks of EMBARGO.

+ *Madison*

PRINTED and for sale by J. K. REMICH, at his Printing Office on Dover Landing.

New England Federalists, who carried on a lively smuggling trade with Canada, were sarcastically reprehended by Republicans to the tune of "Yankee Doodle":

> The Fed'ral Coach went out of town
> With a Nova-Scotia Cargo,
> And all along they sung the Song,
> Oh take off the Embargo.
>
> CHORUS.
> Yankee doodle, with quick steps,
> Take up your Tickets handy;
> The Fed'ralists are in the ditch,
> And that is just the dandy.

And Federalists responded, to the same tune, with a ballad written by a hypothetical sailor, representing the profession most immediately affected by the Embargo. From the *Balance* (November 8, 1808), a periodical published at Hudson, New York:

> A SONG—*Composed by a Sailor.*
>
> Bad news is come from Washington,
> So sailors land your cargo,
> They've now decreed to hem us in,
> By laying an embargo.
>
> The poor old Commerce—haul her up,
> Til stem and stern get rotten,
> While Yankee boys must lay ashore,
> By government forgotten.
>
> With legs as small as marlin spikes,
> I'm wasted to a scare-crow;
> No meat to eat, no grog to drink—
> All by this damn'd embargo.
>
> No more I'll dance, no more I'll play,
> No more drink rum and brandy;
> No more (which grieves me most of all)
> Sing Yankee doodle dandy.
>
> Old Cuffee broke his fiddle-string,
> Which really was a hard blow,
> He could not muster eighteen pence—
> Says Cuffee, damn de bargo!
>
> Amen, says I, amen, says Will,
> Amen, says Dick and Molly;
> I wish the bargo was in h--l,
> Cries weather beaten Polly.
>
> We cant get out, we cant get out,
> With either ships or cargo,
> So here we lay in statu quo,
> By this accurs'd embargo.
>
> I wish they'd hoist their courage off,
> And let us once to war go,
> Nor die ashore like rotten sheep,
> By Jefferson's Embargo.

Jean-Antoine Houdon's noble portrait of Thomas Jefferson

Jefferson declined to run for a third term. Despite the general bipartisan outcry against the Embargo (which Jefferson repealed just before leaving office), the Republicans again overwhelmingly carried the presidential election, and Jefferson's longtime friend, colleague, and protégé, James Madison, succeeded him. Rejoicing in his party's victory, Jefferson attended Madison's inauguration and celebrated it at the Madisons' great inaugural ball. A week later, Thomas Jefferson, the great champion of the people and architect of the democratic American two-party system, mounted his horse and rode home to Monticello.

ELECTION
THE PEOPLE's RIGHT

Written and Composed by John J: Hawkins   March 1801

For Government and order's fake,
   And Laws important fections,
We fhould fupport and pleafure take
   In frequent Free Elections.

Our Agricult'ral int'reft, Marts,
   And Mercantile connections,
With Manufactures, Science, Arts,
   Muft thrive by free Elections.

To thwart the fchemes of Factious bands
   Who for us plan fubjections,
The caufe of Liberty demands,
   Our Votes at all Elections.

Should Enemies befet us round,
   Of foreign fierce complexions,
Undaunted we will ftand our ground,
   Upheld by free Elections.

We'll never from our duty fwerve,
   Let who will make objections,
But while we live, unchanged preferve,
   The Freedom of Elections.

CHORUS
Hail to the Chief
LADY OF THE LAKE,
Composed by Mr. Sanderson,
NEW YORK Published by Wm. DUBOIS.

6. *Hornpipe* *1809-1816*

"Hail to the Chief" is another tune of British origin that came to be "officially" adopted in America. Originally published in London, James Sanderson's musical setting for a section of Sir Walter Scott's "The Lady of the Lake" was first issued in America about 1812 as a three-part chorus. This edition was reprinted from the original plates in 1817 or 1818. Just when "Hail to the Chief" became the American presidential theme song is uncertain, but it is reported to have been played at Martin Van Buren's inauguration.

"I went to the Capitol, and witnessed the inauguration of Mr. Madison as President of the United States," wrote John Quincy Adams in his *Diary* on March 4, 1809. "The House was very much crowded, and its appearance very magnificent." In the evening Adams attended the inaugural ball at Long's Hotel. With characteristic succinctness, he commented: "The crowd was excessive—the heat oppressive, and the entertainment bad. . . ." The first inaugural ball for an American president was indeed an incredible crush. Margaret Bayard Smith vividly described the event in a letter: "The room was so terribly crowded that. . . . it was scarcely possible to elbow your way from one side to another, and poor Mrs. Madison was almost pressed to death. . . . As the upper sashes of the windows could not let down, the glass was broken, to ventilate the room, the air of which had become oppressive." When the former president appeared, "the musick struck up Jefferson's March"; he was soon followed by the Madisons, who were announced by the strains of "Madison's March." Several marches were written for President Madison; this one by Alexander Reinagle is believed to have been published in 1809.

Madison's portrait is an engraving by William Leney after Gilbert Stuart; Mrs. Madison is portrayed in oil by Bass Otis. "Mrs. Madison's Waltz" was published at some time around 1810 to 1812.

At the Madisons' inaugural ball Mrs. Smith remarked that Mr. Jefferson "seemed in high spirits . . . Mr. Madison, on the contrary, seemed spiritless and exhausted." When Madison was asked by the managers of the ball if he would stay to supper, "he assented," adding to Mrs. Smith, "but I would much rather be in bed."

Elegant and vivacious, Dolley Madison socially compensated for her husband's somewhat unprepossessing personality. Introducing a note of gaiety into official Washington life, she entertained lavishly, wore beautiful clothes, and was a great popular favorite. She also appears to have been the first president's wife for whom music was written. Characteristically it was a waltz.

Although both England and France, the belligerent powers in Europe, tried to use America as a weapon against each other during Madison's first administration, it was Britain's unabated aggressions on the high seas that brought many Americans to feel that only through war with England could such stains on the national honor as the *Chesapeake* incident be expunged. Headed by Henry Clay, the "War Hawks," a powerful group of militant young congressmen, hotly agitated for war and the takeover of the adjoining foreign-held territories of Florida and Canada. In June 1812 the Madison government yielded to their pressures and declared war on the greatest power on earth, Great Britain.

IMPRESSMENT OF SEAMEN.

Columbia's sons, your sires address you,

From the tombs hear them complain, Bri-

tain still our sons im-pres-sing,

Ty-ran-ni-zes o'er the main.

Live for ev-er, con-sti-tu-tion,

Live for ever, rights of man, Live for ever, O,

Columbia, Here true Liber-ty began.

Few wars in American history have received a more detailed musical documentation than the War of 1812, "Mr. Madison's War," as the antiwar New England Federalists called it (the prowar Republicans referred to it as the "Second War of Independence"). In the American Patriotic Songbook *(1813), even the painful topic of impressment of American sailors was set to music.*

In 1811 Governor William Henry Harrison of Indiana, with a force of about a thousand men, attacked and subdued an Indian settlement on Tippecanoe Creek during the absence of its chief, the activist Indian leader (and Harrison's adversary) Tecumseh. This exploit, becoming known as the "Battle of Tippecanoe," earned for Harrison the title of hero. An Indian fighter from way back, Harrison had—first under Jefferson and later under Madison—implemented official policy by "negotiating" the cession of millions of acres of land from the Indians in the Northwest Territory. Contemporary Americans believed that Tecumseh's opposition to these wholesale evictions was supported by the British in Canada. This point of view colored the section devoted to the Tippecanoe incident of a fifty-eight-stanza broadside ballad that also presented a rosy-hued progress report on the disastrous 1813 campaign in Canada. In the text, the "Prophet's Town" refers to the Indian village; during his absence Tecumseh had left the village in the care of his brother Tenskwatawa, known as the prophet. No tune was specified.

~~~

Hark, hark ye sons of liberty,
Of what is this we hear?
It is the voice of agony,
It comes from our frontier.
The savage massacre's begun,
Hark, hear the infants cry,
The father, mother and the son,
And daughter slaughtered lie.

Great Britain's tawny brethren,
That cruel savage crew,
Set on by British agents,
This bloody work to do.
The tomahawk and scalping knife
They arm them in with speed.
The bloody weapons to take life,
And do the cruel deed.

Brave Harrison by Congress
Was called into the field,
To make with them a speedy peace
Or fight them till they yield;
He offered them good terms of peace
Nearby the Prophet's Town,
They promised him this to embrace,
And settle on good ground.

He form'd his men in order
To rest and take repose,
Upon their arms with ardor,
And not take off their clothes.
But just before the break of day
The savage cry began,
In secret ambush there they lay
To kill and scalp our men.

A bloody battle did ensue,
With horrid savage yell.
The ground was stained with bloody hue
And many a hero fell.
Brave Harrison inspired his men
With courage bold and free,
Which made the savages to run
And leave him victory.

~~~

THE HARRISON SONG.

Written by

THOMAS POWER, ESQ.

and respectfully dedicated to the

Whigs of the United States.

BOSTON.

Price 25 Cts Nett

Published by PARKER & DITSON, 135 Washington St.

Entered according to Act of Congress in the year 1840 by Parker & Ditson, in the Clerks office of the District Court of Massachusetts

Twenty-nine years after the Battle of Tippecanoe, the names Harrison and Tippecanoe became synonymous. During the sizzling election campaign of 1840, the tremendous popularity of the slogan "Tippecanoe and Tyler too" played an important role in gaining the presidency for Harrison. This sheet music cover of 1840 recalled the famous battle, even down to the tall black hats that Harrison's officers had worn to battle in 1811.

The first great naval victory of the War of 1812 occurred on August 19, when Isaac Hull, commanding the *Constitution*, spectacularly vanquished the British frigate *Guerriere* in the battle that won his ship the name of "Old Ironsides." In announcing the victory, the *Boston Chronicle* (August 31, 1812) foretold America's rapturous response: "This brilliant exploit will excite the liveliest emotions in every American bosom. . . ." Hull's victory and the succeeding naval triumphs during the remainder of 1812 and early 1813 indeed excited deliriously lively emotions in American bosoms, notably in those belonging to balladeers and song-writers. Floods of naval songs were published in broadside and sheet music form; the newspapers were drenched with them, and the theatres presented them embellished with dramatic trappings. It would be difficult to estimate just how many different songs were called "Constitution and Guerriere." This one, from *The American Songster*, parodied a currently popular show tune, "The Landlady of France," alternately known as "Brandy O," an appropriate melody since the song twitted British naval officers on their singular custom of tanking up on brandy during battle situations, something they apparently did just before losing the *Guerriere*.

CONSTITUTION AND GUERRIERE.

TUNE—*Landlady of France.*

It ofttimes has been told,
That the British sailors bold,
Could flog the tars of France, so neat and handy O;
But they never found their match,
'Till the Yankees did them catch,
Oh! the Yankee boys for fighting are the dandy O.

The Guerriere, a frigate bold,
On the foaming ocean rolled,
Commanded by bold Dacres, the grandee O;
With as choice a British crew
As a rammer ever drew,
They could flog the Frenchmen two to one so handy O.

When this frigate hove in view,
Says proud Dacres to his crew,
Come, clear the ship for action, and be handy O;
To the weathergauge, boys, get her,
And to make his men fight better,
Gave them to drink gunpowder, mixed brandy O.

Then Dacres boldly cries,
Make this Yankee ship your prize,
You can in thirty minutes, neat and handy O
Thirty-five's enough. I'm sure,
And if you'll do it in a score,
I'll treat you to a double share of brandy O.

The first broadside we pour'd,
Brought their mainmast by the board,
Which made this lofty frigate look abandoned O.
Then Dacres shook his head,
And to his officers he said,
Lord, I didn't think these Yankees were so handy O.

Our second told so well,
That their fore and mizen fell,
Which doused the royal ensign so handy O.
By George, says he, we're done,
And they fired a lee gun,
While the yankees struck up Yankee doodle dandy O.

Then Dacres came on board,
To deliver up his sword,
Loth was he to part with it, it was so handy O,
Oh! keep your sword, says Hull,
For it only makes you dull,
So cheer up, come let us take a little brandy O.

Come fill your glasses full,
And we'll drink to captain Hull,
And so merrily we'll push about the brandy O!
John Bull may toast his fill,
Let the world say what they will,
But the Yankee boys for fighting are the dandy O.

194

CONSTITUTION AND GUERRIERE.

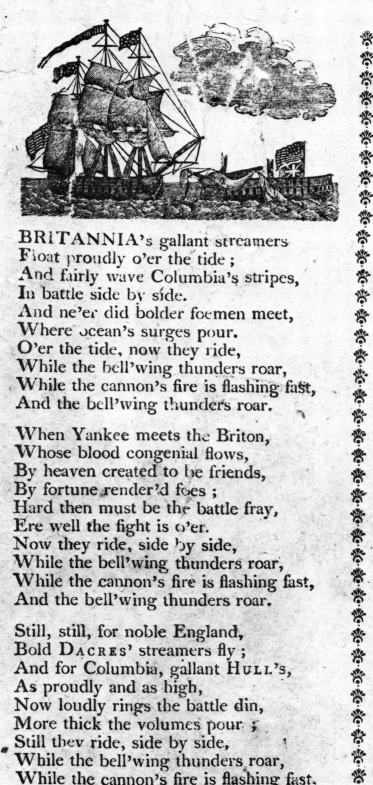

BRITANNIA's gallant streamers
Float proudly o'er the tide ;
And fairly wave Columbia's stripes,
In battle side by side.
And ne'er did bolder foemen meet,
Where ocean's surges pour.
O'er the tide, now they ride,
While the bell'wing thunders roar,
While the cannon's fire is flashing fast,
And the bell'wing thunders roar.

When Yankee meets the Briton,
Whose blood congenial flows,
By heaven created to be friends,
By fortune render'd foes ;
Hard then must be the battle fray,
Ere well the fight is o'er.
Now they ride, side by side,
While the bell'wing thunders roar,
While the cannon's fire is flashing fast,
And the bell'wing thunders roar.

Still, still, for noble England,
Bold DACRES' streamers fly ;
And for Columbia, gallant HULL's,
As proudly and as high,
Now loudly rings the battle din,
More thick the volumes pour ;
Still they ride, side by side,
While the bell'wing thunders roar,
While the cannon's fire is flashing fast,
And the bell'wing thunders roar.

Why lulls Britannia's thunder,
That wak'd the watery war ?
Why stays the gallant Guerriere,
Whose streamer wav'd so fair ?
That streamer drinks the ocean wave !
That warrior's fight is o'er !
Still they ride, side by side,
While Columbia's thunders roar,
While her cannon's fire is flashing fast.
And her Yankee thunders roar.

Hark ! 'tis the Briton's lee gun !
Ne'er bolder warrior kneel'd !
And ne'er to gallant mariners
Did braver seamen yield.
Proud be the sires whose hardy boys,
Then fell, to fight no more :
With the brave, mid the wave,
When the cannon's thunders roar,
Their spirits then shall trim the blast,
And swell the thunder's roar.

Vain were the cheers of Britons,
Their hearts did vainly swell,
Where virtue, skill and bravery,
With gallant Morris fell.
That heart so well in battle tri'd,
Along the Moorish shore,
Again, o'er the main,
When Columbia's thunders roar,
Shall prove its Yankee spirit true,
When Columbia's thunders roar.

Hence be our floating bulwarks,
Those oaks our mountains yield ;
'Tis mighty Heaven's plain decree—
Then take the wat'ry field !
To ocean's farthest barrier then
Your whit'ning sail shall pour ;
Safe they'll ride, o'er the tide,
While Columbia's thunders roar,
While her cannon's fire is flashing fast,
And her Yankee thunders roar.

The Boston Chronicle reported that "a public entertainment at Faneuil Hall was given to capt. Hull, in celebration of his late brilliant achievement on the Constitution frigate . . ."; six hundred people attended and an ode was sung. The ode, first published in the Chronicle, was later issued both as a broadside (above) and in musical notation (left), each time with a different title. The musical version appeared in Polyanthus (1812), a magazine published in Boston.

THE

AMERICAN PATRIOTIC

SONG-BOOK,

A COLLECTION OF

POLITICAL, DESCRIPTIVE, AND

HUMOUROUS SONGS,

OF

NATIONAL CHARACTER,

AND

THE PRODUCTION OF AMERICAN POETS ONLY

Interspersed with

A NUMBER SET TO MUSIC.

To Hull, and such heroes, a garland we raise,
Their valour in battle exultingly praise.

PHILADELPHIA:

PRINTED AND SOLD BY W. M'CULLOCH,
No. 306, MARKET STREET.

1813.

The MERRY SAILORS.

THE

AMERICAN

PATRIOTIC SONG-BOOK

HUZZA, FOR THE AMERICAN TARS;

OR, HULL AND VICTORY.

WRITTEN BY CHARLES HARFORD.

On the capture of the Guerrierre, a British Frigate, of 49 guns, by Captain Hull, of the American Frigate Constitution, of 44 guns, after an action of 30 minutes, when the Guerriere was blown up.

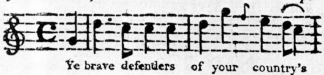

Ye brave defenders of your country's

cause, Receive the triumph of its loud ap-

plause; Your valor put a haughty foe to

4

flight, Who dar'd our tars to meet him in the

ff.

fight: Three cheers proclaim'd the Constitution

ff.

free From vaunting threats of ruthless tyranny.

Allegretto.

Columbia's banners now proclaim her tars Tri-

Second Time Chorus.

umphant ride the sea; And glo-ry swells the

trump of fame, To gallant Hull and vic-to-ry.

NAVAL SONG.
CHARGE THE CAN CHEERILY.

Now coil up your nonsense 'bout England's great Navy,
    And take in your slack about oak-hearted Tars;
For frigates as stout, and as gallant crews have we,
    Or how came her Macedon deck'd with our Stars?
Yes—how came her Guerriere, her Peacock, and Java,
    All sent broken ribb'd to Old Davy of late?
How came it? why, split me! than Britons we're braver,
    And that shall they feel too wherever we meet.

CHORUS.   Then charge the can cheerily;
     Send it round merrily;
   Here's to our country and captains commanding;
     To all who inherit
     Of Lawrence the spirit,
     "Disdaining to strike while a stick is left standing."

Now, if unawares, we should run (a fresh gale in)
    Close in with a squadron, we'd laugh at them all;
We'd tip master BULL such a sample of sailing,
    As should cause him to fret like a pig in a squall:
We'd show the vain boaster of numbers superior,
    Though he and his slaves at the notion may sneer,
In skill, as in courage, to us they're inferior;
    For the longer they chase us the less we've to fear.

     CHORUS.

The *Port Folio* (December 1813)

In 1812 the dazzling succession of sea triumphs over a traditionally all-powerful enemy induced a state of misplaced national euphoria that considerably mitigated the humiliation over General William Hull's ignominious loss of Detroit only a few days before his nephew Isaac conquered the *Guerriere*. The victories of Jacob Jones in the *Wasp* over the *Frolic*, Stephen Decatur in the *United States* over the *Macedonian*, William Bainbridge in the *Constitution* over the *Java*, and James Lawrence in the *Hornet* over the *Peacock* offered songsmiths unparalleled opportunities for salty ditties of jubilation punctuated by puns. Even the title of this song from the *Aurora* (December 15, 1812) is a pun on the name of the vanquished *Frolic*. In the text, "Rodgers" is George Washington Rodgers, brother of Commodore John Rodgers; "Biddle" is James Biddle, a fellow lieutenant with Rodgers on the *Wasp*; "Dacres" is, of course, the British commander of the *Guerriere*.

YANKEE FROLICS—A NEW SONG.

No more of your blathering nonsense,
'Bout the Nelsons of old Johnny Bull;
I'll sing you a song, 'pon my conscience,
'Bout Jones, and Decatur, and Hull.
Dad Neptune has long, with vexation,
Beheld with what insolent pride,
The turbulent, billow-washed nation
Has aim'd to control his salt tide.
    Sing lather-away jonteel and aisy,
    By my soul, at the game hob-or-nob,
    In a very few minutes we'll plase ye,
    Because we take work by the job.

There was Dacres, at vaunting and boasting,
His equal you'll seldom come near;
But Hull, betwixt smoking and roasting,
Dispatch'd his proud frigate Guerriere!
Such treatment, to him, was a wonder,
Which served his proud spirit to choak;
And, when to the bottom our thunder
Had sent her, we laugh'd at the joke.
    Sing lather-away jonteel and aisy,
    Brave Hull, at the game hob-or-nob,
    Is the boy that will surely amaze ye,
    So well he can finish the job.

T'other day, worse than gout, fit, or cholic,
The Wasp, with Rodgers, Biddle and Jones,
So terribly stung the Poor Frolic!
As left her—but bare skin and bones.
She struck, but what could she do better;
For time, there was none to delay,
Indeed it must terribly fret her
To see she could not run away.
    Sing lather-away jonteel and aisy,
    Brave Jones, at the game hob-or-nob,
    Is the lad that will surely amaze ye,
    So well he can work by the job.

Now, to augment our brave little navy,
And add to the strength of each state,
Decatur, without sauce or gravy,
Has dress'd Alexander the Great!
By my soul, to prevent further trouble,
And save a disgraceful downfall,
Since they find all resistance a bubble,
They'll strike without fighting at all.
    Sing lather-away jonteel and aisy,
    Decatur to play hob-or-nob,
    Will in seventeen minutes amaze ye—
    Huzza, 'twas a quick finish'd job.

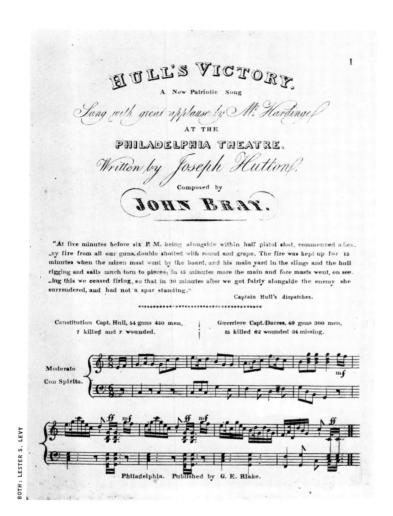

Two show-tunes of the 1812-1813 season

As always, show business reflected the current scene. An advertisement in the *Aurora* (December 11, 1812) announced a bill at the New Theatre to commemorate Decatur's recent victory over the *Macedonian*. The program included a performance by full band of "Decatur's March," especially composed by Mr. Bray; a patriotic sketch, *Return from a Cruise; or, More Laurels for American Tars*, which featured a "grand naval column" and a "superb representation of the Temple of Naval Glory rising out of the sea"; and, as if all this were not enough, an "appropriate Letter Dance—The United States Dance" was performed, and two new patriotic songs, "Columbia's Naval Annals" and "Huzza for the brave Decatur," were sung by Mr. Hardinge.

At a lavish New Year's banquet held in New York to honor the naval heroes, the *Aurora* (January 1, 1813) reported that a song, unimaginatively titled "Decatur, Hull and Jones are Here," was sung after a toast: "To American gallantry—Patriotism is its stimulus: glory its subject: a nation's gratitude its reward." At this point a spectacular transparency with portraits of the American eagle and the three heroes was revealed, "the music at the same moment struck up *Yankee Doodle*, and nine cheers expressed the feeling of the company."

This version of "Yankee Doodle" was published c. 1812.

YANKEE DOODLE

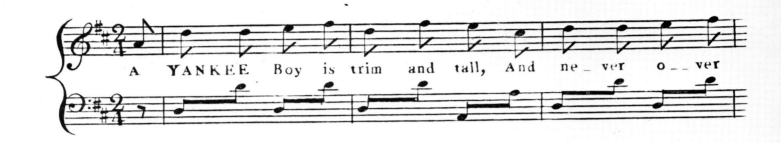

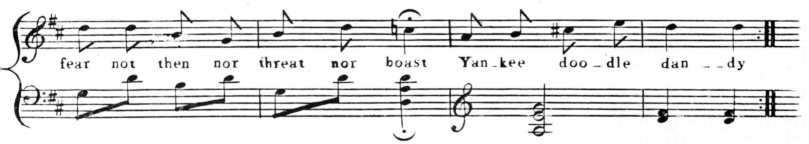

2
He's always out on training day,
   Commencement or election;
At truck and trade he knows the way,
   Of thriving to perfection.
               Yankee doodle &c.

3
His door is always open found,
   His cider of the best, sir,
His board with pumpkin pye is crown'd,
   And welcome every guest, sir.
               Yankee Doodle &c.

4
Though rough and little is his farm,
   That little is his own, sir,
His hand is strong, his heart is warm,
   Tis truth and honor's throne, sir.
               Yankee doodle &c.

5
His country is his pride and boast,
   He'll ever prove true blue, sir,
When call'd upon to give his toast,
   Tis Yankee doodle, doo, sir.
               Yankee doodle &c.

Sold by G. Willig.

A HAPPY NEW-YEAR TO
COMMODORE RODGERS,
OR, HUZZA FOR THE PRESIDENT AND CONGRESS.

A SONG Composed on the arrival of these Frigates in BOSTON, yesterday, (December 31, 1812,)
with a good supply of the READY RHINO.

HUZZA for the seamen undaunted by fear,
May they all of 'em find it a happy New-Year,
May the laurels which cluster on liberty's brow,
For a thousand years hence be as blooming as now.
  CHORUS.
 Columbia's bright name then with glory shall sound,
 And the praise of her heroes be sung the year round.

Our *DECATUR*, our *HULL*, & our *JONES*, on the sea
Have prov'd to Old Nep. that his fav'rites they be,
And the jolly old dog their birth-right to maintain,
His trident gave up, and bade them rule the main.
 Columbia's bright name then with glory shall sound.
 And the praise of her heroes be sung the year round.

Britania's sad genius look'd on with a sigh,
For she saw that the end of her glory drew nigh,
Her tears they flow'd fast as away from her drew,
Daddy Neptune wrapp'd up in his garment of blue.
 Columbia's bright name then with glory shall sound,
 And the praise of her heroes be sung the year round.

New *Hull* soon dispatch'd without trembling or fear,
That proud saucy hussey, the pert Miss *Guerriere*,
And *Jones* at the *Frolic* soon pelted away,
Till the *Frolic* was tir'd of such frolicksome play,
 Columbia's bright name then with glory shall sound,
 And the praise of her heroes be sung the year round,

Next *Decatur* the brave, with a crew full of glee,
Met the fam'd *Macedonian* ploughing the sea,
And though from a *conqueror* she borrowed her name,

To be *conquer'd* she sure to that latitude came.
 Columbia's bright name then with glory shall sound,
 And the praise of her heroes be sung the year round.

The British now thought that the Devil was in't,
As we give them the kick ere they found out the hint,
So in different directions they 'gan soon to ply,
And of late sure it seems that they're been cursed shy.
 Columbia's bright name then with glory shall sound,
 And the praise of her heroes be sung the year round

Bold *RODGERS* has hunted, and hunted in vain,
And but one of their frigates has found on the main,
Who not being fond of his true yankee play,
Ran as fast as she could, and at night ran away.
 Columbia's bright name then with glory shall sound,
 And the praise of her heroes be sung the year round.

But his cruise has successful been, say what you will,
Tho' his bull-dogs no Britons have happen'd to kill,
They were glad to avoid an American dash,
And to purchase whole skins, they left him their cash.
 Columbia's bright name then with glory shall sound,
 And the praise of her heroes be sung the year round.

Now in port safely moor'd, let each brave jolly soul,
To the health of their Commodore toss the full bowl,
For his courage at TRIPOLI sure has been tried,
And he never will run from an enemy's side.
 Columbia's bright name then with glory shall sound.
 And the praise of her heroes be sung the year round.

☞ PRINTED BY N. COVERLY, JUN. PRICE 3 CENTS.

Although the British frigate Belvidera *slipped through his fingers, Commodore John Rodgers received ebullient 1813 New Year's greetings in a broadside ballad (no tune given) because he returned to Boston from his cruise with eight captured merchantmen and a supply of that best of all commodities, "ready rhino" (ready cash).*

WRITTEN AND CORRECTED BY

JAMES CAMPBELL,

LATE OF THE CONSTITUTION:

*IN BEHALF OF THE BRAVE CAPT. JAMES LAWRENCE, AND LIEUT. C. LUDLOW,
OF THE CHESAPEAKE.*
*TOGETHER WITH---LINES ON THE DEATH OF LT. LUDLOW......*TUNE "Disconsolate Sailor."

YE sons of Columbia, O hail the great day,
 Which burst your tyrannical chain,
Which taught the opprest, how to spurn lawless sway,
 And establish equality's reign.
Yes, hail the blest moment when awfully grand,
 Your Congress pronounc'd the decree ;
Which told the wide world, that your pine cover'd land,
 In spite of Coration was free.

Those worthies who fell in the soul cheering cause,
 To the true sons of Freedom are dear ;
Their deeds the unborn shall rehearse with applause,
 And bedew their cold tomb with a tear.
O cherish their names---let their daring exploits,
 And their virtues be spread far and wide,
And if fierce-eye'd Ambition, encroach on your rights,
 Again shall her schemes be destroyed.

As he tills his rich Glebe, the old peasant shall tell,
 While his bosom with gratitude glows ;
How brave *Lawrence* expired, how *Ludlow*, he fell,
 And how WASHINGTON baffled your foes :
With transport his offspring shall catch the glad sound,
 And as Freedom takes root in each breast ;
Their country's defenders with praise shall be crown'd,
 While her plund'rers they learn to detest.

By those fields that were ravag'd, those towns that were
 fir'd ;
 By those wrongs which your females endur'd ;
By those blood sprinkled plains, where your warriors
 exp ;
 O preserve what your prowess procured,

And reflect that your rights is the rights of mankind,
 That to all they are bounteously given ;
And that he who in chains, would his fellow-man bind,
 Uplifts his proud arm against heaven.

How can you who have felt the oppressor's hard hand,
 Who for freedom all perils did brave ;
How can you enjoy ease, while one foot of your soil
 Is disgrac'd by the toil of a slave.
O rouse then in spite of a merciless few,
 And pronounce this immortal decree,
That "what'ere be man's tenets, his fortune, his hue
 He is a man, and shall therefore be free."

On the Death of Augustus C. Ludlow.

GREAT Spirit of the mighty dead,
 Descend a while, and linger here,
And tears, which love and pity shed,
 Shall fall, to grace a Hero's bier.

To thee, thy foes could not refuse
 The meed to Valor justly due,
Nor shall an humble, lowly muse,
 Forget to praise a Patriot true.

What, though no friends, nor kindred dear,
 To grace his obsequies attend :
The foemen---are his brothers here,
 And every Hero--is his friend.

N. COVERLY, Jr. Printer, Milk-Street, Boston.

*In this broadside ballad, a fellow officer mourned the tragic loss of the hero James
Lawrence and his lieutenant, Augustus Ludlow, both of whom perished in the battle
between the* Chesapeake *and the* Shannon *in June 1813. The author chose this unlikely
occasion to voice a strong indictment of slavery, but he failed to mention Lawrence's
immortal last words: "Don't give up the ship!"*

BRILLIANT NAVAL VICTORY.

YANKEE PERRY, BETTER THAN OLD ENGLISH CIDER.

"TUNE---THREE YANKEE PIGEONS."

HUZZA ! for the brave Yankee boys,
    Who touch'd up John Bull on lake Erie,
Who gave 'em a taste of our toys,
    From the fleet of brave Commodore *Perry*.

They were not made of 'lasses but lead,
    And good solid lumps of cold iron,
When they hit JOHNNY BULL in the head,
    They gave him a pain that he'll die on.

Now the *Niagara* bore down,
    To give 'em a bit of a whacking,
The *Lawrence* came up and wore round,
    And set her nine pounders a cracking.

They soon felt the *Scorpion's* sting,
    And likewise the *Æriel's* thunder,
The *Porcupine* give 'em a quill,
    And made the Queen Charlotte knock under.

The *Somers* now gave 'em a touch,
    And the *Tygress* she gave him a shock sir,
Which did not divert Johnny much,
    For it put him in mind of the BOXER.

The *Trip* she was hammering away,
    The *Oris* soon made 'em smell powder,
The brave *Caledonia* that day
    Made her thunder grow louder and louder.

We gave 'em such tough yankee blows,
    That soon they thought fit to surrender ;
That day made 'em feel that their foes,
    Were made in the masculine gender.

Poor Johnny was sick of the gripes,
    From the pills that we gave them at Erie,
And for fear of the stars and the stripes,
    He struck to brave Commodore PERRY.

Now as for poor old Johnny Bull,
    If we meet him on land or on Sea sir,
We'll give him a good belly full,
    Of excellent gun powder tea sir.

Old England is fam'd for her perry and beer,
    Which quickly bewilders the brain,
But such PERRY as she's taken here,
    She never will wish for again.

Huzza ! for our brave Yankee Tars,
    Who pepper'd the British so merry,
Who fought for the stripes and the stars,
    Under brave Commodore PERRY.

☞ Printed by N. COVERLY, Milk-Street.

With the American seagoing ships bottled up in port by the British blockade, in 1813 the principal scene of important naval action shifted to the Great Lakes, where the unsuccessful invasion of Canada was in progress. The first spectacular victory by a homemade fleet, on Lake Erie on September 10, 1813, was succinctly summed up by the victor, Oliver Hazard Perry, who announced to General William Henry Harrison: "We have met the enemy and they are ours."

Among the "considerable . . . public property at the City" that the British burned when they took Washington on August 24, 1814, were the Capitol and the President's House. With the president absent observing the "mortifying scene" at the Battle of Bladensburg, Dolley Madison refused to escape until she was assured that Gilbert Stuart's portrait of George Washington would not fall into enemy hands. When the invaders arrived at the untenanted President's House, they found the presidential table set for forty people, wine in the coolers, and dinner waiting to be served. The British withdrew from Washington after only twenty-four hours to seek more profitable plunder in Baltimore, where instead they met defeat even as they inadvertently assisted at the birth of "The Star-Spangled Banner."

CAPTURE OF WASHINGTON.

On Wednesday, August 24, there was a severe action at Bladensburgh, six miles from the CAPITOL. "Baltimore has acquired immortal honor by the brave resistance of Commodore BARNEY, his sailors and the bold volunteers." The same day "in solid column" the enemy succeeded in taking the CITY OF WASHINGTON. Their number supposed to be from 8 to 13,000 —ours 3 or 4,000. The British destroyed considerable private property and most of the public property, at the City—Navy-Yard, Georgetown, &c. though some was destroyed, by our own citizens. The British Army under the command of Gen. ROSS.—The United States' troops commanded by Gen. WINDER.

BRITANNIA'S arm'd, *Marauders* come,
The cannons' roar, the beating drum,
   Increase the *WAR's* alarms ;
Her fleets *Blockade* and line our coasts,
Of vict'ries won, *Great Britain* boasts,
   —To arms ! to arms ! to arms !
And blest Columbia, with our latest breath,
Our rallying word....be Liberty or Death.

With various insults they oppress,
Our seamen capture and distress,
   Our *RIGHTS* infringe, and *LAWS* ;
Our hopes and benefits curtail,
Our sacred *FREEDOM*, they assail,
   And *vilify* its cause.
But blest Columbia with our latest breath,
Our rallying word....is Liberty or Death.

Negociation oft hast fail'd,
Our hearts have sadden'd and bewail'd,
   And oft in gloom and dread ;
Our wishes do but ill succeed,
Our foes are *Enemies* indeed,
   And "*Havoc*" round us spread.
Yet blest Columbia, with our latest breath,
Our rallying word....is Liberty or Death.

Now hostile troops, and fleets appear,
To jeopardize with threats and fear,
   And all that's dear, destroy :
With depredations far and wide,
Around our shores, on ev'ry side,
   They ravage and annoy.
But blest Columbia, with our latest breath,
Our rallying word....is Liberty or Death.

Now here now there....direct their course,
Barbarians like, they ply their force,
   Against the weaker part ;
But mark ! *New-London, Norfolk* too,
Brave STONINGTON....there's not a few,
   Display the *YANKEE-heart.*
Thus blest Columbia, with our latest breath,
Our rallying word---is Liberty or Death.

In th' *Chesapeake's* expansive bay,
Carnage, and Death---and Fire each day,
   Their tidings to us bring ;
Havre de Grasse was once, in flame,
Hampton and *Frenchtown* share the same,
   Like *Hawks*, they're on the wing.
But blest Columbia, with our latest breath,
Our rallying word....is Liberty or Death.

At last, as *British* pride desir'd
Our *Nation's Capital* is fir'd,
   And all our *Nation's* stores ;
Regret and *Ruin* and *Dismay,*
Terrors and *Threats*, without allay,
   Thus spread, around our shores.
But blest Columbia, with our latest breath,
Our rallying word....is Liberty or Death.

So *ROSS* and his *Marauders* claim,
A triumph 'gainst our *Country's* fame,
   And boast of their success ;
But why brave citizens,... say why ?
Shall *Foes* thus triumph and defy ?
   And *WE*, no *wrongs REDRESS* !
Tho' blest Columbia, with our latest breath,
Our rallying word....is Liberty or Death.

Rich, in resources, why no means ?
And brave in spirit....why these scenes ?
   Why from th' *INVADER* flee ?
WINDER would lead your forces on,
The *Vict'ry* claim'd....he would have won,
   Sacred to *LIBERTY* !
For blest Columbia, with our latest breath,
Our rallying word....is Liberty or Death.

The *Hero BARNEY* would have pour'd,
Whole legions where their cannon roar'd,
   And check'd the *British* pride ;
Stansbury, Pinkney, Sterrett ; all....
Would round their country's standard fall,
   And *Triumph*, where they died !
For blest Columbia, with our latest breath,
Our rallying word....is Liberty or Death.

The *Baltimorean Volunteers....*
Would thrice ten thousand meet, with cheers,
   And with your hearts applause ;
Would *WE*, with *UNION*, but contest,
For all that's dear....to make us blest !....
   Our *FREEDOM, RIGHTS & LAWS* !
When blest Columbia, with our latest breath,
Our rallying word....is Liberty or Death.

Brave are our *Troops* and brave they fall,
Our *Rodgers, Perry, Porter,* all....
   Unite, in our *DEFENCE* ;
O ! then secure our *Country's* fame,
All other interests disclaim,
   Great is our *Recompence.*
As blest Columbia, with our latest breath,
Our rallying word....is Liberty or Death.

Our enemy with pow'rful *Clans,*
Whose vet'ran *Generals* lead their *Vans,*
   With vast munitions stor'd,
Determine all their strength to wield,
To make our great *Republic* yield,
   By dint of *Fire* and *Sword* !
But blest Columbia, with our latest breath,
Our rallying word....is Liberty or Death.

But favor not their desp'rate views,
Our *Rights*, our *Freedom*, they abuse,
   And *Ruin* !....all they seek ;
Rise in full majesty and strength,
" *United Stand*"...rise and at length,
   Their hands and arms are *weak* !
For blest Columbia with our latest breath,
Our rallying word....is Liberty or Death.

New-York the best example gives,
By imitation, *Boston* lives,
   A people *GREAT* and *FREE* !
A *Glory* shall enshrine the name,
Of our *Republic*....rich with fame,
   And blest with *LIBERTY.*
While blest Columbia, with our latest breath,
Our rallying word....is Liberty or Death.

At *Bladensburgh*, the *Foe* they met,
And ev'ry where convince, as yet,
   True *Valor*, on our side.
Ferocious hell-hounds drive away,
Your pow'rs and energies display,
   In all your Nation's *PRIDE* !
While blest Columbia, with our latest breath,
Our rallying word....is Liberty or Death.

Maintain your *Rights*,...." *United Stand,"*
Be prompt and ready at command,
   To sacrifice your all !
No *Sacrifice*....too much to give,
For with our *Country* we all live !
   Or with our *Country FALL* ! ! !
Then blest Columbia, with our latest breath,
Our rallying word....be Liberty or Death.

☞ Printed by Nathaniel Coverly, Jun. Milk-Street—Boston.

*Portrait of Francis Scott Key by D. Clinton
Peters after an original attributed to Rembrandt Peale*

While the British gathered their forces for their ill-fated attack on Baltimore, the well-known Georgetown lawyer and amateur poet Francis Scott Key arrived there on an official mission. He had been sent to negotiate the release of his friend Dr. William Beanes, who had been taken prisoner during the British evacuation of Washington. Accompanied by John S. Skinner, the American agent for flags of truce and the exchange of prisoners, Key embarked aboard a cartel ship on September 5, 1814, for a meeting with no less a personage than Admiral Sir Alexander Cochrane, the British commander in chief. Cochrane courteously invited both men to dine aboard his flagship, the *Tonnant*, but he responded coolly to Key's proposal that he free Beanes. By the time an agreement had been reached, the battle for Baltimore was about to begin, and Cochrane decided for security reasons to detain the three Americans until after the battle.

As captive spectators of the bombardment of Fort McHenry during the night of September 13–14, 1814, the three men shared the unbearable anxiety and suspense that Key immortalized in "The Star-Spangled Banner." He is believed to have conceived his poem during the vigil, noting his impressions and emotions on the back of an envelope and completing the work immediately on arriving at his hotel in Baltimore after being released, probably on September 16.

*Charmingly depicted in J. Bower's aquatint
of the bombardment of Fort McHenry,
the Congreve rockets, by whose "red glare"
Key tried to see whether the flag was still flying
over the fort were a commonly used British
weapon in the War of 1812. They appear to have
had greater psychological than destructive value.*

DEFENCE OF FORT M'HENRY.

☞ [The annexed song was composed under the following circumstances—A gentleman (*Francis S. Key, Esq. of Georgetown, District of Columbia.*) had left Baltimore, in a flag of truce for the purpose of getting released from the British fleet, a friend of his who had been captured at Marlborough.—He went as far as the mouth of the Patuxent and was not permitted to return lest the intended attack on Baltimore should be disclosed. He was therefore brought up the Bay to the mouth of the Patapsco, where the flag vessel was kept under the guns of a frigate, and he was compelled to witness the bombardment of Fort M'Henry, which the Admiral had boasted that he would carry in a few hours, and that the city must fall. He watched the flag at the Fort through the whole day with an anxiety that can be better felt than described, until the night prevented him from seeing it. In the night he watched the bomb shells, and at early dawn his eye was again greeted by the proudly waving flag of his country.]

Tune—ANACREON IN HEAVEN.

O ! SAY can you see by the dawn's early light,   [ing,
   What so proudly we hailed at the twilight's last gleam-
Whose broad stripes and bright stars through the peri-
     lous fight,   [ing ?
O'er the ramparts we watch'd were so gallantly stream-
And the rockets' red glare, the bombs bursting in air,
Gave proof through the night that our flag was still there ;
     O ! say does that star-spangled banner yet wave,
     O'er the land of the free, and the home of the brave ?

On the shore dimly seen through the mists of the deep,
   Where the foe's haughty host in dread silence reposes,
What is that which the breeze, o'er the towering steep,
     As it fitfully blows, half conceals, half discloses ?
Now it catches the gleam of the morning's first beam,
In full glory reflected now shines in the stream,
     'Tis the star-spangled banner, O ! long may it wave
     O'er the land of the free, and the home of the brave.

And where is that band who so vauntingly swore
     That the havoc of war and the battle's confusion,
A home and a country, shall leave us no more ?
     Their blood has wash'd out their foul footsteps pollution ;
No refuge could save the hireling and slave,
From the terror of flight, or the gloom of the grave ;
     And the star-spangled banner in triumph doth wave,
     O'er the land of the free, and the home of the brave.

O ! thus be it ever when freemen shall stand,
     Between their lov'd home, and the war's desolation,
Blest with vict'ry and peace, may the Heav'n rescued
     land,   [nation !
     Praise the Power that hath made and preserved us a
Then conquer we must, when our cause it is just,
And this be our motto—*"In God is our Trust ;"*
     And the star-spangled banner in triumph shall wave,
     O'er the land of the free and the home of the brave.

The ink was scarcely dry when Key's poem, prosaically titled "The Defense of Fort McHenry," was published in Baltimore, first as a broadside and immediately afterwards in two newspapers, the *Baltimore Patriot* (September 20, 1814) and the *Baltimore American* (September 21). The reported naive wonderment over how miraculously the words fitted the tune of the "Anacreontic Song" (it was rumored to be a coincidence) seems silly, since it was common practice to write new texts to existing tunes. Key can hardly have been unaware of what he was doing, having already written another song to the same air in 1805, "When the Warrior Returns," in which even the phrase "the star-spangled flag" had occurred. Legend has it that just after the bombardment the actor Ferdinand Durang, then a private in the army, seized a freshly printed copy and gave a rousing impromptu premiere of the song outside of McConkey's Tavern in Baltimore. Its first documented performance took place on October 19, 1814, when Mr. Hardinge sang the now renamed "Star-Spangled Banner" following a performance of August von Kotzebue's drama *Count Benyowsky: or, The Conspiracy of Kamschatka* at the Holliday Street Theatre, next door to McConkey's. A "military hornpipe," danced by Miss Abercrombie, shared the bill with Mr. Hardinge. The first title appears on this rare 1814 broadside, one of the earliest printings of Key's poem; the explanatory paragraph was reprinted in most contemporary publications of "The Star-Spangled Banner."

Recognizing a hit in the making, the enterprising Baltimore music publisher Joseph Carr, father of Benjamin Carr, lost no time in bringing out sheet music of "The Star-Spangled Banner" in a new two-part harmonization by a younger son, Thomas (the "T. C." credited on the first page of the publication). The edition (following pages) was so hastily prepared that an error in the subtitle was overlooked, leaving a delightful birthmark by which to identify the first edition of "The Star-Spangled Banner": a "pariotic" song.

THE
STAR SPANGLED BANNER

A PARIOTIC SONG,

Baltimore. Printed and Sold at CARRS Music Store 36 Baltimore Street.

Air. Anacreon in Heaven.

O! say can you see by the dawn's early light, What so proudly we hail'd at the twilight's last gleaming. Whose broad stripes & bright stars thro' the perilous fight, O'er the ramparts we watch'd, were so gallantly streaming. And the Rockets' red glare, the Bombs bursting in air, Gave proof through the night that our

(Adap.d & Arr.d by T.C.)

(Pl. 1.)

Flag was still there, O! say does that star spangled Banner yet wave, O'er the

Land of the free, and the home of the brave.

Sym.

L.H.

2

On the shore dimly seen through the mists of the deep,
  Where the foe's haughty host in dread silence reposes.
What is that which the breeze, o'er the towering steep,
  As it fitfully blows, half conceals, half discloses;
Now it catches the gleam of the morning's first beam,
In full glory reflected now shines in the stream
  'Tis the star spangled banner, O, long may it wave
  O'er the land of the free, and the home of the brave.

(3)

And where is that band who so vauntingly swore
  That the havoc of war and the battle's confusion,
A home and a country, shall leave us no more,
  Their blood has wash'd out their foul footsteps pollution.
No refuge could save the hireling and slave,
From the terror of flight or the gloom of the grave.
  And the star spangled banner, in triumph doth wave.
  O'er the Land &c.

(4)

O! thus be it ever when freemen shall stand,
  Between their lov'd home, and the war's desolation.
Blest with vict'ry and peace, may the Heav'n rescued land
  Praise the Pow'r that hath made and preserv'd us a nation!
Then conquer we must, when our cause it is just,
And this be our motto_"In God is our Trust":
  And the star spangled banner, in triumph shall wave,
  O'er the Land &c.

For the Flute.

Con Spirito

Song.

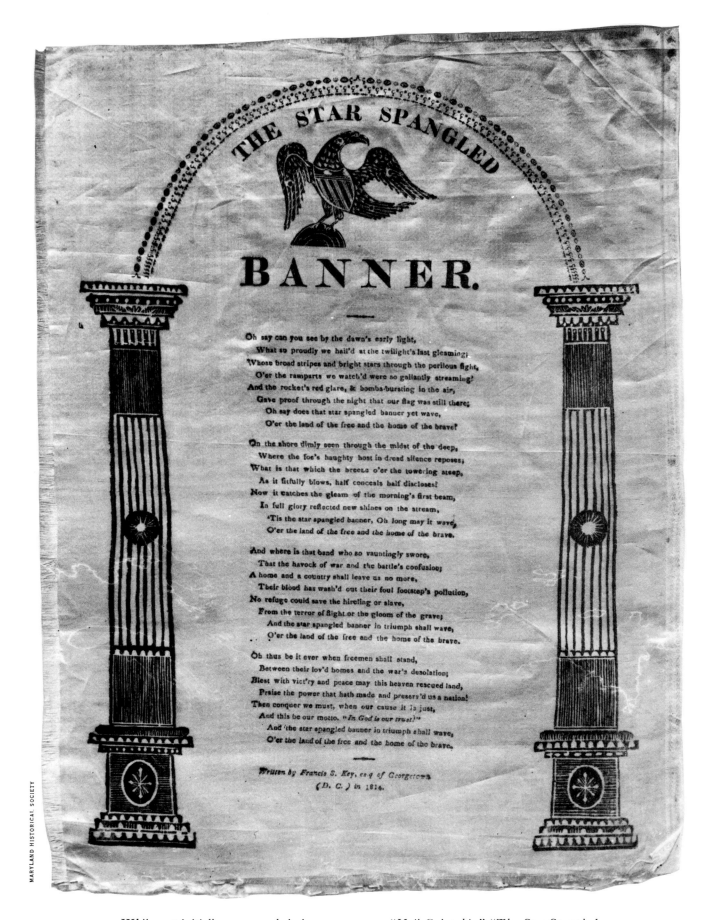

While not initially as overwhelming a success as "Hail Columbia," "The Star-Spangled Banner" nevertheless was widely reprinted in newspapers, magazines, songsters, broadsides, and sheet music. The early sheet music editions and broadsides were often decorated with patriotic emblems. The music page with the flag dates from about 1816; the one with the "toy" soldiers from 1825; the rare broadside printed on silk from between 1815 and 1830. The unfamiliar musical setting of Francis Scott Key's poem was composed in 1816 by James Hewitt.

With the capture of Washington serving as a terrifying example, Baltimoreans of all classes mobilized to oppose the invasion forces that landed at North Point on September 12. General Ross, the British commander, had boasted that he would dine in Baltimore that very evening, but as it turned out he was killed in the battle. An undated ballad of fourteen stanzas found in the *American Songster* (1851) describes the battle of North Point to the tune of the "Anacreontic Song," apparently the accepted theme music for Baltimore's successful participation in the War of 1812. In the selected stanzas that follow, "the plundering Cockburn" is the strutting British Admiral Sir George Cockburn, who ordered the burning of Washington; "brave Armistead" is Lieutenant-Colonel George Armistead, the commander at Fort McHenry.

THE BATTLE OF NORTH POINT.

TUNE—"*Anacreon in Heaven.*"

Hark, hark, was the cry, when *Baltimore* town
Was besieg'd by the plundering Cockburn and Co.
Hear you not the great guns, hear ye not the trump sound;
Haste, haste, was the cry, let us meet the proud foe,
Let us march, heart and hand, let us make a bold stand,
And teach those invaders to cautiously land—
For this ground our fathers declared should be free,
And as dutiful sons we'll enforce their decree.

Our general gave orders for the troops to march down
To meet the proud Ross, and to check his ambition,
To inform him that we have decreed in our town
That here he can't enter without our permission,
And if life he regards, we will not press too hard,
For Baltimore freemen are ever prepar'd
To check the presumptuous, whoever they be,
That may rashly attempt to evade our decree.

〰

We march'd for North Point, and encamped for the night,
Prepar'd for attack by the light of the morning,
Near hand to Bear Creek we prepar'd for the fight;
The fatigues of the field and the danger still scorning,
As this was the day, great Ross was heard say,
He would dine in our town; he'd no longer delay;
So we formed our line in the old Yankee style,
To wait for this lord from the fast anchor'd isle.

〰

Scarce had he spoke, when express brought the news
That Ross was in sight, on his foaming steed prancing,
Then part of the Bladensburg heroes were chose
To wait on his lordship, then boldly advancing,
When lo, their *first* fire brought down great Goliath;
He went down to dine with his aged grandsire;
To dine in our city determined was he,
Or else dine in hell,* so there let him be.

〰

Sixteen hundred bombs, by old Cockburn's command,
At our fort were discharg'd, by his fam'd sons of plunder,
While unmov'd stood brave *Armistead*, and well-chosen band,
Sending back their full charge in red hot Yankee thunder.
'Board the ships that drew nigh, was a dreadful outcry;
'Bout ship, was the word; we from danger must fly,
This d-----d Yankee powder's too strong, you may see,
For his majesty's ships, so, boys, "helm's a lee."

〰

---

* Ross said he would dine in Baltimore on the 12th of September, or in hell, he cared not if it *rained* militia.

Jackson's victory at New Orleans was handsomely commemorated in the sheet music cover art of a gallantly dedicated piano piece published in 1815: "General Jackson's Favorite March" was published just before his first inauguration in 1829.

After seven months of negotiations at Ghent, peace with England was concluded on Christmas Eve, 1814. John Quincy Adams, a member of the American commission, related in his diary that on January 5, 1815, an official banquet was given to celebrate the peace. "As we went into the hall," he wrote, " 'Hail Columbia' was performed by a band of music. It was followed by 'God Save the King,' and these two airs were alternately repeated during the dinner-time until Mr. Goulburn [Adams's British dinner partner] thought they became tiresome. I was of the same opinion." At the time that Adams was being bored by the reiteration of "Hail Columbia" at Ghent, Andrew Jackson's defense of New Orleans against a large British invasion army was well under way. It was not until January 8, 1815—with the adversaries still unaware that peace had been declared—that the main Battle of New Orleans was fought, and at its conclusion Jackson's musicians sounded a triumphant finale to the War of 1812. As the routed British invaders fled, an American band struck up "Hail Columbia." Jackson himself was hailed as a second Washington. His victorious entry into New Orleans was punctuated by triumphal arches, laurel wreaths, white-robed virgins wearing silver stars on their foreheads, the strewing of flowers, and much elaborate ceremonial. Not only was a grand *Te Deum* sung at the cathedral, in which the great throng outside in the square joined, but Jackson was also serenaded to the tune of "Yankee Doodle" by a little girl in white, who stood under a triumphal arch. For many years to come, January 8 was celebrated in America as a national holiday, second in importance only to the Fourth of July.

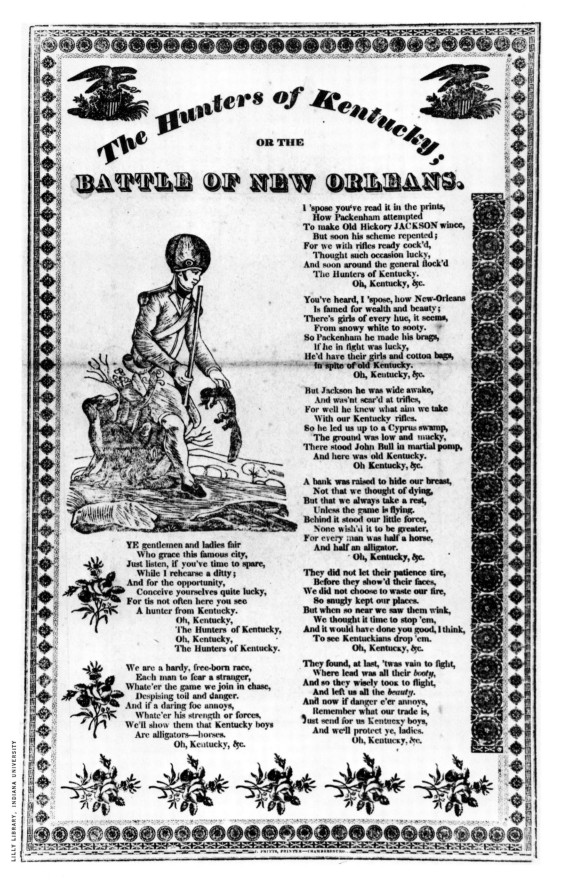

Andrew Jackson's doughty Kentucky riflemen at the Battle of New Orleans are described as a fabulous amphibious combination of horse and alligator in this ballad by Samuel Woodworth. "The Hunters of Kentucky" was later published in sheet music form (see page 227); it was used as a campaign song for Jackson in 1828 and probably also during his unsuccessful bid for the presidency in 1824. In the text, "Packenham" is Sir Edward Packenham, the commander of the British invading army, who was slain at the Battle of New Orleans. His mortal remains were reported to have been sent home preserved in a cask of rum.

GENERAL SPICERS,
GRAND MARCH and QUICK STEP.

Battle of N. Orleans.

Lith'y of Pendleton Wall St.

Composed by
I. ROCA.

Leader of the Jackson Guards Band

And

RESPECTFULLY DEDICATED TO THAT
PATRIOTIC CORPS.

NEW YORK
Published by HEWITT, 137 Broadway.

This spirited delineation of the Battle of New Orleans, probably dating from the 1830s, is the work of John Pendleton, one of the pioneers of lithography in America. With the introduction of lithography in the early 1820s, a distinctive sheet music cover art evolved, adding a rich dimension to the music it decorated.

CHASE CONSTITUTION LEVANT

TO COMMODORE CHARLES STEWART.
"OLD IRONSIDES"
THIS SONG IS CHEERFULLY INSCRIBED BY HIS FRIEND.
THE AUTHOR.

Philadelphia LEE & WALKER 188 Chesnut St

Col'd 4

Plain 2½

T. Sinclair's lith. Phil.

In June 1815 Stephen Decatur led a squadron of ships into the Mediterranean and subdued the forces of the piratical Dey of Algiers. With this victory Decatur terminated the payment of tribute to the Barbary States, exacted reparations for past injuries, and secured the release of American prisoners. On his return to the United States Decatur was enthusiastically wined and dined, and it was at a festive banquet in his honor at Norfolk that he uttered his famous and controversial toast: "Our country! In her intercourse with foreign nations may she always be in the right; but our country, right or wrong." Decatur's victory over the dey was delightfully commemorated in a punning song (undated) found in *The Book of the Navy* (1862).

CARPE DIEM.—SEIZE THE DEY.

The Dey of Algiers, not being afraid of his ears,
Sent to Jonathan once for some tribute;
"Ho! ho!" says the Dey, "if the rascal don't pay,
"A caper or two I'll exhibit."

"I'm the Dey of Algiers, with a beard a yard long,
"I'm a mussulman too, and of course very strong;
"For this is my maxim, dispute it who can,
"That a man of stout muscle's, a stout mussulman."

"They say," to himself one day says the Dey,
"I may bully him now without reck'ning to pay;
"There's a kick-up just coming with him and John Bull,
"And John will give Jonathan both his hands full."

So he bullied our consul, and captur'd our men,
Went out through the Straits and came back safe again;
And thought that his cruisers in triumph might ply
Wherever they pleas'd, but he thought a big lie.

For when Jonathan fairly got John out of his way,
He prepar'd him to settle accounts with the Dey;
Says he, "I will send him an able debater;"
So he sent him a message by Stephen Decatur.

Away went Decatur to treat with the Dey,
But he met the Dey's admiral just in his way;
And by way of a tribute just captur'd his ship;
But the soul of the admiral gave him the slip.

From thence he proceeded to *Algesair's* bay,
To pay his respects to his highness the Dey,
And sent him a message, decided yet civil,
But the Dey wished both him and his note to the devil.

But when he found out that the admiral's ship,
And the admiral too, had both giv'n him the slip,
The news gave his highness a good deal of pain,
And the Dey thought he'd never see daylight again.

"Ho! ho!" says the Dey, "if this is the way
"This Jonathan reckons his tribute to pay;
"Who takes it will tickle his fingers with thorns."—
So the Dey and the *crescent* both haul'd in their horns.

He call'd for a peace and gave up our men,
And promis'd he'd never ask tribute again;
Says his highness, the Dey, "here's the devil to pay
"Instead of a tribute; heigho, well-a-day!"

And never again will our Jonathan pay
A tribute to potentate, pirate, or Dey;
Nor any, but that which for ever is giv'n:—
The tribute to valour, and virtue, and Heav'n.

And again if his Deyship should bully and fume,
Or hereafter his claim to this tribute resume,
We'll send him Decatur once more to defy him,
And his motto shall be, if you please, *Carpe Diem*.

Another postwar triumph—Commodore Charles Stewart's victory in the Constitution *over the British ships* Levant *and* Cyane—*was later remembered in a song (1856) with a beautiful cover of "Old Ironsides" showing the two defeated ships in the background. The fact that the* Levant *eventually slipped out of Stewart's grasp was apparently overlooked in celebrating his victory. Stewart had not known the war was over when he entered the fight, having sailed from Boston in December 1814 before peace was signed.*

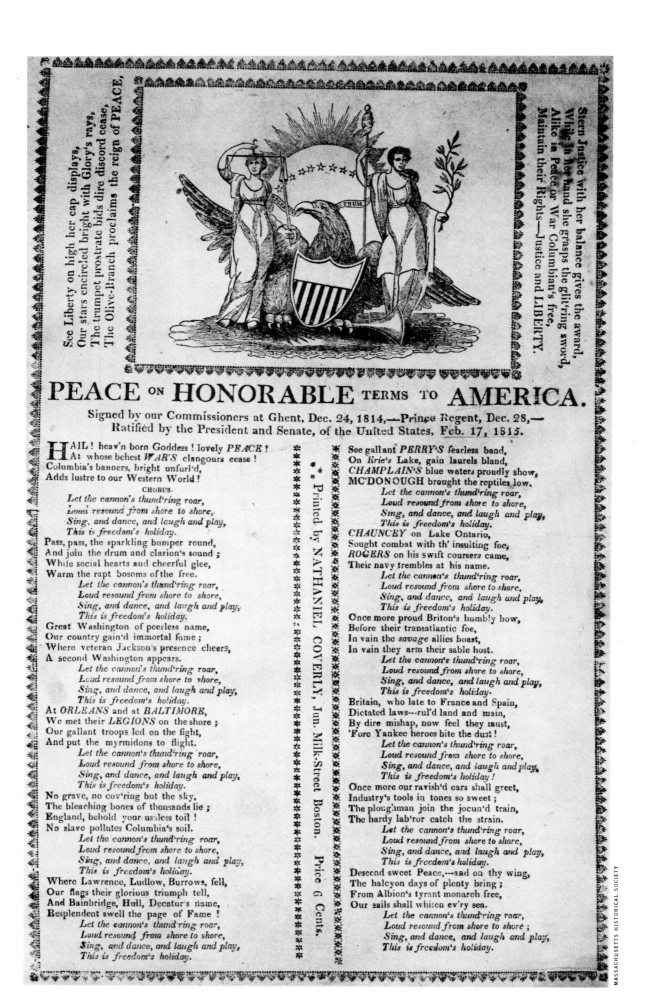

See Liberty on high her cap displays,
Our stars encircled bright with Glory's rays,
The trumpet prostrate bids dire discord cease,
The Olive-Branch proclaims the reign of PEACE,

Stern Justice with her balance gives the award,
While in her hand she grasps the glit'ring sword,
Alike in Peace or War Columbian's free,
Maintain their Rights.—Justice and LIBERTY.

PEACE ON HONORABLE TERMS TO AMERICA.

Signed by our Commissioners at Ghent, Dec. 24, 1814,—Prince Regent, Dec. 28,— Ratified by the President and Senate, of the United States, Feb. 17, 1815.

HAIL! heav'n born Goddess! lovely *PEACE*!
At whose behest *WAR'S* clangours cease!
Columbia's banners, bright unfurl'd,
Adds lustre to our Western World!

CHORUS.
Let the cannon's thund'ring roar,
Loud resound from shore to shore,
Sing, and dance, and laugh and play,
This is freedom's holiday.

Pass, pass, the sparkling bumper round,
And join the drum and clarion's sound ;
While social hearts and cheerful glee,
Warm the rapt bosoms of the free.
Let the cannon's thund'ring roar,
Loud resound from shore to shore,
Sing, and dance, and laugh and play,
This is freedom's holiday.

Great Washington of peerless name,
Our country gain'd immortal fame ;
Where veteran Jackson's presence cheers,
A second Washington appears.
Let the cannon's thund'ring roar,
Loud resound from shore to shore,
Sing, and dance, and laugh and play,
This is freedom's holiday.

At *ORLEANS* and at *BALTIMORE*,
We met their *LEGIONS* on the shore ;
Our gallant troops led on the fight,
And put the myrmidons to flight.
Let the cannon's thund'ring roar,
Loud resound from shore to shore,
Sing, and dance, and laugh and play,
This is freedom's holiday.

No grave, no cov'ring but the sky,
The bleaching bones of thousands lie ;
England, behold your useless toil !
No slave pollutes Columbia's soil.
Let the cannon's thund'ring roar,
Loud resound from shore to shore,
Sing, and dance, and laugh and play,
This is freedom's holiday.

Where Lawrence, Ludlow, Burrows, fell,
Our flags their glorious triumph tell,
And Bainbridge, Hull, Decatur's name,
Resplendent swell the page of Fame !
Let the cannon's thund'ring roar,
Loud resound from shore to shore,
Sing, and dance, and laugh and play,
This is freedom's holiday.

* Printed by NATHANIEL COVERLY, Jun. Milk-Street Boston. Price 6 Cents.

See gallant *PERRY'S* fearless band,
On Erie's Lake, gain laurels bland,
CHAMPLAIN'S blue waters proudly show,
MC'DONOUGH brought the reptiles low.
Let the cannon's thund'ring roar,
Loud resound from shore to shore,
Sing, and dance, and laugh and play,
This is freedom's holiday.

CHAUNCEY on Lake Ontario,
Sought combat with th' insulting foe,
ROGERS on his swift coursers came,
Their navy trembles at his name.
Let the cannon's thund'ring roar,
Loud resound from shore to shore,
Sing, and dance, and laugh and play,
This is freedom's holiday.

Once more proud Briton's humbly bow,
Before their transatlantic foe,
In vain the *savage* allies boast,
In vain they arm their sable host.
Let the cannon's thund'ring roar,
Loud resound from shore to shore,
Sing, and dance, and laugh and play,
This is freedom's holiday.

Britain, who late to France and Spain,
Dictated laws---rul'd land and main,
By dire mishap, now feel they must,
'Fore Yankee heroes bite the dust !
Let the cannon's thund'ring roar,
Loud resound from shore to shore,
Sing, and dance, and laugh and play,
This is freedom's holiday !

Once more our ravish'd ears shall greet,
Industry's tools in tones so sweet ;
The ploughman join the jocund train,
The hardy lab'ror catch the strain.
Let the cannon's thund'ring roar,
Loud resound from shore to shore,
Sing, and dance, and laugh and play,
This is freedom's holiday.

Descend sweet Peace,---and on thy wing,
The halcyon days of plenty bring ;
From Albion's tyrant monarch free,
Our sails shall whiten ev'ry sea.
Let the cannon's thund'ring roar,
Loud resound from shore to shore,
Sing, and dance, and laugh and play,
This is freedom's holiday.

The peace was as copiously serenaded as the war had been, and self-congratulatory ballads often chronicled the events of the recent conflict in astonishing detail.

A NEW SONG

ON THE CAUSES—BEGINNING, EVENTS—END—AND CONSEQUENCES OF THE LATE WAR WITH *GREAT BRITAIN*.

Composed by SILAS BALLOU, *Richmond, New-Hampshire.*

TUNE......"*THE GIRL I LEFT BEHIND ME.*"

OLD England forty years ago,
  When we were young and slender,
She aim'd at us a mortal blow,
But God was our defender.
Jehovah saw her horrid plan,
Great Washington he gave us,
His holiness inspired the man,
With power and skill to save us.
She sent her fleets and armies o'er,
To ravage, kill, and plunder,
Our heroes met them on the shore,
And beat them back with thunder.
Our independence they confess'd,
And with their hands they sign'd it,
But on their hearts 'twas ne'er impress'd,
For there I ne'er could find it.
Ever since that time they have been still
Our liberties invading,
We bore it, and forbore until
Forbearance was degrading.
Regardless of the sailor's right,
Impress'd our native seamen;
Made them against their country fight,
And thus enslav'd our freemen.
Great Madison besought the foe,
He mildly did implore them,
To let the suff'ring captive go,
But they would not restore them.
Our commerce too they did invade,
Our ships they search'd and seized,
Declaring also we should trade,
With none but whom they pleased.
Thus Madison in thunder spake,
We've power and we must use it,
Our freedom surely lies at stake,
And we must fight or lose it.
We'll make Old England's children know,
We are the brave descendants,
Of those who flogg'd their fathers so,
And gain'd our independence.
Our soldiers and our seamen too,
We've put in warlike motion,
Strait to the field our soldiers flew,
Our seamen to the ocean.
They met their foes on tow'ring waves,
With courage, skill, and splendor;
They sunk them down to wat'ry grave,
Or forc'd them to surrender.
Decatur, Hull, and Bainbridge dear,
Did wonders in our navy;
Brave Captain Hull sunk the Guerriere,
And Bainbridge sunk the Java.
Decatur took a ship of fame,
High on the waving water;
The Macedonian was her name,
And home in triumph brought her.

Perry with flag and sails unfurl'd
Met Barclay on lake Erie,
At him his matchless thunders hurl'd,
'Till Barclay grew quite weary.
He gain'd the vic'try and renown,
He work'd him up so neatly;
He brought Old England's banners down
And swept the lake completely.
Proud Downie fell on Lake Champlain,
By fortune quite forsaken,
He was by bold Macdonough slain,
And all his fleet were taken.
Whene'er they met Columbia's sons,
On lakes, or larger waters,
They sunk beneath her thundering guns,
Or humbly cry'd for quarters.
When Prevost saw he'd lost his fleet,
He gave out special orders,
For his whole army to retreat,
And leave the yankee borders.
Through dreary wilds o'er bog and fen,
The luckless gen'ral blund'red,
He fled with fifteen-thousand men,
From Macomb's fifteen-hundred.
Let William Hull be counted null,
And let him not be named,
Upon the rolls of valiant souls,
Of him we are ashamed.
For his campaign was worse than vain,
A coward and a traitor,
For paltry gold his army sold,
To Brock the speculator.
When Proctor found brave Harrison,
Had landed on his region,
Away the tim'rous creature run
With all his savage legions.
But over-taken were, and most
Of them were kill'd and taken,
But Proctor soon forsook his post,
And fled to save his bacon.
At Little York, beneath the guns
Of Chauncey, Dearborn landed,
And quickly made Old England's sons,
Resign what he demanded.
From George's Fort to Erie's beach,
Our savage foes were beaten,
Their naked bones were left to bleach,
When wolves their flesh had eaten.
How often Brown made Drummond fly,
From scenes of desolation,
The terror of his noble eye,
Struck him with consternation.
Brave Miller, Ripley, Jones and Scott,
At Erie and Bridgewater,
At Chippewa in battles hot,
Their bravest foes did slaughter.

At Washington their horrid crimes,
Must tarnish British glory,
Children must blush in future times,
To read this shameful story;
They burnt the volumes which compris'd
The best of information,
Their barb'rous deeds will be despis'd
By every christian nation.
At Baltimore a deadly blow,
The sons of mischief aimed,
The sons of freedom met their foe,
And vict'ry justly claimed.
Amidst their ranks of thunder burst,
Many were kill'd and wounded,
Their chief commander bit the dust,
And all their schemes confounded.
What wonders did brave Jackson do,
When aided by kind heaven,
Their leader and four thousand slew,
And lost but only seven!
Some interposing Angel's hand,
Repell'd their vile intrusion,
The remnant of their broken band,
They fled in sad confusion.
They pass'd thro numerous trying scenes:
In most of them defeated;
Their grand defeat at New-Orleans,
The bloody scene completed.
Soon after this sweet peace arriv'd,
Our armies were disbanded,
Our scatter'd foes who had surviv'd,
The war were home commanded.
What has our infant country gain'd,
By fighting that old nation?
Our liberties we have maintain'd
And rais'd our reputation.
We've gain'd the freedom of the seas,
Our seamen are released,
Our mariners trade where they please,
Impressments too have ceased.
Now in ourselves we can confide,
Abroad we are respected,
We've check'd the rage of British pride,
Their haughtiness corrected.
First to the God of boundless power,
Be thanks and adoration,
Next Madison the wond'rous flower,
And jewel of our nation.
Next Congress does our thanks demand,
To them our thanks we tender,
Our heroes next by sea and land,
To them our thanks we render.
Let us be just, in union live,
Then who will dare invade us?
If any should, our God will give
His angels charge to aid us.

"A British General, su—
ro infect and taken by Ya—
kee light horfe.

Lord Caftlereagh, moun—
ed on a Goat, in the attitu—
of delivering his late " Si—
gua nes" to the British mi—
ifters at Ghent.

Britifh Colonel in a fright,
Loft tail in the fight,
Running off in the night,
What a laughable fight !

Chain of our Union indiffoluble !

UNITED
WE STAND;
DIVIDED—WE FALL.

COLUMBIA, represented
as furrounded by enemies.

Lieutenant-Col. Barret,
To leap up fhout and flide,
Upon a Cam I mounts
And off in fhame b-rides !

The valiant Major Bright,
Afhais the Goose purfued,
And kaffes his Mule
To tell the horrid news!

Battle of Niagara !
OR,
AMERICA again victorious
over her white and red
favage Enemies !

O'ER Huron's wave the fun was low,
The weary foldier watch'd the bow,
Fast fading from the cloud below
Tis dashing of Niagara.

And while the phantom chain'd his fight
Ah ! little thought he of the fight—
The horrors of the dreamless night,
That pofted on fo rapidly.

Soon, soon as fled each fofter charm,
The drum and trumpet found alarm,
And bid each warrior nerve his arm,
For boldest deeds of chivalry.

The burning red crofs, waving high,
Like meteor in the evening sky,
Proclaim'd the haughty foeman nigh,
To try the ftrife of rivalry.

Columbia's banner floats as proud,
Her gallant band around it crowd,
And swear to guard or mrake their fhroud
The starred flag of glory.

"Hafte, hafte thee, Scott, to meet the foe
And let the fcornful Briton know,
Well ftrung the arm and firm the blow,
Of him who strikes for liberty."

Loud, loud is the din of battle rings,
Shrill through the ranks the bullet sings,
And onward fierce each foeman springs,
To meet his peer in gallantry.

Behind the hills defcends the sun,
The work of death is but begun.

City of New-Orleans.

Grand Battle of
N. ORLEANS,
UNDER THE VETERAN
General Andrew Jackson,
The fecond WASHINGTON of America,
On the memorable 8th of January 1815,
In which Yankee fkill & bravery will forever ftand on re-
cord unparalleled in hiftory.

BATTLE OF PLATTSBURGH,
AND
VICTORY ON LAKE CHAMPLAIN,

In which 14,000 *British myrmidons* were defeated and put to flight by 5,000
Yankees and Green-mountain Boys, on the memorable Eleventh of Sept. 1814.

Tune—"Battle of the Kegs."

SIR GEORGE PREVOST with all his hoft
March'd forth from Montreal, Sir,
Both he and they as blithe and gay
As going to a ball, Sir.
The troops he chose were all of those
That conquer'd Marfhal SOULT, Sir,
Who at *Garonne* (the fact is known)
Scarce brought them to a halt, Sir.

With troops like thefe he tho't with eafe
To crufh the Yankee faction :
His only thought was how he ought
To bring them into action.
Your very names, Sir GEORGE exclaims,
Withrur a gun or bay'net,
Will pierce like darts thro'Yankee hearts,
And all their fpirits ftagnate.

Oh ! how I dread, left they have fled
And left their puny Fort, Sir,
For fure MACOMB won't ftay at home,
Good-bye, he faid to thofe that ftay'd,
Keep close as mice, or rats fnug,
We juft run out upon a fcout,
To burn the town of PLATTSBURGH.

Then up *Champlain* with might & main
He march'd with dread array, Sir,
With Fife and Drum to fcare MACOMB,
And drive him quite away, Sir.
And fire by fire their nations pride,
Along the current beat, Sir
Sworn not to fup 'till they eat up
Ma-donough and his fleet, Sir,

Still onward came thefe men of fame,
Refolv'd to give " no quarter !"
But to their felf found out at laft
That they had caught a tartar.
At diftance fhot awhile they fought
By water and by land, fir

With one to ten, I'd fight 'gainft men,
But these are Satan's legions,
With malice fraught, come piping hot
From Pluto's dark-d regions !
Hélas, mon Dieu ! what fhall I do,
I fnell the burning fulphur,
Set Britain's ifle all rank and file—
Such men would foon engulph her.

That's full as bad, oh ! I'll run mad,
Thofe weftern hounds are fummon'd
aines, Scott & Brown are coming down
To ferve me juft like Drummond.
Thuck too as bees the Vermonele,
Are fwarming on the lake, fir ;
And lizard's men come back again,
Lie hid in every brake, fir !

Good Britbane, beat a quick retreat,
Before their forces join, fir,
For fure as fate they've laid a bait,
To catch us like Burgoyne, fir,
All round ab ut, keep good look out,
We'll furely be furrounded,
Since I could crawl my gallant foul
Was never fo afounded."

The rout began, Sir GEORGE led on,
His men ran helter fkelter,
Each cry'd his beft t'out run the reft
To hide their fear they gave a cheer,
And thought it mighty cunning—
He'll fight, fay they, another day,
Who faves himfelf by running !

"Millions for Defence——Not a Cent for

BRITISH LION.

M'DONOUGH'S SHIP.

We won't give up the Ship——We won

CAPT. DOWNIE.

Interefting Sketch.

Extracts of Letters—Official.

New-Orleans, Jan 13, 1815.

"EARLY on the morning of the 8th,
the enemy having been actively employed
the two preceding days in making preparations for a ftorm, advanced in two ftrong
columns on my right and left. They were
received, however, with a firmnefs which,
it feems, they little expected, and which
defeated all their hope.

American Sentinel.

Yankee General, calling for
Volunteers by founding the
Trumpet.

Gen. Drummond attempts
fo efcape by the fleetnefs of
Bear, but is furrounded &
ken prifoner.

General Brifbane, on a
quick retreat, in imitation
of a Monkey on a Pig.

A Coffick, fmoaking his
pipe & thumping his Mule
with a cudgel to keep up
with the reft.

A Vermonter, attacking the veterans of Lord Wellington, while crossing the fatal river.

A British chief from home doth fall.
Brought down by force of Yankee Bull.

Gen. Gen. of the Canadas succeeds for eno candor, and foiled an Elephant.

A Green-Mountain Boy, with his foot on the head of an Indian.

The feeling Matron follows her husband to the field of battle, to avenge the murders, flames and cruelties at Hampton, Havre-de-Grace, and the River Rafin!

The news of Champlain
The Prince Regent receives;
He mounts his old Bull.
'Tis all too too full;
And, frantic with madness,
Most bitterly grieves.

And fouler than Niagara's roar,
Along the line is heard encore,
'On, on to death or victory.'

From time to time with lurid glow,
High wheeling shoots the rocket's bow,
And lights the mingled scene below
Of carnage, death, and misery.

The middle watch has now begun,
The horrid battle fray is done,
Nor longer beats the furious drum,
To death, to death or victory

Ah, 'tis still—with silent tread,
The watchman steals among the dead,
To guard his comrade's lowly head,
Till morning give him sepulchre.

Low in the West, of splendor shorn,
The midnight moon with bloody horn,
Sheds her last beam on him forlorn
Who fell in fight so gloriously.

Oh ! long her crescent wax and wane,
Ere she behold such fray again,
Such dismal night, such heaps of slain,
Foe mix't with foe promiscuously.

COLUMBIA, fiercely victorious
over all her enemies—reclining in
Peace, and surrounded with plenty.

WINDSOR, (Vt.)
Printed for the Flying Book-Sellers.
Jan. 1, 1815.

With pain and woe,
Death strikes the foe
A heavy blow,
And lays him low.

Aloft the Eagle towers,
"We've met the enemy" again—
Again have made them 'OURS !'

Champlain! the cannon's thundering voice,
Proclaims thy waters free ;
Thy forest-waving hills rejoice,
And echo—Victory !

The striped flag upon thy wave,
Triumphantly appears,
And to invested landsmen, brave,
A star of promise bears.

Now to the world Fame's trumpet sounds
The deed with new applause,
While from a Conquer'd Fleet resounds,
Our seamen's loud huzzas.

Britannia, round thy haggard brows
Bind bitter wormwood still ;
For lo ! again thy standard bows
To valiant Yankee skill.

But, O ! what chaplet can be found
Macdonough's brows to grace ?
'Tis done ! the glorious wreath is bound,
Which time can ne'er efface.

And still a just—a rich reward,
His country has to give;
He shall be first in her regard,
And with her PERRY live!

Columbia! though thy cannon's roar
On inland seas prevail,
An't there alone—while round each shore
Outnumbering ships assail.

Yet deed with deed, and name with name
Thy gallant sons shall blend,
Till the bright arch of naval fame,
O'er the broad ocean bend !

A few British Gun Boats barely escape to carry the dismal tidings of defeat and destruction of their Fleet.

——"We have met the enemy, and they are ours."

GEN MACOMB.

GOV. PREVOST.

GENIUS of AMERICA in Combat with OLD JONNY BULL.

[COPY-RIGHT.]

up the Soil.——Free trade, Sailor's rights, and no impressment.

In 30 minutes, said the British Commodore, I will be on board Macdonough's ship; but behold him slain the first fire, and his ship a wreck!

So well the fellow knows us—
Will just as soon jump o'er the moon
As venture to oppose us!
With quick dispatch light ev'ry match,
Man ev'ry gun and swivel,
Crols in a crack the Saranack,
And drive 'em to the Devil !

The Vermont gaoks that lin'd the banks
Then pois'd the unerring rifle,
And to oppose their haughty foes,
They found a perfect trifle.
Meanwhile the fort 'kept up such spart,
They thought the devil was in it,
Their mighty train play'd off in vain—
'Twas silenc'd in a minute.

Sir George amas'd, so wildly gaz'd,
Such frantic gambols acted,
Of all his men not one in ten,
But thought him quite diffracted.
He curs'd and swore, his hair he tore,
Then jump'd upon his poney,
And gallop'd off towards the bluff,
To look for Captain Downie.

But when he spy'd M'Donough ride,
In all the pomp of glory,
He hasten'd back to Saranac,
To tell the dismal story:
"My gallant crews, oh shocking news !
Are all or kill'd or taken !
Except a few that just withdrew
In time to save their bacon.

Old England's pride must now subside,
Oh ! how the news will shock her,
To have her fleet not only beat,
But sent to Davy's locker!
From this sad day let no one say,
Britannia rules the ocean,
We've dearly bought the humbling the't
That this is all a notion.

The God of War mows down the enemy by hundreds, and crimsons the waters of the Saranac with blood !

This ebullient postwar broadside to celebrate Macdonough's victory at Lake Champlain and other successes of the war combined picture, song, and story, as well as a collection of the outstanding American patriotic slogans of the preceding forty years.

If James Madison was hailed as "the wond'rous flower, and jewel of our nation" by the balladeer Silas Ballou in his euphoric song history of the war (page 217), a far different view was taken by members of the expiring Federalist party. Among their valedictory efforts during the virtually uncontested elections of 1816 was a recriminatory parody of the old English song "John Anderson, My Jo," in which old accusations of Madison and Jefferson's complicity with Napoleon were revived. In the text, "Carter's mount" refers to Jefferson's flight to nearby Carter's Mountain thirty-five years earlier, when Monticello was threatened by the British general Banastre Tarleton and his raiders. Apparently the Federalists never tired of belaboring this episode as an example of Jefferson's cowardice. From the *Patriotic Songster* (1816):

NEW SONG.
Tune—"John Anderson my Joe."

James Madison my Joe, Jim, I wonder what you mean,
You proclamate, in chair of state, a vision or a dream,
The war you did begin, Jim, and why did you do so?
You should have found some better ground, James Madison my Joe.

James Madison my Joe, Jim, we find your plans have fail'd;
Ere this you know, that deadly woe, and taxes you've entail'd;
Upon this happy land, Jim, you've brought disgrace also,
That you cant cure, nor we endure, James Madison my Joe.

James Madison my Joe, Jim, 'twas when you first began,
The world did say, and well might they, that you was not the man;
You was a dupe of France, Jim, and Jefferson also:
With gun-boat fleet you'd Britons beat, James Madison my Joe.

Our Capitol you lost, Jim; much wealth with it likewise;
Your fame is fled, your honor's dead; your minions we despise:
In wisdom you're deficient, Jim, in energy also;
Most manfully you ran away, James Madison my Joe.

James Madison my Joe, Jim, you wing'd your flight with speed;
With courage rare, you knew not where you drove your lank old steed,
While British troops were feasting, Jim, on wine and ale you know,
You weary fled, to seek a bed, James Madison my Joe.

I fain would here advise you, Jim, where you must next retreat:
In Carter's mount there is a fount, at Thomas' country seat,
Where you may rest secure, Jim, likewise your friend Monroe,
Free from all harms and war's alarms, James Madison my Joe.

The Museum of Arts, Jim, you fitted up in style,
Where sullen jars about the wars perplexed you awhile;
But soon the noise retires, Jim, and so must you also;
Then Statesmen great shall guide the state, James Madison my Joe.

James Madison my Joe, Jim, no longer we'll withhold,
You barter'd all (at Bona's call) our liberties and gold:
A *Patriot* shall supplant you, Jim, and he shall rule in style,
While you and Tom find asylum on little Elba's Isle.

James Madison my Joe, Jim, when Bona meets you there,
With cap in hand, you all will stand, not knowing where you are;
But regulate your trade, Jim;—full well the world does know,
The firm will be, between you three, *Napoleon & Co.*

At Ghent on Christmas Eve, 1814, John Quincy Adams tells us in his diary, when he and Lord Gambier exchanged the British and American treaties of peace, they both expressed the hope that this "would be the last treaty of peace between Great Britain and the United States." Raynor Taylor's march to celebrate the peace was published c. 1815.

America ⟨and⟩ Brittannia

PEACE.

A NEW MARCH
Composed by
R: Taylor

(and so arranged as to Harmonize perfectly. with **WASHINGTON'S MARCH**
played both together)

PHILADELPHIA Published & Sold at **G**: Willig's Musical Magazine

They screw'd up their pegs, and they shoulder'd their fiddles,
They finger'd the notes of their heigh diddle diddles—
Spectators looked on—they were many a million
To see the performers in this Great Cotillion.

"Presidential Cotillion"
Anonymous
New York Statesman
September 24, 1824

7. Cotillion
1816-1840

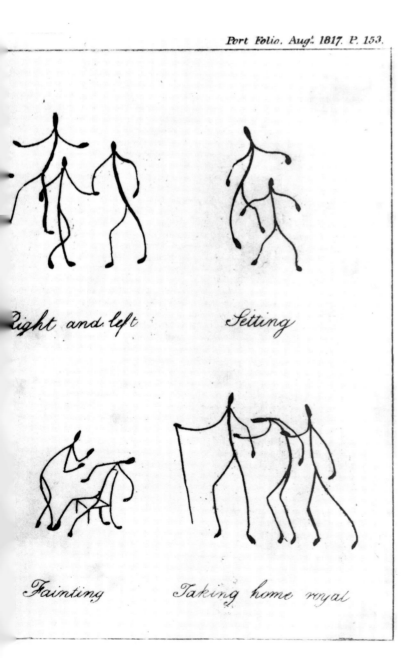

Right and left

Setting

Fainting

Taking home royal

With James Monroe's accession to the presidency in 1817, the political choreography underwent a startling transformation. The demise of the Federalist party effectively diminished political strife, and America basked in the euphoria that caused the Monroe era to become known as the "Era of Good Feelings." Reflecting the balmy political climate, the music of the period tended to be more social than political: lilting waltzes replaced martial tunes, and odes of praise were chanted instead of derogatory political ditties. As a South Carolina bard sang to Monroe in 1819 (see page 225):

> Thrice welcome! since beneath thy feet,
>   Hath *Party Discord* died;
> And now our hearts and feelings meet,
>   In one delightful tide—

During the waltz-captivated Era of Good Feelings, even President Monroe's inauguration march (for his second inauguration) was published together with a "favorite" waltz. The first known presidential waltz music (below) was composed for Monroe and published about 1817.

Shortly after he took office, James Monroe emulated George Washington and set forth on a journey that took him as far north as Portland, Maine, and as far west as Detroit. Like Washington, he was received everywhere by rapturous throngs; and great festivities, accompanied by suitably festive music, were held everywhere. Arriving at New York by steamboat from Staten Island, where he had visited Vice-President Daniel D. Tompkins, Monroe was serenaded on board, according to the *National Intelligencer* (June 17, 1817), by "the elegant band of Colonel Mercier's regiment [playing] a variety of airs." Celebrating the Fourth at Boston, where the famous Era of Good Feelings phrase originated in the *Columbian Centinel* (July 12, 1817), Monroe was greeted by the largest crowds since Washington's visit in 1789. Mounted "on an elegant dun Courser," when he arrived at "State-street, which was fancifully decorated with flags of the United States, a band of Music played on the balcony, fronting the Union Bank, [and] saluted the President as he passed." At Concord, New Hampshire, Monroe heard more water music: he "was received by a large assemblage of ladies and gentlemen on board the pleasure boat 'President,' which had been fitted up and decorated, especially for the occasion . . . and an excellent band of music was provided to enliven the scene. . . ." (*A Narrative of a Tour of Observation*, Philadelphia, 1818). Continuing to follow Washington's pattern, Monroe toured the South in 1819, going as far south as Georgia and as far west as Kentucky and Tennessee.

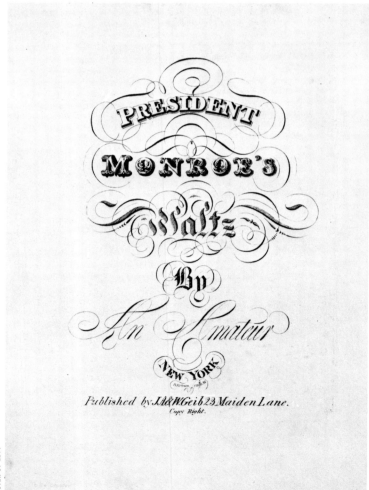

The *Richmond Enquirer* (May 7, 1819) reported on President Monroe's reception at Charleston: "Visited theatre, accompanied by the governor & several other gentlemen, both of the military & civil. When he entered, the orchestra struck up 'Hail Columbia,' and when reaching the Box prepared for him, the audience rose and gave him nine hearty cheers." The *Enquirer* also reported that at Charleston: "The following original song, written by Major Crafts, was received with universal applause, at the Public Dinner in honor of the President. . . ." Major Crafts sang the praises of Monroe, of the recent acquisition of all of Florida through the Adams-Onís Treaty, and of the delights of a partyless regime. No tune was given.

> When Princes through their subject lands
>   Advance in proud array,
> Their path is filled with warlike bands,
>   Who guard them on their way.
> A NATION'S BLESSINGS are thy guard,
> COLUMBIA'S CHIEF, and thy reward.
>
> Welcome! thrice welcome! from the North
>   Whose hills are robed in snow;
> To where the torrid gulf goes forth,
>   And the hot sunbeams glow.
> Welcomed throughout with joy and glee;
> Now CAROLINA welcomes thee.
>
> Thine is Concord's olive wreath,
>   And thine the laurelled brow;
> Since FLORIDA, with fragrant breath,
>   Accords her virgin vow.
> New States, by thee to Freedom given,
> Shall waft thy bloodless praise to Heaven.
>
> Thrice welcome! since beneath thy feet,
>   Hath *Party Discord* died;
> And now our hearts and feelings meet,
>   In one delightful tide—
> While all commend to God above,
> The COUNTRY and the CHIEF we love.

Monroe's travels were musically commemorated by the Italian-born composer Stephen Cristiani in this march, published in 1819, with handsome geographical symbols illuminating its title.

Portrait of James Monroe by Thomas Sully (1820)

PRESIDENT
MONROE'S MARCH
FOR THE
Piano Forte.
Composed by
STEPHEN CRISTIANI.
PHILADELPHIA,
Published by G. E. Blake, No: 13 South 5th Street.

TEMPO DI MARCIA.

No. 27 Blake's Musical Miscellany. — Copy right secured.

Monroe's March.

LESTER S. LEVY

The politically monophonic Era of Good Feelings came to an end with the turbulent presidential election of 1824. To compensate for the disappearance of the opposing Federalist party, a cacophony of conflicting factions broke out within Republican ranks, and no fewer than four contenders for the presidency were backed: William H. Crawford, the secretary of the treasury; Henry Clay, the Speaker of the House; John Quincy Adams, the secretary of state; and Andrew Jackson, the rough-and-ready idol of the people. Despite the wealth of candidates, with their opposing if not downright hostile ideo-logies, the 1824 campaign seems to have been the least musical of presidential elections. But if songs were few, the old bite was not entirely absent. The unknown author of "Presidential Cotillion," a poem that might or might not have been intended to be sung, brilliantly demonstrated that the art of versified political satire still flourished. Translating current political rivalries into choreographic terms, he set the scene at the spectacular ball given at Castle Island for Lafayette shortly after he arrived on his official visit to the United States in 1824. From the *New York Statesman* (September 24, 1824):

PRESIDENTIAL COTILLION.

Castle Garden was splendid one night—tho' the wet
Put off for some evenings the ball for Fayette.
The arrangements were rich—the occasion was pat,
And the whole was in style; but I sing not of that.

Ye Graces attend to a poet's condition,
And bring your right heels to the second position;
I sing of a dance, such as never was seen
On Fairy-tripp'd meadow, or muse haunted green.

The length of the room, and the height of the hall,
The price of the tickets, the cost of the ball,
And the sums due for dresses, I'm glad to forget—
I'd rather pay off the whole national debt.

The fiddlers were Editors, rang'd on the spot,
There were strings that were rosin'd, and strings that were not;
Who furnished the instruments I do not know,
But each of the band drew a *very long bow.*

They screw'd up their pegs, and they shoulder'd their fiddles,
They finger'd the notes of their heigh diddle diddles—
Spectators look'd on—they were many a million,
To see the performers in this Great Cotillion.

One Adams led first Miss Diplomacy out,
And Crawford Miss Money—an heiress no doubt—
And Jackson Miss Dangerous, a tragical actor,
And Clay, Madam Tariff, of home manufacture.

There was room for a sett just below, and each buck
Had a belle by his side, like a drake with his duck;
But the first sett attracted the whole room's attention,
For they cut the capers most worthy of mention.

They bow'd and they courtesied, round went all eight,
Right foot was the word and chassee was the gait,
Then they ballanc'd to partners, and turn'd them about,
And each one alternate was in and was out.

Some kick'd and some floundered, some set and some bounded,
Till the music was drowned—the figure confounded,
Some danc'd *dos a dos*, and some danc'd *contreface*,
And some promenaded—and all lost their place.

In the midst of this great pantomimic ballette
What guest should arrive but the great La Fayette.
The dancers all bowed, and the fiddlers chang'd tune,
Like Apollo's banjo to the man in the moon.

How sweet were the notes, and how bold was the strain!
O, when shall we list to such concord again!
The hall was sky covered with Freedom's bright arch,
And it rung to the music of Liberty's march.

"*The Hunters of Kentucky,*" *written for Andrew Jackson after the Battle of New Orleans (see page 212), was brought out as sheet music in 1822; it was probably used as a campaign song in his behalf in 1824. More atmospherically colorful than politically persuasive, the song was revived again and widely used for Jackson during the campaign of 1828.*

The Hunters of Kentucky.

as Sung in Character
by
Mr PETRIE
with unbounded applause
at
Chatham Garden Theatre
the
Symphonies & Accompaniments.
By
WILLIAM BLONDELL.

Price 25 cts

New York: Published by T. Birch. 235 Chapple near Canal St.

ALLEGRO

Ye Gentlemen and Ladies fair, who grace this famous ci_ty, Just lis_ten, if you've

time to spare, while I rehearse a dit_ty; And for the op_por_tun_i_ty con_

"Corrupt bargain," cried the infuriated followers of Andrew Jackson when John Quincy Adams, who had won the presidency in 1824 despite Jackson's majority of popular votes, appointed his erstwhile antagonist Henry Clay as his secretary of state. In the balloting for president in the House of Representatives, Clay had cast his decisive vote for Adams, and his subsequent appointment by Adams was widely construed as a prearranged deal between the two men to gain the current presidency for Adams and the next one for Clay. Whether or not this accusation was justified, it influenced public opinion against the brilliantly able but personally forbidding Adams during his uneasy presidency and later, in the election campaign of 1828, when the "corrupt bargain" was played up for all it was worth as propaganda against both Adams and Clay.

Adams's victory was, of course, joyfully acclaimed in New England. At inaugural celebrations held in Boston on March 4, 1825, a number of odes were sung saluting the presidential Adamses, John and John Quincy, and hailing the dawn of a new era of northern supremacy now that the quarter-century-long hold of the Virginia "dynasty" had been broken. Three of these songs, preserved in the Adams Family Papers, include "Star of the North, An Ode for the Celebration at Faneuil Hall," to the tune of "Rise Columbia," by Thomas Wells, which began and ended:

> Star of the North!—we greet thy dawn—
> Of Peace, of Arts, the herald bright;
> Millions of Freemen, yet unborn,
> Shall bless the coming of thy light.—
> Sound the Clarion—sound afar—
> Hail the North's ascendant STAR.

A second ode, to an unspecified tune, by the noted poet James Gates Percival, was to be sung at a dinner in honor of Adams's election. The last stanza went:

> To Him, who alike inherits
> The *name*, and the *place* of his sire;—
> Who has won the *rank* he merits,
> By a vigour that cannot tire:—
> Let the hearts of NEW-ENGLAND cherish
> His high, and well-earned fame;
> Till a glory, that cannot perish,
> Be gathered around his name.

The third song, "Adam's Ode" by Charles Sprague, paid homage to the venerable John Adams, then ninety years old. No tune was given.

> Lo! where the SAGE, to Freedom dear,
> Sinks slowly to his honoured rest:—
> One last, glad echo fills his ear,
> One last, proud transport swells his breast.
> Hark! COLUMBIA's sacred voice—
> *Another* ADAMS is her choice!

Portrait of John Quincy Adams
by Thomas Sully (1824)

This march for John Quincy Adams, elegantly embellished with graphic and tonal flourishes, was published about 1825.

John Quincy Adams's presidency brought him no personal satisfaction. Summing up the year 1825 in his diary on December 31, 1825, the congenitally insecure Adams wrote: "The year . . . has witnessed my elevation to the Chief Magistracy of my country; to the summit of laudable, or at least blameless worldly ambition; not, however, in a manner satisfactory to pride . . . ; not by the unequivocal suffrages of a majority of the people; with perhaps two-thirds of the whole people adverse to the actual result." Never one to view the world or himself through rose-tinted glasses, Adams added: "Nearly one year of this service has passed, with little change of the public opinions or feelings." Adams summed up his ineffable boredom in his entry for December 7, 1826: "The succession of visitors from my break-fasting to my dining hour . . . is inexpressibly distress-ing. . . . An hour's walk before daylight is my only exercise for the day [in summer it was a predawn swim in the Potomac]. . . . Then to dress and breakfast I have scarce an hour. Then five-and-twenty visitors, or more, from ten of the morning till five in the afternoon, leave me not a moment of leisure for reflection or writing. By the time evening approaches, my strength and spirits are both exhausted. Such has been the course of this day. Such will be that of how many more?"

*Samuel F. B. Morse's portrait of Lafayette,
painted in Washington in 1825*

On August 16, 1824, the beloved Marquis de Lafayette landed at Staten Island to begin his extraordinary visit as "the nation's guest"; he was to depart sixteen months later laden with tokens of America's enduring affection and gratitude: an official gift of two hundred thousand dollars, a vast grant of lands, and honorary United States citizenship. The apparently inexhaustible supply of jubilation expended in receiving Lafayette everywhere he went—and he went everywhere—must surely have established an all-time record for sustained public emotion. At the first news of his arrival, the streets of New York filled with excited crowds. A New York correspondent writes to the *National Intelligencer* (August 19, 1824): "The streets and windows are lined with the beauty and fashion of the day . . . the thunders of the artillery are roaring around us, mingled with the shrill notes of the fife, the roll of the drum, the ringing of the bells, and the spirit-stirring music of united bands." To complete the picture of the brilliant scene he adds: "The waters are covered with steam boats and barges gaily and beautifully decorated—and almost the entire population of the great city are assembled to receive and welcome, with overflowing hearts, the Soldier and Patriot of the Revolution."

This triumphal arch, reproduced in the Globe *(October 16, 1824), awaited Lafayette in Philadelphia; it was artfully constructed of canvas and painted to simulate marble by the scene painters of the New Theatre.*

230

Lafayette's visit initiated an unprecedented boom in the music-publishing industry.

Lafayette triumphantly toured the length and breadth of the nation—all twenty-four states—with occasional return engagements in major cities; for example, he revisited New York at least four times, each time receiving a tumultuous welcome. Miles of newsprint were consumed in describing the delirious national orgy of welcome, which included banquets, balls, theatrical performances, religious services, resounding eulogies, stately odes, sentimental reminiscences of the Revolution, military escorts, elaborate parades in the grand tradition, triumphal arches, recitations by school-children, illuminations, fireworks, and a great deal besides. When Lafayette arrived at Philadelphia after a tour of New England, he was escorted into the city by a spectacular parade that included veterans of the Revolution riding in brilliantly decorated carriages, and even a portable printing press, from which freshly printed odes in praise of the hero were distributed.

Lafayette was greeted everywhere with specially composed songs and other music. In Baltimore a naval officer, Captain R. T. Spence, serenaded the illustrious visitor to the tune of "The Star-Spangled Banner" in a lofty ode of six stanzas, "Soldier of Fame." Printed in the *National Intelligencer* (November 9, 1824), stanza 2 of Captain Spence's ode went:

> Full of honors and years, he is spared by his GOD
>   To visit the home of the happy once more;
> The path of his glory triumphantly trod,
>   With *Victory* perch'd on the standard he bore,
> Invited, he comes, 'mid the shouts of the world,
>   The shouts of *Ten Millions* who gladden our clime—
> The "Star Spangled Banner" so proudly unfurl'd—
>   The page of his Glory immortal as Time.

And when Lafayette revisited Brandywine, where he had fought at Washington's side in 1777, he was lauded to the tune of "Auld Lang Syne," according to the *National Intelligencer* (August 20, 1825).

LAFAYETTE AT BRANDYWINE.

> Should days of trial be forgot,
>   Although those days have fled?
> Can we neglect the sacred spot
>   Where Patriot Heroes bled?
>   Ah, no! those days of auld lang syne,
>   We never can forget;
>   When with our Sires, to *Brandywine*,
>   Came gallant LAFAYETTE.

The Chivalrous Knight of France

Written on the occasion of General La Fayette's visit to America in 1821.

By Col. W. H. Hamilton

The Music by C. Meineke.

BALTIMORE Published by JOHN COLE No 123 Market Street.

MAESTOSO, ANIMATO.

A Knight of France, with soul of fire, In distance heard the thunder roll, 'Twas

ENTERED ACCORDING TO ACT OF CONGRESS THE 6th DAY OF OCTOBER 1824 BY JOHN COLE OF THE STATE OF MARYLAND.

On June 17, 1825, the fiftieth anniversary of the Battle of Bunker Hill, Lafayette laid the cornerstone of the Bunker Hill Monument (it was completed in 1843), and Daniel Webster addressed a throng of thousands of spectators that included forty Bunker Hill survivors. The *National Intelligencer* (June 25, 1825), reporting the story from a Boston source, reprinted a number of original hymns and odes that were sung there, among them one to the tune of "St. Martin's," which began:

> O Glorious day! that saw the array
> of freemen in their might,
> When here they stood, unused to blood,
> Yet dared th' unequal fight.

~~~

Of the numerous pieces of music inspired by Lafayette's visit, perhaps the most curious is "Massa Georgee Washington and General La Fayette," a precursor of the blackface minstrel song. Written in an all-but-incomprehensible gibberish intended to simulate Negro dialect, the most memorable quality of this song, apart from its curiosity value, is its wonderfully distinctive cover art, representing the actor James Roberts in blackface makeup and the costume of a Continental soldier (Massa Georgee Washington?) he wore when performing the song to "unrivalled applause." Micah Hawkins, who wrote the words and music, was a Long Island composer and playwright who dipped into a number of unrelated professions: coachmaker, hotelkeeper, grocer, performing musician. The text of "Massa Georgee Washington . . ." is notable for its reference to "Unkle Sam," a nickname for the government of the United States that had first come into use during the War of 1812.

"MASSA GEORGEE WASHINGTON"

AND

General La Fayette.

*As Sung in Character by M*r* ROBERTS, with unrivalled applause;*
(at the)

THEATRE, CHATHAM GARDENS.

Written & Composed by,

Micah Hawkins.

NEW YORK,

Engraved, Printed, & Sold, by, E. Riley, 29, Chatham Street

Copy-right secured, according to Law.   October 7 1824. James Dill, Clerk.

"Grand Canal Celebration, View of the Fleet Preparing to Form in Line," by Archibald Robertson (1825)

"Yesterday was a proud day for the state of New York. The GRAND CANAL [Erie Canal], commenced on the anniversary of American Independence, 1817, is completed, and at 10 o'clock yesterday morning, the first boat borne by the waters of Lake Erie, descended into the Canal." This thrilling news story in the *New-York Gazette & General Advertiser* (October 27, 1825) was transmitted from Buffalo to the city of New York in only eighty minutes by the successive firing of cannon placed at intervals within earshot between the two cities. If it was a proud day for New York, it was a day of supreme vindication for New York's governor De Witt Clinton, who over a period of fifteen years had dedicatedly and unswervingly fought for the canal against all odds and ridicule (the canal was popularly referred to as "Clinton's Ditch"). On October 27, 1825, an extra edition of the *Buffalo Journal* reported that on the preceding day: "The 'Seneca Chief' of Buffalo, led off [a procession of vessels] in fine style, drawn by four grey horses, fancifully caparisoned. . . . The whole moved from the shore under a discharge of small arms, from the rifle company, with music from the band, and the loud and reiterated cheers from the throng on shore, which were returned by the companies on board the various boats." Apparently this was only a dress rehearsal, for: "The procession was then reformed and returned . . . to the Court House, where Sheldon Smith, Esq. delivered a well written and highly gratifying address, after which was sung by the Choir to the tune of 'Hail Columbia,' the following Ode, with fine effect:"

CELEBRATION ODE.

Strike the Lyre! with joyous note,
Let the sound through azure float:
The task is o'er—the work complete,
And Erie's waves with ocean meet—
Bearing afar the rich bequest,
While smiling commerce greets the west.
  See where the peaceful waters glide
  Through woodlands wild, as if in pride,
  To mark that learning makes her home,
  Where Solitude had set her throne.
    Strike the Lyre! 'tis envy's knell—
    Pallid Fear, within her cell
    Shrinks aghast—while Truth and Fame
    On glory's scroll 'grave CLINTON's name.

Thousands of spectators lined the shores as the first canal fleet progressed toward New York, and joyous celebrations were held in towns and cities on the way. As for New York City, the *New-York Gazette* (November 4, 1825) reported: "It is calculated that from 40 to 50,000 strangers have already arrived in this city to witness the proceedings—We hope our fellow citizens will afford every accommodation to strangers, for the inns and boarding houses are 'chock full.'" When the fleet reached New York, Governor Clinton performed the ceremony of the "wedding of the waters," pouring a kegful of Lake Erie water into the Atlantic (the Hudson), and at this point, according to the *New-York Gazette* (November 7, 1825), "the fine band attached to the Cyane, struck up with exquisite effect, the appropriate air of 'The Meeting of the Waters.'"

THE MEETING OF THE WATERS
of
HUDSON & ERIE.

Let the day be forever remember'd with pride
That beheld the proud Hudson to Erie allied;
O the last sand of Time from his glass shall descend
Ere a union, so fruitful of glory, shall end.

Yet, it is not that Wealth now enriches the scene,
Where the treasures of Art, and of Nature, convene;
'Tis not that this union our coffers may fill—
O! no—it is something more exquisite still.

'Tis, that Genius has triumph'd—and Science prevail'd,
Tho' Prejudice flouted, and Envy assail'd,
It is, that the vassals of Europe may see
The progress of mind, in a land that is free.

All hail! to a project so vast and sublime!
A bond, that can never be sever'd by time,
Now unites us still closer—all jealousies cease,
And our hearts, like our waters, are mingled in peace.

New York staged a parade to celebrate the birth of the "Empire State" that rivalled the great constitutional parades in grandeur. Representative groups of not fewer than thirty professions marched, led by "four buglemen on Horseback, [followed by] a band of music, [and] the Marshall and his aids. The splendid band, composed of professors, was furnished by the [city] corporation, and played several pieces of music composed for the occasion." The *New-York Gazette* (November 7, 1825) continued: "Preceded by a full band of musicians, in dresses of scarlet and gold, came the members of Columbia College [more professors?] . . . the Typographical Society . . . [marched behind] a car drawn by 4 horses, upon which were two printing presses, handsomely gilt, [upon which] Pressmen were busily engaged in striking off copies of the following Ode, written for the occasion by Mr. S. Woodworth, printer, which were industriously distributed among the public by two Heralds and two Mercuries. . . ."

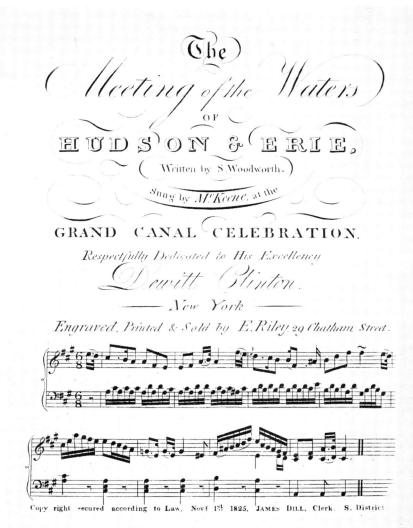

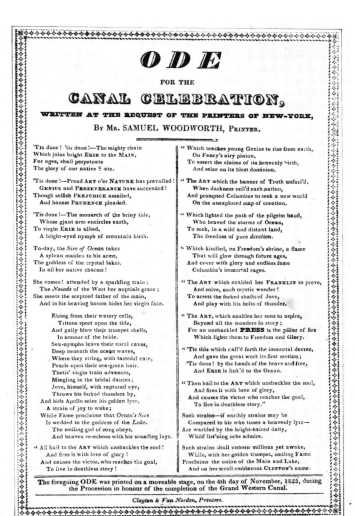

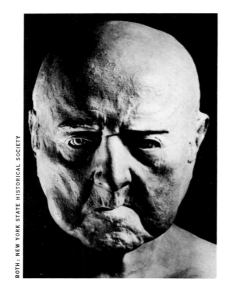

*The sculptor John Browere cast these memorable
life masks of Adams and Jefferson in their old age.*

Festive semicentennial celebrations of American independence became ceremonies of mourning when—by a supremely ironic coincidence—both Thomas Jefferson and John Adams died on the day of the anniversary, July 4, 1826. For most of their long lives—Jefferson lived to be eighty-three and Adams ninety-two—the two men were strongly tied by bonds of alternating conflict and friendship. At the end Jefferson, who had willed himself to survive until the Fourth of July, died asking, "This is the Fourth?" Adams, who was aware that it was the Fourth, expired gasping the prophetic words: "Thomas Jefferson survives."

Funeral Honors by the Town of Salem.

ORDER OF SERVICES

AT THE NORTH CHURCH IN SALEM.....ON THURSDAY, AUGUST 10, 1826,

TO COMMEMORATE THE DEATHS OF

JOHN ADAMS & THOMAS JEFFERSON.

VOLUNTARY ON THE ORGAN.

INTRODUCTORY PRAYER, BY REV. MR. COLMAN.

HYMN FOR THE OCCASION, BY JOSEPH G. WATERS, ESQ.

TUNE——*Burford.*

PP. { In funeral train, in shrouds of woe,
These hallow'd courts we tread,
To pay the grateful debt we owe
To Freedom's honored dead.

P. { We come—to fan the holy flame,
That warms the patriot's breast ;
We come—to point to deathless fame
The memory of the blest.

F. { Yes, kindred spirits ! time shall swell
The splendor of your fame ;

F. { And age to age your deeds shall tell,
Your glorious deaths proclaim.

Mod. { Your shrines shall be the patriot's soul,
The bosom of the free ;
And Heaven born Freedom's golden scroll
Your epitaph shall be.

M. { Here on thy altar, Lord, we lay
Our grateful sacrifice ;

F. { Warmed by thy holy fervor, may
Its incense reach the skies.

EULOGY, BY JOSEPH E SPRAGUE, ESQ.

ANTHEM.

How are the mighty fallen ! They that were great among the Nations, and Rulers of the People.—The People will tell of their wisdom :—The righteous shall be had in everlasting remembrance, and the wise shall shine as the brightness of the firmament.—Their bodies are buried in peace ; but their name liveth evermore.

CONCLUDING PRAYER, REV. MR. WILLIAMS.

DIRGE FOR THE OCCASION, BY MR. JOCELYN.

Pleyel's Hymn.

PP. { SADLY falls the mournful knell ;
Brief those Sable emblems tell ;
Deep a Nation's dirge shall flow,
Death has laid her Sages low.

PP. { Sov'reign Ruler ! to Thy will,
Low we bend, each murmur, still ;
P. { Touch'd by Thee, the mortal breath
F. { Is eloquent,—*PP.* or quench'd in death.

F. { Mighty names, of matchless worth !
Great the deeds ye wrought on earth ;
P. { Rest,—your mortal toils are o'er,—
Hush'd the lips which wisdom bore.

P.P. { Dust to dust, th' unchang'd decree—
F. { Spirits mingle bless'd and free ;—
PP. { Rest in peace, in honor, rest,
Mourn'd in death, in mem'ry bless'd.

BENEDICTION, REV. DR. PRINCE.

W. & S. B. IVES, Printers, Court-Street.

On August 2, 1826, the bereaved John Quincy Adams wrote in his diary: ". . . we went in procession to Faneuil Hall, and heard a eulogy upon John Adams and Thomas Jefferson by Mr. Daniel Webster. . . . The Streets from the State House to the hall were thronged with a greater concourse of people than I ever witnessed in Boston. The hall itself was crowded to the utmost of its capacity. Mr. Webster was about two hours and a half in delivering his discourse, during which attention held the assembly mute." Adams noted that the music included "a funeral symphony, anthem, and dirge" which the *Boston Centinel* (August 5, 1826) partially identified as "a portion selected from a most sublime funeral Anthem, by the great *Handel* . . . also a hymn in sevens, to the popular German air of *Pleyel*." The *Centinel* approved the solid musical fare, taking the opportunity to express some gratuitous music criticism: "It was indeed no time for ingenious chromatic passages, or wildly warbling solos."

Some Account of some of the Bloody Deeds
OF
GENERAL JACKSON.

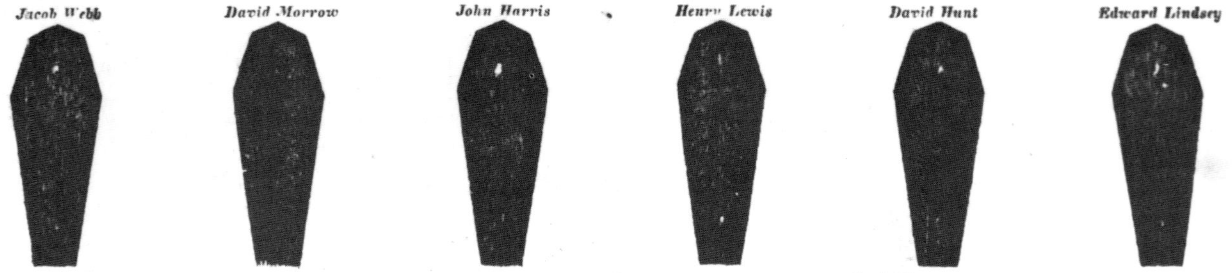

Jacob Webb   David Morrow   John Harris   Henry Lewis   David Hunt   Edward Lindsey

A brief account of the Execution of the Six Militia Men.

As we may soon expect to have the *official* documents in relation to the Six Militia Men, arrested, tried, and put to death, under the orders of General Andrew Jackson, this may not be an improper time to give to the public some of the particulars of their execution, as we have them from—"An Eye Witness," who appeals to Col. Russell, for the truth of every word he relates.

Harris was a Baptist preacher, with a large family. He had hired as a substitute for three months. This was the case with most of them. They were ignorant men, but obstinate in what they believed right, and what they had been told by their officers was right.— They were all sure they could not be kept beyond three months, and they gave up their musquets, and had provisions dealt out to them, from the public stores, before they left the camp.— This confirmed their convictions that they were right and doing what was lawful.

Col. Russel commanded at the execution. The Militia men were brought to the place in a large wagon. The military dispositions being made, Col. Russell rode up to the wagon and ordered the men so descend. Harris was

the only one who betrayed feminine weakness. The awfulness of the occasion; his wife and nine children; the parting with his son; and the fear of a quickly approaching ignominious death! quite overcome him, and he sunk in unmanly grief. No feeling of military pride could brace him up.

Col. Russel, doubtless, felt as a man, but he felt also for the pride of the army, and desired to animate the men with fortitude. "You are about to die, said he, by the sentence of a Court Martial—die like men; *like soldiers.* You have been brave in the field— you have fought well—do no disered— it to your country, or dishonour to the army, or yourselves, by any unmanly fears. Meet your fate with courage."

Harris attempted to make some apology for his conduct, but while he spoke, he wept bitterly. The fear of death, the idea that he should never again behold his wife and little ones, and his son weeping near him, had taken such entire possession of his mind that it was impossible he should rally.

Lewis, the gallant Lewis, said in a clear and manly tone, "Colonel, I have served my country well. I love it dearly, and would, if I could, serve it longer and better. I have fought bravely—*you know* I have, and here I have a right to say so myself. I

"would not wish to die in this way"— here his voice faltered, and he passed the back of his right hand over his eyes —"I did not expect it: But, I am now as firm as I have been in battle, and you shall see that I will die as become a soldier, you know I am a brave man." "Yes, Lewis, said the Colonel, you have always behaved like a brave man." Other sentences were uttered, other declarations were made, and words of comfort spoken, but they were lost on me: my attention, says an Eye Witness, being chiefly directed to Lewis.

Six coffins were ranged as directed, and on each of them knelt one of our condemned American Militia Men— Such a sight was never seen before! I trust to God it never will be seen again! Six soldiers were detailed and drawn up to fire at each man. What an awful duty! Their white caps were drawn over the faces of the unhappy men.— Harris evidently trembled, and I could almost persuade myself that the heart of Lewis was enlarged, and that his bosom rose with manly courage to meet death. The fatal word was given and they all fell.

As we approached the scene of blood and carnage, Lewis gave signs of life; the rest were all dead—he crawled upon his coffin. After the lapse of a few

minutes he said—I give his very words: "Colonel"—the Colonel was close to him—"Colonel, I am not killed, but I am sadly cut and mangled." His body was now examined and it was found that but four balls had wounded him. "Colonel," said he, "did I behave well." "Yes, Lewis"—said the Colonel in the kindest tone of voice—"like a man." "Well sir," said he, "have I not atoned for this offence? *Shall I not live?*" The Colonel was much agitated, and gave orders that the Surgeon should, if possible, preserve his life. They did all that skill and humanity could do— it was all of no avail. Poor Lewis expressed a great desire to live—"not," said he at one time, "that I fear death, but I would repent me of some sins, and I desire to live yet a little longer in the world." He suffered inconceivable agony, from his wounds, and died on the fourth day.

Many a soldier has wept over his grave. He was a brave man and much beloved. He suffered twenty deaths. —I have seen the big drops chase each other down his forehead with pain and anguish. There was much sensibility and sympathy throughout the camp.— I would not have, unjustly and unnecessarily, signed this death warrant for all the wealth of all the Indies. The soldiers detailed to shoot Lewis had,

from strong feelings of sympathy, or mistaken humanity failed to shoot him —but four balls had entered his body.

"An Eye Witness" appeals to Col. Russell, who he thinks now lives in Alabama, for the perfect truth of this sketch. He does not fear but the Colonel will keenly recollect and faithfully depict the horrors of the day on which six Americans were shot to death under his command—but not by his orders.

The order bears date the very day after *General Jackson* returned in triumph to New Orleans, and the day before he joyfully went, under triumphal arches, to the Temple of the living God; where, says the historian, "they crowned their adored General with laurels." The order for the execution of these six unhappy men bears date January 22, 1815. His crown of laurels had not yet withered, when blood, the life's blood of his countrymen, of his fellow soldiers, flowed plentifully by his order. May that order and its consequences, sink deep into the hearts of the American people and steel them against him who had no flesh in his obdurate heart; who did not feel for Man; in the midst of Joy and Revelry, almost in the more immediate presence of his Creator, who issued the fatal order to put his fellow creatures to death, and to make their wives & children, widows and orphans.

MOURNFUL TRAGEDY;

Or, the death of Jacob Webb, David Morrow, John Harris, Henry Lewis, David Hunt, & Edward Lindsey—six militia men, who were condemned to die, the sentence approved by Major General Jackson, and by his order the whole six shot.

O! DID you hear that plaintive cry
Borne on the southern breeze?
Saw you John Harris earnest pray
For mercy, on his knees?

Low to the earth he bent, and pray'd
For pardon from his chief;
But to his earnest prayer for life
Jackson, alas! was deaf.

"Spare me"—he said—"I mean no wrong,
"My heart was always true
"Priest for my country's cause it beat,
"And next, great Chief, for you.

"We thought our time of service out—
"Thought it our right to go;
"We meant to violate no law,
"Nor wish'd to shun the foe.

"Our officers declared that we
"Had but three months to stay;
"We served these three months faithfully.
"Up to the latest day.

"No one suspects intended wrong;
"The judgment only erred:
"In such a case, O noble Chief,
"Let mercy's voice be heard.

"At home an aged mother waits
"To clasp her only son;
"A wife, and little children—this arm
"Alone depend upon.

"Cut me not off from those dear ties;
"So soon from life's young bloom;
"O 'tis a dreadful thing to die,
"And moulder in the tomb!

"Sure mercy is a noble gem
"On every Chieftain's brow;
"More sparkling than a diadem—
"O exercise it now.—"

'Twas all in vain, John Harris' pray'r,
'Tis past the soul's belief:
Hard as the flint was Jackson's heart;
He would not grant relief.

He order'd Harris out to die,
And five poor fellows more!
Young, gallant men, in prime of life,
To welter in their gore!!

Methinks I hear the muffled drum,
And see the column move;
Lo here they come—how sad their looks
Farewell to life and love!

See six black coffins rang'd along—
Six graves before them made;
Webb, Lindsey, Harris, Lewis, Hunt,
And Morrow kneeled and prayed.

They kneel'd and pray'd, and tho't of home,
And all its dear delights.
The deadly tubes are levell'd now—
The scene my soul affrights!

Sure he will spare! Sure Jackson yet
Will all reprieve but one—
O hark! those shrieks! that cry of death!
The dreadful deed is done!

All six militia men were shot;
And O! it seems to me
A dreadful deed—a bloody act
Of needless cruelty.

A short time before the execution of the militia-men, seven regular soldiers were shot near Nashville, by a band of regulars scarcely sufficient to guard the prisoners.— They were confined in a house, and taken out and executed one at a time, there being scarcely enough men for the purpose of executing and guarding at the same moment. An eighth soldier was to have been executed at the same time. He was a young man, who had deserted one month before his time had expired. General Jackson doomed him to die with the others. He was saved by a writ of habeas corpus from Judge M'Nairy, who fell under Jackson's displeasure for snatching this one victim from his blood-stained hands. If Jackson's army had been at hand, no doubt M'Nairy would have shared the fate of Judge Hall and Judge Fromentin. Capital punishments in an army, are designed for example as well as for penalty; but in this case it was a transaction of horror to peaceful citizens: no army was there to witness the bloody tragedy. He has ever been a man of "blood and carnage."

Do not be startled, gentle reader at the picture before you. It is all true and every body ought to know it. Gen. Jackson having made an assault upon Samuel Jackson, in the streets of Nashville, & the latter not being disposed to stand still and be beaten, stooped down for a stone to defend himself. While in the act of doing so, Gen. Jackson drew the sword from his cane and run it through Samuel Jackson's body, the sword entering his back and coming out of his breast. For this offence an indictment was found against Genl. Jackson, by a grand jury, upon which he was subsequently arraigned and tried. But finding means to persuade the petit jury that he committed the act in self-defence, he was acquitted. Gentle reader, it is for you to say, whether this man, who carries a sword cane, and is willing to run it through the body of any one who may presume to stand in his way, is a fit person to be our President.

Poor JOHN WOODS, he was a generous hearted, noble fellow as ever lived, who had volunteered in the service of his country. He was on guard one day at Fort Strother—the officer of the guard had permitted him to go to his tent, and snatch a hasty breakfast; whilst disposing of his scanty meal, seated on the ground beside his skillet, an upstart little officer, who was not Woods' equal at home, ordered him to pick up and scatter off some bones that lay scattered about the place —Woods refused, and the little officer attempted to compel him. At this instant, Gen. Jackson, having heard the dispute, came out of his tent, and without knowing any thing of the merits of the case, repeatedly vociferated—"Shoot the damn'd rascal!—Shoot the damn'd rascal." For this offence, the unfortunate, the gallant Woods, was tried, condemned and shot. Before his trial, Gen. Jackson used this language to the court-martial. *"By the immortal God! if you find him guilty I will not pardon him!"* And he kept his promise, though he did offer a pardon provided he would enlist in the regular service—Thus perished as noble a fellow as ever lived, for as trifling an offence as ever took the life of man!!!

On the 27th day of March, 1814, General Jackson had found at an Indian village, at the bend of the Tallapoosie, about 1000 Indians, with their squaws and children, "running about among their huts." The following is an account of the sanguinary massacre which took place;—it is Gen. Jackson's own, and therefore must be received as sufficient evidence against himself. He says:—"DETERMINING TO EXTERMINATE them, I detached Gen. Coffee with the mounted men, and nearly the whole of the Indian force, early on the morning of yesterday, to cross the river about two miles below the encampment, and to surround the bend in such a manner as that none of them should escape by attempting to cross the river." The result he states details:—"*Five hundred and fifty seven* warriors, and shot. *left dead on the Peninsula, and a great number of them were killed by the horsemen in attempting to cross the river; it is believed that no more than ten escaped. We continu-*

...ed to DESTROY *many of them who had concealed themselves under the banks of the river, until we were prevented by the night. THIS MORNING WE KILLED 16 WHICH HAD BEEN CONCEALED.*"

We ask you to pause and reflect that the above tragic narration of cold-blooded and merciless cruelty, is taken from an official communication made by General Andrew Jackson.

The General, after sleeping (with what composure, we cannot say) thro' the night to witness the tragedy we speak of, awoke the ensuing morning surrounded by the corpses of "five hundred and seventy" fellow creatures, to cause, by way of worthy afterpiece, sixteen others to be dragged from their concealments, and put to death in cold blood. Well may we note the military reputation of our country, has not done enough to disqualify him, in the eyes of the people as virtuous as they are free, for the office he seeks at their hands.

...ning we killed sixteen which had been concealed"—and the man who acts and speaks thus; who has half as much blood upon his conscience, as he has upon his hands,—he, forsooth, is to be called the peer and *like* of Washington, the happy warrior,—

"the
Whom every man at arms could wish to be?"

But it is time to have done with the unpleasant subject. We will observe in addition to the details already given, that the village was burnt, and several women and children killed. In conclusion, we ask our fellow citizens, whether Genl. Jackson, though he has contributed largely—

Gen. Jackson, detailing his progress among the Indians, in the course of which, men, WOMEN and CHILDREN, were indiscriminately "exterminated," their towns burnt and their country laid waste, with the utmost complacency and *sang froid*, says, in his letter dated, "Camp before St. Marks, April 9, 1818"—"Capt. M'Ever having hoisted English colours on board of his boats, Francis *the Prophet*, Hocomohemutcho and *two others*, were *decoyed* on board. *There have been hung to-day*—" Reader, mark the perfect indifference with which Gen. Jackson shoots, hangs or stabs his fellow beings, with or without trial, and the more than callous, aye, even exulting composure, with which he details his horrid and bloody deeds! If the Indians, according to the customs of their nation, put to death a prisoner, all the feelings of our nature rise into indignation against them. With what feelings then should we contemplate the *decoying* and cold-blooded murder of prisoners, by a civilized man, in the face of the laws and customs of his country?

FRANKLIN, Tenn. September 10, 1813.

A difference which had been for some months brewing between Gen. Jackson and myself, produced on Saturday, the 4th inst. in the town of Nashville, the most outrageous affray ever witnessed in a civilized country. In communicating the affair to my friends and fellow-citizens, I limit myself to the statement of a few leading facts, the truth of which I am ready to establish by judicial proofs.

1. That myself and my brother, Jesse Benton, arriving in Nashville on the morning of the affray, and knowing of General Jackson's threats, went and took lodgings in a different house from the one in which he was, on purpose to avoid him.

2. That the General and some of his friends came the house where we had put up, and commenced the attack by levelling a pistol at me, when I had no weapon drawn, and advancing upon me at a quick pace, without giving me time to draw one.

3. That seeing this, my brother fired upon General Jackson, when he had got within eight or ten feet of me.

4. That four other pistols were fired in quick succession; one by General Jackson at me; two by me at the General; and one by Col. Coffee at me. In the course of this firing, General Jackson was brought to the ground; but received no hurt.

5. That daggers were then drawn. Col. Coffee and Mr. Alexander Donaldson made at me, and gave me five slight wounds. Captain Hammond and Mr. Stokeley Hays engaged my brother, who being still under the effect of a severe wound he had lately received in a duel, was not able to resist two men. They got him down; and while Capt. Hammond beat him on the head to make him lie still, Mr. Hays attempted to stab him, and wounded him in both arms, as he lay on his back parrying the thrusts

with his naked hands. From this situation a generous hearted citizen of Nashville, Mr. Sumner, relieved him. Before he came to the ground, my brother clapped a pistol to the breast of Mr. Hays, to thou him through, but it missed fire.

6. My own and my brother's pistols carried two balls each; for it was our intention, if driven to arms, to have no child's play. The pistols fired at me were so near that the blaze of the muzzle of one of them burnt the sleeve of my coat, and the other ashed at my head at a little more than arms length from it.

7. Capt. Carroll was to have taken part in the affray, but was absent by the permission of General Jackson, as he has proved by the General's certificate, a certificate which reflects I know not whether less honor upon the General or upon the Captain.

8. That this certificate was made upon me in the house where the Judge of the District, Mr. Searcy, had his lodgings! Nor has the civil authority yet taken cognizance of this horrible outrage.

These facts are sufficient to fix the public opinion. For my own part, I think it scandalous that such things should take place at any time; but particularly so at the present moment, when the public service requires the aid of all its citizens.—As for the name of courage, God forbid that I should ever attempt to gain it by becoming a bully.—Those who know me, know full well that I would give a thousand times more for the reputation of Croghan in defending his post, than I would for the reputation of all the duellists and gladiators that ever appeared upon the face of the earth.

THOMAS HART BENTON, Lieut. Col. 39th Infantry.

And now a member of the Senate of the United States.

With the resumption of the two-party system, the presidential campaign of 1828 set a standard for character assassination and dirty tricks probably unsurpassed in the history of American presidential elections except for the campaign of 1972. Outrageous personal slanders were hurled at the opposing candidates by the adherents of their newly formed political parties: John Quincy Adams's National Republicans and Andrew Jackson's Democratic Republicans (which later became the Democratic party). Old scandals and rumors of scandals were exhumed and embellished: Adams (like his father) was accused of kingly pretensions, of gambling, political apostasy (he had switched from the Federalists to the Republicans at the time of the *Chesapeake-Leopard* incident in 1807), cheating, bigotry, and even—ludicrously—of pimping for Czar Alexander I when he was minister to Russia. Above all, his rumored "corrupt bargain" with Clay in 1824 was stressed and restressed; Adams was derisively referred to as "a Clay president." In return, Jackson was called an adulterer, a bigamist, a traitor, a murderer, the son of a prostitute mother and a mulatto father, and more besides. The most personally hurtful of these accusations was the charge of adultery stemming from Jackson's marriage in 1791 to Rachel Robards under the mistaken assumption that she had been legally divorced from her first husband; they were remarried when the mistake was discovered two years later. Jackson bitterly believed that his beloved wife's death, shortly before his inauguration, had been caused by the painful scandal. Anti-Jackson cartoons abounded, among them this lurid handbill, complete with multiple coffins and poesy, accusing Jackson of the cold-blooded murder of six militiamen who had served under his command during the Creek War in 1813. The men, in fact, had been found guilty by a court-martial and sentenced to be executed for mutiny, desertion, and robbery, but the "Coffin Hand Bill," published and distributed by John Binns, the publisher of the administration newspaper, the Philadelphia *Democratic Press*, sought to convince Americans that Jackson was a tyrant and a wanton murderer. In a letter published in the pro-Jackson *Richmond Enquirer* (May 8, 1828), an Albany correspondent deplored the "vile slanders against Jackson." He wrote: "The mode in which this official electioneering has been carried on, has kindled a flame, which will singe the whiskers of those members of Congress, who have prostituted their franking privilege, by retailing falsehoods. . . ."

Political bards recovered their muted voices in 1828, and scurrilous ballads were again heard at political functions and read in newspapers, with John Quincy Adams as the special target. For example, he was mercilessly attacked in a series of parodies on "John Anderson, My Joe," in which was reviewed just about every accusation that had ever been made against him, as well as a few against his father. In the installment that appeared in the Philadelphia *Mercury* (August 23, 1828), the old charge that John Quincy Adams had been the author of the unsavory songs in 1803 about Thomas Jefferson and Sally Hemings was revived; even Adams's memorable phrase describing astronomical observatories as "lighthouses in the sky" was ridiculed. Of the three Scottish locutions in the text, *aboon* means above, *baith* means both, and *amaist* means almost.

SONG.

John Adams' son, my jo, John!
  When life ye first began;
Amang the fed'ral crew, John,
  Ye were a leading man;
They did their best to lay, John,
  Our constitution low;
And ye aboon them a' were seen,
  John Adams' son, my jo!

John Adams' son, my jo, John!
  Ye prais'd the British then,
To build up aristocracy,
  Ye plied baith tongue an' pen;
Ye libell'd Thomas Jefferson,
  As "dusky Sal" will show,
Wi' wit lascivious an' profane,
  John Adams' son, my jo!

～～

John Adams' son, my jo, John!
  Yere time is amaist spent—
The people won't be governed
  B' intrigue and management;
Ere one short year goes by, John,
  To Quincy ye shall go,
And "build light houses in the sky,"
  John Adams' son, my jo!

The attack on the president continued in the *Richmond Enquirer* (September 30, 1828):

JOHNNY THE BROKER.

O, Johnny Q. my Jo, John, your father sought a crown,
To deck his brow, and you would now, pull freedom's temple
   down,
Could you but one obtain, John, you ne'er would stand for wo,
You'd seize with joy, the glittering toy, O, Johnny Q. my Jo.

~~~

O, Johnny Q. my Jo, John, the Monticellian sage,
You did oppose, in verse and prose, when party strife did rage;
You then was with the Feds, John, who fain would overthrow
What had been done, by Washington, O, Johnny Q. my Jo.

O, Johnny Q. my Jo, John, when federalism failed
To raise a Throne, 'twas then alone, that equal rights prevailed;
And you, to gain the *loaves*, John, Republicans do know,
Did but pretend to be their friend, O, Johnny Q. my Jo.

~~~

O, Johnny Q. my Jo, John, your honor's deeply stained,
The gem that now hangs on your brow, by bargain was ob-
   tained,—
A bargain made with Clay, John, "as all the world do know,"
And Webster too, was bought by you, O, Johnny Q. my Jo.

~~~

O, Johnny Q. my Jo, John, your race will soon be run,
Nor regal gem, nor diadem, descend upon your son;
You, to your country seat, John, reluctant then must go,
Where time mispent, you will lament, O, Johnny Q. my Jo.

~~~

A continuation of the series in the *Richmond Enquirer* (October 10, 1828) included a reference to the absurd story that the straitlaced Adams, who had privately purchased a billiard table as a gift for his son, was in reality a sinister gambler who had squandered public funds on such sinful gambling instruments as billiard tables and chessmen and, even worse, had introduced them into the hallowed precincts of the White House.

THE BLACK LETTERED LIST.

John Quincy John my Joe, John,
   Before you bid adieu,
To all your regal honors, John,
   And *Billiard Table* too;
Let's tell the reasons why, John,
   The people treat you so,
To take the chair from *Braintree's heir*,
   John Adams Q. my Joe.

John Quincy John, my Joe, John,
   You mind your father's creed,
Was that the rich should govern, John,
   But that the poor should bleed;
And for to silence all complaint
   Enacted laws, you know——
Sedition bills were gagging pills,
   John Adams Q. my Joe.

~~~

The *Richmond Enquirer* later reminisced (August 27, 1830) to the tune of "Yankee Doodle":

He wrote a song, ('twas rather long)
   Of Jefferson and Sally,
And scourged their brats, the Democrats,
   With mighty pith and rally.

PRESIDENCY!!!

This is the House that We built.

TREASURY.

This is the malt that lay in the House that WE Built,

John Q. Adams,

This is the *MAIDEN* all forlorn, who worried herself from night till morn, to enter the House that We built.

CLAY,

This is the *MAN* all tattered and torn, who courted the maiden all forlorn, who worried herself from night till morn to enter the House that We built.

WEBSTER,

This is the *PRIEST*, all shaven and shorn, that married the man all tattered and torn, unto the maiden all forlorn, who worried herself from night till morn, to enter the House that We Built.

CONGRESS,

This is the BEAST, that carried the Priest all shaven and shorn, who married the man all tattered and torn, unto the maiden all forlorn, who worried herself from night till morn, to enter the House that We Built.

CABINET,

These are the *Rats* that pulled off their hats, and joined the Beast that carried the Priest all shaven and shorn, who married the man all tattered and torn unto the maiden all forlorn who worried herself from night till morn to enter the House that We built.

"OLD HICKORY,"

This is the *Wood*, well season'd and good, We will use as a rod to whip out the RATS, that pulled off their hats and joined the Beast that carried the Priest all shaven and shorn, who married the man all tattered and torn, unto the maiden all forlorn, who worried herself from night till morn, to enter the House that We Built.

NEW-YORK.

This is the *state*, both early and late, that will strengthen the Wood well seasoned and good, to be used as a rod to whip out Rats that pulled off their hats, and joined the beast that carried the Priest all shaven and shorn, who married the man all tattered and torn unto the maiden all forlorn, who worried herself from night till morn to enter the House that We Built.

                                        EBONY & TOPAZ.

*The People.

When Mrs. Henry Clay first saw this portrait of her husband, painted in 1838 by Edward Dalton Marchant, it was reported that she was so moved she "actually shedded tears over it."

The signature "Ebony and Topaz" on this anti-Adams broadside satire of the nursery jingle "This is the House that Jack Built" refers to an obscure toast made by President Adams at a political dinner at Baltimore in 1827. After proposing "Ebony and Topaz," he embarked on a convoluted explanation, as mystifying to his contemporaries as it is to posterity. Ebony, he said, symbolized the spirit of darkness, or evil, while Topaz was the emblem for light, or good. From there the president wandered off into the remote domains of Voltaire, Far Eastern folktales, the British general Ross (who had fallen at North Point in 1814), heraldry, patriotic virtue, and other seemingly unrelated topics. The toast offered more grist to the propaganda mill, and "Ebony and Topaz" became a kind of derisive anti-Adams slogan during the campaign.

The controversial secretary of state Henry Clay received his share of tuneful punishment during the brutal 1828 campaign. The pro-Jacksonian *U. S. Telegraph* (July 2, 1828) attacked Clay in a song pretending to be written in the first person that is not without modern parallels.

HENRY CLAY'S REMONSTRANCE.

To the tune of "I won't be a nun."

Now is it not a pity such a cunning dog as I,
Should be turned out of office to pay my debts or fly;
   But I won't be turned out—no, I won't be turned out
   I'm so fond of money that I cannot be turned out.

~~~

I love to eat good dinners and to make a dinner speech;
And when I've got a skinful, why I sometimes love to preach;
   So I won't be turned out—no, I won't be turned out
   I love my place so dearly I cannot be turned out.

~~~

The Jackson party machine, the first to be organized on a national scale, practiced electioneering rites with unprecedented verve and scope in 1828. Establishing a pattern for the uninhibited political extravaganzas that were to enliven the quadrennial American scene for a century to come, constituents—many of them newly enfranchised—were wooed with such blandishments as barbecues, fish fries, picnics, parades, political rallies, planting of hickory trees by "Old Hickory" clubs (the magical Jackson nickname of "Old Hickory," symbolizing his toughness, had somehow become wedded to the Liberty Tree as well), slogans, songs, and free whiskey, to name a few.

As a party bard later sang in 1832:

> No barbacue or steaks from rump,
> No whiskey-punch or egg-nogg,
> No democratic speech from stump,
> We now must go the "whole hog."
>   With Yankee doodle we will *brag*,
>   With Yankee dandy doodle . . .

The charismatic Jackson was not only a larger-than-life hero, but he was also the first bona fide man of the people to run for president and he was popularly adored. Because his party seems to have monopolized the best song-writing talent of the period, most Jackson songs were songs of praise and therefore less arresting than those attacking Adams. The rather bland songs for Jackson tended to be written in Scottish dialect and set to Scottish tunes, doubtless in deference to his Scotch-Irish ancestry. One of these paeans of love appeared in the Philadelphia *Mercury* (April 26, 1828).

THE MAN WE LOVE SO DEARLY.

Tune—"Wha'll be King but Charlie"

Come lads and lasses let us hie
    With dresses neat and gaily,
And watch the time when he'll pass by,
    The man we all love dearly.
        Come through the heather,
        Around him gather,
        You're all the welcomer early,
    Round JACKSON cling with all your kin,
    The man we love so dearly.

~~~

There's not a lass in all the land,
    Who's heard of the brave action,
Who'd give her love, her heart and hand,
    To him who is'nt for JACKSON.
        Come through the heather, &c.

And here's success to JACKSON's cause
    We'er for him late and early,
For freedom and our country's laws,
    And him we all love dearly.
        Come through the heather, &c.

Andrew Jackson's inauguration was attended by countless thousands of his admirers from all over, but not by John Quincy Adams, who followed his father's example and left town. Jackson was nearly mobbed by his well-wishers after his inaugural, and he barely managed to make his way from the Capitol through the "impenetrable living mass" that engulfed him. Margaret Bayard Smith, who had attended the ceremonies with Francis Scott Key, wrote that Jackson was followed up Pennsylvania Avenue by hordes of "country men, farmers, gentlemen, mounted and dismounted, boys, women and children, black and white with carriages, wagons and carts all pursuing him to the President's house." Hours later there were "streams of people on foot and of carriages of all kinds, still pouring towards the President's house." Once there, they crashed the presidential reception en masse, trailing mud and destruction in their wake. When Mrs. Smith finally reached the White House, she found "a rabble, a mob, of boys, negroes, women, children scrambling, fighting, romping. . . . Ladies fainted, men were seen with bloody noses. . . . The President, after having been *literally* nearly pressed to death and almost suffocated and torn to pieces by the people in their eagerness to shake hands with Old Hickory, had retreated through the back way . . . and had escaped. . . ."

It was generally acknowledged that Andrew Jackson was truly "presidential looking," an attribute that was successfully translated in this lithographed sheet music cover portrait of the president, probably published in 1829.

PRESIDENT JACKSON'S

Grand March,

PERFORMED BY THE BOSTON BANDS.

Arranged for the

PIANO FORTE.

BOSTON,

Published by J. L. Hewitt & Co. No. 36 Market St.

Many marches in honor of the new president were published in 1829.

The Scottish motif persisted in victory songs for Jackson. To the tune of "The Campbells Are Coming," the March (1829) issue of *The Casket, or Flowers of Literature* published a song that mingled sadness over Rachel Jackson's recent death with exultation over her husband's triumph.

SONG.

Our Jackson is coming, oh, ho! oh, ho!
  Our Jackson is coming, oh, ho! oh, ho!
Our Jackson is coming, the far echoes swelling
  Resound that he's coming, oh, ho! oh, ho!

Columbia's shout of ecstacy,
The glorious sounds ring far and free;
Thundering abroad—sublime if rude,
A nation's noble gratitude.
    Our Jackson is coming, &c.

Yet hark! shrill rising on the air,
What dirge funereal mingles there?
Sad Triumph droops—her tears are shed
Above the fair, the good, the dead!
    Our Jackson is coming, &c.

But tho' the husband's heart be rent,
The Sage and Chieftain all unbent,
And here to right the helm of state,
And the republic renovate.
  Our Jackson has come, oh, ho! oh, ho!
    Great Jackson has come, oh, ho! oh, ho!
  Our Jackson has come—the cannon deep roaring,
    Proclaim his proud coming, oh, ho! oh, ho!

ALL: LESTER S. LEVY

The mighty conflicts and upheavals of Jackson's presidency appear to have been only sparsely recorded by contemporary balladeers. Frustratingly, persistent research has revealed no songs dealing directly with the major scandal of 1831, the mass resignation, at the president's behest, of his cabinet. This sensational event was precipitated by the cabinet ladies, led by Mrs. Calhoun, the vice-president's wife, who defied Jackson's wishes and adamantly refused to receive the beautiful if morally dubious wife of his friend and protégé, Secretary of War Eaton, into the stratosphere of official Washington society. It was gossiped that Margaret (Peggy) O'Neale Timberlake Eaton, the vivacious daughter of a Washington innkeeper, had enjoyed sinful relations with her present husband even before her former one had met his mysterious death at sea. When a showdown with the cabinet failed to bring the recalcitrant ladies around, Jackson lost his famous temper, and heeding the suggestion of his diminutive secretary of state, Martin Van Buren (who cannily espoused the Peggy cause), he fired the cabinet. Jackson's unceremonious exercise of his imperious will caused his enemies to refer to him quite early in his presidency as "King Andrew," a title that was improvised upon in a purposely obscure satirical fable that appeared in the Boston *Courier* (May 13, 1831) about the time of the cabinet resignations.

KING LOG AND THE FROGS.
A Musical Eclogue not to be found in Aesop or Aristophanes.

FROG.

There once was a donkey a new skin would try on,
But a bray for a roar prov'd him never a lion.
Here's a moral worth gold, and the cream of the story,
Shows redoubtable Log in the blaze of his glory.
   But when Jupiter dozes,
   Mortals bite their own noses,
And wiseacres purchase a pig in a poke;
   Then away, melancholy,
   We grin at their folly,
And cackle a musical croak, croak, croak.
    Chorus.
    Croak, croak!
    Croak, croak, croak!

KING LOG.

Lackaday! What's the cause of this noisy proceeding?
I took you my lieges, for men of more breeding.
   I vow and protest it without any joke,
'Tis vastly uncivil to make such a riot,
So, dear little froggies, I pray you be quiet;
   I never was fond of that croak, croak, croak.

FROG.

The Statesman's race
   An arrant farce is,
Where horses win,
   And sometimes asses.
   Your patriot's craft
    Can't be mistaken,
   'Tis to sink the land,
    And save the bacon.
But hang up patties! Sing away, hearties!
   Long-winded speeches are nothing but smoke.
There's never a gaining in too much complaining,
   'Tis pleasanter music to croak, croak, croak!

KING LOG.

My eyes! what a genius the rogues have for muttering!
Did ever one hear such a pestilent sputtering?
   Have done with your babbling,
   Grumbling and gabbling,
Lest I grapple my sceptre and hit you a poke.
   By my splendor I swear it,
   No mortal can bear it,
Such a noisy, impertinent——
    Chorus.
    Croak, croak, croak.

"Our Union: It must be preserved!" toasted President Jackson at a Jefferson Day dinner in 1830, as he gazed meaningfully at his vice-president and bitter adversary, John C. Calhoun. In the ongoing North-South struggle between the adherents of states' rights and the supporters of federal supremacy, the South Carolinian Calhoun had taken the stand that states had the right to nullify such federal laws as they might find "unconstitutional." The conflict between Jackson and Calhoun culminated in Calhoun's resignation from the vice-presidency in 1832, but not before South Carolina, under Calhoun's leadership, had nullified the hated tariff acts of 1828 and 1832 at a state convention. Alarmed and infuriated at this serious threat of secession, and determined to "preserve the Union" at all costs, Jackson asked for and received the authority to send troops to South Carolina. The dispute was resolved without violence by the adoption of a compromise tariff bill proposed by Henry Clay, who paradoxically had backed the controversial tariff legislation in the first place. The attitude of sister southern states toward the quarrel and its crucial implications was summed up in a song by a Virginian, written in a kind of mock-Negro dialect to the tune of "Clare de Kitchen," a popular "darky" song of the period; it appeared in the *Richmond Enquirer* (October 25, 1833). In the text, "Mas Watkins Leigh" is Benjamin Watkins Leigh, a Virginia lawyer and statesman; "McDuffie" is Governor George McDuffie of South Carolina, a passionate advocate of nullification and no enemy to secession either.

SAVE DE UNION.

"The following Song, written by Mr. LeRoy Anderson, of Virginia, was sung with great taste and spirit during the past season of fashion and gaiety at Saratoga."

A mighty angry quarrel rose
Among the Tariff's friends and foes,
And South Calina, in a fit,
De Union vows to curse and quit.
    But save de Union old folks, young folks,
    Old Virginny never tire.

Virginny love her sister State,
And most as much the Tariff hate,
But while the Tariff she despise,
De Union very much she prize,
    So save de Union, &c.

She send her son Mas Watkins Leigh,
De South Calina folks to see,
To tell em just to wait a while,
And better times will on us smile,
    So save de Union, &c.

The Tariff chief, name Henry Clay,
Who love his country much dey say,
Begin to fear its danger great,
And says I join my native State,
    To save de Union, &c.

Calhoun, a great Calina man,
Abominate the Tariff plan,
But he too say, Oh yes, 'tis right,
And Clay, let's me and you unite,
    To save de Union, &c.

McDuffie too, when he see dat,
Off-hand begin to smell de rat—
He say, no doubt Calhoun is wise,
And we must do what he advise,
    To save de Union, &c.

Den all de folks in Congress Hall,
De ladies, gentlemens an all,
All smile upon Calhoun and Clay,
And say well done, dat is de way
    To save de Union, &c.

And when Calina hear de news,
She come into Virginny's views;
She smile upon Mas Watkins Leigh,
And say my Nullies all agree
    To save de Union, &c.

The first third party in American history also held the first national political convention. In September 1831 the newly formed Anti-Masonic party met in Baltimore and nominated William Wirt, who had been Adams's attorney general, for president (despite his having been a Mason in his youth!). In December the National Republicans convened at Baltimore and nominated the perennially hopeful presidential candidate Henry Clay. And finally, in May 1832, again in Baltimore, the Democrats held their national convention, seemingly only for the purpose of nominating Jackson's protégé, Martin Van Buren, for vice-president; Jackson was not even placed in nomination, so certain was his reelection. Apparently most Democrats felt, as the song in the *Richmond Enquirer* (October 16, 1832) had it, that:

Now every freeman again should pay
On the ensuing Election day,
Their united suffrages to the Chief,
Without the least reluctancy.

And they overwhelmingly did.

Henry Clay's supporters mingled menace with endorsement in a song for their man, to the tune of "Hurrah for the Bonnets of Blue," that appeared in the *Daily National Intelligencer* (July 28, 1832):

Here's a health to the workingman's friend,
Here's good luck to the PLOUGH and the LOOM,
And who will not join in support of our cause,
May light-dinners and ill luck attend.

It's good from *true faith* ne'er to swerve,
It's good from the Right ne'er to stray,
It's good to maintain America's Cause
And stick by our own HARRY CLAY.

But the Demoes unkindly asked, in the Washington *Globe* (September 12, 1832):

HO! WHY DOST THOU SHIVER AND SHAKE, HARRY CLAY?

Air—"Gaffar Gray."

Ho! Why dost thou shiver and shake,
                              Harry Clay,
And why does thy nose look so blue?—
    'Tis my friends, they grow cold,
    And I'm losing the *old*,
While 'tis clear that I cannot get *new*—
                              Well-a-day!

Are not the *high tariff* men thine,
                              Harry Clay,
And will they not help thee along?
    My American System
    Was framed to enlist 'em;
But trick cannot make the weak strong,
                              Well-a-day!

The *Anties* will sure take thee up,
                              Harry Clay,
And their principles drop with their *Wirt*?
    The anties are frantic,
    And in some mad antic,
Will spill me again in the dirt,
                              Well-a-day!

The *Feds*, who live high on the Bank,
                              Harry Clay,
Hate Jackson, and money adore,—
    The folks term them tories,
    And scorn their Bank stories,
And love the *Old Hero* the more—
                              Well-a-day!

Thy chance is but low, 'tis confessed,
                              Harry Clay;
What then? While we can we will give,
    If by bribe and by barter,
    We can get a re-charter;
If not, we must *both* cease to live—
                              Well-a-day!

"THE KING UPON THE THRONE: The People in the Dust!!!" trumpeted a headline in the Daily National Intelligencer *(August 9, 1832), now an anti-administration newspaper. These sentiments were reflected in this cartoon, which appeared at the peak of the 1832 campaign; Jackson is depicted as "King Andrew the First," in full royal regalia, brandishing a veto and trampling upon the Constitution. He was nevertheless reelected by a landslide.*

In 1832 President Jackson, no lover of banks, engaged in mortal combat against the monopolistic Bank of the United States, an institution he pronounced "unconstitutional, un-democratic, and un-American." Vetoing Congress's renewal in 1832 of the Bank's charter, due to expire in 1836, Jackson proceeded systematically to exterminate the "Money Monster" by the withdrawal of its pivotal government deposits, expending two unwilling secretaries of the treasury in the process. With the assistance of the former attorney general and future chief justice Roger B. Taney, he finally succeeded. Taney was a veteran of Jackson's famed "Kitchen Cabinet," the influential group of personal friends and supporters who had unofficially functioned in lieu of the cabinet during the early days of his presidency. The long-continuing "Bank War" (the bank finally went out of existence in 1836 at the expiration of its charter) was the major campaign issue in 1832. Jackson was branded an imperialistic tyrant by the embattled proponents of the Bank.

Calling themselves Whigs, after the party traditionally opposed to absolute monarchy, a formidable coalition of National Republicans, Anti-Masons, disaffected Democrats, remnants of Federalists, and assorted other anti-Jacksonians was organized in the Congressional election year 1834 to do battle with King Andrew. The Whigs sounded their keynote in close harmony at the great Whig Festival at Salem, where, according to the *Hingham Gazette* (August 15, 1834, reprinted from the *Salem Gazette*), "the ample pavilion . . . was filled to overflowing with staunch Whigs, the bone, muscle, and sinew of our society."

Also in close harmony, the brawny Whigs apparently found time, among the speech making and the toasts, to mingle their voices in musical derogation of their archfoe. To identify King Andrew's "trusty squires" and their "pilot

fish" in the text of "King Andrew": "Lou" is most probably
Lewis Cass, the secretary of war, although he might be
Louis McLane, secretary of state in 1834 and former secretary of the treasury; "Ben" is Benjamin Franklin Butler,
attorney general; "Lev" is Levi Woodbury, secretary of the
navy and then of the treasury; "Bill" is William Taylor
Barry, postmaster general; "Roger of Tawney hue" is
Roger B. Taney, who assisted with the United States Bank
withdrawals; "Blair the Book" is Francis P. Blair, publisher
of the tremendously influential pro-Jackson newspaper the
Globe; "Kendall chief cook" is Amos Kendall, the journalist,
who was a major power behind King Andrew's throne; and
"Isaac surnamed the True" is Isaac Hill, a senator and an
alumnus of the Kitchen Cabinet, as were most of the above
cast of characters.

2.
King Andrew had an itching palm
To finger the nation's cash;
Most of 'em thought 'twas just the thing,
But some, it would be rash.
He ask'd Lou. and Ben. &c.

3.
The General took his cook's advice,
And hurried away the Rhino;
But where it went—aye, there's the rub—
I'm sure neither you nor I know.
For there's Lou. and Ben. &c.

HERO'S QUICK STEP.
Twelfth Edition.

Price 25 cts. nett

Boston Published by HENRY PRENTISS Nº 33 Court Street.

Colorful military companies in Boston, such as the Rifle Rangers and the Light Infantry, were great favorites in their community during the 1830s, inspiring local pride, poetic tributes, and a considerable quantity of music—quick steps and marches especially composed for their regimental bands. The Boston *Daily News* (August 27, 1834) reported: "The Company of 'Rifle Rangers' made a parade yesterday in a new and elegant uniform, they were accompanied by the Brigade Band, who performed up State-street, a new march composed by Mr. Comer." The same newspaper had reviewed another of Mr. Comer's compositions earlier that year (June 23): "Mr. Comer, who stands number one, with the Bostonians, as a musical composer, has produced a new piece of music, 'Dedicated to Capt. E. Weston and the Officers and Members of the Boston Light Infantry,' called the 'TIGER QUICK STEP.' The engraved frontispiece represents the company on the march, with 'arms support,' and a Royal Tiger in the act of leaping from a precipice.—The whole is beautifully executed, and does credit to him who designed, as well as the Artist who executed." This accurate art evaluation applies equally to the following graphically superb sheet music covers belonging to a group of pieces especially composed for these two companies (the members of the Light Infantry were known as "Tigers" and the Rifle Rangers as "Roarers") and one for the National Lancers; all were published in Boston in the 1830s.

THE TIGER QUICK STEP.

Pendleton's Lithography, Boston.

Respectfully Dedicated
TO
CAPT. E. WESTON
and the
OFFICERS & MEMBERS
OF THE
BOSTON LIGHT INFANTRY
Performed for the first time at their Anniversary 1834
BY THE BOSTON BRIGADE BAND.
Composed by
T. COMER.

Published for the Author by C. Bradlee & sold by S. H. Parker,
141 Washington St. - Boston.

T. Comer

THE ROARERS.

A Quick Step. Composed Expressly for the

Rifle Rangers

And Humbly Dedicated to

CAPT. CHARLES C. PAINE,

OFFICERS and MEMBERS of the R. R. BOSTON,

BY JOHN HOLLOWAY.

Performed for the first time by the **Boston Brass Band** *at Holloway's Farewell Concert. March 11, 1851.*

Boston: Published by Chs. H. Keith, 67 Court Street.

Rangers' Trip to Westborough

OR

LION QUICK STEP.

Respectfully Dedicated to

CAPT. CHAS. C. PAINE,

and the

OFFICERS AND MEMBERS

OF THE

RIFLE RANGERS, BOSTON

Performed for the first time on their visit to the Lyon Farm by
the Brigade Band at the opening of the Rail Road to West-
borough, November 15th 1834.

Composed by

JAMES HOOTON.

Boston, — Published for the Author by C. Bradlee.

Entered according to act of Congress in the year 1834 by Parker Williams in the clerk's office of the District Court of Mass.

As first performed by the

BOSTON BRIGADE BAND ON THE ANNIVERSARY OF THE

BOSTON LIGHT INFANTRY,

MAY 31ST 1837.

Also the New Nautical Song

A YANKEE SHIP AND A YANKEE CREW,

Sung by

MR. WILLIAMSON.

Words by J. S. JONES *Esq.* — *Melody by* G. M. KING *Esq.*

The whole arranged for the **PIANO FORTE** and dedicated to the

OFFICERS & MEMBERS OF THE B.L.I.

BY. **T. COMER.**

BOSTON Pub'd by PARKER & DITSON, 107 Wash'n St.

Entered according to Act of Congress by PARKER & DITSON in the year 1837 in the Clerks office of the District Court of Mass

T. Moore's Lithography, Boston (successor to Pendleton)

THE LANCER'S QUICK STEP.

~ Respectfully dedicated to

GENERAL DAVIS,

& THE OFFICERS & MEMBERS OF THE

NATIONAL LANCERS.

As performed by

J. BARTLETT'S BRASS BAND, AUG. 30th 1837.

MUSIC BY

F. L. RAYMOND.

Boston. Published by H. PRENTISS, No. 2 Pemberton Hill.

I'LL BE NO SUBMISSIVE WIFE,

A Ballad

BY

ALEXANDER LEE.

NEW YORK,

Published by FIRTH & HALL, No. 1. Franklin Sq.

I'LL BE NO SUBMISSIVE WIFE.

I'll be no submissive wife
No, not I; no, not I
I'll not be a slave for life
No, not I; no, not I.

Think you on a wedding day
That I said, as others say
Love and honor and obey,
Love and honor and obey?
No no no no no no no
No no no, not I.

I to dullness don't incline
No, not I; no, not I
Go to bed at half-past nine
No, not I; no, not I.

Should a humdrum husband say
That at home I ought to stay
Do you think that I'll obey,
Do you think that I'll obey?
No no no no no no no
No no no, not I.

A premonitory blow for women's liberation was struck in 1835 with the publication of an outrageous song with an outrageous title. Apparently it struck a responsive chord in secretly unsubmissive wifely bosoms at the time: the song ran into innumerable editions.

THE FLAG OF TEXAS
A National Song
Composed in honour of the Glorious Victory on the 21 of April 1836.

and respectfully Dedicated to

GENERAL SAM!. HOUSTON

by

A. F. Winnemore

Arranged for the Piano Forte

by

P. M. WOLSIEFFER.

Philadelphia, Geo. Willig N.º 171 Chesnut St.

Allegro Maestoso.

Flow on flow on thou bright young Banner _ _ _ A _ dop _ ted by the free When

at the can _ nonsmouth they swore For Death or Liber _ ty For Death or Lib_er_

General Sam Houston's smashing victory at San Jacinto on April 21, 1836, when he surprised and captured the Mexican dictator Antonio López de Santa Anna, was celebrated in this song. Santa Anna, only six weeks before, had brutally exterminated the heroic American garrison defending the Alamo mission, among whom was the colorful folk hero Colonel Davy Crockett.

'CORN COBS,'

A POPULAR

COMIC SONG & CHORUS

AS SUNG

BY MESS.ʳˢ HILL & BROWER.

WITH RAPTUROUS APPLAUSE

ARRANGED FOR THE PIANO FORTE.

50. cts.

Published by ENDICOTT, 359 *Broadway,* NEW YORK.

In 1836 "Yankee Doodle" spectacularly reappeared in sheet music form with a new title, "Corn Cobs," and a new text, partly composed of earlier versions and partly new. The title was derived from the refrain, in which the "cornstalks" in the mad refrain of the earlier "Yankee Song" (see page 35) had now become "corn cobs." The updated scenario also had "our Jemima," now "our aunt Jemima," perched in a tree and throwing corn kernels down to "our old bob tail rooster." Her eccentric behavior is depicted in the sheet music cover, in the foreground of which is a wondrous "patented" corn-shelling machine operated by a shady-looking character, obviously a city slicker attempting to con an innocent rustic into buying it. The scene probably duplicates the staging of the song, which the sheet music blurb informs us was received with "rapturous applause." The "Captain Crocket" in stanza 10 most probably refers to Davy Crockett.

CORN COBS TWIST YOUR HAIR.

There was a man in our town,
    I'll tell you his condition,
He sold his oxen and plough,
    To buy him a commission.
CHORUS.
Corn Cobs twist your hair,
    Cartwheel run round you,
Fiery dragons take you off,
    And mortar pestal pound you.

When this man a commission got,
    He prov'd to be a coward,
He wouldn't go to Canada,
    For fear he'd get devour'd. Corn Cobs &c.

But he and I we went to town,
    Along with Captain Goodin,
And there we saw the Yankee boys,
    As thick as hasty puddin. Corn Cobs &c.

Now there was Genral Washington,
    With all the folks about him,
He swore they got so tarnal proud,
    They couldn't do without him. Corn Cobs &c.

And there they had a great big thing,
    Big as a log of maple,
And ev'ry time they wheel'd it round,
    It took two yoke of cattle. Corn Cobs &c.

And when they went to fire it off,
    It took a horn of powder,
It made a noise like Daddy's gun,
    Only a nation louder. Corn Cobs &c.

And there they had a little thing,
    All bound round with leather,
With little sticks to beat upon,
    To call the men together. Corn Cobs &c.

And there we saw a hollow stick,
    With six holes bor'd right in it,
And ev'ry time they blow'd upon,
    We thought the devil was in it. Corn Cobs &c.

And there we saw them with big knives,
    Stuck in a piece of leather,
And when the Captain he cri'd draw,
    They all draw'd out together. Corn Cobs &c.

Now brother Ike was very bold,
    As bold as Captain Crocket,
For he sneak'd round on t'other side,
    And held on Daddy's pocket. Corn Cobs &c.

Now I and brother Ike goes hum,
    We wasn't fraid of powder,
For Daddy said he'd learn us both,
    To scream a little louder. Corn Cobs &c.

Our cousin Jim he went to town,
    With a pair of striped trowses,
He swore the town he couldn't see,
    There was so many houses. Corn Cobs &c.

Our aunt Jemima climb'd a tree,
    She had a stick to boost her,
And there she sat a throwing corn,
    At our old bob tail rooster. Corn Cobs &c.

Now cousin Sal she went to town,
    And got upon a steeple,
She took a frying pan of grog,
    And pour'd it on the people. Corn Cobs &c.

Our uncle Ben he lost his cow,
    And didn't know where to find her,
And when the cow she did cum hum,
    She had her tail behind her. Corn Cobs &c.

Now Sister Sue grows very thin,
    And no one knows what ails her,
She us'd to eat nine pound of pork
    But now her stomach fails her. Corn Cobs &c.

Now I've sung you all my song,
    I've told you all the causes
And all that I do want of you,
    Is all your kind applauses. Corn Cobs &c.

Martin Van Buren

Supported by the matchless organization of Old Hickory's political machine, his appointed successor, the "little magician" Martin Van Buren, easily breezed into the presidency in 1836. The unfocused Whigs had vacillated between several candidates, among them Daniel Webster, Senator Hugh Lawson White of Tennessee, and the old hero from North Bend, William Henry Harrison. As the *Globe* (October 22, 1836) taunted, to the air of "A Sailor's life's a life of woe":

> A wiggy's life's a life of woe,
>   He works now late now early;
> From DAN to NORTH BEND forced to go
>   But to be shipwrecked yearly.

Van Buren too received his share of campaign sniping. From the New York *Evening Star* (October 8, 1836) to the tune of "Lilliburlero":

> Buren, Buren, luckless Van Buren,
> Your desperate ambition has met with its doom,
> Your Augean stable and vile kitchen vermin,
> Our freemen will sweep with the Harrison broom.

Four years and hundreds of derogatory songs later, Harrison eventually did defeat Van Buren.

Attended by great pomp and parade, Jackson rode with Van Buren to his inauguration in a "beautiful phaeton built of the wood of the frigate Constitution," reported *Niles' Weekly Register* (March 11, 1837), but that devoted party journal was forced to voice a reservation: "The inaugural address of Mr. Van Buren has disappointed both friends and foes. . . ." The comment was a presage of things to come. Not only did the unfortunate little magician find Jackson a hard act to follow, but he was blamed for the desperate financial panic that occurred soon after he took office. Because no American president has ever been more mercilessly lampooned in song than Van Buren was by the Whigs, it seems incomprehensible that this march for Van Buren was published by the Athens, Georgia, Whig office.

PRESIDENT M. VAN BUREN'S
GRAND MARCH.

COMPOSED AND ARRANGED FOR THE PIANO FORTE, BY

JOHN F. GONEKE.

Printed at the Whig Office. Athens. Ga.

THE AMERICAN BOY.

Father look up and see that flag
    How gracefully it flies,
Those pretty stripes they seem to be
    A rainbow in the skies,

It is your country's Flag, my son,
    And proudly drinks the light,
O'er ocean's wave in foreign clime,
    A symbol of our might.

Father what fearful noise is that
    Like thundering of the clouds!
Why do the people wave their hats
    And rush along in crowds!

It is the noise of Cannonry
    The glad shouts of the free
This is the day to memory dear
    'Tis Freedom's Jubilee.

Francis Johnson, the composer of "The American Boy," was one of the best-known and most highly regarded American musicians of the 1820s and '30s. Principally a composer of social music, the versatile Johnson—he was an accomplished performer on many instruments and apparently a peerless bandleader as well—was in great demand at the most fashionable parties in his native Philadelphia and at Saratoga Springs and other chic watering places. Johnson, who had composed several pieces to welcome Lafayette in 1824, was affiliated with the State Fencibles of Philadelphia and the Philadelphia Grays, for whom he composed military and patriotic music and in whose parades he and his band marched. Enjoying far greater than merely local fame, Johnson and his musicians toured in England and the Continent in 1837. He is rumored to have received a silver trumpet from Queen Victoria after a command performance, and the story—possibly apocryphal—is that he was buried with it when he died in 1844. Johnson was a prolific composer, and his music, seemingly in great demand, was copiously published. His successful life in early nineteenth-century America is altogether extraordinary because Francis Johnson was a Negro.

"My Country! 'tis of Thee," the ultimate American version of "God Save the King," was written in 1831 by Samuel Francis Smith, a young clergyman, whose name does not appear on this undated early sheet music edition of his song. Smith claimed he did not know that he was writing words to the British national anthem. Asked for a school song text by the noted New England music educator and hymnodist Lowell Mason, he had chosen the tune from a German songbook, believing it to be a German patriotic air. "My Country! 'tis of Thee," also called "America," was first sung at a children's Fourth of July celebration at the Park Street Church in Boston in 1831.

MY COUNTRY! 'TIS OF THEE.

TUNE, "GOD SAVE THE KING."

BOSTON: Published by C. BRADLEE Washington Street.

My coun_try! 'tis of thee, Sweet land of lib_ _ _er_ _ty_

Of thee I sing: Land, where my fa_ _ thers died; Land of the

pil_ _grim's pride; From eve_ry mountain-side, Let freedom ring.

2.

My native country! thee—
Land of the noble free—
    Thy name I love:
I love thy rocks and rills,
Thy woods and templed hills;
My heart with rapture thrills,
    Like that above.

3.

Let music swell the breeze,
And ring from all the trees
    Sweet freedom's song:
Let mortal tongues awake,
Let all that breathe partake,
Let rocks their silence break,
    The sound prolong.

4.

Our father's God! to thee—
Author of liberty!
    To thee we sing;
Long may our land be bright,
With freedom's holy light—
Protect us by thy might,
    Great God, our King!

8. Whig Waltzes

and Locofoco Polkas
1840–1841

It was, ironically, a Democrat who provided the magical campaign formula that spectacularly swept the Whigs to victory in the presidential election of 1840. A Democratic newspaperman, attempting to discredit the Whig candidate William Henry Harrison, fatuously suggested giving him a barrel of hard cider and a pension, and "my word for it, he will sit the remainder of his days in his log cabin by the side of a 'sea coal' fire. . . ." Transmuting this inane gibe into purest political gold, the Whigs appropriated the log cabin and cider barrel for their campaign symbols, throwing in a coonskin for good measure. They correspondingly metamorphosed the well-born, well-to-do Harrison (who lived in an imposing mansion) into a suitable tenant for the lowly log cabin: a simple soldier-farmer who hunted the raccoon and cherished a lovable predilection for the common man's potation, hard cider. Log cabins—together with cider barrels and coonskins—became an omnipresent fact of life in America, springing up at every turn and in every conceivable form. In a campaign that was virtually set to music—it was said that Harrison was "sung into the presidency"—the country rang with log cabin songs, marches, quicksteps, and dance tunes.

The distinctive portrait adorning the sheet music cover of "The National Whig Song" (1840) depicts William Henry Harrison as the aristocrat he really was rather than as the rough frontiersman he was supposed to be. Making the best of both worlds, the lyrics combine the two Harrisons—the "fine, true-hearted gentleman" of the old school and the "Farmer of North Bend." In the text, the "arch Magician" is, of course, Martin Van Buren, who bore the burden of a number of uncomplimentary Whiggish nicknames, among them "Martin Van Ruin" and "Sweet Sandy Whiskers."

NATIONAL WHIG SONG.

I'LL sing you now a new Whig song, made to a good old rhyme,
Of a fine, true-hearted gentleman, all of the olden time;
By birth and blood, by kith and kin, a sound, true Whig was he,
For his father signed the charter that made our country free.
    Like a fine, true-hearted gentleman,
    All of the olden time.

In youth, upon the tented field, his laurels he did gain,
No Chief so many battles fought, that never fought in vain;
In peace, the quiet Statesman he; but when grim war arose,
He buckled on his armor then, to meet his country's foes.
    Like a fine, true-hearted gentleman,
    All of the olden time.

And when he'd served his country well, in senate and in field,
The honors that awaited him most freely did he yield;
He turned him to his home again, and sought a Farmer's toils,
for, though he'd *filled the offices*, he never *took the spoils*.
    Like a fine, true-hearted gentleman,
    All of the olden time.

And when the People, in their might, have put their solemn ban
Upon the arch Magician and on all his tory clan,
To manage well their state affairs, with one accord they'll send
For another Cincinnatus,—the Farmer of North Bend.
    For he's a fine, true-hearted gentleman,
    All of the olden time.

~~~

Let every sound, true-hearted Whig now raise his voice on high,
And, for the triumph of the cause, join Freedom's loudest cry;
Come to the fight; we'll win the field—away with doubts and
    fears;
The People's man is HARRISON—let's give him three good cheers,
    For he's a fine, true-hearted gentleman,
    All of the olden time!

The Democrats countered in the Boston *Bay State Democrat* (February 15, 1840) with a somewhat pallid parody of "The National Whig Song," twitting Harrison on his age (he was sixty-seven years old).

I'll sing you a good old song, made by a whiggy great,
Of a weak old *Western Gentleman* who wished to serve the state,
And keep up the *white mansion* at a bountiful old rate,
With a good whig household to receive of spoils a heavy weight,
Like a weak old Western Gentleman all of the olden time.

This uncommonly restrained broadside to promote Harrison refers to his distinguished lineage.

William Henry
HARRISON

Is the son of one of the signers of the Declaration of Independence.

He entered his country's service at the age of 18, as an ensign in an Indian War.
In 1794 he was aid to Gen. Wayne in the famous battle of the Miami, and was conspicuous for his valor.
In 1797 he was made Secretary & Lieut Governor of the Northwestern territory.
In 1799 he was chosen a member of Congress.
In 1800 he was appointed Governor of the Northwestern Territory.
In 1803 Mr. Jefferson appointed him sole Commissioner to treat with the Indians north-west of the Ohio.
His first appointment was made by Mr. Adams,—his second and third by Thomas Jefferson, and his fourth by James Madison.
He commanded at the celebrated battle of Tippacanoe, 7th Nov. 1811---also at Fort Meigs in 1813, and at the Battle of the Thames Oct, 3, 1813.
The Legislatures of Indiana and Kentucky passed resolutions of thanks for his able defence of the country.
In 1812, on the breaking out of the War with Great Britain, he was called into the field as Major General of Kentucky Militia.
Next he was appointed Brigadier General in the Army of the United States.
Next as Commander-in-Chief of the Northwestern Army.
In 1817 Congress passed a resolution, giving him "*a Gold Medal and the thanks of Congress,*" with but one dissenting voice in both Houses.
In '16 he was elected a member of Congress from Ohio.
In '19 he was chosen to the Senate of that State.
In '24 he was elected Senator in Congress from Ohio.
In '28 he was appointed Envoy Extraordinary to Colombia.
Since his return from Colombia, he has lived in comparative retirement in Ohio.
In every station, military or civil, he has shown himself equal to every emergency.
His character is beyond reproach,—while others became rich, he has served his country in times of the greatest trial, and is poor.
This is the candidate for the Presidency of the United States—an able, honest, and talented man. ☞ Let him be sustained in Connecticut.
WHAT CAN BE SAID OF MARTIN VAN BUREN?

M. B. YOUNG, BOOK & JOB PRINTER.

THE NATIONAL WHIG SONG.

B.W. Thayer's Lithog. Boston.

W. H. Harrison.

Written by

WILLIAM HAYDEN, ESQ.

and respectfully dedicated to the

Price 25 cts. nett.

Whigs of the United States.

BOSTON.

Published by PARKER & DITSON, 135 Washington St.

"TIP AND TY"

A New Comic Whig Glee

Respectfully dedicated to the

LOUISIANA WHIG DELEGATION

to the

BUNKER-HILL CONVENTION.

New York, Firth & Hall, 1, Franklin Square.

O what has caused this great commotion, motion, motion, Our country

through, It is the ball that's rolling on, For Tippecanoe and Ty_ler too, For

Tippecanoe and Ty_ler too And with them we'll beat little Van, Van,

Van, Van, oh he's a used up man And with them we'll beat little Van.

In their insistent use of slogans and jingles, the Whigs of 1840 anticipated the mass media techniques of the twentieth century. These Founding Fathers of Madison Avenue recognized in their wisdom that a chanted slogan—or better yet, one set to a catchy popular tune—infected the defenseless public consciousness far more powerfully than one that was merely read. By means of captive mass audience participation, the message was broadcast with a vividness and speed that the printed word simply could not equal. Adopting as a pattern the overwhelmingly successful Democratic image in 1828 of the "Hero of New Orleans," the Whigs contrived a military hero of their own, the "Hero of Tippecanoe," and a slogan to serve him (and his running mate John Tyler as well). The phrase "Tippecanoe and Tyler too" caught on like wildfire; set to the popular tune of "Little Pig's Tail" by Alexander Coffman Ross, a politically conscious jeweler from Zanesville, Ohio, it sent the hypnotized multitudes tripping euphorically to the polls. "Tippecanoe and Tyler Too" became the theme song of the most singing campaign in American history. Reporting the giant Whig convention at Auburn, New York, which had been "attended by about 6,000 of the most intelligent persons in the state, of whom about 300 were of the fairer and better portion of our nature," *Niles' National Register* (November 7, 1840) recounted that during the festive voyage to Auburn from New York aboard "that splendid boat the De Witt Clinton. . . . The band played some 200 or 300 different national airs and beautiful melodies. . . . About a dozen Tippecanoe songs were sung," the *Register* continued, "of which the following ['Tippecanoe and Tyler Too'] was the most prominent and popular." In the text, "the ball a rolling on" refers to gigantic balls of tin or leather, inscribed with the names of the states and campaign slogans and verses, that were rolled from town to town; "locos" were what the Whigs called all non-Whigs—more precisely they were a radical branch of the Democratic party called "Locofocos" after the locofoco friction matches with which they had lighted a meeting at Tammany Hall in 1835 after the opposition had sought to dispossess them by turning out the gaslights; the "Van-Jacks" were Van Buren men, as were the "spoilsmen" and the "leg-treasurers." As printed by *Niles' National Register*:

THE NEW WHIG SONG.

TIPPECANOE AND TYLER TOO.

Tune—*"Little Pig's Tail."*

What has caused this great commotion, motion, motion,
    Our country through?
    —It is the ball a rolling on

CHORUS.
For Tippecanoe and Tyler too—Tippecanoe and Tyler too,
    And with them we'll beat little Van, Van,
      Van is a used up man;
    And with them we'll beat little Van.

Like the rushing of mighty waters, waters, waters,
    On it will go,
    And its course will clear the way
      For Tippecanoe, &c.

See the loco standard tottering, tottering, tottering,
    Down it must go,
    And in its place we'll rear the flag
      Of Tippecanoe, &c.

Have you heard from old Kentuck, tuck, tuck,
    Good news and true,
    Seventeen thousand is the tune
      For Tippecanoe, &c.

Have you heard from old Vermount, mount, mount,
    All honest and true,
    The Green Mountain boys are rolling the ball
      For Tippecanoe, &c.

Don't you hear from every quarter, quarter, quarter,
    Good news and true,
    That swift the ball is rolling on
      For Tippecanoe, &c.

The New York boys turned out in thousands, thousands, thousands,
    Not long ago,
    And at Utica they set their seals
      To Tippecanoe, &c.

Now you hear the Van-Jacks talking, talking, talking,
    Things look quite blue,
    For all the world seems turning round
      For Tippecanoe, &c.

Let them talk about hard cider, cider, cider,
    And log cabins too,
    'Twill only help to speed the ball
      For Tippecanoe, &c.

The latch-string hangs outside the door, door, door,
    And is never pulled through,
    For it never was the custom of
      Old Tippecanoe, &c.

He always has his table set, set, set,
    For all honest and true,
    And invites them in to take a bite,
      With Tippecanoe, &c.

See the spoilsmen and leg-treasurers, treasurers, treasurers,
    All in a stew,
    For well they know they stand no chance,
      With Tippecanoe, &c.

Little Matty's days are number'd, number'd, number'd,
    Out he must go,
    And in the chair we'll place the good
      Old Tippecanoe, &c.

"The lion of the day," pronounced Henry Clay as the colossal ball was rolled in the great parade held on May 4, 1840, in Baltimore, where Whigs from every state had convened to ratify Harrison's nomination. The Democrats estimated the attendance at about eight thousand people; the Whigs claimed at least twenty-five thousand paraders and as many as seventy-five thousand viewers. One onlooker—presumably a Whig—counted a thousand banners in the procession and no fewer than eight ambulatory log cabins. The Baltimore *Patriot* (quoted in *Niles' National Register*, May 9, 1840) reported that the passengers on one of these log cabin floats, the "hard fisted" delegation from Baltimore County, were seen refreshing themselves en route by dipping gourds into the indispensable cider barrel at the cabin door. The parade ball, which had been rolled all the way from the westernmost region in Maryland by the Allegheny County delegation, was described as "immense . . . 10 or 12 feet in diameter . . . upon which various inscriptions were made."

In 1837 the Missouri Democrat Thomas Hart Benton, in trying to persuade the Senate to expunge its censure resolution against Andrew Jackson for doing away with the Bank of the United States, had declared: "Solitary and alone, I put this ball in motion." An inscription on the Allegheny County ball derisively referred to Benton's statement:

> This democratic ball,
> Set rolling first by Benton,
> Is on another track
> From that it first was sent on.

Other stanzas read:

> With heart and soul
> This ball we roll.
> May times improve
> As on we move.

> Farewell, dear Van,
> You're not our man;
> To guide the ship,
> We'll try old Tip.

> As rolls the ball
> Van's reign does fall;
> And he may look
> To Kinderhook;
> His former friends
> To other ends.

> Take care your toes
> Ye loco fo's;
> As ye're in trouble
> Ye may see double;
> Having no bell,
> We roll your knell.

As the campaign went on, balls were rolled from state to state and from convention to convention. They bristled with slogans and catchphrases, often in the form of puns, a recurrent one being the phrase *turn out*. As a song in Horace Greeley's campaign newspaper *The Log Cabin* (August 22, 1840) had it:

> From the White House, now Matty, turn out, turn out,
>   From the White House, now Matty, turn out!
>   Since there you have been,
>   No peace we have seen,
> So, Matty, now please to turn out, turn out!
>   So Matty, now please to turn out!

> All the West is exclaiming, turn out, turn out!
>   All the West is exclaiming, turn out!
>   The South joins the cry,
>   And you'll hear, by and by,
> From the North and the East, turn out, turn out!
>   From the North and the East, turn out!

> The whole Nation is crying, turn out, turn out!
>   The whole Nation is crying, turn out!
>   Of your knaves and defaulters
>   Deserving of halters,
> We've had more than enough, turn out, turn out!
>   We've had more than enough, turn out!

> Make way for Old Tip! turn out, turn out!
>   Make way for Old Tip! Turn out!
>   'Tis the People's decree,
>   Their choice he shall be,
> So Martin Van Buren, turn out, turn out!
>   So, Martin Van Buren, turn out!

As they rolled the ball from the log cabin to the Capitol, both of which are seen in the background of this caption illustration, the Whigs sang: Then haste and turn out, old men, young men, / Haste and turn out new men, true men, / Vote for HARRISON.

TURN OUT! TO THE RESCUE!

"With heart and soul ___ This Ball we roll!"

NEWLY ARRANGED BY T. CARR,

And Inscribed to the Patriots

OF THE

Whole Union.

Philadelphia, G. E. Blake, 13 S? Fifth Street.

Allegretto.

In "Old Kentuck" the People say, That Matty Van has had his day, And

that "Old Tip" he is the man, To rout him out with all his clan, Then

Blake's Log Cabin Music. Copy right secured. 1840.

The Whigs of 1840 were out to win, no matter how—even if it meant assuming a Democratic persona. To bring in the mass vote, the essentially right-wing Whigs retailored their image, just as they had retailored the image of their candidate. In an artfully manipulated confusion of semantics, they claimed to be the only true exponents of Jacksonian equalitarianism, while at the same time they accused the Democrats, whom they called Locofocos, of being elitist exploiters of the workingman. The Whig policy maker Thomas Elder neatly summed up his party's "rationale" when he declared: "Passion and prejudice, properly aroused and directed, would do as well as principle and reason in a party contest." The Whigs, with their superbly executed "image campaign," proved his point. During the unequal struggle (the Democrats were out of their depth), each party accused the other of being turncoats and Federalists, contentions that were mutually set to music. The Whig version of "When This Old Hat Was New," which was handsomely published as sheet music (music publishers mined an unprecedented bonanza from the Whig, but not the Democratic, campaign), went:

WHEN THIS OLD HAT WAS NEW.

When this old hat was new, the people used to say,
The best among the Democrats were HARRISON AND CLAY;
The *Locos* now assume the name, a title most untrue,
And most unlike their party name when this old hat was new.

When this old hat was new, Van Buren was a Fed,
An enemy to every man who laboured for his bread;
And if the people of New York have kept their records true,
He voted 'gainst the poor man's rights, when this old hat was new.

—·—

When this old hat was new, those worthies did oppose
The cause and friends of Liberty, and stood among their foes;
Not so with "Granny" Harrison, for at Tippecanoe
He bravely fought the savage foe, when this old hat was new.

When this old hat was new, the friends to Liberty
Knew well the merits of Old Tip, while fighting at Maumee;
Come now, huzza for Harrison, just as we used to do,
When first we heard of Proctor's fall, when this old hat was new.

The Democrat version, appearing in the Albany *Argus* (August 29, 1840), went:

WHEN THIS OLD HAT WAS NEW.

When this old hat was new, some twenty years ago,
The Fed'ralists began to fear their final overthrow,
And so to keep the Party up and make it look like "blue,"
They've changed their names a dozen times,
    Since this old hat was new.

When this old hat was new, they thought the people fools,
And still they hope for Fed'ral ends to find them willing tools,
But though they've often changed their names as knaves are
        wont to do—
Their doctrines look just as they did—
    When this old hat was new.

When this old hat was new, the Feds despised the poor,
And blushed if ever they were caught within a "cabin" door,
The Democrats alone were found among the toiling crew—
Logs were not rolled in ruffle shirts—
    When this old hat was new.

—·—

When this old hat was new, if I remember well,
Among the heroes of the time, "Old Hickory" bore the bell—
"Dick Johnson" next in honor stood among the noble few—
For Dick was "hero of the Thames"—
    When this old hat was new.

When this old hat was new, the Fed'rals used to boast—
But often found the reckoning to be without their host—
And now they think that Harrison will "run," till all is blue—
Because he used to run so fast—
    When this old hat was new.

When this old hat was new, ere "patent Whigs" were made,
Old Tip was a Federalist and wore the black cockade!
But now he is—the Lord knows what! He's hidden from our
        view!
Though I suspect he's what he was—
    When this old hat was new.

When this old hat was new, Van Buren was the man
The people loved—altho' abused by all the Federal clan,
A Democrat, unmoved, unchanged—still to his country true,
He's ever been her friend and guard—
    Since this old hat was new!

A fire-and-brimstone extract from the Medal Minstrel *was quoted in the sheet music of the Whig version of "When This Old Hat Was New," to the politically well-exploited tune of "John Anderson, My Jo."*

WHEN THIS OLD HAT WAS NEW.

Inscribed to the

Republican Societies.

THROUGHOUT THE UNION.

In the remarks we make in the notes to this admirable song, we do not wish to be understood as casting any reflections whatever upon the majority of those who composed the old Federal party, many of whom were among the purest and brightest patriots in the land; but considering the former party distinctions to have ceased with the last war, we do object to the leading partisans of the "plunder party" denouncing as a Federalist every good patriot who is anxious to stop the leaks in the national treasury; and we do also most strenuously object to the false title of "Democrat," as claimed by those who were among the rankest of the Federalists, and who are now endeavouring to delude the People with the Siren song of Democracy. Out upon such hollow hearted hypocrites!!!

Medal Minstrel.

Printed for the Clubs and for sale at the Music Shops.

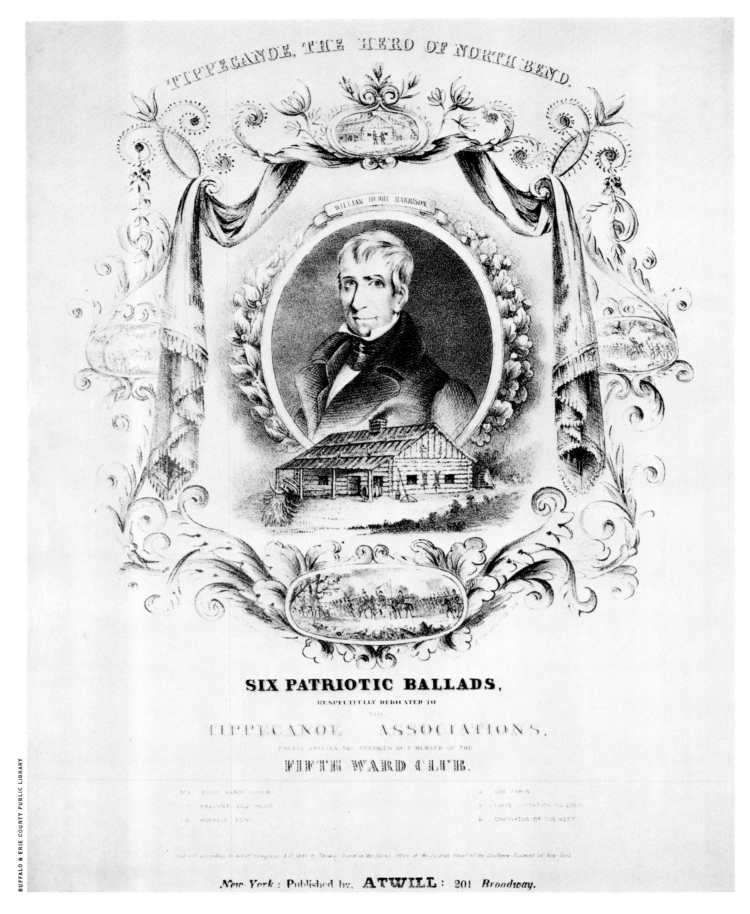

THE GALLANT OLD HERO.

In a little Log Cabin,
    From whose humble door,
Ne'er returns unreliev'd
    The distress'd or the poor,
Where content crowns with plenty,

Her vot'ries so true,
Dwells the gallant old Hero
    Of Tippecanoe.

Tune: "The Campbells Are Coming"
From the sheet music (1840)

BLAKE'S PATRIOTIC

LOG CABIN MUSIC

Respectfully Inscribed to all true Republicans

IN THE

United States.

Philadelphia Published by G.E.Blake. N°. 13, S° Fifth Street.

THE BUCKEYE SONG.

A Favorite Patriotic Ballad
as sung at the TIPPECANOE ASSOCIATIONS.

Oh, I went down to North Bend t'other afternoon,
With my old dog Cato and my double barrel gun,
Oh, I went down to North Bend to give the game a run,
And the first man I met, was Billy Harrison,
Billy Harrison, is the child what can fight,
From the morn's first blushing, till the eve's dark night,
He chucks them in the ribs, and he raps them on the nose,
Till they scarce know which way to look for the blows.
 CHORUS.
 Oh, Tipp a duden duden
 We have trap'd the old sly Fox,
 Oh, Tipp a duden duden
 He shall have some hard dry knocks.
 Oh, Tipp a duden duden
 Nine cheers for the Fox hound,
 Oh, Tipp a duden duden
 He has chas'd the Fox all round.

Far out in the west, where there lives the squatter,
Who hunt with rifle, and trap for mink and otter;
Old Harrison dash'd, when the fuss was just a brewin,
And he made things fly, like a streak of blue ruin:
He knock'd em just as strait, as eels on a platter,
The red skins, or red coats, it made no matter;
He didn't let them stand long, to play or to blubber,
For they had to start soon, either one way or other.
 Oh, Tipp a duden etc.

Then the war being over, he squat him down here,
Rais'd his log cabin first, then began for to clear;
And as long as old Tipp has a scothold there,
The hungry and thirsty, are welcome to a share:
But ev'ry dog, they say has his day,
And the good old hunter ought to have fair play;
Corn dodgers and bacon, are as good as the gold,
But they grow rather tuff, when the teeth gets old.
 Oh, Tipp a duden etc.

There's a sly old rogue, and they say his name is Martin
He's a Fox inside, of that, I'm sartin;
He's been robbin of the hen roost, 'bout long enough,
And·its time old Billy had a turn at the stuff:
While Martin stands hissin the blood hounds on,
In the cold dry trail, where the braves have gone;
The old Fox Hound, has his Tipp eye on him,
And the Fox neck's gone, just as sure as a glim.
 Oh, Tipp a duden etc.

Now Tipps of the Union, let's all be wide awake
We're on the brink of ruin, our all is at stake;
But one hunt more, and 'pon my word depend,
We'll place in the White House, the Hero of North Bend:
Then the old Chief's toils, shall all be well paid,
And his war worn bones on the down bed be laid;
While we sing to the Loco's, good bye to your Fox,
We'll cheer on our Hero, of the dry hard knocks.
 Oh, Tipp a duden etc.

Embellishing the vote-getting techniques that had won the presidency for Andrew Jackson in 1828, the Whigs of 1840, magnificently masterminded by the public relations wizard Thurlow Weed, assaulted the public with a ruthless barrage of political coercion. In his *Diary* (November 3, 1830), the New York lawyer George Templeton Strong described his boredom with the "humbug, lying, spouting, O. K. [the abbreviation of "Old Kinderhook," Van Buren's party nickname], and the Old Hero. Nothing but politics," he complained, "the walls are papered three feet deep with humbug, banners and inscriptions dangle over the street, mass meetings are held in every groggery from National Hall down." The ubiquitous log cabin dominated the scene: people wore log cabin fashions, used log cabin cosmetics, drank from log cabin glasses, read by log cabin lamps, smoked log cabin tobacco, wrote on log cabin notepaper, and even drank log cabin whiskey. Through this last delectable commodity, an enduring term was bequeathed to the American language. The miniature, log-cabin-shaped bottles of whiskey that were distributed by the advertising-conscious E. C. Booz Distillery of Philadelphia became so popular that the firm name came to be the synonym for the product. The latchstring was always out at log cabin party headquarters, which profusely dotted the national landscape; and hospitality from the brimming cider barrel was as freely dispensed as political gospel, usually disguised as community singing.

To counterbalance their resplendent image of Old Tip, the cider-drinking knight of the log cabin, the Whigs invented the corrupt figure of King Matty, the "champaigne"-guzzling despot of the presidential palace. In April 1840, Congressman Charles Ogle of Pennsylvania harangued the House for three whole days, reciting a catalog of outrageous accusations that branded Van Buren as an effete voluptuary who heedlessly squandered the public's money to satisfy his own decadent tastes. Ogle charged Van Buren with having transformed the White House into an "Asiatic mansion" by introducing such un-American exotica as fancy French cooking served on gold plate, French artificial flowers, imported carpets, nine-foot-high, gold-framed mirrors, and—most reprehensible of all—a bathtub. At the presidential open house on New Year's Day, Ogle complained that at the public expense Van Buren always had the Marine Band "stationed in the spacious front hall, from whence they swell[ed] the rich saloons of the palace with 'Hail to the Chief' . . . and other humdrum airs. . . ." Not content with the conformation of the landscape surrounding the White House, "Sweet Sandy Whiskers" was accused of having indulged his unnatural proclivities by having constructed "a number of clever sized hills, every pair of which . . . was designed to resemble and assume the form of AN AMAZON'S BOSOM, with a miniature knoll or hillock on its apex, to denote the ni-ple." Ogle's demagoguery was reprinted in the Whig newspapers and widely circulated among the faithful in pamphlet form as well. Needless to say, Whig voices were soon caroling denunciations of Van Buren's "sickly and vicious tastes." From *The Tippecanoe Song Book* (1840):

HAIL TO OLD TIPPECANOE.

Adapted to the air of "The Mistletoe Bough."

VAN BUREN sits in his marble hall,
And liveried slaves come forth at his call,
The banquet is spread—the silver gleams—
The dark wine flows in purple streams—
Around him bends a servile host,
And loud they shout the welcome toast—
    "Down with Old Tippecanoe!
    Down with Old Tippecanoe!"

"Bring forth," he cries, "the glittering plate,
We'll dine today in Royal state."
He speaks—and on his table soon,
They place the golden fork and spoon;
The dazzling goblets glance around,
And high the joyous shouts resound—
    "Down with Old Tippecanoe!
    Down with Old Tippecanoe!"

But mark! A panic runs through the hall:
They see the handwriting appear on the wall!
The thunder peals from Virginia's shore,
"The dark Magician shall rule no more!"
The Whigs come on with a conqueror's wing,
And the vaulted roof with paeans ring—
    "Hail to Old Tippecanoe!
    Hail to Old Tippecanoe!"

"We stoop to conquer," a banner at the great Whig parade at Baltimore had proclaimed, and this surprisingly truthful admission best describes the Whig hard sell in 1840. In their exchange of the two candidates' identities, Van Buren—in reality a self-made man whose father had been a humble farmer and tavernkeeper in the village of Kinderhook, New York—was persistently represented as a ruthless capitalist whose iniquitous disdain for hard cider made him an object of loathing, contempt, and ridicule. "The poor man is as much entitled to the honors of office and the confidence of the people as the haughty aristocrat with his hoarded millions," bathetically trumpeted the New York *Daily Whig* (quoted in the *Daily National Intelligencer*, January 14, 1840) and in the same outburst accused the Democrats of asking, "with infinite contempt, whether a person who had ever 'drank hard cider' should dare to think of occupying the White House at Washington." Faithful party bards tirelessly translated such irrational propaganda into song, and party artists into appealing scenes such as this idyllic log cabin landscape that decorated the sheet music cover of "The Farmer of North Bend." In the text, "John, Levi, Joel," and "Jim" are the members of Van Buren's cabinet, John Forsyth, Levi Woodbury, Joel Poinsett, and James K. Paulding; "Amos" is Amos Kendall, who had resigned his office of postmaster general to devote his talents entirely to managing the Democratic campaign.

THE FARMER OF NORTH BEND.

A Farmer there was that lived at North Bend,
Esteem'd by his neighbors and many a friend;
And you'll see on a time if you follow my ditty,
How he took a short walk up to Washington City.
Ri tu, di nu, di nu, di nu,
Ri tu, di nu, ri tu, di nu, ri tu na. . . .

His tidy Log Cabin he left with regret,
And he put up a sign that it would be to let;
But whatever rare sights the White House might display,
He'd find none so strange as he'd seen in his day.
    Ri tu, di nu, &c.

The Farmer walked on, and arrived at the door,
And he gave such a thump as was ne'er thumped before;
Master Van thought his rap was the sound of a flail,
And his heart beat with fear and he turned deadly pale.
    Ri tu, di nu, &c.

"Run John and run Levi—run Joel and Jim,"
Said Van, "but leave Amos, I cannot spare him;
There is only one living dares make such ado,
That's the sturdy old fellow called Tippecanoe."
    Ri tu, di nu, &c.

They were all growing merry, and taking champaigne,
And the Farmer impatient rapped louder again;
To the door all the Cabinet Ministers run,
To demand who so boldly had spoiled all their fun.
    Ri tu, di nu, &c.

Says Tip, "my fine fellows get out of my way,
I've routed whole armies like you in my day;
My mind is made up to walk into that chair,
Where Van takes his wine with a swaggering air."
    Ri tu, di nu, &c.

The Patriots home.

A VERY POPULAR WHIG SONG

Respectfully Dedicated to the

LOG CABIN ASSOCIATION OF THE

United States,

BY THE PUBLISHER.   *Pr. 50 Cts*

NEW YORK,

Published by CHARLES T GESLAIN, *357 Broadway.*

Entered according to Act of Congress in the year 1840 by Charles T. Geslain in the Clerks Office of the District Court of the Southern District of N. Y.

Then Amos, who listened, spoke up, "Mister Van,
I know how to tickle that old Farmer man;
I'll ask him politely to come up and dine,
And then we can muddle his wits with the wine."
  Ri tu, di nu, &c.

"Oh! pray Mister Farmer, just walk up this way,
We hardly expected to see you this day;
So many stout swiggers are here at this time,
There's but one bottle left, but you'll find it is prime."
  Ri tu, di nu, &c.

"I tell you what, Amos, I see what you're at,
I wont touch a glass of champaigne, and that's flat;
But a mug of hard cider will answer my turn,
It's getting in fashion up here as I learn."
  Ri tu, di nu, &c.

Then Amos and Van searched the table all round,
Not a drop of hard cider was there to be found;
So the Farmer advised them to lay in a store
By the fourth of next March, if they shouldn't before.
  Ri tu, di nu, &c.

A
MINIATURE
OF
MARTIN VAN BUREN.

I've been a knave—a knave's a fool,
Have ever been the Devil's tool.
Must stand upon contrition' stool,
                                    Van Buren.

WITH A SELECTION OF THE BEST AND MOST POPULAR

TIPPECANOE SONGS.

Amos Kendall's veracity—Tom Benton's honesty—Francis Blair's beauty.

"What is wanting cant be numbered."

Of the avalanche of Whig songbooks that descended in 1840, none rivalled in unmitigated malignity the anonymous collection called *A Miniature of Martin Van Buren.* Some of the songs were a distillation of Ogle's "Omnibus of Lies"; others —set to German tunes—derided Van Buren's Dutch derivation; still others lampooned Van Buren's Democratic henchmen nearly as mercilessly as they did the president. *A Miniature of Martin Van Buren* may very well represent the nadir of sung political abuse.

KING MATTY AND BLAIR.

Tune—"Lord Lovell and Nancy Bell."

King Matty he sat in his big "white house,"
    A curling his whiskers fine,
And the Globe man Blair sat at his side,
    A drinking his Champaigne wine, wine, wine,
        A drinking his Champaigne wine.

Then awful shook King Matty's locks,
    And fearful glanced his eye,
And he stamped his foot upon the floor,
    And he heaved a monstrous sigh, sigh, sigh,
        And heaved a monstrous sigh.

Oh! What's the matter King Matty, said Blair,
    Oh! What's the matter? said he;
I'm a gwyine to go to Kinderhook,
    My family for to see, see, see,
        My family for to see.

Says Blair, you are a good hearted man,
    And love your family dear;
I'd thought that you would not go back,
    'Till after another four year, year, year,
        'Till after another four year.

Nor would I go back, my dearest Blair,
    But what the deuce can I do!
The people say I must make room
    For the Hero of Tippecanoe, noe, noe,
        For the Hero of Tippecanoe.

Then the Globe man's cheek sunk on his breast,
    And his eyes fell to the floor,
And his nether lip hung on the ground,
    And it couldn't drag any lower, ower, ower,
        And it couldn't drag any lower.

Alack and alas! said Globe man Blair,
    We're deep in the mud and the mire;
Alack and alas, said Matty the King,
    The Sub-Treasury fat's in the fire, ire, ire,
        The Sub-Treasury fat's in the fire.

Now Matty and Blair they raised their eyes,
    Each other's face to see,
And they placed their thumbs upon their nose,
    And their fingers twirled twiddle de-de-de-de,
        And their fingers twirled twiddle-de-de.

OH! OH! WHERE SHALL I FLY TO.

Tune—"Thou, thou, reign'st in this bosom."

Oh! oh! where shall I fly to,
    I, I, can't live alone;
No, no, I must apply to
    Those who are fondly my own.
        Yes, yes, yes, yes,
        Those who are fondly my own.

A, A, Amos, oh hear me—
    Don't, don't go for to go;
Do, do, do linger near me,
    It's cruel t'abandon me so.
        Yes, yes, yes, yes, &c.

Van, Van, cease your soft soapin'
    A, A, Amos replies;
Soon, soon, you will see slopin'
    A chap just about my own size.
        Yes, yes, yes, yes, &c.

Blair, Blair, you will stand by me,
    Van, Van, cries in despair;
You, you, surely can *lie* me
    Safe in the President's chair.
        Yes, yes, yes, yes, &c.

Off, off, Blair he has gone too,
    Rats, rats, leave a doom'd ship;
Tom, Tom Benton—Calhoun too—
    All give poor Matty the slip.
        Yes, yes, yes, yes, &c.

I, I, I've liv'd in clover,
    Oh! oh! sighs little Van;
Tip, Tip, Tip's tip'd me over,
    "I am a used up man."
        Yes, yes, yes, yes
        I am a used up man.
        Van, Van, Van, Van.
        Van is a used up man.

NON-COMMITTAL SONG.

Tune—"German Air."

A Dutchman came over from Kinderhook—snapoo,
A Dutchman came over from Kinderhook—snapoo,
  A Dutchman came over from Kinderhook,
  When ask'd for his name he replied with shy look,
Snapooter, snapeeter, philantro, kiksheeter, snapoo.

Oh, where are you going, you little Dutchman?—snapoo,
Oh, where are you going, you little Dutchman?—snapoo,
  He nodded his head but he stuck to his plan,
Of snapooter, snapeeter, philantro, kiksheeter, snapoo.

He got on a stump and palaver'd away—snapoo,
He got on a stump and palaver'd away—snapoo,
  In a very mysterious obfuscated way,
About snapooter, snapeeter, philantro, kiksheeter, snapoo.

The people all wonder'd and opened their eyes—snapoo,
The people all wonder'd and opened their eyes—snapoo,
  But thought there was something exceedingly wise
In snapooter, snapeeter, philantro, kiksheeter, snapoo.

He cast a sheep's eye at the President's chair—snapoo,
He cast a sheep's eye at the President's chair—snapoo,
  You must answer some questions before you get there,
Mr. snapooter, snapeeter, philantro, kiksheeter, snapoo.

Whatever you ask I am ready to *hear*—snapoo,
Whatever you ask I am ready to *hear*—snapoo,
  And the answer I make you shall prove quite as clear
As snapooter, snapeeter, philantro, kiksheeter, snapoo.

Oh, what's your opinion of *this* and of *that*—snapoo,
Oh, what's your opinion of *this* and of *that*—snapoo,
  With a cringe and a bow quick replies little Mat,
Snapooter, snapeeter, philantro, kiksheeter, snapoo.

Some said he meant *yes*, and some said he meant *no*—snapoo,
Some said he meant *yes*, and some said he meant *no*—snapoo,
  But resolved to the White House the Dutchman should go.
With his snapooter, snapeeter, philantro, kiksheeter, snapoo.

For three or four years we have tried the Dutchman—snapoo,
For three or four years we have tried the Dutchman—snapoo,
  And we've found to our cost what he meant by his plan
Of snapooter, snapeeter, philantro, kiksheeter, snapoo.

So Matty to Kinderhook, march, march away—snapoo,
So Matty to Kinderhook, march, march away—snapoo,
  Says Van "If you will but allow me to stay,
I'll snapooter, snapeeter, philantro, kiksheeter, snapoo."

VAN BUREN.

Who, while but a little boy,
Was counted crafty, cunning, sly,
Who with the wily fox could vie!
                Van Buren.

Who, when an urchin, young at school,
Would of each classmate make a tool,
In cheating, who the roost would rule?
                Van Buren.

Who with a Sophist's subtle art,
Could act the politician's part,
And either party aid or thwart?
                Van Buren.

Who when his peers in heart and mind,
To scant and frugal fare confin'd,
From gorgeous, golden service din'd?
                Van Buren.

Who when distress and want was ours,
Profusely scattered golden showers?
To buy French Artificial Flowers?
                Van Buren.

Who finds his own a sinking ship,
And sadly hangs his nether lip,
And vents his spleen upon "Old Tip?"
                Van Buren.

Who when November shall come round,
Shall hear reverberate the sound,
Magician! Thou art wanting found?
                Van Buren.

Who then shall take his final look,
At toys in which such pride he took,
Next March—shall *march* to Kinderhook?
                Van Buren.

Now rally at the Ballot Box,
And vote the *Patriot Farmer's Prox*,
So shall absquatulate the *Fox*.
                Van Buren.

Who was faithless from his youth,
Who hates the light and scorns the truth,
And worst of Sophists is forsooth?
                Van Buren.

Who never did a noble deed,
Who of the people took no heed,
But followed worst of Tyrants' creed?
                Van Buren.

Who like the wily serpent clings,
Who like the pois'nous adder stings,
Who is more base than basest Kings?
                Van Buren.

Who tried to climb ambition's ladder,
At ev'ry step grew mad and mader,
And now is dwindled to a shadow?
                Van Buren.

Who rules us with an iron rod,
Who moves at Satan's beck and nod,
Who heeds not man, who heeds not God?
                Van Buren.

O Lord! Have mercy on us Whigs,
And drive away the Loco Pigs,
And he who ran so many rigs,
                Van Buren.

Who would his friend, his country sell,
Do other deeds too base to tell,
Deserves the lowest place in Hell?
                Van Buren.

THE TIPPEC

Published by SA

HOE QUICK STEP
CARUSI Baltimore

In the tidal wave of Whig conventions that swept over the nation, the attendance was so great that crowds were estimated by the acre: "Fifteen acres of men" and six thousand "females" was the male chauvinist, Whig reckoning of the meeting held on May 29–30, 1840, at Tippecanoe battleground, and we are told by Robert Gray Gunderson (*The Log Cabin Campaign*, 1957) that "thirty cider dispensaries contributed to the roar." At the great Bunker Hill convention held at Boston in September, the Whigs reported that sixty thousand shouting, chanting, cheering, singing Whigs marched from Boston Common to Bunker Hill amid the floats and the banners and the blaring bands of music and cheering spectators (see page 298). The Boston *Notion* (September 12, 1840) commented that "the procession was magnificent beyond description. The long line of mounted men, and coaches, and emblems, and delegations, with their beautiful banners, and bands of music, were nearly two hours passing a given point . . . as far as the eye could reach, the streets were closely thronged with citizens, and the houses were lined to the very tops with ladies and children." The *Notion* added that the cheers and shouts "must have rent the very concave of the skies." As they marched the Whigs chanted slogans like:

> Old Tip he wears a homespun coat
> He has no ruffled shirt-wirt-wirt.
> But Mat he has the golden plate
> And he's a little squirt-wirt-wirt.

The "wirt" sound was made by spitting through the teeth, a sobering thought when multiplied by sixty thousand.

For social diversion at Whig conventions, the evenings were mostly spent at log cabin clubs and headquarters "in singing Tippecanoe songs, and shouting, and hurraing," *Niles' National Register* (November 7, 1840) tells us. A song performed at one of these soirees during the Bunker Hill convention was so "heartily" performed, commented the Boston *Notion* (September 12), where the "Harrison Song" was printed, that "Old Tip might almost have heard it at the North Bend." In the text, "Johnson" is Richard Mentor Johnson, the incumbent vice-president and the reputed slayer of Tecumseh at the Battle of the Thames in 1813. In a feebleminded attempt to compete with the zingy Whig slogans, the Democrats had concocted for Johnson: "Rumpsey-dumpsey, rumpsey-dumpsey/Colonel Johnson killed Tecumpsey."

HARRISON SONG.

Tune—YANKEE DOODLE.

On seventy six, our minds we'll fix
    And take it for our text, sir,
I now declare, our nation's chair
    William shall take it next sir.

HALF CHORUS.
Old Tip ca nu, he has been true,
    So says our country's spoiler,
So now my boys, without much noise
    A health to Tip and Tyler.

FULL CHORUS.
    Roll away, Roll away
        Keep the ball in motion,
    Roll away, Roll away
        From Rocky Hill to ocean.

~~~

For little Van, is not the man
    For our next President sir,
But Harrison, he is the one
    For him our course is bent sir.
        Old Tip &c. Roll away &c.

And Jackson he may live to see,
    With one sad solem look sir;
Little Van Bu, and Johnson too
    Going home to Kinderhook sir.
        Old Tip &c. Roll away &c.

Ye voters all, both great and small,
    I'd have you to Remember,
The time's at hand, come take your stand,
    And don't forget November.
        Old Tip &c. Roll away &c.

And when that day, has past away,
    We'll then lay by our fighting,
And every one, both old and young
    Will see us all uniting.
        Old Tip &c. Roll away &c.

Then if Old Tip, should take a trip,
    To see our farms grow wider,
We'd take him to our log cabin,
    And treat him with hard cider.
        Old Tip &c. Roll away &c.

"Amidst the spirit-stirring sounds of martial music, and the enlivening shouts of the spectators, they commenced their triumphant march through the decorated streets" (Niles' National Register, *September 19, 1840, on the Bunker Hill Convention parade*).

WHIG GATHERING,

SONG AND CHORUS

respectfully dedicated

TO THE WHIGS OF THE

UNITED STATES.

BOSTON.

Published by HENRY PRENTISS, 33 Court St.

Entered according to Act of Congress in the year 1840 by H. Prentiss in the Clerks office of the District Court of Massachusetts

The beautiful girls, God bless their souls, souls, souls,
The country through,
Will all to a man do all that they can,
For Tippecanoe and Tyler too, &c.

Although women continued mainly to be onlookers in 1840, they nevertheless participated more actively in this campaign than they had yet dared to do. Lucy Kenney, an articulate Whig lady, contributed a landmark political tract by an American female. And at the mammoth Dayton Convention parade (by Whig reckoning, one hundred thousand people), ten thousand Tippecanoe ladies, thrilling deliciously to the proximity of their hero, greeted Old Tip with the fluttering of "thousands of white handkerchiefs" as he rode by. It was repeatedly observed within the party that Old Tip would have been unanimously elected if women had been allowed to vote. Even so, Whig women were credited with having influenced the election in no small way: they refused to have anything to do with Locofoco swains, and many a lovelorn Democrat was blackmailed into casting a Whig vote in 1840. "Whig husbands or none" was the motto inscribed on campaign sashes worn by politically conscious Tennessee women, reports Robert Gunderson, who also quotes an Ohio newspaper's report of a local women's Fourth of July celebration where the celebrants genteelly toasted Harrison with gourds of cold water and cups of tea.

Mostly, however, Whig women performed women's tasks, sewing prodigious numbers of campaign banners and preparing literally tons of food that were devoured at gargantuan Whig banquets, barbecues, clambakes, fish fries, party anniversaries, July Fourth celebrations, log cabin raisings, and innumerable other party festivities.

In 1840 the Democrats made their own enduring contribution to the language when they bestowed on their man the nickname of "Old Kinderhook," hoping to offset the powerful hold on the public imagination of "Old Tip." Abbreviating it to "O. K.," they considered that they had devised a zesty and vote-getting sobriquet for Van Buren, but the Whigs characteristically turned it around. George Templeton Strong tells his diary (May 1, 1840): ". . . we'll be O. K. by and by, perhaps according to the new Whig interpretation: out of kash, out of kredit, out of karacter, and out of klothes. . . ." On May 6 he writes that at an interminable Whig parade in New York, with "banners, log cabins on wheels, [and] barrels supposed to be full of cider. . . . The Locos, of course, disgraced themselves as usual, by a fierce attack on one banner in particular—representing Matty shinning away from the White House with O. K. under it, i.e., 'Off to Kinderhook.' " Van Buren's rapid gallop "off to Kinderhook" is probably what the "O K Gallopade," dedicated to the Whig ladies, was meant to suggest.

Symptomatic of their party's generally impotent performance in the campaign, the once-puissant Democrat bards appear to have been rendered all but inarticulate by the Whig steamroller. Instead of trading blows, the Democrats complained querulously of the avalanche of abusive songs, the raucous and insistent hurrah, the rampant alcoholism, and the floods of Whig words with which the electorate was ceaselessly assaulted (more than five thousand orators stumped for the Whigs, among them such luminaries as Henry Clay and Daniel Webster). Under the heading "Making Proselytes by Music," the Albany *Argus* (June 25, 1840) ineffectually grumbled: "A new light has dawned upon the political world. The power of reasoning and argument is to give place to the irresistible influence of poetry and song." The Washington *Globe*, gleefully quoted in the Whig *Madisonian* (June 25, 1840), protested more passionately, giving a furious annotated catalog of the hated Whiggish electioneering apparatus: "Signs and badges . . . to *excite the passions* and STULTIFY THE JUDGEMENTS of the people; songs, *inspired by the* FURIES AND WRITTEN *with* FIREBRANDS, *and rabidly clamoured* through the streets; the waving of *itinerant pageants* of banners bearing STUPID MOTTOES. . . . And lastly, to complete these *ignoble saturnalia*, INTEMPERANCE *itself, evoked as an auxiliary* FIEND *in a* FIENDISH CAUSE, in the form of a BARREL!! *on which are written the words* HARD CIDER!!!" With an apology for the "hard swearing, which is the natural result of hard cider revels," the *Globe* (October 7, 1840) printed a ballad apocryphally reported to have been sung at dedication ceremonies for a "Log Cabin, near Centre Market."

ODE TO MUSIC.

> Spirit of cider hard! we raise
> An altar sacred to thy praise!
> O give us store of apple toddy,
> And then we don't fear any body;
> We'll drink, and sing, and brag, and war,
> And swear that sense shall be no more.

CHORUS.
> D--n Democrats, d--n the Administration;
> D--n argument, d--n demonstration;
> D--n common sense, d--n human reason,
> They're little better than high treason.
> Give us a gourd of right good stuff,
> And "d--n'd be he cries hold enough!"

~~~

Harping on the same solitary string, the Albany *Argus* (July 17, 1840) published a sardonic "lullaby" preceded by a note in dubious taste, captioned "sentimental": "A whig paper says Tippecanoe cradles are becoming fashionable among whig ladies (married or single the editor sayeth not). We recommend the following nursery ditty as an accompaniment":

> Hushaby baby,
> Daddy's a whig;
> Before he comes home,
> Hard cider he'll swig;
> Should he get tipsey,
> Together we'll fall,
> Down will come daddy,
> Tip, cradle and all.

Criticizing Harrison for his noncommittal speeches—he was the first presidential candidate actively to stump in his own behalf—the Democrats dubbed him "General Mum." Harrison's public utterances were in fact carefully screened by his party managers, who preferred to restrict Old Tip—no political or intellectual giant—within the safe confines of the classical references he loved to cite. If he was a less than inspiring orator, he was nevertheless rapturously received by his bewitched constituents—after all, he was Old Tip. A stanza of the *Globe*'s "Ode to Music" went:

> Another gourd for General *Mum*,
> Whose fame is like his fav'rite drum,
> Which when most empty makes most noise,
> Huzza for General Mum, my Boys.

Campaign songs were regularly printed in Horace Greeley's newspaper The Log Cabin. *This one, lampooning Amos Kendall, appeared in the July 25, 1840, issue.*

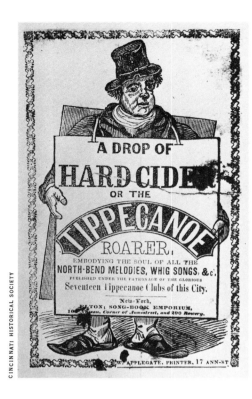

The Whig singing marathon was nourished and replenished by a plethora of songsters and sheet music, in which were endlessly reiterated—usually to popular tunes—the incredibly simpleminded theme that served the Whigs in lieu of a platform: the virtues of Old Tip, log cabins, and hard cider, as opposed to the depravities of the evil Little Magician and his lawless crew. "The Abortive Van Buren Convention" lampoons the Democratic nominating convention in Baltimore in May, at which no candidate for vice-president had been nominated. In the text, "Polk" is James Knox Polk, the future president of the United States; "Tecumseh" is another nickname for old Rumpsey-Dumpsey Johnson.

From *The Tippecanoe Song Book*:

THE ABORTIVE VAN BUREN CONVENTION.

Tune—"Pretty Betty Martin, Tiptoe Fine,
Couldn't Get a Sweetheart to Please Her Mind."

Pretty little Martin, tiptoe, tiptoe,
Pretty little Martin, tiptoe fine,
Couldn't get a candidate for Vice-President,
Couldn't get a candidate to please his mind.
Old Dick Johnson he wouldn't answer,
He was too rough for a President so fine;
Pretty little Martin, tiptoe, tiptoe,
Couldn't get a candidate to please his mind.

Pretty little Martin, tiptoe, tiptoe,
Couldn't make the loco-focos toe the line,
Some were for Polk and some for Johnson,
But no one but Polk could please his mind.
The Tennessee loco-focos they wanted Polk in;
To poke him in for President next in the line;
Pretty little Martin, tiptoe, tiptoe,
Couldn't get a candidate to please his mind.

Pretty little Martin, tiptoe, tiptoe,
He couldn't coax old Tecumseh to decline;
Old Tecumseh's friends would not leave him;
To go for Mr. Polk did not please their minds.
Polkites and Johnsonites wouldn't pull together,
The split was too wide, and they couldn't make it join;
Pretty little Martin, tiptoe, tiptoe,
Couldn't get a candidate to please his mind.

Pretty little Martin, tiptoe, tiptoe,
The jig is up with him, as he will find:
His legs are not long enough to follow in the footsteps;
He can't make the party all go the whole swine.
Now every loco-foco has to pick a candidate,
And run him for himself on his own hook and line.
Pretty little Martin, tiptoe, tiptoe,
Couldn't get a candidate to please his mind.

From *Harrison Melodies*:

SONG FOR THE WORKING MEN.
Tune—"*Yankee Doodle.*"

That Matty loves the Working man,
　No working man can doubt, sirs;
For well doth he pursue the plan
　That *turns* the workies *out*, sirs;
He turns them out of *Whig* employ,
　He turns them out of bread, sirs;
And *middle* men doth he annoy,
　By striking business dead, sirs;
　　For Matty is a Democrat,
　　　Sing, Yankee Doodle dandy,
　　　With spoons of *gold*, and English coach,
　　　And servants always handy.

And doth he not his love display,
　While pressing *Labor* down, sirs,
By showing, in his pleasant way,
　A shilling's worth a crown, sirs;
　　For Matty is, &c.

Quoth he, a shilling soon shall buy
　As much of bread and meat, sirs,
As *two*—when wages were so high.
　If not—*you must not eat, sirs*;
And then, for all the *little things*
　They are but "*luxuries*," sirs,
And if, like riches, they take wings,
　Why eat—*more bread and cheese, sirs.*
　　For Matty is, &c.

But time is short to tell of all
　The love of little Van, sirs,
He is the friend—doubt not at all—
　Of every working man, sirs;
And if he scrimps your daily food
　By docking down your pay, sirs;
'Tis only for *his own* best good;
　Then what have you to say, sirs?
　　For Matty is, &c.

Now if you do not like such love
　But vote for *Harrison*, sirs,
All I can say, is,—*Van must move*,
　For then his race is run, sirs.
　　Still Matty is a Democrat
　　　By Yankee Doodle dandy;
　　　His golden spoons and English coach,
　　　And *serfs* are always handy.

YE JOLLY YOUNG LADS OF OHIO.
Tune—Old Rosin The Beau.

Ye jolly young lads of Ohio,
 And all ye sick Jackson men too,
Come out from among the Van party,
 And vote for old Tippecanoe,
CHORUS.
And vote for old Tippecanoe,
 And vote for old Tippecanoe,
Come out from among the Van party,
 And vote for old Tippecanoe.

The great Twenty-Second is coming,
 And the Vanjacks begin to look blue,
They know there's no chance for poor Marty,
 If we stick to old Tippecanoe.
  If we stick, etc.

I therefore will give you a warning,
 Not that any good it will do,
For I'm certain you all are a going,
 To vote for old Tippecanoe.
  To vote, etc.

Then let us be up and a doing,
 And cling to our cause brave and true,
I'll bet you a fortune we'll beat them,
 With the hero of Tippecanoe,
  With the Hero, etc.

Good men from the Vanjacks are dying,
 Which makes them look kinder askew,
For they see they are joining the standard,
 With the Hero of Tippecanoe,
  With the Hero, etc.

They say that he lived in a cabin,
 And lived on old hard cider too,
Well, what if he did, I'm certain,
 He's the Hero of Tippecanoe,
  He's the Hero, etc.

Then let us all go to Columbus,
 And form a procession or two,
And I tell you the Vanjacks will startle,
 At the sound of Old Tippecanoe,
  At the sound, etc.

As for one I'm fully determined,
 To go, let it rain, hail or snow,
And do what we can in the battle,
 For the Hero of Tippecanoe,
  For the Hero, etc.

And if we get any ways thirsty,
 I'll tell you what we can do,
We'll bring down a keg of Hard Cider,
 And drink to Old Tippecanoe,
  And drink, etc.

Many 1840 campaign songs were sung to the tune of "Old Rosin the Beau" (also spelled "Bow"), a ditty of obscure origin that had taken the country by storm after it appeared at some time during the 1830s. The tune was to become a campaign song staple in ensuing elections.

From *The Tippecanoe Song Book*:

LITTLE VANNY.
Tune—"Rosin the Bow."

You can't make a song to Van Buren,
 Because his long name will not do;
There's nothing about him *allurin'*,
 As there is about Tippecanoe!

He never was seen in a battle,
 Where bullet and cannon shot flew,
His nerves would be shocked with the rattle
 Of a contest like Tippecanoe!

While Harrison march'd to the border—
 Sly Van staid at home as you know,
Afraid of the smell of gun-powder—
 Then hurrah for Old Tippecanoe!

Little Matt was too tender a dandy,
 To shoulder a musket and go
Where Harrison battled so handy,
 As he did when at Tippecanoe;

But snug in his pretty silk stockings,
 And dressed in his broadcloth all new,
He roasted his shins in a parlour—
 Not fighting like Tippecanoe.

And now with his gold spoons and dishes,
 He lives like a king with his crew;
He'll feast on the loaves and the fishes,
 Till we put in Old Tippecanoe.

NORTHERN VOLUNTEERS QUICK STEP,

Composed & dedicated to

CAPT. SAM^L S. MILLS

and the

OFFICERS AND MEMBERS OF THE CORPS;

And arranged for the

PIANO FORTE

by

Maximilian Zuboff.

CHARLESTON. S.C.

Published by DEMING, BULKLEY & Cº, *King Street.*

Entered according to Act of Congress, AD 1840 by Deming, Bulkley & Cº in the Clerks Office of the District Court of the Southern District of New York.

This arresting sheet music cover art depicting a northern volunteer company on parade in Charleston, South Carolina, was lithographed by Nathaniel Currier in 1840, ten years before he formed his partnership with J. Merritt Ives.

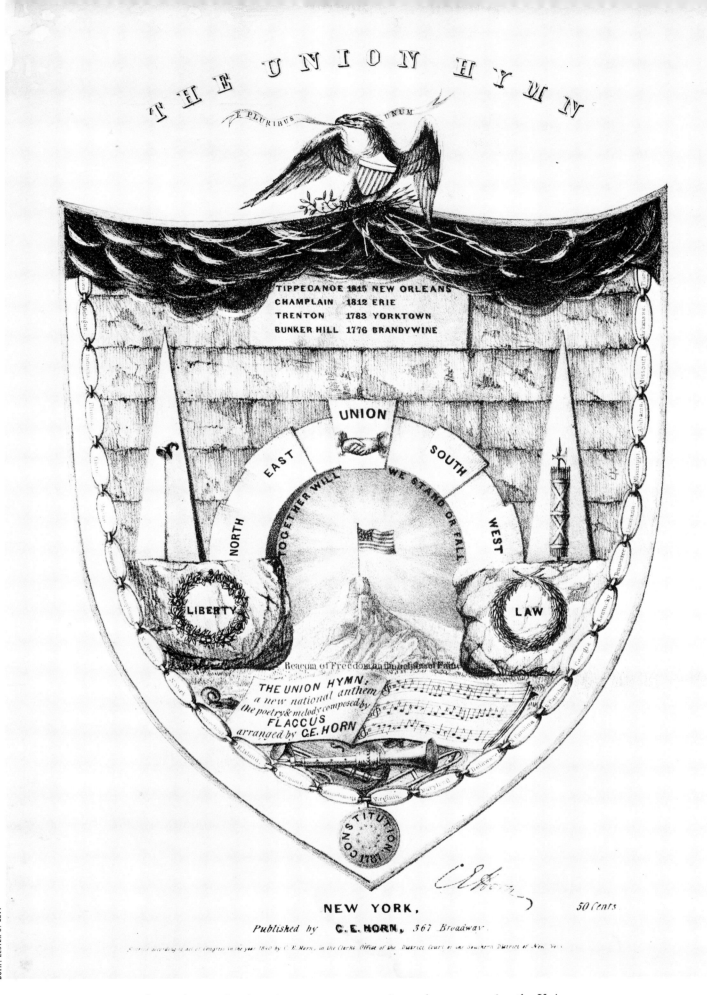

Increasing sectional tensions were a source of growing concern for the Union, as this striking, symbolic sheet music cover of 1840 illustrates.

Beautiful graphics adorned publications of military music in 1840.

HEWITT'S QUICK STEP:

PIANO FORTE.

Respectfully dedicated to

L. JAMES L. HEWITT.

AND THE OFFICERS AND MEMBERS OF THE

NEW YORK LIGHT GUARD;

by

T. REBHUN.

Pr 25 cts Nett

NEW YORK:
Published by *HEWITT & JAQUES*, 239 Broadway.

Entered according to Act of Congress A.D. 1840 by Hewitt & Jaques, in the Clerks Office of the District Court of the Southern District of New York

Even social music bore the party imprint.

HARRISON & TYLER

Sinclair Lith. Phila.

GRAND MILITARY WALTZ,

Dedicated with Respect to

PRESIDENT HARRISON.

Composed in Honor of the

GRAND BALL,

Given by the Citizens of Phila

by the

PUBLISHER.

Price 25 Cts. nett.

PHILADELPHIA,

OSBOURN'S MUSIC SALOON, 30, SOUTH FOURTH STREET.

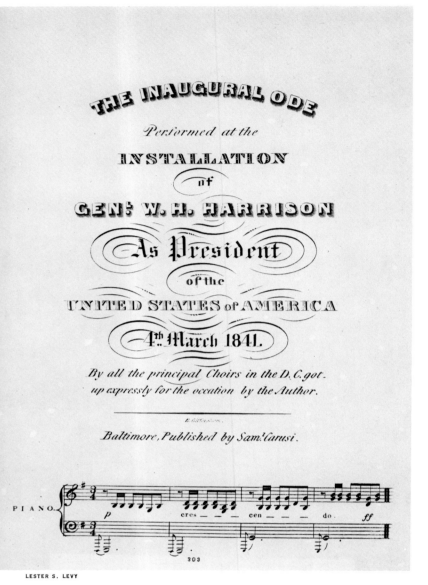

LESTER S. LEVY

William Henry Harrison rode to his inauguration on horseback, "as the Roman Emperors were wont to pass along the Appian Way," floridly recalled the Washington newspaperman who eccentrically signed his name Ben: Perley Poore (*Perley's Reminiscences of Sixty Years in the National Metropolis*, 1886). Perley's description of Harrison's mount as a "spirited white charger" is worlds removed from John Quincy Adams's evaluation of the animal. Calling it a "mean-looking white horse," Adams characteristically found the procession otherwise a "showy-shabby" affair, "consisting of a mixed military and civil cavalcade . . . Tippecanoe clubs, students of colleges and schoolboys, with about half a dozen veterans who had fought under the hero in the War of 1812, with sundry awkward and ungainly painted banners, and log cabins. . . ." Not so the Whigs, who reveled in their final victorious hurrah, despite having to undergo the agonizing ordeal of being exposed to the freezing weather for nearly two hours while the overcoatless Harrison spun out his tiresome inaugural address, composed chiefly of classical allusions and quotations. Even the most fanatical Whigs admitted that Old Tip's oratory left much to be desired. Braving Harrison's displeasure, Daniel Webster had tactfully attempted to edit the inaugural address; he is quoted by Perley as having pleaded guilty to the assassination of "two Roman Emperors and a pro-Consul" in the process. Not one, but three, lavish inaugural balls were given in Washington on March 4, 1841, at which Harrison celebrated. Exactly one month later he was dead.

SMITHSONIAN INSTITUTION

Special tickets were issued to admit Whig ladies to the inaugural ceremonies on March 4, 1841.

THE INAUGURAL ODE.

Come, let our voices join
And young and old combine
  To raise the song;
We hail this joyous day
Congratulations pay,
And cast our cares away
  And shouts prolong.

Let freemen's voices raise
A Hymn of grateful praise
  For Harrison,
Our love is his just claim—
Our hearts enshrine his name—
History records his fame
  Brave Harrison!

No log cabin, but an elegant lithograph of the Capitol, decorated "President Harrison's Grand Inauguration March" (1841).

PRESIDENT HARRISON'S

Lith of Ed. Weber & Cº Baltº

GRAND INAUGURATION MARCH

COMPOSED BY

HENRY DIELMAN

BALTIMORE

Published by G Willig Jr

Sinclair lith. Phil.

PRESIDENT HARRISON'S FUNERAL DIRGE

As performed on the occasion of his burial at

Washington City,

April, 1841.

Composed by

HENRY DIELMAN.

Price 25 Cts. Nett.

Philadelphia, OSBOURN'S MUSIC SALOON, *30 S. Fourth St.*

Harrison was the subject of what may be the unique programmatic funeral march. In "President Harrison's Funeral March," a running scenario accompanies passages musically descriptive of funerary rites: "Descending into the grave" (octaves in the bass in a stepwise downward progression); "The last trumpet peal" (a fanfare in triplets); "The lamenting bugle" (the same fanfare transposed a third lower); and "The Widow's Shriek" (two diminished seventh chords, fortissimo).

Six white horses, each led by a black groom dressed in white, "with white turban and sash," drew the hearse bearing William Henry Harrison's remains. The funeral procession, Ben: Perley Poore tells us, was two miles long, eclipsing in size "the inaugural pageant which had so recently preceded it." Encircling the black grooms, as they marched, were the pallbearers (presumably white), dressed in black with black scarves, and Perley observes that the starkness of this striking black and white design contrasted dramatically with the brilliant colors of the military uniforms marching in the procession. Harrison had died of pneumonia, believed by many to have resulted from exposure to the cold when he had stubbornly refused to wear an overcoat or a hat at his inaugural. His sudden death, following so soon after the "phenomenal commotion" of the campaign, was the subject of a goodly amount of sanctimonious moralizing about the transience of human glory. Perley tells us that at the Congressional Burying Ground, after Harrison's body had been temporarily placed in a vault, the troops fired three volleys in a "ludicrously straggling manner," after which "the drums and fifes struck up merry strains, the military marched away, and only the scene of the public bereavement remained."

Sketched on the spot, by W. Sharp.

Remark's — As this print will remain long after all who beheld the brilliant spect
"10th of September" a Fair was held by Ladies in the City of Boston, for the purpose of c
entirely successful. This drawing was taken from Mr. Phipps' house, South East of the Monument, a
portion only of the Delegates on foot

FREEME

As performed on the "Glorio

BUNKER-HILL WH

GE

Published by

shall have passed away, it may not be amiss to stamp upon it the interesting fact, that on this same

ing funds for the completion of the Monument (which is here presented in its unfinished state) the object was

resents the moment of time when the Cavalcade having countermarched, are about returning to the City; while a

have yet reached the hill.

Printed by Sharp, Michelin & Co.

IS' QUICK STEP.

th of September" Composed and dedicated to the

elegates

TO THE

CONVENTION of 1840.

—BY—

GE HEWS.

OSTON

KER & DITSON 135 Washington St.

25 cts. nett.

Like the keys of a forte-piano,
  They are now arranged for the action;
The black and white spread one banner—
  The rag-tag-and-bobtails of faction!

A Song for Cass and Butler
The Daily Union
October 18, 1848

9. Counterpoints

1841-1860

First published in 1843 as "Columbia the Land of the Brave," this famous patriotic song did not become "Columbia, the Gem of the Ocean" until it was reprinted the following year; it was also known as "Red, White, and Blue." Its authorship, credited in the first edition to the actor-singer David T. Shaw, was later claimed by its arranger, Thomas A. Beckett (or Thomas à Beckett), a Philadelphian of British origin. The song was the subject of transatlantic controversy as well, being claimed in England as a totally British production with words by an Irishman, Stephen Meany, and music (the same music) by an Englishman, Thomas Williams. Neither Meany nor Williams was credited when the song was first published in England during the late 1840s or early 1850s under various titles: "Britannia, the Gem of the Ocean," "Britannia, the Pride of the Ocean," "The Pride of the Ocean," and "The Red, White, and Blue." Who really wrote it has never been proved.

COLUMBIA THE LAND OF THE BRAVE.

O! Columbia the gem of the ocean,
  The home of the brave and the free;
The shrine of each patriot's devotion
  A world offers homage to thee.
Thy mandates make heroes assemble
  When Liberty's form stands in view,
Thy banners make tyranny tremble
  When borne by the red white and blue.
    CHORUS.
    When borne by the red white and blue,
    When borne by the red white and blue
      Thy banners make tyranny tremble;
    When borne by the red white and blue.

~~~

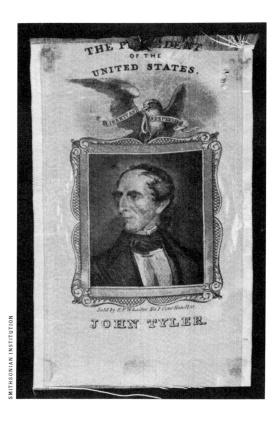

THE PRESIDENT OF THE UNITED STATES.

JOHN TYLER.

SMITHSONIAN INSTITUTION

Other recriminations of Tyler in *The Clay Club Coon Songster* (1844), where the preceding lines appeared, included:

THE TREACHEROUS HEARTED PRESIDENT.
TUNE—*Fine old English Gentleman.*

I'll sing you a true Whig song, made to a fine old rhyme,
Of a treacherous hearted President, one of the modern time—
By act and deed, and Veto too, a Whig he's ceased to be;
For he would'nt sign the Charter to aid our Currency.
    Like a treacherous hearted President,
      All of the modern time.

A President by chance is he, the People's choice is dead;
The brave old hearted HARRISON sleeps in his narrow bed—
And when Whigs think of what they've lost, and who assumes his place,
They feel that "Captain Tyler" fills it only with disgrace!
    Like a treacherous hearted President.
      All of the modern time.

When into office first he went, he swore he would be true,
And every Whig throughout the land huzza'd for "Tyler too!"
But now he wears a traitor's coat, we'll "head him," if we can,
And of all the Whigs to do it right, JOHN BOTTS is just the man.
    Oh, this treacherous hearted President,
      All of the modern time.

Unequivocally rejecting Congress's proposal that he be called "Vice President of the United States, Acting President," John Tyler demanded and got the full title and powers due to an elected president when he succeeded William Henry Harrison on April 6, 1841. "His Accidency" soon made it clear that he intended to use those powers without inhibition or interference from the Whig party. An uncompromising states' rights man, he was, in the estimation of John Quincy Adams, who disapproved of both Tyler and his title, "a political sectarian, of the slave-driving, Virginian, Jeffersonian school . . . with all the interests and passions and vices of slavery rooted in his moral and political constitution. . . ." (*Diary*, April 4, 1841). Adams wisely observed that this "first instance of a Vice President's being called to act as President of the United States [would] bring to the test that provision of the Constitution which places in the Executive chair a man never thought of for it by anybody." Obviously the Whigs responsible for John Tyler's vice-presidential nomination in 1840 had not anticipated that he might one day fill that chair. As its unexpected occupant, Tyler so unbendingly opposed the predominantly Whig Congress and its all-powerful leader, Henry Clay, that a state of political warfare soon developed. Not only was the president excommunicated from the Whig party, but a resolution for his impeachment "for gross usurpation of power" was proposed by his fellow Virginian and bitter antagonist, John Botts. Tyler's bid for renomination in 1844 was summarily rejected by the Whigs, who bitterly sang, to the tune of "Sea Snake":

    By accident to the White House he went,
      There his traitorous work began,
    In '44 to the shades he'll be sent
      Because he's a used up man.

On June 17, 1843, President Tyler attended the ceremonies held in Boston to celebrate the completion of the Bunker Hill Monument. Daniel Webster delivered the oration, just as he had done in 1825, when Lafayette had laid the cornerstone. The great champion of freedom John Quincy Adams, who had witnessed the battle sixty-eight years earlier, was greatly moved by the significance of Bunker Hill in the "annals of mankind," but he greatly deplored both the "burlesque" of an oration by Webster, whom he characterized as "a heartless traitor to the cause of human freedom," and the "pilgrimage by John Tyler and his cabinet of slave-drivers, to desecrate the solemnity by their presence" (*Diary*, June 17, 1843). With his customary intolerance of falsehood, Adams was incensed at the mockery of "a dinner at Faneuil Hall in honor of a President . . . hated and despised by those who invited him to it, themselves as cordially hated and despised by him." The Boston *Daily Evening Transcript* (June 19, 1843), on the other hand, fairly vibrated with excitement over the "all-glorious occasion," where from the hillside "covered with a multitudinous assembly of bravery and beauty; shouts rent the air; hurrah! hurrah! swept over the plain . . . [and Webster's voice] awakened their love of country, and made them drink deeply from the wellspring of his own patriotism."

The Boston Daily Evening Transcript *(June 15, 1843) announced the publication of several musical pieces specially written for the Bunker Hill Monument celebration. Among them was the* "'76 Quickstep, *an excellent composition, which [would] be played by the Brass Band, on the 17th, with a vignette view of the Monument, and the countless host upon the old battlefield."*

"'76"
QUICK STEP,

As Performed by the BOSTON BRASS BAND, on the anniversary

OF THE BATTLE OF BUNKER HILL, AND THE

GREAT MONUMENTAL CELEBRATION,
17TH JUNE 1843.

Most Respectfully Dedicated to the

BUNKER HILL MONUMENT ASSOCIATON,

— BOSTON. —

Published by CHAS H KEITH, 67 & 69 Court St.

Thayer & Co Lith.

Price 25 cts net

Entered according to act of Congress in the year 1843 by Chas H Keith in the clerk office of the District Court of Massachusetts

During the Bunker Hill Monument festivities, the *Daily Evening Transcript* (June 15, 1843) announced a concert by the famed Hutchinson Family, at which President Tyler and his entourage were expected. His attendance would have been most awkward: the singing Hutchinsons were passionately committed Abolitionists who used the concert platform as a sounding board to disseminate antislavery propaganda. At a time when singing families were the rage, the New Hampshire Hutchinsons, Judson, John, Asa, and their sister Abby, had taken the country by storm with their appealing performances of popular music, accessible to the most unsophisticated musical tastes. Borrowing the propagandizing techniques that had served the Whigs so successfully in 1840, "the tribe of Jesse," as the Hutchinsons called themselves, tirelessly reiterated their political credo in simple words set to tunes that everybody knew. Until the Civil War, they exerted a major influence on American thinking in behalf of Abolition; after emancipation they raised their voices in support of women's suffrage.

First edition sheet music cover (1843) of the
Hutchinson Family's theme song, "The Old Granite State,"
set to the revivalist tune "The Old Church Yard."

MUSIC DIVISION, THE NEW YORK PUBLIC LIBRARY

THE OLD GRANITE STATE.

We have come from the mountains,
We have come from the mountains,
We have come from the mountains,
 Of the "Old Granite State."

~~~

With a band of music,
With a band of music,
With a band of music
 We are passing 'round the world,

~~~

Liberty is our motto,
Liberty is our motto,
Equal liberty is our motto
 In the "Old Granite State."

We despise oppression,
We despise oppression,
We despise oppression,
 And we cannot be enslaved.

Yes we're friends of emancipation,
And we'll sing the proclimation,
Till it echoes through our nation,
 From the "Old Granite State."

That the Tribe of Jesse,
That the Tribe of Jesse,
That the Tribe of Jesse,
 Are the friends of equal rights.

~~~

Now three cheers altogether,
Shout Columbia's people ever,
Yankee hearts none can sever,
 In the "Old Sister States."

Like our sires before us,
We will swell the chorus.
Till the Heavens o'er us,
 Shall rebound the loud hussa.
  Hurrah! hurrah! hurrah!

The Hutchinsons were ardent teetotalers as well:

We are all teetoatlers,
We are all teetoatlers,
We are all teetoatlers,
 And have signed the Temperance Pledge.

In 1844 the Hutchinson Family contributed a memorable campaign song to the antislavery Liberty party, whose presidential candidate, James G. Birney, paradoxically succeeded in deflecting enough votes away from the Whig candidate, Henry Clay, to put James K. Polk, a slavery man, in the White House. In common with a number of other 1844 campaign songs of various political persuasions, the words of "Get Off the Track" were set to the recently published popular tune "Old Dan Tucker," claimed by Daniel Decatur Emmett to have been written in 1830 or 1831. Emmett, who was to gain immortality in 1859 as the composer of "Dixie," was one of the founding fathers of the blackface "minstrel show," a form of musical entertainment that remained popular until the twentieth century.

"Get off the Track" was a dynamic allegory, treating Abolitionism in up-to-date terms of the railroad, then in its exciting infancy.

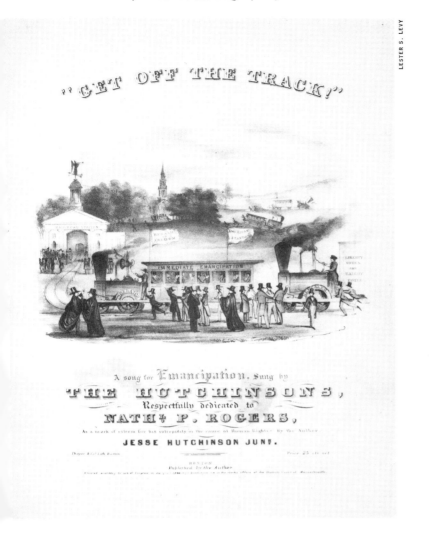

When the Hutchinsons sang "Get Off the Track" at an antislavery meeting at Salem, Massachusetts, in April 1844, both the song and the stirring performance were eulogized in the New Hampshire Abolitionist periodical *Herald of Freedom*, whose banner is seen flying from the railroad car "Emancipation" on the song's sheet music cover. The *Herald*'s editor, Nathaniel P. Rogers, to whom the song was dedicated, wrote:

[It] represented the railroad with all its terrible enginery and speed and danger. . . . When they [the Hutchinsons] cried to the heedless pro-slavery multitude that they were stupidly lingering on the track, and the engine 'Liberator' coming hard upon them, under full steam, and all speed, the Liberty Bell all ringing, and they standing like deaf men right in its whirlwind path, the way they cried 'Get off the Track,' in defiance of all time and rule, was magnificent and sublime.

GET OFF THE TRACK!

Ho! the Car Emancipation,
Rides majestic thro' our nation
Bearing on its Train, the story.
Liberty! a Nation's Glory.
    Roll it along, thro' the Nation
    Freedom's Car, Emancipation.

First of all the train, and greater,
Speeds the dauntless *Liberator*
Onward cheered amid hosannas,
And the waving of Free Banners.
    Roll it along! spread your Banners
    While the people shout hosannas.

Men of various predilections,
Frightened, run in all directions:
Merchants, Editors, Physicians,
Lawyers, Priests and Politicians.
    Get out of the way! every station.
    Clear the track of 'mancipation.

Let the Ministers and Churches
Leave behind sectarian lurches;
Jump on board the Car of Freedom
Ere it be too late to need them.
    Sound the alarm! Pulpit's thunder!
    Ere too late, you see your blunder.

Politicians gazed, astounded,
When, at first our Bell resounded:
Freight trains are coming, tell these Foxes,
With our *Votes* and *Ballot Boxes*.
    Jump for your lives! Politicians,
    From your dangerous false positions.

Rail Roads to Emancipation
Cannot rest on *Clay* foundation
And the *tracks* of *"The Magician"*
Are but *Rail Roads* to perdition.
    Pull up the Rails! Emancipation
    Cannot rest on such foundation.

All true friends of Emancipation,
Haste to Freedom's Rail Road Station;
Quick into the Cars get seated,
All is ready and completed.
    Put on the Steam! All are crying,
    And the Liberty Flags are flying.

Now, again the Bell is tolling,
Soon you'll see the car wheels rolling;
Hinder not their destination.
Chartered for Emancipation.
    Wood up the fire! keep it flashing,
    While the Train goes onward dashing.

Hear the mighty car wheels humming!
Now look out! *The Engine's coming*!
Church and Statesmen! hear the thunder!
Clear the track! or you'll fall under.
    Get off the track! all are singing,
    While the *Liberty Bell* is ringing.

On triumphant, see them bearing,
Through sectarian rubbish tearing;
Th' Bell and Whistle and the Steaming,
Startles thousands from their dreaming.
    Look out for the cars! while the Bell rings,
    Ere the sound your funeral knell rings.

See the people run to meet us;
At the Depots thousands greet us;
All take seats with exultation,
In the Car Emancipation.
    Huzza! Huzza! Emancipation
    Soon will bless our happy nation.
    Huzza!—Huzza!!—Huzza!!!—

As always, dashing members of the military
establishment were musically acclaimed in the 1840s.

John Tyler, an ardent slavery man and expansionist,
brought to a head the stormiest issue of the presidential
campaign of 1844 when he submitted for the Senate's approval his treaty for admitting the republic of Texas into
the Union. Not only was the annexation of Texas a certain
provocation to war with Mexico, but it was also a source of
growing sectional conflict: as a prospective slave state,
Texas was hotly desired by the South and as vehemently
opposed by the North. At first rejected, Tyler's annexation
treaty was later passed by joint congressional resolution
and signed by him on March 1, 1845, just before he left the
presidency. Publicly expressed disapproval of the admittance
of Texas to the United States cost Martin Van Buren the
Democratic nomination in 1844, as it ultimately deprived
Henry Clay of the presidency he had so tirelessly pursued
since 1824.

Spirited military quicksteps and songs contributed to the
argument for annexing Texas. From the *Richmond Enquirer*
(August 23, 1844):

BEHOLD THE LONE STAR.

Air—"The American Star."

From battles terrific and war's desolation,
    Where blooming savannas were crimson'd with gore;
There valor and vic'try gave birth to a nation,
    And hushed the dread rifle and cannon's loud roar.
The heroes of Texas have shown great devotion;
    The fame of their deeds has been sounded afar;
And millions behold with a friendly emotion
    The flag that displays the lone Texacan Star.

THE TEXAS QUICK STEP
TO TEXAS
Wade, del.
As performed by the
MILITARY BANDS
arranged for the
PIANO FORTE
25 Cts. Nett.
NEW YORK
Published by FIRTH & HALL 239 Broadway
& No. 1 Franklin Sq.

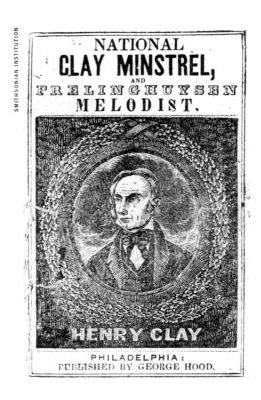

Under the caption "Coon Conventions in Baltimore," a sharp reporter for the Democratic *Richmond Enquirer* (May 17, 1844) described the big doings at the Whig nominating and ratifying conventions on May 1 and 2. He wrote: "I had not been in the city two hours, when my attention was attracted by the sound of music. The band consisted of some eight or ten musicians, dressed in deer skins, with coon skin caps." In 1844 the raccoon supplanted the log cabin and cider barrel as the Whig party emblem. Coons and music seemed to be everywhere: "Moving about the city . . . I would see at the corners of the streets crowds engaged in the laudable and patriotic task of singing what they call Coon songs, taken from that great text-book of the Whig party, 'the Clay Minstrel,' [frontispiece right] to the tunes of Rosin the Beau, Old Dan Tucker, &c." He added sardonically: "The Whigs now say that the people have decided that Clay shall be the President . . . and it is only necessary that they should sing him into the Presidency." The convention nominated Clay by acclamation—since 1842, when he had resigned from the Senate following his clash with Tyler, he had been chosen for president by one Whig state convention after another. All that remained was to nominate Theodore Frelinghuysen of New Jersey for vice-president and to hold a rip-snorting parade, replete with floats, banners, emblematic animals, "noise, hurrah, music, &c."

"Hurrah! hurrah! the country's risin'/For Harry Clay and Frelinghuysen," resourcefully rhymed the Whigs of 1844 to the tune of "Old Dan Tucker." Apparently the doggerel sank into the public consciousness. George Templeton Strong, a devout Whig, referred to the possible outcome of the Democratic convention in his diary: "Don't much care; 'country's risin,' Clay and Frelinghuysen, quite surprisin, give the Loco pisen,' and so on."

The Whig Banner Melodist *(1844) illustrated its version of the favorite Whig hurrah with a cartoon depicting an insouciant raccoon perched atop a parade ball, beneath which a Tyler-headed serpent is being crushed. The "little red fox," representing Van Buren, is seen fleeing in the background.*

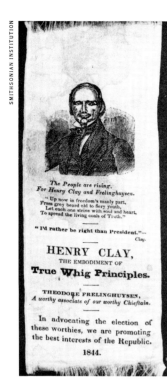

Campaign ribbons served as effective vehicles for highly concentrated party propaganda.

In the text of another version of "Clay and Frelinghuysen," published as sheet music (1844), "Kendall" is the Democrat publicist, Amos Kendall; *wires* denotes the hallowed political tradition of wire-pulling.

HARRY CLAY AND FRELINGHUYSEN.

The skies are bright, our hearts are light,
As one man all the Whigs unite;
We'll set our songs to good old tunes,
For there is music in these Coons.
    Hurra! Hurra! the people's rising,
    For HARRY CLAY and FRELINGHUYSEN!
    Hurra! Hurra! the people's rising,
    For HARRY CLAY and FRELINGHUYSEN!

The Loco's hearts are very sore,
To see the Whigs in Baltimore;
And they begin to think with reason!
That this will be a great "Coon season!"
    Hurra! Hurra &c.

O Frelinghuysen's a Jersey blue,
A noble Whig and honest too,
And he will make "New Jersey" feel
Whigs pay respect to her broad seal.
    Hurra! Hurra &c.

He is a man of truth and candour,
That even Kendall dare not slander,
And when he gets into a fight,
Lord! how the Jersey Coons will bite.
    Hurra! Hurra &c.

The "Coon" now looks around with pride,
For who is here dare touch his hide,
The "Locos" thought asleep to cross him
But found him only "playing possum."
    Hurra! Hurra &c.

Sly Matty Van's a man of doubt,
He wires in and he wires out,
You cannot tell when on the track,
If he's running on, or coming back.
    Hurra! Hurra &c.

United heart and hand are we,
From northren lake to southren sea,
From east to west, the people's rising,
For Harry Clay and Frelinghuysen,
    Hurra! Hurra &c.

21

CHORUS.

And it's hurrah! the country's rising for Harry Clay and Freling-
Hurrah! hurrah! the country's rising for Harry Clay and Freling
huysen! Hurrah! Hurrah! the country's rising For Harry Clay and
huysen! Hurrah! Hurrah! the country's rising For Harry Clay and
Frelinghuysen!
Frelinghuysen!

The locos hate to hear us sing,
And Shakspeare says a very true thing,
"Men who no music have in them,
Are fit for *spoils* and *stratagem.*"
    Hurrah, &c.

No doubt they'd rather hear us groan,
But that we'll leave to them alone;
For with good Clay and Frelinghuysen,
The way we'll beat them is surprising.
    Hurrah, &c.

There's no two names that can be found,
Although you search the country round,
More terror to that clan comprising,
Than *Harry Clay* and *Frelinghuysen.*
    Hurrah, &c.

The loco's cause is out of season—
For it has neither rhyme nor reason;
The people tried and found it lacking,
Their promises had not good backing.
    Hurrah, &c.

Clay's a patriot, through and through,
And so is Frelinghuysen, too;
They are men of truth and candor,
Who can't be hurt by loco slander.
    Hurrah, &c.

When locos see them on our ticket,
'Tis a sight which they grow sick at—
For any thing from humbug free
With locos' systems don't agree.
    Hurrah, &c.

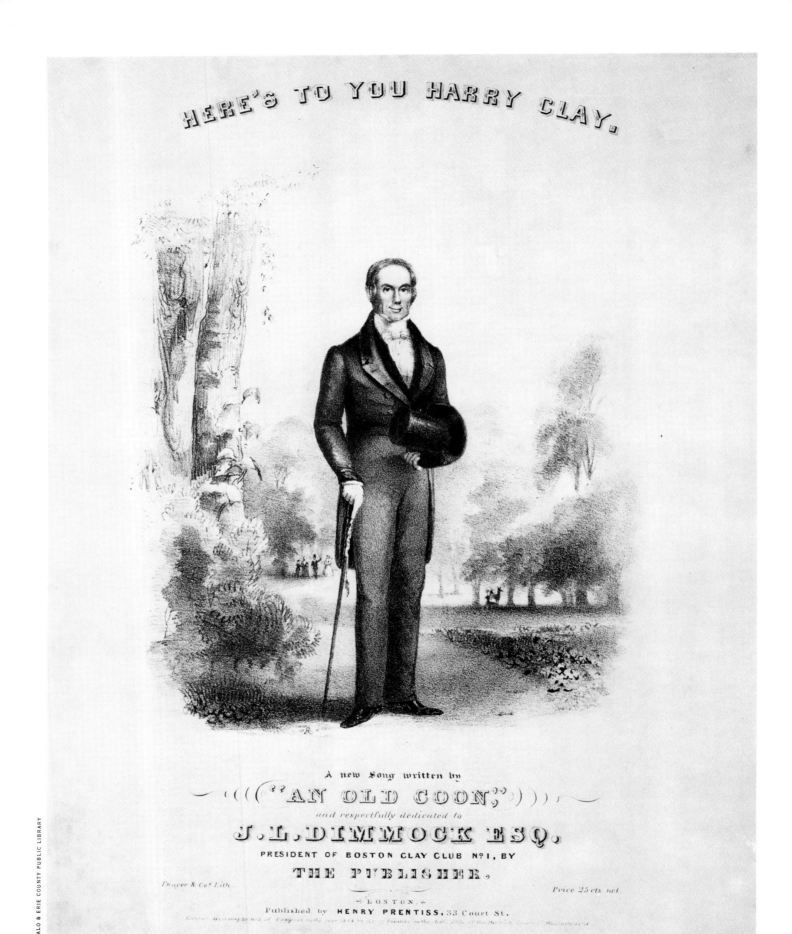

HERE'S TO YOU HARRY CLAY.

A new Song written by
"AN OLD COON,"
and respectfully dedicated to
J. L. DIMMOCK ESQ.
PRESIDENT OF BOSTON CLAY CLUB Nº1, BY
THE PUBLISHER.

Thayer & Cos Lith.   Price 25 cts net.

BOSTON.
Published by HENRY PRENTISS, 33 Court St.

For Henry Clay our candidate,
Hurrah, Hurrah, Hurrah!
To place him in the Chair of State,
Hurrah, Hurrah, Hurrah!

"God's noblest work—an honest man,"
A nobler show us if you can!
Hurrah, Hurrah, Hurrah, Hurrah,
Hurrah, Hurrah, Hurrah!

The Clay Club Coon Songster *(1844)*

The cover art for this musical toast to Henry Clay elegantly portrays the charismatic Clay standing on the grounds of his famous Kentucky estate, Ashland. Besides hailing Clay, the song derides the cast of characters that performed at the Democratic convention at Baltimore on May 27, 1844. It had been expected that Martin Van Buren would be unanimously nominated by the Democrats, as Clay had been by the Whigs, but by the time the convention was held, party feeling had turned violently against him. The publication a month earlier of his letter to Congressman W. H. Hammett, in which he stated his disapproval of the annexation of Texas, had created so great an uproar within the predominantly expansionist Democratic ranks that his candidacy was dropped. (A similar letter of Clay's published at about the same time had caused no such reaction among the Whigs.) With the expunction of Van Buren as a certain nominee, a number of would-be candidates briefly surfaced at the Democratic convention, among them Lewis Cass, the former minister to France; the perennially available Rumpsey-Dumpsey Johnson; James Buchanan; and the tireless Southern expansionist and secessionist, John C. Calhoun. But the Democratic wire-pullers produced a surprise: the first victorious "dark horse" in American presidential convention history, James K. Polk of Tennessee. Polk, a protégé of Andrew Jackson, was just what was wanted: he was expansionist, not opposed to slavery, and he could and did deliver the problematical Southern vote.

NEW-YORK HISTORICAL SOCIETY

THE POLKA.
A NEW NATIONAL DANCE ADOPTED by the DEMOCRATIC CONVENTION at BALTIMORE May 29th 1844.

In this visually punning, politico-choreographic cartoon, Polk's dancing partner is his running mate, George Mifflin Dallas; the musicians are Andrew Jackson and the hapless Van, once again a "used up man."

HERE'S TO YOU HARRY CLAY.

Written by "An Old Coon."

Why what a host of Candidates
And how the party prates
As to who shall be next President
Of these United States.
    CHORUS.
    Here's to you Harry Clay,
    Here's to you my noble soul,
    Here's to you with all my heart
    And you will be the people's choice,
    And that before we part,
    Here's to you Harry Clay.

Their hopes are all in vain
For deny it if they can,
The people's voice has made its choice
And Harry Clay's the man
    Here's to you Harry Clay &c.

The first upon the list,
Is that Arch Magician Martin,
"He's a very nice old Man"
But he can't come in for sartin.
    Here's to you Harry Clay &c.

The next is Gineral Cass,
And he's just come home from France,
He'll only do, to parley vous,
He hasn't got a chance.
    Here's to you Harry Clay &c.

Colonel Johnson has a claim,
But 'tis very humpsey dumpsey,
He wears 'tis said, a waistcoat red,
Because he killed Tecumseh.
    Here's to you Harry Clay &c.

The most able of the Party,
Is the Southern Man Calhoun
But 'tis plain to see,—tho clever—he
Cant come it o'er that Coon.
    Here's to you Harry Clay &c.

And last upon the list
Is President Captin Tyler
Tho' now he's strong, 'twill not be long
Before he'll burst his Biler.
    Here's to you Harry Clay &c.

The Loco's all, both great and small,
Have had their ipse dixit,
They cant come in, aint it a sin,
Not nohow they can fix it.
    Here's to you Harry Clay &c.

In forty five the Whigs will thrive,
And Loco's put to rout.
There'll be a call, from Faneuil Hall,
"Does you mother know you're out?"
    Here's to you Harry Clay &c.

And having thus disposed of all,
From Beersheba to Dan,
The People's voice, will make its choice,
And Harry Clay's the man.
    Here's to you Harry Clay &c.

This Whig campaign newspaper, named after the party catchphrase, carried on its front page—in addition to Clay's summation of the Whig platform and a withering report on the "Locofoco" Baltimore convention—the words and erratically notated music of still another song called "Hurrah for Henry Clay." The ornamental border surrounding the page (unfortunately marred) is composed of a garland of raccoons and roosters (the rooster was at that time the symbol of the Democratic party).

The Whigs sang:

Let Locofocos ever fret,
   At midnight or at noon,
For we have some Hard Cider yet,
   Log Cabins and a Coon.
CHORUS.
   'The same old cunning Coon,' my boys,
   The same old cunning Coon;
We'll rout the Locofoco camp,
   With that old cunning Coon.

     "Up Salt River"
    The Clay Club Coon Songster *(1844)*

The Democrats sang:

Come all ye jolly hunters,
   The time is not too soon—
To make full preparation
   *To hunt that "*SAME OLD COON!*"*
It is the same "old varmint," boys,
   That fooled us once before—
    Then let's prepare,
    The sport to share
In Eighteen forty-four!

     "The Coon Hunter's Song"
    Richmond Enquirer *(January 9, 1844)*

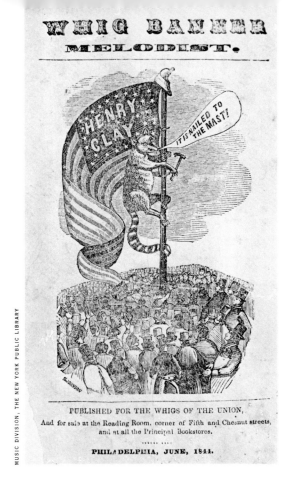

After Polk's surprise nomination, the Whigs sloganized the question: "Who is James K. Polk?" and frolicsome Whig songwriters reveled in making puns on his name. From the *Whig Banner Melodist* (1844):

A PIG-IN-A-POLK.

Alas! For Van Buren, "Great Leader," Alas!
Alas! For Tecumseh, and Stewart, and Cass,
You are all pushed aside as if 't had been a joke,
And your friends are all off for a pig-in-a-Polk.

A true pig-in-a-Polk, both in name and in action,
Ne'er heard of before but as leading a faction,
And whose greatest merit, if merit it be,
Is to come like the Hero from Old Tennessee.

But we welcome the issue—we join it with gladness,
Poor Cass, and Van Buren will look on in sadness,
And you'll find in the end, as the triumph we carry,
That your Polk was too Polky to run against Harry.

THE LOCO POLK-O CONVENTION.

Tune—"Tee-total Society."

Ah! Matty, how hard is your lot,
Short sighted magician and wizard;
That ill-pointed Texas blank shot,
Struck each Loco down deep in his gizzard.
"What! shall we lose Texas?" they say,
That magnificent valley of vagabonds?
No! we'll *Polk* down the man that says nay,
With "the party" no more shall he drag his bones.
    Then Whigs let's huzza for the day
    When they up Salt River are ferrying,
    We'll stick them all under the Clay,
    And next fall have a general *Polk-burying*.

WHIG QUODLIBET.

Oh Polk! Oh Polk!
Don't you know you'll end up in smoke!
For up Salt River you must go, Polk!
And the way you go up won't be slow, Polk.

The *Melodist* had harsh words to spare for President Tyler. To the tune of "Away with Melancholy" was sung:

AWAY WITH THE TRAITOR TYLER.

Away with the traitor Tyler!
Down with the Veto King,
Our party's base reviler;
Whilst the people cheerily sing,
    Hurrah!

Though for years of sorrow
We've cursed that traitor's crime,
Yet we wait a glorious morrow,
And sternly, sternly "bide our time,"
    Hurrah!

Now as each hour is falling,
Thorns strew the traitor's path;
And to his ears appalling,
Sounds the people's long pent wrath;
    Hurrah!

But as from the horizon,
Now breaks our triumph's day;
Behold our Frelinghuysen,
And glorious Harry Clay,
    Hurrah!

The Whig farmers and mechanics made a special bow to the ladies:

HURRAH FOR HENRY CLAY.

Air—"Lucy Neal."

The Farmers and Mechanicks,
  A Patriotic band,
Will elect for President,
  The farmer of Ashland.
CHORUS.
Hurrah for Harry Clay,
  Hurrah for Harry Clay,
He's bound to be next President,
  I've heard the people say.

The Ladies, bless the lovely band,
  Our Country's Joy and Pride,
They go for Harry hand and hand,
  Maid, matron, belle and bride,
    Hurrah, &c.

To gain *Protection* for themselves,
  They'll marry and marry away,
And tell their lovers, husbands, sons,
  To vote for Harry Clay.
    Hurrah, &c.

From the sheet music (1844)

The coy reference to "protection" in the preceding song is a pun having to do with the high tariff that Clay proposed as "a fair protection to American industry." The Democrats maintained that this measure would inflict hardships on the workingman, an attitude they set to music. The sheet music subtitle of "Oh, Coony, Coony Clay" tells us that it was "Sung with Unbounded Applause by the President and Members of the Empire Club," a vivid organization mentioned by Perley in his description of Polk's inauguration parade. He wrote: "The pugilistic Empire Club from New York, led by Captain Isaiah Rynders, had with it a small cannon, which was fired at short intervals as the procession advanced." In the text of their song, "Two dollars and roast beef per day" refers to a Whig campaign slogan of 1840, not unlike the Herbert Hoover slogan of 1932: "A chicken in every pot."

OH, COONY, COONY CLAY.

Oh, coony coony Clay,
    The rich man is your god,
You raise the manufacturer,
    But doom the poor to plod.
CHORUS.
Oh, coony, coony Clay,
    Oh, coony coony Clay,
All for to be the President,
    You'll never see the day.

Oh, coony, coony Clay,
    You'd starve the working man,
And press his children to the earth
    With tyrant's iron hand. Oh, coony, &c.

Oh, coony, coony Clay,
    Your tariff's mighty high,
You make the poor man dearly pay
    For clothes to keep him dry. Oh, coony, &c.

Oh, coony, coony Clay,
    You tax our salt and bread,
You double tax our garments too,
    And the blankets that we spread. Oh, coony, &c.

Oh, coony, coony Clay,
    What care you for the poor,
What care you though the hungry wolf
    Is ent'ring at his door. Oh, coony, &c.

Oh, coony, coony Clay,
    Your bank ain't worth a pin,
You issue promises to pay,
    But never call them in. Oh, coony, &c.

Oh, coony, coony Clay,
    Your promises are sham,
Two dollars and roast beef per day,
    We've found it all a flam. Oh, coony, &c.

Oh, coony, coony Clay,
    We'll do without you sure,
For POLK and DALLAS are the boys
    Your tyranny to cure. Oh, coony, &c.

Then pull, away, my boys,
    Pull on the lab'ring car,
For POLK will give us better times
    To smile upon the poor. Oh, coony, &c.

When Polk captured all of Maine's electoral votes, the Georgia *Federal Union* celebrated with a sharp little song deriding the Whigs, their pompous reference to Clay as the "Great Embodiment" of Whig principles, and Clay's well-publicized prowess as a gambler and a duelist. The song was reprinted in the Democrat campaign newspaper the *Dollar Globe* (October 18, 1844).

THE DYING COON.
Air—"Araby's Daughter."

"Farewell to thee, land of the coon's ruthless slaughter"—
    Thus warbled a coon who apostrophized Maine—
"You know that you haint done by us as you'd oughter,
    And the way we once come it, we can't come again.

"I feel the sharp knife o'er my furry hide going;
    I feel its sharp point in my very heart's core,
Good bye, my dear patrons, I feel that I'm going,
    And shortly the coon will be heard of no more.

"Oh! give my respects to our darling old Harry;
    Conjure him to give up his pistols and dice,
And then die with honor: one State he may carry—
    But, sure as I'm dished, the 'embodiment' dies."

From the *Richmond Enquirer* (July 26, 1844):

DEMOCRATIC ODE.
Air—"Rosin the Bow."

November election is coming,
    To arms, all true Democrats, rise;
Fear not the loud braying and drumming,
    In which all Whig argument lies.

All over the country, the rally,
    Of Democrats gladdens the land;
They gather from mountain and valley—
    Whole armies are on every hand.

Our Polk is the Joshua blowing,
    The blast that to victory calls;
Around the last time he is going,
    And tumbling are Whiggery's walls.

The sun in his course need not tarry,
    For Polk to encompass his foe;
One moment to charge—*and Old Harry*
    Is sent to the regions below.

The Whigs obtained power and station,
    By thousands of promises made;
Deceived and defrauded the nation,
    And its best interests betrayed.

To millions they promised in '40,
    Roast beef and two dollars per day;
And many a working man thought he
    Might trust in the promise of Clay.

But when the election was over,
    Hear how the duped voter laments;
The lead nags were rolling in clover—
    The others outside of the fence.

Americans in the 1840s disguised their ravenous appetite for territorial expansion under the cloak of Manifest Destiny, a sanctimonious phrase adopted from an editorial in the *United States Magazine and Democratic Review* (July–August 1845), in which the journalist John L. O'Sullivan proclaimed that it was "our manifest destiny to overspread the continent allotted by Providence for the free development of our yearly multiplying millions." When President Polk, a devout exponent of Manifest Destiny, failed in his attempts to negotiate with an understandably hostile Mexican government for new boundaries to the recently annexed Texas territories and for the purchase of California, the long-expected war with Mexico was declared. But even before hostilities began, Polk had dispatched Brigadier General Zachary Taylor, popularly known as "Old Rough and Ready," to Texas, and by the time war was formally declared in May 1846, Taylor had already won his initial engagements with the Mexicans at Palo Alto and Resaca de la Palma. The troops—largely volunteers—who fought the Mexican War appear to have been motivated by their own interpretation of Manifest Destiny, if this song by "an American Officer," published in *The Rough and Ready Songster* (c. 1848) is an indication.

WE'RE THE BOYS FOR MEXICO.

Air—"Yankee Doodle."

The Mexican's are doomed to fall,
 God has in his wrath forsook 'em,
And all their goods and chattels call
 On us to go and hook 'em.
  CHORUS.
  We're the boys for Mexico,
   Sing Yankee Doodle Dandy,
  Gold and silver images,
   Plentiful and handy.

Churches grand, with altars rich,
 Saints with diamond collars,
(That's the talk to understand,)
 With lots of new bright dollars.
  We're the boys for Mexico, &c.

The Mexicans have cut up high,
 And we have let 'em do it,
'Till they have got our "dander riz,"
 And now they'll have to rue it.
  We're the boys for Mexico, &c.

We'll have a corps of Editors,
 Each with a mighty bellows,
To strike a mortal terror in
 Them tarnal Spanish fellows.
  We're the boys for Mexico, &c.

And when we've laid aside our arms
 With nothing more to vex us,
We'll vote ourselves extensive farms,
 Each one as big as Texas.
  We're the boys for Mexico, &c.

And when our flag has been upheld,
 And crushed lies each presumer,
We'll open "free and easy's" in
 The "Halls of *Montezumer*."
  We're the boys for Mexico, &c.

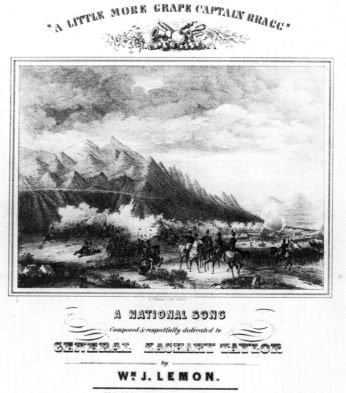

"A LITTLE MORE GRAPE CAPTAIN BRAGG"

A NATIONAL SONG
Composed & respectfully dedicated to
GENERAL ZACHARY TAYLOR
by
WM. J. LEMON.

Although General Winfield Scott won the definitive victories of the Mexican War, it was his rival, Zachary Taylor, who captivated the public imagination. After his spectacular victory over Santa Anna at Buena Vista in February 1847, Old Rough and Ready became a national idol, and his well-publicized command during the battle, "A little more grape, Captain Bragg," was quoted universally. The Battle of Buena Vista was musically commemorated in many forms: as a lengthy battle sonata, whose scenario bristled with heroism and Manifest Destiny; as a jaunty little march by the talented young composer Stephen Collins Foster; and in the following song based on Taylor's famous words.

"A LITTLE MORE GRAPE CAPTAIN BRAGG."

The old hero stands on the brow of the hill,
With his heart in the thick of the fray,
Where his squadrons beneath him are bat'ling still,
On the eve of that terrible day;
His quick eye has numbered the mustering bands,
And he points to the enemy's flag,
While the battery answers the old man's commands,
"A little more grape, Captain Bragg."

The foe men charge home with a thundering shock,
And a touch of Castillian pride;
They dash on our lines like the wave on the rock,
When the storm is abroad on the tide;
The wave falleth back but the rock standeth still—
There is heat in that bristling crag—
And the old man stands yet on the brow of the hill—
"A little more grape, Captain Bragg!"

SANTA ANNA'S RETREAT FROM BUENA VISTA.

Composed by. ————————— S. C. Foster Esq.ᵣ

Entered according to Act of Congress, in the year 1848, by W.C. Peters, in the Clerk's office of the District Court of Ky.
1185, 4.

Zachary Taylor, a Louisiana plantation owner, was lionized when he visited New Orleans in 1847. Special music was written for a gala performance in his honor at the Saint Charles Theatre by its orchestra leader.

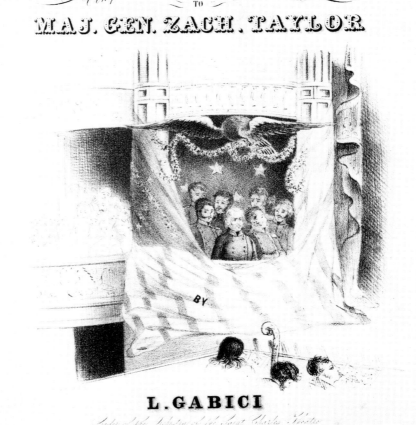

A daguerreotype of the Capitol, where John Quincy Adams died, taken by John Plumbe in 1846

"A mournful and agitating event occurred in the house of representatives yesterday," reported the *National Intelligencer* (February 22, 1848). "Just after the yeas and nays were taken on a question, and the speaker had risen to put another question to the house, a sudden cry was heard . . . 'Mr. Adams is dying!'" The eighty-one-year-old John Quincy Adams of Massachusetts had collapsed. Unconscious, he was carried to the Speaker's chamber where he died two days later, being too ill to be moved. Adams momentarily recovered consciousness and uttered his memorable last words: "This is the last of earth; I am content."

John Quincy Adams had rarely allowed himself contentment during his long and great life. Always a prey to gnawing self-doubts and merciless self-criticism, he had resigned himself—after the termination of his unpopular presidency—to an old age of oblivion. Instead, Adams was elected in 1831 as a representative from Massachusetts, and in this post he accomplished the crowning achievements of his unique career of more than a half century's service to his country. At the end, Adams enjoyed the high regard of his contemporaries, who affectionately called him "Old Man Eloquent."

An undated lithograph of John Quincy Adams's collapse at the House of Representatives on February 21, 1848

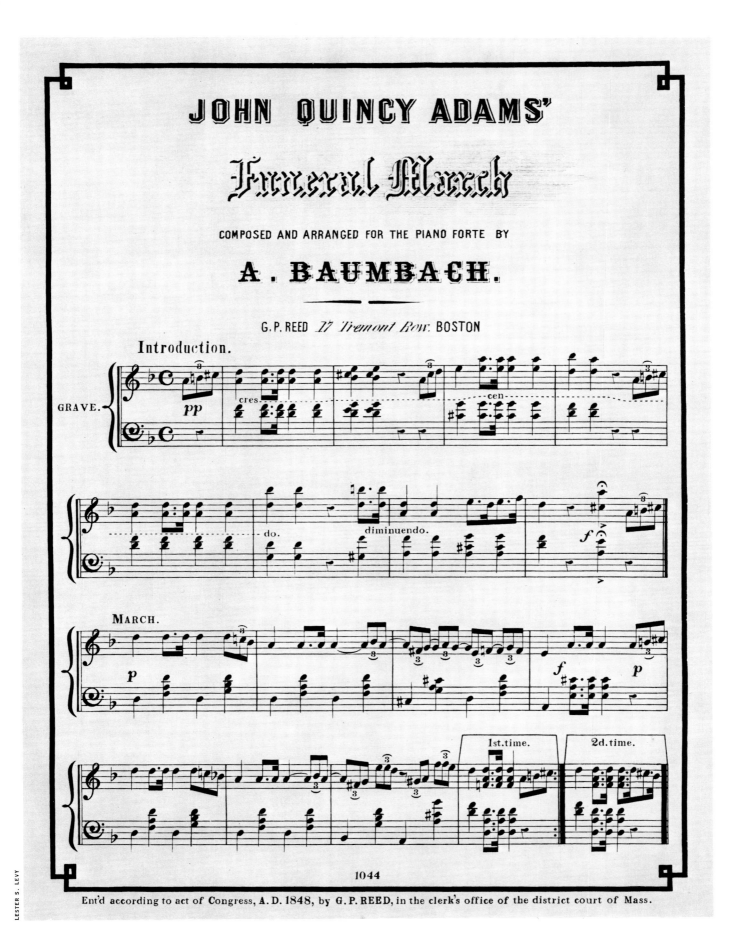

JOHN QUINCY ADAMS'

Funeral March

COMPOSED AND ARRANGED FOR THE PIANO FORTE BY

A. BAUMBACH.

G.P. REED 17 Tremont Row. BOSTON

1044

Elaborate state funerals were held for John Quincy Adams in Washington, in New York, and, of course, in Boston; and between these cities, mourners lined the route of his black-draped funeral train. Among the countless traditional dirges and dead marches performed at the Adams obsequies was this original funeral march, presumably played at his Boston funeral.

On the sheet music cover of this Zachary Taylor campaign song are listed his military triumphs and the names of some of his officers who fell in battle.

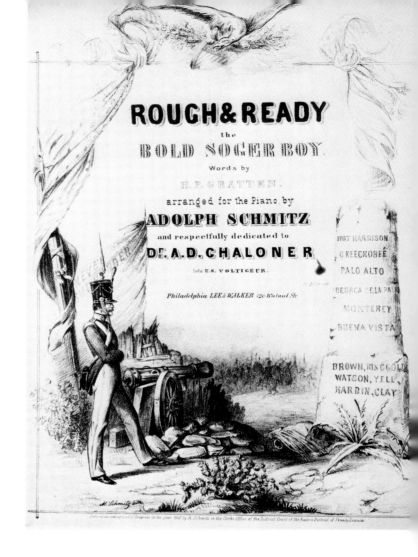

Following his Mexican successes, Zachary Taylor, "the toast of America," played a coy game of political possum as the presidential election of 1848 approached. While ingenuously disclaiming that he had any qualifications whatsoever for the presidency, at the same time he made it unmistakably clear that he was both tremendously available and tremendously willing. Taylor's self-depreciation was not unjustified: at the age of sixty-four, Old Rough and Ready was a political virgin. Not only had he never been affiliated with any party, but he had never even voted. His nomination at the Whig convention in Philadelphia on June 7, 1848, over such seasoned political masters as Daniel Webster and Henry Clay—and over his Mexican War rival, Winfield Scott—testifies to the consummate virtuosity of the president-maker Thurlow Weed, who had been playing political Pygmalion to Taylor's presidential Galatea since 1846.

Zachary Taylor's extraordinary silence on being notified that he had been chosen as the Whig nominee for president caused a good deal of mystified apprehension among his nominators. It was discovered that Taylor, tired of paying for masses of postage-due mail, had returned the letter of notification, together with other unpaid-for letters, to the Baton Rouge dead letter office, where it had lain for nearly a month before it was retrieved and answered.

Although the Whigs invoked the tried and true electioneering paraphernalia of former years, their lyric muse undeniably suffered a setback in 1848: the old fire was no longer there. Perhaps the blandness of the Whig campaign songs in 1848 was a presage of the impending decline of Whiggery in 1852. The twilight period of the Whig campaign ballad is exemplified in this song for Taylor in the New York Whig campaign newspaper *The Grape-Shot* (August 26, 1848). In the text, "the old WHITE HORSE" apparently is a nickname referring to both Taylor and his famed battle-steed, "Old Whitey" (which he is reported sometimes to have ridden sidesaddle). Here they are combined in a single, centaurlike personification.

OUR FLAG IS UP.

Tune—"Old Dan Tucker."

Come Whigs and Patriots, one and all,
Our Suffering Nation gives a "call,"
The Constitution's gone to rust,
Scarce seen beneath the dirt and dust;—
    The flag is up and there we'll nail her,
    Bright with stars and stripes and TAYLOR.

The Loco ranks have thinned to naught,
The old "WHITE HORSE" begins to snort;
They're on "the go"—they're put to rout,
They have not time to look about;—
    The flag, etc.

Old "ZACK" has raised a smoke so quick,
It floats about the land so thick,
The Locos in a "fog" can't see,
They wonder what "that shout" can be;—
    The flag, etc.

Our foes are sick—they're in a scrape,
We'll give them help—a dose of "*grape*,"
With cheers and huzzas loud and long,
We'll entertain them with the song;—
    The flag, etc.

The old "WHITE HORSE" is on the race,
The "Loco-*motive*" can't keep pace;
Old "Zack" sits firmly on his seat,
They all know he "can't be beat;"—
    Then up the flag and there we'll nail her,
    Bright with stars and stripes and TAYLOR.

A benign "Old Zack" is portrayed on this sheet music cover (1847).

THE BOAT HORN
by
GEN? WILLIAM O. BUTLER

Most Respectfully dedicated to
Mrs JAMES K. POLK
And composed by
H. THORBECKE.

Published for the Author by A. Fiot Philad?

William Orlando Butler, the Democratic vice-presidential nominee in 1848, was an accomplished poet. This musical setting of one of his poems appeared during the campaign year; it was probably intended as a form of electioneering propaganda, although the poem itself had no political implications.

Taylor's nomination created bitter resentment among the defeated Whig candidates, and the ugly clash of discord was heard within the ranks of the "harmonious coons." Daniel Webster is reported by Perley to have "denounced the nomination as one 'not fit to be made,'" although he later "was induced, by the payment of a considerable sum of money, to make a speech in favor of the ticket." Perley also observed that "the friends of Mr. Clay made a desperate rally in his behalf, knowing that it was his last chance." Both Taylor's incompetence and the party's disharmony were satirized by an anonymous Democrat bard in a parody of "Dame Durden" published in the *Richmond Enquirer* (September 22, 1848). In the text, "Clayton" is John Middleton Clayton, who became Taylor's secretary of state; "Cass" is, of course, Lewis Cass, the Democratic candidate for president.

HARMONIOUS COONS.

The coons they had five candidates,
  From which their chief to choose,
And all of them had principles
  But Zack—he had no views!
    There was old black Dan,
    With traitor clan,
And Zachary with his sword;
    Clayton and Scott,
    By friends forgot,
And Clay, spurned and abhorred!
    Scott's claim enhanced,
    And Dan advanced:
    Clayton's descending,
    While Clay's unbending,
And Zachary claims reward,
  Because he's most available,
By reason of his sword!

Now when the candidate was named,
  And Zachary was the man,
The *old coons* were so much inflamed,
  That from the scene they ran!
    Hold on black Dan,
    Said Taylor's clan—
Help Taylor with his sword—
    Clayton and Scott,
    Back out must not,
And Clay, you shall accord!
    Dan said he wouldn't
    Clay said he couldn't
    Clayton was flurried,
    And Scott was worried,
And Zachary claimed reward,
  Because he was available
In nothing but his sword!

Harmonious coons are in a plight;
  To grasp official spoil
Their principles they put to flight,
  And raise an angry broil!
    But when they aim
    To win the game,
With Zachary and his sword;
    Cass on the track
    Will drive them back,
And cleanly sweep the board!
    Now coons may truckle,
    And loudly chuckle;
    But we'll not follow,
    Nor will we swallow
Old General Taylor's sword;
  And principles more stable are
Than Zachary's unpledged word!

If the Democrats twitted the Whigs on their disunity, they had more reason to be concerned over the alienation within their own party. At the Democratic convention in Baltimore on May 22, 1848, after it had been decided to seat the delegates of both the Hunkers and the Barnburners, two violently conflicting New York factions who had sent separate delegations, both groups refused to share the split vote, and New York consequently went unrepresented in the balloting. Like the Whigs, the Democrats were divided into numerous groups and subgroups representing the countless shades of opinion and feeling toward the escalating problem of slavery and its abolition or its extension. The Hunkers, presumably so called because they "hunkered" (or hankered) after office, were conservative Democrats who, among other things, were opposed to any form of agitation against slavery. The Barnburners, named for a legendary farmer who preferred burning down his barn to allowing the rats to live in it, were on the other hand outspoken supporters of antislavery and of the Wilmot Proviso, David Wilmot's controversial measure to prohibit the extension of slavery to the free soil of the vast territories gained from Mexico, over which Congress had been deadlocked for two years. Seceding from the party, the Barnburners organized the Free Soil party and nominated Martin Van Buren for president and Charles Francis Adams as his running mate on a Wilmot Proviso platform. In November the Free-Soilers polled enough votes to bring about the defeat of the Democratic nominees, Lewis Cass of Michigan and William Orlando Butler of Kentucky.

At a noisy Democratic mass meeting in Washington the *Daily Union* (October 18, 1848) reported that some two hundred guns were fired and that the following song by an anonymous New York party poet was sung.

A SONG FOR CASS AND BUTLER.

The whigs and the tories unite,
    The barnburners join in the van,
The Clay-men are ready to fight
    And beat Lewis Cass—if they can.
Then, democrats, arm for the shock,
    And gird up your loins for the battle,
Your cause will resist, like a rock,
    The shot that the enemy rattle.

We hear the fantastical throng,
    "War, famine, and pestilence" shout!
By hook or by crook, right or wrong,
    The *ins* they intend to turn *out*.
With Taylor, Van Buren, and Clay,
    They move on in column unsteady,
Resolved o'er their corduroy way
    To *Rough* it in search of the *Ready*.

The rights we possess we demand,
    Unshackled by federal decrees:
In safety to dwell on the land,
    In freedom to roam on the seas.
If this opportunity pass,
    The chain of the UNION may sever:
Preserve it, then, freemen, in CASS
    And BUTLER, for ever and ever.

The enthusiasm that characterized the Free-Soilers' convention at Buffalo in August 1848 was reflected in their exhilarating motto "Free Soil, Free Speech, Free Labor, and Free Men." A coalition of the Abolitionist Liberty party and antislavery elements from the Whig and Democratic parties, they nominated the Democrat Martin Van Buren and the "Conscience Whig" Charles Francis Adams by acclamation. To those opposing slavery and its threatened extension, the Free-Soilers offered an answer to the subterfuges and evasions of the other two parties, neither of which had dared to make a commitment on these explosive issues. "The best possible feeling prevails," quoted Horace Greeley's *New-York Daily Tribune* (August 11, 1848) from a telegraphed dispatch continuing, "the enthusiasm is immense. Three cheers were given for the candidates, 3 for [John P.] Hale and the Liberty party [they had turned over their votes to the Free-Soilers]—3 for the Radical Whigs—3 for [David] Wilmot—3 for Preston King [Wilmot's staunch supporter]—3 deafening yells for John Van Buren [Martin Van Buren's brilliant son]. Then a universal scream for five minutes for everybody." The next day the *Tribune* reported that, following the unanimous confirmation of the nominations, "there were songs from the Hutchinsons. . . ." It is likely that they sang the following spicy songs from the songster *Free Soil Songs for the People* (1848).

MARTIN VAN OF KINDERHOOK.

Air—"Dandy Jim of Caroline."

Come, ye hardy sons of toil,
And cast your ballots for Free Soil;
He who'd vote for Zacky Taylor,
Needs a keeper or a jailor.
And he who still for Cass can be,
He is a Cass without the C;
The man on whom we love to look,
Is Martin Van of Kinderhook.
    CHORUS.
    Martin Van's the one we'll go,
    He is the man for the people O,
    I look around and find it so,
    Just as they said in Buffalo.

THE NEW PARTY.

Air—"Dan Tucker."

Come all ye who're fond of singing,
Let us set a song a-ringing,
Sound the chorus loud and hearty,
And we'll make a Free Soil Party.
    Get out o' the way, Cass and Taylor,
    You can't come to the White House ever.

Some want Cass and some want Taylor,
But we say we won't have either;
We've a man that's far above them,
He's the man that's pledged for Freedom.
    Get out, etc.

What has Zachary Taylor done,
That he should to the White House come?
He's good for fighting, we'll allow,
But we don't want him "anyhow."
    Get out, etc.

The institutions of the South
Must be supported by the North;
If the North like it, very well,
But if they don't why "just as well."
    Get out, etc.

And now it is proposed, you know,
To make Slave States in Mexico,
And General Taylor's just the man
To carry out that Southern plan.
    Get out, etc.

And then there's Lewis Cass, they say,
Is with every one, in every way;
He's what the people of this place
Denominate a great doughface;
    Get out, etc.

Now for the Buffalo nomination,
Made by men of every station,
They're the men to go before us,
And they'll always shout the chorus,
    Get out o' the way, with your Slavery,
    Get out o' the way, with your Slavery,
    Get out o' the way, Cass and Taylor,
    You can't come to the White House ever.

For the second time in less than a decade, the Whigs suffered the shock of political bereavement when President Taylor suddenly died on July 9, 1850. The president succumbed to a gastric ailment contracted from consuming a surfeit of fresh fruit and iced drinks after he had been exposed to the broiling sun during an interminable July Fourth ceremony at the unfinished Washington Monument.

With Millard Fillmore's accession to the White House began the twilight of the Whig party and the succession until 1861 of the presidential "doughfaces," a term of contempt for Northerners who supported Southern principles; John Randolph is believed to have coined the expression in 1819. In opposition to his party—and in the name of preserving the Union—Fillmore upheld and promptly signed into law the separate acts that comprised Henry Clay's great Compromise of 1850. A plan designed to pacify

dissidents in all sections, the Compromise offered conciliatory partial concessions to the demands of both the North and the South; without satisfying either section, it served to maintain an uneasy and artificial peace until slumbering sectional strife was reawakened by the passage of the Kansas-Nebraska Act in 1854.

Millard Fillmore's Unionist credo is quoted in this sheet music cover, on which his portrait is encircled by a chain of the thirty-one states, the thirty-first being California, recently admitted as a free state under the Compromise of 1850. "If there be those, North or South, who desire an administration for the North as against the South, or for the South as against the North, they are not the men who should give their suffrages to me. For my own part, I know only my whole country, and nothing but my country."

California, gained from Mexico in 1848, set the world agog that same year when the discovery of gold precipitated the most phenomenal boom in American history. A self-made free state in 1849—the year the gold rush erupted—California was formally admitted to the Union in 1850. When the celebrated eccentric French musician Louis Antoine Jullien concertized in the United States in 1852 and 1853, he included this quadrille named for California in his famed set of "American Quadrilles" for twenty virtuoso soloists and orchestra.

"A Barnum set to music" is how a contemporary characterized Jullien. He enthralled audiences on both sides of the Atlantic with his sensational onstage antics, his gorgeous attire, and his superextravaganzas. Jullien refused to conduct Beethoven (which he is reported to have done superbly) except with a jewelled baton and wearing white kid gloves presented to him at the podium on a silver salver. He augmented his "monster" orchestra with auxiliary military bands when he gave his "Fireman's Quadrille" at the Crystal Palace in New York; and ladies are reported to have fainted as realistic smoke poured into the hall and three companies of New York firemen rushed in carrying operational firehoses. George Templeton Strong, who was present, wrote in his diary (June 10, 1854) that it was "a pleasure to see humbug so consistently, extensively, and cleverly applied: military bands beginning to play in the distance, drawing nearer and nearer and finally marching into the orchestra; red and blue fire visible through the windows of the dome; a clamorous chorus shouting 'Go it, 20,' 'Play it away, 49,' 'hay-hay,' and so on." Despite his flamboyance, Jullien was universally respected for his uncommonly fine musicianship.

By the time the last installment of Harriet Beecher Stowe's earthshaking story of *Uncle Tom's Cabin* appeared in the April 1, 1852, issue of the Washington antislavery weekly the *National Era*, where it had been running serially for more than a year, the complete novel had also been published in book form in Boston. More than ten thousand copies were reported to have been sold during the following month. In a year the sales exceeded three hundred thousand copies, and by 1860 more than a million. A flaming indictment of the institution of slavery, with particular immediate focus on the Fugitive Slave Act—the section of the Compromise of 1850 designed to pacify the South—*Uncle Tom's Cabin* exerted an unprecedented impact on all parts of the nation: in the North it was hailed as revelation; in the South (where its circulation was widely banned) it was shunned as anathema. Mrs. Stowe's book was rightly or wrongly credited with having accelerated the outbreak of the Civil War, if not having directly caused it. Translated into innumerable languages and transposed to every conceivable medium from tent shows to motion pictures, for more than a century *Uncle Tom's Cabin* continued to occupy a unique place in American culture. Although its title has been invested with a new and contrary significance in the latter part of the twentieth century, the work, for all its quaintness, is still capable of arousing an emotional response.

The first successful dramatization of *Uncle Tom's Cabin* was presented at the National Theatre in New York in 1852 by George C. Howard, who also acted the role of St. Clare; his wife played Topsy, and to round out the family circle, their fetching four-year-old daughter, Cordelia, wrenched susceptible heartstrings as Little Eva. Apart from its powerful social message, *Uncle Tom's Cabin* played heavily upon the extravagant sentimentalism of the period. A commentator in the *New-York Tribune* (August 8, 1853) described it as a veritable "*pièce de mouchoir*," with floods of tears being unashamedly shed by men as well as by women and children. Besides several songs that Howard had composed for his production, a profusion of *Uncle Tom's Cabin* songs of all sorts appeared in print—political, comic, and, as in this example by the noted Abolitionist poet John Greenleaf Whittier (published in 1852), almost embarrassingly saccharine.

LITTLE EVA.

Dry the tears for holy Eva,
With the blessed angels leave her,
Of the form so sweet and fair,
Give to earth the tender care.
For the golden locks of Eva
Let the sunny south land give her
Flowery pillow of repose
Orange bloom and budding rose.

～～～

A caustic dialect song dedicated to "the estimable wife of Ex-President Tyler, and the other estimable and Union loving ladies of Virginia," by the composer John Hill Hewitt (James Hewitt's son), a Southerner by adoption, expressed the repugnance in which Mrs. Stowe was held in the South.

AUNT HARRIET BECHA STOWE.

I went to New York city a month or two ago,
A hunting for dat lady, Aunt Harriet Becha Stowe;
I see'd de Abolitions, dey said she'd gone way,
Dey told me in de city it was no use to stay.
She take away de dollars, and put 'em in her pocket,
She lai'd her hand upon it, and dar she safely lock it,
Dey said if Massa come for me, den dey would quickly meet,
Dey'd make a lion of me, and gib me 'nuf to eat.
    CHORUS.
Oh! Oh! Oh! Aunt Harriet Becha Stowe!
How could you leave de Country and sarve poor nigga so.

Dey treated dis here child, as doe I was a Turk,
Den tole me for to leave dem and go away to work;
I could'nt get no work, I could'nt get no dinner,
And den I wish dis Fugutive was back to ole Virginny,
Oh! when I was a picanin, Ole Uncle Tom would say,
Be true unto your Massa, and neber run away,
He tole me dis at home, he tole me dis at partin,'
Ned, don't you trust de white folks,
For dey am quite unsartin.
    CHORUS.

～～～

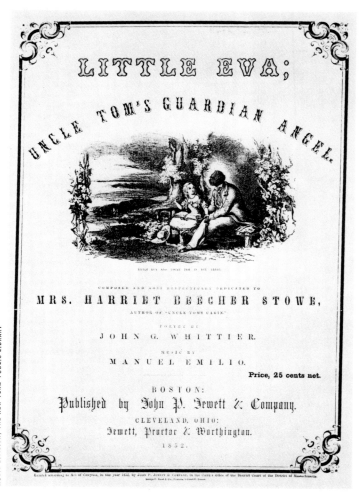

Mrs. Stowe was not the only American housewife to create a universal furor in the 1850s. Amelia Jenks Bloomer, a modest and mild matron of Seneca Falls, New York, set the world by its ears in 1851 when she launched a kind of symbolic pants suit for women. As editor of *The Lily*, a women's magazine devoted chiefly to the edifying topics of temperance and literature, she hurled her first spear in defense of women's rights when she made the following comment on a news story concerning two fashionably dressed New York women who had been seen openly smoking cigars on the street: "Surely we have an equal right to do it." This liberated attitude was doubtless fostered by her friendship with the feminist leaders Susan B. Anthony and Elizabeth Cady Stanton. Adding the topic of women's rights to the subject matter of *The Lily*, in 1851 Mrs. Bloomer embodied her advanced editorial policy by appearing on the streets of Seneca Falls in a pair of Turkish-looking trousers topped by a knee-length overdress or tunic. Taking off like wildfire, the audacious fashion soon stirred up prodigious controversy on both sides of the Atlantic. In the *New-York Tribune* (June 12, 1851), a male chauvinist fulminated against "that shocking Mahomedan movement in dress," which, he darkly prophesied, "would do much to unhinge our reverence for the best of mothers and stifle our affection . . . for the most amiable of wives . . . should we ever see this heathenish caricature of masculinity associated with their sacred persons."

Among a plethora of waltzes, polkas, schottisches, and songs inspired in 1851 by the bloomer craze was:

THE BLOOMER'S COMPLAINT.
A Very Pathetic SONG.

Dear me, what a terrible clatter they raise,
Because that old gossip Dame Rumor
Declares, with her hands lifted up in amaze
That I'm coming out as a Bloomer,
That I'm coming out as a Bloomer.
I wonder how often these men must be told
When a woman a notion once seizes,
However they ridicule, lecture or scold
She'll do, after all, as she pleases,
She'll do, after all, as she pleases.

They know very well that their own fashions change
With each little change of the season,
But Oh! it is "monstrous" and "dreadful" and "strange"
And "out of all manner of reason,"
And "out of all manner of reason."
If we take a fancy to alter our dress,
And come out in style "a la Bloomer,"
To hear what an outcry they make, I confess
Is putting me quite out of humor,
Is putting me quite out of humor.

I'll come out, next week, with a wide Bloomer flat
Of a shape that I fancy will fright them,
I had not intended to go quite to that,
But I'll do it now only to spite them,
But I'll do it now only to spite them.
With my pants "a la Turque," and my skirts two feet long,
All fitting of course most completely,
These grumblers shall own after all, they are wrong,
And that I, in a Bloomer, look sweetly,
And that I, in a Bloomer, look sweetly.

Franklin Pierce, the dark horse presidential candidate in the lusterless campaign of 1852, was characterized by the diarist George Templeton Strong as a "galvanized cypher," whose "talent for silence . . . will serve him far better than his antagonist's electioneering." Strong added, quoting a current joke: "It is not impossible that the Locos will pierce their enemies in 1852 as they poked them in 1844."

The songs for the presidential campaign of 1852 are a fair reflection of the campaign itself, conceded to have been just about the dullest in the annals of American history. At the Whigs' final national convention in Baltimore on June 16, 1852, they followed the pattern of their earlier successes and nominated a military man, the alternate hero of the Mexican War, General Winfield Scott, unfelicitously nicknamed "Old Fuss and Feathers." Two weeks before, the Democrats had repeated their own winning formula at their Baltimore convention by nominating another dark horse, Franklin Pierce, a good-looking lawyer from New Hampshire who had contrived to remain virtually unblemished by any sort of political reputation. Since both party platforms endorsed the Compromise of 1850, generally believed to be the ultimate solution to sectional dissentions, the substantial absence of issues offered campaign songwriters sparse inspiration. "Ratification Song" to celebrate Scott's nomination, sardonically set to a tune that more appropriately would have served his rival, illustrates the extent to which Whig songwriting vitality had waned. From *The Signal* (July 18, 1852), a Whig newspaper published in Washington:

PRESIDENT PIERCE'S,

March and Quick Step.

Composed and arranged for the

PIANO FORTE.

and respectfully dedicated to

MISS C. C. P. LEARNED

BY

B. R. LIGNOSKI.

Price 37½

Published by G. WILLIG J. Baltimore, Orange. G. LIGNOSKI, KENER & C.

RATIFICATION SONG.

Tune.—*The Old Granite State.*

Hark! it thunders from the mountains,
And pours down through all their fountains;
Yea! it reaches the tall fountains
 Of far off Mexico.
  CHORUS.
 We're a band of soldiers,
 We're a band of soldiers,
 We're a band of soldiers,
And our leader's name is Scott.
 With his banner streaming,
 And our weapons gleaming,
 And fresh glory beaming,
 We are fighting as he fought.

He is mighty in the battle,
And, 'mid war's iron rattle,
Drives the foe like frightened cattle,
 Before his conquering march.
  CHORUS.
 With his band of soldiers,
 With his band of soldiers,
 With his band of soldiers,
 He has won his mighty fame.
  Hurra! hurra!! hurra!!!
  Hurra! hurra!! hurra!!!
 Then, 'mid banners streaming,
 And old weapons gleaming,
 We see glory beaming
Round our Hero's honored name.

Like their songs, the Whigs' campaign techniques in 1852 were but a pale reflection of their vivid tactics in the halcyon days of 1840. A disgusted Democrat wrote in the *Richmond Enquirer* (August 17, 1852): "The log-cabins, coonskins, gourds and hard-cider . . . are now substituted by the exciting theme of 'Soup.'" And indeed soup had become the Whigs' new party symbol. Since 1846, Old Fuss and Feathers had been the butt of many unkind jokes because he had made an irrelevant reference to "a hasty bowl of soup" in a letter to William Learned Marcy, then the secretary of war. Perversely adopted in 1852 as the Whigs' electioneering device, soup was understandably derided by the Democrats. *The Campaign*, a Democratic party newspaper, observing that "the Whig creed is now typified by a soup bowl," reprinted (August 17, 1852) a Whig report of a Scott meeting in Pennsylvania, at which had been paraded "an immense 'soup bowl,' on wheels, containing a band, glee club, with flags, banners, and three or four live coons. . . ." The Whigs lamely stood up for their unfortunate symbol in a punning song titled "Hasty Soup" to the tune of "Auld Lang Syne," printed in *The Signal* (September 4, 1852). Continuing the alimentary image, in the text "Graham Bread" refers to Scott's running mate, William Alexander Graham, the incumbent secretary of the navy.

Ye lovers of good Hasty Soup
 Well spiced with Graham Bread;
See how the startled Locos droop
 Before the war-horse tread.

As in former elections, word-games continued to be played by both parties, each of which protested the inferiority of the other's puns. For purposes of ridicule, a stanza of a Whig song was reprinted in the *Richmond Enquirer* (June 29, 1853). "Old Chippewa" was another of Scott's nicknames, referring to his heroism at the Battle of Chippewa back in 1814.

> The hero that can't lose a battle.—
> *Win-field* wins the field in each fray;
> We'll be—while Scott fights for our freedom—
> *Scott Free*, with our old Chippewa.

Heavy-handed irony was mutually indulged in. A bathetic electioneering tale, delivered in Pierce's behalf by a golden-tongued orator, was lampooned to music in the *New Orleans Campaign Republic* and reprinted in *The Signal* (October 23, 1852).

INCIDENTS IN THE LIFE OF PIERCE.

Tune—"Northfield."

> Frank Pierce was born, in early life,
>   Down in the Granite State,
> And growed to be a General,
>   When he reached man's estate.
>
> Before he riz so very high,
>   A Congressman he went;
> And, many years before, he gave,
>   An unknown boy a cent.
>
> The facts are these, as Gov. Steele
>   Related in his speech:—
> Two boys were sucking, by the road,
>   A stick of candy each.
>
> A third sat blubbering on a stone,
>   His eyes brim full of water;
> Says Pierce, my nasty little friend.
>   You feel wuss than you ought to.
>
> I want to suck, the boy replied,
>   And have not got a cent;
> Says Pierce, producing that amount,
>   Now, stranger "let her went!"
>
> The boy looked up and blowed his nose,
>   And, with prophetic fire,
> Said, you shall be President
>   For giving me that 'are.
>
> Strange boy, said Pierce, I am surprised,
>   That you should think a cent
> Is cash enough to make a Dem-
>   Ocratic President.
>
> The boy replied—a cent, I own,
>   Is not a heavy price,
> But Democratic Presidents
>   Are not upon the rise!

～～～

The Whigs' final defeat at the polls in 1852 supplied the closing cadence to a three-part dirge that had begun earlier that year with the deaths of the two Whig giants, Henry Clay in June and Daniel Webster in October. Each in his different way had personified the party since its inception in 1834; each had wielded great power and achieved the highest possible status short of the presidency. Because they had not attained this ultimate goal, which both had passionately coveted, Daniel Webster and Henry Clay, two of the towering figures of nineteenth-century America, died frustrated, disillusioned, and embittered old men.

Apparently there were favorites among the funeral marches played at funerals for Henry Clay in many cities, North and South.

The evanescent Sam was at least musically captured during the heyday of Know-Nothingism.

In the chaotic political scene of the early 1850s, the Know-Nothings, originally founded in 1849 as a secret society called the "Order of the Star-Spangled Banner," speedily developed into a political party of national importance. Perpetuating the racial and religious intolerance of earlier nativists who had rioted against foreigners and Catholics, the Know-Nothings attracted discontented and confused remnants of the Whig party and dissidents of other political complexions. Calling themselves "Sams," the Know-Nothings practiced elaborate ritualistic mumbo jumbo,

with secret lodges, codes, passwords, and handshakes. Their initiation ceremonies were referred to as "seeing Sam," and they exacted vows of strictest secrecy from their members, constraining them, under penalty of expulsion or worse, to deny all knowledge of—or affiliation with—the party and to make one standard reply to all questions: "I know nothing." Only pure-blooded, native-born, racially superior American Anglo-Saxons were eligible and even then only if they were "untainted" by Catholic connections or sympathies.

The quest for Sam was translated into a kind of musical travelogue that even included a visit to Phineas T. Barnum's Museum in New York, but nobody anywhere could give a clue to Sam's whereabouts or even to his identity. In the text, the anachronistic reference to Joice Heth has to do with Barnum's first foray into the world of flimflam, when in 1835 he had exhibited an aged Negro woman, claiming that she was at that time 161 years old and that she had been the infant George Washington's nurse; the "wooly horse" pertains to another bit of Barnumesque apocrypha, a wondrous wooly-coated animal, combined of equal parts of elephant, deer, buffalo, camel, sheep, and horse. The wooly horse, also called a "nondescript," was purported by Barnum to have been discovered by John C. Frémont on his travels in the Far West. As the first presidential candidate of the newly formed Republican party in 1856, Frémont was frequently lampooned with the wooly horse. "Croton," in the text, is a contemporary synonym for the pure water that, since 1842, had been dispensed to New Yorkers from the Croton Reservoir, located at Fifth Avenue and 42nd Street.

HAVE YOU SEEN SAM?

I floated down the river
  On the schooner Polly Ann;
I landed on York Island,
  A very verdant man;
I gather'd up my baggage
  In a shocking crowd and jam,
When a fellow jump'd before me
  Saying "Have you seen Sam"?
    CHORUS.
    I don't know Sam,
    I don't know Sam,
    Confound this noise and bother
    Who is this fellow Sam?

I thought the fellow crazy,
  And fled before the wind:
The Astor rose before me,
  My coat tail stream'd behind:
Soon up the steps I scrambled,
  And shouted "Here I am"
Another fellow tapp'd me
  And ask'd "Have you seen Sam?"
    CHORUS.

I then went straight to Barnum's
  To see the mighty show:
The Shanghais and the Babies,
  How loudly they did crow!
I stood and gaz'd about me,
  To see if 'twas a sham:
I smooth'd the bearded lady's cheek,
  She sigh'd "Have you seen Sam?"
    CHORUS.

I hunted through each corner,
  Till nearly out of breath:
I ask'd about the wooly horse,
  The mermaid and Joice Heth;
Men laugh'd, the Shanghais cackled,
  I left old Captain Sham:
And as I turn'd to leave the place,
  The monkey's chatter'd Sam!
    CHORUS.

I went up to Albany,
  To see the wires at play:
'Twas pulling here 'twas bawling there
  Has Sam been here to day?
To Washington I went to see,
  The Senatorial jam:
I told them of the war in York,
  They ask'd if I'd seen Sam?
    CHORUS.

I told them horns and bugles blew
  A fearful warlike blast:
That crotchets, quavers, fiddles flew
  In bloodless conflict past:
The fifers scream'd their piercing notes,
  The drummer's beat their flam:
While high above the noise and din,
  The cry was "Where is Sam?"
    CHORUS.

I'm going up the river,
  My purse is running down:
No matter whom I chance to meet,
  They ask if Sam's in town:
It's Sam around above me,
  In Croton or in dram:
With luck, I'm off to morrow,
  Who is this fellow Sam?
    CHORUS.

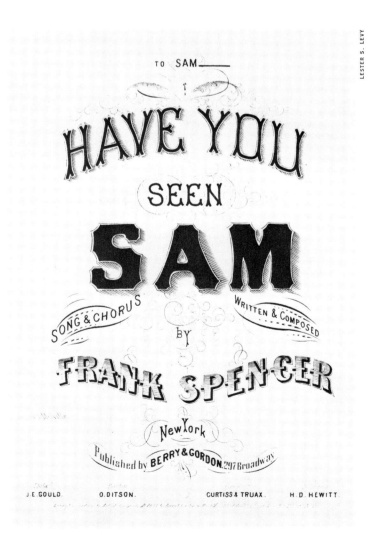

TO SAM

HAVE YOU SEEN SAM

SONG & CHORUS

WRITTEN & COMPOSED

BY

FRANK SPENCER

New York

Published by BERRY & GORDON, 297 Broadway

J. E. GOULD.   O. DITSON.   CURTISS & TRUAX.   H. D. HEWITT.

The Republican party was born out of the savage sectional conflict that was unleashed by the passage in May 1854 of the Kansas-Nebraska Act. Chiefly engineered by the opportunistic "Little Giant," Stephen A. Douglas, to implement the construction of a railroad from Chicago to the Pacific coast, the explosive law repealed the Missouri Compromise, which since 1820 had safeguarded the Louisiana Purchase territories above 36°30' north latitude from the inroads of slavery. At the same time, the law created two new territories, Kansas and Nebraska, to be governed by "popular sovereignty," less elegantly known as "squatter sovereignty," a system that allowed the voters themselves to decide whether or not they wanted slavery. Reacting with horror, antislavery elements of all shades and political denominations swiftly coalesced into a party pledged to resist the inevitable extension of slavery that the Kansas-Nebraska Act invited. The new party is believed to have adopted the name of Thomas Jefferson's Republican party for the first time at a local political meeting held in Ripon, Wisconsin, on February 28, 1854, and to have formally adopted it at a state meeting at Jackson, Michigan, on July 6.

"Free Soil, Free Speech, Free Men, and Frémont," chanted the Republicans, incorporating their aptly named first presidential candidate into their slogan, inherited from the campaign of 1848. Frémont was the very embodiment of a glamorous hero—young, handsome, and romantic. Known as "the Pathfinder," Frémont had made several notable trips of exploration to the Far West, where in 1846 he had played an important role in claiming California for the United States. The sheet music cover of this campaign song for Frémont (1856) depicts thrilling scenes from his western adventures (some were shared with Kit Carson) and an even more thrilling vista of the Capitol yonder, not the White House.

THERE IS THE WHITE HOUSE YONDER,

OR

THE FREMONT CAMPAIGN SONG

By 1856 the white-hot sectional passions exacerbated by the Kansas-Nebraska Act had erupted into bloody violence on the plains of Kansas, where a miniature civil war was raging between slavery and antislavery forces. And with the fate of the Union in jeopardy, the campaign for the presidency was waged with scarcely less vehemence by the three contending parties, two of which were competing for the first time. Abandoning all secrecy, the Know-Nothings, now calling themselves the American party, ushered in the 1856 campaign with a meeting at Philadelphia on Washington's birthday, doubtless to confirm the purity of their Americanism. They nominated the Unionist former president Millard Fillmore, with Andrew Jackson Donelson as his running mate; the Democrats met at Cincinnati on June 2 and chose another doughface, James Buchanan of Pennsylvania, and an authentic Southerner, John C. Breckinridge of Kentucky; and the Republicans at their maiden national convention in Philadelphia on June 17 named John C. Frémont and William Dayton. Frémont, a former Democrat, had been approached by both the Know-Nothings and the Democrats as a possible candidate.

Recalling the excitement of the contest of 1840, but with far more crucial issues at stake, electioneering in 1856 was fiery, and a correspondingly fiery crop of campaign songs reflected the intensity of the three-cornered battle. For example, Franklin Pierce, whose bid to be renominated was denied, was execrated in the *Republican Campaign Songster* (1856) for his acquiescence in the passage of the calamitous Kansas-Nebraska Act.

FRANK PIERCE'S SOLILOQUY.

Air—"Jordan is a hard road to travel."

Of all the tricks that have been played of late,
  The dirtiest and worst, every man says,
Was the one I played myself, in the hope of fame and pelf.
  It was helping the South to pilfer Kansas.
    Pack up my duds and take my leave,
      Hard work to travel back to Concord,
    For all my broken pledges these sighs I heave,
      It's a hard road to travel back to Concord, I believe.

The reign of terror in Kansas was paralleled in the halls of Congress, where, according to Ben: Perley Poore, "acrimonious altercations, with threats of personal violence by the excited Southerners," reached so high a pitch in 1856 that "Northern Congressmen went about armed with revolvers, and gave notice that while they would not fight duels, they would defend themselves if attacked." This aggravated hostility was kindled by the disgraceful assault on Senator Charles Sumner of Massachusetts by Congressman Preston S. Brooks of South Carolina on May 22, 1856.

Exercising a prerogative of Southern "chivalry," Brooks had attacked Sumner as he sat working at his desk in the Senate chamber, and had beaten him over the head with a heavy gutta-percha cane until the cane snapped and the bleeding senator was unconscious. Two days earlier, Sumner, an impassioned Abolitionist, had delivered a violent tirade to Congress on "The Crime Against Kansas," in which he had unreasonably and offensively attacked Brooks's uncle, Senator Andrew Pickens Butler, also of South Carolina. Sumner was incapacitated for the following two years, and it is believed that he never completely recovered. The episode added fuel to the already raging sectional flames. In the North Brooks was anathematized; in the South he was eulogized.

In New York, George Templeton Strong wrote in his diary (May 28, 1856): "North and South [are] farther alienated than ever before. I believe civilization at the South is retrograde and that the Carolinas are decaying into barbarism." On September 30 Strong poured his feelings into a sardonic song to the tune of "Bonnets of Bonny Dundee," after Sir Walter Scott, and on October 2 he delightedly noted: "Sent my doggerel to the *Evening Post*, which published it to my surprise. . . ." The New York *Evening Post* (October 2, 1856) had changed its title from "Southern War-Song" to "Scalp Song" and attributed its authorship to one Maria Jane Peytoun Middletonne Fitz-Fysshe, a pseudonym that could only have been fabricated by Strong. In the text, "the wild Quattlebum" is Paul Quattlebaum, a fire-eating South Carolina senator who supported slavery, nullification, and secession.

SCALP SONG.

To the base churls of Congress 'twas Brooksy who spoke:
"Ere the West shall be free, there are heads to be broke;
"So let each southern gent who loves niggers and me,
"Come follow the bludgeon of Chevalier B."
    CHORUS.
    Go finish your cocktail, go borrow a ($)10,
    Go lock up your niggers and count up your men:
    We'll pepper the Yankees for talking so free,
    And it's room for the bludgeon of Chevalier B.

Bold Brooks is excited, he strides down the street,
The children drop senseless, the dogs they retreat;
But the judge (well-bred man) says, "It isn't for me
To confine a *real gent* like the Chevalier B."

With free free-soil *canaille* the hotel steps were filled,
As if half of New York had come South to be killed,
There was buttoning of pockets and trembling of knees,
As they watched for that bludgeon of Chevalier B.'s.

He strode to the bar through saliva and smoke,
And with the wild Quattlebum gaily he spoke:
"Our district alone will raise regiments three,
"For the love of buck-niggers, big bludgeons and me."

The Quattlebum asks, "The campaign! Is it planned?"
"The spirit of Arnold our march shall command!
"You shall soon hear of Boston surrendering to me,
"Or, that high swings the *corpus* of Chevalier B.

"There are streams besides Hudson, (with swamps as their
    mouth),
"If they've men in New England, we've gents at the South.
"And loyal 'white trash' (they can't read, don't you see?)
"Who will bite, scratch and gouge for the Chevalier B.

"There are whips and revolvers that lie about loose;
"There are dogs in our kennels we've trained up for use.
"The pistols shall shoot and the bloodhounds run free,
"At a sign from the bludgeon of Chevalier B.

"Away to the bogs—to the hills—to the moon!
"Ere I bow to John Frémont I'll couch with the coon—
"And tremble, false snobs, as you sit at your tea,
"You'll catch fits before long from my bludgeon and me."

He "waved his proud hand" and the toddies were brewed,
The glasses were clinked, and the chieftains were "stewed";
And in slight incoherence, chivalric and free,
"Died away the wild war notes" of Chevalier B.
    CHORUS.
    Go finish you cocktail, go borrow a ($)10,
    Go mortgage your niggers and muster your men—
    It's Death to the North where the workies are free,
    And hurra for the bludgeon of Chevalier B.!

"Is Freedom Worth a Song?" an advertisement in the New York *Evening Post* asked, and it went on to announce that the first ten thousand copies of the *Republican Campaign Songster*, "a collection of Thrilling Original Lyrics, Pasquinades, &c., especially prepared for the Friends of Freedom in the Campaign of Fifty-Six," had been sold out in five days and that a new printing was now available. Not a few of the thrilling pasquinades consisted of personal invective against the opposing candidates. In the following example, an old anti-Democratic declaration of James Buchanan's was dredged up; he was reminded that he had been a Federalist back in the early days of the century; his bachelorhood was inelegantly ridiculed; and he was openly accused of being a tool of the South. "Buck" (also "old Buck") was a party nickname for Buchanan; the Democrats called themselves "Buchaneers."

BUCK'S PRIVATE CONFESSION PUBLICLY REVEALED.
Air—"Lucy Long."

"If I thought I had one drop of Democratic blood in my veins, I would open every one of them to eject it," said James Buchanan, some years ago.

    "Oh, if I thought that I had got
      One drop of a Democrat's blood,
    My jugular vein I'd rip in twain,
      And spill *the filthy flood*."

(*Chorus of*   Don't let that annoy you!
"*Loafers*")   We say, old buffer, stop!
           If they boiled you down in a chandler's vat
           They couldn't raise a drop.

    "I don't believe in marriage—
      A curse on 'wives and weans'—
    I love myself too much to share
      With them my pork and beans!"

(*Chorus*   But don't let that alarm you,
hilariously)   A "cuckold" he was born,
           And since he left his "Federal wife,"
           Oh hasn't she given him "*a horn*?"

    "No more I'm James Buchanan—
      I sold myself down South;
    Henceforth I'll do what my masters please,
      And speak what they put in my mouth!"

(*Chorus*   But don't let that alarm you,
solemnly)   Forgive his slavish tone;
           Can you ask a man to stand up straight
           Who was "*born without a backbone?*"

In keeping with their new image, in 1856 the Know-Nothings allowed Sam to emerge from his secret hiding place and they absolved him of his oath of silence. He raised his newfound voice in the service of his party in a song directed against Frémont that appeared in the songster *Fillmore and Donelson Songs for the Campaign* (1856). In the text, "Jacky Free of Caroline" is, of course, Frémont, who was born in Virginia but educated in Charleston, where his unwed mother had emigrated when he was a child; "Bullion" is a nickname for Thomas Hart Benton, a stalwart advocate of hard money, with whose seventeen-year-old daughter, Jessie, Frémont had romantically eloped when Benton had refused to permit their marriage (they were married by a Catholic priest, providing the Know-Nothings with still more ammunition against Frémont); and Thurlow Weed was now devoting his extraordinary political talents to the Republicans, having accurately read the handwriting on the Whig wall.

WHAT SAM TELLS THE PEOPLE.

Air—"Dandy Jim."

I've heard how Black Republicans
Were figuring out their traitorous plans—
The Northern States they would combine
With Jacky Free of Caroline.
    But SAM has told the people—O!
    That sixteen States are a very poor show,
    The Woolly Horse will never go,
    For SAM has told the People so.

The good old South Carolina State
This Jacky Free did educate—
But now he thinks it very fine,
To curse the name of Caroline.
    But SAM has told the people—O!
    That Jacky has a very poor show;
    The Woolly Horse will never go,
    For SAM has told the People so.

This Dandy Jack was a trooper wild,
He ran away with Bullion's child;
Quoth he "I'll make this *heiress* mine,
For I'm Jack Free of Caroline."
    But SAM has told the People—O!
    That a trick like that makes very poor show;
    The Woolly Horse will never go—
    For SAM has told the People so.

~~~

This Jack he used to go to mass,
And the holy water he never could pass,
Till his fingers crossed had made the sign
Of Catholic Jack of Caroline.
    But SAM has told the People—O!
    That a Jesuit President has no show;
    The Woolly Horse will never go—
    For SAM has told the People so.

~~~

O ! Jacky Free, my counsel heed—
Don't trust too much in Thurlow Weed—
The knaves who now for Freedom whine,
Will sell you out to Caroline.
    For SAM has told the People—O !
    That Kansas is a juggler's show ;
    The Wooly Horse is made of dough ;
    O ! SAM has told the People so.

This spooky-looking sheet music cover (c. 1856) pictures Know-Nothing political symbolism with a Whig raccoon and a Democratic rooster looking helplessly on as their inanimate counterparts are dangled from a sinister banner carried in a shadowy Know-Nothing parade.

If the Know-Nothings lashed out at Frémont, the Democrats bestowed unbiased animosity on both their adversaries in this song printed in the *New York Weekly Times, and National Democrat* (July 26, 1856):

CLEAR THE TRACK!

Music—"Begone, dull care!"

Begone, Fillmore!
    I prithee, begone from me—
The President
    You never again, sir, can be!
Your former friends
    Their voices will not give for you;
And so here ends
    The visions the Know-Nothings drew!
    CHORUS.
    So the people all say,
    "Give us only fair play!
    And we'll soon hold at bay
    All the pack!
We'll put Old Buck and Breckinridge through!
    Clear the track!

Begone, Frémont!
    I prithee, begone from me!
The President
    You never, oh never, can be!
You turn from the South—
    The region in which you were born—
To humbug the North,
    With a hope that you know is *forlorn*!
    So the people, etc.

~~~

In one regard, James Buchanan was uniquely honored among American presidents. Stephen Foster, whose sister Ann Eliza was married to Buchanan's brother Edward, wrote a number of Buchanan campaign songs in 1856. Of these, only two are known to have been found: "The Great Baby Show, or The Abolition Show," a mild spoof of a Republican parade at Pittsburgh, for which Foster wrote words to the tune of "Villikens and his Dinah"; and "The White House Chair," an exquisite miniature for solo and four-part chorus, for which he wrote both the words and music.

THE WHITE HOUSE CHAIR.

Let all our hearts for Union be,
    For the North and South are one;
They've worked together manfully,
    And together they will still work on.
CHORUS.
Then come ye men from every State,
    Our creed is broad and fair;
Buchanan is our candidate,
    And we'll put him in the White House chair.

We'll have no dark, designing band,
    To rule with secret sway;
We'll give to all a helping hand,
    And be open as the light of day.
CHORUS.
We'll not outlaw the land that holds
    The bones of Washington,
Where Jackson fought and Marion bled,
    And the battles of the brave were won.

Stephen Foster's campaign song for James Buchanan, "The White House Chair," was not published until twenty-one years after Foster's too-early death, when it appeared in the Pittsburgh Dispatch (September 20, 1885). The editor apologized for having omitted the title and the second stanza and chorus, "due to an accident, such as is liable to happen in any office, no matter how well regulated."

THE WHEELBARROW POLKA.

J.H.Bufford's Lith.

Photograph by Turner & Cutting

MAJOR BEN. PERLEY POORE OF NEWBURY,

Made a bet, with Col. Robert I. Burbank of Boston, on the Presidential vote in Massachusetts. The bet doomed the loser to wheel a barrel of apples from his house to the house of the winner. The Colonel won the bet, and the Major started the next morning from Newbury (36 Miles from Boston) with the apples (notwithstanding the Col. had promptly released him from the Conditions of the bet) and arrived at the Tremont House the third day at 2½ o'clock—where in presence of at least 30,000 enthusiastic spectators the most interesting ceremonies took place between the parties.

Composed and dedicated to
MAJOR BEN. PERLEY POORE.

BOSTON
Published by **OLIVER DITSON** 115 Washington St.

National Song

STAR SPANGLED BANNER

Written during the

Bombardment of Fort McHenry

(BALTIMORE)

by the late

FRANCIS S. KEY Esq.

Published by MILLER & BEACHAM Baltimore
Successors to F.D. Benteen

Entered according to Act of Congress in the Year 1855 by Miller & Beacham in the Clerks Office of the District Court of M.d.

No less an artist than Winslow Homer perpetuated Ben: Perley Poore's exploit with this sheet music cover (1856) for "The Wheelbarrow, or Cider Polka," by a composer calling himself "A. Barrel Apples."

The eminent biographer of politics, Major Ben: Perley Poore—to give him his full title—spectacularly paid off a losing bet after he had backed the wrong man, Millard Fillmore, to win in Massachusetts in 1856. Manfully fulfilling his singular obligation, described in the sheet music cover of "The Wheelbarrow Polka," Perley was cheered along the entire distance of his journey by delighted spectators. When he reached Boston, he was welcomed not only by cheering, flag-waving throngs, who lined State Street and hung from windows, balconies, and rooftops, but also by a great military parade, in which he promptly joined, wheelbarrow and all. "Flanked by an honor guard of six on each side consisting of citizens of Charlestown and Boston," according to a quotation in Lester S. Levy's book *Grace Notes in American History* (1967), and serenaded by the Boston Cornet Band, Perley did not relinquish his load until he and his escort reached the Tremont House, where he was regally wined and dined.

THE UNION MUST AND SHALL BE PRESERVED.

Tune, "The Star-Spangled Banner."

Oh! say, can a thought so vile and base come
  To the mind of a dweller on Columbia's soil,
That the work of our fathers should now be undone,
  And unwound should now be the proud national coil?
And that traitors should sway and rule o'er this proud land,
  With tyranny's lash, and the plunderer's brand!
No, never! Freemen, never! With the right, our arm nerved,
  The Union it must and shall be preserved!

And though traitor may spring from 'mong kindred and friends,
  Let them look to themselves, to the Union we're true;
If their hearts will prove false let its blood make amends,
  And the stain we'll wash off while our hands we imbue!
Neither love of friends false or kindred shall save
  Them the terror of flight, and the gloom of the grave;
Let them look to themselves, with the right our arm nerved,
  The Union it must and shall be preserved!

If a son or a father prove false to the flag,
  Then sever the tie with which nature has bound you,
And remember, though anguish your own heart may drag
  To despair, that the love of your country has found you.
And whatever the issue be of this foul strife,
  Be sure that it cost not fair Liberty's life.
Then let traitors beware! with the right our arm nerved,
  The Union it must and shall be preserved!

Oh! thus be it ever when freemen shall stand
  Between their loved homes and fraternal blood spilling;
May they ever be guided, great God, by thy hand,
  To obey thy just laws and commandments be willing,
And a prosperous nation we ever shall be,
  With true love for our Country and full trust in thee.
Grant these blessings, Jehovah! with the right still us nerve,
  While the Union we rush to uphold and preserve!

The Camp-Fire Songster (1862)

THE FLAG OF OUR UNION
A NATIONAL SONG

POETRY BY Geo. P. MORRIS.
MUSIC BY Wm. VINCENT WALLACE.

Lith of H.Holt N.Y.

Price 25 Cts. Nett.
in Colort 38 Cts.

NEW YORK
PUBLISHED BY Wm. HALL & SON 239, BROADWAY
NEW ORLEANS W. I. MAYO.

"A song for our banner," the watch word recall,
  Which gave the Republic her station:
"United we stand, divided we fall!"
  It made and preserves us a nation!

The union of lakes, the union of lands,
  The union of States none can sever—
The union of hearts, the union of hands,
  And the flag of our Union for ever!

UNION WAR GALOP

composed by

WILLIAM DRESSLER.

LITH. OF EHRGOTT, FORBRIGER & CO. CIN.

CLEVELAND.
Published by S. BRAINARD & Co 203 Superior Str.

Entered according to act of Congress in the year 1861 by S. Brainard & Co in the Clerks office of the District Court of the Northern District of Ohio.

10. Dirge
1860-1865

The American propensity for musical self-expression reached its highest fulfillment during the terrible years of the Civil War. From Fort Sumter to Appomattox the war was recorded and reflected in a phenomenal outpouring of songs (more than two thousand were reported published during the first year alone). A commentator observed in the *New York Weekly Review of Music, Literature, Fine Arts, and Society* (November 19, 1864): ". . . all the phases through which this dreadful struggle has gone . . . are duly represented in the songs . . . there is not an event, whether political or on the battle field, which does not find its echo in them." Apart from its documentary value, this extraordinary translation of history into music acts as a unique instrument for transmitting to us at first hand the immediate emotions and reactions of the time as well as its foibles.

People on both sides of the battle lines placed great reliance on the songs, finding in them a source of strength, courage, solace, hope, much-needed laughter, and a general escape valve for the unbearable tensions of their lives at a time of fratricidal slaughter. Everybody sang everywhere—at home, at work, in school, in church, at rallies, in camp, on the march, in retreat, in victory, in defeat, in reunion, in sorrow, in jubilation. Paradoxically, the belligerents of both sides often adopted the selfsame tunes to express their conflicting ideologies as well as their common emotions.

Furious Southern extremist delegates staged a dress rehearsal for secession in April 1860 when they walked out of the Democratic national convention in Charleston after having failed to win a plank in the platform that would assure federal protection to slavery in the territories. With balloting deadlocked because of their defection, the convention was adjourned to Baltimore in June, when Stephen A. Douglas, the "Little Giant," was duly nominated with Herschel V. Johnson of Georgia as his running mate, but not before a replacement set of dissenting Southerners had irrevocably split from the party. Still in Baltimore, the splinter group met later that month and nominated their own Democratic candidates, John C. Breckinridge of Kentucky and Joseph Lane of Oregon, and by so doing they presented the Republicans with the election.

Between the Charleston and Baltimore episodes, the Republicans held their mammoth convention in Chicago and nominated Abraham Lincoln of Illinois and Hannibal Hamlin of Maine, a former Democrat. To round out the populous political picture, the Constitutional Union party, a new name for remnants of the old Whigs and the Know-Nothings, convened in Baltimore early in May and nominated John Bell of Tennessee for president with Edward Everett of Massachusetts for vice-president.

Like the music it adorned, American sheet music cover art, both in black and white and in color, reached its most eloquent expression during the Civil War years.

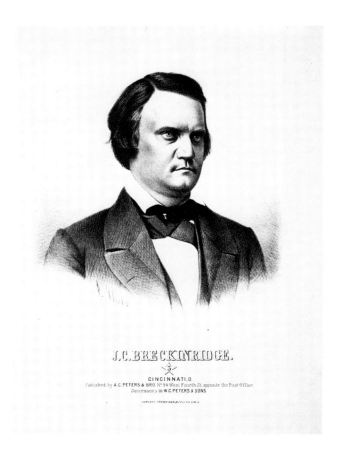

Through thick and thin, Douglas persistently backed the concept of popular sovereignty (squatter's rights) as the solution to the apparently insoluble problem of the extension of slavery to the territories; but at the Baltimore convention he came out in support of the Dred Scott decision, which in 1857 had officially relegated the Negro to the status of a chattel. These questions and the Charleston fiasco were objects of irony in a Republican campaign song appearing in *The Wide-Awake Vocalist; or, Rail Splitters' Song Book* (1860).

SING A SONG OF CHARLESTON.

Air, "Sing a Song of Sixpence."

Sing a song of Charleston!
   Bottle full of Rye!
All the Douglas delegates
   Knocked into pi!
For when the vote was opened
   The South began to sing,
"You little Squatter Sovereign
   Shan't be our King!"
CHORUS.
Hi diddle, diddle! the Dred Scott riddle!
   The delegates scatter like loons!
The little Dug swears to see the sport,
   And the Southerners count their spoons.

There was a little Senator,
   Who wasn't very wise,
He jumped into Convention,
   And scratched out both his eyes.
And when he found his eyes were out,
   With all his might and main,
He bolted off to Baltimore
   To scratch them in again.
   CHORUS.—Hi diddle, diddle! &c.

In this song for Breckinridge and Lane from the New York *Herald* (August 30, 1860), "Bill Seward" is William Seward, Lincoln's future secretary of state, who had been in the running for the presidential nomination at the Chicago convention; "Horace" is Horace Greeley, who had vehemently opposed Seward's nomination.

PRESIDENTIAL ASPIRANTS.

Air—"Ho! For the White House."

Honest Abe, Honest Abe,
   You are only a babe,
To dream of the Presidential chair;
   Not even Bill Seward,
   Whom Horace sent leeward,
Could ride on the nigger in there,
     Honest Abe,
Could ride on the nigger in there.

Little Giant, Little Giant,
   Though bold and defiant,
Your time for the White House ain't come;
   It may ill suit your taste,
   But for four years at least,
You must play the squatter at home,
     Little Giant,
You must play the squatter at home.

Breck and Lane, Breck and Lane,
   Tried and true are the twain—
Statesmen—not splinters of timber—
   Who, as captain and mate
   Of the great ship of State,
The people will ship in November,
     Breck and Lane,
The people will ship in November.

Expectedly, many puns on John Bell's name were made by both his supporters and detractors. Supportive Constitutional Union party organizations were called the "Bell Ringers," the "Bell-Everetters," and the "Clapperites." "The Tennessee Bell will toll the death-knell of Sectionalism wherever it is heard," wishfully proclaimed a banner at a Bell and Everett meeting at Lancaster, Pennsylvania, the New York *Evening Express* (June 30, 1860) reported; and the apparently politically nonsectarian New York *Herald* printed a less than inspired Bell song set to an intriguingly titled tune.

VOTE FOR BELL OF TENNESSEE.

Air—"Harlem National Union Glee Club No. 1."

Don't you hear that rumbling sound;
Those deep toned murmurs all around,
The people's voice 'tis known to be,
For old John Bell of Tennessee.
Sound the tocsin, strike the drum;
The people have resolved to come;
Shouts of gladness and of glee
Are raised for Bell of Tennessee.
　　U li, a li, o la e,
　　Vote for Bell of Tennessee.

Flags are spread and banners fly,
Union men are now to try
And win a glorious victory
With old John Bell of Tennessee.
For Abraham the chance is lost;
He quails before the Union host;
And Breck, and Dug, and all will be
Used up by Bell of Tennessee.
　　U li, a li, o la e,
　　Vote for Bell of Tennessee.

～～～

This appealing campaign portrait of a youthful-looking Lincoln belies both his political nickname of "Old Abe" (he was fifty-one years old in 1860) and the opposition's customary ridicule of his physical appearance: his unusual height and his homely face. As a satirical Democratic campaign song in the New York *Herald* (August 30, 1860) had it:

OLD ABE AND HIS FIGHTS.

Air—"Roger de Coverly."

Tell us of his fight with Douglas—
　　How his spirit never quails;
Tell us of his manly bearing,
　　Of his skill in splitting rails.

Tell us he's a second Webster,
　　Or, if better, Henry Clay;
That he's full of genial humor—
　　Placid as a summer day.

Call him Abe, or call him Abram—
　　Abraham—'tis all the same;
Abe will smell as sweet as either;
　　We don't care about the name.

Say he's capable and honest—
　　Loves his country's good alone—
Never drank a drop of whiskey—
　　Wouldn't know it from a stone.

Tell us he resembles Jackson,
　　Save he wears a larger boot,
And is broader 'cross the shoulders,
　　And is taller by a foot.

Anything you care to tell us
　　We will take without a stricture;
But, oh, don't!—we beg and pray you—
　　Don't, for God's sake—show his picture!

343

To the tune of Daniel Decatur Emmett's popular "walk-around" (a minstrel show finale), "Dixie's Land" (see pages 352-353), Republicans sang:

At Chicago they selected
Lincoln, who will be elected,
    Abraham, Abraham,
    Abraham, Abraham.
As Honest Abe the people know him,
And all his actions go to show him
    A true man, a true man,
    A true man, a true man.

Because the people do demand
    A hero, a hero,
As leaders of their Spartan band,
They'll take him from his "prairie-land,"
    Away, away,
Across the line of Dixon.

Hutchinson's Republican Songster,
for the Campaign of 1860

DEDICATED TO THE
Republican Presidential Candidate
HON. ABRM. LINCOLN.
BOSTON
Published by OLIVER DITSON & CO. 277 Washington St

DEDICATED TO THE
PRESIDENT OF THE UNITED STATES.
HON. ABRM. LINCOLN.
BOSTON
Published by OLIVER DITSON & CO. 277 Washington St

At some time between his nomination and his inauguration, Lincoln acquired his beard, reportedly in response to a letter from a young lady admirer suggesting that a beard made a man look more distinguished. Exhibiting traditional publishers' frugality, the music house of Oliver Ditson ingeniously affixed a beard to a campaign song portrait of a clean-shaven Lincoln and used the same plate again for an "Inauguration Grand March" the following year. The "Wigwam" refers to the vast wooden structure that was built to house the 1860 Republican convention at Chicago.

At Lincoln's inauguration, the *New-York Times* (March 5, 1861) reported that ". . . the Marine Band . . . played several patriotic airs before and after the reading of the address." Later: "Mr. Lincoln and Mr. Buchanan, arm in arm, and followed by a few privileged persons, proceeded at a measured pace to the Senate Chamber, and thence to the President's Room, while the Band played 'Hail Columbia' 'Yankee Doodle' and the 'Star Spangled Banner.'" Still later: "The thirty-four little girls who personated the several States of the Union, and rode in a gaily decorated car in the procession, halted at the door while they sang 'Hail Columbia,' after which they were received by the President. . . ."

The inaugural ball was held in a specially constructed building adjacent to the Washington City Hall. The *Times* commented: "The ball is a decided success. The room is very tastefully decorated with shields and flags, and is lighted with gas. . . . At 10¾ o'clock the Presidential party came in. . . . The Band struck up 'Hail Columbia,' and the party marched from one end of the hall to the other, amid inspiring strains of the national air, causing an era of tremendous good feeling. . . ." The *Times* failed to mention that "Hail to the Chief" was repeatedly played, both at the inaugural ceremonies and in the ballroom.

In a follow-up story the next day, the *Times* colorfully reviewed the preinaugural doings: "There was a good band, a car-load of pretty girls, thirty-four in all . . . militia-men, who walked like country paupers on a semi-diluted spree, and that climax of absurdities, 'citizens in carriages.'" Of the music, the reporter wrote: "The brass band exhausted its capabilities and the endurance of the throats of the musicians. Patriotic airs were generally played, though I noticed that 'Way down South in Dixie' was a great favorite with anybody who knew what a good tune was, and, as slowly the procession moved on, the President elect was obliged, in response to repeated calls, to rise and bow with hat in hand."

Little more than one month later, the *New-York Times* (April 13, 1861) reported: "The Disunion conspiracy, which has for the last twenty years been gnawing at the heart-strings of the great American Republic, has at last culminated in open war upon its glittering and resplendent flag." And on April 15: "The curtain has fallen upon the first act of the great tragedy of the age. Fort Sumter has been surrendered, and the Stars and Stripes of the American Republic give place to the felon flag of the Southern Confederate."

The historic moment of secession was captured in the first Confederate sheet
music, published only a few days after the event it commemorated.

THE PALMETTO STATE SONG.

All hail to the dawn of this glor'ous morning,
The genius of liberty lights from the skies,
Points to the Palmetto, our banner adorning,
And bids us at once from our slumbers to rise!

Shall we bend to the power that threatens our peace,
Or stand for our country till being shall cease?
Then beneath the Palmetto, the pride of our story,
Like freemen we'll stand, or we'll perish in glory.

Southern states are symbolized by bales of cotton, tobacco leaves, a palmetto, and a cask (of rum?) in this undated, allegorical Confederate sheet music cover.

THE FIRST GUN IS FIRED!

The first gun is fired.
　May God protect the right;
Let the freeborn sons of the north arise
　In power's avenging might;

Shall the glorious Union our fathers made,
　By ruthless hands be sundered,
And we of freedom's sacred rights
　By trait'rous foes be plundered?

Arise! Arise! Arise!
　And gird ye for the fight,
And let our watchword ever be,
　"May God protect the right."

Words and music by George Frederick Root (1861)

TO THE HERO OF SHILOH & CHARLESTON

BEAUREGARD'S CHARLESTON

QUICKSTEP

COMPOSED BY L. SCHREINER

PUBᵉᵈ BY J.C. SCHREINER & SON. MACON

AND SAVANNAH GA

The first shots were fired when the Confederate hero General Pierre Gustave Toutant Beauregard ordered the bombardment of Fort Sumter in Charleston harbor on April 12, 1861. It was reported that the band played "Yankee Doodle" as the Union troops evacuated Sumter on April 14. On April 14, 1865, the day Lincoln was assassinated, Major Anderson, who had surrendered Sumter to Beauregard, restored the Stars and Stripes over Fort Sumter to the rousing accompaniment of George F. Root's "The Battle Cry of Freedom."

FAREWELL TO THE STAR SPANGLED BANNER.

Let tyrants and slaves submissively tremble
   And bow down their necks 'neath the juggernaut car;
But brave men will rise in the strength of a nation,
   And cry give me freedom or else give me war.

Farewell forever the Star spangled banner
   No longer shall wave o'er the land of the free.
But we'll unfurl to the broad breeze of Heaven
   Thirteen bright stars round the Palmetto tree.

OUR NATIONAL CONFEDERATE ANTHEM

GOD SAVE THE SOUTH

THE TEXT BY ERNEST HALPIN
COMPOSED BY C.T. DE CŒNIÉL RICHMOND Vᵃ

PUBLISHED BY THE COMPOSER AND MAY BE HAD
AT HIS RESIDENCE GRACE Sᵀ COR 1ˢᵀ & OF ALL THE PRINCIPAL BOOK & MUSIC STORES IN THE CONFEDERACY

LITH. BY E. CREHEN 146 MAIN Sᵀ
Entered according to the act of congres by C.T. De Cœniel Richmond Vᵃ

GOD SAVE THE SOUTH.

God save the South! God save the South!
Her altars and firesides! God save the South!
Now that the war is nigh, Now that we're arm'd to die
Chanting our battle cry Freedom or Death!

God make the right Stronger than the might!
Millions would trample us, Down with their pride!
Lay· thou their legions low, Roll back the ruthless foe.
Let the proud spoiler know, God's on our side.

~~~

351

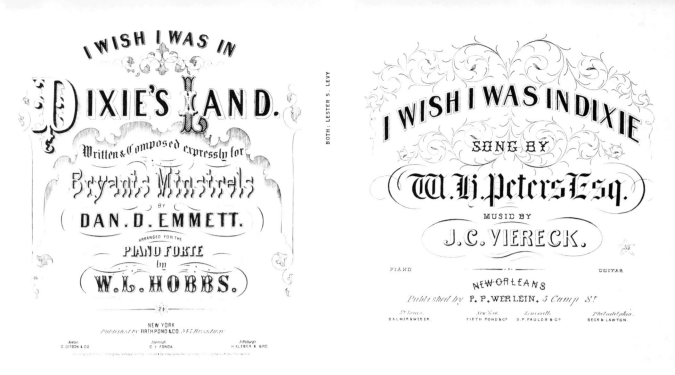

*The first edition of Daniel Decatur Emmett's walk-around, published in New York
in 1860 (left), and the first pirated edition, which preceded it, issued in New Orleans.
In the ensuing controversy over the piracy, the New Orleans publisher offered
to pay Emmett five dollars for the copyright.*

Ironically, it was a Northern song that became the definitive Southern "anthem" for all time, although great Confederate effort was expended in attempting to disprove this discomfiting fact. Beginning life on the New York stage in 1859 as a walk-around, or finale, for a production by Bryant's Minstrels, the words and music of "Dixie's Land," as it was first called, were written by a member of the company, Dan Emmett (the composer of the great hit of 1843, "Old Dan Tucker"). "Dixie's Land" was a tremendous spontaneous success, spreading so rapidly that by the time it was published in New York in 1860 a pirated version, with the music credited to one J. C. Viereck, had already appeared in New Orleans.

With flamingly patriotic texts, "Dixie" served as a powerful war song for both sides during the war; but Emmett's original words were apolitical, and they are the ones that are best remembered.

The derivation of the word *Dixie* remains as mystifying as when the song was new; it was variously believed to refer to the Mason and Dixon Line, to be a synonym for a Negro, to refer to a utopian paradise for blacks, to signify the South. In this last context, Dixie became as enduring a part of the American language as the song is a symbol of the South.

"Dixie" first took the South by storm shortly before the war when, as Richard B. Harwell (*Confederate Music*, 1950) tells us, forty ladies in Zouave costumes performed a drill to it in a production of *Pocahontas* at the Varieties Theatre in New Orleans. W. H. Peters's words for the pirated edition, which soon followed, were as innocent of overt political implications as Emmett's had been, but a good deal less talented.

DIXIE'S LAND.

I wish I was in de land ob cotton,
Old times dar am not forgotten;
 Look away! Look away!
 Look away! Dixie Land.
In Dixie Land whar I was born in,
Early on one frosty mornin,
 Look away! Look away!
 Look away! Dixie Land.

Den I wish I was in Dixie,
 Hooray! Hooray!
In Dixie Land, I'll take my stand,
To lib an die in Dixie,
 Away, away,
Away down south in Dixie,
 Away, away,
Away down south in Dixie.

I WISH I WAS IN DIXIE.
Corrected Edition!

Come along, boys, come out in the fields,
The moon is bright and shines right cherily,
 ho, boys, for
 the days of yore;
Bring along the girls and we'll have a merry time,
Never mind the dew, but come along merrily,
 ho, boys, for
 the days of yore.

I wish I was in Dixie
 yo ho, yo ho,
There is no land like Dixie
All the wide world over.
 The land, the land,
The happy land of Dixie,
 The land, the land,
The happy land of Dixie.

When the tune of "Dixie" became the official Southern battle hymn in 1861, it was sung to many different sets of warlike words. The renegade Confederate poet-general Albert Pike contributed one of the more memorable lyrics.

Southrons! hear your country call you!
Up lest worse than death befall you!
    To arms! To arms!
    To arms, in Dixie!
Lo! all the beacon fires are lighted,—
Let all hearts be now united!
    To arms! To arms!
    To arms, in Dixie!
Advance the flag of Dixie!
    Hurrah! Hurrah!
For Dixie's land we take our stand,
And live or die for Dixie!
    To arms! To arms!
And conquer peace for Dixie!
    To arms! To arms!
And conquer peace for Dixie!

In a curious musical subwar, many of the same tunes were enlisted by both North and South. "Dixie" especially was hotly claimed by both sides. Despite its having become synonymous with the South, "Dixie" was played and sung in the North until well into 1863. In 1861 Northerners sang:

DIXIE FOR THE UNION.

On! ye patriots to the battle,
Hear Fort Moultrie's cannon rattle;
Then away, then away, then away to the fight!
Go meet those Southern Traitors,
With iron will.
And should your courage falter, boys,
Remember Bunker Hill.
    Hurrah! Hurrah!
    The Stars and Stripes forever!
    Hurrah! Hurrah!
    Our Union shall not sever!

A minstrel show walk-around is brilliantly depicted on this broadside of "Dixie's Land" in a variant version of Emmett's original text.

LINCOLN QUICK STEP.

DEDICATED TO

ABRAHAM LINCOLN
PRESIDENT OF THE UNITED STATES.

Philadelphia LEE & WALKER 722 Chesnut St.

"Dixie" was played at the inaugurations of both American presidents in 1861.

MOST RESPECTFULLY DEDICATED TO PRESIDENT
JEFFERSON DAVIS.
CONFEDERACY MARCH.

Jeff'n Davis
Miss

BY
ALFRED F. TOULMIN.
OF PATAPSCO INSTITUTE.
Published by GEORGE WILLIG, Baltimore.

ELLSWORTH.

A BATTLE HYMN FOR ELLSWORTH'S ZOUAVES.

Who is this ye say is slain?
Whose voice answers not again?
Ellsworth, shall we call in vain
On thy name today?

No! from every vale and hill
One response all hearts shall thrill:
"Ellsworth's fame is with us still,
Ne'er to pass away!"

Harper's Weekly (*June 8, 1861*)

Vignettes portraying incidents in the life and death of Colonel Elmer Ephraim Ellsworth encircle his full-length portrait, adapted from a Mathew Brady photograph, on the sheet music cover of a requiem in his memory. Ellsworth, who commanded the New York Fire Zouaves, was the first notable Northern fatality of the war. On May 24, 1861, he was shot dead by the secessionist proprietor of the Marshall House, a hotel in Alexandria, Virginia, from whose roof Ellsworth had torn down a Confederate flag. Young Ellsworth's tragic and wasteful death—he was only twenty-four years old—was nationally mourned, and he was given a state funeral from the White House. In 1860 Ellsworth had studied law in Abraham Lincoln's law office in Springfield, and it was said that Lincoln was as affected by Ellsworth's death as if he had been his own son.

With their exotic, fancy dress uniforms and their intricate, almost choreographic drills, patterned after those of the French Zouaves, both Northern and Southern Zouave companies captured the public imagination during the early days of the war. But their extravagant trappings were soon discarded when the horrors of war became reality. (For Zouave uniforms, see pages 377-379.)

Surprisingly, the John Brown for whom the stirring "John Brown Song" was originally named was not the martyr of Harpers Ferry, whom the song came to immortalize, but a Sergeant John Brown who served in a vocally accomplished Massachusetts volunteer regiment stationed at Fort Warren in the spring of 1861 and known as "The Tigers." Begun by his messmates as a light-hearted spoof of Sergeant Brown, the song soon began to spread spontaneously, and when the future world-famed bandmaster Patrick Sarsfield Gilmore carried it to Boston, it really took off like the proverbial wildfire.

The lyrics of the "John Brown Song" were communally improvised to an old Methodist hymn tune of uncertain origin with a rousing, rememberable chorus that went, "Glory, Glory, Hallelujah!" By the time they were published in the summer of 1861, first as a penny broadside, and then, on immediately selling out, as a broadside with music, the words had undergone many changes and some refinements. For example, according to the Civil War authority Boyd B. Stutler (*Civil War History*, September 1958), an earlier version of the line about hanging Jeff Davis "to a tree" (later, for reasons of meter, "a sour apple tree") at first was the more vivid: "We'll feed him on sour apples till he has the di-ar-ree!" Stutler says that the commander of the Tigers, fearing political feedback, vainly suggested substituting an uncontroversial martyr, Colonel Ellsworth, for John Brown, and that among many discarded lines for the song were some for Ellsworth: "We lament the death of Colonel Ellsworth," and "Colonel Ellsworth's death we will avenge." In other versions, which were myriad, Ellsworth's name was substituted for Brown's. Stutler reports some sixty-five different sheet music editions of the "John Brown Song," to say nothing of incalculable numbers of penny broadsides and songsters.

The rare second broadside of the "John Brown Song," copyrighted in July 1861.

To
Albert G. Pike, Esq.
The Poet Lawyer of Arkansas

THE

Bonnie Blue Flag

COMPOSED, ARRANGED,
And Sung
AT HIS

PERSONATION CONCERTS
BY

HARRY MACARTHY

THE ARKANSAS COMEDIAN.

NEW ORLEANS
Published by A.E. BLACKMAR & BRO. 74. Camp St.

The first edition sheet music cover of "The Bonnie Blue Flag" bore a dedication to General Albert Pike, himself a writer of patriotic song texts. Macarthy contributed only the words to his great song hit; the tune was a jiggy ditty of the 1850s, "The Irish Jaunting Car."

A broadside with Northern words to "The Bonnie Blue Flag"

Johnson, Song Publisher, No. 7 N. 10th St., Phila.

BONNIE BLUE FLAG.

Copied by permission of S. T. Gordon, Music Publisher, 538 Broadway,
New York, owner of the copyright.

We are a band of patriots,
  Who each leave home and friend,
Our noble Constitution
  And banner to defend;
Our Capitol was threatened,
  And the cry rose near and far,
To protect our country's glorious flag,
  That glitters with many a star.

CHORUS.—Hurrah, hurrah, for the union, boys, hurrah!
  Hurrah for our forefathers' good old flag,
    That glitters with many a star.

Much patience and forbearance
  The North has always shown,
Toward her Southern brethren,
  Who had each way their own;
But when we made our president,
  A man whom we desired,
Their wrath was roused, they mounted guns,
  And on Fort Sumter fired.   (Chorus.)

They forced the war upon us,
  For peaceful men are we,
They steal our money, seize our forts,
  And then as cowards flee;
False to their vows, and to the flag
  That once protected them,
They sought the union to dissolve,
  Earth's noblest brightest gem.   (Chorus.)

We're in the right and will prevail,
  The Stars and Stripes must fly,
The "bonnie blue flag" be hauled down,
  And every traitor die;
Freedom and peace enjoyed by all,
  As ne'er was known before,
Our Spangled Banner wave on high,
  With stars just thirty-four.   (Chorus.)

See Johnson's New Catalogue of Songs.

Even before "Dixie" made its sensational conquest of the South, another show tune, "The Bonnie Blue Flag," was having a sweeping success in the Confederacy. First introduced in the spring of 1861 by its author, the actor and songsmith Harry Macarthy, known as "the Arkansas Comedian," at his popular "Personation Concerts" (one-man shows at which he was assisted by his wife), "The Bonnie Blue Flag" was another example of the musical spontaneous combustion so characteristic of the period. The New Orleans and Augusta music publishing house of Blackmar is said to have issued no less than eleven editions of the song, to say nothing of the innumerable pirated editions that appeared in both the Confederacy and the Union, where, of course, Northern words were sung.

Such great importance was placed on the power of Macarthy's words to incite Southern emotions that publication and performance of "The Bonnie Blue Flag" in New Orleans were reported proscribed by the controversial commander of the occupation, General Benjamin Franklin Butler, after the city was taken in 1862.

607

The Bonnie Blue Flag.

The Words and Music of this Song will be sent to any address, post-paid, on receipt of 40 cents, by H. J. Wehman, P. O. Box 1823, New York City.
A complete Catalogue of Songs sent free to any address.

We are a band of brothers, and native to the soil,
Fighting for the property we gained by honest toil;
And when our rights were threatened, the cry rose near and far:
Hurrah! for the bonnie blue flag that bears a single star.

CHORUS.

Hurrah! hurrah! for Southern rights! hurrah!
Hurrah! for the bonnie blue flag that bears a single star

As long as the Union was faithful to her trust,
Like friends and like brothers, kind were we and just;
But now, when Northern treachery attempts our rights to mar,
We hoist, on high, the bonnie blue flag that bears a single star.
Hurrah! hurrah! for Southern rights! &c.

First gallant South Carolina nobly made the stand,
Then came Alabama who took her by the hand;
Next, quickly Mississippi, Georgia and Florida,
All raised, on high, the bonnie blue flag that bears a single star.
Hurrah! hurrah! for Southern rights! &c.

Ye men of valor, gather 'round the banner of the right,
Texas and fair Louisianna join us in the fight;
Davis, our loved President, and Stevens, statesman rare,
Now rally 'round the bonnie blue flag that bears a single star.
Hurrah! hurrah! for Southern rights! &c.

And here's to brave Virginia, the old Dominion State,
With the young Confederacy, at length, has linked her fate;
Impelled by her example now other States prepare
To hoist, on high, the bonnie blue flag that bears a single star.
Hurrah! hurrah! for Southern rights! &c.

Then cheer, boys, cheer, raise the joyous shout—
For Arkansas and North Carolina now have both gone out;
And let another rousing cheer for Tennessee be given—
The single star of the bonnie blue flag has grown to be eleven.
Hurrah! hurrah! for Southern rights! &c.

Then here's to our Confederacy—strong we are and brave,
Like patriots of old, we'll fight our heritage to save;
And rather than submit to shame, to die we would prefer—
So cheer for the bonnie blue flag that bears a single star.
Hurrah! hurrah! for Southern rights! &c.

Apparently the Southern words of "The Bonnie Blue Flag" were available in the North.

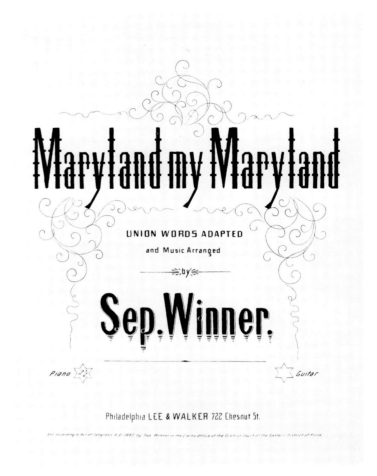

Another important Southern song with a borrowed tune that led an active double life on both sides of the battle lines was "Maryland, My Maryland," written by James Ryder Randall, a young Baltimore professor of English teaching at a Louisiana college. Aroused by a newspaper account of the fighting in Baltimore on April 19, 1861, when a Massachusetts regiment passing through the city had been attacked by angry local Southern sympathizers, Randall was moved to write his impassioned resistance verses. First published in a New Orleans newspaper, "My Maryland" was wildly acclaimed and reprinted throughout the South. When it reached Baltimore, it was excitedly hailed by a group of pro-Confederate ladies, one of whom—Miss Jennie Cary—was responsible for its being set to the well-known German collegiate tune "Tannenbaum, O Tannenbaum" and for its subsequent publication by the pro-Southern Baltimore music publishers Miller and Beacham. The cover of their first edition (1861) bore the Maryland coat of arms, but the author and the arranger of the music were not identified because the song was highly subversive.

MARYLAND! MY MARYLAND.

The despot's heel is on thy shore,
  Maryland, My Maryland!
His touch is at thy temple door,
  Maryland, My Maryland!
Avenge the patriotic gore
That flecked the streets of Baltimore,
And be the Battle Queen of yore,
  Maryland, my Maryland!

If the success of Randall's song prompted a large number of Northern parodies in 1861, the invasion of Maryland in 1862, led by Robert E. Lee and "Stonewall" Jackson after the Rebel victory at the first Battle of Bull Run, elicited a fresh batch of Union texts. Among these was a version by Septimus Winner, one of the most successful and prolific songwriters of the nineteenth century. He is perhaps best remembered for "Listen to the Mocking Bird," which was published under one of his many pseudonyms, Alice Hawthorne. Winner's invocation of Maryland, lacking Randall's pristine passion, bears the unmistakable copying-machine flavor of the imitator.

MARYLAND MY MARYLAND.

The rebel horde is on thy shore,
  Maryland! my Maryland!
Arise and drive him from thy door,
  Maryland! my Maryland!
Avenge the foe thou must abhor,
Who seeks thy fall, oh Baltimore,
Drive back the tyrant, peace restore,
  Maryland! my Maryland!

Hark to a nation's warm appeal,
  Maryland! my Maryland!
And sister states that for thee feel,
  Maryland! my Maryland!
Gird now thy loins with arms of steel,
And heavy be the blows they deal,
For traitors shall thy vengeance feel,
  Maryland! my Maryland!

A less hackneyed Northern parody of Randall's song, referring to the Confederate incursion into Maryland, shuns mock heroics, but vividly conveys the bitterness and rancors of war. From *Beadle's Dime Knapsack Songster* (c.1862):

OUR MARYLAND.

Air—My Maryland.

The rebel thieves were sure of thee,
    Maryland! our Maryland!
And boasted they would welcome be,
    Maryland! our Maryland!
But now they turn and now they flee,
With Stonewall Jackson and with Lee
And loyal souls once more are free!
    Maryland! our Maryland!

With plundered guns and stolen swords,
    Maryland! our Maryland!
On thee they came in ruffian hordes,
    Maryland! our Maryland!
With raving oaths and roaring words,
And pirates' knives and hangmen's cords,
They swarmed across the border fords,
    Maryland! our Maryland!

Through passways of the mountain crags,
    Maryland! our Maryland!
They bore their vile secession flags,
    Maryland! our Maryland!
Like beggar troops, in filthy rags,
Barefooted men and spavined nags,
Their voices hoarse with Southern brags,
    Maryland! our Maryland!

Like dogs all raving for a crumb,
    Maryland! our Maryland!
They madly rushed for bread and rum,
    Maryland! our Maryland!
But backward ran, with voices dumb,
And drooping hands, and faces glum,
They ran from Union's rolling drum,
    Maryland! our Maryland!

Before its sheet music publication to the tune of "Tannenbaum, O Tannenbaum," "Maryland, My Maryland" was sung to "My Normandy," as this broadside illustrates.

BATTLE HYMN OF THE REPUBLIC

Adapted to the favorite Melody
OF
"Glory, Hallelujah,"

WRITTEN BY

Mrs. Dr. S. G. Howe,

FOR THE

ATLANTIC MONTHLY.

BOSTON.
Published by Oliver Ditson & Co. 277 Washington St.

Firth Pond & Co. N. York.   J. Church Jr. Cin.   J. C. Haynes & Co. Boston   J. E. Gould Philad.a   C. C. Clapp & Co. Boston.

Mine eyes have seen the glo-ry of the coming of the Lord: He is trampling out the vintage where the grapes of wrath are stored; He hath loosed the fateful lightning of His ter-ri-ble swift sword: His truth is march-ing on.

The Battle-Cry of Freedom.

SONG & CHORUS
by GEO. F. ROOT.

CHICAGO:

PUBLISHED BY ROOT & CADY.

95 CLARK STREET.

THE BATTLE CRY OF FREEDOM.

(RALLYING SONG.)

GEO. F. ROOT.

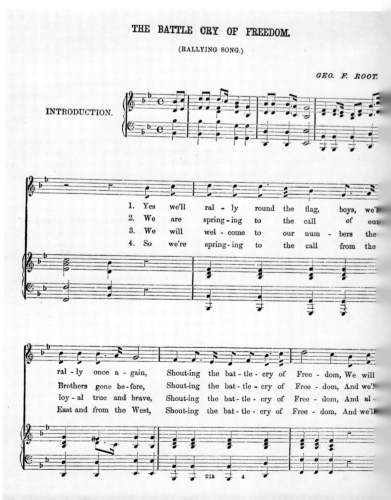

INTRODUCTION.

1. Yes we'll ral - ly round the flag, boys, we'll
2. We are spring-ing to the call of our
3. We will wel - come to our num - bers the
4. So we're spring-ing to the call from the

ral - ly once a - gain, Shout-ing the bat-tle-cry of Free - dom, We will
Brothers gone be-fore, Shout-ing the bat-tle-cry of Free - dom, And we'll
loy - al true and brave, Shout-ing the bat-tle-cry of Free - dom, And al -
East and from the West, Shout-ing the bat-tle-cry of Free - dom, And we'll

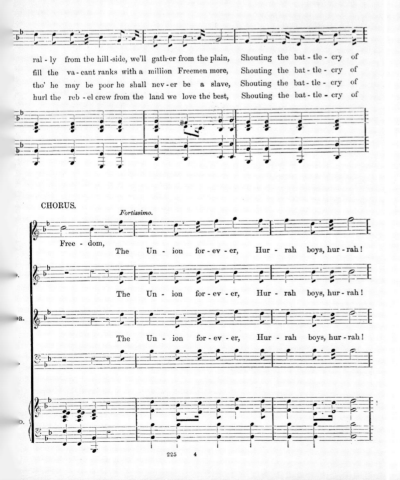

"Good martial, national music is one of the advantages we have over the rebels," stated an editorial in the New York *Herald* (January 11, 1862). And indeed it was true. In all the flood of patriotic music published in the Confederacy, there was nothing to compare with the great Northern marching songs. Contemporaries attested to their importance both at home and on the battlefield: ". . . we boys used to yell at the band for music to cheer us up when we were tramping along so tired that we could hardly drag one foot after the other," reminisced a Union veteran (quoted by Frank Rauscher in *Music on the March*, 1892). Another veteran, Richard Wentworth Browne, recalled a musical party in Richmond just after peace had been declared, at which Confederate officers on parole had asked to hear some of the Northern army songs. "We gave them the army songs with unction," wrote Browne, "the 'Battle Hymn of the Republic,' 'John Brown's Body,' 'We're Coming, Father Abraham,' 'Tramp, Tramp, Tramp, the Boys are Marching' . . . and closed with 'Rally Round the Flag, Boys.' When the applause subsided, a tall, fine-looking fellow in a major's uniform exclaimed, 'Gentlemen, if we had your songs, we'd have licked you out of your boots'" (*Century Magazine*, December 1887). "Rally Round the Flag, Boys" was another name for George Frederick Root's phenomenally popular song "The Battle Cry of Freedom," written in 1861 in response to President Lincoln's second call for troops.

Also written in 1861, but published early the following year, was Julia Ward Howe's inspired "Battle Hymn of the Republic," set to the tune of the "John Brown Song." Mrs. Howe was moved to write her powerful verses after having witnessed an army review near Washington being disrupted by an actual enemy attack.

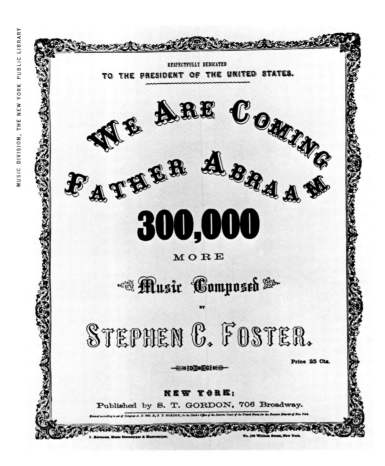

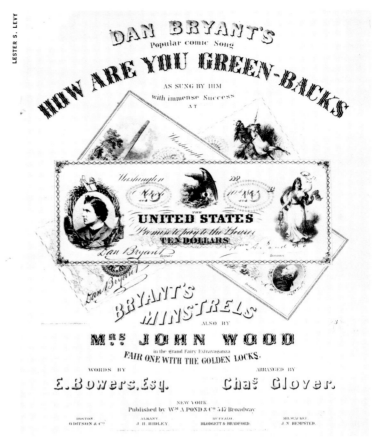

In 1862 no less than sixteen different composers, among them Stephen Foster, wrote musical settings for John Sloan Gibbons's poem "We Are Coming, Father Abraham, Three Hundred Thousand More." Gibbons, a financial expert by profession and a Quaker by religion, had been moved to write the poem by Lincoln's call in July 1862 for three hundred thousand more troops after McClellan's disastrous failure in the Peninsular Campaign. The poem was anonymously published in the New York *Evening Post* (July 16, 1862), and because the author was not identified, it was generally assumed that it had been written by the editor of the *Evening Post*, William Cullen Bryant, himself a distinguished poet; a number of the composers credited Bryant with the text.

WE ARE COMING, FATHER ABRAHAM.

We are coming, Father Abraham,
  Three hundred thousand more,
From Mississippi's winding stream,
  And from New England's shore;
We leave our plows and workshops,
  Our wives and children dear,
With hearts too full for utterance,
  With but a silent tear;
We dare not look behind us,
  But steadfastly before—
We are coming, Father Abraham,
  Three hundred thousand more!
We are coming, we are coming,
  Our Union to restore;
We are coming, Father Abraham,
  Three hundred thousand more.

~~~

To help finance the war, Congress passed the Legal Tender Act in February 1862, and some 450 million dollars in paper currency was issued without a specific commitment for redemption. At treasury secretary Salmon P. Chase's suggestion, the backs of the new bank notes were printed in green ink; they came to be called "greenbacks," and Chase was nicknamed "Old Greenbacks." With Lincoln bearing the brunt of public dissatisfaction over the disappointing progress of the war, the unpopular inflationary currency was lampooned in a satirical parody of "We Are Coming, Father Abraham," titled "How Are You Green-Backs." Its 1863 sheet music cover, printed in green, satirized a ten-dollar bill, on which the handsome, actor's features of Dan Bryant, who performed the song with his Minstrels, substituted for the stern official visage of Secretary Chase. "How are you" appears to have been contemporary slang for a derisive form of address.

HOW ARE YOU GREEN-BACKS.

We're coming, Father Abram,
  One hundred thousand more,
Five hundred presses printing us
  From morn till night is o'er;
Like magic, you will see us
  Start and scatter thro' the land,
To pay the soldiers or release
  The border contraband.
With our promise to pay,
  How are you Secretary Chase?
Promise to pay,
  Oh! dat's what's de matter.

~~~

Illustrating what was apparently an excellent intelligence system, a Southern parody of "We Are Coming, Father Abraham," published in 1863, ridiculed recent events in the North, particularly emancipation. In the text, "de Conscript bill" refers to the Conscription Act, passed in 1863 (the South had enacted its own less than successful conscription law the year before); "contraband" was a slang term for an escaped slave—a term used by both sides and attributed to General Benjamin F. Butler, who had refused to return three slaves to their master when they had escaped to Fortress Monroe, Virginia, in 1861, claiming them as contraband of war; "de kingdom comin" and "de jubilo" are references to Henry C. Work's great emancipation song, "Kingdom Coming" (see page 392); "in a horn" appears to have been a term of derision.

WE'RE COMING FODDER ABRAHAM.

We're coming Fodder Abrahan,
From de distant shore,
We're coming Fodder Abrahan
Dis nation to restore,
We're from de East and from de West,
From ebber odder quarter
Day got de Nigger on de brain,
And dat's what de matter.
> CHORUS.
> We're coming Fodder Abrahan,
> Sure as you are born,
> We're coming Fodder Abrahan,
> Coming *in a horn*.

De Conscript bill passed de house,
From de top, to bottom,
To send us down to Dixie Land
To Confiscate de Cotton,
We're coming Fodder Abrahan,
To make de army bigger.
Come white folks behave yourself's,
And be good, as any Nigger. (CHORUS.)

We're coming Fodder Abrahan,
To do, de best we can
To make de Nigger just as good
As any odder man—
Dis rebellion must be crushed.
We're de boys to do it,
We're coming Fodder Abrahan,
But I tell you, we can't see it. (CHORUS.)

We're coming Fodder Abrahan,
But don't be made a fool,
We're all a lot of Contrabands,
As stubborn as a Mule.
De kingdom coming, am play'd out,
Wid us some time ago,
You can't fool de Nigger longer.
About de jubilo. (CHORUS.)

To the new American Citizens of AFRICAN DESCENT.

WE'RE COMING FODDER ABRAHAM

WE'RE COMING—IN A HORN

COMIC SONG.
BY AN "INTELLIGENT CONTRABAND"

LESTER S. LEVY

C. T. BEAUMAN.
Nashville, Tenn.

TRIPP & GRAGG.
Louisville, Ky.

In 1862, wrote Perley (*Perley's Reminiscences*, 1886): "The people responded gloriously to the demand for more troops, and by the middle of August, 1862, they were pouring into Washington at the rate of a brigade a day. The regiments, on their arrival, were marched past the White House, singing, 'We are coming, Father Abraham, three hundred thousand more.'"

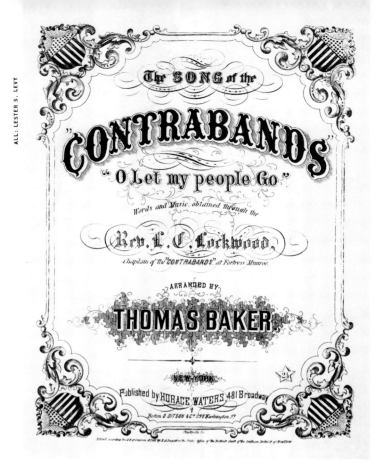

The Continental Monthly, a New York magazine, reviewed an offbeat song in July 1862:

We are indebted to Clark's *School-Visitor* for the following song of the Contrabands, which originated among the latter, and was first sung by them in the hearing of white people at Fortress Monroe, where it was noted down by their chaplain, Rev. L. C. Lockwood. It is to a plaintive and peculiar air, and we may add has been published . . . in "sheet-music style," with piano-forte accompaniment, by Horace Waters, New York.

The Reverend Lockwood had assisted in the landmark publication of the great spiritual "Go Down, Moses" in a variant version.

THE SONG OF THE "CONTRABANDS."
"O! LET MY PEOPLE GO."

The Lord by Moses to Pharaoh said:
  "O let my people go!
If not, I'll smite your first-born dead,
  Then let my people go!"
    O go down, Moses,
    Away down to Egypt's land,
    And tell King Pharaoh,
    To let my people go!

No more shall they in bondage toil,
  O let my people go!
Let them come out with Egypt's spoil,
  O let my people go!
    O go down, (&c.)

Haste, Moses, 'till the sea you've crossed,
  O let my people go!
Pharaoh shall in the deep be lost,
  O let my people go!
    O go down, (&c.)

The sea before you shall divide,
  O let my people go!
You'll cross dry-shod to the other side,
  O let my people go!
    O go down, (&c.)

Fear not King Pharaoh or his host,
  O let my people go!
They all shall in the sea be lost,
  O let my people go!
    O go down, (&c.)

The firey cloud shall lead the way,
  O let my people go!
A light by night, a shade by day,
  O let my people go!
    O go down, (&c.)

Jordan shall stand up like a wall,
  O let my people go!
And the walls of Jericho shall fall,
  O let my people go!
    O go down, (&c.)

Your foes shall not before you stand,
  O let my people go!
And you'll possess fair Canaan's land,
  O let my people go!
    O go down, (&c.)

O let us all from bondage flee,
  O let my people go!
And let us all in Christ be free,
  O let my people go!
    O go down, (&c.)

This world's a wilderness of woe,
  O let my people go!
O let us all to glory go,
  O let my people go!
    O go down, (&c.)

first born dead, Then let my peo - ple go!"

O! go down, Mo - ses, A - way down to E - gypt's land, And

tell King Pha - raoh, To let my peo - ple go!

THE OLD CONTRABAND.

I'se a contraband from de old plantation,
I think I hab work'd out my own salvation,
I'se citizen now ob dis glorious nation
Freedom! freedom! de old slave is free.
  CHORUS.
  Den hurrah, den hurrah,
  I am a slave no longer,
  Den away, den away,
  To de land ob de free. (CHORUS.)

Long I hab hoed in the field ob cotton,
So many de years I'se almost forgotten,
I leave dem behind me dey all may be rotten.
Freedom! freedom! de old slave is free. (CHORUS.)

When dis rebellion was fust beginnin;
I golly it set all darkies a grinnin;
Cause we knowed afore long we all would be singin;
Freedom! freedom! de old slave's free. (CHORUS.)

We spend our time now singing an' playin,
Old massa spends his in swearin an' prayin,
He'd drink whiskey too, but he can't without payin;
Freedom! freedom! de old slave's free. (CHORUS.)

Den farewell de cabin whar I was born in,
Farewell de fields wid de cotton an' corn in,
'Spec' we'll be off for de broke ob de morning.
 Freedom! freedom! de old slave's free. (CHORUS.)

In both the North and the South, contrabands and music about them were very much in the air.

Music by the "Contra-Band."

Sold by S. C. Upham, 310 Chestnut St.

Enterprising stationers on both sides enlivened their envelopes and notepaper with cartoons of timely interest. This one appeared on an envelope printed in the North.

Skedaddle, a word of uncertain origin, but of Southern extraction, meaning to run away, to take flight in a panic, became another favorite colloquialism during the Civil War. Mostly used derisively against the South—but also denoting the escape of slaves—the word captured the fancy of Northern songwriters. In the text of "The New Skedaddle Song," from *Beadle's Dime Song Book* (1864), "Gen'ral Price" is Sterling Price, a turncoat Missourian; "Ole Ben" could be one of a number of Confederate Bens; "Bragg" is General Braxton Bragg, of "A little more grape, Captain Bragg" fame; "Polk" is General Leonidas Polk.

THE NEW SKEDADDLE SONG.

I'll sing you now de last new song
    I heard down in Secessia;
I'll change de words a little mite,
    And hope dey won't distress you;
'Twas Gen'ral Price fus' pitched de tune,
    "Ole Ben" struck in sonorous,
While Bragg and Polk took up de strain,
    And all jined in de chorus.
      CHORUS.
      We hear it by night, we hear it by day,
        On foot or in de saddle;
      Dey used to sing de Dixie song,
        But now, "Skedaddle," "Skedaddle."

De rebels dey am husky boys,
    Quite fond of tune and rhyme, sah;
Dey sing dis one to double-quick,
    While toes and heels keep time, sah;
De darkies, too, dey lub to sing,
    And so be in de fashion;
De way dey promulgate dis ting,
    "Skedaddle," am a passion. (CHORUS.)

Secesh and contrabands unite,
    Like brodders all before us,
Dough one go souf de oder north,
    'Tis all to dis same chorus;
De locomotives cotch de tune,
    De steamboat as dey paddle,
And keep dar wheels a goin' round,
    To dis same tune, "Skedaddle." (CHORUS.)

Jeff. Davis wants to learn de song,
    De Richmond papers tell us;
But dar's no music in his soul;
    I know dey're trying to sell us;
Den darkies run and darkies sing,
    "Skedaddle" am de chorus;
We'll neber fear but always keep
    De norf star right before us. (CHORUS.)

Both skedaddle and contrabands were translated into brilliantly imaginative graphics.

To the
Colonel of the Stuyvesant Guards

SKEDADDLE

CLASSICALLY DEFINED *and* MUSICALLY ILLUSTRATED

GEO. DANSKIN.

BOSTON.
Published by Oliver Ditson & Co. 277 Washington St.

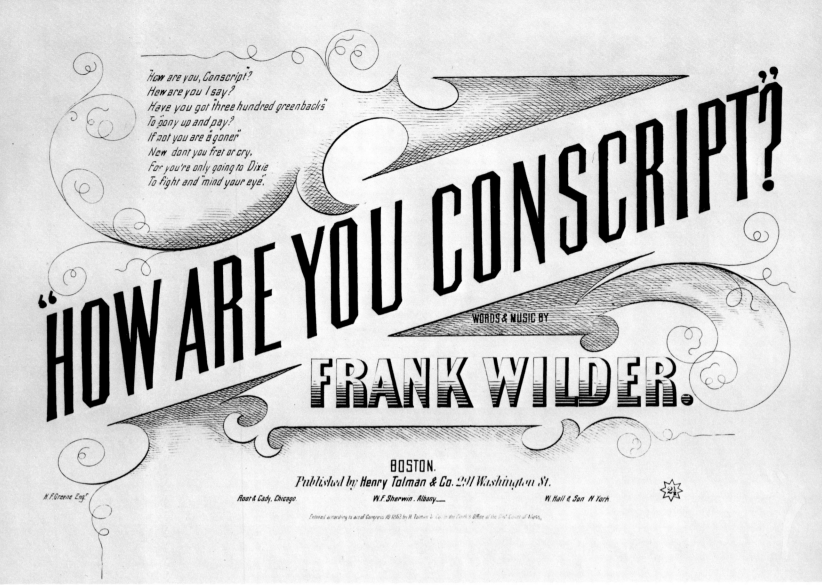

"How are you, Conscript?
How are you I say?
Have you got "three hundred greenbacks"
To pony up and pay?
If not you are a "goner"
Now dont you fret or cry,
For you're only going to Dixie
To fight and mind your eye".

"HOW ARE YOU CONSCRIPT?"

WORDS & MUSIC BY

FRANK WILDER.

BOSTON.
Published by Henry Tolman & Co. 291 Washington St.

Root & Cady, Chicago.   W.F. Sherwin, Albany.   W. Hall & Son, N York.

Entered according to act of Congress AD 1863 by H. Tolman & Co. in the Clerk's Office of the Dist. Court of Mass.

H.F.Greene Eng.r

"How are you Exempt;
I 'spose you are all right.
As the Doctor said you'd never do
To take your gun and fight.

HOW ARE YOU EXEMPT?

you git out

WORDS & MUSIC BY

FRANK WILDER.

BOSTON.
G.D. Russell & Company 126 Tremont,
Opposite Park St.

Entered according to act of Congress AD 1863 by G.D.Russell & Company in the Clerk's Office of the Dist Court of Mass.

Greene Eng

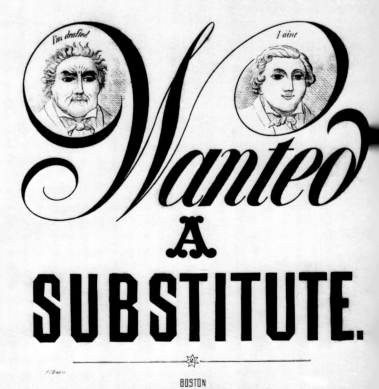

I'm drafted   I aint

Wanted A SUBSTITUTE.

H.F.Green

BOSTON
Published by Oliver Ditson & Co. 277 Washington St.

Cin.   St. Louis   Boston   Phila.
J. Church Jr.   Holt Ford & Co.   J.C.Haynes & Co.   J.E.Ditson

The malapropish mom in Henry C. Work's hit song about the draft provided comic relief when it was desperately needed.

The first national draft law, enacted by Congress in March 1863, permitted a draftee to purchase his exemption by hiring a substitute for three hundred dollars. This curious provision (also permitted in the South) inspired an outpouring of sardonic lyricism.

WANTED—A SUBSTITUTE!

Wanted—a Substitute!
Show me the man
That will buckle on his armor
And fight for Uncle Sam!
He must have an arm of power,
And a heart of courage too,
He must love his native country,
And the Red, the White and Blue!

Wanted—a Substitute!
Three hundred I'll pay!
If you know of one that wants it,
Just send him 'long this way!
What glory he'll inherit
When Rebellion is put down,
No greater mark of merit
Could any mortal crown!

Wanted—a Substitute!
None need apply
Unless he's sound from head to foot,
With perfect teeth and eye.
Now, such a one is wanted,
Then who will go for me,
To fight his country's battles
In the land of Dixie.

CRAFTED
Into the Army.

Our Jimmy has gone for to live in a tent,
  They have grafted him into the army;
He finally pucker'd up courage and went,
  When they grafted him into the army.
I told them the child was too young, alas,
At the captain's fore quarters, they said he would pass—
They'd train him up well in the infantry class—
  So they grafted him into the army.

CHORUS.

Oh, Jimmy farewell! Your brothers fell
  Way down in Alabarmy :
I thought they would spare a lone widder's heir,
  But they grafted him into the army.

Dressed up in his unicorn—dear little chap;
  They have grafted him into the army ;
It seems but a day since he sot in my lap,
  But they grafted him into the army.
And these are the trousers he used to wear—
Them very same buttons—the patch and the tear—
But Uncle Sam gave him a bran new pair
  When they grafted him into the army.
    CHORUS.—Oh, Jimmy farewell, &c.

Now in my provisions I see him revealed—
  They have grafted him into the army ;
A picket beside the contented field,
  They have grafted him into the army.
He looks kinder sickish—begins to cry—
A big volunteer standing right in his eye l
Oh what if the ducky should up and die
  Now they've grafted him into the army.
    CHORUS.—Oh, Jimmy farewell, &c.

Johnson & Co. Song Publishers, 18 N. 10th St, Phil.

Comic topical ditties were not the only relief to tightly stretched emotions; people also turned for escape to the hundreds of sentimental ballads that inundated the Civil War scene and that were as popular around the campfire as they were around the parlor piano or harmonium. While many of these songs remain valid and affecting expressions of parting and loss and of hope, the larger part are unbelievably melodramatic, tear-jerking mother-songs that appear today to be travesties of the emotions they apparently earnestly sought to express. In an editorial on the war songs in the *New York Weekly Review* (November 19, 1864), a contemporary evaluated the significance of the mother-songs: "Where motherhood, the source of all that is pure and good in this world, is constantly appealed to, there must be strength and fortitude in a nation. Who can read all those appeals to mothers . . . as from week to week we see them published in the songs, and not be touched by them?" Some of the titles—they are innumerable—that touched people were: "Rock Me to Sleep, Mother," "Oh! Mother, Hear My Dying Call," "Mother Kissed Me In My Dream," and "Kiss Me Goodbye for Mother." Occasionally other relatives were added, as in "Brother's Fainting at the Door" and "Will My Father Come Again," also called "Mother, Is the Battle Over?"

Published by Chas Magnus, 12 Frankfort St NY

Tell Mother, I die happy,

The last words of Lieut. CROSBY, who was killed in his battery at Salem Heights
in the Fight of Sunday Evening, May 2d, 1863.
Words by C. A. Vosburgh, Music by Jabez Burns.
Published by S. T. Gordon, 538 Broadway.

I am dying, comrades dying,
  As you hear me lightly tread
Soon ah soon I shall be lying
  With the silent sleeping dead
I am dying comrades dying
  Still the battle rages near,
Tell me are our foes a flying
  I die happy mother dear.

Chorus.

Tell my mother I die happy,
  That for me she must not weep,
Tell her how I long'd to kiss her,
  Ere I sank in death to sleep.

I am going, comrades going,
  See how damp my forehead's now
Oh, I see the angels coming,
  With bright garlands for my brow.
Bear this message to my mother,
  How in death that God was near,
He to bless and to support me
  I die happy mother dear.

Chorus.

Lay me comrades, 'neath the willow,
  That grows on the distant shore,
Wrap the starry flag around me,
  I would press its folds once more.
Let the cold earth be my pillow
  And the "Stars and Stripes" my shroud
Soon, oh soon I shall be marching,
  Amid the heavenly crowd.

Chorus

Ten illustrated Songs on Notepaper, mailed to any Address on
receipt of 50 cts. Published by Chas. Magnus, 12 Frankfort St., N Y

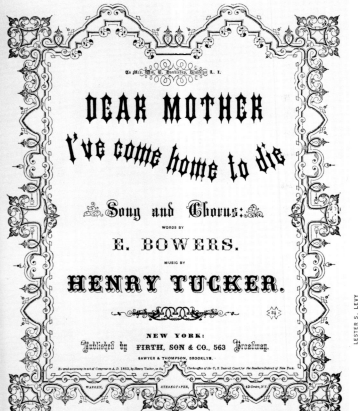

To Mrs. Wm. H. Banbledge, Brooklyn, L. I.

DEAR MOTHER I've come home to die

Song and Chorus:

WORDS BY

E. BOWERS.

MUSIC BY

HENRY TUCKER.

NEW YORK:
Published by FIRTH, SON & CO., 563 Broadway.
SAWYER & THOMPSON, BROOKLYN.

Luridly illustrated broadsides of mother-songs were profusely published; they were often backed with lined notepaper, presumably for sending cheering messages to the boys at the front.

Mother, I've come home to die.

Words by E. Bowers, Music by Henry Tucker, author of "When this Cruel War is over, "Star of the Evening," etc. Music to be had at FIRTH, SON & CO., 563 Broadway, New York, owners of the copyright.

Dear mother, I remember well
  The parting kiss you gave to me,
When merry rang the village bell,
  My heart was full of joy and glee:
I did not dream that one short year
  Would crush the hopes that soar'd so high!
Oh, mother dear, draw near to me,
  Dear mother, I've come home to die.
        CHORUS.

Call sister, brother to my side,
  And take your soldier's last good-bye;
Oh, mother dear, draw near to me,
  Dear mother, I've come home to die.

Hark! mother, 'tis the village bell,
  I can no longer with thee stay;
My country calls to arms, to arms,
  The foe advance in fierce array!
The vision's past—I feel that now
  For country I can only sigh:
Oh, mother dear, draw near to me,
  Dear mother, I've come home to die.
    Chorus—Call brother, &c.

Dear mother, sister, brother, all,
  One parting kiss, to all good-bye:
Weep not, but clasp your hand in mine,
  And let me like a soldier die!
I've met the foe upon the field
  Where kindred fiercely did defy,
I fought for Right. God bless the Flag!
  Dear mother, I've come home to die.
    Chorus—Call brother, &c.

In a premonitory, pre-Freudian flash, one Eugene T. Johnson in 1865 summed up the rampant momism of the period with "Mother on the Brain," a song whose text was made up of mother-song titles with a few asides thrown in.

MOTHER ON THE BRAIN.

Mother songs are all the rage of course you all do know,
You will hear these touching ditties wherever you may go,
In the cot, in the parlor, even on the battle plain,
Our soldier boys all seem to have "Mother on the brain."
This mania is increasing most fearful I avow,
Ever since the appearance of "Who'll care for mother now?"
I've arranged a list of mother songs together in a string,
And with your kind permission, them to you I will sing.

What is home without a mother (in a garret near the sky,)
Courage mother, I am going, mother, I've come home to die.
Mother, is the battle over, have our soldiers gained the day?
I can't mind my wheel, mother (what will Mrs. Grundy say.)
It was my mother's custom, my grandmother's advice,
The song my mother loved to sing (a big thing on ice,)
Kiss my mother dear for me, mother, I've come home again,
Break it gently to my mother, I've got mother on the brain.

Write a letter to my mother send it when her boy is fled,
Tell mother I die happy, (is Joe Muggin's dog long dead.)
Is that mother bending o'er me, 'tis the ring my mother wore.
Rock me to sleep mother (on the old Virginy shore.)
Let me kiss him for his mother, let me kiss his infant brow,
Bless me mother ere I die . . . who will care for mother now?
My dear kind old mother, (her name was Mary Blane,)
I cannot call her mother, I've got mother on the brain.

Just before the battle mother, I was thinking most of you,
Be quiet do, I'll call my mother (for an old Irish stew,)
Mother dear would comfort me if she were here,
I'm lonely since my mother died (from drinking lager beer)
A mother's love can never change (picking a ham bone,)
I'll not forget thee mother wherever I may roam:
O sing me to rest mother, (Joe Bowers is my name,)
Kiss me good-night, mother, with mother on the brain.

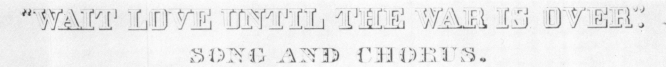

WAIT LOVE UNTIL THE WAR IS OVER.

'Twas gentle eve, the stars were bright,
　All nature hushed, seemed lonely;
I wandered in the moon's pale light,
　With the maid I loved so fondly.

Our vows renewed, our spirits free,
　Our hearts with joy ran over;
But ah! a sad smile said to me,
　"Wait love until the war is over."

Wait love, wait love, wait love until the war is over.

THE SOLDIER'S GOOD BYE.

Good-by to you, mother! Though hard to the parting,
   Though sad is the picture that gleams in your eye,
Let your love for your boy check the tear at its starting;
   Here's my hand with my heart to be faithful. Good-by!
Let your love for your boy check the tear at its starting;
   Here's my hand with my heart to be faithful. Good-by!

Good-by to you, father! Remember and cherish
   My vow that has cost perhaps many a sigh
To be zealous and loyal and then, should I perish,
   You'll remember I died for my country. Good-by!
To be zealous &c.

Good-by to you, sister! The sun on the morrow
   May be laden with gladness in every ray,
Yet no joy will suffice in dispelling the sorrow
   Of thus parting with you, my dear sister, to-day.
Yet no joy &c.

Good-by to you, brother! The deepest dejection
   Comes crowding upon me in taking your hand;
But a solace I find in the single reflection
   That I leave you for service in liberty's band.
But a solace &c.

Good-by to you, darling! The vows that we've spoken
   Will be sealed with my love for you down in my breast;
I hope to return with those pledges unbroken,
   And find, with you, home for a soldier to rest.
I hope to return &c.

Good-by to you, friends! Should my ardent devotion
   Decree for me death and a patriot's grave,
You'll remember I lived for my country's promotion,
   And died for the liberty Washington gave.
You'll remember &c.

THE VACANT CHAIR.
(Thanksgiving, 1861.)

We shall meet, but we shall miss him,
   There will be one vacant chair;
We shall linger to caress him,
   While we breathe our evening prayer;
When a year ago we gathered,
   Joy was in his mild blue eye;
But a golden cord is severed,
   And our hopes in ruin lie.
     CHORUS.
   We shall meet, but we shall miss him,
     There will be one vacant chair;
   We shall linger to caress him,
     When we breathe our evening prayer.

At our fireside, sad and lonely,
   Often will the bosom swell,
At remembrance of the story,
   How our noble Willie fell;
How he strove to bear our banner
   Through the thickest of the fight,
And uphold our country's honor,
   In the strength of manhood's might.
     CHORUS.

True, they tell us wreaths of glory
   Evermore will deck his brow,
But this soothes the anguish only,
   Sweeping o'er our heart-strings now;
Sleep today, O early fallen,
   In thy green and narrow bed,
Dirges from the pine and cypress
   Mingle with the tears we shed.
     CHORUS.

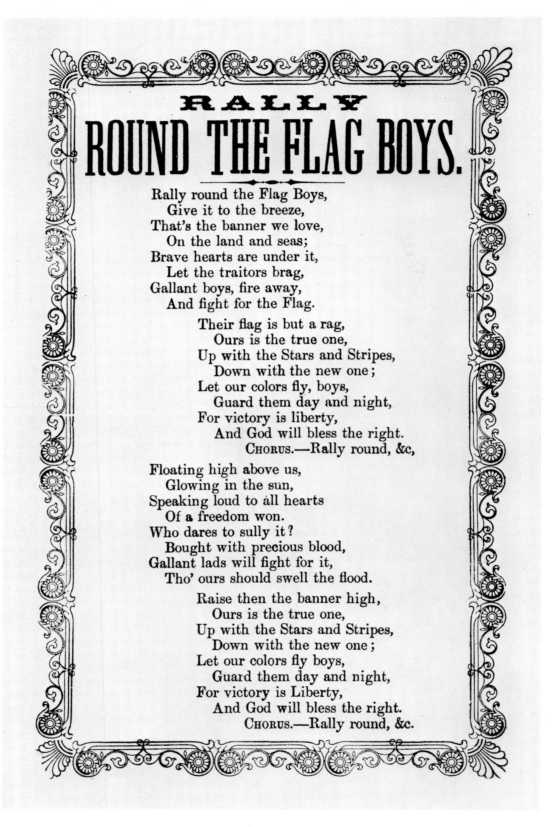

RALLY
ROUND THE FLAG BOYS.

Rally round the Flag Boys,
Give it to the breeze,
That's the banner we love,
On the land and seas;
Brave hearts are under it,
Let the traitors brag,
Gallant boys, fire away,
And fight for the Flag.

Their flag is but a rag,
Ours is the true one,
Up with the Stars and Stripes,
Down with the new one;
Let our colors fly, boys,
Guard them day and night,
For victory is liberty,
And God will bless the right.
CHORUS.—Rally round, &c,

Floating high above us,
Glowing in the sun,
Speaking loud to all hearts
Of a freedom won.
Who dares to sully it?
Bought with precious blood,
Gallant lads will fight for it,
Tho' ours should swell the flood.

Raise then the banner high,
Ours is the true one,
Up with the Stars and Stripes,
Down with the new one;
Let our colors fly boys,
Guard them day and night,
For victory is Liberty,
And God will bless the right.
CHORUS.—Rally round, &c.

Military dress uniforms of the period provided a rewarding subject for sheet music cover art in brilliant color, which reached its highest development during the Civil War years.

ZOUAVE GRAND PARADE MARCH
DUETT FOR
FOUR HANDS.
COMPOSED BY
Solo ☆   Duett ☆
S. D. S.
PHILADELPHIA. LEE & WALKER 922 CHESTNUT ST.

TO
CAPT. LUCIUS SLADE
NATIONAL LANCERS, BOSTON.

ELLSWORTH ZOUAVES' AND NATIONAL LANCERS'

GREETING

GRAND MARCH

COMPOSED BY

Adolph Baumbach.

PUBLISHED BY

Root & Cady, 67 Washington St., Chicago.

UNITED STATES
ZOUAVE CADETS
CHICAGO.
PUBLISHED BY ROOT & CADY

MILWAUKEE LIGHT GUARD

CAPT J. C. STARKWEATHER.

LIGHT GUARD
POLKA & SCHOTTISCH

COMPOSED BY FRANZ STAAB & DEDICATED TO

Capt. Wyman. the Officers & Members of the
CHICAGO LIGHT GUARD.

PUBLISHED by GEO. P. REED & Cº 13 TREMONT ST. BOSTON.

POLKA 50 Cents net.　　　　SCHOTTISCH 50 Cents net.

LOUISVILLE CITIZEN GUARDS

DAGUEREOTYPED BY WEBSTER & BRO. LOUISVILLE KY

MARCH ┊ QUICK STEP

Each 50cts. Nett

LOUISVILLE KY. D. P. FAULDS & Cº 539 MAIN ST.

WM HALL & SON   GEO. WILLIG.   C. FRITZ

MARYLAND GUARD GALLOP.
53
Lith. by A. Hoen & Co. Balto.
5
Entered according to Act of Congress A.D. 1861. By Miller & Beacham in the Clerks Office of the Dt. Ct. of Md.
Published by MILLER & BEACHAM, Baltimore.

384

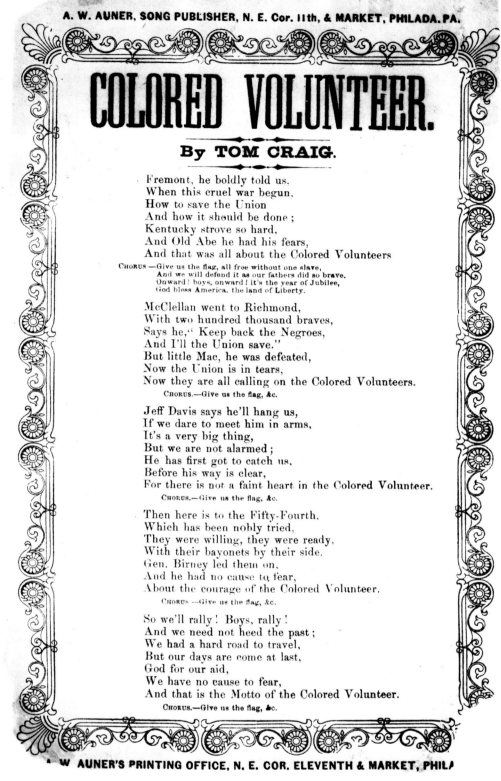

A. W. AUNER, SONG PUBLISHER, N. E. Cor. 11th, & MARKET, PHILADA. PA.

COLORED VOLUNTEER.

By TOM CRAIG.

Fremont, he boldly told us.
When this cruel war begun,
How to save the Union
And how it should be done;
Kentucky strove so hard,
And Old Abe he had his fears,
And that was all about the Colored Volunteers

CHORUS—Give us the flag, all free without one slave,
And we will defend it as our fathers did so brave.
Onward! boys, onward! it's the year of Jubilee,
God bless America, the land of Liberty.

McClellan went to Richmond,
With two hundred thousand braves,
Says he," Keep back the Negroes,
And I'll the Union save."
But little Mac, he was defeated,
Now the Union is in tears,
Now they are all calling on the Colored Volunteers.

CHORUS.—Give us the flag, &c.

Jeff Davis says he'll hang us,
If we dare to meet him in arms,
It's a very big thing,
But we are not alarmed;
He has first got to catch us,
Before his way is clear,
For there is not a faint heart in the Colored Volunteer.

CHORUS.—Give us the flag, &c.

Then here is to the Fifty-Fourth.
Which has been nobly tried,
They were willing, they were ready,
With their bayonets by their side.
Gen. Birney led them on,
And he had no cause to fear,
About the courage of the Colored Volunteer.

CHORUS —Give us the flag, &c.

So we'll rally! Boys, rally!
And we need not heed the past;
We had a hard road to travel,
But our days are come at last,
God for our aid,
We have no cause to fear,
And that is the Motto of the Colored Volunteer.

CHORUS.—Give us the flag, &c.

W AUNER'S PRINTING OFFICE, N. E. COR. ELEVENTH & MARKET, PHILA

This ballad broadside refers to Frémont's rash unilateral emancipation proclamation, issued in Missouri in 1861 and revoked by Lincoln. Negroes, who volunteered for military service from the inception of the war, were officially recruited into the Federal army in 1862 after Lincoln issued the Proclamation of Emancipation.

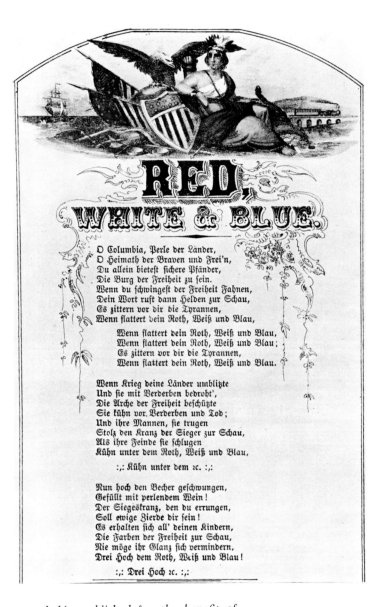

These German language broadsides were most probably published for the benefit of the troops of German origin, who constituted the largest ethnic contingent in the Union army. The German-born general Franz Sigel even inspired a song, "I'm Going to Fight mit Sigel," attributed to one "O. N. E. Schnapps."

THE SOUTH:

A Parody on "*Scots Wha Ha'e*," etc.

By C.: Feb'y 1st, 1862.

I.

Sons of SECESSIA glorious *land!*
Sons of THE SOUTH—noble band;
Proudly keep your gallant stand,
    On to Victory.

II.

Now's the day, and now's the hour;
See the front of battle lower;
See approach fanatic Lincoln's power,
    Chains and Slavery.

III.

By the dearest human ties,
By the starving ORPHAN's cries,
We must strike for FREEDOM, and rise—
    And they shall be FREE.

IV.

Lay those Vandal hordes low;
Tyrants fall in every foe;
Liberty's in every blow—
    Strike for Victory!

V.

Who, will be a TRAITOR knave?
Who, will fill a COWARD's grave?
Who, so base as be a Yankee's slave?
    Let him turn and flee!

VI.

Who, in this STRUGGLE would pause?
Let him read *Our Righteous Laws*—
Let him join our Southern Cause,
    For we SHALL be Free!

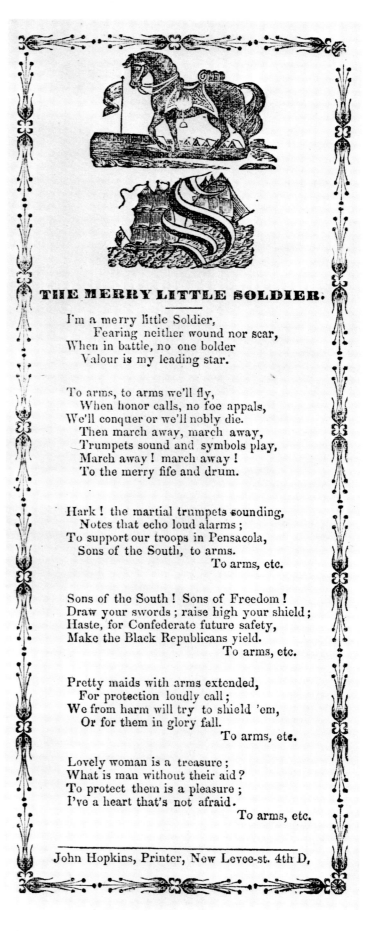

THE MERRY LITTLE SOLDIER.

I'm a merry little Soldier,
    Fearing neither wound nor scar,
When in battle, no one bolder
    Valour is my leading star.

To arms, to arms we'll fly,
    When honor calls, no foe appals,
We'll conquer or we'll nobly die.
    Then march away, march away,
    Trumpets sound and symbols play,
    March away! march away!
To the merry fife and drum.

Hark! the martial trumpets sounding,
    Notes that echo loud alarms;
To support our troops in Pensacola,
    Sons of the South, to arms.
                To arms, etc.

Sons of the South! Sons of Freedom!
Draw your swords; raise high your shield;
Haste, for Confederate future safety,
Make the Black Republicans yield.
                To arms, etc.

Pretty maids with arms extended,
    For protection loudly call;
We from harm will try to shield 'em,
    Or for them in glory fall.
                To arms, etc.

Lovely woman is a treasure;
What is man without their aid?
To protect them is a pleasure;
I've a heart that's not afraid.
                To arms, etc.

John Hopkins, Printer, New Levee-st. 4th D.

Two ballad broadsides printed in the Confederacy

WE'LL GO DOWN OURSELVES.

SONG AND CHORUS

BY

HENRY C. WORK.

3

CHICAGO.

Published by ROOT & CADY, 95 Clark Street.

WM. HALL & SON, FIRTH, POND & CO., New York.   HENRY TOLMAN & CO., Boston.   S. BRAINARD & CO., Cleveland.
H. N. HEMPSTED, Milwaukee.   J. H. WHITTEMORE, Detroit.

The militant threat made by the dissatisfied women in Henry C. Work's 1862 song was no idle boast. According to Frank Moore (*Women of the War*, 1867): "During all periods of the war, instances occurred of women being found in the ranks, fighting as common soldiers. . . ."

WE'LL GO DOWN OURSELVES.

"What shall we do, as years go by,
  And Peace remains a stranger
With Richmond yet in rebel hands,
  And Washington in danger?
What shall we do for leaders,
  When Old Age this race is cropping?"
I asked some ladies whom I met
  And didn't it set them hopping!
    CHORUS.
    "What shall we do?
      What shall we do?
    Why, lay them on the shelves,
      And we'll go down ourselves,
    And teach the rebels something new,
    And teach the rebels something new."

"What shall we do when armies march
  To storm the rebel quarters
If as of yore, their marches end
  Beside Potomac's waters?
May not we call our soldiers home?
  May not we think of stopping?"
I strove to frame the question fair
  But didn't it set them hopping!
    CHORUS.

"What shall we do when all the men
  For battle have enlisted
And yet the rebels hold their ground,
  And law is yet resisted?"
Instead of doing as I should,
  The theme politely dropping,
I ventured yet one question more;
  Oh didn't it set them hopping!
    CHORUS.

But knitting needles, not guns, were the acceptable womanly weapons. From *Beadle's Dime Song Book* (1864):

THE KNITTING SONG.

Knit! Knit! Knit!
  For our Northern soldiers brave!
Knit! Knit! Knit!
  While the Stars and Stripes they wave!
While they the rebels in battle meet,
Be yours to fashion with fingers fleet,
The nice warm socks for weary feet.
    Knit! Knit! Knit!
      CHORUS.
    For our boys on Southern hills,
      Our boys in Southern vales,
    By the woods and streams of Dixie's land,
      Are feeling the wintry gales.

Knit! Knit! Knit!
  The socks and mittens and gloves!
Knit! Knit! Knit!
  Each one that her country loves!
Lay by the useless, though beautiful toy,
With which you many an hour employ,
And knit, instead, for the soldier boy.
    Knit! Knit! Knit!
      CHORUS.

Knit! Knit! Knit!
  Narrow, and widen, and seam,
Knit! Knit! Knit!
  Till the flying needles gleam.
Knit till the mitten lies complete,
Knit till the socks for the weary feet
The eye of each patient soldier greet.
    Knit! Knit! Knit!
      CHORUS.

Knit! Knit! Knit!
  And knit with many a prayer!
Knit! Knit! Knit!
  Pray God the lives to spare
Of loved ones, soon on the battle-field
The deadly weapons of war to wield,
And pray that the foe before them yield.
    Knit! Knit! Knit!
      CHORUS.

This "Emancipation March," published in 1862, followed Lincoln's preliminary
Proclamation of Emancipation; the final proclamation was issued on January 1, 1863.

THE OLD UNION WAGON.

In Uncle Sam's Dominion, in Eighteen Sixty-one,
The fight between Secession and Union was begun;
The South declared they'd have the "rights" which Uncle Sam
   denied,
Or in their Secesh Wagon they'd all take a ride!
  Hurrah for the wagon—the old Union wagon!
  We'll stick to the *wagon* and *all take a ride!*

The makers of our wagon were men of solid wit,
They made it out of "Charter Oak" that would not rot or split.
Its wheels are of material, the strongest and the best,
And two are named the North and South, and two the East and
   West.

Our wagon *bed* is strong enough for any "revolution,"
In fact, 'tis the "hull" of the "old Constitution,"
Her coupling's strong, her axle's long, and any where you get
  her,
No Monarch's frown can "back her down"—no Traitor can
  upset her.

This good old Union wagon, the nation all admired;
Her wheels had run for four score years and never once been
  "tired,"
Her passengers were happy as along her way she whirled,
For the good old Union Wagon was the glory of the world!

But when old Abraham took command, the South wheel got
  displeased
Because the *public fat* was gone that kept her axle greased;
And when he gathered up the reins and started on his route,
She plunged into secession and knocked some "fellers" out!

Now while in this secession mire the wheel was sticking tightly,
Some Tory passengers got mad and cursed the driver slightly;
But Abraham "could see it"—so he didn't heed their clatter—
There's too much *black mud* on the wheel, says he—"that's
  what's the matter."

So Abram gave them notice that in eighteen sixty-three,
Unless the rebels "dried it up," he'd set their niggers free;
And then the man that led the van to fight against his nation,
Would drop his gun and *home* he'd run, to fight against starva-
  tion.

When Abram said he'd free the slaves that furnished their
  supplies,
It opened Northern traitors' *mouths* and Southern traitors' eyes.
"The slaves," said they, "will run away if you thus rashly free
  them!"
But Abram "Guessed, perhaps they'd best *go home and oversee
  them!*"

Around our Union wagon, with shoulders to the wheel,
A million soldiers rally, with hearts as true as steel;
And of all the Generals, high or low, that help to save the nation,
There none that strikes a harder blow than *General Emancipation!*

A lively symbolic political cartoon decorated the sheet music cover of this song to commemorate the Emancipation Proclamation, set to the popular tune from the 1850s, "Wait for the Wagon."

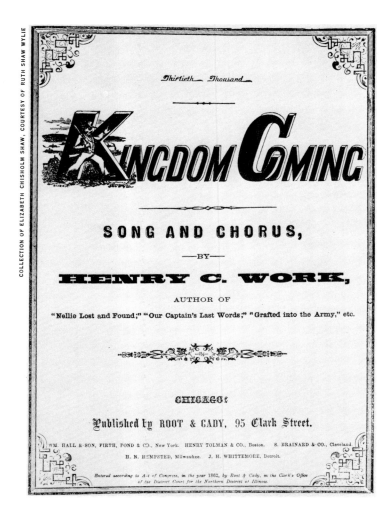

When Henry Clay Work, a confirmed Abolitionist, followed the suggestion of his publisher, the composer George F. Root, that he write Civil War songs, he turned out one great hit after another. Among his most successful songs, besides "Kingdom Coming" and "Wake Nicodemus," were "Babylon is Fallen" and—most spectacularly—"Marching Through Georgia" (see page 423).

KINGDOM COMING.

Say, darkeys, hab you seen de massa,
　Wid de muffstash on his face,
Go 'long de road some time dis mornin',
　Like he gwine to leab de place?
He seen a smoke way up de ribber,
　Whar de Linkum gumboats lay;
He took his hat, an' lef' berry sudden,
　An' I spec' he's run away!
　　　　CHORUS.
　De massa run? ha, ha!
　　De darkey stay? ho, ho!
　It mus' be now de kingdom comin',
　　An' de year ob Jubilo!

He six foot one way, two foot tudder,
　An' he weigh t'ree hundred pound,
His coat so big, he couldn't pay de tailor,
　An' it won't go half way round.
He drill so much, dey call him Cap'an,
　An' he get so drefful tanned,
I spec' he try an' fool dem Yankees,
　For to t'ink he's contraband.
　　　CHORUS.—De massa run? ha, ha! etc.

De darkeys feel so lonesome libing
　In de log-house on de lawn,
Dey move dar t'ings to massa's parlor,
　For to keep it while he's gone.
Dar's wine an' cider in de kitchen,
　An' de darkeys dey'll hab some;
I s'pose dey'll all be cornfiscated,
　When de Linkum sojers come.
　　　CHORUS.—De massa run? ha, ha! etc.

De oberseer he make us trouble,
　An' he dribe us round a spell:
We lock him up in de smoke-house cellar,
　Wid de key t'rown in de well.
De whip is lost, de han'-cuff broken,
　But de massa'll hab his pay;
He's ole enough, big enough, ought to know better,
　Dan to went, an' run away.
　　　　CHORUS.
　De massa run? ha, ha!
　　De darkey stay? ho, ho!
　It mus' be now de kingdom comin',
　　An' de year ob Jubilo!

WHERE'S STONEWALL JACKSON?

Know ye, boys, where Jackson goes,
 "Stonewall," the wiry?
if he's among his friends or foes,
 Jackson, bold and fiery?

Is he South or is he North,
 Stonewall, the wiry?
Or to the West has he gone forth,
 Jackson, bold and fiery?

Is he to Abraham's bosom gone,
 Stonewall, the wiry?
Or has he taken Richmond town,
 Jackson, bold and fiery?

Where'er he be, the devil's near him,
 Stonewall, the wiry!
And may the devil this way steer him,
 Jackson, bold and fiery!

Beadle's Dime Knapsack Songster (1862)

General Thomas Jonathan Jackson, most dauntless and dashing of Civil War heroes, gained his legendary nickname at a parlous moment of the first Battle of Bull Run in July 1861, when a colleague, General Barnard E. Bee, just before dying, cried out: "There is Jackson, standing like a stone wall!"

When Jackson died of pneumonia on May 10, 1863, after he had inadvertently been shot by one of his own men in the treacherous visibility of twilight, he was deeply mourned in the South, where he was adored. Many musical memorials to Jackson were published, among them a setting of his "last words" (1866) and another of a poem, "My Wife and Child," attributed to him, but actually written by Henry Rootes Jackson, another Confederate general.

STONEWALL JACKSON'S LAST WORDS.

"Come, let us cross the river,
 Those who have gone before,
Crush'd in the strife for freedom,
 Wait us on yonder shore.
So bright the sunshine sparkles,
 So merry hums the breeze:
Come, let us cross the river,
 And rest beneath the trees."
 CHORUS.
 Life's war for him is over;
 The warrior takes his ease:
 We left him across the river,
 At rest beneath the trees.

Stationed in occupied New Orleans, where he had been sent in 1863 to reorganize the state military bands, Patrick Sarsfield Gilmore, the dynamic, Irish-born, Bostonian bandmaster, composed "When Johnny Comes Marching Home" under the pseudonym of Louis Lambert. Gilmore's song is another of the extraordinary musical legacies of the Civil War, a sweeping success in its time and an accepted classic in ours. It was first published in Boston in 1863 with the handsome cover shown above.

WHEN JOHNNY COMES MARCHING HOME.

Music of this Song published by TOLMAN & Co., 291 Washington st., Boston.

When Johnny comes marching home again,
       Hurrah! hurrah!
We'll give him a hearty welcome then,
       Hurrah! hurrah!
The men will cheer, the boys will shout,
The ladies they will all turn out,
      And we'll all feel gay
      When Johnny comes marching home.

The old church bell will peal with joy,
       Hurrah! hurrah!
To welcome home our darling boy,
       Hurrah! hurrah!
The village lads and lassies say,
With roses they will strew the way,
      And we'll all feel gay
      When Johnny comes marching home.

Get ready for the jubilee,
       Hurrah! hurrah!
We'll give the hero three times three,
       Hurrah! hurrah!
The laurel wreath is ready now,
To place upon his loyal brow,
      And we'll all feel gay
      When Johnny comes marching home.

Let love and friendship on that day,
       Hurrah! hurrah!
Their choicest pleasure then display,
       Hurrah! hurrah!
And let each one perform some part
To fill with joy the warrior's heart,
      And we'll all feel gay
      When Johnny comes marching home.

Johnson, Song Publisher, 7 N. 10th St., Phila.

An unbelievable oriental fantasy decorated this broadside of Gilmore's song. The parody on the right, bitterly berating Lincoln for the unsuccessful war and the hardships of conscription and inflation, probably was a Copperhead song for the presidential election campaign of 1864.

In 1864, while still in New Orleans, the Barnumesque Patrick S. Gilmore staged a dress rehearsal for his later prodigious peace jubilees of 1869 and 1872. To celebrate the inauguration of a federal governor in Louisiana, Michael Hahn, Gilmore recruited a chorus of five thousand, and with the merged bands of the area—about five hundred musicians —masses of auxiliary trumpet and drum corps, and mingled church bells and cannon shots to augment the percussion, he presented a mammoth concert of patriotic music in Lafayette Square.

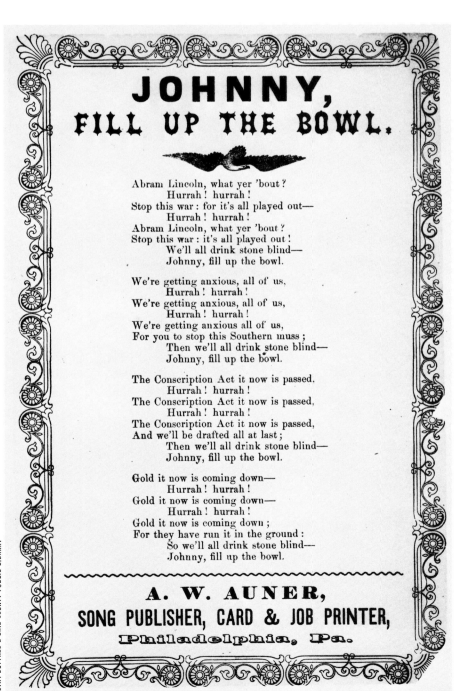

JOHNNY, FILL UP THE BOWL.

Abram Lincoln, what yer 'bout?
    Hurrah! hurrah!
Stop this war: for it's all played out—
    Hurrah! hurrah!
Abram Lincoln, what yer 'bout?
Stop this war: it's all played out!
      We'll all drink stone blind—
      Johnny, fill up the bowl.

We're getting anxious, all of us,
      Hurrah! hurrah!
We're getting anxious, all of us,
      Hurrah! hurrah!
We're getting anxious all of us,
For you to stop this Southern muss;
      Then we'll all drink stone blind—
      Johnny, fill up the bowl.

The Conscription Act it now is passed,
      Hurrah! hurrah!
The Conscription Act it now is passed,
      Hurrah! hurrah!
The Conscription Act it now is passed,
And we'll be drafted all at last;
      Then we'll all drink stone blind—
      Johnny, fill up the bowl.

Gold it now is coming down—
      Hurrah! hurrah!
Gold it now is coming down—
      Hurrah! hurrah!
Gold it now is coming down;
For they have run it in the ground:
      So we'll all drink stone blind—
      Johnny, fill up the bowl.

A. W. AUNER,
SONG PUBLISHER, CARD & JOB PRINTER,
Philadelphia, Pa.

To his Excellency,
ANDREW G. CURTIN.
Governor of Pennsylvania

DIRGE

SUNG AT THE CONSECRATION

— OF THE —

Soldiers' Cemetery at Gettysburg:

(NOV: 19TH 1863)

Composed and arranged for Four Voices,

— BY —

ALFRED DELANEY.

Geo. F. Swain

Philadelphia. LEE & WALKER. 722 Chesnut St.

DIRGE

SUNG AT THE CONSECRATION OF THE

SOLDIERS' CEMETERY. GETTYSBURG, PA.

O! it is great for our Country to die,
  whose ranks are contending,
Bright is the wreath of our fame;
  glory awaits us for aye;
Glory, that never is dim,
  shining on with a light never ending,
Glory, that never shall fade,
  never, O! never away!

O! it is sweet for our Country to die,
  how softly reposes
Warrior youth on his bier,
  wet by the tears of his love,
Wet by a mother's warm tears:
  they crown him with garlands of roses,
Weep, and then joyously turn,
  bright where he triumphs above.

Not in Elysian fields,
  by the still oblivious river,
Not in the Isles of the blest,
  over the blue rolling sea;
But on Olympian heights
  shall dwell the devoted forever;
There shall assemble the good,
  there the wise, valiant, and free.

O! then how great for our Country to die,
  in the front rank to perish,
Firm with our breast to the foe,
  victory's shout in our ear;
Long they our statues shall crown,
  in songs our memory cherish;
We shall look forth from our heaven,
  pleased the sweet music to hear.

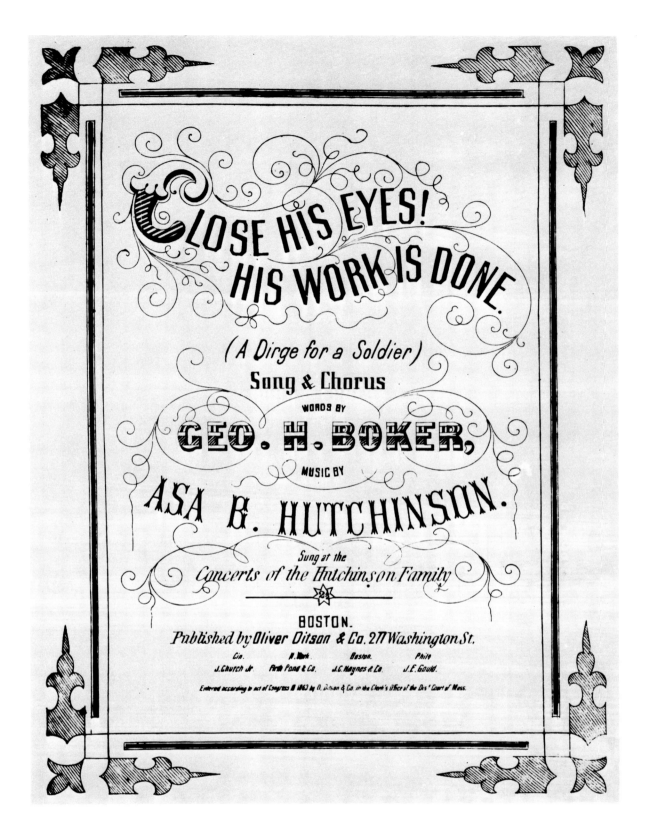

CLOSE HIS EYES! HIS WORK IS DONE.

(A Dirge for a Soldier.)

Close his eyes; his work is done!
  What to him is friend or foeman;
Rise of moon, or set of sun,
  Hand of man or kiss of woman!
    CHORUS.
    Lay him low, lay him low,
      Under the clover or under the snow;
    What cares he! he cannot know;
      Lay him low.

As man may, he fought his fight,
  Proved his truth by his endeavor;
Let him sleep in solemn night,
  Sleep forever and forever. (CHORUS.)

Fold him in his country's stars;
  Roll the drum and fire the volley!
What to him are all our wars,
  What but death bemocking folly! (CHORUS.)

Leave him to God's watching eye;
  Trust him to the Hand that made him.
Mortal love weeps idly by:
  God alone has pow'r to save him. (CHORUS.)

A mighty North-South controversy raged over the authorship of "All Quiet Along the Potomac," claimed by Lamar Fontaine in the South and Ethel Lynn Beers in the North. In truth. Mrs. Beers's moving poem had first been published in *Harper's Magazine* (November 30, 1861) about a year before it appeared anonymously in a Southern newspaper. At first two Southerners, Fontaine and Thaddeus Oliver, claimed authorship, but Fontaine was credited with the words when "All Quiet Along the Potomac To-night" was first published with John Hill Hewitt's music in Richmond (1864). With Mrs. Beers's authorship now unquestionably established, it is ironic that this unwitting collaboration between enemies should have contributed one of the truly memorable songs of the war.

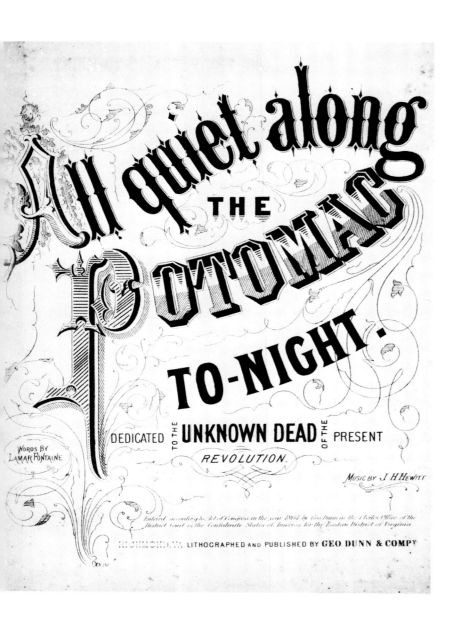

"ALL QUIET ALONG THE POTOMAC TO-NIGHT."

"All quiet along the Potomac to-night,"
   Except here and there a stray picket
Is shot, as he walks on his beat to and fro,
   By a rifleman hid in the thicket:
'Tis nothing, a private or two now and then,
   Will not count in the news of the battle:
Not an officer lost, only one of the men,
   Moaning out all alone the death rattle,
"All quiet along the Potomac to-night."

"All quiet along the Potomac tonight,"
   Where the soldiers lie peacefully dreaming,
And their tents in the rays of the clear autumn moon,
   And the light of the camp fires are gleaming.
A tremulous sigh, as the gentle night wind
   Thro' the forest leaves slowly is creeping,
While the stars up above, with their glittering eyes,
   Keep guard o'er the army while sleeping.

There's only the sound of the lone sentry's tread,
   As he tramps from the rock to the fountain,
And thinks of the two on the low trundle bed,
   Far away in the cot on the mountain.
His musket falls slack—his face, dark and grim,
   Grows gentle with memories tender,
As he mutters a prayer for the children asleep,
   And their mother—"may Heaven defend her."

Then drawing his sleeve roughly over his eyes,
   He dashes off the tears that are welling;
And gathers his gun close up to his breast,
   As if to keep down his heart's swelling.
He passes the fountain, the blasted pine tree,
   And his footstep is lagging and weary:
Yet onward he goes, thro' the broad belt of light,
   Toward the shades of the forest so dreary.

Hark! was it the night wind that rustles the leaves?
   Was it the moonlight so wondrously flashing?
It looked like a rifle! "Ha! Mary, good-bye!"
   And his life-blood is ebbing and plashing.
"All quiet along the Potomac to-night,"
   No sound save the rush of the river;
While soft falls the dew on the face of the dead.
   "The Picket's" off duty forever.

Drawn from the Original Statuette by permission of the Sculptor John Rogers.

ON PICKET DUTY.

F.H.CARTER. LITH. BOSTON

BOSTON,
C.D.RUSSELL & COMPANY.
126 TREMONT, OPPOSITE PARK STR!

INTER'D ACCORDING TO ACT OF CONGRESS IN THE YEAR 1864 BY C.D.RUSSELL&COMPANY IN THE CLERKS OFFICE OF THE DISTRICT COURT OF MASSACHUSETTS

*John Rogers's powerful sculpture group, "On Picket Duty," was translated
into a sheet music cover for another 1864 song about pickets.*

BOTH: LESTER S. LEVY

First published in Brooklyn in 1863 in sheet music form as "Weeping, Sad and Lonely; or, When This Cruel War Is Over," this sentimental ballad was a great success on both sides; it was elegantly issued in the South as sheet music and in the North in broadside versions as well.

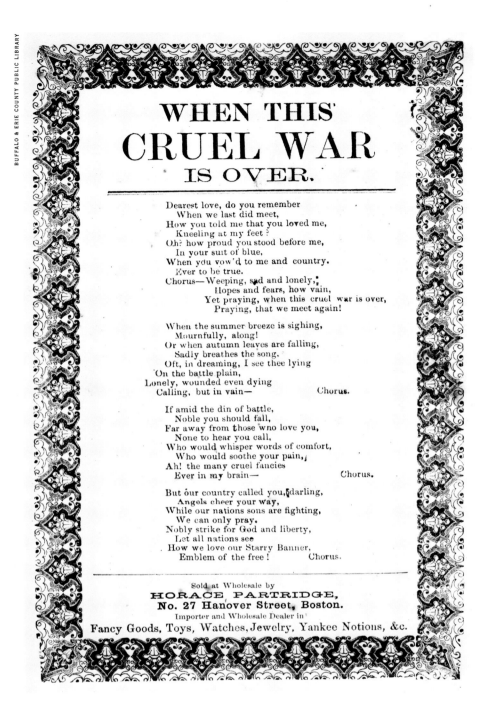

WHEN THIS CRUEL WAR IS OVER.

Dearest love, do you remember
　When we last did meet,
How you told me that you loved me,
　Kneeling at my feet?
Oh! how proud you stood before me,
　In your suit of blue,
When you vow'd to me and country.
　Ever to be true.
Chorus—Weeping, sad and lonely,
　　Hopes and fears, how vain,
　　Yet praying, when this cruel war is over,
　　Praying, that we meet again!

When the summer breeze is sighing,
　Mournfully, along!
Or when autumn leaves are falling,
　Sadly breathes the song.
Oft, in dreaming, I see thee lying
On the battle plain,
Lonely, wounded even dying
　Calling, but in vain—　　　　Chorus.

If amid the din of battle,
　Noble you should fall,
Far away from those who love you,
　None to hear you call,
Who would whisper words of comfort,
　Who would soothe your pain,
Ah! the many cruel fancies
　Ever in my brain—　　　　Chorus.

But our country called you, darling,
　Angels cheer your way,
While our nations sons are fighting,
　We can only pray.
Nobly strike for God and liberty,
　Let all nations see
How we love our Starry Banner,
　Emblem of the free!　　　　Chorus.

Septimus Winner's sequel, or "answer," to "When This Cruel War Is Over" became nearly as popular as the song it answered.

YES, I WOULD THE WAR WERE OVER.

Yes, I would the war were over,
　Would the cruel work were done;
With my country undivided,
　And the battle fought and won;
Let the contest now before us,
　Be decided by the sword,
For the war can not be ended
　Till the Union is restored.
　　CHORUS.
Yes, I would the war were over,
　Would the cruel work were done;
With my country still united,
　And the many States in one.

Dead upon the field of battle,
　Husbands, sons and brothers lie;
Friends are waiting, wives and mothers.
　Looking for them, by-and-by;
Far away from home forever,
　Many a noble boy lies slain;
Look not for thy child, fond mother,
　Thou shalt see him not again. (CHORUS.)

Yes, I would the war were ended,
　And the cruel struggle o'er,
But our flag must be defended,
　And our country as before;
Peace, indeed, is heaven's blessing,
　Though its joys are easy lost,
Still we'll battle for our nation,
　Whatsoe'er it yet may cost. (CHORUS.)

Beadle's Dime Song Book (1864)

RIDING A RAID

J. W. RANDOLPH RICHMOND Vᴬ
LITH BY E CREHEN

This magnificently mounted, dashing Confederate officer, his peacock plume blowing in the breeze, is General "Jeb" Stuart, next to Stonewall Jackson the most romantic and adored hero in the Confederacy.

RIDING A RAID.

'Tis old Stonewall the Rebel that leans on his sword,
And while we are mounting prays low to the Lord:
"Now each cavalier that loves Honor and Right,
Let him follow the feather of Stuart to night."
   CHORUS.
  Come tighten your girth and slacken your rein;
  Come buckle your blanket and holster again;
  Try the click of your trigger and balance your blade,
  For he must ride sure that goes Riding a Raid!

Now gallop, now gallop to swim or to ford!
Old Stonewall, still watching, prays low to the Lord:
"Good Bye dear old Rebel! the river's not wide,
And Maryland's light's in her windows to guide."
   CHORUS. Come tighten, &c.

There's a man in a white house with blood on his mouth!
If there's knaves in the North, there are braves in the South.
We are three thousand horses and not one afraid;
We are three thousand sabres, and not one dull blade;
   CHORUS. Come tighten, &c.

Then gallop, then gallop by ravines and rocks!
Who would bar us the way take his toll in hard knocks;
For with these points of steel, on the line of Penn,
We have made some fine strokes—and we'll make 'em again;
   CHORUS. Then tighten, &c.

NO SURRENDER.

Ever constant, ever true,
  Let the word be, No Surrender;
Boldly dare and greatly do!
  They shall bring us safely through.
No Surrender! No Surrender!
  And though fortune's smiles be few,
  Hope is always springing new,
  Still inspiring me and you
With a magic, No Surrender!

Constant and courageous still,
  Mind, the word is, No Surrender!
Battle, tho' it be up hill,
  Stagger not at seeming ill.
No Surrender! No Surrender!
  Hope, and thus your hope fulfill,
  There's a way where there's a will,
  And the way all cares to kill,
Is to give them, No Surrender!

Confederates satirized their woes in so-called "comic" songs. "Short Rations," published in Augusta in 1864, made a somewhat bitter joke about the lack of sufficient food for the army. "Ye Tragic," its author, wrote from firsthand experience; he was a poet-soldier, John Alcée Augustin, who served in the underfed Confederate Army of Tennessee in 1863.

SHORT RATIONS.

Fair ladies and maids of all ages,
    Little girls and cadets howe'er youthful.
Home-guards, quarter-masters and sages,
    Who write for the newspapers so truthful!
Clerks, Surgeons and Supes, Legislators,
    Staff Officers (fops of the Nation),
And even you dear speculators,
    Come list to my song of starvation!
        CHORUS:
        For we soldiers have seen something rougher,
        Than a storm, a retreat, or a fight,
        And the body may toil on and suffer,
        With a smile, so the heart is all right!

Our bugles had roused up the camp,
    The heavens look'd dismal and dirty,
And the earth look'd unpleasant and damp,
    As a beau on the wrong side of thirty.
We were taking these troubles with quiet,
    When we heard from the mouths of some rash ones,
That the army was all put on diet,
    And the Board had diminished our rations.
        CHORUS. For we soldiers, etc.

Reduce our rations at all?
    It was difficult, yet it was done,
We had one meal a day, it was small,
    Are we now, oh! ye gods! to have none?
Oh! ye gentlemen issuing rations,
    Give at least half her own to the State,
Put a curb on your maddening passions,
    And commissaries commisserate!
        CHORUS. For we soldiers, etc.

~~~

Erewhiles we had chickens and roasters,
    For the fowls and pigs were ferocious,
We would send them to short Pater Nosters,
    And the deed was not stamped as atrocious;
But since men have been shot for the same,
    We parch corn, it is healthier, but tougher—
The chickens and pigs have got tame,
    But the horses and mules have to suffer.
        CHORUS. For we soldiers, etc.

But the "Corn-fed" is proof to all evils,
    Has a joke for all hardships and troubles,
In honor and glory he revels,
    Other fancies he looks on as bubbles!
He is bound to be free, and he knows it,
    Then what cares he for toil and privation!
He is brave, and in battle he shows it,
    And will conquer in spite of starvation.
        CHORUS. For we soldiers, etc.

HOW ARE YOU? JOHN MORGAN.

A famous Rebel once was caught,
    With sabre bright in hand,
Upon a Mule he never bought,
    But press'd in Abram's land,
The Yankees caught his whole command,
    In the great Ohio State;
And kept the Leader of the band,
    To change for Colonel Streight.
        CHORUS.
        Then raise the shout, the glorious shout,
        John Morgan's caught at last,
        Proclaim it loud, the land throughout,
        He's into prison cast.

A felon's cell was then prepared,
    At David Tod's request,
And in Columbus prison shared
    The convict's *shaven crest*.
And thus the Rebel chieftain's pride,
    They sought to humble low,
But Southern valor don't subside
    Nor less in prisons grow. (CHORUS.)

But Prison fare he did not like,
    And sought a time to leave,
And with Greenbacks and pocket knife
    The keepers did deceive.
They say he dug a tunnel 'neath
    Its grated walls so grand,
And from the North he took "french leave"
    Away for Dixie's land. (CHORUS.)

John Morgan's gone like lightning flies,
    Through every State and Town;
Keep watch, and for the famous prize
    Five Thousand dollars down.
But he is gone, too late, too late,
    His whereabouts to find,
He's gone to call on Col. Streight
    Way down in Richmond town.
        CHORUS.
        Upon his Mule, he's gone they say
        To Dixie's promised Land,
        And at no very distant day
        To lead a new command.

HOW ARE YOU? JOHN MORGAN.

COMIC SONG,

A SEQUEL TO HERE'S YOUR MULE.

Published by **C. D. BENSON**, Nashville, Tenn.

3½

A. C. PETERS & BRO.	R. DE ROOD & CO.	C. D BENSON.	TRIPP & CRAGG.	E. A. BENSON.
Cincinnati. O.	*Lexington. Ky.*	*Nashville. Tenn.*	*Louisville. Ky.*	*Chicago. Ill.*

The famed Confederate raider John Morgan is gaily depicted astride the mule he had
" 'press'd" from a dim-witted Yankee farmer in a previous tongue-in-cheek comic song,
"Here's Your Mule." Published in Union-occupied Nashville in 1862, a pro-Confederate
final stanza to the song, having to do with Morgan, had been privately distributed.
In 1864 its sequel, "How Are You? John Morgan," brought the John Morgan story up
to date, relating, in gleeful, non-too-thinly-veiled subversive implications, the story
of Morgan's capture and imprisonment in Ohio in 1863 and how he ran away to raid
again some other day. In the text, Colonel Streight is Colonel Abel D. Streight, a raider
in his own right; David Tod is the federal governor of Ohio.

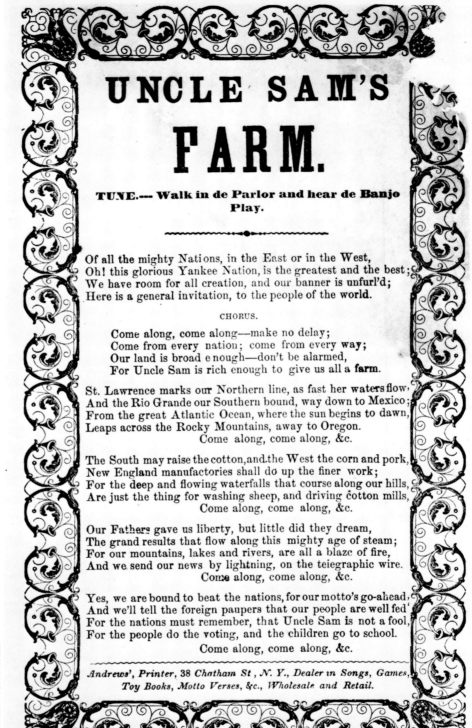

The Civil War—its battles and sentiments and its heroes, grand and humble—is recorded in a procession of brightly colored sheet music covers.

DEDICATED TO THE PEOPLE
OF THE UNITED STATES OF AMERICA.

LIBERTY AND UNION NOW AND FOREVER

OUR COUNTRY AND FLAG.
A NATIONAL SONG & CHORUS. WORDS & MUSIC BY
RICHARD CULVER,
Philadelphia LEE & WALKER, 722 Chestnut St.

OUR GENERALS GRAND MARCH.
New York, Published by HORACE WATERS, 481 Broadway.
Boston, O DITSON & C°

RISING OF THE PEOPLE

"The Drum-Tap rattles through the Land."

PATRIOTIC SONG.

Words by N. P. BEERS.

Music by M. COLBURN.

NEW YORK,

Published by FIRTH, POND & Co. 547 Broadway

BOSTON. O.DITSON & Co   ROCHESTER. J.P.SHAW   MILWAUKEE H.N.HEMPSTED.   PITTSBURGH H.KLEBER & BRO.

Entered according to Act of Congress in the year 1852 by Firth, Pond & Co in the Clerks Office of the District Court of the Southern Dist of N. Y.

THE SOLDIER'S RETURN
SCHOTTISCH

BY

T. VAN BERG.

ST LOUIS.
Published by **Endres & Compton**, 52 Fourth St.

PHILADELPHIA, **LEE & WALKER.**   CHICAGO, **ROOT & CADY.**   CINCINNATI, JOHN CHURCH, JR

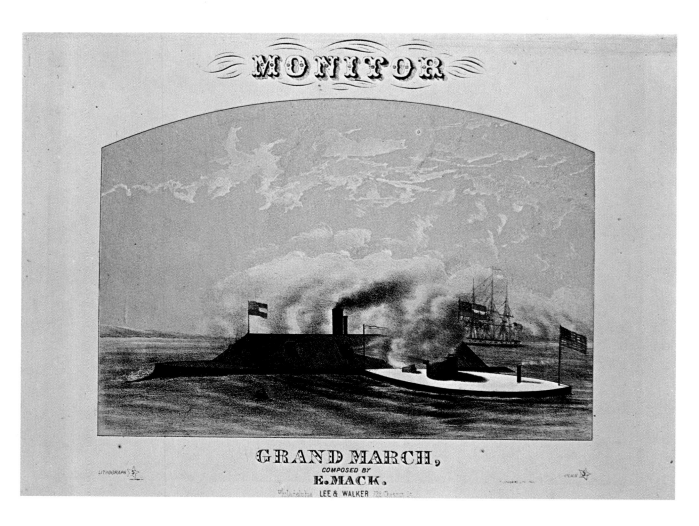

MONITOR

GRAND MARCH,
COMPOSED BY
E. MACK.

Philadelphia LEE & WALKER 722 Chestnut St.

THE
BATTLE OF NEW ORLEANS

Philadelphia LEE & WALKER 722 Chestnut St

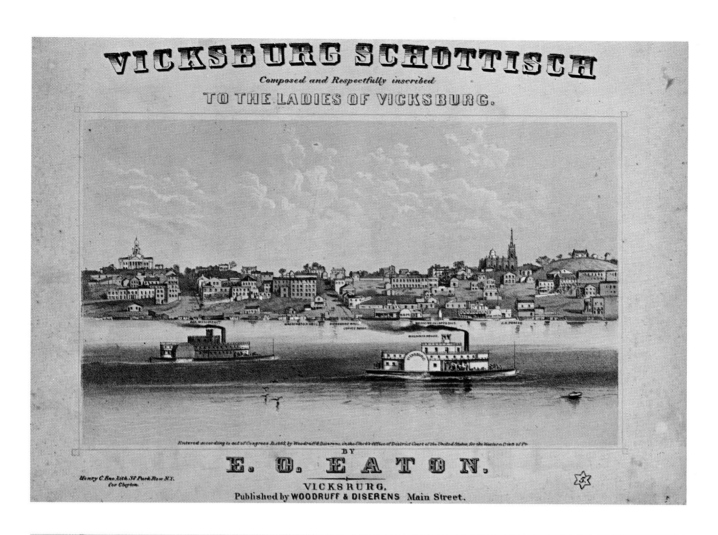

Dedicated to
MISS PRICE.

SOUTHERN CONSTELLATION

WORDS BY

ROBT. F. CARLIN.

⑤ Surgeon 5th Confederate Regt C.S.A.

Published By SCHREINER & SONS Macon, Ga.

Blackmar & Bro,
VICKSBURG, MISS.

Schreiner & Sons
MONTGOMERY, ALA.

To GENERAL M^c CLELLAN

GENERAL M^c CLELLAN'S
GRAND MARCH,
COMPOSED BY
E. MACK.

Philadelphia. LEE & WALKER 722 Chesnut St.

Published by Chas Magnus. 12 Frankfort St. N.Y.

McClellan
FOR PRESIDENT.

Air: Pompey Moore.—By John C. Cross.
Sung by Cool Burgess, of Sam Sharpleys Minstrels.

Kind folks if you will listen I'll sing to you a song,
  It's all about the peoples nomination :
Of the present Back-woods lawyer the Country's had enough,
  And we want a true Statesman for that station.
    Who shall we nominate ?
    To save the ship of state
  From wrecking in the sea of dissolution,
The people shout McClellan he has proved himself a man,
  That will stand by the Laws and Constitution !

It's now three years and more since this bloody war began
  And as yet there's no sign of its ending :
Now Union folks do know that Abe Lincoln don't want peace,
  But to ruin he is fast our Country sending ;
    He can't have his own way,
    The people soon will say—
  Who shall hold the reins of power ;
For spades will soon be trumps, how are you Abraham ?
  And "Little Mac" the nation's right bower.

McClellan soon will stand with extremes in his hand,
  To bring back the South to the Union ;
It will be the greatest time in our history's page
  To live once more in sweet communion ;
    With the Olive Branch he'll say,
    Now throw your arms away
  And I'll grant you all the rights of Constitution ;
If then they won't come back, he will say then clear the
          track,
  For the Swoad will end the work of dissolution !

The handsome sheet music cover portrait of General George Brinton McClellan and his noble steed was transposed to a campaign song broadside when "Little Mac" was nominated for president by the Copperhead-dominated Democratic national convention at Chicago in August 1864. Their platform, seeking to capitalize on the general despondency in the North about the war, called for immediate peace and restoration of the Union, slavery notwithstanding. McClellan, who had been removed in 1862 from his army command because of his ineffectual leadership, found himself in the anomalous position of an army man opposing war. The Republicans satirized his dilemma to the tune of "Oh Susanna."

Poor Mac! he tried to climb the hill,
  But it was too steep and high;
A pipe of peace was in his mouth,
  And a tear was in his eye;
One foot upon a war-horse placed,
  The other on an ass;
But the brutes ran off in opposite ways,
  And he fell on the grass.

  CHORUS.
  O McClellan! you cannot follow me;
  You're going up Salt River,
  With the platform on your knee.

Albany *Evening Journal* (October 27, 1864)

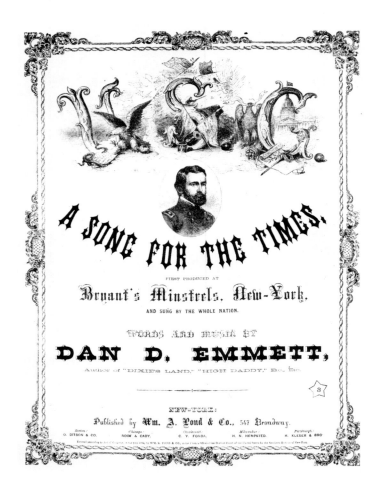

Great numbers of virulent defeatist and racist anti-Lincoln songs were sung in 1864 by the Copperheads, a name at first applied to the Peace Democrats, but later to all members of the party. Many Copperhead sentiments were vocalized to the tunes of the great war songs, "The Battle Cry of Freedom," and "Battle Hymn of the Republic," and even to "We Are Coming, Father Abraham."

Lincoln, who had been the butt of merciless intrigue and attack since entering the presidency—not only from Democrats but from foes within his own administration—was pessimistic about the outcome of the election. The string of smashing Northern victories during the summer and autumn of 1864 turned the tide both militarily and politically, however, and Lincoln's reelection was assured. These providential events were exultantly enumerated to the old tune of "Tippecanoe and Tyler Too" and published in the Albany *Evening Journal* (October 13, 1864).

> What has caused this great commotion, motion, motion,
> The country through?
> It is the ball that's rolling on
>   For honest Old Abe and Johnson too,
>   For honest Old Abe and Johnson too,
> And with them we'll beat Little Mac, Mac, Mac,
> Mac is off the track;
> And with them we'll beat Little Mac.
>
> Have you heard the news from Mobile, Mobile, Mobile,
> So good and true?
> FARRAGUT is a-pushing on
>   For honest Old Abe and Johnson too, &c.

> Have you heard the booming cannon, cannon, cannon,
> Atlanta through?
> Our soldier boys are fighting on,
>   For honest Old Abe and Johnson too, &c.
>
> On this line we'll fight it out, out, out,
> Though all looks blue;
> Meade and Grant will have Richmond yet,
>   For honest Old Abe and Johnson too, &c.
>
> We have whipped Mac's friends on the Shenandoah, doah,
> And that will do;
> Sheridan has been bagging them
>   For honest Old Abe and Johnson too, &c.

> The Chicago Platform is going down, down, down,
> The country through;
> So is little failure Mac
>   For honest Old Abe and Johnson too, &c.

> Have you heard the news from Maine, Maine, Maine,
> So good and true,
> That all the world seems turning round
>   For honest Old Abe and Johnson too, &c.
>
> Copperheads are in commotion, motion, motion,
> What can they do?
> War Democrats are coming round
>   For honest Old Abe and Johnson too, &c.

Lincoln was unanimously nominated, with Andrew Johnson as his running mate, when the Republicans met in Baltimore in June 1864 at what was called the Union National Convention. There had been a flurry for Grant, and Dan Emmett prematurely celebrated his nomination in a campaign song, which apparently was performed as a production number by Bryant's Minstrels. In the text, "Chase" is Salmon P. Chase. who intrigued to gain the presidency while serving as Lincoln's secretary of the treasury.

U. S. G.

NATIONAL WALK'ROUND.

> I suppose you've heard of the great commander,
>   He's second to none but Alexander;
> Then U. S. G.'s the man for me,
>   Three cheers for your old Uncle Sam.
> He comes from the West with the spangled banner,
>   A mudsill and by his trade a tanner,
> Goodbye Chase, you'll lose the race,
>   He can distance Abraham.
>   CHORUS.
>   U. stands for uncle,
>   U. S. for Uncle Sam,
>   But U. S. G., it just suits me,
>   Or any other man;
>   He dug a trench at Vicksburg,
>   And sure as you're alive;
>   He'll dig one more, round the White House door,
>   In eighteen sixty-five.

Lincoln, who was popularly loved despite the ugly political attacks, was the subject of a prototypal spot commercial, presumably published around election time. An enterprising tobacco manufacturer used his likeness (but not his endorsement) to promote sales through the medium of music.

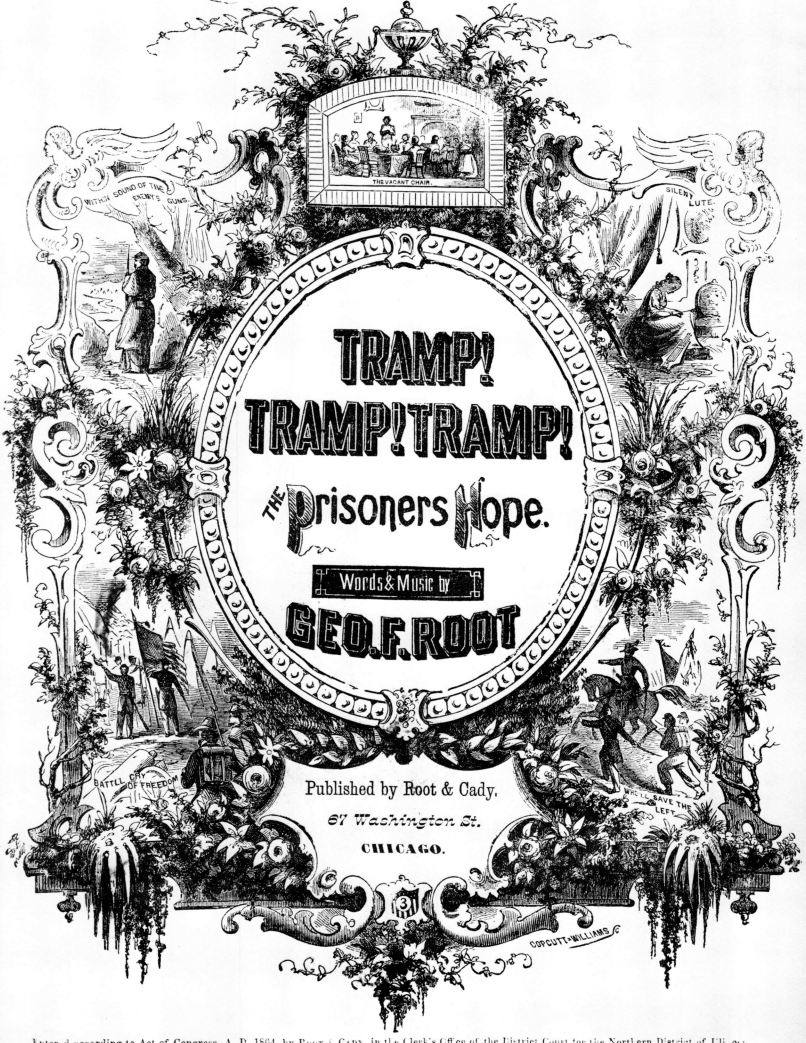

THE VACANT CHAIR.

WITHIN SOUND OF THE ENEMY'S GUNS.

SILENT LUTE.

TRAMP! TRAMP! TRAMP!

THE Prisoners Hope.

Words & Music by

GEO. F. ROOT

BATTLE CRY OF FREEDOM

WHO'LL SAVE THE LEFT.

Published by Root & Cady.

67 Washington St.

CHICAGO.

COPCUTT & WILLIAMS

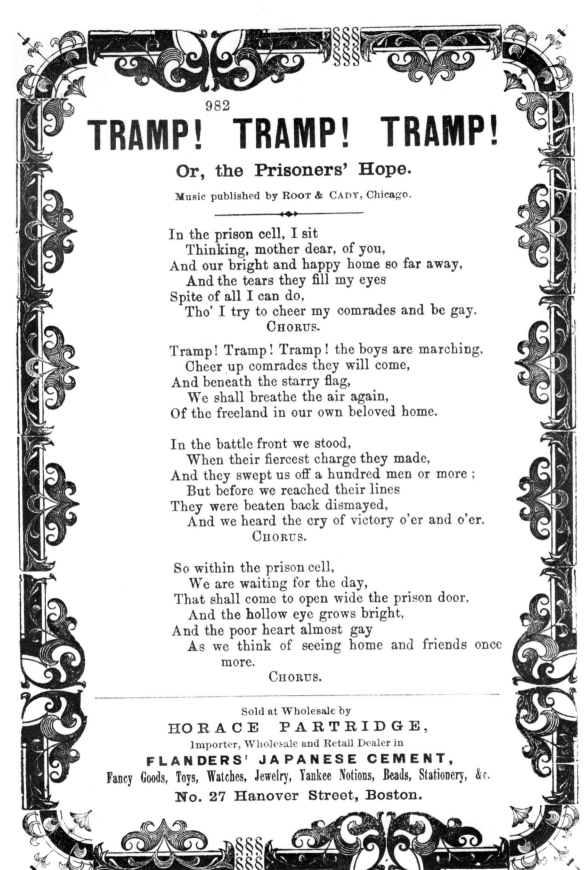

Ornately engarlanded vignettes representing some of his many famous songs decorated the sheet music cover of George F. Root's great marching song "Tramp! Tramp! Tramp!" when it was first published in 1864. Despite its having appeared toward the end of the war, the song became tremendously popular in the North, and it was widely issued in broadside form, of which this is a handsome example.

MAJ. GEN. W. F. SHERMAN'S

GRAND MARCH.

COMPOSED BY

J. VAL. HAMM.

BOSTON

Published by OLIVER DITSON & CO 277 Washington St

W. A. POND & CO.   J. C. HAYNES & CO   J. E. GOULD   JOHN CHURCH Jr

To Cousin Mary Lizzie Work,   Of New Washington, Indiana.

MARCHING THROUGH GEORGIA

SONG AND CHORUS:

Words and Music by

HENRY CLAY WORK.

CHICAGO:

PUBLISHED BY ROOT & CADY, No. 95 CLARK STREET.

Entered according to Act of Congress, 1865, by Root & Cady, in the Clerk's Office of the District Court for the Northern District of Illinois.

General William Tecumseh Sherman's capture of Atlanta on September 1, 1864, and his subsequent ravaging march to the sea was jubilantly acclaimed in the North, where it was recognized as the beginning of the end of the war. But in the South Sherman became the object of a loathing so intense that Henry C. Work's song "Marching Through Georgia" was proscribed there until well into the twentieth century, being regarded as a greater insult to Southerners than "Yankee Doodle" had been to New Englanders before the Revolution.

JOHNSON & CARTLITCH, 18 N. Tenth St.

MARCHING
THROUGH GEORGIA

Words and Music by HENRY C. WORK.

Published by ROOT & CADY, No. 95 Clark Street, Chicago.

Bring the good old bugle, boys! we'll sing another song—
Sing it with that spirit that will start the world along—
Sing it as we used to sing it, fifty thousand strong,
　While we were marching through Georgia.
　　CHORUS.—Hurrah! hurrah! we bring the Jubilee!
　　　　　Hurrah! hurrah! the flag that makes you free!"
　　　　　So we sung the chorus from Atlanta to the sea,
　　　　　　While we were marching through Georgia.

How the darkeys shouted when they heard the joyful sound!
How the turkeys gobbled which our commissary found!
How the sweet potatoes even started from the ground,
　While we were marching through Georgia.
　　Hurrah! Hurrah! etc.

Yes, and there were Union men who wept with joyful tears,
When they saw the honor'd flag they had not seen for years;
Hardly could they be restrained from breaking forth in cheers,
　While we were marching through Georgia.
　　Hurrah! hurrah! etc.

"Sherman's dashing Yankee boys will never reach the coast!"
So the saucy rebels said, and 'twas a handsome boast,
Had they not forgot, alas! to reckon with the host,
　While we were marching through Georgia.
　　Hurrah! hurrah! etc.

So we made a thoroughfare for Freedom and her train,
Sixty miles in latitude—three hundred to the main,
Treason fled before us, for resistance was in vain,
　While we were marching through Georgia.
　　Hurrah! hurrah! etc.

JOHNSON'S
CARD AND JOB
PRINTING ESTABLISHMENT,
No. 7 North Tenth St., Philad'a.

N. B —Get the two New Songs—"There's Somebody Waiting for Me." and "Somebody is Waiting for Me."
Printing of all kinds done as cheap as at any Office in town.

More than for its rousing tune, Henry C. Work's classic "Marching Through Georgia," published in 1865, was embraced in the North for precisely the same reason that it was hotly shunned in the South: its words.

The face attached to the tail of the serpent encircling a Richmond in flames presumably was meant to represent Jefferson Davis, who did not tarry to receive General Grant when he entered the burning city on April 3, 1865.

RICHMOND HAS FALLEN.

Richmond has fallen!
  Hurrah, boys, hurrah!
Old Jeff and his traitors
  Have skedaddled afar;
They better "go to Halifax"
  Or some other place,
For the Yankee boys are after them,
  And won't give up the chase.

Grant and his heroes
  Stormed the rebel town,
Showed them the Stars and Stripes
  Felled the traitors down!
He marched in triumphantly,
  And hoisted our flag,
And from the rebel Capitol
  "Doused" the secesh rag.

THE CONQUERED BANNER.

Furl that Banner! furl it sadly,
 Once ten thousands hailed it gladly,
And ten thousands wildly, madly
 Swore it would forever wave,
Swore the foeman's sword could never
 Hearts like theirs entwined dissever,
Till that flag should float forever
 O'er their freedom or their grave.

Furl that Banner softly, slowly!
 Treat it gently, It is holy,
For it droops above the dead!
 Touch it not! unfold it never,
Let it rest there, furled forever!
 For the people's hopes are dead!

Respectfully dedicated to General U.S. Grant.

General Grant's Quick Step

E. MACK.

Philadelphia. LEE & WALKER 722 Chestnut St.
Wᵐ H. BONER & Cᵒ 1102 Chestnut St.   CHAS. W. HARRIS, Troy, N.Y.

On April 9, 1865, as General Grant approached the McLean house in the village of Appomattox Court House, Virginia, to receive General Lee's surrender, "one of our bands, near by, through the generous impulse of the moment, struck up the appropriate air of 'Auld Lang Syne,' " Union officer Major E. M. Woodward recalled later (*History of the One Hundred and Ninety eighth Pennsylvania Volunteers*, 1884). After the brief ceremony, Major Woodward continued,

"When the news of the surrender became known to the army, the enthusiasm of our men burst all bounds, and arose to the zenith of perfect frenzy. The boys screeched, yelled, danced, tossed their caps in the air and rolled upon the ground. Even the bands that attempted to play our national anthems broke into discordant medleys, and cut short their jumble in wild shouts and frantic waving of their instruments."

In its coverage of the wild jubilation in Washington at the news of Lee's surrender, the *New-York Times* (April 11, 1865) reported: "Thousands assembled in front of the Executive mansion. The bands played and many in the crowd sang ['The Star-Spangled Banner' and 'Rally Round the Flag, Boys'] in unison with the music." The president, who had just returned from Richmond, was deliriously "greeted with huzzas, clapping of hands and waving of hats." To conclude the serenade, the president requested " 'Dixie,' one of the best tunes I ever heard." He added: "I had heard that our adversaries had attempted to appropriate it. I insisted . . . that we had fairly captured it . . . it is our lawful prize." The band then played "Dixie" with "extraordinary vigor, when three cheers and a tiger were given, followed by the tune of 'Yankee Doodle.' "

Pres. Lincoln's

FUNERAL MARCH

BY
E. M. BROWN.

SAINT LOUIS.
Published by ENDRES & COMPTON. 52 Fourth Str.

J. MEEAN. LITH.

Jubilant victory hymns soon gave way to dirges and the muffled drums of funeral marches as a shocked and grieving nation mourned for Abraham Lincoln, assassinated on April 14, exactly four years after the surrender of Fort Sumter.

FAREWELL FATHER, FRIEND AND GUARDIAN.

(Written on the Death of Abraham Lincoln.)

Words by L. M. Dawn. Music by George F. Root.

All our land is draped in mourning,
  Hearts are bow'd and strong men weep;
For our lov'd, our noble leader,
  Sleeps his last, his dreamless sleep,
Gone forever, gone forever,
  Fallen by a traitor's hand;
Tho' preserv'd his dearest treasure,
  Our redeem'd beloved land.
    CHORUS.
  Farewell father, friend and guardian,
    Thou hast join'd the martyr band,
  But thy glorious work remaineth,
    Our redeem'd beloved land.

Thro' our night of bloody struggle,
  Ever dauntless, firm and true,
Bravely, gently forth he led us,
  Till the morn burst on our view—
Till he saw the day of triumph,
  Saw the field our heroes won;
Then his honor'd life was ended,
  Then his glorious work was done. (CHORUS.)

When from mountain, hill and valley,
  To their homes our brave boys come,
When with welcome notes we greet them,
  Song and cheer and pealing drum;
When we miss our loved ones fallen,
  When to weep we turn aside;
Then for him our tears shall mingle—
  He has suffer'd—he has died. (CHORUS.)

Honor'd leader, long and fondly
  Shall thy mem'ry cherish'd be;
Hearts shall bless thee for their freedom,
  Hearts unborn shall sigh for thee;
He who gave thee might and wisdom,
  Gave thy spirit sweet release;
Farewell father, friend and guardian,
  Rest forever, rest in peace (CHORUS.)

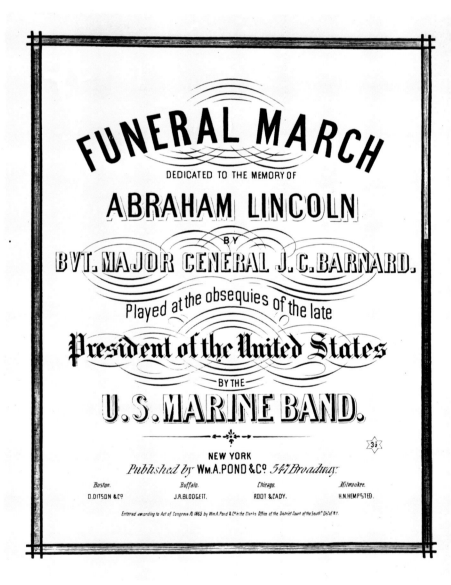

429

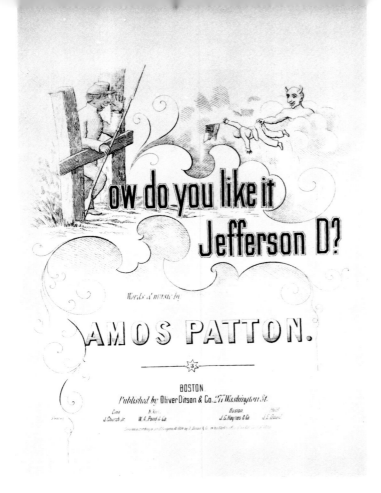

In 1864, as Union victories proliferated, Jefferson Davis was cruelly taunted in a vindictive song with an expressive cartoon on its cover.

HOW DO YOU LIKE IT, JEFFERSON D?

Oh, how do you like it as far as you've got,
  Jefferson D! Jefferson D!
Are you glad you began it, or d'ye wish you had not?
  Jefferson D! Jefferson D!
People say (though of course I don't know that it's so),
That your spirits are getting decidedly low,
And you're sick and discouraged, and I don't know what;
But say, though, do you like it as far as you've got?
  CHORUS. Oh, ho! Jefferson D!
    Things look rather shaky now,
    'Twixt you and me.

If I were in your place I'd try foreign air,
  Jefferson D! Jefferson D!
And at once for a short trip to Europe prepare,
  Jefferson D! Jefferson D!
But as things are at present I don't think I'd sail
From Charleston, Savannah, New Orleans or Mobile;
But in order, though absent, to retain my command,
I'd just take an ox-team and go round by land.

You can't think how sorry I was when I heard,
  Jefferson D! Jefferson D!
That your visit to Washington had been deferred,
  Jefferson D! Jefferson D!
I hope that you'll find it convenient to come,
When Abe and the rest of the boys are at home;
But I trust you won't mind it, they're such a queer lot,
If they ask you how you like it as far as you've got.

After the surrender Northern songsmiths had a field day with the scandalous tale that Jefferson Davis had attempted to escape disguised as a woman. When Davis was apprehended in Georgia, the shawl and waterproof coat he had snatched up in his haste to get away turned out to be his wife's. The Northern newspapers soon had him wearing one of his wife's dresses, and this juicy story was repeatedly set to music.

THE SOUR APPLE TREE.

The Yankee boys have caught him—
The traitor, Old Jeff D!—
I wonder if they'll hang him
To the "Sour Apple Tree!"
Don't you think it will be right?
And justice, I declare!
To hang him up "to dry," my boys,
And dangle in the air.

O when our Soldiers found him,
I'll bet he did "look rich"
With the "petticoats" around him
As he stood in the "last ditch!"
Old Jeff, he wasn't wise
With "boots" on! don't you see!
It was a splendid sight, I'm sure,
Such "Southern Chivalry!"

Now if they hang him, it will be
A moral lesson taught
To those who might in future time
Like him be evil fraught.
Some think it will be right—
Whatever it may be,
I really think they'll hang him
To the "Sour Apple Tree!"

How intensely Jefferson Davis was loathed in the North can be seen from this symbolic sheet music cover for a sardonically named polka, in which the former president of the Confederacy is savagely caricatured as a rat in a cage. In 1865 Davis was imprisoned at Fortress Monroe, Virginia, where he remained for two years.

WHEN THE BOYS COME HOME.

Words and Music by CHARLES CARROL SAWYER.

The Music of this song can be obtained at the celebrated Music-Establishment of
SAWYER & THOMPSON, 59 Fulton Avenue, Brooklyn. N, Y.

The boys are coming home again,
　This war will soon be o'er :
The North and South again will stand
　United as of yore ;
Yes, hand in hand, and arm in arm
　Together we will roam ;
Oh ! won't we have a happy time,
　When all the boys come home !
　　Chorus :
We'll hoist the good old Flag again,
　On Freedom's lofty dome,
And live in peace and happiness,
　When all the boys come home.

We'll have no more false hopes and fears,
　No more heart-rending sighs—
The Messenger of peace will dry
　The weary mourner's eyes :
We'll laugh and sing, we'll dance and play
　Ah ! wait until they come,
And joy will crown the happy day
　When all the boys come home !
　　Chorus—We'll hoist, &c.

How proud Our Nation then will stand !
　United ever more,
We'll bid defiance to the foe
　That dare approach our shore ;
We'll hoist the good old Flag again,
　On Freedom's lofty dome,
And live in peace and happiness
　When all the boys come home !
　　Chorus—We'll hoist, &c.

Ten illustrated Songs on Notepaper, mailed to any Address on
receipt of 50 cts. Published by Chas. Magnus, 12 Frankfort St., N. Y.

Songs of rejoicing that greeted the peace—at least in the North—optimistically envisioned a utopian, reunited land, a sentiment exemplified in both the evocative broadside of Charles C. Sawyer's song above and in the words and sheet music cover of a prizewinning jubilee song, apparently published for the first postwar July Fourth celebration.

NATIONAL JUBILEE.

PRIZE SONG.

Words by Carlos Wilcox.
Music by Konrad Treuer.

Fling forth the Nation's banner
　In its glory on the air!
'Tis the ancient Flag of Freedom,
　Not a star is missing there:
Our triumph and redemption,
　For the people all are free;
And the Jubilee hath sounded—
　Universal Liberty.
CHORUS.
Shout! the good time has come,
　Our Nation now is free;
Echo the chorus wide,
　Proclaim the Jubilee!

The Dove of Peace is brooding
　O'er the desolated earth,
And the flowers again are springing
　In our Freedom's second birth.
Ring out the bells of glory,
　Call our noble veterans home;
From the fields of war and carnage,
　Greet the heroes as they come.
CHORUS.

Upon the brow of millions
　God hath placed the crown of light,
And the host of their oppressors
　He hath 'whelmed in endless night.
We'll shout aloud the triumph
　Through the world, from pole to pole.
Be the boon for all defended
　As the birth-right of the soul.
CHORUS.

The starry flag is floating
　In its glory on the air;
'Tis the spotless flag of freedom,
　Not a star is missing there;
Eternal truth and justice,
　All mankind exulting see
Shout the universal chorus
　Of our country's Jubilee
CHORUS.

PEACE ON EARTH

GOOD WILL TO MEN.

THE NATIONS JUBILEE July 4th 1865

CIVILIZATION.

CHRISTIANITY.

'TIS FINISHED!
or
SING HALLELUJAH.

Words and music by Henry C. Work.

'Tis finished! 'tis ended!
  The dread and awful task is done;
Tho' wounded and bleeding,
  'Tis ours to sing the vict'ry won,
Our nation is ransom'd—
  Our enemies are overthrown
And now, NOW commences,
  The brightest era ever known.
    CHORUS.
      Then sing hallelujah! sing hallelujah!
        Glory be to God on high!
      For the old flag with the white flag
        Is hanging in the azure sky.

Ye joy bells! ye peace bells!
  Oh never, never music rang,
So sweetly, so grandly,
  Since angels in the advent sang,
Your message is gladness
  To myriads of waiting souls,
As onward and world-ward
  The happy, happy echo rolls.
    CHORUS.

Come patriots! come free men!
  Come join your every heart and voice;
We've wept with the weeping—
  Now let us with the blest rejoice,
With armies of victors
  Who round about the white throne stand—
With LINCOLN, the Martyr
  And Liberator of his land.
    CHORUS.
      Then sing hallelujah! sing hallelujah!
        Glory be to God on high!
      For the old flag with the white flag
        Is hanging in the azure sky.

PEACE

" HARK IN THE DISTANCE, WHAT SOUND WE HEAR "
"'TIS THE VOICE OF THOUSANDS, AS THEY COME."

⬦6

MUSIC BY

CHARLES MOULTON

NEW YORK, SCHARFENBERG & LUIS 758 BROADWAY.

RECONSTRUCTION!

AS IT SHOULD BE

AS IT IS!

Entered according to act of Congress A.D. 1867 by A.E. Blackmar in the Clerks Office of the Dist. Court of the Eastern Dist. of La.

Grand March

BY

CHARLES YOUNG.

Published by J. L. PETERS, 599 Broadway, N.Y.

Instead of speech making to satisfy wrong,
All will join the glad chorus to sing Freedom's song.
And if the millennium is not a pretence,
We'll all be good brothers a hundred years hence.

Song: "A Hundred Years Hence"
Frances Gage
1850–1860

11. *Walk-Around*
1865-1876

Wishful early peace songs hailed a blissfully reunited land, wherein all past differences would be magically erased and all men joined together as brothers in a vast, euphonious chorus of common purpose. But this was not to be. Instead, the postwar North was torn by violent political strife and the uncontrite South was subjected to the excruciating afflictions of Reconstruction. The resulting chorus was a cacophony of hideous discord.

The essence of unreconstructed rebeldom was distilled into this song, credited to Major Innes Randolph, a Virginia lawyer, who not only flagrantly defied the victors and their rule, but satirically dedicated his resistance song to Thaddeus Stevens, the vengeful Radical Republican author of the most repressive Reconstruction measures.

O I'M A GOOD OLD REBEL.

O I'm a good old rebel,
  Now that's just what I am,
For this "Fair Land of Freedom"
  I do not care a dam;
I'm glad I fit against it—
  I only wish we'd won;
And I don't want no pardon
  For any thing I done.

I hates the Constitution,
  This Great Republic, too,
I hates the Freedmen's Buro,
  In uniforms of blue;
I hates the nasty eagle,
  With all his braggs and fuss,
The lyin', thievin' Yankees,
  I hates them wuss and wuss.

I hates the Yankee nation
  And everything they do,
I hates the Declaration
  Of Independence, too;
I hates the glorious Union—
  'Tis dripping with our blood—
I hates their striped banner,
  I fit it all I could.

I followed old mas' Robert
  For four year, near about,
Got wounded in three places
  And starved at Pint Lookout;
I cotch the roomatism
  A campin' in the snow,
But I killed a chance o' Yankees,
  I'd like to kill some mo'.

Three hundred thousand Yankees
  Is stiff in Southern dust;
We GOT three hundred thousand
  Before they conquered us;
They died of Southern fever
  And Southern steel and shot,
I wish they was three million
  Instead of what we got.

I can't take up my musket
  And fight 'em now no more,
But I aint a going to love 'em,
  Now that is sarten sure;
And I don't want no pardon
  For what I was and am,
I won't be reconstructed
  And I don't care a dam.

Like John Tyler in 1840, Andrew Johnson, also a Southerner and a states' rights Democrat, was regarded as political window dressing when he was chosen by the Union party to run as Lincoln's vice-president in 1864; nobody expected that he would ever get to be president. When he did—again like Tyler—he was soon locked in mortal combat with an intensely hostile Congress. The Radical Republicans, led by the fanatical Abolitionist Thaddeus Stevens, solidly opposed Johnson, overriding fifteen of his record twenty-nine vetoes. When they eventually impeached him in 1868, he barely escaped conviction by the frail margin of a single vote.

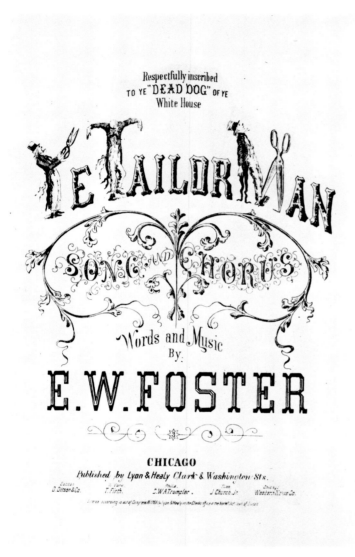

A disrespectful sheet music cover to set the mood for an equally disrespectful song published in 1866 about President Andrew Johnson, who had begun his career as a tailor in Tennessee

Johnson was not a loved president. He had gotten off to a bad start, having been scandalously intoxicated when he took his vice-presidential oath. Generous people, among them Lincoln, excused him on the grounds of ill health (Johnson had just recovered from typhoid fever), but the general reaction was one of disgust. Feeling faint and nervous before the ceremony, Johnson had asked for a drink. When a bottle of brandy was produced, he had gulped down two large tumblerfuls, "drinking it down like water," wrote Perley (*Perley's Reminiscences*, 1886), who continued: "To the surprise of everybody, the Vice-President, when called on to take the oath of office, made a maudlin, drunken speech. . . . in the most incoherent, and in some instances offensive, manner. The Republican Senators were horror-stricken, and . . . vainly endeavored to make him stop his harangue; but he would not be stopped . . . the brandy had made him crazily drunk. . . ."

Johnson's foibles and his humble beginnings were often reviewed by irreverent songsmiths, as in "Ye Tailor Man." In the text, *sound upon the Goose* means to be sound on the question of slavery from the Southern point of view; "Moses" was what Negroes called Lincoln, who had led them "out of the land of bondage." The application of the term to Johnson, no friend to blacks, was satirically meant.

YE TAILOR MAN.
Words and music by E. W. Foster.

Now, once there was a tailor man,
    That lived in Tennessee,
His name they say began with J,
    A Tailor good was he;
He prosper'd as good Tailors do,
    Who use no Shoddy mean and loose,
For then the people said he was
    Quite "sound upon the Goose"!
        CHORUS.
    Come! Moses lead the way,
        O show the promised land to us!
    Strike the flinty rock,
        And let the waters gush!
    Hurrah! for Union ever,
        The Freeman's former chains
    We'll keep to shackle Traitors,
        As long as one remains!

Alas! for him, this tailor man,
    For Office 'gan to seek,
From selling "close," he nat'rally
    Became a "Moses" meek;
And many then did follow him,
    And fain would act as he did utter,
Save when he undertook to spread
    For them their "bread and butter"!
        CHORUS.
This humble individual
    A balm for all your scars,
"Presents the Constitution with
    Its six and thirty stars!"
But 'twixt the many and the few,
    That fill the Gover'ment Caboose.
Alas! for him, I know they mean
    To cook the Tailor's Goose!
        CHORUS.

PRESIDENT JOHNSON's
GRAND UNION MARCH

CHICAGO, Ill.

4.

Published by LYON & HEALY cor. Clark & Washington Sts.

Entered according to Act of Congress A.D. 1865 by Lyon & Healy in the Clerks Office of the U.S. District Court of the North.ⁿ Distr. of Ill.ˢ

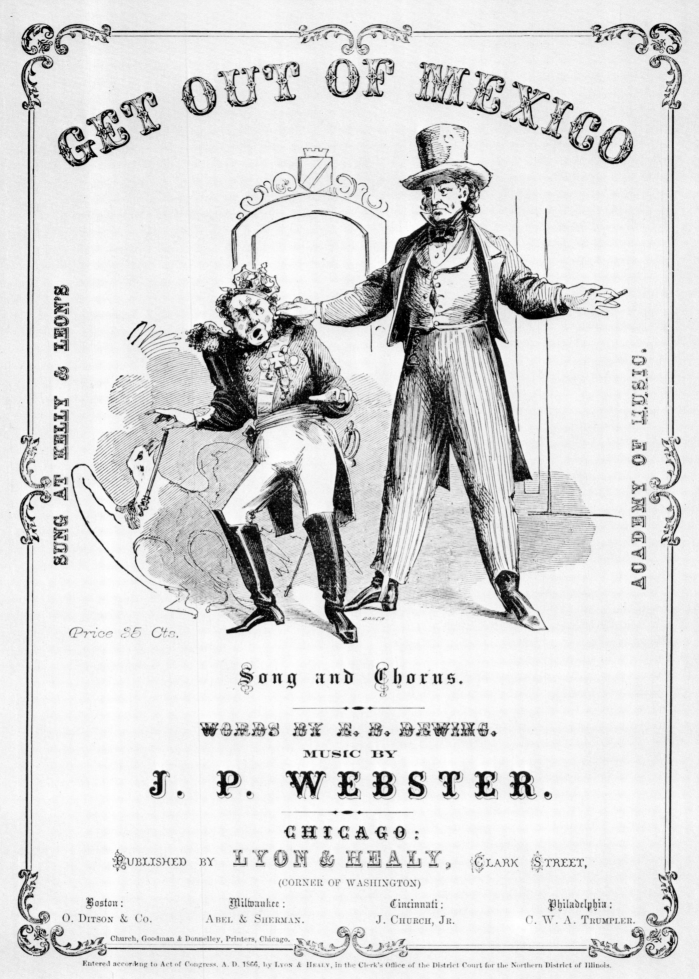

Uncle Sam and an indignant-looking American eagle are forcibly evicting
Emperor Maximilian from Mexico in this sheet music cover of 1866.

At the outset of the Civil War, Napoleon III of France, with the connivance of England and Spain (all supporters of the Confederacy), violated the Monroe Doctrine and sent an invading army into Mexico. Interested in carving a slice of America for himself, Napoleon ousted the Mexican president, Benito Juárez, and in 1864 installed the ill-fated Archduke Maximilian of Austria as the puppet emperor of Mexico. The episode, a sorry blend of sordid international intrigue, comic-opera plot, and human tragedy, came to an end in 1867, when the French withdrew from Mexico after receiving a forceful warning from Secretary of State William Seward. The vulnerable but stubborn Maximilian, who unreasonably insisted on remaining behind to protect his "throne," was captured by Juárez's men, and despite official efforts by the United States government to secure his release, he was court-martialed and executed in June 1867. Maximilian died like a prince. As he faced the firing squad, he pointed to his heart and said, "*Muchachos* ["boys"], aim well, and aim right here."

MAXY!

by Silex.

On the other side the ocean they have lords and grand dukes
  plenty,
And vacancies are getting scarce for more than one in twenty,
So one of them call'd Maxy, has come out here to settle,
And squatted down right on the peak of Popocatepetl!
  CHORUS.
  Oh Maxy! Maxy! Maxy! oh Maximilian! oh! ho! ho! ho!
  Right upon the crater of Popocatepetl!
  Oh Maxy! Maxy! Maxy! oh Maximilian, well! well!
  Don't you feel a little warm on Popocatepetl?

He went to see the Pope of Rome and got a dispensation,
To quench the fires of freedom in that great volcanic nation,
While all the kings and emperors are in an awful pucker,
To see how royalty would fare rigged out in bib and tucker.
  CHORUS.

Why Maxy didn't you know it how America departed,
From all that kind of policy when Yankee Doodle started?
And foreigners that come out now, round here to cut their
  capers,
Before they go to bossing things, must first take out their
  papers!
  CHORUS.

And don't you know how Uncle Sam gave royalty its clearance,
And stuck a pin right there and said, "No foreign interference!"
And when he gets Jeff Davis hung you ought to know full well
He'll touch your great volcano off, and send you straight to Austria!
  CHORUS.
  Oh Maxy! Maxy! Maxy! oh Maximilian! oh! ho! ho! ho!
  Won't you have a fast time getting out of Mexico!
  Oh Maxy! Maxy! Maxy! oh Maximilian oh! ho! ho!
  Won't you have a fast time *then* getting out of Mexico!

The public's reaction to Maximilian's presence in Mexico was set to music by no less a composer than Joseph Philbrick Webster, whose sentimental ballad of lost love, "Lorena," was one of the most popular and influential songs of the Civil War (see page 414). So powerful had been its subversive influence that some Southern officers blamed the loss of the war on "Lorena." No soft sentiment was wasted in Webster's song about Maximilian, however.

GET OUT OF MEXICO!

Words by E. B. Dewing. Music by J. P. Webster.

While old Uncle Sam was busy
  Not so very long ago
With his dear rebellious children,
  There crept into Mexico
From across the bright blue water,
  Under "Nap's" imperial wing,
A young scion of the Hapsburgs,
  Who was spoiling to be King.
    CHORUS.
    Oh, poor Max, there's no use talking
      So pack up your kit and go,
    For the Universal Nation says,
      "Get out of Mexico!
    Get out of Mexico!
    Get out of Mexico!"
    For the Universal Nation says,
      "Get out of Mexico!"

Now political tradition,
  Since the time of James Monroe,
Had prevented interference
  In affairs of Mexico,
By the crowned heads of Europe,
  Until just the moment when
Uncle Sam had both his hands full
  With some desp'rate naughty men.
    Get out, &c.

"Nappy" thought the great Republic
  So by war and faction torn,
That no more in pride and triumph
  Would the starry flag be borne;
But in spite of British cruisers,
  Notwithstanding French intrigue,
Proudly floats that tri-hued banner
  Over every native league.
    Get out, &c.

Now our "cruel war is over,"
  We're united all once more,
Universal peace and freedom
  Haply reign from shore to shore—
Uncle Sam has thirty million
  Loyal hearts, who want to know
If the vagrant, Maximilian,
  Won't get out of Mexico.
    Get out, &c.

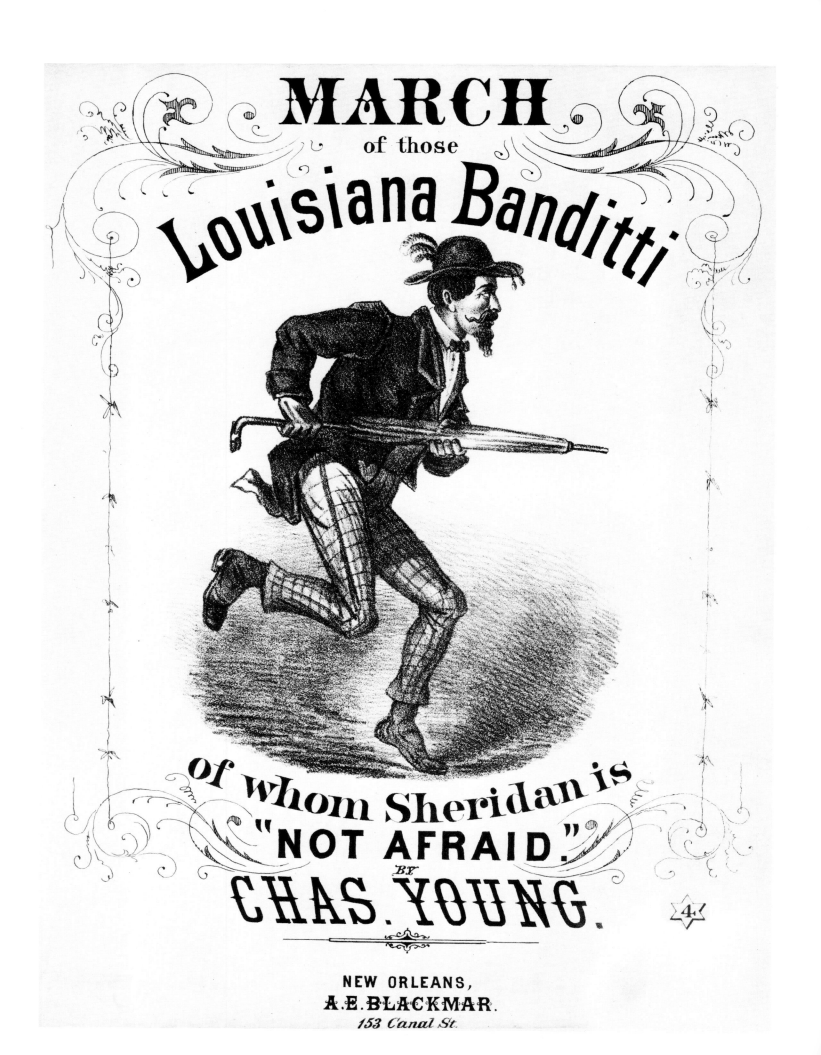

O I'M A GOOD OLD REBEL

*Two sheet music covers illustrating Southern resistance to Reconstruction: a
tongue-in-cheek reference to General Philip Sheridan, who was military administrator
for the district of Louisiana and Texas under the Reconstruction Act, passed in
1867 over President Johnson's veto; and the rugged rebel on the cover of
Innes Randolph's song (page 437)*

The pro-Johnson cartoon decorating the cover of "The Veto Galop" depicts people cheering on the sidelines as Andrew Johnson, astride the noble steed Constitution and brandishing a veto, tramples his adversaries, identified as "dead ducks." They are the journalist John Wien Forney, the Radical congressmen Thaddeus Stevens and Benjamin Franklin Wade, and the Abolitionists Wendell Phillips and Frederick Douglass. The Freedmen's Bureau, seen toppled at the right, was the official federal agency formed after the war for aiding Negroes in the South; it was extended and expanded in 1866 over Johnson's veto.

IMPEACHMENT SONG.

The "Rumps" are all assembling,
  Impeachment is at hand.
And Johnson is a coming
  To be put on the stand.

  CHORUS.
  This is a funny play,
  And all of us can say:
  That there is no right
  In this Impeachment fight!

The father of the "Greenbacks,"
  Will occupy the chair,
And all the other Cossacks,
  Will judge or foul or fair,

But hush, they are commencing—
  Now, hear the idle tale,
It just amounts to nothing
  And smelleth very stale!

'Tis all about Ned Stanton,
  Enough to make one sick,
Why not send him to Canton,
  And tell him there to "Stick."

Hear Sumner, the "Athenian,"
  Discuss this bogus case—
He fighteth like a Fenian,
  For Sambo and his race!

Old Thad, the fierce "Dictator,"
  Who brought about this scene,
Is every way a traitor!
  And wants the Guillotine.

The "Rumps" keep busy gaping,
  As jurors always will,
They rather would be tapping
  At Uncle Sammy's till.

But Johnson, my dear fellow,
  They'll never put you out,
Though Wade may want your pillow
  To rest his ugly snout!

Now let them give their Verdict,
  And be it, what it may,
The people in this conflict
  Will have the final say!

In February 1868 Andrew Johnson furnished his enemies in the legislative branch with the pretext they sought to impeach him when he violated the Tenure of Office Act (passed over his veto in March 1867) by dismissing Secretary of War Edwin M. Stanton without the advice and consent of the Senate. Defining this action as a "high misdemeanor," the House of Representatives voted 126 to 47 to impeach the president; but at his trial, despite unrelenting attack and pressure by Radical Republicans, he managed to scrape by with only one vote under the two-thirds majority needed to convict him.

Johnson had his supporters as well, one of whom, L. A. Dochez, was impelled to translate his support into song. In his "Impeachment Song," "the father of the 'Greenbacks'" is Chief Justice Salmon P. Chase, who presided at the impeachment trial; "Ned Stanton," whose banishment to Canton is suggested, is the controversial war secretary, who came from Ohio; "Sumner, the 'Athenian'" is the eloquent Boston Abolitionist Charles Sumner, who with "Old Thad, the fierce 'Dictator,'" worked tirelessly for Johnson's downfall; "Wade" is Benjamin F. Wade who, as president pro tempore of the Senate, was the hotly eager heir designate to the presidency.

Andrew Johnson was not present at his impeachment trial, but so many others clamored for admittance that it was necessary to issue tickets.

THE FATHERHOOD OF GOD
AND
THE BROTHERHOOD OF MAN.

What will the bigots do
 When they see the hosts advance,
With banners streaming high,
 And its motto shall entrance,
As the golden words they read,
 They will quickly join the van,
And vote for equal suffrage,
 And brotherhood of man.
  CHORUS.
For the Fatherhood of God,
 And the brotherhood of man,
With universal suffrage
 Is spreading thro' the land,
For the Fatherhood of God,
 And the Brotherhood of man,
We'll talk and sing while on the wing,
 And ring it thro' the land.

Columbia's sons now lead the way,
 And rally to the standard
Of equal rights for one and all,
 Though once to slavery pandered,
Our country shall this banner bear,
 Free suffrage is its motto,
For liberty we'll work you see,
 And vote the way we ought to.
  CHORUS.

Now peace on earth, the hosts above
 Proclaim the nation's free,
And all both black and white enjoy
 The boon of liberty,
We claim no creed for class or clan,
 But cherish all the good,
While round the world
 There soon will be our common brotherhood.
  CHORUS.

List ye sorrow stricken sisters
 To the voice of truth today,
On the world the sun is rising,
 Error's clouds shall flee away,
True hearts waiting for the dawning
 Earnest seers their joys foretold,
Look! oh look! the field of promise
 White with harvest rich as gold,
Ever hopeful, never doubting,
 Always working for the right,
Loving, waiting, watching, longing
 For the millennial dawn of light.
  CHORUS.
For the Fatherhood of God,
 And the brotherhood of man,
This message that the angels bring,
 We'll sing it thro' the land,
For the Fatherhood of God
 And the brotherhood of man,
We'll talk and sing for woman's cause,
 Do all the good we can.

"For the Fatherhood of God and the Brotherhood of Man,
We'll talk and sing while on the wing, and ring it through the land."

BY

JOHN W. HUTCHINSON,

AUTHOR OF

"One Hundred years hence," "Clear the Way, for Woman Voting," "Will the New Year come to night Mother," "Freemen, let your shouts arise," "Vote right along," "No Tear in Heaven."—CHANT.

PUBLISHED BY JOHN W. HUTCHINSON.

Entered, according to act of Congress, A. D., 1868, by J. W. Hutchinson, in the Clerk's office of the Dist. Court of the U. S. for the Northern Dist. of Illinois.

While idealistic Northern reformers in the late 1860s envisioned an equitable new world wherein all men—and even some women—were brothers, Southerners in the throes of Radical Reconstruction—and therefore perhaps less attuned to universal brotherhood—were being invaded by political and material fortune hunters from the North, contemptuously known as "carpetbaggers." The name referred to a current fashion in hand luggage.

THE CARPET-BAGGER.

I'm a gay old Carpet-Bagger!
 O! don't you understand?
'Mong the color'd folks I swagger
 Down in the cotton land.
Now I got no eddication;
 Of brains I does not brag,
But I owns a big plantation
 All in my carpet bag.
  CHORUS.
 I'm a gay old Carpet-Bagger!
  O! can't you understand?
 'Mong the color'd folks I swagger
  Down in the cotton land.

In the North I was Nobody,
 O! don't you understand?
Now I drinks my wine, and toddy,
 King of the cotton land!
For I drives the old slave master;
 He calls me scallawag
While he cusses fast, and faster,
 I fills my carpet bag.
  CHORUS.

General Grant was nominated by acclamation at the Republican national convention in Chicago on May 20, 1868. When the hero's name was submitted, pandemonium broke loose, and the musicians we see in the orchestra pit of the handsome theater, where the convention was held, anticipatively struck up "Hail to the Chief."

Since General Grant—in common with other glamorous military heroes singled out for the presidency—possessed an exceedingly sparse political background, the Republican bards of 1868 were largely forced to promote him with catalogs-in-song of his great Civil War achievements. Ignoring the crucial current issues of Reconstruction and Negro suffrage, the pro-Grant songs consisted predominantly of refought battles, to which were added lauds of Grant's lovable characteristics—his reticence and his fondness for cigars.

In the following song, "Foote" is Commodore Andrew Hull Foote, who aided Grant in his capture of Fort Donelson, Tennessee, in 1862; "the doughty Pem." is John Clifford Pemberton, the Northern-born Confederate general who surrendered Vicksburg to Grant on July 4, 1863; "no more WAR" refers to Grant's letter of acceptance of his nomination, which he ended with the celebrated words that became the great Republican campaign slogan of 1868: "Let us have peace." The lyricist's identity was disguised by a suitably military-sounding pun.

FOR PRESIDENT, ULYSSES GRANT, A-SMOKING HIS CIGAR.

Words by Ason O'Fagun. Music by J. P. Webster.

At Donelson the rebel horde
　　Had gathered in their might,
Determined there with fire and sword
　　To make a dreadful fight.
But gallant Foote, with his command,
　　Went "in" by water route,
While Grant besieged upon the land,
　　And smoked the rebels "out."
　　CHORUS.
　　Where volleyed thunder loudest pealed,
　　　　Along the front of war,
　　The Gen'ral calmly viewed the field,
　　　　A-smoking his cigar.

And Beauregard did swear, methinks,
　　Upon his bended knee,
That his good horse should have some drinks,
　　All from the Tennessee;
But ah! a "slip twixt cup and lip"
　　That sweet illusion broke;
For Grant just smote 'em thigh and hip,
　　And made the rebels smoke. (CHORUS.)

The doughty Pem. at Vicksburg, too,
　　Did naught of Yankees fear;
Grant passed his guns in quick review,
　　And gained the city's rear.
He pitched his tent, deployed his force,
　　And lighted cigar;
Said he, "Misguided lads, of course
　　You know just where you are." (CHORUS.)

— — —

And now, let politicians wait,
　　There's work for men to do;
We'll place one in the Chair of State
　　Who wears the army blue;
The people know just what they want—
　　Less TALK, and no more WAR—
FOR PRESIDENT, ULYSSES GRANT,
　　A-SMOKING his CIGAR!

Continuing in John Tyler's pattern, Andrew Johnson vainly sought to be renominated in 1868. As early as 1866 he had made his celebrated "swing around the circle" as far as Chicago, during which his unfortunate "electioneering" speeches had not only added fuel to the growing congressional conflagration but had also gained him legions of new enemies.

When Johnson was finally repudiated by his own party at the Democratic convention, opening on July 4, 1868, at New York's new Tammany Hall, the Republicans serenaded him with a cruel farewell song. From the *Grant Campaign Songster* (1868):

GOOD-BY! ANDY!

Air, "Jim Crack Corn."

Good-by, Andy, clear the way,
　　You're a dog that's had his day,
Your other days you'd better spend
　　In thinking of your latter end.
　　CHORUS.
　　Good-by, Andy, good-by!
　　Good-by, Andy, good-by!
　　Good-by, Andy, good-by!
　　　Git! and clear the way!

Maybe, down in Tennessee,
　　You'll find folks that will agree,
You're the same old chap they sent
　　From Alderman to President.
　　Good-by, Andy, good-by! &c.

Go it! You're not wanted here,
　　We've got a man to fill "that cheer,"
All your usefullness is o'er,
　　So grope around and find the door!
　　Good-by, Andy, good-by! &c.

Now, old fellow, don't get mad,
　　Swearing is so awful bad!
Just take it easy as you can,
　　And try to be a better man!
　　Good-by, Andy, good-by! &c.

Don't be troubled by your fears,
　　Take again the same old shears,
You're better in your tailor shop,
　　Than of the government on top.
　　Good-by, Andy, good-by! &c.

Keep your temper! Draw it fine!
　　Slide on down your greased incline!
You slipped your neck Impeachment through
　　But cannot dodge election too!
　　Good-by, Andy, good-by! &c.

Go it, Andy, slide on down!
　　Go it, to your native town!
And think, at last, when you get there,
　　You're the man we all could spare.
　　Good-by, Andy, good-by! &c.

　　CHORUS.
　　Good-by, Andy, good-by!
　　Good-by, Andy, good-by!
　　Good-by, Andy, good-by!
　　　Git! and clear the way!

The Democrats' nominee for president was Horatio Seymour, the wartime governor of New York, around whose name floated reverberations of Copperheadism; for vice-president they chose the fiery and problematical General Francis P. Blair, Jr., of Missouri, a committed Abolitionist, whose opposition to Radical Reconstruction, however, had caused him to break violently with the Republican party. Like many of his political contemporaries, Blair had a reputation for being a heavy drinker, and opposition propagandists did not allow the electorate to forget it.

Apart from Andrew Johnson, disappointed Democratic presidential aspirants included two Ohioans, "Gentleman George" Pendleton, who advocated the redemption of government bonds in greenbacks rather than specie, and Chief Justice Salmon P. Chase, whose unquenchable lust for the presidency was exceeded only by his daughter's ambition to be first lady. These characters were sharply lampooned in an unusual, satirical campaign song pretending to have been written by a popular fictitious Democrat, Petroleum V. Nasby (its real author was W. W. Bridewell). Nasby was an outrageous caricature of an ignorant, homespun, Copperhead preacher, whose grossly misspelled political imbecilities turned a merciless spotlight on the evils and corruptions of current Democratic politics. Nasby's creator was David Ross Locke, the most gifted and influential political satirist of his time; he had been greatly admired by Lincoln.

NASBY'S LAMENT
OVER THE NEW YORK NOMINATIONS.

I'm weeping, feller dimmycrats,
  A sorry tale I'll tell
About the New York nomenees,—
  About the Yankee sell;
I bet a hat on Pendleton—
  Was certain I would win;
I feel that I have been picked up
  And badly taken in.

They couldn't get enuff uv men
  To nominate in full,
They tuk an abolitionist,
  To make the ticket whole.
I swore I woudn't vote for Chase
  To ask it wasn't fair,
But then I'd rather vote for him
  Than vote for Mister Blair.

Our idol was a western man,
  And whiskey rather high,
And greenbacks getting up to par,
  And Dimmycrats were dry;
We thot we had a ded shure thing,
  But O, what made 'em go
And nominate a crazy man?
  It hurts my feelings so!

The Yankees play'd the game tu strong,
  And dimmycrats ar sold,
The late unpleasantness in mind
  Is not so very old;—
To take a man that salt won't save,
  So orful hard to keep,—
Who used to butcher dimmycrats,
  Is going most tu steep.

The corners now are hung with crape,
  The winder blinds ar down,
I feel dimmocracy is ded
  As any nail in town;
I'll seek a place whar whiskey flows,
  And lay me down to die,—
Demmocrisy must shut up shop—
  O how I want to cry!
    CHORUS.
    O, how I want to cry,
     I am so orful dry;
    We've been picked up and taken in,—
     Demmocrisy will die.

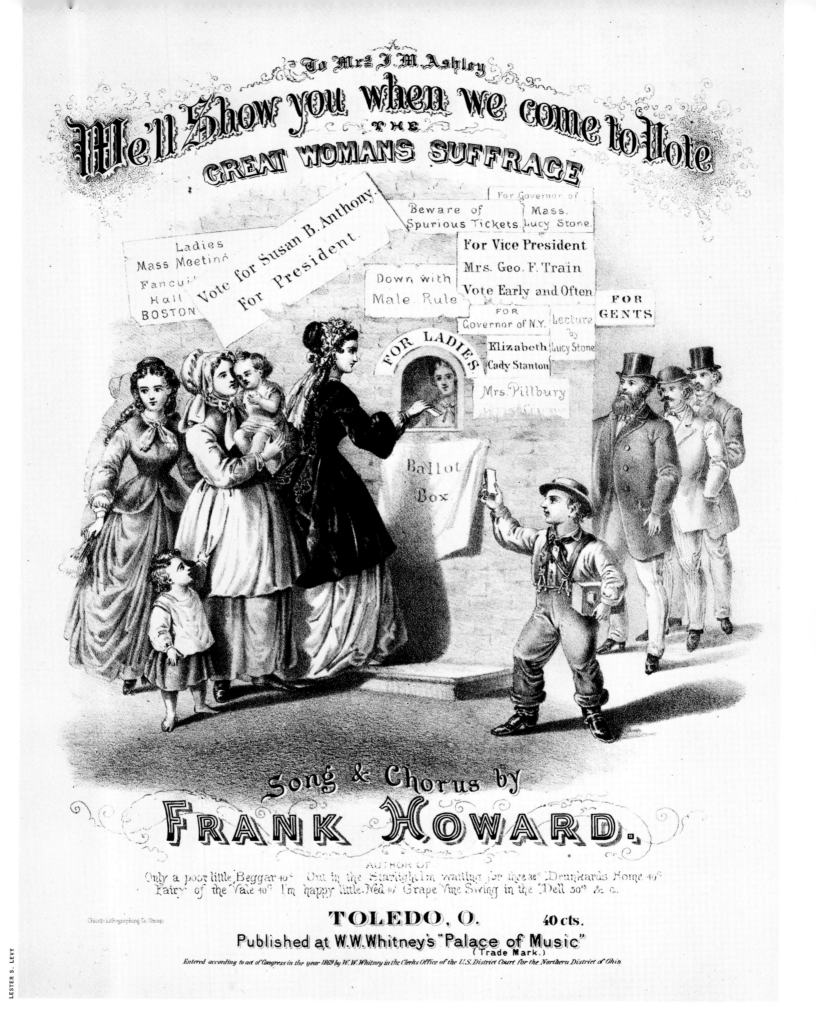

The sheet music cover for this song satirizing women's suffrage projected the balloting place of the future, with segregated his-and-hers voting booths and the walls plastered with feminist posters.

Not one, but two, women's suffrage conventions met in Chicago on February 11 and 12, 1869, when dissenting members of the Sorosis Society split from the main convention and held their own meeting. The *New-York Times* (February 12) reported, with a faint tinge of sarcasm: "The Sorosis Division No. 1, aristocratic branch, met in Crosby's Music Hall, and Division No. 2 in the Library Hall, the latter meeting being the stronger." There was good reason for the superior strength of Division No. 2. Perhaps more accurately designated as the National Woman Suffrage Association, it was led by Susan B. Anthony and Elizabeth Cady Stanton, the principal pioneers in the nineteenth-century struggle for women's rights. Their enlightened concepts continued to guide their successors in the ongoing struggle more than a century later. On consciousness raising (according to the *Times*), "Miss Anthony . . . rejoiced at the agitation and division of the Chicago Sorosis as the proof that women were asserting their rights." And on the balanced benefits to be derived from equality of the sexes, Mrs. Stanton declared that "the best way to develop a high manhood [was] to elevate woman."

Editorial reaction to the women's movement was composed equally of indignation and heavy-handed ridicule, with perhaps a slight tilt toward the ridicule. In a long, anti-feminist *New-York Times* editorial (February 25, 1869), titled "The Woman Question," the author concluded with a tongue-in-cheek offer to support women's rights, but only if he were "knighted with the Order of the Garter and the Cross of the Dishcloth." This reprehensible level of satire —and worse—was translated into male-chauvinist-oriented comic songs, of which the following example by Frank Howard, making women out to be silly, vain, and selfish creatures, is perhaps more revealing of men than it was meant to be.

WE'LL SHOW YOU WHEN WE COME TO VOTE.
The Great Womans Suffrage.

Oh, how we suffer, maids and wives,
Although our wants are very slight;
How sad and dreary pass our lives,
Now who can say it's right?
We're snubbed at night and we're snubbed at morn,
And looked upon the same as slaves;
We're treated oft with contempt and scorn,
By the men, the cruel knaves.
    CHORUS.

Oh, Sad is the life of womankind,
Trod under foot we've always been,
But when we vote, you soon will find
That we'll fix these "terrible men."

~~~

Of course we know each word is false,
That's said of Mistress William Brown,
That she so dearly loves to walk
And flirt about the town;
They say she leaves Mister B. alone,
And out to "suffrage circles" goes,
While he the little ones rocks at home,
Which I'm sure quite plainly shows. (CHORUS.)

~~~

The first woman to run for president was the notorious Victoria Claflin Woodhull, who in 1872 virtually nominated herself as the candidate of the so-called Equal Rights party. Mrs. Woodhull, one of the more flamboyant apparitions of nineteenth-century America, had arrived at this eminence by devious paths—as a practitioner of the exotic arts of spiritualism, mesmerism, and clairvoyance; as a pitchperson for travelling medicine shows; and as a participant in a number of alliances, matrimonial and otherwise. With her sister and faithful collaborator, Tennessee Claflin, Mrs. Woodhull made her way to New York, where, under the impartial, benevolent wing of Commodore Cornelius Vanderbilt, both ladies made a spectacular killing on Wall Street. Far from reticent about her advocacy and enthusiastic practice of free love, Mrs. Woodhull took to the concept of women's liberation like a fish to water. Attempting to seize control of the National Woman Suffrage Association, but foiled by the ever-watchful Miss Anthony, Mrs. Woodhull managed to engineer her own nomination, and she promoted it with articles and campaign songs in *Woodhull and Claflin's Weekly*, a newspaper created expressly for the purpose.

Apparently Frederick Douglass, the great black reformer, discovered that he had been named as Mrs. Woodhull's running mate only when he read about it in the papers. Horrified, he promptly disclaimed the nomination in an open letter to the press. Douglass is named in the following Woodhull campaign song from *Woodhull and Claflin's Weekly* (June 1, 1872). The Grundys in the title are the classic personification of prudery—particularly Mrs. Grundy.

THE GRUNDYS.
Air—"Comin' thro' the Rye!"

If you nominate a woman,
  In the month of May;
Dare you face what Mrs. Grundy
  And her set will say?
How they will jeer, frown, and slander,
  Chattering night and day;
Oh! did you dream of Mrs. Grundy
  In the month of May?

If you nominate a Negro
  In the month of May;
Dare you face what Mr. Grundy
  And his chums will say?
How they'll swear, and drink, and bluster,
  Raging night and day;
Oh! did you dream of Mr. Grundy
  In the month of May?

Yes! Victoria we've selected,
  For our chosen head:
With Fred Douglass on our ticket
  We will raise the dead.
Then around them let us rally
  Without fear or dread:
And, next March, we'll put the Grundys
  In their little bed.

THE PRESIDENT'S MARCH.

COMPOSED AND DEDICATED TO
GENERAL U.S. GRANT
by FEDERICO GENNARI.

WASHINGTON. D.C.
Published by JOHN F. ELLIS, 306 Penn: Ave.

LESTER S. LEVY

Considering his sorry record, Grant's unanimous renomination at the Republican national convention in Philadelphia on June 5 was scarcely less bizarre. And to complete the curious political picture, the Democrats, meeting at Baltimore on July 9, adopted the Liberal Republican ticket, albeit unwillingly. A Southern delegate summed up the nomination by saying: "If the party puts Greeley into our hymn book we'll sing him through if it kills us."

Electioneering songs in 1872 tended more toward vitriolic character assassination than self-praise, no doubt with good reason. Greeley songs dwelt on Grant's nepotism and his corrupt appointees, and they often resorted to feeble word-play, addressing Grant as "Useless." Grant minstrels countered by calling Greeley a "Chappaquack" (Greeley's farm was at Chappaqua, New York) and making fun of his idiosyncratic mode of dress (he affected a long white duster and a white hat, garb that his adherents regarded as endearing, if not downright admirable).

Grant's relatives and henchmen offered endless grist to the mills of opposition songwriters. For example, in the text of a "Greeley and Gratz Campaign Song" from *The Farmer of Chappaqua Songster* (1872), "the Dents" are Colonel Frederick Dent, Grant's father-in-law, a frequent visitor at the White House, and Frederick Tracy Dent, Grant's brother-in-law, who served as his military secretary after he became president; "Murphy" is Thomas Murphy, an odorous New York politician, who wrought spectacular political corruption at the New York Customhouse after having been appointed as its head by the New York State political boss, Roscoe Conkling, one of Grant's preferred henchmen.

Hero though he was, Ulysses Simpson Grant proved to be a dismal failure as a president. Lacking the essential qualities and qualifications to administer his office adequately, Grant displayed consistently poor judgment in choosing his associates; he stubbornly persisted in surrounding himself with men of such deplorable political and moral caliber that his administration came to be regarded as the most corrupt in American history—at least until the days of Richard Milhous Nixon. The peculations of Grant's friends and relatives, with whom he filled the key government posts, cast a shadow over the president, who himself was accused of having no objections to receiving nice gifts.

By the time the election season of 1872 came around, a group of liberal Republicans had broken away from the parent party, and on May 1 they held an independent convention at Cincinnati, where they made their bizarre nominations of Horace Greeley, the eminent but eccentric editor of the New York *Tribune*, for president and Benjamin Gratz Brown, the alcoholically inclined governor of Missouri, as his partner.

GREELEY AND GRATZ CAMPAIGN SONG.

Air—"Not for Joseph."

When Useless came to Washington
    He wore a jaunty plume,
The Dents and Murphys crowded in
    And drove him to his doom.
His nephews and his cousins all
    Came up to win the race,
And every man who gave a dog
    Was sure to get a place.

And therefore, so, accordingly, all the people say and sing:

Down with Grant, Useless Grant!
Up with Greeley, good old Greeley!
Down with Grant, Useless Grant!
Hurrah for Greeley! Old White Hat!

The "Hiram" addressed in this song from *The Sun's Greeley Campaign Songster*, "published from the offices of the New York *Sun*" (1872), is none other than President Grant, who was baptized Hiram Ulysses. In the text, George Robeson is Grant's venal secretary of the navy, whose dealings in that office were so reprehensible as to prompt Congress to conduct an investigation of them; "the Rev. Cramer" is Michael John Cramer, another of Grant's innumerable brothers-in-law, who had been appointed United States consul to Leipzig by Andrew Johnson, but who was elevated by Grant to the ambassadorship to Denmark; "Ben Butler" is the former Civil War general, now a congressman, who was apparently as mighty a bottleman as his chief; "Forney" is the journalist John Wien Forney, seemingly as antagonistic to Grant as he had been to Johnson.

HIRAM'S MENAGERIE.
Air—The Battle-Cry of Freedom.

Hiram had a little *lamb*,
George Robeson was his name,
  Shouting the battle-cry of plunder:
And every time the master robbed,
The lamb would do the same,
  Shouting the battle-cry of plunder.
CHORUS.
Greeley forever! Hurrah, boys, hurrah!
Pack off Ulysses to dwell with his pa.
We'll rally round our flag, boys,
We'll rally round our flag,
Shouting for Greeley and the Union!

Hiram had a wicked *goat*,
The Rev. Cramer named,
  Shouting the battle-cry of plunder;
But he got flogged in Leipzig
By a man he had defamed.
  And that made Grant's parson swear "By th-nd-r!"
CHORUS.

Hiram had a *bison* bold,
Ben Butler, fierce and grim,
  Shouting the battle-cry of plunder;
But Hiram "bottled" Butler, and
Ben Butler bottled him—
  May both bottles never burst asunder!
CHORUS.

~~~

Hiram had a sly *fox*,
Who two papers edited,
  Shouting the battle-cry of plunder;
But Forney soon will bury Hiram
Deep among the dead,
  For this good fox hates to make a blunder.
CHORUS.

Now all ye honest people, do
Come in and see the show,
  Shouting the battle-cry of Greeley!
For when November fifth comes round
These *animules* must go,
  Shedding their briny tears right freely.
CHORUS.

The following song, a popular success, varied the usual theme of Grant's nepotism with a reference to his country place at Long Branch, New Jersey, a kind of Camp-David-cum-Key-Biscayne of the 1870s, where the president liked to relax by driving a team of spirited horses. A derisive mention of Grant's aborted attempt in 1871 to annex Santo Domingo is thrown in for good measure.

HORACE AND NO RELATIONS.

There was a jolly President,
  Who should have been a resident
Of Washington the Cap'tol of the Nation;
  At Long Branch he did reside,
  With Tom Murphy by his side,
To help increase the profits of his station.

  CHORUS.
  O no we don't belong,
  And we'll never sing a song,
To Ulysses and the office holder's party;
  For Horace and no relations
  To fill the public stations,
We'll work and vote with pleasure true and hearty.

First they tried on San Domingo,
  But they couldn't make the thing go.
For the people open'd their eyes and saw clear thro' it.
  So they dropped that little job,
  The Nation's purse to rob,
For they knew the day would come when they would rue it.
  CHORUS.

Next their eyes so very wistfull,
  Cast around to get a fist full
Of the needful cash to fill their empty purses;
  And they fell on cheap relations,
  Who soon filled the public stations—
Carpet-baggers, Uncle's, Aunts and e'en their Nurses.
  CHORUS.

~~~

Respectfully Inscribed
TO THE
Hon: Horace Greeley.

HORACE GREELEY'S GRAND MARCH

Arranged for the
PIANO FORTE
BY
CHARLES GLOVER,
NEW YORK,
Published by Wm. A. Pond & Co. 547 Broadway.

Horace Greeley's eccentric personality and his odd appearance offered a ready-made target for abusive caricaturists and songwriters in 1872. His baby face, incongruously framed by white throat-whiskers (usually pictured carelessly tucked into one side of his collar), his straggly white locks haloing a shiny bald head, his unconventional long white overcoat and hat, and his thousand-and-one other quirks and fads were unmercifully lampooned to make him appear ridiculous in the eyes of the electorate. Greeley was quoted as sometimes wondering whether he was running for the presidency or the penitentiary.

Despite his offbeat characteristics and his unsuitability for the presidency, Horace Greeley made a matchless contribution to nineteenth-century America. As founder and editor of the innovative and influential New York *Tribune*, Greeley for thirty years devoted his powerful editorial gifts to furthering liberal causes and combating social and political inequities. He fought slavery, monopolies, capital punishment, and other ills of his times, while he supported human rights, laborers' rights, and even—mildly—women's rights. A patchwork of contradictions, Greeley also espoused a wide gamut of crackpot schemes and fads, from spiritualism and health foods to free love. Perhaps his greatest failing was his unappeasable and unappeased desire for political office, for which he was in every way unfitted.

Tragically, Greeley survived his overwhelming defeat at the polls on November 5 by only a few weeks. Emotionally exhausted and succumbing to depression over his wife's death on October 30, his political annihilation, and the shock of learning that he had lost control of his beloved *Tribune*, Greeley suffered a mental collapse and died on November 29, 1872. President Grant attended his funeral.

During the heat of the campaign, the *New-York Times* (September 26, 1872) published the following anti-Greeley song and reported it as having been sung by the Union Glee Club at a Grant Republican rally at Cooper Institute. In the text, *Free Love* and *Free Farms* refer to Greeley enthusiasms. A committed disciple of agrarianism, Greeley's zeal for farming had culminated in a book published in 1871, *What I Know of Farming*, used by both sides for their separate political purposes. *Free-trade* is a sardonic reference to an area of unresolved dissension among Liberal Republicans; "Bill Seward and Weed" (Thurlow) were formerly—but no longer—Greeley's colleagues and supporters. "Doolittle" is James Root Doolittle, a former Republican, who had cast his lot with the Democrats in 1871; "Banks" is Nathaniel Prentiss Banks, a Republican congressman who, as a result of a quarrel with President Grant, changed sides and supported Greeley; "honest Bill Tweed" is the infamous archcrook and Tammany boss, William Marcy Tweed; "Belmont" is August Belmont, a powerful New York Democrat; "Schurz" is Senator Carl Schurz, a chief motivator of the Liberal Republican heresy; "sore-headed Fenton" is Reuben Eaton Fenton, governor of New York in 1864, and now an opponent of Grant and a supporter of Greeley; "one Burr" is unidentified.

THE GREELEY PILL.
Mixed at Cincinnati and taken at Baltimore,
July 10, 1872.

Air—"The Mistletoe Bough."

There was an old doctor who wore a white hat;
He made pills of Free Love and Free Farms and all that;
Patent pills of pig-iron and copper and wool,
And expected to cure Free-trade with 'em, the fool.
And, first to be seen like a quack at a fair,
That Chappaquack mounted an editor's chair,
With one pant in one boot and he sung but one tune,
That the pill for all ill was his daily *Tribune*.
 Oh, the *Tribune* old pill!
 Oh, the Greeley old pill!

Then he politics tried, and sought as Republican
To feed at the public crib, drink from the public can.
Bill Seward and Weed took him in as a partner,
But the share that pill brought wasn't what he was arter;
For the fee that he sought was an office of trust,
To be of the upper political crust.
For this he called all Southern Democrats knaves,
And he hated them more than he loved their poor slaves.
 Oh, the political pill!
 Oh, the Greeley old pill!

So he cut the concern, and to farming he went;
What he knew about farming wasn't worth a red cent,
He grew broom-corn to get the broom-handles for lumber;
He planted a cow, and he milked the cow-cumber.
But although in his farming things looked rather mixed,
He in politics soon got himself snugly fixed
By not knowing, when Tammany Rings were in vogue,
A Republican saint from a Tammany rogue.
 Oh, the farming old pill!
 Oh, the Greeley old pill!

When the plague of secession broke out this quack cried,
"Oh, this plague may kill some one; the Union must slide."
So the Democrats said, "You're the doctor we want;
Doctor Lincoln we killed, but our death is this Grant.
His practice with Kuklux is thorough and bold,
And he leaves the big rebels all out in the cold.
Help, Tammany friends in Republican ranks!
Come, Greeley, Doolittle! we'll take even Banks."
 Oh, the Tammany pill!
 Oh, the Greeley old pill!

Then Seymour and Belmont and honest Bill Tweed,
Schurz, Sumner and sore-headed Fenton, agreed
To follow the war-path no more, but instead
To bury the hatchet in Doctor Grant's head;
And while dying Democracy's blood was yet warm
Let Greeley prescribe his new pill called Reform:
Reform poor Democracy up on her feet,
Reform himself into good Doctor Grant's seat.
 Oh, the reforming old pill!
 Oh, the Greeley old pill!

Democracy lay on her Baltimore bed,
No mortal could tell whether living or dead.
Doctor Greeley appeared, and said, "My dear friend,
My ends will be served by postponing your end,
Just settle your stomach to settle my bill,
And take me down quickly, for *I* am the pill."
Belmont shuts her eyes and one Burr holds her nose;
A gasp opens her mouth, and down Greeley goes.
 Oh, that Baltimore pill!
 Oh, that Greeley old pill!

Our Next President

Horace Greeley's March

as played by

GRAFULLAS SEVENTH REG.T BAND.

NEW YORK **HORACE WATERS** 481 BROADWAY,
Publisher of Sheet Music, Music Books &c.

MANUFACTURER & DEALER in PIANOS MELODEONS & ORGANS.

On April 22, 1874, while the country was in the throes of severe economic depression following the drastic financial panic of the year before, President Grant, after a certain amount of vacillation, vetoed the Inflation Bill, which had proposed as a relief measure to maintain a permanent circulation of four hundred million dollars in greenbacks, not supported by specie reserve. The antigreenback New York *Tribune* (January 19, 1874), now edited by Whitelaw Reid, had waxed passionate against the impending bill, resorting to parable: "If a healthy man cuts his finger, experience teaches that the wound will heal. It is not essential to the cure that the wound be wrapped in greenbacks. . . . Yet as long as there are quacks and fools the former will be able to persuade the latter that the greenback is a marvelous specific for cut fingers." Other inflations, other cures.

Inflationary dance music appeared with an inspired political cartoon on its cover depicting, on the left (according to Lester S. Levy), Senators Oliver P. Morton of Indiana and Matthew H. Carpenter of Wisconsin, who, with Senator Benjamin F. Butler of Massachusetts, are busily blowing up the inflation balloon. Sprawled on its top is Senator Carl Schurz of Missouri, desperately straining to hold it down, while at the right stands an undecided-looking Grant, with cigar in mouth and air hose in hand.

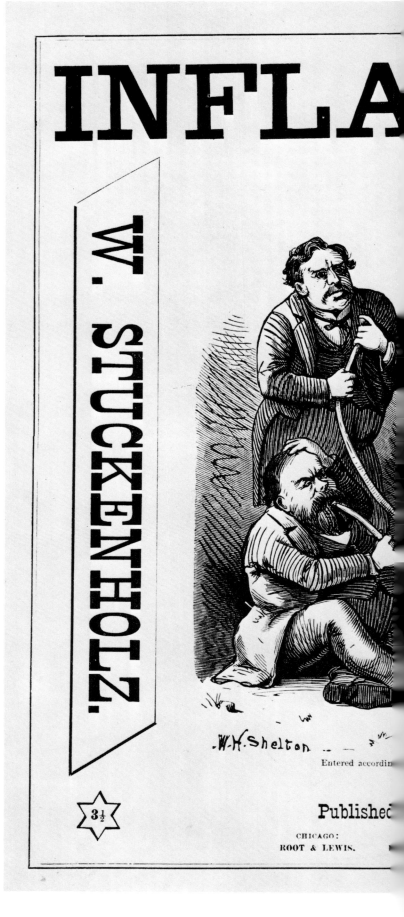

INFLA

W. STUCKENHOLZ.

.W.H.Shelton.

Entered accordin

3½

Published

CHICAGO:
ROOT & LEWIS.

458

TION GALOP!

COMPOSED BY

NEW YORK:

WM. A. POND & CO., 547 Broadway and 39 Union Square.

RGH:	SAN FRANCISCO:	MILWAUKEE:	ST. PAUL:	SAVANNAH:
& BRO.	M. GRAY.	H. N. HEMPSTED.	JOHN A. WEIDE.	LUDDEN & BATES.

Yes, Grant from out the White House
With his thieving crew must "get";
"Addition, division and silence"
Must no longer reign, "you bet."

Tune—"Tommy, Make Room for Your Auntie."

"General Grant's Administration was not an unalloyed success," tactfully understated Ben: Perley Poore. More realistically he continued: "The [Republican] party had sunk under the combined effects of political money making, inflated currency, whiskey rings, revenue frauds, Indian supply steals, and pension swindles. General Grant, though himself honest, appeared unable to discern dishonesty in others. . . ." The president's seemingly unlimited lack of discernment was manifested not only in his impervious tolerance of the outrageous political immoralities that had poisoned his administration but by his expressed desire to continue for a third term. By 1876, however, it was abundantly clear to both parties that massive reform was drastically needed and that a pure candidate would be required to effect it. To this end, the Republicans, at their convention at Cincinnati on June 4, nominated for president Rutherford Birchard Hayes, a comparatively blameless Civil War veteran and third-term governor of Ohio, and for vice-president they picked William Almon Wheeler, a New York congressman. On June 27, at St. Louis, the revivified Democratic party chose as their presidential candidate Samuel Jones Tilden, the multimillionaire governor of New York, who was acclaimed for his successful prosecution of the notorious Tammany ringleader, "Boss" Tweed; and for Tilden's running mate they nominated the Indiana governor Thomas Andrews Hendricks.

Reform was the dominant theme of both parties in 1876, and reform dominated their campaign songs as well. Both sides branded opposing candidates as "sham reformers," and the Democrats implied that all Republican contenders were in some way implicated in the abominations of Grant's regime, which were frequently catalogued. For example, in the following song from the *Hayes and Wheeler Campaign Song Book* (1876), the list of scandals includes *Whiskey rings and revenue robbers*, a reference to the infamous tax fraud known as the "Whiskey Ring," in which millions of dollars in illicit tax abatements were pocketed by distillers in St. Louis and treasury officials in Washington. Grant's private secretary, Orville E. Babcock, was implicated, but the president interceded in his behalf and he was acquitted. *Salary grabbers* refers to the "Salary Grab Act," by which Congress voted itself a fifty-percent salary increase and then voted itself two years of back pay at the new rate. Public indignation brought about the repeal of the Salary Grab, also known as the "Back-Pay Steal." "Railroad robbers" were the vast army of crooked manipulators and wheeler-dealers who dispensed showers of gold into the eager hands of greedy legislators in return for contracts and preferments.

WE'LL VOTE FOR HAYES AND WHEELER.
Air—"Dixie."

In the land of corn and the land of cotton,
Democrats are rife and rotten,
    Look away! look away!
Never again shall the rascals rule us,
Gobble our cash, and trick and fool us,
    Look away! look away!
CHORUS.
So we'll vote for Hayes and Wheeler,
    The statesmen true;
On their brave side we'll stand with pride,
    And vote for Hayes and Wheeler,
We'll vote, and shout, and work for Hayes and Wheeler.

Honesty is what's the matter,
All the ring there is we will scatter,
    Look away! look away!
Driving the rats of the Tammany buildin'
Beating their sham reformer, Tilden,
    Look away! look away! (CHORUS.)

Whiskey rings and revenue robbers,
Salary gobblers, and railroad jobbers,
    Look away! look away!
Leeches that stick to the public pockets,
All must go up and away like rockets,
    Look away! look away! (CHORUS.)

Justice and Truth have long been scanted,
Honesty now is the thing that's wanted,
    Look away! look away!
Look alive then, be sure to remember,
To vote for our Hayes, boys, next November,
    Look away! look away! (CHORUS.)

HAYES
THE TRUE
AND
WHEELER
TOO!
Campaign Song and Chorus.

Adapted from the immensely popular Whig Song of 1840,

"TIPPECANOE AND TYLER TOO."

ARRANGED BY

R. E. PUBLICAN.

NEW YORK:
Published by WM. A. POND & CO., 547 Broadway,
And 39 UNION SQUARE.
Copyright, 1876, by Wm. A. Pond & Co.

The cockaded, three-cornered hat surmounting this campaign portrait of the Democratic candidates is a reminder that the election year coincided with the Centennial of American independence.

The dignified Democratic nominee, Samuel Tilden, incongruously nicknamed "Uncle Sam" for campaign purposes, had enjoyed a distinguished reputation as a political reformer long before the popular pressure for reform in 1876. His vanquishment of the corrupt Tammany boss, William Marcy Tweed, and its attendant events were cruelly distorted in a song in the *Hayes and Wheeler Campaign Song Book*, in which Tilden was made out to have been Tweed's accomplice before becoming his accuser. In the text, "William" is the redoubtable Tweed; "the facile Hoffman" is John Thompson Hoffman, a former Tammany politician, who had become governor of New York through Tammany manipulation but later repudiated the Tweed Ring; "O'Brien" is James O'Brien, a former sheriff and Tammany man who, unsatisfied with his cut of the take, brought the damning evidence of Tweed's gargantuan swindles to the *New-York Times*; "Jones" is George Jones, the publisher of the *Times*, who refused a Tammany bribe of five million dollars and published the facts about Tweed; "Dix" is John Adams Dix, a Republican and Tilden's immediate predecessor as governor of New York; "Canal Rings" refers to a powerful group of crooked politicians and contractors who defrauded the State of New York on repairs and improvements of the state canal system and whom Tilden had put down; the "ugly baby made of rags" refers to inflationary paper money (Hendricks was a "soft money" man).

THE PSALM OF SAMMY TILDEN.

Air—"Auld Lang Syne."

In good Boss Tweed's successful days
 I ruled the State Committee;
But when they found our crooked ways
 O, wasn't it a pity?
CHORUS. I stuck to William fast and true,
   I spent the money stolen;
   I put the facile Hoffman thro'—
   O, wasn't I a cool one?

But when O'Brien gave the *Times*
 Those all convincing figures,
And Jones began to ring the chimes,
 By Jove! I got the rigors! (CHORUS.)

I took the water—dived in fact,
 Played possum for a season,
And, when all safe, came up intact,
 And charged Old Tweed with treason. (CHORUS.)

This plan I've followed all thro' life,
 To keep one eye to leeward,
And when your brother falls in strife
 Haul off awhile to seaward. (CHORUS.)

If he comes up throw out a stick,
 And clasp your arms around him;
If he goes down, give him a kick
 And let him sink, confound him. (CHORUS.)

When Dix had made an easy path,
 I went in for Reform,
Uncorked the vials of my wrath,
 And bared my awful arm. (CHORUS.)

I smote the Canal Rings hip and thigh,
 And marked in this connection,
Your uncle kept a wary eye
 For effect on the election. (CHORUS.)

At last, by hook or crook, I've got
 The longed-for nomination;
But then there is a dreadful blot
 That mars the situation. (CHORUS.)

That ugly baby made of rags
 That Hendricks keeps on nursing,
Out-squalls my most vociferous brags
 And almost sets me cursing. (CHORUS.)

And then to have the people cry
 "Hurrah for Sammy Tilden,
And Tommy Hindrance!" may I die
 And my little bed be filled in! (CHORUS.)

If I don't fear the game is up
 For this old double-dealer!
For men may dine, and men may sup.
 But they'll vote for Hayes and Wheeler! (CHORUS.)

461

Campaign propagandists in 1876 overindulged their predilection for puns and punning imagery, as the symbolic cartoon and the words of this Hayes and Wheeler song illustrate. Even the pseudonymous lyricist, Thomas Peppergrass, relates to the load of "Hayes" that is being "Wheelered" to the White House. The "composer," "Y. D., Esq.," is "Yankee Doodle," who contributed the tune.

ROLL ALONG! ROLL ALONG!
Words by Thomas Peppergrass. Music by Y. D., Esq.

O, in the East and in the West,
  The crop is finely growing,
We wait without a thought of fear
  The days of frost and snowing.

  CHORUS I.
  O, the brisk November days!
    We'll shout the Harvest home, sir,
  When with this honest load of Hayes
    To Washington we come, sir.

  CHORUS II.
  Shout the campaign battle song!
    A mighty load of Hay, sir,
  We roll along, we roll along,
    To Washington this day, sir.

We farmers feel the nation's weal
  Cannot be saved by buildin'
On friends of former Tweedy rings,
  On Hendricks, or on Tilden.
    CHORUS.

We crave no bags of paper rags,
  But love the *golden* grain, sir,
And think hard cash the kind of hash
  We'll feed on in the main, sir.
    CHORUS.

Then Wheeler round your mammoth cart,
  As big as all the town, sir,
And here's a mighty load of Hayes,
  Just fresh and newly mown, sir.
    CHORUS.

"THE GREAT UNKNOWN".

RESPECTFULLY DEDICATED TO THE

REPUBLICAN CENTENNIAL PRESIDENTIAL

CANDIDATE,

Hon RUTHERFORD B. HAYES. OF OHIO.

J.E.BAKER

MACK'S GRAND CENTENNIAL MARCH.

Song. "HURRAH FOR HAYES & HONEST WAYS".

Mixed Quartette
Male

E.W. Foster.

BOSTON, Published by JOHN F. PERRY & CO. opp. Boston Theatre. 538 Washington St.

Rutherford B. Hayes eventually won the hotly disputed election of 1876 by arbitration (and some prearrangement) when—only two days before he was inaugurated—a specially formed (predominantly Republican) electoral commission awarded him the bitterly contested votes of four states. The unresolved election aroused so great a degree of public feeling that civil war was feared. Samuel Tilden, who originally polled the majority of votes, maintained to the end of his life that he had wrongfully been deprived of the presidency. Throughout Hayes's administration—and beyond—the controversy continued.

Vividly recreating the first festive moments of America's great birthday party, Perley wrote (*Perley's Reminiscences, 1886*):

The Centennial year of the Republic was ushered in at Washington with unusual rejoicings. . . . Just before twelve o'clock, the chime of bells of the Metropolitan Methodist church played "Pleyel's Hymn." The fire alarm bells then struck 1–7–7–6 a few moments later, and as the Observatory clock sounded the hour of twelve, the fire alarm bells then struck 1–8–7–6; at the same moment the brilliant light in the tholus which surmounts the dome of the Capitol was lighted by electricity, casting its beams over the entire metropolis. . . . The Metropolitan bells chimed a national centennial march, introducing the favorite tunes of this and other nations, and there was general ringing of bells, large and small, with firing of pistols and blowing of horns.

On the surface, it might seem that America's festive birthday mood was unjustified and inappropriate. The year 1876 found the nation deeply enmeshed in the toils of economic depression, unemployment, inflation, political corruption in high places, and the evil aftereffects of war. Yet America was bent on a bang-up birthday party and—despite the forbidding disapproval of gloomy Cassandras who didn't see what there was to celebrate—a bang-up birthday party was had, complete with music, fireworks, flags, feasting, and a mammoth spectacle in Philadelphia, formally called the International Exhibition of Arts, Manufactures, and Produces of the Soil and Mine, to which people from all over flocked in multitudes.

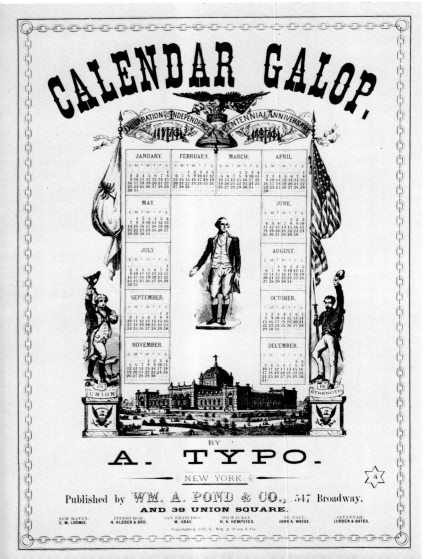

"UNCLE SAM'S A HUNDRED."

Oh, ye Powers! what a roar.
Such was never heard before—
Thundering from shore to shore:
  "Uncle Sam's a hundred!"

Cannons boom and trumpets bray,
Fiddles squeak and fountains play—
'Tis his great Centennial day—
  "Uncle Sam's a hundred!"

Stalwart men and puny boys,
Maids and matrons swell the noise,
Every baby lifts its voice:
  "Uncle Sam's a hundred!"

Nervous folks who dote on quiet,
Though they're half distracted by it,
Can't help mixing in the riot:
  "Uncle Sam's a hundred!"

Brutes that walk and birds that fly,
On the earth or in the sky,
Join the universal cry:
  "Uncle Sam's a hundred!"

Centennial Songster (1876)

The building seen on the sheet music cover for this anniversary dance music is Memorial Hall, one of the principal buildings at the Centennial Exhibition, the grounds of which covered some two hundred and forty acres.

A HUNDRED YEARS AGO.

A little band of earnest men,
  Who knew no law but right,
We just a century ago
  Set freedom's torch alight,
We fought and fell and ages tell
  The story which you know,
Of how the sun of glory rose
  A hundred years ago.

CHORUS.
A hundred years ago we stood in fight arrayed, boys,
  And boldly met the foe, for truth and liberty:
Our voice is living still, and we should be obeyed, boys,
  Who gave our lives to make you free a hundred years ago.

Centennial Songster (1876)

The unlikely-looking title page for the music that officially opened the American Centennial celebration

Despite rain earlier on the morning of May 10, 1876, by nine-thirty a crowd of more than one hundred thousand people in holiday mood had gathered in front of Memorial Hall in Philadelphia, where the opening ceremonies of the Centennial Exhibition were to take place. The *New-York Times* (May 11) reported that among the first arrivals were the "750 fair creatures of the Women's Committee, each of whom was adorned with a beautiful bright star of silver, pendent from a clasp containing the initials of their organization." The surging, milling mass of people cheered and applauded as brilliantly uniformed and bemedalled domestic and foreign dignitaries appeared, but in the general crush the arrival of President and Mrs. Grant was not noticed until "a handkerchief was waved frantically from the centre of the platform where Dom Pedro [of Brazil] and his Empress were seated, and the orchestra burst into 'Hail to the Chief.'" While waiting for the president to arrive, the orchestra, under the direction of the eminent German-born conductor who made music history in America, Theodore Thomas, played a medley of eighteen national airs—American and foreign—beginning with "The Washington March" (which one?) and concluding with "Hail Columbia." An anonymous *New-York Times* music critic found that the predominance of strings, combined with Mr. Thomas's "exceedingly tranquil" style of conducting, lacked the "color and force" and the "roughness and warmth" that a brass band more appropriately would have brought to the occasion. Patrick Sarsfield Gilmore and his famous band did perform there on the Fourth of July, and another, even greater bandmaster—a future one—was heard at the exhibition, but as the young first violinist of Jacques Offenbach's Orchestra, John Philip Sousa.

Apparently the *Times* critic understood the popular musical taste better than did Theodore Thomas, whose notable series of orchestra concerts attracted such pitifully sparse audiences that they were terminated by order of the Philadelphia sheriff, who seized Thomas's priceless music library and sold it at auction for a pittance to pay the musicians.

Indicative of American nineteenth-century inferiority feelings and subservience to Germany insofar as "good" music was concerned, the Women's Centennial Committee, doubtless at Theodore Thomas's suggestion, handsomely if incongruously commissioned Richard Wagner, for a fee of five thousand dollars, to compose a march for the Centennial. Given the place of honor, the work opened the inaugural ceremonies on May 10, at which two other specially, if less munificently, commissioned works by Americans (both educated in Germany) were heard. Wagner's piece, gallantly dedicated to the ladies who had paid for it, proved to be a dismal failure. The *Times* critic wrote that its obviously expert orchestration did not "make amends for the lack of thought" it exhibited. Thomas, who was the devoted early champion in America of Wagner's music, never forgave Wagner for the insult of this bad composition. And Wagner himself was quoted as having said that the best thing about the piece was the money he had received for it.

CENTENNIAL HYMN.

Words by JOHN G. WHITTIER.   Music by JOHN K. PAINE.

Copyrighted 1876, by JOHN K. PAINE.

1776—1876.

BY APPOINTMENT OF THE U. S. CENTENNIAL COMMISSION.

THE

CENTENNIAL

MEDITATION OF COLUMBIA.

A CANTATA

FOR

THE INAUGURAL CEREMONIES

AT

PHILADELPHIA, MAY 10, 1876.

POEM BY

SIDNEY LANIER,

OF GEORGIA.

MUSIC BY

DUDLEY BUCK,

OF CONNECTICUT.

NEW YORK:

G. SCHIRMER, 701 BROADWAY.

Performed between speeches and prayers, the two other specially written works on the opening program met with greater approval than Wagner's march had done. The *Times* writer found that the "Centennial Hymn" by the distinguished New England composer John Knowles Paine, while it did not attempt "originality of theme or form . . . [was] wedded in the elegance of the treatment" to John Greenleaf Whittier's poetry, itself not notably original.

CENTENNIAL HYMN.

Our fathers' God! from out whose hand
   The centuries fall like grains of sand,
We meet today, united, free,
   And loyal to our land and Thee,
To thank Thee for the era done,
   And trust Thee for the opening one.

~~~

Oh! make Thou us, through centuries long
   In peace secure, in justice strong;
Around our gift of freedom draw
   The safeguards of Thy righteous law,
And, cast in some diviner mould,
   Let the new cycle shame the old.

Of the three works commissioned for the Centennial opening ceremonies, Dudley Buck's cantata to Sidney Lanier's distinctively titled poem "The Centennial Meditation of Columbia" was adjudged "unquestionably the most successful effort of the day." The praise was restricted to Buck's music, however. Lanier's unconventional, mystical poetry both puzzled and irritated contemporary listeners, and the criticism it aroused impelled the poet to write a lengthy letter to the press in defense of his poem and its suitability for being set to music. Lanier was well qualified to speak: he was as gifted a musician as he was a poet. And a gifted poet he undeniably was.

THE CENTENNIAL MEDITATION OF COLUMBIA.

~~~

Long as thine Art shall love true love,
Long as thy science truth shall know,
Long as thine eagle harms no dove,
Long as thy law by law shall grow,
Long as thy God is God above,
Thy brother every man below,
So long, dear land of all my love,
Thy name shall shine, thy fame shall grow.

O Music, from this height of time my Word unfold;
In thy large signals all men's hearts Man's Heart behold;
Mid-heaven, unroll thy chords as friendly flags unfurled,
And wave the world's best lover's welcome to the world.

It had been expected that Frédéric Auguste Bartholdi's statue "Liberty Enlightening the World," then being cast in France, would be completed in time to be displayed at the Centennial Exhibition in Philadelphia, but visitors had to be content with only a fragment: the right forearm and hand grasping the torch. The colossal proportions of this detail excited great astonishment and admiration, but not from the *New-York Times* (September 29, 1876), which ridiculed Bartholdi's grandiose concept, calling the statue "a combined goddess and lighthouse," consisting of "several hundred feet of bronze female with a practicable staircase in her left leg and a balcony in her back hair," and with a thumbnail that "afforded an easy seat for the largest fat woman in existence."

More tactfully and appreciatively, the popular composer Harrison Millard collaborated with the equally popular lyricist George Cooper in a song, "America and France," with bilingual words and a visual projection of the completed Statue of Liberty on its cover. Its actual completion and installation did not occur until a decade later, when after great financial vicissitudes, the Statue of Liberty was unveiled by President Cleveland on October 28, 1886.

AMERICA AND FRANCE.

Behold thy pure, sacred shrine, blessed Freedom!
  Mark the names there like bright jewels set!
In living lustre, their glory unfading:
  Noble Washington, Brave Lafayette!
O'er Rochambeau's grand and Fame-laurel'd pillow
  Is thy tri-color brightly unfurl'd!
One noble purpose our fortunes uniting,
  Fair Republic, of yon olden world!
CHORUS.
Let songs arise 'neath Freedom's skies!
  In Fame's advance
Twin daughters fair, America and France!

On, on to triumphs yet grander and prouder,
  Still united in heart and in hand!
The hope, the joy of earth's down-trodden millions,
  In the sunlight of Freedom ye stand!
Oh, in the lapse of ages so glorious,
  May our bond be belov'd Liberty!
As now our flags in sweet sisterhood twining,
  Fair Republic, far over the sea!
CHORUS.

SONG OF "1876."

'Tis the Centennial year,
  A goodly time for cheer.
America now welcomes every nation,
  For our flag it is unfurled
  In friendship to the world,
And a beacon to the down-trod of creation.
  CHORUS.
    For the battle has been won
    By our glorious Washington,
  In whose name we feel a growing exultation.
    And the stars and stripes shall be
    The emblem of the free,
  And the pride of every coming generation.

  In our Centennial year,
  We'll all be of good cheer,
And stretch a friendly hand to every nation,
  Who may send across the sea
  To our home of liberty,
To which the exile looks in expectation. (CHORUS.)

Centennial Songster (1876)

468

Let this universal grand display,
Your feelings not to mar.

As the triumph of a nation's age,
By Phil-a-del-phi-a.

In the troubled 1850s, the reformer and feminist Frances Gage—to John Hutchinson's music—wrote a timeless song for entering a new century.

A HUNDRED YEARS HENCE.

One hundred years hence what a change will be made,
In politics, morals, religion and trade;
In statesmen who wrangle or ride on the fence,
These things will be altered a hundred years hence.

Our laws then will be non-compulsory rules,
Our prisons converted to national schools,
The pleasure of sinning—'tis all a pretence,
And the people will see it a hundred years hence.

Lying, cheating and fraud will be laid on the shelf,
Men will neither get drunk nor be bound up in self;
But all live together as neighbors and friends,
Just as good people ought to a hundred years hence.

Then woman, man's partner, man's equal shall stand,
While beauty and harmony govern the land,
And to think for one's self will be no offence,
The world will be thinking a hundred years hence.

Oppression and war will be heard of no more,
Nor the blood of a slave have its print on our shore;
Conventions will then be a needless expence,
The world will be thinking a hundred years hence.

Instead of speech making to satisfy wrong,
All will join the glad chorus to sing Freedom's song.
And if the millennium is not a pretence,
We'll all be good brothers a hundred years hence.

GRAND MARCH, D. L. DOWNING ⑥ **CENTENNIAL ODE.** H. MILLARD. ㊵

NEW YORK
Published by **C. H. DITSON & CO.** 711 Broadway.

BOSTON.	CHICAGO.	BOSTON.	PHILADA.
O. DITSON & CO.	**LYON & HEALY.**	**J. C. HAYNES & CO.**	**J. E. DITSON & CO.**
451 WASHINGTON STREET.			SUCCESSORS TO LEE & WALKER.

POSTLUDE

To avoid reiteration of information already supplied throughout the text of this book and again in the Index, no separate bibliography is given of primary sources: newspapers, periodicals, almanacs, tune-books, songsters, memoirs, diaries, and other contemporary published materials. The provenance of archival materials—broadsides, portraits, prints, cartoons, electioneering devices, and other visual items—is given in their accompanying credits. The sheet music carries its own bibliographic information in its titles, composer and author credits, imprints, and copyright notices.

The following titles are selected from among the innumerable secondary sources consulted in the preparation of this book. Offering general information and historical background on some of the music and its composers are Gilbert Chase, *America's Music* (1966 edition); and John Tasker Howard, *Our American Music* (1965 edition). Early American sheet music bibliography to 1800 is listed in Oscar George Theodore Sonneck, *Early American Secular Music*, revised and enlarged by William Treat Upton (1945); the bibliography is continued from 1800 to 1825 in Richard J. Wolfe, *Secular Music in America* (1964); for general music bibliography, see Julius Mattfeld, *Variety Music Cavalcade* (1971 edition); and James J. Fuld, *The Book of World-Famous Music* (1966).

Four of our national songs are exhaustively examined in O. G. T. Sonneck, *Report on "The Star-Spangled Banner," "Hail Columbia," "America," and "Yankee Doodle"* (1909). Other information on "Yankee Doodle" is found in S. Foster Damon, *Yankee Doodle* (1959); and the history of "The Star-Spangled Banner" is thoroughly investigated and beautifully illustrated in P. W. Filby and E. G. Howard, *Star-Spangled Books* (1972).

Token selections from the huge literature dealing with Civil War songs and composers are Kenneth A. Bernard, *Lincoln and the Music of the Civil War* (1966); and Richard B. Harwell, *Confederate Music* (1950). Bibliographic information is found in Marjorie Lyle Crandall,

Confederate Imprints, vol. 2 (1955); and Louis A. Warren, *Lincoln Sheet Music* (1940). The innumerable writings on the songs include Brander Matthews, "The Songs of the War," *Century Magazine*, vol. 34 (1887); Hans Nathan, "Dixie," *Musical Quarterly* (1949); and a group of articles appearing in the magazine *Civil War History* (September 1958), among them: Dena J. Epstein, "The Battle Cry of Freedom"; Richard B. Harwell, "The Star of the Bonnie Blue Flag"; and Boyd B. Stutler, "John Brown's Body." Interesting references to the music are contained in autobiographical works by three major figures of the Civil War music scene: Julia Ward Howe, *Reminiscences* (1899); George Frederick Root, *The Story of a Musical Life* (1891); and Louis Moreau Gottschalk, *Notes of a Pianist* (1881).

For general history information, see T. Harry Williams, Richard N. Current, and Frank Friedel, *A History of the United States to 1877* (1969 edition); Samuel Eliot Morison, *The Oxford History of the American People* (1965); and Norman A. Graebner, Gilbert C. Fite, and Philip L. White, *A History of the American People* (1970). Capsulized historical facts are found in the *Dictionary of American History* (1968 edition); and in Tim Taylor, *The Book of Presidents* (1972); and for concise biographical information, see the *Dictionary of American Biography* (1964 edition).

Outstanding among great masses of political writings are Eugene H. Roseboom, *A History of Presidential Elections* (1972 edition); Arthur M. Schlesinger, Jr., and Fred L. Israel, eds., *History of American Presidential Elections*, vols. 1 and 2 (1971); Lillian B. Miller, *If Elected* (1972); and Robert Gray Gunderson, *The Log-Cabin Campaign* (1957).

For information on graphics, see Wendy J. Shadwell, *American Printmaking, The First 150 Years* (1969); and for sheet music covers, see Nancy Davison, "The Grand Triumphal Quick-Step; or, Sheet Music Covers in America," *Prints in and of America to 1850* (1970).

INDEX